PARLIAMENTARY HISTORY: TEXTS & STUDIES
15

Anglo-Irish Politics, 1680–1728

The Correspondence of the Brodrick Family

of Surrey and County Cork

VOLUME ONE, 1680–1714

Alan Brodrick as Speaker of the Irish house of commons (British Horological Institute).

Anglo-Irish Politics, 1680–1728

The Correspondence of the Brodrick Family

of Surrey and County Cork

VOLUME ONE, 1680–1714

Edited by

David Hayton and Michael Page

WILEY
for
THE PARLIAMENTARY HISTORY YEARBOOK TRUST

John Wiley & Sons

Registered Office
John Wiley & Sons Ltd, The Atrium, Southern Gate, Chichester, West Sussex, PO19 8SQ, UK

Editorial Offices
101 Station Landing, Medford, MA 02155, USA
9600 Garsington Road, Oxford, OX4 2DQ, UK
The Atrium, Southern Gate, Chichester, West Sussex, PO19 8SQ, UK

For details of our global editorial offices, for customer services, and for information about how to apply for permission to reuse the copyright material in this book please see our website at www.wiley.com/wiley-blackwell.

ISBN 9781119564096

A catalogue record for this title is available from the British Library
Set in 10/12pt Bembo
by Aptara Inc., India
Printed and bound in Singapore
by C.O.S. Printers Pte Ltd

1 2019

Parliamentary History: Texts & Studies

CONTENTS

ACKNOWLEDGMENTS

First and foremost, we must acknowledge the gracious permission of the Viscount Midleton to print these letters and to cite and quote from other papers in the family archive. For permission to make use of other manuscript materials, we are grateful to: the duke of Abercorn; the marquess of Bath; Lieutenant-Commander H.W. Drax, the keeper of western manuscripts of the Bodleian Library; Bristol Archives; the British Library Board; the clerk of the records of parliament; the comptroller of Her Majesty's Stationery Office; the Hardiman Library; National University of Ireland; the Kenneth Spencer Research Library, University of Kansas; the librarian, Lambeth Palace Library; Leicestershire, Leicester and Rutland Record Office; the keeper, Marsh's Library; the director, National Archives of Ireland; the director, National Library of Ireland; North Yorkshire Record Office; the deputy keeper of the Records of Northern Ireland; the librarian, Nottingham University Library; Southampton Archives Services; the board of Trinity College Dublin and University College Cork, Archives Service. We must also thank the Viscount Midleton and the British Horological Institute for permission to reproduce the portrait of Alan Brodrick, 1st Viscount Midleton which appears on the cover and as a frontispiece. We owe a particular debt of gratitude to the staff of the Surrey History Centre, and its predecessor, the Surrey Record Office (Guildford Muniment Room) for their assistance over many years, especially the late Miss G.M. Beck and the late Mrs Shirley Corke at Guildford. Friends and colleagues have helped us by supplying references and elucidating problems, notably Toby Barnard, John Bergin, Eveline Cruickshanks, Karst de Jong, Clyve Jones, Ivar McGrath, Daniel Szechi, and James Woolley. But our greatest debt, and one which is shared by all those interested in the history of this period, in Ireland and England, is to Simon Meade, who over a half-century ago rescued the volumes of Brodrick letters from almost certain destruction, preserved them for future generations and enabled them to be consulted, studied and quoted by those interested in Anglo-Irish politics and in the social life of the protestant ascendancy in County Cork.

ABBREVIATIONS

Add. MS(S)	Additional Manuscript(s)
Al. Dub.	*Alumni Dublinenses: A Register of the Students, Graduates, Professors and Provosts of Trinity College in the University of Dublin 1593–1860*, ed. G.D. Burtchaell and T.U. Sadleir (new edn, Dublin, 1935)
Ball, *Judges*	F.E. Ball, *The Judges in Ireland 1221–1921* (2 vols, London, 1926)
BL	British Library, London
Bodl.	Bodleian Library, Oxford
CTB	*Calendar of Treasury Books*
CJ	*Commons Journals*
CJI	*The Journals of the House of Commons of the Kingdom of Ireland* (2nd edn, 19 vols, Dublin, 1753–76)
Cork Council Bk	*The Council Book of the Corporation of the City of Cork, from 1609 to 1643, and from 1690 to 1800*, ed. Richard Caulfield (Guildford, 1876)
Cotton, *Fasti*	Henry Cotton, *Fasti Ecclesiae Hibernicae: The Succession of Prelates and Members of the Cathedral Bodies of Ireland* (5 vols, Dublin, 1847–60)
CSP Dom.	*Calendar of State Papers, Domestic Series*
DIB	*Dictionary of Irish Biography*, ed. James McGuire and James Quinn (9 vols, Cambridge, 2009)
ECI	*Eighteenth-century Ireland*
[E]	England
[GB]	Great Britain
Hayton, *Ruling Ireland*	D.W. Hayton, *Ruling Ireland, 1685–1742: Politics, Politicians and Parties* (Woodbridge, 2004)
HC 1690–1715	*The House of Commons 1690–1715*, ed. Eveline Cruickshanks, D.W. Hayton and Stuart Handley (5 vols, Cambridge, 2002)
Hist. Ir. Parl.	Edith Mary Johnston-Liik, *History of the Irish Parliament 1692–1800: Commons, Constituencies and Statutes* (6 vols, Belfast, 2002)
HL 1660–1715	*The House of Lords 1660–1715*, ed. Ruth Paley (5 vols, Cambridge, 2016)
HMC	Historical Manuscripts Commission (reports)

IHS	*Irish Historical Studies*
ILD	Irish Legislation Database (http://www.qub.ac.uk/ild)
[I]	Ireland
K. Inns Adm.	*King's Inns Admission Papers, 1607–1867*, ed. Edward Keane *et al.* (Dublin, 1982)
Lib. Mun.	*Liber Munerum Publicorum Hiberniæ,* ed. Rowley Lascelles (2 parts, 1824–30)
LJ	*Journals of the House of Lords*
LJ.	*Journals of the House of Lords [of Ireland]* (8 vols, Dublin, 1779–1800)
M. Temple Adm.	*Register of Admissions to the Honourable Society of the Middle Temple from the Fifteenth Century to the year 1944*, ed. H.A.C. Sturgess (3 vols, 1949)
McGrath, *Constitution*	C.I. McGrath, *The Making of the Eighteenth-century Irish Constitution: Government, Parliament and the Revenue, 1692–1714* (Dublin, 2000)
NAI	National Archives, Dublin
NLI	National Library of Ireland, Dublin
n.s.	new series
OED	*Oxford English Dictionary* (online edition: http://www.oed.com)
Oxf. DNB	*The Oxford Dictionary of National Biography* (online edition: http://www.oxforddnb.com)
Perceval Diary	'An Irish Parliamentary Diary from the Reign of Queen Anne', ed. D.W. Hayton, *Analecta Hibernica*, xxx (1982), 97–149
Phillimore, *Indexes*	*Indexes to Irish Wills*, ed. W.P.W. Phillimore and Gertrude Thrift (5 vols, 1909–20)
PRONI	Public Record Office of Northern Ireland
Reg. Deeds	Registry of Deeds, Dublin.
Reg. Deeds, Wills	*Registry of Deeds, Dublin: Abstracts of Wills*, ed. P.B. Eustace and Eilish Ellis (3 vols, Dublin, 1954–84)
SHC	Surrey History Centre
TCD	Trinity College Dublin
TNA	The National Archives [of the U.K.]
UL	University Library
Vicars, *Index*	*Index to the Prerogative Wills of Ireland, 1536–1810*, ed. Sir Arthur Vicars (Dublin, 1897)

Introduction

1

The letters of the Brodricks, viscounts and earls of Midleton, of Ballyannan, near Midleton in County Cork and Peper Harow, near Godalming in Surrey, were first quoted in a work of history as far back as 1798, when Archdeacon Coxe published material from the correspondence relating to English politics in his three-volume edition of the *Memoirs of the Life and Administration of Sir Robert Walpole*. Only in the last few decades have the papers been used systematically by historians. The existence of the collection, in nine bound volumes covering the period 1627–1728, was briefly noticed in the appendix to the first report of the Historical Manuscripts Commission in 1872. The eighth Viscount Midleton (1830–1907) had brought a 'schedule' of the archive into the Public Record Office so that the commission could record its existence.[1] But after Coxe the papers were not cited again until the History of Parliament Trust published its volumes on *The House of Commons 1715–1754* in 1970. Here a few original letters were referenced, merely as 'Midleton mss', with no hint of their location.[2]

When the Historical Manuscripts Commission compiled its report, the family archive was presumably kept at Peper Harow House. The 9th viscount (1856–1942), who became earl of Midleton in 1920, was an active Conservative politician, successively secretary of state for war and for India in 1902–5. He led the Irish unionist alliance until the Irish Convention of 1917, when his willingness to compromise over home rule in order to avoid partition alienated supporters and prompted his removal. In response he seems to have abandoned Ireland for Surrey. His successor, the second and last earl (1888–1979), sold Peper Harow, which became a residential community for disturbed adolescents, and retired to Jersey. The bound volumes of letters were held in the offices of a family solicitor until they were taken away for safekeeping by the earl's nephew Simon Meade, in whose Welsh farmhouse David Hayton was permitted to consult them in the early 1970s. Subsequently they were deposited with Surrey County Council, in the Guildford Museum and Muniment Room, the branch of the Surrey Record Office which was closest to the old Brodrick family home, before being transferred to the newly built Surrey History Centre in Woking, which also holds a substantial deposit of unbound Brodrick estate papers (G145).

[1] HMC, *1st Report*, app., 44.

[2] Romney Sedgwick, *The House of Commons 1715–1754* (2 vols, 1970), i, 492.

2

The connection of the Brodrick family with Ireland went back to Henry VIII's reign, and the military career of Captain Thomas Brodrick, who was killed there in 1547. The same fate befell Thomas's grandson Edward during the Elizabethan conquest of the country. However, Edward's nephew William followed a safer, as well as more decorative and profitable career, becoming King's Embroiderer to James VI and I. He moved from his ancestral home in Yorkshire down to London, acquiring property at Wandsworth in Surrey and building a house there which remained the family's principal English seat for the following century.[3] It was in the next generation but one that the connection with Ireland was resumed. William's son Thomas became lieutenant of the Tower of London under Charles I, and was knighted. In his will he gave his address as Wandsworth, and he was buried in the parish church in 1642.[4] Of his seven sons, Allen and St John (referred to as St John I whenever it is necessary to distinguish him from his son and grandson), involved themselves in Irish affairs and acquired Irish estates, though the paths they followed to membership of the Anglo-Irish governing class were very different.

Allen, the eldest son, was sent to Oxford and Gray's Inn, where he was called to the Bar.[5] Thomas, the second surviving son, became a merchant in London, dying in the early 1690s.[6] St John, Sir Thomas's third surviving son, acquired an army commission, and was in Ireland in 1641 as a captain in the king's forces.[7] He remained there, taking the Parliamentarian side, and serving as provost marshal to Roger Boyle, Lord Broghill, during the Munster campaigns of the early 1650s.[8] His reward came in 1653 with a grant of property in County Cork, centred on the demesne of Ballyannan, whose ruined castle he rebuilt as a fortified manor house. In the same year St John married Alice Clayton of Mallow. His choice of wife was another indication of his close association with Broghill and the conservative 'Old Protestant' interest within the Cromwellian establishment in Ireland: her family had acquired their Irish property during the Munster plantation and were tenants to the Boyles.[9] Meanwhile, Allen was on a very different political trajectory. His sympathies were royalist, and while he did not fight for King Charles, he refused to take the covenant when called to the Bar in 1648; and so, disqualified from legal practice, he went abroad, first to France and

[3] The family history of the Brodricks has been drawn principally from *Genealogical Memoranda Relating to the Family of Brodrick* (1872); and *Visitation of England and Wales,* ed J.J. Howard and F.A. Crisp (35 vols, 1893–1921), xxv (Notes, vi), 9–14. For William Brodrick see *Issues of the Exchequer: Being Payments made out of His Majesty's Revenue during the Reign of James I*, ed. Frederick Devon (1836), 84. His portrait, in the dress of a Jacobean courtier, is held in the Battersea Arts Centre Moving Museum, Wandsworth Collection.

[4] TNA, PROB 11/198/185; Daniel Lysons, *The Environs of London* … (4 vols, 1792–6), i, 515.

[5] Details of Allen's life can be found in the entries in *Oxf. DNB*, *DIB*, i, 849–50, and *The History of Parliament: The House of Commons 1660–1690*, ed. B.D. Henning (3 vols, 1983), i, 721–4.

[6] A copy of his will (dated 7 May 1690 and proved 13 July 1693) is TNA, PROB 11/415/121.

[7] There is a brief entry for St John in *Hist. Ir. Parl.*, iii, 270. See also John Lodge, *The Peerage of Ireland* … (4 vols, 1754), iii, 228.

[8] Aidan Clarke, *Prelude to Restoration in Ireland: The End of the Commonwealth 1659–1660* (Cambridge, 1999), 220–1.

[9] J.P. Rylands, 'The Claytons, of Thelwall …', *Transactions of the Historic Society of Lancashire and Cheshire*, xxxii (1879–1880), 40–2. For the divisions in Irish politics in the 1650s, see T.C. Barnard, 'Planters and Policies in Cromwellian Ireland', *Past and Present*, no. 61 (Nov. 1973), 31–69; Patrick Little, *Lord Broghill and the Cromwellian Union with Ireland and Scotland* (Woodbridge, 2004), ch. 3.

then to Italy. On returning in 1654, he immediately engaged in royalist conspiracy, acting as secretary to the 'Sealed Knot'. This brought him into a regular correspondence with Sir Edward Hyde, the future earl of Clarendon, a connection which was to serve him well. After a scare in July 1659, when he was arrested and committed to the Tower, he secured his release by suing for a writ of habeas corpus, and as the commonwealth regime collapsed was elected to the convention for the borough of Orford in Suffolk.

Allen's friendship with Hyde brought handsome dividends when Charles II resumed the throne. He was knighted in August 1660 and appointed surveyor-general for Ireland, and subsequently a commissioner for executing the land settlement. He also acquired for himself the Irish estates of the regicides Daniel Axtell and John Hewson, though he was later obliged to surrender these to Clarendon's brother-in-law, the duke of York, in exchange for other forfeited properties. York then made Sir Allen receiver-general of his Irish revenues.[10] At the same time Sir Allen remained active in English politics, as one of Clarendon's closest allies in the house of commons, until the fall of his patron (and the conclusion of the business of the Irish land settlement) prompted his withdrawal from public affairs in general, and from Irish affairs in particular. A typical Restoration rake in his morals and manners, he never married, and died at Wandsworth in 1680.

St John, despite his Cromwellian past, also prospered after 1660. He too was knighted, after receiving (with Orrery's help) a pardon for past indiscretions,[11] and his land grants were confirmed. His brother's relationship with Clarendon may have had some part to play, but Sir St John had a powerful patron of his own in Broghill, who was created earl of Orrery in 1660 and made lord president of Munster. The two men were always close, Sir St John overseeing the absentee Orrery's Irish estate, and managing his political interest. At the same time, Sir St John was extending his own influence in County Cork, developing the estate at Ballyannan and building up the neighbouring town of Midleton, which was incorporated as a parliamentary borough in 1671, with a corporation franchise, and Sir St John himself named as its first sovereign.[12]

Marriage and procreation were important instruments of family aggrandizement, and Sir St John used both to great effect; indeed, he seems to have put material advantage above all things in considering his children's domestic arrangements.[13] Dynastic strategies were focused on County Cork. He himself married a Clayton cousin, reinforcing the alliance between the two families. To drive the point home, he named one of his sons Randal after his father-in-law. Sadly, Randal died young. The eldest son, Thomas, was married into the family of the Pigotts of Innishannon, in the west of the county, while the second, Alan (I), was provided with a bride in another extensive county family, the Barrys. Sir St John's daughter Katherine Brodrick seems also to have been intended for a local husband until she slipped the halter and married an English clergyman.[14]

Sir St John did not lose sight of the wider picture, for he would naturally have assumed that his unmarried elder brother (whose health was significantly weakened by a lifetime

[10]SHC, 1248/1/327: petition of Sir Allen Brodrick to the duke of York, n.d.

[11]SHC, 1248/1/104: warrant, 11 July 1661.

[12]Toby Barnard, *Irish Protestant Ascents and Descents, 1641–1770* (Dublin, 2004), 68.

[13]See below, Letter 7.

[14]See below, Letters 3–4.

of courtly dissipation) would wish to use his testamentary dispositions to consolidate the family's English and Irish landholdings. To further assist the advancement of his children Sir St John put four of his surviving five sons to the law, while the youngest, Laurence, went into the Church. Thomas, as the eldest, inherited the lion's share of the family estates, and in due course gave up his barrister's gown for a purely parliamentary career, but Alan, St John II and William all continued to pursue their professional calling, alongside their political ambitions, and with considerable success. Alan returned to Ireland, combining his legal work with a parliamentary career and rising to become lord chancellor of Ireland; St John remained at the Middle Temple, where he was a successful and sought-after advocate until his death in 1707; William, the most mercurial of the three, went out to the West Indies, becoming attorney-general of Jamaica, and of the Leeward Islands, and a controversial figure in Caribbean politics.[15]

It is in the aftermath of Sir Allen's death in 1680 that we hear for the first time of tensions in the relationships between Sir St John and his sons, though it is perfectly possible that this kind of unpleasantness was already a feature of family life, given the frequent disputes and eruptions of ill-feeling in later years.[16] Much, though not all, of the trouble may be laid at Sir St John's door, since he was a man who tested the patience of everyone connected with him.[17]

The provisions of Sir Allen's will seem to have provoked resentment. Apart from a small house in the parish of Wandsworth, which went to the only son of Sir Allen's other brother, the merchant Thomas Brodrick, all the Surrey properties, including some recent purchases, together with the Irish lands, were left to St John's eldest son, Thomas, and his heirs, with remainders first to Alan I and then to St John II. Their father received for himself the residue of the English property, together with Sir Allen's plate, books, and household goods.[18] It was not long before a peevish Sir St John was making difficulties for his offspring. In 1683 he took exception to his son St John's choice of bride, and managed to prevent the wedding; the following year, professing that poor health meant that he would not have much longer to live, and despairing of Thomas's failure to produce an heir, he proposed to settle his own property in County Cork on Alan, a decision that was bound to sow discord between the brothers.[19]

As Sir St John grew older, he became even more difficult and at one time or another fell out with almost all his children. He exasperated his son St John II beyond measure by his extravagance, which scuppered St John's second attempt at marriage; clashed with Thomas over property boundaries in County Cork, to a point of 'open war' between them; and drew Alan into his quarrels, until the three brothers themselves were almost at daggers drawn.[20] Sir St John's insistence on building a wall around his demesne at Cahermone, adjacent to Ballyannan, not only encroached on Thomas's lands but also on the public

[15] Karst de Jong, 'The Irish in Jamaica during the Long Eighteenth Century 1698–1836', Queen's University Belfast PhD, 2017, pp. 75–82.

[16] See below, Letter 7.

[17] SHC, 1248/1/183–4: Laurence Clayton to St John II, 31 Aug. 1683.

[18] TNA, PROB 11/364/132–3; Victoria County History, *Surrey*, iv, 114.

[19] See below, Letter 7; SHC, 1248/1/200–1: Sir St John to Thomas, 1 Nov. 1684.

[20] SHC, 1248/1/305–7: St John II to Alan I and Thomas, 22, 27 Dec. 1698; SHC, 1248/2/11–14, [Alan I] to Thomas, 11 Oct., 2 Nov. 1700; below, Letters 27, 30–3.

highway, and threatened to inflame 'the country' into seeking a grand jury presentment against him.[21] In Katherine's case he seems to have been disgusted by her choice of husband, and as late as 1698 was refusing to see her. It was only through the intercession of a daughter-in-law, Alan's first wife, that he could be brought to a reconciliation.[22]

The sins of this cantankerous and emotionally unpredictable father were visited on his sons. The Brodrick brothers grew up to be highly-strung, quick-tempered and quarrelsome. Alan I's observation that 'our family is naturally melancholy' is borne out by letters laden with prophecies of doom. Misfortunes were exaggerated: any setback, whether personal, financial or political, was considered a potential, if not an actual, disaster.[23] But 'melancholy' in the modern sense is not really the appropriate word: there is a kind of overwrought desperation about these lamentations which reveals the passionate, even violent, temperament which was considered by contemporaries to be a family trait. Political opponents often characterised Alan I and Thomas, and indeed Alan's son St John (III), as bitter, vindictive and intractable, with their 'unruly passions' and 'malicious hot tempers'.[24] Allied to a shared sense of entitlement, fierce ambition, and a watchfulness over financial interests that bordered on the avaricious, this intensity of feeling naturally exploded from time to time into domestic conflict.[25] Alan frequently complained about his long-absent brother William, and was capable of writing to his own eldest son in such a 'severe, angry unkind manner', that the wounded recipient complained, 'I protest the bare reading of it puts me so far beside myself that I am not able to recollect my thoughts so as to write common sense'. Outside Alan's immediate family, there is evidence of friction with a brother-in-law over inheritance issues, and a fine example of short temper in the threat to have nothing more to do with a nephew who failed to take advice. Thomas proved just as irritable, quick to upbraid close relations for not paying rents promptly, and just as insensitive, criticizing Alan's treatment of his children at a time when the eldest of them, St John III ('Senny') was in the grip of a mortal illness.

Yet paradoxically, for such a quarrelsome crew the Brodricks appeared to the outside world as a close-knit family. The brothers worked intimately together, helping to run each other's estates, and presenting a united front in politics. They expected other siblings, relations and marital connections to follow suit. Laurence's high church tendencies were a constant worry, since, as a clergyman based in England, he was subject to what were considered undesirable influences.[26] Otherwise, Alan and Thomas seem to have been able to rely on their brothers and brothers-in-law to do their bidding, as well as a host of 'cousins' (a

[21] SHC, 1248/1/305–7: St John II to Alan I and Thomas, 22, 27 Dec. 1698; SHC, 1248/2/10,13–14: Alan I to Thomas, 8 Oct., 2 Nov. 1700; below, Letters 27, 30–1.

[22] SHC, 1248/1/303–4: Katherine to Sir St John, 6 Dec. 1698; SHC, 1248/1/288–9: same to Lucy Brodrick, 21 Jan. 1698[/9].

[23] This replicated their father's behaviour: see, for example, SHC, 1248/1/200–1: Sir St John to Thomas, 1 Nov. 1684.

[24] PRONI, D/638/167/12: earl of Drogheda to Lord Coningsby, 11 Oct. 1697; BL, Add. MS 47027, ff. 58–9, Edward Southwell to Sir John Perceval, 6 Dec. 1713. See also Jonathan Swift, *Journal to Stella: Letters to Esther Johnson and Rebecca Dingley 1710–1713*, ed. Abigail Williams (Cambridge, 2013), 243.

[25] For what follows see D.W. Hayton, 'A Presence in the Country: The Brodricks and their "Interest"', in Hayton, *The Anglo-Irish Experience: Religion, Identity and Patriotism* (Woodbridge, 2012), 89.

[26] See below, Letters 100, 169. Laurence was named in a pamphlet of 1701 as one of many members of Oxford and Cambridge colleges who had written congratulatory poems on the birth of the prince of Wales, James Francis Edward Stuart, in 1688 (*The Congratulations of Several Kings and Princes of Europe to King James the II, on the Birth of the Prince of Wales …* (1701), 13).

term which also covered uncles and great-uncles, nephews and great-nephews) in Cork and the neighbouring counties.[27] One family of 'cousins', the Bettesworths, acted as local agents for the Brodricks in east Cork: Richard Bettesworth, senior, who lived at White Rock, a part of the Cahermone estate belonging to Sir St John and settled on Alan I, managed Alan's various interests in the county, financial and political, and provided accommodation for occasional visits. In return, Alan paid for the schooling of Richard's son. Other forms of patronage doled out to local clients included, inevitably, recommendations for preferment, and the deployment of political influence to assist in election to parliament. Alan was particularly conscious of family connection, and his three marriages – to Catherine Barry, Lucy Courthope and Anne Hill, afforded him a range of contacts. The Courthope marriage was particularly advantageous: having brought a portion of £1,000 on marriage, Lucy then inherited half her father's estate when her childless brother died fighting with King William's troops in Flanders.[28] But it also provides a fine example of Alan's heightened sense of family obligation, since he took over responsibility for his late brother-in-law's widow, Rachel, his wife's sister Anne, and an unmarried aunt, Martha Courthope, all of whom he called his 'sisters'. This relationship continued even after Lucy had died and he had married again. He provided homes for the three women in England; indeed his own estate in Surrey was purchased in the name of Martha Courthope, who acted as its chatelaine.[29]

3

As well as being acutely conscious of their family responsibilities, the Brodricks used their many connections by blood and marriage as an important resource in the development of their power and prestige. An equally important asset was their landed property. Indeed, the two were often linked: family members or connections were granted leases on parcels on the Brodrick estate, which cemented the relationship and added another layer of obligation. Not only did Richard Bettesworth manage Alan Brodrick's property, he and other Bettesworths were also tenants, as were several Barrys, and the Irish MP Bartholomew Purdon, who represented several County Cork constituencies between 1699 and his death in 1737, and who could claim a distant kinship to the Brodricks through their Jephson cousins.[30] The rentals of Alan's estate include the names of other tenants who were themselves country gentlemen, with political ambitions of their own.[31]

While the core of the Cork estate had come through acquisitions in the Cromwellian and Restoration land settlements, Alan and Thomas continued to expand their holdings, principally in the east of the county, and coalescing around Midleton. As always, profitable marriages played a part. But the Brodricks also continued to buy land whenever it became available, reinvesting the profits from their legal practice and official appointments. Alan was particularly keen to translate his earnings into real estate, ensuring that his local contacts gave

[27] Alan's brother-in-law by his first marriage, James Barry of Rathcormac, Co. Cork, was a rare exception, though even then his flirtation with opposing political interests did not prove permanent: see below, p. 217.

[28] SHC, G145/box95/1: marriage settlement, 1695.

[29] Hayton, *Anglo-Irish Experience*, 87 (where Martha is incorrectly described as Alan's sister-in-law).

[30] *Hist. Ir. Parl.*, vi,131.

[31] SHC, G145/box102/4: rent account book, 1712–28.

him early notice of any suitable properties coming onto the market.[32] He and his brothers could afford to spend. When Alan began his career as a barrister in the 1680s he earned £120 (Irish) a year; by the 1690s this figure had risen to £1,000.[33] St John II and Thomas, who both practised at the English Bar, could hope to do even better, since £3–4,000 a year was a reasonable expectation for a successful counsel in England,[34] and St John, who never married, left an estate worth £10,500.[35] By 1713 Alan's landed income was thought to be about £2,000, which put him close to the highest stratum of Irish landowners, though still short of the very wealthiest, such as his colleague in the Irish house of commons (and future political rival) William Conolly, whose rent-roll was estimated by the same source at £5,500.[36]

Conolly makes an interesting contrast with the Brodricks in the way he managed his estates and extended his influence. There are some similarities in the means by which he and the Brodricks made their money, through legal fees (Conolly was originally an attorney), marrying well, and obtaining high political office, but significant differences in the way the money was spent. Conolly owned property across Ireland, but focused his interests in and around Dublin, with a handsome city mansion, and various estates in the hinterland of the capital. One, Castletown House, in the Liffey valley in County Kildare, was built in the 1720s (by which time Conolly's annual income had rocketed to £16–17,000) by the fashionable young architect Edward Lovett Pearce, and decorated lavishly in the latest style. It would serve as the scene of political house-parties in the manner of Sir Robert Walpole's 'Norfolk congresses' at Houghton.[37]

Conspicuous consumption on such a grand scale was not something in which the younger generation of Brodricks were inclined to indulge. Sir St John had been responsible for the extension of the house at Ballyannan, from its origin as a small, late medieval, castle into a substantial fortified house, with gardens and a deer park. In old age, when Thomas had possession of Ballyannan and Sir St John had relocated himself to the neighbouring castle of Cahermone the old man was still busying himself with projects of 'improvement', such as imparking his estate. Thomas, on the other hand, although making sure that he was well informed about the stables at Ballyannan, as horse racing was one of his passions, seems to have paid no attention to the house or demesne. He allowed the gardens to become overgrown, the house to be denuded of furniture and linen by the depredations of the agent and servants, and the deer park to be abandoned. There was a brief renaissance when Thomas's nephew, St John III, returned to live there with his family in the 1720s,

[32]SHC, G145/box98/1: Nicholas Grene to Alan I, 28 Feb. 1720.

[33]T.C. Barnard, 'Lawyers and the Law in Later Seventeenth-century Ireland', *IHS*, xxviii (1992–3), 276–7; and more generally, Toby Barnard, *A New Anatomy of Ireland: The Irish Protestants, 1649–1770* (New Haven, CT and London, 2003), 115–28.

[34]Geoffrey Holmes, *Augustan England: Professions, State and Society 1680–1730* (1982), 124–34; David Lemmings, *Gentlemen and Barristers: The Inns of Court and the English Bar 1680–1730* (Oxford, 1990), 155–6.

[35]SHC, G145/box165: abstract of title of 2nd Viscount Midleton to manor of Dunsford, Surrey; 1248/2/286–78: estimate of assets of, and liabilities on, the estate of St John II, [1707].

[36]BL, Add. MS 6167A, ff. 3, 5: printed list of peers and MPs [I], with MS annotations. For Conolly see Patrick Walsh, *The Making of the Irish Protestant Ascendancy: The Life of William Conolly, 1662–1729* (Woodbridge, 2010), 80, and for Irish landed incomes in general, Barnard, *A New Anatomy*, 60–2. In 1725, Alan's rental income from his property in Co. Cork amounted to around £1,500 *p.a.* (SHC, G145/box 102/4: rent rolls).

[37]Walsh, *Making of the Irish Protestant Ascendancy*, ch. 9; Toby Barnard, *Making the Grand Figure: Lives and Possessions in Ireland, 1641–1770* (New Haven, CT and London, 2004), 69–76.

and spent money 'in making the place habitable, and beautifying it, and in planting and improving the land', but Ballyannan never rivalled Castletown or became in any sense a great house.[38]

This is not to say that the Brodricks neglected the management of their estates; far from it. The evidence of their correspondence and estate papers proves that Alan in particular kept a very keen eye on the upkeep of his lands, the terms of the leases, and the returns from his tenants.[39] He and his brothers regarded property as an engine of income rather than an opportunity for indulgence and display. Theirs was a more hard-headed, less imaginative, approach to the way in which landed property could be exploited to create a political 'interest'. While Conolly and his friends built country houses within easy reach of Dublin in which to parade their wealth and good taste, and entertain their political friends, the Brodricks concentrated their attention on consolidating their ancestral power-base.

4

There was a further paradox: while firmly anchored in County Cork, the Brodricks never forgot that they were an Anglo-Irish family, so much so that in 1712, when explaining why he was reluctant to consider election to the house of commons at Westminster, Alan gave as one of his reasons, besides his unfamiliarity with the forms of the British parliament, that he was afraid of being regarded by English colleagues 'and perhaps told that I am (what of all things I would last choose to be) an Irishman'.[40] Although Alan's primary residence was in Dublin he travelled to England frequently, and in September 1712 purchased an English estate at Peper Harow in Surrey: as always, when the Brodricks bought land, it was close to their existing property. Later Alan would talk of retiring there.[41] His brothers based themselves in England, or in William's case, in the English plantations in the Caribbean. Laurence, the clergyman, made his career entirely within the Church of England, while St John II resided in London, bought land at Reigate in Surrey, and insisted in his will on being buried with his forefathers at Wandsworth.[42]

Thomas, as the eldest son, inherited property on both sides of the Irish Sea but preferred to make Wandsworth rather than Ballyannan his principal seat. He too was eventually buried there.[43] Although chosen at every general election in Ireland between 1692 and 1713, and attending parliamentary sessions regularly in Dublin until 1711, he eventually sensed greater opportunities at Westminster, and in 1713 relinquished his seat in the Irish parliament to be returned instead in England, for the notoriously venal borough of Stockbridge.[44] In 1715, after Alan had been raised to the Irish lord chancellorship, Thomas agreed to do his duty by the family and resumed his place as one of the MPs for County Cork, but also

38 Below, Letter 30; Hayton, *Anglo-Irish Experience*, 93; Barnard, *Making the Grand Figure*, 235.

39 Hayton, *Anglo-Irish Experience*, 94.

40 Below, Letter 184.

41 SHC, G145/box3/1: 'sale particular' of the Peper Harow estate; SHC, G145/box1: book relating to Peper Harow estate; Hayton, *Anglo-Irish Experience*, 96.

42 TNA, PROB 11/495/204–5: will of St John II, 2 Sept. 1700.

43 TNA, PROB 11/640/97: will of Thomas Brodrick, 5 Aug. 1728.

44 *HC 1690–1715*, ii, 248–51.

retained his seat in the British parliament and even persuaded Alan (now Baron Brodrick) to put aside previous reticence and join him at Westminster in February 1717.

The brothers had all been brought up with a strong sense of their English heritage. All had been educated in England: Thomas, Laurence and William at Cambridge University, Alan and St John II at Oxford. And the four lawyers had attended London Inns of court. Thomas, Alan and St John went to the Middle Temple, a favourite resort of Irish students,[45] while William entered the Inner Temple. They made the most of these experiences, making valuable friendships, even though in 1685 Alan declared himself to be 'so very little obliged by the Middle Temple that I owe the society no service'.[46] The letters between Thomas, Alan and St John II, regularly mention fellow Middle Templars who had risen to positions of importance in England in the law, parliament and government. Thus it was natural that Alan should send his own sons to England to be educated: St John III began at Eton, where, he may have become acquainted with Robert Walpole, and went on to Cambridge University and the Middle Temple. In due course Alan's younger son (by his third marriage), Alan II, whom his father called 'Nally', followed suit. He also went to Cambridge. By this time (in 1717) there was evidently some pressure on Alan, as lord chancellor, to set an example and send his son to Trinity College, Dublin. The explanation for his refusal to do so, in a letter to Thomas, is revealing:

> Many here would persuade me to place him in this college, and give for reason that now there is a good provost and the education and discipline will not be as it was of late. This I own to be very true, but beside other reasons this weighs so with me as not to be capable I think of an answer: whoever proposes to come to anything considerable hereafter must make England the theatre he resolves to appear on: and this is so true that I see little fellows of this country by only spending some of their time there make themselves thought to be men of consequence, while others of real merit fare like our best clergymen and never rise by attending their cures.[47]

5

In terms of party politics, the Brodricks came to be synonymous with the whig interest in Irish politics, but their identification with 'the Good Old Cause' was a relatively recent phenomenon, a product of the Glorious Revolution and its aftermath in Ireland. In the early years of the Restoration their political alignment was determined to a great extent by Sir Allen Brodrick's close friendship with the first earl of Clarendon, and the family remained close to the Hydes even after Clarendon's death in 1674, and Sir Allen's six years later. Sir St John Brodrick's Cromwellian past did not prove an insuperable problem, for in 1685 the second earl of Clarendon told his brother Laurence Hyde, earl of Rochester, that despite Rochester's scepticism he himself believed Sir St John to be a good friend, and in 1690 Sir St John and Alan I visited the non-juring Clarendon when he was temporarily

[45] Barnard, *A New Anatomy*, 121.

[46] Quoted in Lemmings, *Gentlemen and Barristers*, 42.

[47] Quoted in Hayton, *Anglo-Irish Experience*, 96.

incarcerated in the Tower of London on suspicion of jacobite plotting.[48] Among Sir St John's children his namesake was perhaps the most sympathetic to Clarendon's brand of Stuart loyalism and high churchmanship (though there were also doubts about Laurence's politics). St John II may well have been the 'Mr Brodrick' spoken of as being close to the Hydes in 1689; certainly his correspondence shows him to have been on terms of personal intimacy with such well-known Oxford high churchmen as Henry Aldrich, the dean of Christ Church, and Aldrich's young colleague Francis Atterbury, the future jacobite.[49] He shared their devotion to the church of England and even, it would seem, their attachment to the tory side in English party politics, at least at the time of the 1690 general election.[50] He also owned a substantial theological library, including books by Hooker and Laud;[51] and his will, drawn up in 1700, included a small legacy to his fellow Middle Templar Constantine Phipps, a high tory who had already made a reputation for himself in defending jacobites and crypto-jacobites in the courts, and who, as lord chancellor of Ireland 1710–14, would become the great bugbear of Irish whigs in general, and St John's own brothers and nephew in particular.[52]

To some extent, Sir St John's own attachment to the earl of Orrery may have acted as a counterweight to the gravitational pull of the Hydes. One historian has suggested that there was 'more than a germ of the whig ideology of the next generation' in Orrery's politics, both before and after the Restoration.[53] But although it was probably true to say that the Boyles as a family leaned towards whiggism, this was not a pronounced partisanship, and Orrery's grandson, the 4th earl, eventually became a tory. The Boyle connection lasted until at least the Glorious Revolution – arrangements for the education of the young Charles Boyle (later the 4th earl) at Christ Church formed one subject of the correspondence between St John II and Henry Aldrich. Moreover, the letters printed below show that Thomas Brodrick and his brothers continued to be on amicable terms with the principal representatives of the Boyle family, most of whom were resident in England. There was, however, a gradually increasing distance. In Queen Anne's reign, when Alan sought to influence the disposition of the electoral interest of the earl of Burlington, the senior branch of the Boyles, he was obliged to employ a third party to approach the dowager Lady Burlington, who was managing the affairs of her young son.[54]

[48] *The Correspondence of Henry Hyde, Earl of Clarendon and His Brother Laurence Hyde, Earl of Rochester* ... ed. S.W. Singer (2 vols, 1828), i, 200; ii, 321; SHC, 1248/1/243–4: Clarendon to St John II, 22 Sept. 1690. Some indication of Sir St John's political orientation in the aftermath of the Exclusion Crisis is suggested by the fact that when he was chosen in 1684 to serve as a juror at the trial of the nonconformist Thomas Rosewell for supposedly preaching sedition, his nomination was challenged by the defence (T.B. Howell, *A Complete Collection of State Trials* ... (34 vols, 1816–28), x, 155).

[49] *Clarendon Correspondence*, ed. Singer, ii, 25; SHC, 1248/1/ 217–18, 233–4, 235–6: Aldrich to St John II, 16 Jan. 1686/7, 11 Feb., 13 Mar. 1689/90; SHC, 1248/1/219: St John II to [Aldrich], 8 Feb. 1686/7; SHC, 1248/1/213–14, 211–12, Atterbury to St John II, 12 July[1687], 26 Oct. [1688]; SHC, 1248/1/226: St John II to [Atterbury], [1687]. See also *The Entring Book of Roger Morrice 1677–1691*, ed. Mark Goldie et al. (7 vols, Woodbridge, 2007–9), iii, 349. For Aldrich and Atterbury, see their entries in *Oxf. DNB*; and G.V. Bennett, *The Tory Crisis in Church and State: The Career of Francis Atterbury, Bishop of Rochester* (Oxford, 1975), ch.2.

[50] SHC, 1248/1/239–40: Arthur Charlett to St John II, 20 Feb. 1689/90.

[51] SHC, 1248/2/290: list of theological works owned by St John II, [1707].

[52] TNA, PROB 11/495/204–5; SHC, 1248/2/276–7: additional instructions, [2 Sept. 1700].

[53] David Dickson, *Old World Colony: Cork and South Munster 1630–1830* (Cork, 2005), 48.

[54] See below, Letters 88, 144, 180, 214.

The events of James II's reign in Ireland, especially after the intervention of the prince of Orange, seem to have decisively affected the political outlook of Sir St John and his children. Sir St John and Alan, both of whom were in England, were attainted *in absentia* by King James's parliament in Dublin in 1689, together with Thomas, who was in County Cork trying to preserve the family estates.[55] In London father and son worked with other émigré Irish landowners to press King William and the English parliament to intervene on behalf of the protestant interest, and both were elected by these 'gentlemen of Ireland' as representatives from Munster on an ad hoc committee which co-ordinated lobbying activities.[56]

Evidently Sir St John offered on more than one occasion to raise troops at his own expense, especially for a Williamite invasion of Munster. This brought him unwillingly into a public controversy. Another refugee Irishman, Sir Richard Bulkeley, published early in 1690 a pamphlet which argued that Irish protestants in England should be forced to return to Ireland to support the protestant cause, with financial support from government if necessary. This comment was aimed at the London committee, whom Bulkeley considered were shirking their duty, and he singled out Sir St John Brodrick, whose personal integrity and loyalty to the Williamite cause were brought into question. Bulkeley alleged that Sir St John had balked at leading troops against the jacobites out of cowardice, that he had attempted to pocket for himself the funds raised for an expeditionary force, and even that, before the revolution, he had joined the county lieutenancy and commission of the peace for Surrey under James II 'when few honest men would accept it'.[57] Naturally Sir St John was full of righteous indignation. He went into print himself with a detailed defence, which pointed out, in relation to the jacobite slur, that he had been a deputy lieutenant and justice long before 1685, and had in fact resigned after refusing to give his consent to the removal of the penal laws against catholics.[58] Even though there were no repercussions the incident continued to rankle, and Sir St John went so far as to seek a legal remedy, to no avail.[59]

The Williamite victory at the Boyne in 1690, and the final capitulation of the jacobite commanders at Limerick the following year did not quell the Brodricks' discontents. Their estates in County Cork had suffered not only from the spoliation committed by jacobite troops and the rural bandits – 'tories' or 'rapparees' – who followed behind them, but also from the burdens imposed by the Williamite army, especially the Danish contingent, which made itself particularly obnoxious to the inhabitants.[60] Alan complained in November 1691

[55] *The Acts of James II's Irish Parliament of 1689*, ed. John Bergin and Andrew Lyell (Dublin, 2016), 99, 101, 148; 1690: SHC, 1248/1/252–2: Thomas to Sir St John, 16 Dec. 1690.

[56] *Journal of the Very Rev. Rowland Davies, LL.D., Dean of Ross* ... ed. Richard Caulfield (Camden Soc., ser 1, lxviii, 1857), 21, 28, 57, 60. The Thomas Brodrick mentioned in Dean Davies's diary as being in London (13) was almost certainly Sir St John's brother.

[57] [Bulkeley], *The Proposal for Sending Back the Nobility and Gentry of Ireland* ... (1690), 8–9, 19–20. Bulkeley has an entry in *DIB*, i, 979–80.

[58] *Animadversions on the Proposal for Sending Back the Nobility and Gentry of Ireland* ... (1690); *Sr St. John Brodrick's Vindication of Himself from the Aspersions Cast on Him in a Pamphlet Written by Sir Rich. Buckley* [sic] *Entituled, The Proposal for Sending Back the Nobility and Gentry of Ireland* ... (1690).

[59] SHC, 1248/1/241–2: Sir St John to ——, Mar. 1689/90; SHC, 1248/1/231: —— to Sir St John, Mar. 1689[/90].

[60] D.W. Hayton, 'The Williamite Revolution in Ireland, 1688–91', in *The Anglo-Dutch Moment: Essays on the Glorious Revolution and Its World Impact*, ed. Jonathan Israel (Cambridge, 1991), 207; and in general, Alan Smyth, 'The Social and Economic Impact of the Williamite War on Ireland, 1689–91', TCD PhD, 2012.

that 'our part of the Country is in the most miserable condition possible'.[61] Moreover, the articles of Galway and Limerick, which had enabled the conclusion of hostilities, were regarded by many Irish protestants as far too lenient: some, including the Brodricks, would have preferred a wholesale expropriation of catholic landowners and a serious attempt to plant the forfeited lands with a new generation of English settlers.[62]

It seems that the Brodricks envisaged nothing short of a new Munster plantation, from which they themselves would naturally benefit. In 1695, Thomas put himself at the head of a consortium of Cork gentry who made an unsuccessful bid to acquire the forfeited Muskerry estate for just such a purpose.[63] The family's attitude in this regard is clear from their own leasing policy: although Alan did have a handful of catholic tenants, the leases he issued included covenants specifying that subletting must be to protestants only.[64]

Dissatisfaction with the government's failure to treat the defeated catholics severely enough, or to take measures necessary to enable the Irish economy, and especially the landlord class, to recover from the after-effects of warfare, focused on the administration in Dublin Castle, especially the lords justices, Lord Coningsby, an English Court whig, and the Irish lord chancellor Sir Charles Porter, a tory. They were accused of corruption, and in Porter's case of favouring 'papists' and protestants who had collaborated with the jacobite regime. The Castle apartments were said to be 'crowded' with catholics, 'almost … as in Tyrconnell's time'.[65]

The upshot was that when the lord lieutenant, Lord Sydney, called his first Irish parliament in 1692, the first sitting since 1666 (if we exclude King James II's parliament), he was unable to get business done.[66] The house of commons in particular bared its teeth on the catholic question: the articles of Limerick were denounced; the government could make no progress with its indemnity bill; and resolutions were passed against admitting catholics to office and allowing them to bear arms. More specifically, a body of MPs, including many of those who had served on the unofficial Irish committee in London in 1689, launched a campaign to pursue grievances, expose wrongdoing and punish the individuals responsible. Charges of corruption were brought against the revenue commissioner William Culliford, and threats were made against Porter and Coningsby.

The same group of malcontents, who could perhaps be described as an 'opposition' party, took grave exception to the money bill which the Irish privy council had prepared in advance of the session. Strictly speaking, all Irish bills were prepared in the privy council in Dublin before being sent over to the English privy council for approval and, if necessary, amendment. Once returned, bills would be presented to the Irish parliament, which could do no more than pass or reject them. Such were the provisions of Poynings' Law of 1494. In practice the Irish parliament had evolved a system whereby one house or the other would

[61] Below, Letter 10.

[62] BL, Add. MS 78452: [John Evelyn, jr] to John Evelyn, sr, 18 June 1694; PRONI, T/3406/4/1: presentment of Co. Cork grand jury 1694 (original in University College Cork, Southwell MSS).

[63] BL, Add. MS 38153: [Sir Richard Cox] to [Edward Southwell], [July 1695]; HMC, *Buccleuch MSS*, ii, 276–7; Dickson, *Old World Colony*, 62; Walsh, *Making of the Irish Protestant Ascendancy*, 45–6.

[64] SHC, G145/box102/4: rent account book, 1712–28.

[65] TCD, MS 2008a/190: Bishop William King to James Bonnell, 4 Dec. 1691.

[66] For what follows see J.I. McGuire, 'The Irish Parliament of 1692' in *Penal Era and Golden Age: Essays in Irish History, 1690–1780*, ed. Thomas Bartlett and D.W. Hayton (Belfast, 1979), 1–31; Hayton, *Ruling Ireland*, 443–8; McGrath, *Constitution*, 74–90.

prepare 'heads' of a bill, which would then be sent to the Irish privy council to be turned into form and transmitted to England. The council continued to prepare some bills of its own, to begin a session, and especially a new parliament, but most legislation originated as 'heads', and, as with the English parliament, it was accepted that heads of money bills would begin life in the house of commons. The 'opposition' members now decided to claim a 'sole right' for the Commons to initiate all supply legislation. This was too much for Sydney, who prorogued the session. The parliament was then dissolved.

Sir St John and his two elder sons, Thomas and Alan, all belonged to the 'opposition' grouping in the 1692 parliament. The principal grievance which underlay the attacks on ministers, namely that the Castle administration had been soft on popery, resonated strongly with their concerns as landowners in a province where protestant landlords had peculiarly powerful reasons to worry about the claims of dispossessed catholic gentry, while at the same time itching to exploit the opportunity of further confiscations. Whether the Brodricks were committed to claims for a greater degree of parliamentary independence is much less clear. Even if, as Sydney claimed, the more excitable MPs talked about 'freeing themselves from the yoke of England and taking away Poynings' Law', this was not a realistic prospect.[67] But there was an advantage in withholding or restricting supply, by whatever means, in order to force regular parliamentary sessions, and this was a strategy that the Brodricks always endorsed. There would be no repeat of the mistake made by the Restoration Irish parliament, in granting Charles II 'additional' taxes for life to supplement the royal hereditary revenues.

All three Brodricks were prominent among opposition speakers in 1692 but they were not yet ranked among the leaders of what had become known as the 'country party'. None could be found among the MPs who petitioned the English house of commons early in 1693 requesting that action be taken 'for the security of the Protestant interest' in Ireland, and who were summoned to give evidence at Westminster about allegations of maladministration in Ireland: this was in any case largely an Ulster initiative.[68] Nor was any Brodrick singled out by the lord lieutenant for particular opprobrium as Sydney's parliamentary management collapsed.[69] And the notion of the 'sole right', which was to become a vitally important question in future parliamentary sessions, and with which Alan Brodrick would subsequently become identified, to his own discomfort, was evidently a spontaneous invention of another oppositionist, Robert Rochfort.[70] However, in the aftermath of the failed parliament of 1692 their political profile became much higher.

The key to their advancement was the replacement of Sydney as chief governor of Ireland in the summer of 1693 by a commission of lords justices. At first Porter had been included, but a second commission shortly afterwards dropped him and established a triumvirate in which the most significant figure was Henry Capel, Lord Capell, an English whig politician closely associated with the emerging whig junto. The strength of Lord Capell's political support in England, which became even more powerful over the following two years as the junto tightened their grip on government, enabled him to surmount the difficulties caused

[67] *CSP Dom.*, 1695 and Addenda, 213.

[68] *The Rawdon Papers …* ed. Edward Berwick (1819), 371–4; *CJ*, x, 823, 826–33; *The Parliamentary Diary of Narcissus Luttrell 1691–1693*, ed. Henry Horwitz (Oxford, 1972), 436–43.

[69] *CSP Dom.*, 1695 and Addenda, 209, 213; PRONI, D/638/18/2: Porter to Coningsby, 18 Nov. 1692.

[70] Below, Letter 74.

by chronic ill-health and establish a dominance over his colleagues which culminated in May 1695 in the dissolution of the commission of lords justices and Capell's appointment as lord deputy, with instructions to recall the Irish parliament.[71] He had already prepared the ground for a new general election by negotiating with some sections of the previous opposition, seeking to find a way in which a compromise could be agreed over the 'sole right' in return for concessions over the passage of 'good laws' to strengthen the protestant interest, principally by further penal legislation against the catholic interest, clerical and lay, and by a reconstruction of the Irish ministry.

The Brodricks were among those most intimately involved in these discussions. Sir St John sent the deputy a letter in August 1694, in which he reported canvassing the gentlemen of County Cork, Limerick and Kerry. He had found them willing to come into an agreement with government over money provided that Capell undertook to do 'those previous things … before the meeting of a parliament, which I mentioned to your lordship'. Sir St John also declared that he was speaking not just for himself but for 'our party', a reference which seems to have been to the Munster protestants in particular rather than the former 'country party' in general.[72] The emphasis on 'good laws', which also coloured Alan's opinions at this time, certainly fitted with the priorities of the Munstermen, as did the desire to find a way around the issue of the 'sole right' and not become embroiled in futile constitutional wrangling when it was clear that the security of Irish protestants depended on the maintenance of English military support.[73] As Capell's plans matured, the part played by the Brodricks in brokering the deal became more important and more obvious, facilitated by their deepening involvement with the whig junto in England. Alan and his brothers were already acquainted with Lord Keeper Somers through a Middle Temple connection, and in 1695 Alan was employed by the comptroller, Thomas Wharton, in a lawsuit involving an estate in Tipperary (although Wharton also had other clients in Ireland).[74] They received their rewards when Capell pushed through his ministerial reconstruction in the spring and early summer of 1695: Thomas became an Irish privy councillor, while Alan was promoted from the comparatively minor place of third serjeant to solicitor-general.

6

When Capell's Irish parliament met, in August 1695, Alan and Thomas acted in effect as Capell's parliamentary managers or 'undertakers' (the first example of Irish politicians fulfilling this role, 'undertaking' to secure the passage of the supply in return for privileged access to patronage and a voice in the making of policy). At this stage Thomas seems to have been the senior partner, taking responsibility for the supply bills and conducting a private correspondence with the English secretary of state, the duke of Shrewsbury, to report on the progress of the session.[75] Their nearest rival, Robert Rochfort, allegedly the author of

[71] *HL 1660–1715*, ii, 459–60. For what follows, see C.I. McGrath, 'English Ministers, Irish Politicians and the Making of a Parliamentary Settlement in Ireland, 1692–5', *EHR*, cxix (2004), 596–610.

[72] HMC, *Buccleuch MSS*, ii, 110, 115.

[73] See below, Letter 15.

[74] *LJ*, xi, 276; below, Letters 16, 17.

[75] McGrath, *Constitution*, 114; HMC, *Buccleuch MSS*, ii, 225–6, 228, 233–4, 248–51, 256, 259–64, 271–4, 281–2; BL, Add MS 28879, f. 157, J.F. to John Ellis, 28 Sept. 1695.

the concept of the 'sole right', had been advanced to attorney-general in Capell's reshuffle. He was then elected as speaker of the Commons, frustrating Thomas's ambitions in this respect, but his victory proved pyrrhic:[76] Rochfort was unable to exploit the advantages of the Speakership (which gave him, for example, control over the conduct of business in the House) to build up his own personal influence and standing, probably because he did not have close allies – family members, cronies, or dependants – to do the work in debates while he presided in the chair.

In taking on the leadership of the court or 'Castle' party, Thomas and Alan had eclipsed not only Rochfort and other opposition orators from 1692, but also their own father. During the run-up to the general election of 1695 some observers still considered Sir St John to be one of the moving spirits in Irish politics and to stand at the head of his family's interest, but when parliament met it was clear that the initiative had passed to his sons.[77] Ill-health was the prime cause of Sir St John's decline: the previous year gout had prompted the cancellation of one projected journey to Dublin, and soon his physical 'weakness' was causing his children grave concern, despite, or even because of, the difficult relationships he now had with them all.[78] It would not be long before he was confined to his residence in County Cork, where from the late 1690s onwards he spent his time meddling in his children's affairs, settling and resettling property, and squandering money on faddish 'improvements'. In this way he would linger on until January 1712, physically feeble but mentally active and as much of a thorn in everyone's side as he could contrive to be.

The 1695 session could generally be accounted a success. Parliament gave the king a supply; the issue of the 'sole right' was fudged, and the king's prerogative preserved, by the expedient of the privy council preparing in advance a 'short' money bill, which extended the additional excise duties for one year, and allowing the remainder of the supply to be granted by means of 'heads of bills'.[79] Some of the more ideologically committed of the former opposition, with political principles akin to 'country whigs' in England, had bridled at the compromise over the 'sole right' and had brought forward a radical and libertarian agenda, including a draft bill of rights, but their initiative had been forestalled.[80] Some of the 'good bills' the Brodricks had envisaged as necessary were brought to the statute book: an act to annul the attainders passed by the jacobite parliament in 1689, and a raft of penal laws including measures 'to disarm papists', to prevent catholics from sending their children abroad to be educated, and to banish the regular clergy.[81] An attempt to secure a toleration act for protestant nonconformists proved unsuccessful; predictably, for few MPs were sympathetic.[82] Nor did the parliament do much for the economic infrastructure of the country, since almost every measure introduced relating to agriculture, trade or industry

[76] BL, Add. MS 288879, f. 96: William Burgh to John Ellis, 27 Aug. 1695; f. 98, J.F. to same, 28 Aug. 1695.

[77] BL, Add. MS 38153, ff.12–13: [Sir Richard Cox] to [Edward Southwell], [July 1695].

[78] BL, Add. MS 15857, f.74: Sir St John Brodrick to [John Evelyn], 5 Apr. 1694; SHC, 1248/1/298–301: Katherine Whitfield to Sir St John, 14 Apr., 4 Aug., 1698.

[79] McGrath, *Constitution*, 101–17.

[80] Hayton, *Ruling Ireland*, 59–60.

[81] C.I. McGrath, 'Securing the Protestant Interest: The Origins and Purpose of the Penal Laws of 1695', *IHS*, xxx (1996–7), 25–46.

[82] *The Hamilton Manuscripts* ... ed. T.K. Lowry (Belfast, [1867]),152; J. S. Reid, *History of the Presbyterian Church in Ireland* (new edn, 3 vols, Belfast, 1867), ii, 453–6.

was lost, including a proposal for a bill to regulate the woollen manufacture (a staple of the Munster economy). But when Thomas Brodrick complained to Shrewsbury that the kingdom remained 'distracted and unsettled' his principal concern was not to put right the damage done to the Irish economy by the consequences of war; it was the necessity, as he and his family perceived, to safeguard the protestant interest and destroy the potential for a catholic resurgence.[83]

As far as Capell was concerned his 'cabinet council' had done well. There was only one episode that required him to explain himself to the king: the attempted impeachment of the lord chancellor, Porter, which had not only been an embarrassment in itself, as some senior office-holders were involved, but had also provoked an outburst of factional conflict that resulted in a second impeachment, stirred up by Porter's friends against Capell's chief secretary, Richard Aldworth. Capell's expressions of regret over the impeachment of Porter, and his claims that in these matters he had no control over the Brodrick brothers, may or may not have been genuine. As far as contemporary observers were concerned, responsibility for the campaign against the lord chancellor, and for attacks on Sydney and Coningsby, whose names were also dragged through the mud, lay firmly with Thomas and Alan, aided and abetted by Speaker Rochfort.[84] Opponents thought that it was all a ploy to have Porter dismissed so that Thomas could take his place.[85] More likely, the impeachment stemmed from simple vindictiveness, personal and partisan, for which the family were notorious.

Had there been an element of calculation, one possibility might be that the Brodricks were trying to rally those MPs of a whiggish cast of mind – which in the atmosphere of post-jacobite Ireland would have been a substantial majority in the Commons – by accusing Porter of closet Jacobitism. The chancellor had, after all, served King James in a private capacity early in his legal career, and had originally been made lord chancellor of Ireland in 1686 before eventually falling foul of Lord Tyrconnell.[86] If this had been the intention behind the impeachment the tactic did not pay off in the short term, though there may have been some long-term consequences. The emergence in the post-Revolution decades of a two-party system in Irish politics closely paralleling the English cannot be dated precisely, and in 1695 one important factor was still to make itself felt, namely the rise of a distinctively tory interest, sparked by the reaction of loyal anglicans against the threat they apprehended from presbyterians in Ulster. But the evidence of a surviving division-list relating to the votes for and against Porter suggests a strong correlation with the whig and tory parties as they existed a decade later; so it may be that the impeachment provided a catalyst.[87]

Alan and Thomas were now at the centre of political controversy in Ireland, and the objects of considerable personal animosity. The first occasion on which this became obvious was on Lord Capell's death in May 1696, when a dispute arose in the Irish privy council over whether the deputy had the power to nominate lords justices to succeed him, as Capell had attempted to do from his deathbed. Porter led the faction arguing that the council was

[83] HMC, *Buccleuch MSS*, ii, 251.

[84] PRONI, D/638/18/51: Porter to Capel, 22 Sept. 1695; Nottingham UL, Portland (Bentinck) MSS, PwA 252: Capel to Portland, 6 Nov. 1695; PwA 255: Capel to Portland, 17 Dec. 1695; Hayton, *Ruling Ireland*, 56–7.

[85] BL, Add. MS 28879, ff. 184–5: Arthur Bushe to John Ellis, 5 Oct. 1695.

[86] *DIB*, viii, 227.

[87] Hayton, *Ruling Ireland*, 58, 96–105.

legally entitled to elect, but it was clear that this constitutional principle took second place to the determination of the chancellor and his friends to thwart the Brodricks.[88]

To the mounting frustration of their rivals and enemies, Thomas and Alan seemed invulnerable, supported as they were by powerful figures in England. Thomas now had immediate access to King William's court, as one of the managers of the very extensive grants of Irish forfeited estates handed over by the king to his Dutch favourite Lord Albemarle, and to his English mistress Elizabeth Villiers, Lady Orkney.[89] To some extent this was a double-edged weapon, as it opened up for his enemies another possible angle of attack for Thomas's enemies. There was even a possibility that some evidence of wrongdoing against both brothers might be rooted out from investigations into the administration of the charity school which Lady Orkney established at Midleton, and for which Thomas and Alan acted as trustees.

The continued whig complexion of the government in Dublin Castle protected the Brodricks from their political foes. By the time the 1695 parliament resumed in August 1697, the chief governorship was in commission again and the lords justices were the veteran Huguenot military commander Lord Galway, the junto nominee Lord Winchester, and Edward, Lord Villiers, who happened to be Lady Orkney's brother. Just as important was the appointment as Irish lord chancellor of an English whig, John Methuen, regarded as a reliable junto man.[90] Despite some early problems, when Winchester fell briefly under the influence of the Irish chancellor of the exchequer, the Dublin barrister Philip Savage, the lords justices followed Lord Capell's political strategy and retained the 'Brodericians' as their parliamentary managers, even though Galway considered the brothers to be '*des gens assez difficile*'.[91]

Savage, a politician every bit as ambitious as Thomas or Alan, was an inveterate intriguer: he had defended Lord Chancellor Porter in 1695, but according to Alan Brodrick had only done so because he was a 'creature' of Thomas Wharton and hoped to engineer Capell's dismissal.[92] Savage now wormed his way into Winchester's confidence, and from what he assumed was a position of safety launched attacks on the Brodricks in the Irish privy council and in the house of commons, where he tried to evict them from the chairmanship of the committees of privileges and supply. It took all Methuen's persuasive talents to effect a compromise, whereby Alan relinquished the chair of the committee of privileges but took his brother's place on supply, arguably the more important of the two. A key factor in both Savage's original scheme and Methuen's response was the attitude of the 'country whig' element in the Commons, men who had advocated the 'sole right' in 1692, had been unhappy at the compromise of 1695, and had backed various measures in that session to restrict the power of the executive and defend the liberties of the subject. Because Methuen himself shared an attachment to these principles and was particularly close to a leading 'true Whig' in Ireland, Robert Molesworth, he was able to bring those who were suspicious of the Brodricks back into the government fold.[93]

[88] Hayton, *Ruling Ireland*, 61.

[89] Walsh, *Making of the Irish Protestant Ascendancy*, 47.

[90] *HC 1690–1715*, iv, 802.

[91] *HC 1690–1715*, v, 187; *HL 1660–1715*, iv, 181; HMC, *Buccleuch MSS*, ii, 551, 567.

[92] Below, Letter 19.

[93] HMC, *Buccleuch MSS*, 551, 567; Hayton, *Ruling Ireland*, 63–4; *HC 1690–1715*, iv, 802–3, 829–30.

In this session Alan and Thomas seem again to have pursued a strongly anti-catholic policy. This had two elements: the first and most important was to secure the forfeiture of as much property as possible from jacobite families, whether they had been in arms against King William in 1689–91 or had subsequently sought refuge abroad; the second to extend the penal laws excluding catholics from participation in political and economic activity and diminishing the presence in Ireland of the catholic church and clergy. The Irish parliament had yet to ratify the Articles of Limerick, and when it finally did so, by means of a bill prepared in the Irish privy council and passed in 1697, the terms were deliberately contrived to be as unfavourable as possible to the catholic lobby, so much so that a significant opposition arose in the house of lords, which protested against the passage of the bill as inconsistent with King William's honour.[94] Contemporaries attributed the success of the bill largely to the efforts of the Brodricks,[95] and their hands can also be detected in the three major penal laws added to the statute book in 1697, all of which originated in the Irish privy council, not to mention several unsuccessful bills, most obviously the sets of 'heads' designed to promote further protestant settlement, and 'to prevent Protestants turning papists, and converts from being reconciled to the Church of Rome' both of which Thomas Brodrick had sponsored.[96]

Despite the belief of their political opponents that the tide had turned, the Brodricks' political position seemed secure at the end of the 1697 parliamentary session.[97] But it was soon to come under a very serious threat; not from within Ireland, but from England. On the one hand the junto whig ministry was being forced increasingly onto the defensive by a resurgent tory interest, now headed by two former whigs, Paul Foley and Robert Harley, who combined their interest with the tory chieftains to form a 'new country party'. Foley and Harley mounted a campaign against the ministers over the maintenance of a standing army after the conclusion of the Treaty of Rijswijk, and, having achieved some success in the English general election of 1698, opened up a second front on the issue of ministerial corruption, which was so successful that by the end of 1699 they had forced all the members of the junto out of office.

At the same time, the parliamentary tactics followed by the 'new country party' opposition created a major crisis in Anglo-Irish relations in 1699. Tories at Westminster obtained a statutory restriction on Irish woollen imports (which was expected to have a significant negative impact on the Munster economy), and then turned their attention to the question of the Irish forfeited estates, as a prime example of the way in which whig ministers and courtiers had enriched themselves at the expense of the English taxpayer, who, it was argued, had borne the cost of the defeat of James II and the restoration of the protestant establishment. In 1699, an English act of parliament set up a commission of inquiry to report on the extent of the forfeitures and the way they had been administered. This had ominous implications for Thomas Brodrick. Moreover, the commissioners included several

[94]J.G. Simms, *War and Politics in Ireland, 1649–1730*, ed. David Hayton and Gerard O'Brien (1986), 213–14; Wouter Troost, 'William III and the Treaty of Limerick (1691–1697): A Study of His Irish Policy', Leiden D Lett, 1983, 168–83.

[95]BL, Add. MS 70303: newsletter, 25 Sept. 1697.

[96]James Kelly, 'Sustaining a Confessional State: The Irish Parliament and Catholicism' in *The Eighteenth-century Composite State: Representative Institutions in Ireland and Europe, 1689–1800*, ed. D.W. Hayton, James Kelly and John Bergin (Basingstoke, 2010), 49–51; ILD.

[97]HMC, *Portland MSS*, iii, 586.

individuals of whom the Brodricks had every right to be suspicious: the earl of Drogheda, who had nursed an enmity to them ever since the conflict over the appointment of lords justices in 1696, Sir Richard Levinge, the Speaker of the 1692 parliament, who had been a thorn in their side in the 1698–9 parliamentary session in Ireland, and Sir Francis Brewster, a quondam ally whom they now considered an enemy.[98]

The problems faced by the Brodricks were twofold: first there was the danger that Thomas's agency for Lord Albemarle and Lady Orkney would expose him to public and parliamentary opprobrium; and second, any conflict between the English and Irish parliaments would naturally place the ministry's Irish 'undertakers' in a delicate position. Relations were already difficult: the claim of the English house of lords to exercise an appellate jurisdiction over Irish causes, superior to that of the Irish house of lords, had produced tension, and a previous attempt by the English woollen lobby to secure legislative restrictions over Irish imports, in 1697–8, had prompted John Locke's Irish friend William Molyneux to publish his argument for constitutional autonomy, *The Case of Ireland Being Bound by Acts of Parliament in England, Stated* ..., which the English house of commons declared to be 'of dangerous consequence'.[99]

When the commissioners of inquiry reported in December 1699, Thomas's name did indeed appear, as having acted as an agent for Albemarle, and having assisted a cartel headed by William Conolly to purchase forfeited estates at a low price; there was also a suggestion that Thomas had abused his position as a privy councillor.[100] Alan was furious, and blamed the commissioners as a body, taking no notice of the fact that Levinge, Brewster and the earl of Drogheda had publicly dissented from the decision to include Lady Orkney's grant in the report (because the lands concerned came from James II's private estate).[101] Worse was to come in 1700 with the passage of an act for the resumption of the forfeitures and their resale by trustees for the benefit of the English treasury, an English intervention in Irish affairs which was potentially even more damaging to the protestant propertied elite than the Woollen Act had been.

The Brodricks now had to pick their way even more carefully: the angry response from Irish protestants, including many MPs who had supported the administration in 1695–9, could easily shade off into reiterations of the argument made by Molyneux, that Ireland should not be governed by laws made by a parliament which Irishmen had no part in electing. In general, those objecting to the resumption were careful not to push their arguments so far, though there were occasional indiscretions – including, to the Brodricks' embarrassment, a printed attack on the trustees published by Sir St John, who claimed that he was himself 'a sufferer by the late bill for resumption' and expressed his outrage that Ireland should be 'bound by a law made by persons never chosen to represent her'.[102] It

[98]Below, Letters 20–21; McGrath, *Constitution*, 149; Hayton, *Ruling Ireland*, 73–4.

[99]Hayton, *Ruling Ireland*, 68.

[100]*The Report Made to the Honourable House of Commons, Decemb. 15 1699. By the Commissioners Appointed to Enquire into the Forfeited Estates of Ireland* (1700), 11, 24; Walsh, *Making of the Irish Protestant Ascendancy*, 48–9.

[101]'The Memorial of the Earl of Drogheda, Sir Francis Brewster and Sir Richard Leving ...', in *A Collection of State Tracts, Publish'd on Occasion of the Late Revolution of 1688, and during the Reign of William III* ... (3 vols, 1705–7), ii, 709–22; J.G. Simms, *The Williamite Comnfiscation in Ireland 1690–1703* (1956), 98–109; below, Letter 25.

[102]Sir St John Brodrick, *Short Remarks upon the Late Act of Resumption of the Irish Forfeitures and upon the Manner of Putting That Act in Execution* (1701), 3.

was comments of this kind that enabled English writers like the trustee John Trenchard to allege that the Irish were aiming at independence. This in turn opened the way for a vulgarisation of the public debate, with English sneers at 'Irish understandings' and the extension to Irish protestants of the derogatory English stereotyping that had previously been reserved for Irish catholics.[103]

Unlike their father, Thomas and Alan orchestrated their response carefully. Involvement in the 'paper war' over the resumption was likely to be more risky than profitable, and Thomas was fortunate, given his high profile, that his name was rarely mentioned by the rival sets of pamphleteers.[104] But passivity was not an option. Public anger in Ireland was not to be assuaged: it reached an even higher pitch when the trustees began their work in Dublin, with accusations flying against them of corruption and pro-catholic bias. Personal attacks were also being made by the trustees on the Brodricks themselves, and on close political allies like William Conolly,[105] which provided an additional spur to action, if one was needed. Alan, who was always prone to over-dramatise, characterised the trustees as the 'mortal enemies' of Ireland. So, from a combination of political necessity – that they should appear to be in the forefront of the popular reaction – and private outrage, the Brodricks set about organising a counter attack: a country-wide petition to the king from his loyal protestant subjects in Ireland.

Involvement in the so-called 'national remonstrance' of December 1701, a set of addresses to the king from each Irish county, was not without its dangers.[106] Alan and Thomas had been able to survive the fall of the junto in 1700 and the appointment of a tory ministry in England for the simple reason that the incoming chief governor of Ireland, this time a lord lieutenant, was not the duke of Ormond, who had made a return to the Irish political scene in 1697 and was accounted the head of the tory interest in Ireland, but their old family friend Laurence Hyde, earl of Rochester. In later years it would be a commonplace in Irish whig circles that Rochester had been personally responsible for introducing the virus of party into Ireland: it was said that before his arrival the only distinction had been between protestant and papist; afterwards Irishmen had been divided into whigs and tories.[107] But although Rochester did advance a few tories and high churchmen, he made no significant changes to the Castle administration and seems to have looked for a balance of opinions. Alan could not complain at the way Rochester behaved towards him and indeed felt obliged to 'pay all duty and gratitude for the great favour my Lord hath done me'.[108] In any case, the English ministers unwillingness to recall the Irish parliament – understandable given the current state of Anglo-Irish relations – avoided a choice between retaining office and maintaining his reputation as a man of 'revolution principles'.

[103]See, for example, [John Trenchard], *A Letter from a Souldier to the Commons of England* … (1702); *The Several Addresses of Some Irish Folks to the King and the House of Commons* [1702].

[104]For two examples, see *A Letter to a Member of Parliament Relating to the Irish Forfeitures* (1701), 14; John, Lord Somers, *Jus Regium; or, The King's Right to Grant Forfeitures, and Other Revenues of the Crown, Fully Set Forth and Trac'd from the Beginning* … (1701), 50.

[105]Walsh, *Making of the Irish Protestant Ascendancy*, 51–60.

[106]For the remonstrance, see Simms, *Williamite Confiscation*, 125-6; Hayton, *Ruling Ireland*, 82–3.

[107]See, for example, Centre for Kentish Studies, U1590/O141/11: Henry Maxwell to [James Stanhope], 23 Nov. 1703, 25 Mar. 1705, 6 Dec. 1713 [*recte* 6 Jan. 1714].

[108]Below, Letter 59.

Alan's involvement in the 'national remonstrance' could still have made his position a difficult one. He was involved in planning and co-ordinating the addresses, though he was at pains to explain to St John II, in an account that was presumably intended for wider circulation, that the objectionable aspects of the enterprise had originated with others. Nor is it clear whether or not he signed the Cork address – probably not, for he felt obliged to deny a rumour that he had struck his name out after having signed, and instead insisted that he had signed 'the general address' to the lords justices. This explanation was not communicated to the English house of commons, which debated the remonstrance in February 1702 and cross-examined Lord Abercorn and James Topham, MP [I], who were depicted as the principal organisers.[109]

King William's death in March 1702 and the accession of Queen Anne put Alan firmly on the spot. While the king lived, there was a possibility of a tack back towards the whigs, but Anne made it clear from the outset that her administration would have a strongly tory complexion. For the time being, Rochester remained as lord lieutenant. Alan was sanguine about his own prospects: he wrote to St John in London to assure him that while he would never decline the queen's service:

> if such alterations are worth making here, as with you, I do not think myself of long continuance; nor shall be surprised or displeased at being put out of an employ which I neither got into nor can hold on any terms but what consist with the good of the English interest of this kingdom.[110]

As Rochester did not request his resignation, Alan did not resign, though he clearly became increasingly uncomfortable. In January 1703, the lords justices deputising for Rochester in the lord lieutenant's absence in England, summoned the law officers to seek their advice on when a new Irish parliament should be called and the preparations to be made for it (the previous parliament having been dissolved on the death of the sovereign). Alan (and not the attorney-general, Rochfort, who might have been expected to say something about the 'sole right' that he had supposedly invented), was the only individual present who was against the privy council preparing a money bill in advance. He argued on grounds of political expediency that responsibility for supply should be left to the house of commons, given the discontent in country against the forfeiture trustees, which was accentuated by a short-term economic depression.[111]

7

The day that the Brodricks had long feared dawned in February 1703, when Rochester was dismissed and replaced by the duke of Ormond. The Irish administration immediately took on a more strikingly tory colouring, as John Methuen was replaced as lord chancellor

[109]Below, Letters 51–3, 58; *CJ*, xiii, 718, 743–6; *The Parliamentary Diary of Sir Richard Cocks, 1698–1702*, ed. D.W. Hayton (Oxford, 1996), 214–16.

[110]Below, Letter 59.

[111]BL, Add. MS 9715, ff. 39–40: Thomas Keightley and Lord Mountalexander to Rochester, 30 Jan. 1702/3.

by Ormond's client, Sir Richard Cox, himself a Corkman and an opponent of the Brodrick interest in the county.[112] Alan kept his place as solicitor-general, having done nothing before Ormond's parliament met in the autumn of 1703 that could have justified his removal. However, he cut an increasingly isolated figure in the administration, in which his bitterest political enemies now enjoyed public recognition and private influence, especially Philip Savage and Robert Rochfort (whose refusal to condemn the forfeiture trustees had provoked a final break with the Brodricks).[113]

Political divisions in protestant Ireland were now settling into a two-party system on English lines, and Alan and Thomas found themselves at the head of a faction which, though it was sometimes referred to in personal terms ('the Brodericians'), was more likely to be considered as the Irish equivalent of the whig junto.[114] The Brodricks were at this point the undisputed leaders of Irish whiggery, ably supported in the Irish house of commons by a rising generation of politicians, which included their ally in the forfeitures campaign, William Conolly, the recorder of Dublin, John Forster, and other up-and-coming lawyers like William Neave and George Gore.

The preparations for the calling of an Irish parliament in 1703 were bound to create problems, given Alan's stated position on the issue of supply, and Ormond's determination to secure the longest possible grant of 'additional duties' for the queen. In the event Alan played his hand skilfully. In return for vague, and almost certainly disingenuous, promises on his part to work towards 'promoting her majesty's affairs and carrying all with moderation and temper', he secured Ormond's recommendation for the Commons Speakership, ahead of Rochfort, whom the lord lieutenant persuaded to step aside.[115] At the same time, Alan was not a party to the pre-sessional planning by Ormond's parliamentary managers, and their decision to ask for what amounted to a three-year supply, by proposing that parliament pay the debts incurred by treasury in the absence of a parliament since 1699 and support the establishment for two more years. At any rate, he did not consider himself bound by it. While the Commons waived the 'sole right' claim and agreed to the government's 'short' money bill, which had been prepared by the privy council along the lines of the constitutional fudge accepted by Capell in 1695, the government's advance towards a more substantial supply measure was subjected to guerrilla attack in the accounts committee, chaired by Alan's brother-in-law and close political associate Laurence Clayton, and then a frontal assault in the crucial debates on 13 and 14 October in the committee of supply, when Alan himself, seconded by his brother Thomas, led demands to restrict the grant of additional duties to a single year, in a display of party 'violence' that outraged Ormond's friends.[116] The attempt was unsuccessful, but the fact that it had been made at all was an embarrassment to the lord lieutenant.

The supply debate may have been the most flagrant instance of Alan having broken his promise to Ormond, but it was not by any means the only example. One tory MP reported to an English correspondent that from the very beginning of the session 'the Speaker and

[112] For Cox, see *DIB*, ii, 937–8.

[113] *CSP Dom.*, 1703–4, 27.

[114] HMC, *Ormonde MSS*, viii, p.xliii; Hayton, *Ruling Ireland*, 89–90.

[115] McGrath, *Constitution*, 161.

[116] McGrath, *Constitution*, 163–9; BL, Add. MS 28891, f. 139: Benjamin Chetwood to John Ellis, 17 Oct. 1703.

his party' had 'given all possible opposition to the court'.[117] The inquiries made by the committee of accounts offered another series of insults to the viceroy, culminating in the denunciation of the deputy vice-treasurer, Sir William Robinson, another of Ormond's clients, who was imprisoned in Dublin Castle on the orders of the Commons for allegedly misrepresenting the state of the public debts.[118] But while tories considered the Brodricks' behaviour as merely the latest manifestation of an addiction to partisan 'violence', there was also a strategic rationale. Doubtless an element of factional vindictiveness was present in their pursuit of Robinson, and of the former trustee, the tory MP Francis Annesley, who was expelled from the House. On the other hand, seeking to expose corruption in government, and giving a parliamentary expression to the simmering resentment at the forfeitures resumption, presented the Brodricks as champions of the 'public interest' and conversely put government spokesmen on the defensive.

Despite the increasing reality of whig and tory party divisions, many contemporaries continued to talk of the two sides in the Irish parliament as the 'court' and the 'country',[119] and to represent 'the country' was an obvious means of maximising support, and in particular of copper-fastening the allegiance of 'country whigs' like Robert Molesworth who had been suspicious of the Brodricks' links to the whig administrations of 1695–9. Thus Alan and Thomas gave strong support to a 'representation' of grievances, highlighting Ireland's economic difficulties, and pleading for the kingdom to be included in the current negotiations for an Anglo-Scottish union, an initiative which had the added advantage of embarrassing Ormond and his English cabinet colleagues.[120] And in a different way, Thomas's persistent efforts to promote the idea that there was still a serious catholic threat to the protestant establishment, which extended to embroidering, if not entirely manufacturing, reports of popish conspiracies, served an additional purpose in rallying Irish MPs to what was fast becoming a distinctively whiggish cause.[121] Irish tories as a body were not really 'soft' on popery, or sympathetic to the jacobite cause; nevertheless, the excesses of their English counterparts made it easy to paint them as less than wholly committed to 'revolution principles' and to the maintenance of the Williamite settlement.

If the 'Orange card' seemed to be a trump in the hands of the whigs, the tories thought they had one of their own in the shape of their self-definition as the 'Church party'. In the same way that an overwhelming majority of Irish MPs had a stake in defending the

[117]BL, Add. MS 28891, ff. 185, 218: William Steuart to John Ellis, 9, 27 Nov. 1703. Alan's conduct during this session is analysed in C.I. McGrath, 'Alan Brodrick and the Speakership of the Irish House of Commons, 1703–4' in *People, Politics and Power: Essays in Irish History 1650–1850 in Honour of James I. McGuire,* ed. James Kelly, John McCafferty and C.I. McGrath (Dublin, 2009), 70–93.

[118]Below, p. 161. For Robinson, see *DIB*, viii, 552–3.

[119]See, for example, PRONI, T/2812/9/34: Toby Caulfield to Kean O'Hara, 2 Nov. 1703. The terms whig and tory were also being used, but predominantly by tories: see BL, Add. MS 9712, f. 51: Robert Echlin to Edward Southwell, 23 Nov. 1703.

[120]BL, Add. MS 29589, f. 308: Sir Richard Cox to Lord Nottingham, 6 Nov. 1703; D.W. Hayton, 'Ideas of Union in Anglo-Irish Political Discourse, 1692–1720: Meaning and Use' in *Political Discourse in Seventeenth- and Eighteenth-century Ireland,* ed. D.G. Boyce, R.R. Eccleshall and Vincent Geoghegan (2001), 157–60; C.I. McGrath, 'The "Union" Representation of 1703 in the Irish House of Commons: A Case of Mistaken Identity', *ECI*, xxiii (2008), 11–35.

[121]SHC, 1248/2/76–7: statement by Thomas Brodrick of what took place in the house of commons and privy council in relation to tories in Co. Limerick, 12 Jan.1703/4; Longleat House, Thynne MSS, 15, f. 286: Edward Southwell to Lord Weymouth, 17 Jan. 1703/4; NLI, MS 991, pp. 254–5: same to Nottingham, 18 Jan. 1713–14.

revolution and supported further penal laws against catholics, parliamentary opinion was united against the perceived threat to the established church from the growing number of presbyterians in Ulster. The concentration of protestant dissent in the north-east of the country had given rise to friction with the established church in the early 1690s, but the flood of immigrants from western Scotland into Ulster between 1694 and 1697 ratcheted up tensions to an unprecedented degree. Churchmen, both clerical and lay, looked to the events of 1689–90 in Scotland, which had seen the re-establishment of presbyterian control of the Kirk and the marginalisation of episcopalianism. In their darkest moments they feared that the same fate might await them. The General Synod of Ulster, the governing body of Ulster presbyterianism, appeared to represent a 'state within a state', and any local incident which seemed to exemplify aggressive tendencies within the synod, such as the attempt to set up a new (and therefore illegal) congregation at Drogheda in County Louth in 1708, would be magnified and publicised.[122]

Tories in the Irish house of commons were quick to raise the presbyterian question when under pressure in the accounts committee in October 1703, refocusing the committee's scrutiny of civil list pensions on to the '*regium donum*', the annual sum granted by the crown to the General Synod for stipends to presbyterian ministers. Their florid denunciations of presbyterian expansionism aroused a muted response from leading whigs, and those who did defend the grant only felt able to do so half-heartedly: Laurence Clayton said that he would 'give a negative because of the posture of affairs in Europe', which required protestant unity at home, and neither Alan nor Thomas Brodrick appears to have said anything at all.[123] Something similar happened later in the session, when the bill 'to prevent the further growth of popery', a landmark measure in the erection of the 18th-century penal code, returned from England with the addition of a clause imposing a sacramental test on all holders of crown and municipal office, a test that Ulster presbyterians, who abominated the practice of occasional conformity, could never take. For a majority in both houses of parliament there could be no question of losing such a bill for the sake of the dissenters, and Alan Brodrick in particular responded very carefully, wishing neither to endorse publicly the imposition of the test, nor to take up too robustly the cause of Ulster presbyterians. The arguments he and his friends laid against the test related to the supposed constitutional impropriety in the manner of its imposition and the risk of creating divisions among protestants at a critical time in domestic and international affairs.[124]

Not surprisingly, Alan's behaviour in the Speaker's chair brought repercussions. tory resentment was such that a cabal of MPs meeting in the Fleece Tavern in Dublin devised a plan to avoid paying the Speaker the customary end-of-session compliment of a vote of thanks from the House.[125] Ormond and his closest advisers were determined to be done with him, but given the difficult session they had undergone, and the financial necessity for

[122]Raymond Gillespie, 'The Presbyterian Revolution in Ulster, 1660–1690' in *Studies in Church History*, xxv: *The Churches, Ireland, and the Irish*, ed. W.J. Sheils and Diana Wood (Oxford,1989), 168–70; S.J. Connolly, *Religion, Law and Power. The Making of Protestant Ireland 1660–1760* (Oxford, 1992), 79–80, 159–71; Phil Kilroy, *Protestant Dissent and Controversy in Ireland 1660–1714* (Cork, 1994), chs.7–8.

[123]D.W. Hayton, 'A Debate in the Irish House of Commons in 1703: A Whiff of Tory Grapeshot', *Parliamentary History*, x (1991), 157–62 (printing notes on the debate in Alan's hand in SHC, 1248/4/360).

[124]J.G. Simms, 'The Making of a Penal Law (2 Anne, c. 6), 1703–4', *IHS*, xii (1960–1), 105–18; BL, Add. MS 9715, ff. 66–70: memorandum on the conduct of the Speaker, c.1704.

[125]SHC 1248/9/88: notes by Alan I, [c.Feb.1704].

parliament to meet again in the spring of 1705, had to proceed carefully. Both Alan and Thomas were in England in the summer of 1704 (Thomas to enjoy the horse-racing at Newmarket) and Alan in particular conducted himself with 'greater mettle and assurance than at any time heretofore', being received politely by the queen and pluming himself on his apparent immunity from tory reprisals.[126] But in August Ormond came to a decision. Alan was dismissed as solicitor-general, his place being taken by Sir Richard Levinge, and the lord lieutenant resolved to see out the next session with the Speaker in open opposition.[127]

This political drama took place against a background of domestic tragedy. Alan's wife, Lucy, had been taken ill in 1702, after the birth of her second child, a boy named after his father. Despite going to Bath with her husband in an effort to restore her health, she died the following year.[128] Alan was heartbroken. He was, however, by nature uxorious, and, as ever, keenly aware of the material advantages of matrimony. By June 1707 he was being spoken of as the likely husband of the dowager Lady Shelburne,[129] and although this match did not come off, he was not to remain unmarried for long. After his eldest son, St John III, married Anne Hill of Hillsborough, County Down, in 1710, Alan soon became close to her widowed mother, and in due course fastened the family connection by marrying the elder Mrs Hill.

At first Alan's loss of office in 1704 proved a serious political setback for the family. Although supporters of the Brodricks were in a bullish mood before parliament reassembled in February 1705 they were unable to make good the boasts that they would persuade the Commons to address for Alan's reinstatement.[130] In fact the session was a success for Ormond's tory managers, who secured a supply for two more years, and avoided embarrassments: the principal hope of the opposition, that the English privy council might amend the money bill and therefore give them an occasion for 'patriotic' outrage, went unfulfilled.[131]

But while Ormond's administration was secure in Ireland, and the Brodricks were reduced to trying to stir up discontent in the privy council and through local grand juries, over spurious grievances and imaginary conspiracies,[132] the pendulum was swinging in English politics. The resignation of Lord Nottingham, and the removal of other high tories in April 1704 left the ministry of the 'duumvirs', Lord Treasurer Godolphin and the duke of Marlborough, reliant on an uneasy coalition of moderate tories, headed by Robert Harley, and 'Lord Treasurer's Whigs', buttressed by placemen and other court dependants. The 1705 general election in England weakened the tory party and enhanced the influence of the whig junto, who began to press for a greater share in government. The appointment of a whig, William Cowper, as lord keeper (later lord chancellor) in 1705 was followed by an even more significant gain in December 1706 when Marlborough's son-in-law, the young earl of Sunderland, himself a member of the junto, was made secretary of state for the northern department.

[126] HMC, *Ormonde MSS*, n.s., viii, 93–4, 106.

[127] HMC, *Ormonde MSS*, n.s., viii, 102–3, 113–14,122.

[128] BL, Add.MS 37531, f. 38: lords justices to Rochester, 11 Aug. 1702.

[129] NLI, MS 41508/22: Catherine O'Brien to Jane Bonnell, 30 June 1707.

[130] HMC, *Ormonde MSS*, n.s. viii, 137.

[131] McGrath, *Constitution*, 183–90.

[132] HMC, *Ormonde MSS*, n.s. viii, 199, 201–2.

With every whig advance the position of the Harleyites became weaker, and the junto's increasing influence over Godolphin encouraged them to make greater and greater demands. They were known to have their eyes on the Irish viceroyalty, on behalf of Thomas (now Lord) Wharton, who had a connection by marriage in Ireland and a long-standing ambition to preside at Dublin Castle. This boded well for the Brodricks, as Thomas, whose career ambitions were increasingly focused in England, had established a close relationship with Wharton, enough for him to be appointed in 1706 as comptroller of the salt duties in England, one of the earliest whig promotions after the reconstruction of Godolphin's ministry.[133]

Wharton evidently considered his own appointment as lord lieutenant a formality,[134] but he was to be disappointed. Ormond's eventual replacement, named in April 1707, was the earl of Pembroke, that rarity in early 18th-century English politics, a non-partisan politician. A man of mild tory sympathies, Pembroke was capable of working with any administration.[135] The junto were unhappy with his appointment, even though indications were made of a modest change of direction in the ministry's Irish policy. There were changes in personnel, the most important of which were the replacement of Cox as lord chancellor by an English whig, Richard Freeman, and the restoration of Alan Brodrick to office, this time as attorney-general; promises were made that Pembroke would attempt to repeal the test; and a staunch, if unsophisticated, junto follower, George Dodington, was made chief secretary.[136]

The Brodricks shared the junto's dissatisfaction: Alan's letters show that he wanted more thorough-going changes, a complete clear-out of the old Irish ministry, in fact. 'There will be lesse satisfaction then were to be wished if the Chariot keep the same track, and only changes the Driver.'[137] He also hoped for a new election, which was not forthcoming.[138] Pembroke's coolly reserved demeanour, and studied neutrality in his relations with Irish politicians, made for an unsatisfactory beginning.[139] Privately, the Brodricks were struck by the hammer-blow of another family bereavement. The death of St John II, in London in June 1707, must have been of particular significance, as he was the first of the brothers to die.

It says much for the resolve of both Alan and Thomas, and their dedication to the pursuit of political power, that they were not put out of their stride. They strove, with the aid of Dodington, to monopolise the viceroy's attention, and to persuade him that they, rather than the old tory managers, could deliver the supply that Pembroke wanted.[140] The problem was that the viceroy was asking for a grant of a further two years. This was something Alan felt that he could not himself propose, being compromised by previous resistance to similar demands from Ormond; nor was it something his followers would accept, as for many

[133] *HC 1690–1715*, iii, 336; vi, 842; *HL 1660–1715*, iv, 904–5.

[134] Below, Letter 129.

[135] Geoffrey Holmes, *British Politics in the Age of Anne* (1967), 253; *HL 1660–1715*, iii, 336–52.

[136] Christ Church, Oxford, Wake MSS, Epist. xvii, f. 165: White Kennett to [Bishop Wake], 17 Apr. 1707; BL, Add. MS 9710, f. 65: Nicholas Price to Edward Southwell, 20 Aug. 1707; TNA, SP 63/366, f. 97: Dodington to Sunderland, 8 Oct. 1707.

[137] Below, Letter 136.

[138] Below, Letter 132.

[139] TCD, MS 750 (3), 143: Archbishop King to Francis Annesley, 16 Aug. 1707.

[140] BL, Add. MS 9710, f. 63: Nicholas Price to Edward Southwell, 4 July 1707; Add. MS 9715, ff. 170, 181: Anderson Saunders to same, 5, 24 July 1707.

of them one-year grants constituted a 'fixed principle'. After prolonged negotiations, the Brodricks and their friends settled on a year and three quarters, which saved face and satisfied the lord lieutenant.[141] The settlement did not satisfy all whigs, however, and the Speaker found himself criticized in the Commons for 'quitting the sole right, and his principle of one year'.[142]

Once the thorny matter of the supply was out of the way, things went more smoothly. Pembroke tentatively suggested a repeal of the test, but the idea was rejected on a Commons vote, with two thirds of those present voting against.[143] The whigs, and more particularly the Brodricks, had again avoided embarrassment. Then, as the session entered its closing stages, junto pressure on Godolphin began to make itself felt in Ireland. Godolphin himself told Lord Chancellor Cowper that there would be soon be more 'encouragements' to Irish whigs, including preferments, 'where safe', and it was noted in Dublin that Pembroke was openly showing more favour to the whigs.[144]

This was not enough to save his viceroyalty, however. In the winter following his return to England the tensions within the Godolphin-Marlborough ministry reached crisis point, and with the fall of Robert Harley in February 1708, the lord treasurer was no longer able to resist the junto's demand for Wharton to be given the Irish lord lieutenancy, something which had loomed increasingly large in their calculations throughout the previous year.[145] Godolphin managed to postpone the decision as long as he could, but by December 1708 further foot-dragging was impossible, and Wharton secured the prize he had been seeking for over a decade.

For Alan and Thomas, Wharton's appointment opened a mouth-watering prospect. Thomas had already been translated to a more lucrative government office in England, as joint comptroller of army accounts, and presumably the family hoped for more patronage in the months to come. Alan was therefore much more indulgent of Wharton than he had been of previous viceroys. He made no complaints at the continuation of tories in office, despite his previous demands, under Pembroke, for a wholesale purge.[146] From the first, Alan's prime concern was to do what he could to make Wharton's tenure of office as smooth as possible, even if that meant sacrificing principles or letting down allies.

One likely obstacle was the lord lieutenant's commitment to repealing the test. The Brodricks had never been among the more enthusiastic advocates of the interests of protestant dissenters and were keenly aware of the unpopularity of repeal in the Irish house of

[141] McGrath, *Constitution*, 195–203; HMC, *Ormonde MSS*, n.s., viii, 302–3.

[142] McGrath, *Constitution*, 208.

[143] BL, Add. MS 9715, ff. 163, 168, 170: Anderson Saunders to Edward Southwell, 10 June, 1, 5 July 1707; Leicestershire, Leicester and Rutland Record Office, Finch papers, DG7: same to [same], 10 July 1707; HMC, *Ormonde MSS*, n.s., viii, 303–5.

[144] William Coxe, *Memoirs of John, Duke of Marlborough* (6 vols, 1820), iii, 365; H.L. Snyder, 'The Formulation of Foreign and Domestic Policy in the Reign of Queen Anne: Memoranda by Lord Chancellor Cowper of Conversations with Lord Treasurer Godolphin', *Historical Journal*, xi (1968), 157, 160; BL, Add. MS 9715, f. 225: Anderson Saunders to [Edward Southwell], 4 Nov.1707.

[145] *The Private Correspondence of Sarah, Duchess of Marlborough* … (2 vols, 1838), ii, 251; TCD, MS 1995–2008/1276: Francis Annesley to Archbishop King, 28 Oct. 1707.

[146] L.A. Dralle, 'Kingdom in Reversion: The Irish Viceroyalty of the Earl of Wharton, 1708–10', *Huntington Library Quarterly*, xv (1951–2), 393–5.

commons. But at the same time, they recognized the political importance of satisfying the aspirations of some whig MPs on this issue and, more important, perhaps, the potential electoral dividend for whig candidates in boroughs with a strong dissenting presence. To that extent, repeal was a good thing, provided that they themselves were not seen to be responsible. Alan's favoured scheme, according to Jonathan Swift, was to have the test removed by some action of government or parliament in England. But when Swift stated this publicly in a pamphlet published in London, Alan was driven to fury, lamenting the indiscretions of Ulster presbyterians and denying that he or his family had any concern in their difficulties.[147]

Fortunately for his managers, Wharton followed Alan's advice to some degree and settled with cabinet colleagues that repeal was to be achieved in the same manner that the test had originally been imposed, through an addition in the English privy council to an Irish popery bill. Perhaps even more fortunately for the Brodricks, the junto ministers then reneged on their promise, sparing Alan and Thomas from the embarrassment of having to excuse and explain away the kind of constitutional provocation that they had previously denounced.[148] In another instance where the English privy council did interfere with an important Irish bill, they had no choice, for this was no less than the principal supply bill. In the matter of money Wharton had made life easier for his parliamentary 'undertakers' by asking for no more than a year's worth of additional duties, but the enabling bill included an appropriating clause, against which the English law officers took exception. The debate on the returned bill became the great set-piece of the session. Alan was in the chair, but Thomas and St John III, who had only recently been elected to the Irish parliament for the first time, both spoke in favour, bringing most whigs with them.[149]

Such service deserved a return, and Alan was duly given a plum appointment, as lord chief justice of queen's bench in Ireland. He was succeeded as Speaker in Wharton's second session, in 1710, by John Forster. Even Laurence benefited, despite his possible tory leanings, being made a chaplain to the house of commons at Westminster and recommended for further ecclesiastical preferment.[150] More generally, the Irish whigs belatedly reaped the rewards they had always expected from a viceroy of their own kidney: Forster succeeded Alan Brodrick as attorney-general, William Whitshed came in as solicitor-general, and the revenue commission was reorganised, with William Conolly at its head. The result was a second session more comfortable than Wharton's first, at least until the latter stages, when the political news from England cast a shadow over whig triumphalism.[151] To begin with the Brodricks had been able to relish their success: tories complained of Alan's *hauteur* in his treatment of political opponents who now had to plead before him in court, and they also took particular exception to young St John's conduct in the Commons, where he was

[147] Below, Letter 145.

[148] D.W. Hayton, 'Divisions in the Whig Junto in 1709: Some Irish Evidence', *Bulletin of the Institute of Historical Research*, lv (1982), 209–12.

[149] BL, Add. MS 34777, f. 67: 'List of those who spoke pro and con in the money bill'; McGrath, *Constitution*, 226–7. For Thomas's key role in forwarding supply business, see *The Letters of Joseph Addison*, ed. Walter Graham (Oxford,1941), 144.

[150] *CJ*, xvi, 153.

[151] McGrath, *Constitution*, 233–46.

said to show 'all the heat and rancour of his father without any mixture of his sense or learning'.[152]

8

In England the political tide had turned. The impeachment of the high church firebrand Henry Sacheverell in February–March 1710 rebounded badly on the Godolphin/junto ministry, producing a torrent of popular tory enthusiasm. At the same time Robert Harley was using his backstairs influence to dismantle the administration from within. Sunderland was dismissed in June; Godolphin in August. Harley himself took over as chief minister, and a British general election in October (in which the Brodricks did all they could to assist the whig interest in Surrey) produced a tory landslide.

The effect on Alan was startling: he was genuinely shocked by the news from England, and in typically melodramatic style likened the situation to that in 1688, before the prince of Orange's expedition. He seems genuinely to have believed that the tories, in England and in Ireland, were at bottom jacobites, and that their political victory heralded a revival in the fortunes of the Pretender, and by extension Irish catholics. 'In short I can see nothing drawing on, but what we have for more than twenty years past been … endeavouring to prevent; and the consequences of such an event, which I need not name.'[153] He considered that his own career was over, and in despair suggested to Thomas that they should sell up in England and hunker down to 'live privately' in the provincial seclusion of County Cork.

These assumptions about his own political future were justified in the short term, as the queen reappointed Ormond to the viceroyalty, and the duke initiated a purge of whigs from office in Ireland. Not only was Alan dismissed as lord chief justice, replaced by Sir Richard Cox, but he and Thomas, together with William Conolly, were also removed from the Irish privy council at Ormond's express request, a rarely inflicted ignominy.[154] At the same time, tories who had suffered Wharton's displeasure, including Sir Richard Levinge, were restored to office. But the most important tory appointment was that of St John II's friend, the English barrister Sir Constantine Phipps, who was named as lord chancellor after the death of Richard Freeman. Phipps was an extreme partisan, with genuinely jacobite leanings, and a temper to match the Brodricks. He was a dangerous adversary, who at the same time embodied all of Alan's worst apprehensions of tory government.[155]

At first the whigs seemed to be cowed. Ormond was given an enthusiastic welcome when he returned to Ireland in July 1711, and the expected whig opposition in the Irish parliament took time to materialise. Many whigs simply did not attend parliament during the first weeks of the session.[156] St John III was the only Brodrick to be present: Alan had been obliged to give up his seat on being raised to the judicial bench, and Thomas stayed in England. Alan was not even in Dublin to watch events unfold, having gone down to Cork

[152]BL, Add. MS 47026, ff.10–11: Philip Crofts to Sir John Perceval, 4 Apr. 1710; f. 26: William Perceval to same, 29 Aug. 1710.

[153]Below, Letters 153–4.

[154]TNA, SP 63/367, ff. 49, 58: Ormond to Dartmouth, 31 May, 14 June 1711.

[155]For Phipps, see the biographical entries in *Oxf. DNB* and *DIB*, viii, 112–4.

[156]HMC, *Lonsdale MSS*, 119.

to attend his ailing father, a departure some interpreted as a manifestation of defeatism (although said to be on his last legs, Sir St John did not in fact die until January 1712). Such was Alan's importance to his party that Ormond's chief secretary Edward Southwell took the former Speaker's absence as a conclusive indication that there would be no real opposition.[157] And so it proved, at least until the recess.[158]

In October 1711, when the bills were returned from England and parliament resumed sitting, the whigs attended in force. They raised various issues which enabled them to parade their attachment to the Williamite revolution and by implication to question the allegiance of the tories; attacked the Irish privy council for amending 'heads of bills' sent up from the Commons before engrossing them and sending them to England for approval; and expressed a particular outrage at what they alleged was an abuse of power by the privy council in interfering with the government of borough corporations.[159]

The so-called 'new rules' of 1672 required that the election of chief magistrates in a number of named corporations had to be approved by the council. Previous administrations had occasionally exercised this power, and Wharton had been accused of intervening in the affairs of one parliamentary borough, Trim in County Meath, on behalf of one of his supporters.[160] But Phipps's arrival in Dublin inaugurated a systematic campaign by the tory-dominated council to disapprove the election of whig magistrates, reminiscent of Lord Tyrconnell's efforts in 1687–8 to remodel corporations in order to 'pack' an Irish parliament.[161] The most notorious instance was in Dublin, where the council disapproved no less than seven elections in order to uphold the claim of a tory alderman.[162] Eventually, after a petition to the queen, the council and corporation agreed on a compromise candidate in Dublin, but the damage was done, and whigs pursued their grievance in the Commons, so effectively that they were able to push the ministry close in a series of highly contested divisions.

The consequences of the 1711 parliamentary session were profound. Not only was whig morale uplifted, the party's spokesmen had succeeded in spreading alarm about the intentions of the tory ministry among those moderate members of the 'Church party' who had welcomed Ormond with open arms only a few months before but were nervous of any hint of Jacobitism. When Ormond returned to England, leaving Phipps at the head of the Dublin Castle administration, as a lord justice alongside the archbishop of Tuam, John Vesey, the political atmosphere became even more frenetic. The Dublin mayoral dispute went into a second round in 1712, then a third in 1713, which could not be resolved; and whig politicians and pamphleteers brought up a range of complaints against the administration, focussing on Phipps, which built into a narrative depicting the lord chancellor as a second Tyrconnell.

[157]HMC, *Portland MSS*, v, 30; TNA, SP 63/367, f. 80: Southwell to Lord Dartmouth, 5 July 1711; SHC, 1248/3/53, Katherine Whitfield to [Alan Brodrick], July 1711.

[158]McGrath, *Constitution*, 251–7.

[159]*Perceval Diary*, 108–20.

[160]See below, p. 235.

[161]BL, Add. MS 47087, ff. 2–4: Sir John Perceval's journal, Aug. 1711; TNA, SP 63/367/204–5: petition of the lord mayor and aldermen of Dublin, Sept. 1711.

[162]On the extended Dublin mayoral dispute, see Sean Murphy, 'The Corporation of Dublin, 1660–1760', *Dublin Historical Record*, xxxviii (1984), 22–35; C. M. Flanagan, '"A Merely Local Dispute?" Partisan Politics and the Dublin Mayoral Dispute of 1709–1715', Notre Dame PhD, 1983.

As well as interfering in borough corporations, Phipps was said to have deliberately neglected the militia; intruded crypto-catholics into office, in both central and local government; and protected jacobites, while at the same time pursuing 'honest' protestants with the full rigour of the law.[163] One prominent victim was none other than St John Brodrick III, who during his short parliamentary career had quickly made a reputation for himself as a hothead, and in January 1712 was reported to the lords justices for having supposedly slandered the queen during an argument in a Dublin coffee-house over the recent block creation of peerages in order to push the ministry's peace policy through the British house of lords.[164] That particular allegation was eventually dropped, although some felt it had damaged Alan's reputation (which may have been the intention).[165] More significant was the prosecution of Dudley Moore, a brother of the prominent whig MP John Moore, for his part in a riot at a Dublin playhouse on King William's birthday in November 1712. Moore was brought to trial, in front of Sir Richard Cox in queen's bench in June 1713, with Alan Brodrick and several other leading whig politicians as his counsel. The defence made every effort to turn the occasion into a political protest, accusing the government of a witch-hunt, and of attempting to stack the jury against Moore, which had the effect of presenting the young man as a political martyr.[166]

By the summer of 1713, when it would soon be time for the Irish parliament to reconvene to pass a further supply, the Irish political world was in uproar. The hearing on the Moore case, combined with a third successive impasse between the privy council and the Dublin aldermen over the mayoralty, had raised party passions so high that Robert Molesworth thought it impossible for an Irish parliament to meet.[167] Certainly something would have to be done to allay the fears of whigs and moderate men more generally about the trajectory of government policy in Ireland. Harley, who had now been raised to the peerage as earl of Oxford, and had become lord treasurer, thought that the answer might lie in the kind of 'project of comprehension' – a bringing together of men of goodwill from all parties – that he had himself attempted (without success) in England in 1708 and 1710.

Sending Ormond back to Dublin was not an option, given the torrid time the duke had endured in the latter stages of the 1711 session. Instead, Oxford appointed one of his remaining whig allies, the duke of Shrewsbury, who was sent to Ireland with the express purpose of winning over whigs to support the court with offers of protection and favour, and uniting the kingdom in the service of the queen.[168] Before leaving for Ireland in the autumn of 1713 Shrewsbury contacted Alan Brodrick, and through an intermediary was able to get some idea of the scale of the difficulties he would face, when Alan made it clear that there could be little hope of silencing whig protests while the lord chancellor remained in office.[169]

[163] Hayton, *Ruling Ireland*, 163–5.

[164] See below, Letters 172–3. For another example, see NAI, M/2447, p.138: lords justices to Ormond, 13 Nov.1712.

[165] BL, Add. MS 47026, f. 112: Emmanuel Moore to Sir John Perceval, 7 Feb. 1711/12.

[166] D.W. Hayton, 'An Image War: The Representation of Monarchy in Early Eighteenth-century Ireland' in *Ourselves Alone? Religion, Society and Politics in Eighteenth- and Nineteenth-century Ireland: Essays Presented to S.J. Connolly*, ed. D.W. Hayton and A.R. Holmes (Dublin, 2016), 35–6; below, Letters 188, 194–5.

[167] HMC, *Various Collections*, viii, 262.

[168] Hayton, *Ruling Ireland*, 166–9; BL, Add. MS 70260: Shrewsbury to Oxford, 4 Apr. 1712.

[169] Below, Letter 197.

The decision to call a general election in Ireland in October 1713 did not make Shrewsbury's task any easier: quite the reverse. The electoral process itself encouraged a furious public debate and aggravated personal animosities through competition for seats. Attempts by Phipps and others at Dublin Castle to deploy the resources of government systematically on behalf of tory candidates only enraged whigs the more. A great deal was also made of the appearance on the tory side of a number of candidates who were recent converts from popery.[170] Archbishop King of Dublin considered that the end result was to render the country 'in a high ferment, higher than ever I saw it except when in actual war'.[171]

The Brodricks were secure in their control of the corporation of Midleton, but for reasons of personal prestige, and for the greater good of their party, preferred to leave the borough to nominees and to stand themselves for more open constituencies.[172] Thomas, who had held one of the county seats, was unwilling to seek re-election after being returned to the Westminster parliament in October 1713. So Alan took his place, though not without alarums; for the family's position in the county constituency, which had been comfortable in the 1690s, had come under pressure in Queen Anne's reign as political allegiances in Cork were polarised by the rise of party.[173] It was a similar story in Cork city, where Alan had been returned in 1692, 1695 and again in 1703. St John III had replaced his father as recorder of Cork in 1708 and duly took a parliamentary seat in 1713, but the election was not a formality, and there is evidence of the appearance of a tory faction in the borough. The reverberations of party conflict had reached the corporation of Cork as early as 1708, when there were 'great animosities in the election of magistrates', as opponents of the ruling oligarchy disputed the right of the outgoing mayor and sheriffs to nominate a panel of candidates, which would perpetuate whig control over the corporation offices.[174] Then in November 1711 a tory was removed from the roll of freemen for calling St John III 'a rascal' and afterwards insulting the aldermen who went to their young recorder's defence. The following year a second vote was necessary in the mayoral election, while the mayor chosen in 1713 was evidently a man of tory sympathies.[175]

When he arrived in Dublin Shrewsbury quickly realized the impossibility of the task he had set himself.[176] In fact he was ground between two millstones. On the one side the tory majority on the privy council refused all proposals for a compromise over the Dublin mayoral dispute. They seemed in thrall to Phipps and the recently arrived earl of Anglesey, a tory from a prominent Anglo-Irish family who had made a name for himself at Westminster and had designs on the lord lieutenancy for himself. On the other side the Irish whigs were determined to force Phipps from office, even to the extent of withholding a supply. In simple party terms the result of the election had probably given the tories a narrow majority, but there were a number of disputed contests, where the adjudication of

[170] F.G. James, *Ireland in the Empire, 1688–1770: A History of Ireland from the Williamite Wars to the Eve of the American Revolution* (Cambridge, MA, 1973), 76–8; J.G. Simms, 'The Irish Parliament of 1713' in *Historical Studies, iv: Papers Read Before the Fifth Irish Conference of Historians*, ed. G.A. Hayes-McCoy (1963), 85–6.

[171] TCD, MS 2532, pp. 222–3: King to Francis Annesley, 14 Nov. 1713.

[172] BL, Add. 34777, f. 24: analysis of constituencies, [1713].

[173] BL, Add. MS 46964A, f. 53: William Burton to Sir John Perceval, 1 Dec. 1710; Add. MS 469654B, ff. 77–8: Francis Smyth to same, 1 Mar. 1713/14; *Post Boy*, 28–30 Jan. 1713/14.

[174] *Cork Council Bk*, 331.

[175] *Cork Council Bk*, 350, 354; *Post Boy*, 23–25 Feb. 1713/14.

[176] For what follows, unless otherwise stated, see Hayton, *Ruling Ireland*, 171–6.

election petitions might gain valuable votes; and there were also moderate tories who were out of sympathy with the administration and fearful about the succession.

Alan took full advantage of both opportunities. His first aim was to secure the Speakership for himself: Shrewsbury's slowness in recommending a candidate enabled Alan to steal a march, organising his friends and followers to be ready for the opening of parliament and convincing others that he was standing with the viceroy's backing.[177] When the viceroy did eventually recommend Sir Richard Levinge, Alan benefited from his opponent's reputation as a man of lukewarm principles who lacked sincerity and aimed only 'to keep fair with both the parties'.[178] In the crucial division on the first day of the session, after the galleries had been cleared, Alan was elected Speaker by 131 votes to 127. A few days later the whigs carried the chairmanship of the committee of privileges, where election petitions were heard, in favour of John Forster over the tory Anderson Saunders, by 127 to 121. Not only were they now in a position to control proceedings in the Commons, they had achieved an apparent ascendancy over the tories, and a vital momentum in carrying forward their campaign against the ministry.[179]

Observers were struck by the tenor of Alan's disabling speech, which emphasized not his own inadequacies, but his determination not to disappoint those who had voted for him.[180] While he and his friends seem to have made no objection to the government's 'short' money bill, the interim measure prepared by the Irish privy council in advance of the session according to the practice established in 1695, the main business of supply did not progress smoothly, and it seems a reasonable inference that the whigs were deliberately holding up proceedings to give themselves leverage.[181] Their main focus was on undertaking a programme of inquiries into what they saw as the abuses of power committed since 1711: the council's interference with municipal elections, especially in Dublin, the lords justices' failure to prosecute Edward Lloyd, and the contrasting persecution of Dudley Moore. They were also keen to profit from any scrap of evidence which might add to the picture of an administration, and especially a lord chancellor, whose loyalty to the Williamite settlement and the Hanoverian succession could not be trusted, such as the events of the tumultuous parliamentary election for Dublin city, where catholics were alleged to have formed part of the tory mob, and a member of the chancellor's staff could be identified as a ringleader.[182] The underlying purpose was revealed on 18 December, when St John reported from the committee appointed to investigate the cases of Moore and Lloyd, and the House voted a resolution that Phipps 'had acted unfaithfully to his trust, and contrary to the Protestant interest of Ireland'.[183]

St John had taken a leading role in this parliamentary campaign. A tory pamphlet published after the session singled out the Brodricks, father and son, for particular criticism. Making an elaborate analogy between the beleaguered Phipps and the Athenian statesman

[177] BL, Add. MS 38157, ff. 26, 27: Sir Richard Cox to Edward Southwell, 21, 26 Nov. 1713; *The Correspondence of Jonathan Swift*, ed. Harold Williams (5 vols, Oxford, 1963–5), i, 408.

[178] BL, Add. MS 47087, ff. 17–18: Sir John Perceval's journal, 18 Mar. 1713.

[179] *Perceval Diary*, 124–8.

[180] *Perceval Diary*, 125; NLI, MS 50545/2/18; Henry Rose to David Crosbie, 26 Nov. 1713.

[181] McGrath, *Constitution*, 274–5.

[182] Below, Letter 199.

[183] *Perceval Diary*, 134–6, 140–3.

Aristides, the author introduced Alan in the character of 'Ericos', a man with 'a certain livid paleness of aspect' and possessed of 'a very boisterous and precipitate eloquence', whose son was heir to all the malignity of his [*father's*] nature'.[184]

Phipps had his supporters, in the Irish house of lords, where the presence of a squadron of high church bishops stiffened the tory majority, and in the Irish convocation, but the situation in the Commons was crucial for Shrewsbury, since the money bill which parliament had passed only extended the additional duties until Christmas. It was quite clear that the whigs in the lower house had in effect issued an ultimatum, that Phipps must be dismissed if there was to be any hope of a further supply. Shrewsbury made one last attempt to secure a compromise, inviting the whig leaders to the Castle during the Christmas recess, but they would make no promise to 'lay aside heats' and 'do the queen's business' so long as Phipps remained in office.[185] And the dynamics of English politics made the removal of the lord chancellor impossible. The parliament was prorogued, and after a decent interval, Shrewsbury returned to England.

The failure of the 1713 parliament left Irish politics in limbo: tory interests in various counties and boroughs, including County Cork, joined in addresses in vindication and praise of the lord chancellor.[186] But all eyes were now on the situation in England. A sharp deterioration in the queen's health over the winter brought the issue of the succession to the forefront of the public mind, and the whig opposition at Westminster, which included Thomas Brodrick, lost no opportunity to make political capital from it.[187] At the same time, Oxford's dominance over the ministry was slipping away as his long-term friend, and now rival, Henry St John, Viscount Bolingbroke, made a bid for power on the back of high tory dissatisfaction with Oxford's preference for moderate policies. Should Bolingbroke succeed it was likely that the Irish viceroyalty would either be given to Ormond again, or to Anglesey. So far as Irish whigs were concerned there was little to choose between them: although Anglesey was known in England as a 'Hanoverian tory', his association with Phipps made him appear quite the reverse in Ireland. As the political crisis deepened, the Brodricks could see nothing but disaster ahead: the discovery that French agents were active in Ireland recruiting catholics for the armies of Louis XIV further upset their jangling nerves.[188] In June Alan Brodrick wrote from Dublin that:

> The resentments, apprehensions, and fears which may be observed among people are not to be expressed: I doe not take on me to say how well grounded they are, but am convinced the hopes of the papists and apprehensions of most of the protestants with whom I converse were never greater in my memory.[189]

Finally, on 27 July, with the queen on her deathbed, Oxford was at last ordered to break his white staff. Two days earlier, Anglesey had been given a commission to remodel the army

[184] [Patrick Delany] *The Life of Aristides, the Athenian; Who Was Decreed to be Banish'd for His Justice* … (Dublin, 1714), 8–9, 11–12. See also PRONI, D/623/A/3/7, Lord Abercorn to Edward Southwell, 22 Dec.1714.

[185] Below, Letter 209.

[186] Below, Letter 212.

[187] *HC 1690–1715*, iii, 336.

[188] Below, Letters 215, 222, 224.

[189] Below, Letter 223.

in Ireland, but by the time he reached Ireland the queen had already died.[190] Her last act had been to appoint Shrewsbury as lord treasurer, ruining Bolingbroke's plans. So despite Alan Brodrick's fears, the transition to Hanoverian rule, both in Ireland and England, passed off peacefully.[191] A new political world opened. In Dublin Sir Richard Cox was disgusted to see the whigs 'exceeding insolent, and fancy they have all in their power, and can turn in and out whom they please'.[192] For their part, Alan and Thomas were already in London, seeking to make as much profit as they could from their reputation and connections among the English whigs.[193]

[190] Hayton, *Ruling Ireland*, 183.

[191] TNA, SP 63/371/86: lords justices to Bolingbroke, 14 Aug. 1714.

[192] BL, Add. MS 38157, f. 110: Cox to Edward Southwell, 17 Aug. 1714.

[193] *The Correspondence of Richard Steele*, ed. Rae Blanchard (Oxford, 1941), 305.

Note on Editorial Principles

The bound volumes of Brodrick papers contain a variety of materials: letters to and from various correspondents belonging to or connected with the Brodrick family, together with assorted papers. In order to give some system to the selection of letters and to reduce as far as possible the element of subjectivity, we have chosen to print only the correspondence between Alan Brodrick I and his siblings and offspring: his brothers St John II and Thomas, his sons St John II and Alan II and his daughter Alice. There is one exception to this rule: sometimes, in order to evade the prying eyes of political and personal enemies, Alan I addressed letters to his wife's aunt Martha Courthope in England, who was clearly expected to pass them on to his brothers or son. Such letters have therefore been included in the edition. We have also exercised a limited discretion in omitting material of an entirely domestic nature, including references to the management of property and the pursuance of cases at law, where these have no discernible relevance to the political and public lives of the principals. We have indicated such abridgments by ellipses.

In presenting the text, we have generally sought to preserve the original spelling and punctuation, including underlinings. We have silently modernised thorns, extended standard contractions (including ampersands), and lowered superior letters. (Contemporary material quoted in footnotes and in the introduction, has, however, been modernised throughout). A full point has been added at the end of each sentence where the writer has omitted to do this (usually when the sentence ends with a closing bracket). We have not reproduced subscriptions, superscriptions and signatures to the letters. Square brackets have been used to indicate editorial interpolations: doubtful readings are printed in roman type, editorial extensions in italics. Dates are given, in letter-headings and in footnotes, in the customary fashion, that is to say in Old Style (the Julian calendar) but with the year beginning not on 25 March but on 1 January (which was the case with New Style, under the Gregorian calendar). Where a letter is dated using both year-dates, as for example 1 Mar. 1712/13, this has been preserved; where the year-date given is only in Old Style, the New Style year-date has been added in square brackets.

Every effort has been made to identify persons who figure in the letters, but not always successfully; the Brodricks often wrote allusively or elliptically, in the hope of mystifying those in the Irish post office (in particular the postmaster-general Isaac Manley) whom they suspected of attempting to intercept their correspondence. To prevent repetition in the footnotes, biographical information relating to family members and connections, and to members of the Irish house of commons, has been gathered into appendices. On occasions where the letter-writer provides a full name, and the context makes it clear that the person concerned was an Irish MP, no footnote reference is given. Similarly, in order to conserve space, an individual mentioned by his or her full name in the text is identified in a footnote only on their first appearance. A full index will appear at the end of the last volume in the edition. Unless otherwise stated, basic biographical details (dates of birth and death, place of residence, offices held, constituencies represented) have been drawn from standard sources, such as the *Complete Peerage* and *Complete Baronetage*; the relevant volumes produced by the History of Parliament Trust; Edith Mary Johnston-Liik's *History of the Irish Parliament*; the *Dictionary of Irish Biography*; and the *Oxford Dictionary of National Biography*.

Correspondence 1680–1714

1. *Alan I, Cork, to St John II, at the Black Boy, Fleet Street, 7 Sept. [1680]*

(1248/2/146–7)

I have wrote but seldom in the Circuit which was the cause of not doing it to you: I will not trouble you with any thing of businesse, that will be uneasy; only you shal have an account how I spent my time since I left Cork. Going into Kerry the only direction we had to find our way over a certain mountain of some eight miles acrosse (they call it Slieve lohir[1]) were certain posts set in sight one of the other, but very hard to be found out partly through the foggynesse of the weather and partly by reason of the strange posicion of them; for whereas the first post stood soe as you went from it to the second N.W. you must goe to the second S. etc. all this occasioned by the frequent interposicion of bogs. When we had passed the mountain we swam some fords, but that I looked on as a trifle being through wet before. At Trallee[2] I had good lodging tho very scanty with others: for I lay in Ned Dennys[3] house: the town is very poor and uncapable of receiving the great concourse of people the Assises bring together. The last night the Judges stay in any little town it is the constant practice to pull all the Councell and Atturnies (that will not goe serenading voluntarily) out of their beds, make them dance in their shirts, sconce[4] them 3 or 4 bottles of wine, then force them to dresse and go with you; thus they did in Trallee and I rather chose to be active than passive in the thing. We roused o'Sullevan More[5] and some 35 of his scullogues[6] out of one house, who sent for 20 bottles of sack and we might have drained them if we pleased. Going from Kerry to Limrick my horse carried me well, and in recompence Tom and I some six times lifted him out of bogs where he would have stuck till doomsday without help; but when we came of from the mountain we saw a very pleasant Country much like England; the ways are in the County of Limrick soe deep as not to be passed but by help of Causeways occasioned by the richnesse of the soil. Limrick is a pretty gentile town, but poor: here I was very kindly used by Coghlans mother, Major Macguire[7] and his Lady, and

[1]Slieve Logher, on the border of Counties Cork and Kerry.

[2]Tralee, Co. Kerry.

[3]Edward Denny (1652–1712), of Tralee, Co. Kerry, MP [I] Co. Kerry 1692–9.

[4]Levy a fine upon.

[5]Daniel MacOwen O'Sullivan More (*d.* 1699) of Dunkerran Castle, Kenmare, Co. Kerry (William Betham, *The Baronetage of England* … (5 vols, 1801–5), v, 562).

[6]Farm labourers.

[7]Richard McGuire, major in Lord Le Poer's regiment of foot (Charles Dalton, *Irish Army Lists of King Charles II, 1661–1685* (1907), 50–1).

my Couzen Jephson[8] who all remember them to my father and Mother. Nothing hapned remarkable on the Crown side in the whole circuit, besides a womans condemnacion for killing a bastard child who died at Cork, and a young Irish stubborn rogue for killing a Scotch pedlar boy; discovered by Major Macguire. He at first was obstinate but confessed at the Gallows. The reason the woman gave for killing her bastard was that it was begotten by an Irish rogue, and she was unwilling to rear any of the breed. What feats the serenaders did at Ennis I cannot yet acquaint you, leaving the town the day foregoing in order to my going to Clonmel Assises: but they have made a song in which I among 6 or 7 Councel and Attornies are named: but there is no harm in it. I should have told you that at breaking up the serenade at Trallee about 20 went into the Court house, held a formal Court, arraigned a prisoner, charged a Jury with him, who found him guilty, whereon he was condemned: George Crofts[9] lay under the Court and hearing them proceed regularly looked out, and finding it (in his mind) very dark mistrusted his eyes till he had twice or thrice rubbed them: at last he conjectured the Judges had a mind to hasten out of town and soe sate before day, whereon he dresses in great hast but ere he was half dressed opens his doors where he met his own Atturny whom he asked whether his businesse were coming on; he humoured the thing and told him he was just then called on; goe in (saith Crofts to his Atturny) and if possible defer its coming on but a moment; up went he, told the story; and then the Court rung of nothing but George Crofts come and appear, make your defence etc. which noise soe alarmed him that unbuttoned, his knee strings untied, head uncombed, and without a Cravat he run up stairs crying and bellowing ere he came to sight, my Lord here I am, heres Crofts my Lord, I hope your Lordshipp will consider the time of the day and not let me suffer by the Courts sitting at this early unusual hour; he perceived his error by a loud laughter of all the Court, and would have getten to his chamber again, but was seised, hooted at, sconced in wine, then dismissed. Sir Phil. Percival is ill of a feavor.[10]

2. *Alan I, Dublin, to St John II, 31 May [1681]*

(1248/1/197)

Your account of Fitz.H[*arris*][11] I have and am obliged to you for it; pray in your next send me word how the Cheif Justice[12] is thought and talked of, and if you can get me some new songs you will doe what is most gratefull to me; goe to Carrs[13] for them, and there pick out such as be new, and have sence in them if a little roguish they take never the worse

[8]Probably John Jephson, MP [I], who was sheriff of Co. Limerick in 1682 (*Hist. Ir. Parl.*, iv, 482). A John Jephson of Limerick appears in a number of deeds between 1708 and 1720 (Reg. Deeds, 2/417/541, 2/555/629, 3/3/442, 3/28/498, 23/319/13540, 31/80/18260).

[9]George Crofts (c.1640–98), of Churchtown, Co. Cork, MP [I] for Charleville, 1692.

[10]Sir Philip Perceval, 2nd Bt., of Burton, Co. Cork, died on 11 Sept., 1680 (*Complete Baronetage*, ed. G.E.C[okayne] (5 vols, Exeter, 1900–6), iii, 315).

[11]Edward Fitzharris (c.1646–81), the Irish informer and agent provocateur, executed in England in July 1681.

[12]Sir William Davys (*d.* 1687), of Merchant's Quay, Dublin, named chief justice of king's bench [I] in Mar. 1681 (Ball, *Judges*, i, 357–8).

[13]The London bookseller John Carr, who specialised in music books.

here: what they cost I will justly discount for: Laur. Cl.[14] will soon after Trinity term when Mr Worth[15] can be there to draw the writings be happy in the arms of his long admired Mistrisse Katy Tynte.[16] One song I desire tho not new; I have heard Gething[17] sing it often; it begins with Mrs Mosely,[18] the sence is to shew the convenience of kept Misses to keep men to doe their businesse and support them with their pensions; in it are these words, let the wealth of the Cully, be reward of the Bully, Soe y'are sure of a man when you need one.[19] …

[*PS.*] I hold my self so very little obliged by the Middle Temple that I owe the society no service; Mr Whitlock[20] I have great respect for and will doe all that is proper in what he desires.

3. *Alan I, Cork, to St John II, at the Black Boy, Fleet Street, 25 Oct. [1681]*

(1248/1/198–9)

It is long since I wrote to you; I now will acquaint you how things goe here: I beleive Katy[21] is in a fair way to alter her name for H[*enry*] T[*ynte*]s[22] tho I know there daily are and will be more endeavours to prevent it: Of this say nothing, when terms are agreed on you shal know them. I hope soon too to be wedded, I mean to the Recordership of Cork; great have been the endeavours to supplant me but I think we have fairly given them the goeby: Evans[23] had a letter from my Lord Lieutenant,[24] Will FitzGerald[25] by means of Will Hanway[26] had made a good interest among the Merchants; neither Cox[27] nor Farsen had

[14] Laurence Clayton, MP [I], who eventually married Anne, the youngest daughter of Alan Brodrick I.

[15] William Worth (c.1646–1721), of Aungier St., Dublin, and Rathfarnham, Co. Dublin. 2nd baron of exchequer [I] Sept. 1681–9 (Ball, *Judges*, i, 358–9).

[16] Clayton's first wife Catherine, daughter of Sir Henry Tynte.

[17] Unidentified.

[18] Mistress Mosley, a notorious woman of the town, probably a brothel-keeper, whose name was often linked in popular literature with that of the 1st earl of Shaftesbury (*Poems on Affairs of State: Augustan Satirical Verse 1660–1714,* ed. G. de F. Lord *et al.* (7 vols, New Haven, CT, 1963–75), ii, 106).

[19] Thomas Duffett, *New Songs and Poems A-la-mode* … (1677), 47, printed 'A song set by Mr Hart' with the line 'Let the wealth of the cully, provide for thy bully, then his weapon will always be ready'. A 'cully' was a rake; a 'bully' a whore's protector.

[20] Carleton Whitlock (1652–1705), sixth son of Bulstrode Whitlock, and a barrister of the Middle Temple (Ruth Spalding, *Contemporaries of Bulstrode Whitlock 1605–1675* … (Oxford, 1990), 414–15; *Middle Temple Records,* ed. C.H. Hopwood (4 vols, 1904–5), iii, 1274).

[21] His sister Katherine. She eventually married a clergyman, William Whitfield.

[22] Henry Tynte (c.1660–c.1692), son of Henry Tynte of Cork (*Al. Dub.*, 830; Vicars, *Index*, 464).

[23] George Evans, sr, MP [I].

[24] James Butler (1610–88), 1st duke of Ormond.

[25] William Fitzgerald (*d.* c.1700) of Cork (R.G. FitzGerald-Uniacke, 'The Fitzgeralds of Castle Dodd', *Journal of the Royal Society of Antiquaries of Ireland*, ser. 5, iv (1894), 293; Vicars, *Index*, 171).

[26] William Hanway (c.1640–c.1688). Tax farmer and revenue commissioner [I], 1675–6, collector of customs at Cork by 1678. *London Marriage Licences, 1521–1869,* ed. Joseph Foster (1887) 622; TNA, PROB 11/391, f. 283; *Lib. Mun.*, pt 2, p. 132; *Calendar of the Orrery Papers,* ed. Edward McLysaght (Dublin, 1941), 205.

[27] Sir Richard Cox (1650–1733), 1st Bt, of Clonakilty, Co. Cork. Elected recorder of Kinsale in 1680; subsequently justice of common pleas [I] (1690), chief justice (1701) lord chancellor [I] (1703–6) and lord chief justice of queen's bench [I] (1711–14).

been idle, but perhaps tho I now act as Councel to the Mayor and Sherifs I in time may succeed Baron Worth till which time he never will quit. Under the rose[28] this. Buy me two short perrukes of about 30s each; you soon shal have that mony and more I have took very handsome and convenient lodgings in Baron Worths house … [*PS.*] The fourth of next month I shal be in Dublin. Could you send the Perrukes to Dublin and that very suddenly it were well, for I mightily want them.

4. *Alan I, to St John II, at the Black Boy, Fleet Street, 11 Nov. 1681*

(1248/1/202–3)

I have not lately wrote more then once to you, and in it told you somewhat of a match designed for Katy of which as I then did so I now continue to desire your silence; whether any advances will be made till I return by reason of the absence of some whom the Gentlemans freinds much relye on I cannot say; his estate you know is considerable as well as family, but some advantages he wanteth, and some qualities he hath gotten of which I could wish him free, as well as endowed with the advantages I think he wants; however he is capable of acquiring what by being bred still at home he is short in, and I perswade my self easily to be brought of from any idle disposicion (for I cant call them habits) he may be inclined to. I hope to be Recorder of Cork soon tho the Devil, Evans and FitzGerald would say nay; Baron Worth is to that degree just and kind as well as prudent and vigilant they will find the matter hard to bring in any one against his will. If I can but one year or two keep even with the world I shal after (I speak it without vanity) have as much businesse as any one here of my standing, and more then many of far greater: and it is but need knew you how things stand here: before God I think had not Sir A[*llen*] died as he did things would so apparently have gone to ruine I doubt he might have been induced to have in a great measure altered what he left my brother. The businesse between Capt Barry and my Father[29] is left to Baron Worths decision who will one way or other so decide the matter that it never shal come to a Chancery suit, of which you may be sure I am heartily glad. On the Barons promocion[30] I had from him several good clients recomended; as the Countesse of Orrery,[31] Clancarty,[32] Lord Kingstone,[33] and two or three trusts; Sir R. Gethin[34] hath at last signed my annuity as standing councel to my Lord Insiquins[35] businesse which with the Salary and Recorders seal of Cork of which I have the benefit (tho under the rose) makes

[28] 'sub rosa': privately, or in secret.

[29] In 1672 Redmond Barry (*d.* c.1690) of Rathcormac, Co. Cork (Vicars, *Index*, 24), had been made a trustee of the marriage settlement of Thomas Brodrick, but the settlement had been revoked the following year (deed of revocation, 14 June 1673 (SHC, G145/box 95/1)).

[30] Worth had been appointed a baron of the Irish exchequer a month before.

[31] Either Margaret (1623–89), née Howard, widow of Roger Boyle, 1st earl of Orrery, or Mary (1648–1710), née Sackville, wife of Roger Boyle, 2nd earl.

[32] Either Donough MacCarthy (1668–1734), 4th earl of Clancarty, or possibly his mother Elizabeth (*d.* 1698), née Fitzgerald, widow of Callaghan MacCarthy (*d.* 1676), 3rd earl.

[33] Robert King (*d.* 1673), 2nd Baron Kingston.

[34] Sir Richard Gethin (c.1615–c.1685), 1st Bt, of Mallow, Co. Cork.

[35] William O'Brien (1640–92), 2nd earl of Inchiquin.

£70 per annum: my last I might too have said too [*sic*] my first years practice brought me in £120 and upwards; should not these addicions make it better then £200 this year I should be sorry: of this tho a single man and forty times more covetous then you thought I ever could be I shal not save 6d. The chamber rent I pay amounts to £41 per annum; I have two Clerks one I wanted the other I could not avoid taking coming under the recomendacion and character of Baron Worth and Alderman Dunscomb of Cork[36]; my Groom and Mr Webster:[37] could I but sow the rogues mouths up it were well. Pray think of what I told you of perrukes and let me have them; for I want them much and soe you will beleive when you hear that the only one I have is one I carried over hither in August two years. My brother Will is I think past hopes of ever being what he ought to be; all I can doe shal be used to prevail with my Father to send him to sea; he may make a good tarpawlin,[38] and nothing good else. Remember me to Turner and Burton and if any else there be of our Irish acquaintance worth mencioning whom I knew; St John let me give you one peice of advice, save mony if you can, for it is a good freind in time of necessity, and no one knows how near that may be. If any thing very remarkable happen, in writing which you can come to no trouble, it will be kind to me to send it. You wrote formerly to me to know when I was at Dublin; you may take it for granted that each term I am in Dublin; they are the same as with you save that Michaelmas term begins not till Nov. 6. the Assises I constantly attend; of which I still acquaint you by letter when they are appointed. At other times I generally am in Cork …

5. *Alan I to St John II, at the Black Boy, Fleet Street, 9 May [1682]*

(1248/1/193-4)

What you say of Suxberys[39] not needing any letter was true, I knew him too well to need be told what he was or had been at the Inns of Court, and you may rest assured that I will keep your word as to giving him a just character when it lies in my way. There is nothing in that of my courting the young Lady you mencion but I would be glad to know from whom it was you were told I was a fool if I did not. Pray whenever you can inform your self of any new Governour to succeed here let us know it with the first for it is greatly our interest, especially if as the Irish here[40] seemed pretty confidently to report his Royal Highnesse[41] should succeed. Sir Richard Reeves Recorder of Dublin[42] is Sollicitor to the Duke[43] soe as that affair is at an end. How long my father hath been in Ireland you are

[36]Noblett Dunscomb (*d.* c.1695), sheriff of Cork 1659–60, and mayor 1665–6 (Phillimore, *Indexes*, ii, 36; *Cork Council Bk*, 1174).

[37]Edward Webber (*d.* c.1695), mayor of Cork 1684–5 (Phillimore, *Indexes*, ii, 113; *Cork Council Bk*, 1175).

[38]A tarpaulin: a career naval commander, who had risen through the ranks.

[39]Anthony Suxbery (bef.1671–c.1702), of Dublin, MP [I] Waterford 1692–9.

[40]Unless qualified, the term 'the Irish' was used throughout the correspondence to mean the *catholic* Irish.

[41]James, duke of York, later King James II.

[42]Sir Richard Ryves (c.1643–93), of Capel St., Dublin, recorder of Dublin 1680, 3rd serjeant [I] 1683–7, 2nd serjeant [I] 1690–1, commissioner of the great seal [I] 1690, baron of the exchequer [I] 1692–3.

[43]Presumably the 1st duke of Ormond. Ryves was already recorder of Kilkenny (Ball, *Judges*, ii, 60), and in about 1682 became second justice and master of the rolls in the duke's palatinate of Tipperary (W.P. Burke, *History of Clonmel* (Waterford, 1907), 443).

sensible and yet I can assure you that he is as far not to say farther from putting any good end to those affairs he came over about as ever, for he hath not proceeded one step towards the doing of it.

6. *Alan I, Dublin, to St John II, at the Black Boy, Fleet Street, 13 May [1682]*

(1248/1/195-6)

I received one from my father of the fifth past, by it he orders me to supply what he designed by that post to have wrote to you but was forced to omit it through multiplicity of businesse as you may conceive … I will pay for any pretty new song if the words be good and the air pleasing, and the rather if to comply with the females fancys it be pretty bawdy, get them at Cars and I will pay for them. Mrs Worth[44] had her Chocolate and I my Wigs. She hath a young son.[45] Suxbery is called to the bar[46] and will inform Dick and you how lamentable dull trade is with us young men at the bar; he shakes daintily on making a mocion, but Crow[47] and Ward[48] doe it most confidently (relying I beleive on merits and skill in the Laws which they know themselves to have beyond him, for I am loath to impute it to unapprehensivenesse of the Auditorys greatnesse which ought to strike some terror in them, or to impudence.) … Send word how the first and second Addresses of the County of Cork[49] were received, and what impressions they made in the minds of Whig and Tory. …

7. *Alan I, to St John I, 9 Nov. 1683*[50]

(1248/1/330–1)

Your other matters I will answer if I have room but will postpone them till I have offered you my sence in a matter that nearly concernes us all. I beg you, Sir, to consider it well and to give your thoughts of what I write together with your Pardon for my freedom in venturing to advise without your commands to doe it. My Brother St John and I having

[44]Mabel or Mabella, da. of Sir Henry Tynte of Ballycrenane, Co. Cork, and the second wife of the exchequer baron William Worth.

[45]James Worth (later Tynte), MP [I].

[46]Anthony Suxbury was called to the Bar at the Inner Temple in Feb. 1682 (*Calendar of the Inner Temple Records*, ed. F.A. Inderwick *et al.* (9 vols, 1896–2011), iii, 172).

[47]Probably William, son of Thomas Crowe of Dublin, who was called to the Bar at the Middle Temple in 1681 (*M. Temple Adm.*, i, 189). He seems to have returned to reside in Dublin: *The Irish Statute Staple Books, 1596–1687*, ed. Jane Ohlmeyer and Éamonn Ó Ciardha (*Calendar of Ancient Records of Dublin*, supp. 3, Dublin, 1998), 84.

[48]Probably Charles, son of Richard Ward of Newport, Salop, who was called to the Bar at the Middle Temple in 1681 (*M. Temple Adm.*, i, 193). He was evidently practising in Dublin in 1699 (TNA, C/110/80/I: John Rotton to Alice, Countess of Drogheda, 12 May 1699, including a copy of a draft of assignment of a decree against the earl of Antrim signed by Charles Ward).

[49]The grand jury of Co. Cork, meeting at the assizes in early Apr., had on their own initiative subscribed a loyal address (John Keating and Arthur Turner to Ormond, 3 Apr. 1682 (*CSP Dom.*, 1682, 153)). A month later another loyal address was sent from the county and city, 'subscribed by a multitude of hands' (HMC, *Ormonde MSS*, n.s., vi, 363). It was reported that when the former was presented at court the reaction was one of laughter (HMC, *Hastings MSS*, ii, 392).

[50]Copy in hand of St John II.

been always bred together had added to our relation a strict tie of freindship beyond what is usually seen in brothers; wee parted with great concern, and finding our occasions forced us to live at a distance from one another wee were very constant in conversing by letter, till of late I hardly hear from him and when I doe his style so differs from what I remember it, his sentences are so abrupt and freedome so constrained that I find hee labours under some great disquiet of mind. Nothing can cause it unless what I have often heard discoursed here tho without much certainty his inclinacions to Mrs O. The world allows you as good (not to say the best) father that lives in it; and you will not now doe what may make as deserving a child as you have miserable. What the Ladies fortune is I know not, but will take the thing at the worst and suppose to his and her disadvantage shee had not a groat; if shee bee (as I cannot question it, since hee likes her) a well born and vertuous woman, and consequently one that never can bee a disgrace to you or yours, if hee love her I should humbly offer to you that you would please to comply with his inclinacions. No one better understands the circumstances of your Family than I doe, nor hath better and more advisedly considered them on this subject; Admit it were not onely probable but certain that hee might get a woman with thrice her fortune (which is not every days chance) if you put his satisfaction into one scale and the money into the other you must allow the former ought to outweigh. Our family is naturally melancholly and hee in a great measure soe, and that is a distemper that grows very dangerous when considerably encreased. For you to say you give him your consent to marry, without setling an Estate on him as far as your circumstances can admit is really a way rather to heighthen then abate his concern; this is a matter that were I as fond of as I am the contrary I never could move to you on my own behalf, but am bold to bee free on account of my dearest Brother and freind: and least any of my other brothers should think I have been their enemy I beg you what you doe to the prejudice of any other of your younger children may fall as an incumbrance on what your care and kindness hath designed for mee. I am in such circumstances as I am not like to want, and resolve never to create my self a charge without prospect of supporting it; so my inconvenience (if I should survive you which I neither hope nor much expect) will bee the lesse. Your own prudence will tell you this is a matter my Mother ought to know to whom I offer it as well as you: If shee consent, I beg you to speak to my brother, for I doubt his concern or modesty, will hardly admitt him to speak to you, else sure 'ere now hee had done it; but in this you may observe his intire obedience, that since hee may have hitherto observed you or my mother averse to his marrying hee hath (I beleive barely on that account) forbore it. Please to lett mee know of your receipt of this letter, and to beleive my whole design is the health and happyness of my Brother whose welfare I much wish and beleive in great measure depends on the event of this matter.

8. *Alan I, Dublin, to [?Thomas], 15 Feb. 1685[/6]*

(1248/1/190)

… Not long since Baron Worth was speaking to me about your making interest to succeed Clayton[51] in the Sherivalty of Cork[52] in which you may relye on his assistance; but Lady

[51] Laurence Clayton.

[52] The office of county sheriff.

Orrery hath this time been Jemmy Barrys[53] freind and will continue soe therefore it will be an hardship put on her to speak in your own behalf to her: Really it were well for your affairs here that you came over. If you aim at it you must doe it in time and with all privacy …

9. *Thomas, Cork, to St John I, Wandsworth, 16 Dec. 1690*

(1248/1/251–2)

I am forc't to bee here for a little time contrary to my inclinations, the Countrey being all mett in order to putt the militia in such a posture, as that they may bee able to defend the frontiers and all within our line, when the army shall be drawne of; and for the giving their best assistance att this time, when the greatest part of the forces quarterd in this Countrey are leaving us. Lt Generall Ginkle[54] is now on his march (and I beleive att this time hee may bee neer Limerick) in order to reduce the County of Kerry and the westerne parts of this County. Wee have two entire Regiments of Horse and the kings of Dragoons; who are to bee joined by strong Detachments of all the Regiments both of horse and foote in these parts whoe march by the way of Muccromp[55] and soe through Beare[56] and Bantry into Kerry. The successe of this enterprize will strike a great stroake in the affaire both of Limerick and Gallaway; for if wee can beate them[57] out of this County and Kerry they cannott long subsist; these being the onely places where they have good forrage, Connaught is soe destitute of itt, that they every day turne their cattle over the Shanon, and if this affaire succeed wee shall ease them of the trouble and care of a great number of them; besides their want of forage in Conaught they are in Limerick reduc't to great necessityes having broken open the late kings stores there, and the rabble have seizd the greatest part of them; soe that the consequences of this expedition must I thinke inevitably bee either their fighting the Lieutenant Generall or being soe streighned that twill bee impossible for them to subsist long; and I beleive they have noe thoughts of the former, Sir James Cotter[58] Maxwell[59] the two Luttrells[60] and some others of noate being gone of;[61] this you may depend uppon is soe; and to strenghthen this conjecture of their beginning to despaire they have turned out of Limerick great numbers of the poore english whoe were there prisoners, keeping

[53]James Barry, MP [I].

[54]William's Dutch general Godard van Amerongen-Van Reede (1644–1703), seigneur of Ginckel, subsequently 1st earl of Athlone.

[55]Macroom, Co. Cork.

[56]Castletownbere, Co. Cork.

[57]The jacobite forces.

[58]Sir James Cotter (c.1630–1705), of Ballinsperry, Carrigtohill, Co. Cork, a lieutenant-colonel in King James's army and formerly the jacobite governor of Cork city (*DIB*, ii, 904–5).

[59]Thomas Maxwell (*d.* 1693), a major-general in the jacobite army.

[60]Simon Luttrell (1643–98), of Luttrellstown, Co. Dublin, and his younger brother Henry (c.1655–1717), both officers in the jacobite army (*DIB*, v, 605–6, 607–8).

[61]Maxwell and the two Luttrells, along with Nicholas Purcell and the catholic bishop of Cork, Peter Creagh, had been sent by the more militant elements on the jacobite side as a deputation to James II in France to request the removal of the earl of Tyrconnell from his position as James's viceroy (J. G. Simms, *Jacobite Ireland 1685–91* (1969), 185).

onely a few of the most considerable men. I have this day talkt with severall whoe are just arriv'd from thence, and they all agree in what I have told you; they have noe expectation of men from france butt ammunition and provisions they are promisd which I beleive will nott bee sufficient props to support their drooping spiritts should they arrive soone; which if they doe nott I am sure they will come too late; The villains in protection in this Countrey are those whoe doe us the greatest harme; these and our being forc't to subsist the troops quarterd with us makes this part yett poorer then ever itt has been in the worst of the late times. However the people are setling on their farmes, and resolve to begin the world againe. The enemy make frequent inroads into our frontier quarters and in two or three places have done us some prejudice. Att Castletowne neer Inisheene[62] they surprisd a Lieutentant and 30 Dragoons, putting fire to the house, the Lieutenant and four were killd the rest prisoners; butt neither this nor any of their other feats have gone unrevenged; for uppon my word wee are allways quitts with them. Yesterday went from hence three hundred prisoners towards Limerick they having proposd to exchange those of ours which they had; and they amount to soe many. This place begins to grow much healthier then twas, and were mony enough sent over for the paying the army (some is come) wee should in a short time bee in a very good condition, our people being very hearty and seeme desirous of falling to their buisnesse once more; I can yett say nothing to you of your estate more then that your Tenannts are all on their farmes, and when ever any are able to pay rent they will. The buisnesse of the Array[63] will keep mee longer then I expected; however I hope in a short time to bee looking towards you.

I came from Bristoll before the post came in, though I waited soe long in expectation of itt, that I was forc't in a fisher boate to follow the ship almost to the Homes. I told you in my last from thence I had made use of my creditt for the releife of some of them; a great many of them are landed; butt wee want four ships from Bristoll and one from Minehead whoe wee hope are putt back; for wee doe nott yett heare of any Privateers on these coasts.

I have yours and my owne Tenannts allowd mee; and shall bee able to make a very good double troope of men, for horses wee have none butt I thinke I shall nott have them, till I see them well mounted, and I hope that will nott bee long first. Some few armes wee have orderd out of the stores; and I have directions to take what I can find among the Irish within my precinct; they had I am sure enough; and I resolve they shall produce them, or buy new ones for mee. All your freinds here are well and give you their humble services. I have mett with an extreme kind reception and wellcome among them, butt I dare nott yett breake the suddainenesse of my designe back to them. Assoone as the buisnesse of our Array is over theyle better beare itt.

Please to give my humble service to all my freinds, perticularly to Good Mr Fermin;[64] whose health, and Sir Thomas Cookes[65] are as constant as our dinners; where wee have yett good meat, butt very little bread or beere, butt what comes out of England in corne.

[62]Enniskeane, Co. Cork.

[63]Of the militia.

[64]Probably the London businessman and philanthropist Thomas Firmin (1632–97).

[65]Sir Thomas Cooke (c.1648–1709), of Lordshold, Hackney, Middx., deputy governor of the East India Company.

10. *Alan I, Dublin, to St John II, at Lamb Buildings, Middle Temple, 11 Nov. 1691*

(1248/1/255–6)

I have yours of the 31 Oct. and thank you for your trouble in the matter of Cranage etc[66] but your thoughts came long after the hearing at Councel board,[67] where it is hard for any man to stem the current of Mr Cullifords (I should have said the Kings) interest:[68] but in a Court of common Law things will go otherwise; and there the suit will be immediately commenced; and because it will come to be finally determined in England the persons concerned will begin it in the Kings Bench here. As for what judgement is given it is not expected it will be final to either side soe you may expect to hear of it by error about this time 12 months. You may tell Mrs Alice How she may come over when she pleases; there are noe raporees[69] here now to ravish or murder her and as for her cause I will tell her more of it when I know more of it my self. In short it is wholly out of my mind, being a thing I was entertained in before the revolution, nor have I seen her many letters nor desire to see them: If she writes to any freind here to speak to me I will that way send her my thoughts, but can not be at the trouble and charge of writing and receiving letters: tell her this in as soft words as you please … If the term afford it I will send you a little bill with directions how to employ the mony: but our part of the Country is in the most miserable condicion possible, the Danes quartered on us[70] and the Irish to be shipped of from the great Island;[71] soe as we are infested by the worst of men and greatest of enemyes. Several murthers have been committed thereabouts one very barbarous one on Will White a considerable merchant of Corke[72] near the town; another in the great Island etc. several robberies of houses, stripping and plundring in the high wayes, nay in the Streets

[66]The duty payable at ports (as part of the Irish customs) for loading and unloading goods by crane.

[67]The Irish privy council.

[68]William Culliford (*d.* 1724) of Encombe, Dorset, revenue commissioner [I] 1684–8, 1690–2. Culliford was unpopular among Irish protestants because of his service under King James II's government, his overbearing manner and obvious self-enrichment. Accused of corruption, and of favouring catholics in his administration of the revenue and over the disposal of forfeited estates, he was the subject of complaints in the English house of commons in Feb. 1692, and in the Irish Commons in the following autumn (*DIB*, ii, 1077–8; *HC 1690–1715*, iii, 800–3).

[69]Rapparees: Irish rural brigands, particularly active in the latter stages of the 'war of the two kings', their numbers swollen by deserters and disbanded men from the two royal armies. The term 'rapparee' was often used as a synonym for 'tory', to indicate criminal elements of the Gaelic Irish population, but Smyth, 'Social and economic impact of the Williamite War' suggests a distinction between the two and identifies 'rapparees' with larger groups of unsettled people, perhaps kinship groups, roaming the Irish countryside, and appropriating goods and livestock for their sustenance.

[70]The Danish contingent of the Williamite army, comprising eight battalions, for which see *The Danish Force in Ireland 1690–1691*, ed. Kevin Danaher and J.G. Simms (Dublin, 1962). For local complaints against the behaviour of the Danes, see BL, Add. MS 38847, f. 274: Lord Orrery to Sir Robert Southwell, 26 Aug. 1690; *The Council Book of the Corporation of Youghal* … ed. Richard Caulfield (Guildford, 1878), 387. On 27 Oct. 1691 Secretary Nottingham had informed the Irish lords justices that orders for the embarkation of the Danes were imminent (*CSP Dom*., 1690–1, 553).

[71]Those jacobite troops who had opted to go to France rather than stay on in Ireland. A substantial contingent left from Limerick in Oct. 1691, the remainder with Patrick Sarsfield from Cork in Dec. (Simms, *Jacobite Ireland*, 259–60). The 'Great Island' was the largest island in Cork harbour.

[72]Possibly William White of Castle White, Rochfordstown, Co. Cork.

of Carigtowhil:[73] some English as Robin Serjeant[74] etc. forced from their dwellings (the little Island[75]) where they have been safe during the whole rebellion till now: the army pay nothing, the countrey calls it living on free quarter we must give it a more gentle name. Last night all the Kings Councell[76] were summoned to meet on a letter of the governement to Serjeant Osborn[77] which follows:

Sir, The Lords Justices command me to send you the enclosed Copy of the articles of Limrick[78] to the end you with the rest of the Kings Councel in town (whom you are to summon to meet with you for that purpose) may forthwith consider of such an order or such method to be used for giving possession pursuant to the articles as may be proper for the Lords Justices to grant to the several persons concerned.[79] I send you the draught of an order formerly designed to be given out. You must give all possible dispatch etc. John Davis.[80]

We are not yet agreed on our answer. If I understand the thing right, the Justices have a mind to pull the thorn out of their own foot and put it into ours; that is if there be any thing in the articles which relates to the giving possessions not consistent with our Laws, that the blame shal be laid at our doors if they are not fully executed by reason that we give our opinions they cannot be restored by Law to their possessions in such maner as the articles require; If we shal advise their being put into possession in as large speedy and beneficial maner as the articles seem to promise, then we are accountable for any illegal methods that shal be used in execucion or pursuance of our advice: Our answer is as follows.

To the right honourable the Lords Justices of Ireland. May it please your Lordships In pursuance of a letter from Mr Secretary Davis of the 9th of this instant November directed to Jn Osborn Esqr their Majesties prime Serjeant at Law signifying your Lordships pleasure that he should summon the rest of their Majesties Councel in town and with them consider of such an order or such method to be used for giving possession pursuant to the articles of Limrick as may be proper for your Lordships to grant to the several persons concerned: We whose names are underwritten doe humbly certifye your Lordships that we have twice met together and considered of the said letter and that we have carefully perused the Copy of the articles of Limrick sent inclosed together with the draught of an order formerly designed to be given out to the persons restorable by the said articles to their possessions, and are of opinion that several persons concerned in and restorable by the said articles stand in different circumstances the one from the other, some of them having (as we are informed) never been indicted, others altho indicted are not yet outlawed, and others actually outlawed of high treason. As to those persons whose estates of Inheritance

[73]Carrigtohill, three miles east of Midleton.

[74]Possibly Robert Sargent (*d.* c.1716) of Castle Grace, Co. Tipperary (Vicars, *Index*, 415).

[75]An island in Lough Mahon (itself an expansion of the River Lee), five miles east of Cork.

[76]Privy councillors, rather than King's Counsel.

[77]John Osborne, prime serjeant and MP [I].

[78]The articles of peace signed by the lords justices with the jacobite forces at Limerick on 3 Oct.

[79]By the terms of the articles the garrison and inhabitants of Limerick, and any other towns still held by the jacobite army, those officers and soldiers still in arms, and those under the protection of the jacobite army in Counties Clare, Cork, Kerry and Mayo, were to be pardoned and restored to their property notwithstanding any previous outlawry or attainder.

[80]John Davys (Davis) (1665–1743), of Carrickfergus, Co. Antrim, MP [I] 1692–1714, chief secretary to the lords justices [I].

and freehold (Note that Leases for years and chattels are of another consideration being in a distinct article) have been seised or leased by the Commissioners of their Majesties revenue or by the Subcommissioners for seisures, who have not been indicted or altho indicted are not yet outlawed, we are of opinion that inasmuch as their said estates have never been legally vested in their Majesties your Lordships may grant an order to the Commissioners of their Majesties revenue requiring them to permit such person or persons (intitled to the benefit of the said article) to enter on and enjoy their said real estates; and that the draught of the said intended order is sufficient in that behalf (Note the order is by the Lords Justices to the Commissioners of the revenue to require them to permit the proprietors to enter where the Lands are in the Kings hands and that they shal write to the Kings tenants to quit possession, the proprietor first giving securitye by recognisance not to demand any thing for the time past (which agrees with the articles) and to permit the tenants who have sowed the Lands to reap etc. paying the Custom of the Country) Altering only the words November last and inserting in their stead November instant: Provided that care be taken that such order given to persons not outlawed for possessing of their said former real estates may not be so executed as to oust any Creditor in possession of such estate or any part thereof by vertue of any mortgage judgement or other Legal incumbrance. As to those persons who stand actually outlawed of high treason whose estates are legally and actually in their Majesties hands we are of opinion that while such outlawryes stand unreversed, there can be no legal order framed or conceived by your Lordships for dispossessing the Crown of the estates of the persons so outlawed or putting the former owners into the possession thereof: But the most proper method which we can find to be used in that behalf is that the said persons may forthwith reverse their said outlawries which may be done assoon as their Majesties shal order the same, after which they will be immediately restored to their said possessions of course. And we humbly submit to your Lordships consideration, that no order may be granted in favor of any person intitled to the benefit of the said articles for the putting him into or permitting him to enter on the possession of any estate of Inheritance or freehold upon pretence that the same descended to him or to which he claims any right by vertue of any settlement Remainder Reversion or any other way whatsoever, unlesse the said person was in actual possession of the said estate at the time when he went into rebellion. All which is humbly submitted to your Lordships. Signed Jo*[hn]* Osborn, Alan Brodrick, John Mead[81] Nehemiah Donelan,[82] Thomas Pagenham,[83] Robert Dixon,[84] Tho: Coote.[85]

I know not whether the above return will please, and fear the contrary. Sir John Mead and I were for granting Custodiums[86] to some freinds of the persons outlawed that were restorable in trust for them under several qualificacions too long to be here inserted, but the rest were soe violently against it and apprehended such fatal consequences to Creditors etc. by that course, and shewed us some other reasons that we joined with them. Let not this be

[81] Sir John Meade, MP [I].

[82] Nehemiah Donnellan (1649–1705), KC [I]; later baron of the exchequer [I] (1695), and chief baron (1703).

[83] Sir Thomas Pakenham, KC [I], MP [I].

[84] Robert Dixon, MP [I].

[85] Hon. Thomas Coote (1663–1741), of Cootehill, Co. Cavan, King's Counsel [I] and MP [I] 1692–3; appointed a justice of king's bench [I] in Mar. 1693.

[86] Custodiams: grants by the exchequer of lands in the possession of the crown.

publick. I formerly wrote to my father about Coghlans[87] being either dead or irrecoverably ill; since I hear he (contrary to all mens expectacions) is mending; desire my father not to stir farther in that matter then he hath already done, only if he could secure that place[88] on his death or removal as Hartstongue hath that of Ryves[89] by having a warrant under Lord Ormonds hand[90] to grant him a Commission for it when the other dies or is removed, it might prevent his interposing there by means of his brother who is a menial servant to Lord Ormond; promises we know are forgotten and Coghlan is not long lived. I wish to God now matters are quiet you could contrive to send me my Law books and my common place and papers hither, for here my cheif businesse will for the future be. Consider which is the best way by Chester or Longsea:[91] but the sooner the better: for I shal very soon want my books when businesse comes in …

11. *Alan I, Dublin, to St John II, 6 May 1693*

(1248/1/259–60)

Since my name hath been lately mentioned before the house of Lords in relacion to my giving up or losing my patent for being one of their Majesties Serjeants at Law in this Kingdome,[92] I hold my self obliged to give you a succinct and candid relacion of that matter, which you may communicate to any freind of mine or yours that desires a sight of it; and if it vary from the Copy I have of a narrative, I will take care it shal not be in any point but where there is good reason for its soe doing. The thing was thus: On Monday the 7th November Mr Pulteney[93] came to my chamber early in the morning and let me know that he was commanded by my Lord Lieutenant[94] to acquaint me his Excellency had heard I had given out, that I had carried my patent for being one of their Majesties Serjeants at Law to the Castle with a design to deliver it up to his Excellencye; but I doe not remember that he told me his Excellencye heard that I said I stil had it: he added that his Excellencye looked on this proceeding as a slighting the patent and service, and that he had it in commands from his Excellencye to come for my patent, which was his errand: or words to this effect. I must take leave to affirm that if his orders were to inform himself of the truth of the report from my mouth, he forgot that part of his Excellencyes commands: for I should then have readilye said (as the truth of the fact was) that I had been told by a member of the house of Commons above a week before the prorogacion, that

[87] Joseph Coghlan, MP [I].

[88] Attorney-general of the palatinate of Tipperary.

[89] Standish Hartstonge, jr, MP [I], succeeded Sir Richard Ryves in about 1692 as second justice and master of the rolls in the palatinate of Tipperary (Burke, *Hist. Clonmel*, 443).

[90] James Butler (1665–1745), 2nd duke of Ormond.

[91] Anglesey.

[92] James Sloane (MP [I]) in evidence to the English house of lords on 2 Mar. 1693, in relation to alleged miscarriages in Ireland, had drawn attention to the dismissal of Alan Brodrick and the prime serjeant John Osborne in the immediate aftermath of the prorogation of the Irish parliament of 1692, as an example of oppressive government. John Pulteney, the chief secretary, replied with a full, explanatory, account (*LJ*, xv, 265, 269–70).

[93] John Pulteney, MP [I], chief secretary.

[94] Henry Sydney (1641–1704), Lord Sidney, lord lieutenant [I] 1692–3; later 1st earl of Romney.

a Gentleman of good qualitye and station had assured him great notice was taken (among others) of my acting and voting in the house contrarye to what was thought by some to be for their Majesties service and the publick good; and that I must not expect to continue an immediate servant to the Crown, while I acted in opposition to its interest, as he said I was looked on to doe. Upon this informacion given me I discoursed three or fowre Gentlemen that were my freinds, what was fit for me to doe: and after hearing their opinions went the next morning to the Castle before I went to the house of Commons, and had the honour to be admitted to my Lord Lieutenants presence, and told his Excellencye that something of the nature of what is above mentioned had been hinted to me, that I did not apprehend it came from the Castle; that to the best of my understanding I alwayes had acted for their Majesties service and the interest of this Kingdome, and should ever continue soe to doe: that my not having soe clear or right a sense of things as others was my misfortune, not my fault; but that my being an immediate servant to the Crown did not (as I conceived) lay me under any obligation to act in the house of Commons conformable to other mens reason, where they differed from my own: nor did I beleive his Excellencye expected such a servile compliance from me who had not received nor could hold the employment on such condicions, and rather then I would disappoint a confidence reposed in me (if such things were expected) I would quit the honor of their Majesties service in that station, and had brought my patent to lay at his Excellencyes feet, if I might not hold it but on those terms. His Excellency was pleased to say that nothing was expected by him from any one of the house of Commons but a readinesse to doe and consent to such things as should be for their Majesties service and the good of the Kingdome; which I expressed a great willingnesse to join in, and his Excellencye saying noe more then that he should see me again, I came away. I cannot say these words then passed, but if need were would appeal to his Excellencye (no body being then present besides) that this is the truth in substance. From the Castle I went to the Parliament house where some few dayes after hapned those votes of which his Excellency took notice in the speech he made at the prorogacion of the Parliament,[95] in the passing of both which votes I own that I was fully convinced the house was in the right, and the more I consider the matter the more am I confirmed in my opinion: And what ever some mens sentiments may now be, who would seem to have been only passive in the matter I must take leave to say both passed nemine contradicente,[96] and that I doe not remember one of those arguments used that are mentioned in the narrative, and I have discoursed others, whose memories are as bad as mine, if such reasons were offered: on the contrarye a Gentleman now and alwayes in very good esteem here was one of the great assertors of those votes; he is of our Countye. The Fryday or Saturday after the prorogacion I heard that Lord C.[97] had treated Mr Serjeant Osborne very freely at the Council board in relacion to the part he bore during the late Session of Parliament, and was told that probably neither he nor I should be long within the bar: This put me in

[95] Sidney's closing speech referred to the entrenchments made on the royal prerogative in the Commons' votes of 27 and 28 Oct. affirming their 'sole right' to initiate supply bills (in defiance of Poynings' Law) (*CJI*, ii, 614, 615, 629).

[96] Literally, 'nobody contradicting'.

[97] Either, Sir Charles Porter (1631–96), lord chancellor [I] 1686–7, 1690–*d*., or his colleague as lord justice from Dec. 1690 to Mar. 1692, Thomas Coningsby (1657–1729), 1st Baron Coningsby, and later 1st earl of Coningsby). A subsequent reference in this letter to Coningsby as 'Lord C.' suggests that he is probably the person meant.

mind of what Mr F.[98] whispered into my ear before the prorogation that I should find Mr Osborne would not continue Prime Serjeant long, and of what passed at a Committee of grievances, where the new duty collected in the City of Corke by or under colour of an order of the Councel board made in the end of the raign of King Charles the second or in the beginning of the reign of the late King James for paying Cranage etc. was debated: by colour of which order the merchants of that port informed me (who was elected one of the Citizens for that City) that they have been forced by the Custom house officers to pay Cranage for goods where the Crane is not used and which may better be laden and unladen by hand, and to pay Keyage[99] for Landing at the Custom house key where they are obliged by a Statute Law and an order of Councel founded thereon to Land their goods upon penalty of forfeiture, and is conceived to be a publick key: against which order or the execucion thereof, or both, the said City had peticioned the Lord Chancellor Porter, and the now Lord C[*oningsby*] being then Lords Justices and the Privy Councel, and after long delayes interposed by the Commissioners of the revenue came at last to an hearing before the board, but found no redresse there.[100] Upon debate of that matter I endeavoured to shew to the Committee the illegalitye and unreasonablenesse of the order, and how great an invasion it was on the propertye of the subject and the Laws of the Land, as well as a discouragement to trade: Immediately after speaking my sense of this matter I was asked by Mr P[*ulteney*] who sate next me this short question, Whether I was not one of their Majesties Serjeants: to which I replied that I was a Commoner of Ireland too, and acted under that character there. It could not be for informacion the question was put, but to give me an hint (as I judge) that in his opinion I had not acted conformable to the duty of my place. And laying all matters together I did concur in opinion with the Gentleman that I should not probably continue long within the bar and said I had formerly made a tender of my patent in maner before sett forth and should not be surprised to be superseded considering how those votes were resented and how far I was concerned in them; in this maner I made a tender of my Commission and have alwayes owned to have done soe. As to that part of the narrative wherein it is said Mr P[*ulteney*] told me he was sent to accept of a surrender of my patent, and that if I was willing to part with it he had directions to receive it I must desire to be excused for saying, that tho I stood at due distance I heard nothing to that purpose, and I am told that he used no such words to Mr Osborne yet the narrative saith he said the same thing to both: On the contrarye his words were (as near as I remember them) that by his Excellencyes command he came for my patent: I was surprised to find that method taken and said the legal course was to determine their Majesties pleasure by writ under the Great Seal: Mr Pulteney replied that his Excellencye was apprised of that,

[98]Possibly Robert Foulke, MP [I], who had acted in opposition alongside the Brodricks in 1692 (*Hist. Ir. Parl.*, iv, 231).

[99]More usually referred to as wharfage; like cranage. a duty payable at ports on loading and unloading goods.

[100]In Nov. 1689 the corporation of Cork discussed the excessive demands being made in the port for cranage, especially the fact that this was being imposed when the merchants themselves had not requested that the crane in the port be used to unload their goods. In the following Feb. they sent a petition to their recorder, Alan Brodrick, to be laid before the lords justices and privy council. This proving fruitless, Alan, as MP for the city, then raised the issue in the Commons' committee of grievances, which reported on 26 Oct. 1692 that the source in this complaint lay in the self-interested actions of William Culliford, who, through a trustee, had taken a lease of the cranage duties from the revenue commissioners and was seeking to maximise his return from it. (*Cork Council Bk*, 211, 214; *CJI*, ii, 613.)

but would not order a supersedeas[101] to be sealed till farther directions out of England, as I understood him: and added that he had been with Mr Osborne just before and had his patent in his pockett. I then considered that altho I had been near two years one of their Majesties Serjeants, yet had I not (that I remembred) been advised with more then once, nor had I ever had any oportunitye to act in any their Majesties concerns, save once that by order from the Lords Justices I had a letter wrote to me by Mr Secretarye Davis to take care to indict and prosecute for rebellion and treason such as were liable to prosecucion within the intention of that letter in the Munster circuit, which I was ready to have done, but how that matter stopt is not necessarye to my purpose to insert: soe as I needed not the patent for my justificacion, never having had oportunitye to act under it: I thought too that having once made a tender of it, the denying it when sent for would be improved to my disadvantage and an occasion of railerye; thereupon I asked Mr P[*ulteney*] whither it were not proper for me to carry it to the Castle, who was soe far from saying I might if I pleased, that to the best of my memorye his answer was that it would be by no means fit. Upon recollection I was of the same mind, and delivered it into his hands with a desire that he would give his Excellencye my humble service: and soe we parted. My memorye is very faulty if this be not the true state of the matter, but I am confirmed that I have not mistaken the thing; because I repeated what passed between Mr Pulteney and me to my father, Mr Dean Jephson,[102] and Mr Riley (in whose house I lye)[103] as soon as Mr Pulteney went out of my study, they being then in my outward room: and perswade my self they remember the matter noe other wise then I now tell it. Upon the whole matter I own that several of my freinds have told me I was in the wrong in tendring my patent as I did: I can easilye submit my judgement to theirs, and doe it soe far that I doe declare and have often done it publickly, I noe way resent the losse of my employment: whatever the motive is that makes a servant declare a readinesse to be discharged his service, I think the master may well take him at his word: but I must protest to have had no ill intent in doing what I did, much less to have insulted over or put the Governement at defiance. The summe is, and I must and alwayes will affirm that I never had a willingnesse to give up my Commission or patent, provided I might have been permitted to have held it on such terms as I thought were consistent with the obligacions I lay under as a member of the house of Commons, and with my reputacion. This is written with no other intent then to justifye me if there be occasion, therefore to that use only I desire you will put it.

12. *Alan I, Dublin, to St John II, Lamb Buildings, Middle Temple, 26 June 1693*

(1248/1/261–2)

It is one of the many misfortunes this unhappy Country labours under, that their inclinations and actions are generally represented in England by persons whose interest it is to have both

[101] A writ to stay legal proceedings.

[102] Michael Jephson (c.1655–94), dean of St Patrick's, Dublin (*Al. Dub.*, 439; Cotton, *Fasti*, ii, 57–8, 102) or William Jephson (c.1658–1720), dean of Lismore (*Al. Dub.*, 439; Cotton, *Fasti*, i, 47).

[103] Edward Ryley or Reilly (*d.* c.1720) of Dublin (Reg. Deeds, 1/215/134; Vicars, *Index*, 395). He acted as a trustee for Alan I's in a land purchase in 1703 (SHC, G145/box 99: document in the hand of Alan I giving an account of the acquisition of 'Glenane and Ballyfines', 13 Sept. 1703).

ill thought of for by ends of their own: And it is to be feared the characters they give, have taken too deep impression, when any of them are soe hardy to affirm that it is our desire and resolution to act independent of England; a charge they dare not maintain the truth of when the representative body of the nation is assembled, who know the loyalty of the Protestants of this Kingdome to the Crown of England and will vindicate themselves from such malicious imputations. The design now on foot is to justifye the usage the Commons mett with at their prorogacion in November, and the opinions the Judges here are said to have given in opposicion to the vote of that house asserting the sole right that the heads of mony bills should be prepared in the house of Commons:[104] You tell me that you never received any account of our proceedings or any reason or grounds that we went on for passing that vote, tho you wrote for them; this is another unhappinesse, that when any matter thwarting the sense of those on this side is transmitted it seldome comes to hand: thus are we misrepresented by others and barred by particular persons but I am sure without order of any oportunitye of doing ourselves right. Depend on it, I sent you in three sheets of paper what at that time occurred on the subject to me and men of much better understanding, which having not come to your hand is certainly fallen into worse;[105] but the paper will bear the light, and let the inquisitive make their own use of it: It was not so methodical as an account I shal at the bottom of this direct you to, but for substance did in great measure agree with it. If the matter in debate seem a contest between the King and Queen and the Commons of Ireland, it will upon serious consideration appear to be nothing of that kind: No man can shew any advantage the Crown can reap by the construction the Judges are said to have put on Poynings act[106] and the 3 and 4 Ph. and Mar.[107] together with the other acts in Queen Elizabeths time relating thereto,[108] that mony bills may arise originally from the Councel board here; since they who allow us very little else have yet been soe favourable as to say we may reject such a mony bill and frame one or the heads of one that will better please us. But as far as I can apprehend matters, the true difference is between the house of Commons and the Councel board here; and the doctrine that Lord Strafford held (which you may find in the 4th article of his impeachment) That he would make all Ireland know while he had the Governement there any act of State there made or to be made should be as binding to the subjects of that Kingdome as an act of Parliament,[109]

[104]See above, pp. 13–15, 51.

[105]This has not survived in the Brodrick papers at SHC.

[106]'Poynings' Law', the Irish act of 1495 (10 Hen. VII, c. 22), named after Lord Deputy Poynings, stipulating that a licence for the calling of an Irish parliament be issued by the English privy council, which would approve bills prepared for the purpose by the Irish privy council.

[107]The Irish act of 1556 explaining Poynings' Law (3 and 4 Phil. and Mary, c. 4).

[108]Two Irish acts of 1569: 11 Eliz., sess. 2, c. 1, authorising statutes, and 11 Eliz., sess. 3, c. 8, against the English act suspending Poynings' Law. On this subject, see in general R.D. Edwards and T.W. Moody, 'The History of Poynings' Law: Part I, 1494–1615', *Irish Historical Studies*, ii (1940–1), 415–24.

[109]Not in fact in the fourth article (John Rushworth, *Historical Collections of Private Passages of State* … (8 vols, 1721–2), viii, 8), but expounded in the answers Strafford had given on 24 Feb. 1640 to the twenty-eight 'special articles' (ibid., 23), in which he stated that 'he would make … all Ireland know that so long as he had the government there, any act of state there made [in the privy council] or to be made should be as binding to the subjects as an act of parliament …' (*Proceedings in the Opening Session of the Long Parliament*, ed. Maija Jansson (3 vols, Rochester, NY, 2000–2001), iii, 13). Sir Allen Brodrick's papers included a notebook with jottings on the impeachment proceedings against Strafford (SHC, 1248/9/1–30).

relishes soe well with some persons that just after the prorogacion in November[110] I was told by a Privy Councellor we were governed and should be governed by the Councel board and that they would give us Law: And the truth is the Gentleman in my sense seemed to ground himself on the practice of that board in time past, and alsoe to look forward and to foresee a great improbabilitye of its being otherwise for the future: He was of our house and well knew how unanimous we were in that vote and how unlikely it was we should ever recede from it: He saw how far the Lord Lieutenant was advised to insist on what they said was the Kings prerogative, and in what maner he had done it: and I beleive knew that some here (whose interest it was the Parliament should then be prorogued and in such a maner) would not omit using all possible arguments and endeavours to represent our vote as a great invasion on the Prerogative, and soe render our meeting inadvisable: and then of course we are to goe in our old rode by orders of that board, where there is a necessitye to remedye incoveniencyes not before provided for by Statute Laws: which the Councell board here have sometimes formerly done during the recesse of Parliaments in times of war or soon after the appeasing disturbances and quelling rebellions: soe that what Lord Strafford saith pag.160. of his trial is in fact true, that Ireland is governed (I mean hath some times but I will not say is at present) by proceedings att Councel board in a different maner from the Laws of England:[111] and tho what he offers pag.179. be true that the authoritye of the Councel board for reasons of State must be preserved, yet times are soe altered that his reason now fails;[112] for I dare boldly affirm that the English planters (I mean the Protestants of this Kingdome) and I beleive the Clergy of it too look on the known Laws of the Land to be the best place of resort for their protection and defence, and that much of the businesse of the Councel board would be taken off their hands if Parliaments may be permitted to sit and to hear the peticions complaints pressures and greifs of the people, where they think they should meet as certain speedy and effectual redresse as at the Privy Councell. This position that when Parliaments are not sitting (which by some is phrased cannot sit) the Councel Board may frame orders which shal have the force of a new Law hath almost brought forth another; that since matters may be done without them where is the great need of their meeting at all: and puts me in mind of what Thuanus[113] writes that the convention of estates in France (who till then much resembled our Parliaments in England) devolved a power on the French King, who never till that time enjoyed it to raise mony by his own edict in Case of necessitye but not else; but he being made judge of the necessitye, the French monarchs found it very convenient and absolutely necessarye to raise it that way ever since:[114] You may apply this. It is the nature of all Courts to enlarge

[110] 1692.

[111] *The Tryal of Thomas Earl of Strafford* … (1680), 160: 'The kingdom of Ireland (as I conceive) is governed by customs and statutes, and execution of martial law, and proceedings at council board in a different manner from the laws of England.'

[112] *The Tryal of Thomas Earl of Strafford* … (1680), 179: 'That my care to preserve the authority of the deputy and council, is not a subversion of the laws: only it directs it, and puts the execution of the law another way. That for reasons of state, it must be preserved, being the place of report for protection and defence of the English planters and Protestant clergy.'

[113] Jacques-Auguste de Thou (1553–1617). An edition of his *History and Memoirs* … was published in London in 1674.

[114] Probably the passage at the end of book xx, relating to the estates-general of 1558 (*Monsieur de Thou's History of His Own Time*, trans. Bernard Wilson (2 vols, 1729), ii, 246–7).

their jurisdiction, and the Councel board here hath formerly done it to some purpose, and if it should happen to doe soe hereafter where is our remedye: If we flye to the Courts of Common Law we have five of our nine Judges of the board,[115] and the others have alwayes shewn a just veneration for the awfull edicts of that Court: Our only hopes is in a Parliament, and there is as little likelyhood that many of the board will freely concur in the expediencye of calling one as that the Pope will be fond of assembling a General Councel; where not only the exorbitancies of his Court may be taken into consideracion, but his power is lessened and lustre eclipsed while such an assembly is sitting. The King no doubt wants as much mony as we can give, but the way to supply those wants best is to let us judge where we can spare it: what can bear a tax and what cannot: now besides the nature of the thing that the Commons who give, best know how to lay the tax, is it probable that the Councel board who transmitted such acts last Sessions as no man could speak for or tell the drift intent or use of them, will model acts much more out of their observacion (as mony bills must necessarilye be) to a sober assemblyes good liking, when the confirmacion of the Settlement of Ireland[116] fell one would think under the Judges immediate knowledge, and other acts under the consideracion of the whole Councel, yet such were transmitted that I blush at; and fear posteritye will have but an indifferent opinion of the nation, when they find those bills to be the result of that great board. I have endeavoured to shew it is no benefit to the Crown to have mony bills rise at the Councel board but a prejudice: that the right is barely contested between the Commons and Council board; and that if it be ruled with the Councel, that in probabilitye it will turn to the prejudice of the Crown, since it is morally certain the bills they shal frame will have such objections to them that they will not passe and soe the Crown will be disappointed of a seasonable supply: for if ever the Commons take such bills into their consideracion it is certain they ought not to proceed on other methods of raising mony till they find those proposed by the Councel board impraticable; and that will probably take up a good part of the Session: whereas if we be left to our own way of raising mony, it will be the first thing we shal enter on to prepare heads or bills to that purpose; and when they are transmitted we may enter on other businesse read bills necessarye to be passed into Laws, and enquire into mismanagement of the revenue, corruption in officers, freequartering the army, levying mony on the Country without Law or colour of it, by fine force: not paying quarters when the Souldiers have been subsisted; not allowing mony advanced on the Credit of proclamacions out of hearth mony or other duties as excise etc. payable to the Crown:[117] the proclamacion I have not by me soe cannot be precise on what branch of the revenue we are promised to have credit,

[115]The nine judges alluded to are the chief baron and two barons of the exchequer, the chief justice and two judges of king's bench, and the chief justice and two judges of common pleas. In Feb. 1693 the Irish judges had reported to Sidney, on request, an opinion endorsing his interpretation of the Commons claim to a 'sole right' of initiating supply bills (McGrath, *Constitution*, 91).

[116]Presumably the Irish act of 1692 recognising William and Mary's title to the crown of Ireland (4 Will. and Mary, c. 1).

[117]Here and in the following passage Alan was to some extent recapitulating the complaints made by the administration's Irish parliamentary critics, both in the brief session of 1692, and to an English parliamentary inquiry in Feb. 1693 (for which see *CJ*, x, 823, 826–33; *The Parliamentary Diary of Narcissus Luttrell, 1691–1693*, ed. Henry Horwitz (Oxford, 1972), 436–43).

but I doe affirm it is but indifferently performed.[118] We might enquire into the reason of pressing horses and never returning them, laying and receiving new duties against Law in several ports by the Commissioners of the revenue under colour of an order of the Councel board for wharfage Cranage etc. and indeed into the practice and proceedings of Courts of Justice and particularly of the Councel board, whence in my sense many things take their rise: and till the Jurisdiction of that board be circumscribed by some Statute Law, and its practice not permitted to warrant illegall proceedings I am of opinion it will be an hard matter for any man to say what is or is not his own. The dread of these inquiries makes it in some mens thoughts not advisable Parliaments should meet and if they doe, that they should have nothing to doe but hastilye to passe two or three mony bills ready prepared, under the notion of an absolute necessitye the Crown is then in of the mony which can admit of no delay; and when that is done you shal be heard in your other matters at a more convenient season. We know that in the best reigns Good Laws are bought, and we are willing to be sure of something for our mony which never will be while the Councel board transmits us mony bills which will be sure to come at the beginning of the Sessions. This and other consideracions makes us beleive it absolutely necessarye for us to retain the little remaining power that is left us by those Laws, which were never calculated for times when English men were at the helm, and no man sate in either house of Irish extraction or the Popish religion. It will be hard to have opinions given ex parte,[119] when we neither are ordered to appear and attend, nor can be prepared with the rolls journals and records to justifye our proceedings: so much falsitye hath been already broached by the other side in matters of fact that there is no depending on the truth of what they say, this I speak of some of them of my own knowledge. Let the event be as God pleaseth; if ever we meet we shal publickly to the world avow and justifye our proceedings and give the reasons of our soe doing, and the consequence of an opinion of those on your side concurring with those here will (if I judge right) be an irremovable and perpetual bone of dissension and render it impossible for a Parliament ever to sit here; but this one comfort remains to us, that tho we are represented as persons bent to act independent of England, yet we may reasonably hope that if Parliaments may not sit here we may by a certain number to be elected here be represented in the house of Commons of England, which many of us heartilye wish:[120] but this will be too great a check to the immense power exercised by some here and will be vigorously opposed on that side. As to the right upon exposicion of the Statutes and usage since, I would have you go to Mr Slone[121] who will let you see a paper called Some consideracions upon the late vote etc.[122] I have just got a Copy of the Judges argument or opinion: Next post shal bring my thoughts and other mens upon it, in few words.

[118]Presumably the proclamation of the lord lieutenant and privy council of 3 May 1693, issuing regulations for exemptions from hearth money (earl of Crawford and Balcarres, *A Bibliography of Royal Proclamations of the Tudor and Stuart Sovereigns ... 1485–1714* (2 vols, Oxford, 1910), ii, 158).

[119]On one side only.

[120]A reference to a possible Anglo-Irish Union. For early 18th-century unionism see James Kelly, 'The Origins of the Act of Union: An Examination of Unionist Opinion in Britain and Ireland, 1650–1800', *IHS*, xxv (1986–7), 236–63; Jim Smyth, 'Anglo-Irish Unionist Discourse, c.1656–1797: From Harrington to Fletcher', *Bullán*, ii (1995), 17–34; D.W. Hayton, 'Ideas of Union in Anglo-Irish Political Discourse, 1692–1720: Meaning and Use' in ed. D.G. Boyce, R.R. Eccleshall and Vincent Geoghegan, *Political Discourse in Seventeenth- and Eighteenth-century Ireland*, ed. D.G. Boyce, R.R. Eccleshall and Vincent Geoghegan (2001), 142–68.

[121]James Sloane, MP [I].

[122]No surviving printed copy has been identified.

13. *Alan I, Waterford, to Thomas, Wandsworth, 25 Sept. 1693*

(1248/1/264–5)

I have not wrote lately to you not having either news or businesse worth the postage … My father no doubt hath at large given you an account of the speeding the Commission at Middleton; the truth is he was (as he usually is when he acts for another) over anxious and sollicitous in the matter if what both your Commissioner Robin Rogers[123] and those of the adverse party told me were true; for they complained of his examining numbers of witnesses to the same point when it was sufficiently proved before: but it is better to err on that hand then the other: the matter will come before the Court and I think must bring the articles of Limrick under debate as well in relacion to his being in Kerry, as whether the Chancerye will take a rise from them to stop suits at Law for private trespasses done during the war. In the mean time pray shew this to my brother St John and tell him that there hardly happens a mocion in Chancerye wherein the articles of Limrick are mencioned but that my Lord Chancellor puts us in mind of a Case but tells not the name of it nor the term nor before what Chancellor it was heard; but the Case is to the following purpose.[124] That the effects of English merchants were seised by the King of Denmark upon a war between the two Crowns in the hands of their Danish correspondents; that a Dane owing an English merchant mony the King obliged him to pay it into his Exchequer; that one article of the peace made afterwards was that the debts due by the subjects of each Prince to those of the other should be cancelled and forgiven; the Dane comes afterwards into England and is arrested for the debt and flies into equitye and (as my Lord Chancellor saith) had a perpetual injunction against the suit at Law. I must say I doe not beleive such a decree was ever made; this was since the return of Charles 2d so must be about the time of the first Dutch war; my brother by discoursing Chancerye practices will find out the Case meant and I think it will be worth while to have the precedent sent over; but if it be for us, as I presume it is; mention it not till the hearing, for we certainly shal have it again cited as a Case in point decreed and settled: now I am told the Chancerye declared they were no Court of state but of equitye and that the Plaintif had no equitye against the Defendant, but [r]eleif must be in some other place …

14. *[Alan I], Dublin, to St John II, Lamb Buildings, 29 Nov. 1693*

(1248/1/266–7)

By the date of this letter you will see the term is over, of which I hear many at the bar complain; but I have no reason to doe soe: Our term begins not as yours on 23d Oct. but the 5th of November, which hapning this year on a Sunday we had just twenty sitting dayes, and in them I made a shift to get (for I have cast up my terms profit) in ready mony £198=17–6. and there are due to me ten fees which will well make up the odd two and twenty and six pence; soe that one day with another this term I have received £10, which is

[123]Robert Rogers, MP [I].

[124]Sir Charles Porter was accused of consistently favouring catholics in applying in chancery his interpretation of the various articles that had ended the Williamite war (*HC 1690–1715*, v, 178).

very fair; but I have worked hard for it and came soe weak out of Court yesterday that I was ready to faint and hardly able to speak, occasioned by much businesse and a most excessive cold I took coming up, of which I have not been able to gett rid tho I endeavoured it all I could, and in order to it have been very temperate, kept early hours; been abstinent in my meat and lett blood. If I continue to have my health some few years I shal be able much to sett all things at ease in our familye, which I confesse to be much the aim of my life ... Let not Senny[125] want any thing that is necessarye, convenient or handsome; I will remit mony constantly to answer those ends: try to perswade him to spare soe much time from his play as will finish another letter and be sure give him a new years gift from me, and let him not be without mony, which you know is a heartbreaking to a sparke of his age. I am really very ill, and weak, and beleive I shal be forced to tell you I am worse before I can with truth pretend to be on the mending hand ... Pray let me know whether when the Atturnye General[126] puts in an informacion in the Crown office for an offence at Common Law, as our Case was for assault batterye and wounding; doth he lay it Done [*sic*] in what County he pleaseth, or is he obliged to lay it in the proper County and if he doe not will the Court on the usual affidavit (that if any assault etc. was done, it was in such a County) alter the venue without his consent: this matter was debated and your practice affirmed to be one way by some, and another by others. This is the great Case about cutting Sir Toby Butlers nose by Nich. FitzGerald:[127] they have had a trial at the Common pleas bar this term, where the defendant pleaded de son assault demesne[128] and proved the issue by five witnesses, honest Protestants and men of substance of the City of Waterford where the fact was done; but Butler had the fortune to have freinds on the jury and they found for him on the oath of one Brogadeer and gave £500 damages: and no doubt if the informacion be tried here, they will also convict him on that too. If he plead de son assault demesne, it will be to no purpose (admit the Law to be that the informacion ought to be in the proper County, which I confesse I take it not to be tho that is the matter that is best for my Client) to give in evidence that the assault was done in Waterford ... I hear nothing of the Danish merchants Case I wrote to you of long since

15. *Alan I, Dublin, to Thomas, Wandsworth, 5 May 1694*

(1248/1/268–9)

I have yours of this day sennights date from Wandsworth to which it is fit I return an immediate answer, considering you say you resolve not to leave London till you hear from me, and that you are ready to leave it as soon as my answer comes to hand: if it were not for this your resolucion I should not more willingly be silent in any matter then in answering

[125] St John III.

[126] Sir Edward Ward (1638–1714), appointed attorney-general [E] in March 1693.

[127] In 1693 Sir Theobald ('Toby') Butler (c.1650–1721), a noted catholic lawyer and formerly solicitor-general to James II in Ireland, had accused Nicholas Fitzgerald of attempting to murder him, following a quarrel in a Waterford tavern (*DIB*, ii, 181).

[128] Literally pleading 'his own first assault'; a plea of self-defence.

your letter. As for your concern with Mrs V.[129] and the late Kings[130] entring on the estate conveyed by him to Sir A[*llen*] B[*rodrick*][131] my next must and shal bring you an answer: for by that time I shal have said as much to and done all with Mr Rotchfort[132] and Pooley[133] that is fit and shal have their answer: The other matter depends on this question whether my sense be that a Parliament is indispensably necessarye in this Kingdome soon? My thoughts are little to be regarded in a matter of such weight, but since you desire to know them, take what my sentiments are off hand; on which I would not have you in any sort depend, much lesse let any body know that what I now write is my sense; for I confesse I have not had time since I received your letter to consider an affair of this nature as it ought to be: soe shal not be bound to maintain or abide by the opinion I now am of, when I at any time hereafter shal see or hear reasons to alter me. I suppose you doe not understand indispensably in the strict import of the word, for soe every body must see that a Parliament here is far from being indispensably necessarye: but if you would know my thoughts whether the meeting of a Parliament here upon the terms you say they must meet, that is by relinquishing what I stil think to be the just right of the Commons to prepare heads of money bills and receave one offered by the Governement of the Councel boards framing; will be of publick use to this Kingdome: I must say that matter depends on the disposicion of the Court of England, and the Laws that will be offered us to passe which may be some equivalent to this great concession of ours, for soe I take it to be. If I consider the Governement here as it is in the hands of the three Lords Justices or two of them[134] I have no reason to doubt but that there is at least a quorum of them sincerely freinds to the true interest of this Kingdome the British Protestant interest; then which people I mean the Protestants of Ireland I am morally certain there are not under the Sun a more affectionately dutiful body of men to their now Majesties Governement. How far the Lords Justices may be crampt by instructions I know not, but fear we have too many and too powerful enemyes on your side the water; who knowing they have already used us ill, think the only way to prevent being told of it will be to continue doing soe: but for my part I shal be of opinion if we doe meet that since there is no hopes to redresse things past it will be our prudence to look forward and prevent future mischeifs; and with this resolucion I doe declare to you I shal come into the house, if a Parliament be called and I happen to be of it. Beside this point yeilded, little to our reputatacion and I think much to our detriment hereafter: mony will be expected which we are not able to give with out greatly pressing the poor Country; yet good Laws will be an equivalent and be a good exchange for our mony and for ought I know our sole right of preparing heads of bills for mony: but what Laws we may expect I know not: none of

[129] Elizabeth Villiers (1657–1733), later Countess of Orkney; acknowledged mistress of William III.

[130] James II.

[131] Part of James II's Irish landed estate, which became forfeit after the Revolution and was granted by William III to Mrs Villiers, had been purchased from Sir Allen (SHC, G145/box 94/1: 'Abstract of the duke of York's conveyance to Sir Alan Brodrick').

[132] Robert Rochfort, MP [I].

[133] Henry Poley (1654–1707), barrister of Lincoln's Inn, but formerly of the Middle Temple, to which he had been admitted in 1673 (*HC 1690–1715*, v, 168).

[134] Henry Capel (1638–96), 1st Baron Capell, William Duncombe (c.1647–1704), and Sir Cyril Wyche (c.1632–1707). In separate letters to the English ministry in July 1694 Lord Capell recommended recalling the Irish parliament, while Wyche and Duncombe argued against (BL, Add. MS 21136, ff 25–8: Duncombe and Wyche to Sir John Trenchard, Capell to same, 14 July 1694; HMC, *Buccleuch MSS*, ii, 103).

any publick advantage that are considerable can I hear to be transmitted from hence for England: there were several pointed out as fit to be enacted by the last house of Commons, and a bill to repeal the Acts which erect the Star chamber and high Commission Court in this Kingdome will I think be very useful and not soe only but in my sense necessary.[135] Whether we may hope such bills or any of them will be hence transmitted I know not, but till I can have some reasonable assurance the Country may be the better and not the worse for our meeting I shal never desire a Parliament may be summoned: Now i[t w]ill be much the worse if we meet and part in heat, or doe no[t] comply with their Majesties expectacions: but to meet [and sole]ly to u[n]say what the last house voted, to give a tax and passe three or fowre insignficant acts and then to goe home seems to me soe little for the service of the Country that I shal think it is better not to meet then to meet to soe little purpose. I would not therefore advise, nor can I wish to see a Parliament called till I have some tolerable assurance what we may hope for: If good bills are not already sent over, or doe not come to Whitehall before issuing writs for summoning a Parliament here I despair of seeing such transmitted; for the Councel board have been told I mean the late house of Commons hath sufficiently hinted what acts of force in England we want to be enacted here; there needs no great trouble to draw them, being done to their hands in such maner that I presume they will not take it ill to be told they are not easily to be mended: if they do not send them, it is in my sense a tacite allowance that by their good wills they shal not be enacted as Laws here: if we are put off to framing bills of that kind ourselves, in my opinion that is an open confession nothing but delay is meant, and before they can be framed, transmitted, sent back, and passed, the Session will be over …

[*PS*.] After all if you foresee that a Parliament will in some few years be called (as I think it necessarily must) I shal think it to be for the good of the Kingdome that it be summoned during this Governement rather then another, that we may own the admirable care taken by the Lords Justices in governing the Kingdome, and redressing many things that were amisse, particularly the army.

16. *Alan I, Limerick, to Thomas, Wandsworth, 31 Mar. 1695*

(1248/1/271–2)

I find by rumor and an account that is come by letter to this town that I am looked on to have broken the priviledge of the house of Commons of England in moving for a trial in ejectment wherein Mr Wharton took defence.[136] It is a sin of ignorance, and therefore I hope will not damne me; I confesse I never did think that the Parliament of England

[135] Two separate sets of heads were introduced in the 1695 session to abolish 'the court commonly called the Star Chamber or Castle Chamber', one in the Lords and the other in the Commons. The former was dropped after being presented; the latter was sent to the lord deputy but proceeded no further than the Irish privy council. No legislative action seems to have been taken against the court of high commission in Ireland. In any case, neither court had operated since the revolution.

[136] On 19 Mar. 1695 a complaint was made to the English house of commons that two named individuals had moved 'declarations in ejectment for an estate in the county of Tipperary, in the kingdom of Ireland, in the possession of the right honourable Thomas Wharton' (1648–1715), later 1st Earl Wharton; and that Alan Brodrick 'had moved the court there against allowing the privilege of the said Mr Wharton, in breach of the privileges of this house' (*CJ*, xi, 276). Alan was summoned, but the session ended before the matter could be taken any further.

had judged trials of titles of Land in this Kingdome to be any invasion of their priviledges and was the more induced to think soe by having heard many such mocions made sitting the Parliament in England without any notice taken of it by the house: beside I thought that the word of an Attorney that Mr Wharton was a member of the house of Commons (for there was noe more, neither plea nor affidavit) was not sufficient proof or notice of his being soe; nor had I really any knowledge of it, farther then that knowing him to be a man of great estate and qualitye I had cause to beleive him a member of Parliament. But I doe not contest its being a breach of priviledge, nor having competent notice since the house have ordered me to attend and answer the matter and that the suit doe stay in the meantime: The later part of the order will be performed the first day of Clonmel Assises when the Atturney[137] will withdraw the rule for trial: And tho I have not yet been served with any summons yet I resolve forthwith to leave this town and if any shipping be ready at Corke to goe thence to the first port I can make in England, if by any means I may overtake the Parliament before it rises: Nothing can fall out more unluckilye at this time, for my wife is extreamly sick, the term is at hand and we talk of a Parliament here;[138] but all these consideracions apart I will assoon as I have prepared my self with mony for such a voyage and journey begin it: but hope that this being the first president that ever was in this Kingdome I shal not be condemned for a crime I never knew was o[?ne] till the vote hath informed me: and to proceed with rig[?our] against me (if I may say soe) looks like condemning a man upon a penal Law not promulgated.

17. *Alan I, Dublin, to St John II, Wandsworth, 21 Sept. 1695*

(1248/1/274–5)

I think my last to you was directed to the Bath about your writing to the Speaker to have a new member for Middletown elected in your roome,[139] which Sir Joseph Williamson opposed on pretence such a thing had never been done; but I shewed several precedents in our journals which overruled his assumed authoritye of determining all matters according to what he alledged the usage was in England, much to his mortificacion who expressed his resentment some little time afterward that his precedents were not regarded: but if I mistake not, there was another reason in the wind: for you must know he is one of the heads of a party, who look on us of an interest utterly opposite to that they drive, and probably was unwilling to strenghthen it so much as by one vote;[140] but honest Charles Oliver is chosen in your stead. I have for near a fortnight past been extraordinarilye ill, of a cold, feavorish, and soe hoarse as not to be heard a yard but am now on the mending hand: this hath hindred my giving you an account of our proceedings: never were greater endeavours used to break us by insisting on the sole right, nor to lesse purpose: they that knew how little good it was

[137]Sir John Temple (c.1632–1705) served as attorney-general for Ireland until May 1695.

[138]The Irish parliament reconvened (after a general election) in Aug. 1695.

[139]On 6 Sept. 1695 the Speaker of the Irish house of commons reported receipt of a letter from St John Brodrick (from England) requesting permission to resign his seat 'by reason of his great indisposition of body'. A writ was ordered to be issued for the seat. (*CJI*, ii, 509).

[140]For Williamson's prominence in the 'party' that supported Lord Chancellor Porter see SHC, Somers papers, 371/14/F/5: Capell to Shrewsbury, 28 Aug. 1695.

to the Crown to frame money bills at Councel Board, and of what importance it was to have them arise in the house of Commons considered too a rupture would be of more fatal consequence which in most mens judgements must have been the end of our disagreeing to receive a money bill from the Lord Deputye and Councel, and chose the least evil:[141] This was the sheet anchor our enemies depended on that we should split on that rock; their next method was since we had carried that point they would clog it soe that the King should not have reason to think my Lord Deputye[142] had done him such signal service in weathering this great affair; to effect which extraordinarye bills were moved for; the hab. corp. act and several others which are all good in themselves; but in my mind tacking on these demands immediately upon the other (for I must observe to you Mr Savage our Chancellor of the Exchequer[143] and a great creature of Mr Whartons[144] the next moment after receiving the mony bill moved for the hab. corp. bill to be brought in) look as if they would tell the King that my Lord Deputye had bought the point of the sole right very dear.[145] In short we want not influences and refined politicks from your side the water, whither Mr Savage is now hastning in hopes of being chosen at Colchester (but I hope he will meet another disappointment)[146] Sir Joseph hath not forgot how a Courtier ought to manage; Lord Ranelagh,[147] Normanbye[148] and Coningesbye have their friends etc. but I am of opinion poor dull honest Irish understandings[149] will bring matters to passe as they ought. I may mistake in my judgement, but I apprehend the cheif design of each party was and is to have a cheif Governor of their own, such an one as for their own private ends they can like; for there is not the least pretence of misgovernement by this Gentleman since his receiving the sword; but I fancy it will be difficult to doe his businesse at Whitehall who doth that of the King at Dublin soe very well as Lord Capel doth …

18. *Alan I, Dublin, to St John II, Lamb Buildings, 13 Nov. 1695*

(1248/1/276–7)

I have read and well considered your letter intended to my father but superscribed to me that I might read it: I doe not think it will overtake him in Munster tho sent by the next post, soe I keep it to be delivered in town and the rather since from it I will take a rise to presse him to the same purpose your letter doth. Your impressions of our affairs and

[141] On this general issue, see McGrath, 'Making of a Parliamentary Settlement in Ireland', 585–613.

[142] Capell had been appointed lord deputy on 9 May.

[143] Philip Savage.

[144] Thomas Wharton.

[145] In a letter to King William III on 26 Oct. 1695 Capell gave an account of his attempts to prevent the passage of the habeas corpus bill (Nottingham UL, Portland (Bentinck) MSS, PwA 251). See also James Kelly, *Poynings' Law and the Making of Law in Ireland 1660–1800* (Dublin, 2007), 74, 79.

[146] At the English general election in Oct. Savage seems to have based his aspirations on the interest of his kinsman Richard Savage, 4th Earl Rivers, but did not press his candidature as far as a poll (*HC 1690–1715*, ii, 186–7).

[147] Richard Jones (1641–1712), 1st earl of Ranelagh.

[148] John Sheffield (1648–1721), 1st marquess of Normanby, and later 1st duke of Buckingham.

[149] An ironical use of what in England was a common pejorative phrase.

proceedings, and the issue and event of them are all made by the same party: the story is told you and others much different from what it is and the consequences you apprehend are like those of men in real concern much greater then the thing can occasion; tho if those very matters you seem to foresee as our utmost misfortunes should happen, the mischeif would not be such as you imagine to the Protestant interest of this Kingdome. I have several reasons for not sending you an entire narrative of our proceedings; perhaps it may fall into other hands, and he that will tell the whole truth of this affair must say some things not fit for the publick, considering what was done in the house of Commons: if I should be obliged to shew the reasons of some of our actions and the motives that occasioned some of our votes (which I allow deserve the epithetes you say some people give some of our proceedings) there would be enough upon producing my letter to censure it as a libel and a scandalous one, tho I related not one tittle but truth. But this is not my only reason; I am not able to give a true account of the whole matter upon my own knowledge, being sick for ten dayes about the beginning of the Session and not in the house when the matter began in that General vote when the house had the state of the Nation in its consideracion and had resolved into a Committee of the whole house on that occasion: That vote was to this effect That among others the favour the Irish Papists had received during the late Governements since the year 1690 was one occasion of the miserye of the Kingdome.[150] I am as well convinced this is nicely true as I was and am that it was very unseasonable: Slone[151] was either by design or accident the occasion of it: the maner is too tedious to mention, but the thing is true: and I hear it was presently taken up and pressed by Poets and Painters[152] - After the house was up several of the members came to see me and told me what they had done: My answer was they had a zeal but not according to knowledge and I gave them reasons to think these matters were better forgotten, and to the intent I might judge for my self and not by others representacions I went to the house tho sick the next day that matter came on which was Friday the 13th of September (If I remember right) with a full intent to endeavour to compose matters; I was ill and in particular was soe hoarse as not to be heard but with difficulty and resolved not to speak; but no sooner was my Lord Chancellor named but Mr Savage[153] and Mr Sloane[154] (among others) acted soe as altered all my measures: I thought it might with ease have been ended by saying it was no proper time to enquire into things that were past when we had a prospect of good things to come, for fear of losing what we were almost in possession of and could not be disappointed of

[150]Alan's chronology in this letter is awry. The committee of the whole house on the state of the nation had met first on 18 Sept., and the resolutions reported the next day focused on the period before 1690, in relation to the long absence of parliaments and the encouragement given to catholics 'during the two last reigns' (*CJI*, ii, 524–6). On Monday, 23 Sept., the committee met again and produced the resolution mentioned here, that the countenance and favour shown to catholics by the government in Ireland since 1690 had been another cause of 'the miseries of the kingdom' (*CJI*, ii, 531). A further meeting on Friday the 27th reported progress and was adjourned to the following Monday (30 Sept.), but on that day, before the committee could be constituted, Colonel William Ponsonby, MP for Co. Kilkenny (and later Viscount Duncannon), presented 'articles of high crimes and misdemeanours' against Lord Chancellor Porter. On Porter's impeachment, see Hayton, *Ruling Ireland*, 56–9.

[151]James Sloane. For his superficially erratic behaviour in this session, see BL, Add. MS 28879, f. 157: [J.F.] to John Ellis, 28 Sept. 1695.

[152]Presumably an allusion to the discussion of mimesis in Aristotle's *Poetics*. Alan's meaning would be the following speakers merely imitated what had been said before.

[153]Philip Savage.

[154]James Sloane.

but by impatience etc. Instead of this their behaviour was other then I expected or beleived suited with the occasion: nothing but Panegyricks of the good man, some were I think for Statues: one sett speech was made,[155] but by misfortune the Gentleman by offering it unseasonably was taken down to orders and being put out could never gett in again, soe that was lost. However in that dayes work tho my Lord Chancellors action then in debate was not (in my opinion) to be justified, yet I handled it with great tendernesse and soe as I since repent it since it was followed by such actions in his freinds as it soon produced. For as on Fryday nothing but a justificacion (not a passing by) of the matter in debate would serve, we were assured on Saturday that they intended on Munday to give him thanks for his very good administracion: If I were asked the author of this I cannot name him but verily beleive some of the hot ones of that party intended it: I confesse I was unwilling to have a man thanked for those things which in my opinion would in the eye of the Law had another return; I thought that would be to own all he had done was just and good and Legal and fit to be made a precedent to posteritye; how far it will be soe I know not, if it be I know how many hours sail it is to another part of the world: they were not content to be cleared of one matter which did not look very well neither, but must triumph and this put men on endeavouring to shew him more clearly and at large and this I am confident produced the articles against him: which how they come to be rejected I will not trouble you with an account now but it will be told in story, not worse in favour of us who were for them (as I own to have been) whatever it may be for his freinds.[156] I can not think that among the many who are gone over hence, there will not be one or two found to doe the Country right by giving this affair another face then it bears (as you say) among many with you: this I have heard observed, and I beleive truly that in the whole house there was not one man that had sate in the Irish Parliament, had served in employ civil or militarye under the late King since the abdicacion, had been suspected for having too favourable an opinion of his proceedings or almost lived in the Irish quarters but were of the same opinion: and if they were thus unanimous in the house and had a majoritye (as they had) I assure you so they have in the Countrey: this is not very politick to own, but to one that hath a concern in the Kingdome and knows where the majoritye of this nation lyes it will not seem strange that we are outnumbred in the Country as well as the house; and his Lordship hath the best fortune of any good minister living or that ever was in this Kingdome, that no Irish man ever yet opened his mouth against him, and indeed if they should I think it were wrong done him. My last told you that beside the honour of the employment I hold under the Crown[157] I never did covet, nor am I fond of it: I never aimed at it, nor sought nay I declined it and every publick station: if I am succeeded by a more confiding person I shal be no way uneasy, I took it at the Kings pleasure which I knew once before determined on much lesse ground (if the same interest hold stil) but I will never decline serving the King and Country for the sake of an office of never so great consideracion: You may beleive as you will, but nothing lesse then omnipotence can perswade men here of the good qualities

[155] A prepared speech, recited from memory (P.D.G. Thomas, *The House of Commons in the Eighteenth Century* (Oxford, 1971), 203).

[156] The Commons eventually agreed on 25 Oct. that Porter be heard in his own defence, and a resolution was passed declaring his answers satisfactory 'without proof [*being needed*]' (*CJI*, ii, 584–5). Among those who earlier 'took upon themselves the proof of the articles' were Brodrick himself, his father, brothers-in-law James Barry and Laurence Clayton, and friends Henry Conyngham, Robert Foulke and George Rogers (*CJI*, ii, 549, 584).

[157] As solicitor-general.

and few faults this Gentleman is supposed by some of your side to have. What the Devil was or can be beleived to have been the motive of so many men to attemt so difficult a task as removing a minister? So dangerous an one as to disoblige an omnipotent Lord Chancellor? for the power of that Minister here bears no proporcion to what it does among you: One thing in your letter is pleasant: A very good freind of ours you say told you it is apprehended we pressed hard in our bills on the King considering his alliances, which are most valuable to his Majestye of all things:[158] now to us safety is the most valuable thing on earth, and without the passing the bills transmitted and others we beleive and know ourselves not safe, not withstanding the taking of Namur[159] and greater successes which God grant: Excuse therefore us for obeying self preservacion …

19. *Alan I, Dublin, to St John II, Lamb Buildings, 17 Dec. 1695*

(1248/1/278–9)

This comes by a safe hand, by Colonel Cuningham[160] who is a very worthy man and intimately my freind: I would have you contract some acquaintance with him if you have a mind to have a sensible and impartial account of our proceedings in Parliament here. Tho I am to take Coach for Munster in an hour I will not omit writing, since I may venture to speak more boldly then prudence will permit where the letter goes by post. Take then this summary account of this Session of Parliament. There were some who abhorred the thoughts of a Parliaments meeting here at all, among which were all the Irish and those who had enriched themselves by the spoil and ruine of this unhappy Country; the former for fear of Laws being made against them, the later least their actions should be pried into and be censured if not punished: I may be suspected to speak with prejudice to the Lord Chancellor, but (whatever was his motive) he certainly advised against calling a Parliament as warmly as any: You cant think Lord Rumney[161] could be fond of a Parliament succeeding well under Lord Capel, when during his Governement a former had been so warmly dismissed and so fatally miscarried. Mr Wharton[162] had an eye on this Governement and was intended to be joint in Commission with Lord Capel as Lords Justices but that would not be accepted: You may guesse how far any of these persons or their freinds and dependants would contribute to carry things on easilye; and I assure you, tho none of them had a very considerable party yet all joined together (as they seldom or never failed to do) made a formidable body. Mr Savage[163] was the head of Whartons freinds, and I beleive he thought whatever tended to the removing Lord Capel (as an abrupt breaking up the Parliament must have done) put

[158]A reference to measures introduced into the Irish parliament to tighten up the penal laws against catholics — notably the Bishops' Banishment Act (9 Will. III, c. 1), the Disarming Act (7 Will. II, c. 5), the Education Act (7 Will. III, c. 4), and the act to prevent intermarriage between protestants and catholics (9 Will. III, c. 3) — which embarrassed the king with his catholic allies, especially the Habsburg Emperor Leopold I.

[159]The recapture of Namur in Sept. 1695 had been hailed as marking a decisive turn in the European war.

[160]Henry Conyngham, MP [I].

[161]Henry Sydney (Lord Sidney) had been created earl of Romney in 1694.

[162]Thomas Wharton.

[163]Philip Savage.

Mr Wharton nearer and next to the possession of his wishes. His[164] interest in Leinster (which province sends most burgesses) is generally good, and in particular in Wexford and Carlow; beside what influence he had as Chancellor of the Exchequer and Clerk of the Crown in the Kings Bench: Slone[165] was a great bawler and stickler too for Wharton but his underling: yet made some small interest in the North. Sir Joseph Williamson was the head of the Chancellors party[166] which consisted of trencher[167] freinds (for he[168] kept a very good table, and is a courteous well bred man, and a very boon companion) of persons having Causes depending before him, of Clerks of Chancerye and Lawyers, and of all that are supposed not much disaffected to the Irish or Jacobitism.[169] I need not tell where Sir Donogh o'Brien,[170] Sir John Mead,[171] Robin FitzGerald[172] or some beside Sir John Meade who have Papist wifes[173] and breed their children or some of them in that religion went. Lord Sydneys party I think owned Mr Dering[174] for one of his zealous freinds, but I cannot beleive they esteemed him head of their party; he had also two menial servants one Jones[175] and one Carter[176] (both Atturnyes of the Kings Bench) in the house; and all who belong to the Treasurye or Custom house were wondrously concerned for him, Lord Coningesbye and the Chancellor. Besides these all the freinds of those who were lately displaced (as Sir Standish Hartstonges[177] son in Law Brownlow[178], his own son[179] and grandson both of his own name[180] and Capt Corry,[181] Napper[182] and others who were Levinges[183] freinds) were

[164]Savage's.

[165]James Sloane.

[166]Confirmed in BL, Add. MS 28879, f. 104: [J.F.] to John Ellis, 6 Sept. 1695.

[167]Those who shared with him the pleasures of the table.

[168]Lord Chancellor Porter.

[169]This description of Porter's party echoes that sent by Capell to Shrewsbury, 28 Sept., 6 Oct. 1695 (HMC, *Buccleuch MSS*, ii, 229, 235). Details are provided in a contemporary list of the Commons in 1695, marked to indicate supporters and opponents of the lord chancellor (TCD, MS 1179, pp. 37–9, printed in Hayton, *Ruling Ireland*, 96–105). The factional affiliations ascribed to individuals by Alan in the present letter are confirmed by this list.

[170]Sir Donough O'Brien, 1st Bt., had been a jacobite in 1690 (*Hist. Ir. Parl.*, v, 367).

[171]MP for TCD in James II's Irish parliament in 1689.

[172]Son of Garrett Fitzgerald of Corkbeg, Co. Cork and descended from a cadet branch of the Geraldine earls of Desmond.

[173]Meade was married three times: his current wife (m. 1688) was Elizabeth (1669–1757), whose father, Pierce Butler, 2nd Viscount Ikerrin (1637–c.1680), had been brought up a catholic but had conformed to the established church to secure the recovery of his lands after the Restoration. Ikerrin's father, the 1st viscount, had been a prominent member of the Catholic Confederacy in the 1640s.

[174]Charles Dering. He may have been identified as an opponent of Porter on the list cited above, n. 169.

[175]Probably Edmond Jones. Edward Jones, MP Old Leighlin 1692–5, was an attorney, but was dead by 21 Oct. 1695 (*Hist. Ir. Parl.*, iv, 500).

[176]Thomas Carter.

[177]Sir Standish Hartstonge (1630–1700), 1st Bt, baron of exchequer [I] 1680–6, 1691–5.

[178]Arthur Brownlow (formerly Chamberlain), MP [I], who had married Hartstonge's daughter Jane (*Hist. Ir. Parl.*, iii, 291).

[179]Standish Hartstonge, sr.

[180]Standish Hartstonge, jr (later 2nd Bt).

[181]James Corry.

[182]Either James Napper or William Napper.

[183]Sir Richard Levinge, Speaker of the Commons in 1692.

not very fond of him that caused it: Envy of the preferments conferred on Rotchfort and me[184] and making the new Privy Councellors[185] and displacing Sir Richard Cox and Sir John Jefreyson[186] added their freinds to the number; and you may be sure the new relacion between Lord Coningesbye and Sir Thomas Southwell[187] secured him and his Cousen Southwell[188] and their freinds. Lord Clifford[189] (tho I observed him much to conceal it) had his resentments, I beleive, upon being informed what resolucions Lord Deputye had taken, if (as it was for one while talked) his brother Harry had come over and aimed at the Chair,[190] in which my brother was used to oppose him and I suppose by that means he is no freind to any of us. The first great point was the sole right, in defence of which (after five or six had spoken against it) neither Mr Savage nor Sir Joseph Williamson (tho of the Privy Council) ever opened their mouthes. I was the first that took it up and I may truly say turned that matter; however upon the question for receiving the mony bill from the Councel board the noes desired a division in expectacion of the silent mens coming over to them, and I have been told by some of them that they had a promise of such a defection in that party if they saw their assistance was like to carry it; but being too few the bill was received and that great point ended contrary to their wishes if not expectacions. The next game they plaid was to possesse the King that Lord Capel must give more for the thing then it was worth, and Mr Savage the moment after receiving that bill moved for the habeas corpus act and tho my brother and I with others proposed that it should not extend to non Jurors during the war it could not be obtained: the disarming bill, and that to prevent foreign educacion[191] were represented as ill drawn and of noe great consequence: nothing would serve turn but the bill of rights,[192] the same Act to regulate the Privy Council here that is in England which is not practicable in this Kingdome:[193] Quartering on private houses and the right of it must be enquired into and if possible voted illegal, which of course must starve and ruine the Army especially on their marches where it is impossible to find publick houses to receive them: Besides they knew the more hard things any one moved against the Irish the more popular they who moved them became by soe doing: and when those who were concerned for the Governement shewed the ill policye of pressing things to extremitye and of demanding all things at once against Irish men th[ey] were represented

[184]In June 1695 Robert Rochfort had been appointed attorney-general and Alan Brodrick solicitor-general.

[185]For Capell's remodelling of the Irish judiciary and privy council in the spring of 1695, see Hayton, *Ruling Ireland*, 54–5.

[186]Sir John Jeffreyson (1635–1690), justice of common pleas [I] 1690–*d.* (Ball, *Judges*, ii, 58–9).

[187]Sir Thomas Southwell, 2nd Bt, MP [I], was Coningsby's son-in-law.

[188]Edward Southwell, MP [I].

[189]Charles Boyle (1660–1704), Baron Clifford [E], who succeeded his grandfather as 3rd earl of Cork in 1698.

[190]Hon. Henry Boyle, later 1st Baron Carleton, sat for Co. Cork 1692–3 and Youghal 1695–9. *Hist. Ir. Parl.*, iii, 240–1, mistakenly suggests that the MP for Youghal was an unidentifiable namesake, an error followed in *HC 1690–1715*, iii, 291. Boyle was absent (in England) at a call of the Irish house of commons on 25 Sept. 1695, and ordered to attend (*CJI*, ii, 537).

[191]See above, p. 66.

[192]Heads of a bill of rights were sent to the lord lieutenant from the house of lords in Oct. 1695 but suppressed by the Irish privy council. See W.N. Osborough, 'The Failure to Enact an Irish Bill of Rights: A Gap in Irish Constitutional History', *Irish Jurist*, n.s., xxxiii (1998), 392–413.

[193]Heads of a bill 'For regulating the privy council, and for taking away the court commonly called the Star Chamber or Castle Chamber', originating in the Commons, were sent to the lord deputy on 27 Sept. 1695 but were lost in the Irish privy council.

as Courtiers who had lost all regard for the Country. It is true that my brother and I had a great hand in carr[?ying] the matter of the sole right, and for this at the beginning of the Sess[ion] they called it the Brodricks Parliament to create envy to u[s] and were enraged to see things succeed as they did. How the articles against Lord Chancellor came in and were rejected I formerly have told you: Since that Mr Coghlan[194] moved the house on the peticion of one Geohoghan an Irish Papist that he might be interceded for by the Parliament to have his outlawrye for rebellion reversed (tho not within any articles) on pretence of ill usage by our army,[195] but in that they were disappointed and outvoted, as they were in the mentioning the Lord Deputye in our addresse at the Close of the Session,[196] which was furiously opposed by Sir John Mead, the Recorder of Dublin,[197] Mr Dering,[198] Mr Maurice Annesley,[199] Mr Eyres[200] and good Sir Joseph;[201] and indeed most of the party were in their minds against it but upon the division of the house finding the majoritye against them they all come out that it might not be known who would have staid in. In short the Session is over, the King has had the money given him which he demanded, his sole right is either asserted or given up to him which were the terms on which the Parliament was to sit: the Country hath had such Laws passed as they long have wanted and wished for but never expected to have had granted but by such a King and under such a Cheif Governor; we have regulated the measures and fees in the Exchequer in the Collection of quitrent[202] and in the Custom house: and pray what harm have the articles against Lord Chancellor done; if they succeeded I think we had laid a foundacion for an English establishment for ever.

20. *Alan I, Dublin, to St John II, Wandsworth, 25 Feb. 1695/6*

(1248/1/282–3)

I think of going in a day or two toward Munster and cant leave the town without telling you soe: My brother shewed me a letter from you in which you say a Gentleman whom you will not name (but give entire credit to) saw a letter under Mr Neves[203] hand to Sir

[194] Joseph Coghlan.

[195] Edward Geoghegan of Castletown, Co. Westmeath. A motion was made on 2 Dec. for leave to bring in a petition on his behalf, but defeated on a division (*CJI*, ii, 611). Letters to the duke of Shrewbury confirm that Joseph Coghlan ('the head of my lord chancellor's party') brought in the petition, and that Sir Joseph Williamson and Sir John Meade spoke in favour of its reception (HMC, *Buccleuch MSS*, ii, 272–3). See also J. G. Simms, *The Williamite Confiscation in Ireland, 1690–1703* (1956), 80–1.

[196] On 13 Dec. 1695, on a motion to omit mention of the lord deputy from the address to the King thanking him for the legislation passed in this session (*CJI*, ii, 636–7).

[197] William Handcock.

[198] Charles Dering.

[199] A teller in favour of Lord Chancellor Porter in the crucial division on 25 Oct. that had terminated the proceedings against him (*CJI*, ii, 585).

[200] Either Edward Eyre or John Eyre.

[201] Williamson.

[202] A tax on freehold land granted by the crown; in origin, a monetary composition for the various services obligatory under feudal tenure.

[203] William Neave, MP [I].

Francis Brewster[204] giving him and me very ill characters: I taxed Neve with it in presence of Mr Wingfeild[205] at Kilmainham[206] who utterly disownes it: In few words I know not your Author, but is not that Gentleman you hint at my sister Patty Barry or some body from her?[207] Tho I ever thought ill of Sir Francis Brewster, and constantly (but to no purpose) told my brother his saint would appear a Devil, and his man of money and integritye a beggarly knave;[208] yet it is hard to beleive he could forge and then produce such a letter; yet if he produced such an one I beleive it to be counterfeit, for I am confident the other could never be soe ill a man … I am sure you have a real concern for me therefore I give you a constant account of my own affairs; depend on it you never shal find me guilty of an ill thing; pride and insolence or haughtinesse which you say I am taxed with is a very sencelesse charge, nothing is so remote from my nature. I confesse I cannot cringe to a knave for his being great, nor court a villain tho he have interest at court. When I hear a favourite fool talk long at the bar and fancy he is very wise I love to humble him, especially if he be pert and saucy which is sometimes the Case. Be not troubled for any thing can befall me; I took up the emploiment I am in unwillingly, by force; my Lord Deputy would take no denial: I doe not expect honesty will or can long support a man in emploiment in some parts of the world, and I never will be of the accursed crew to gain all their favours. If Lord Deputy were bereft of his Secretarye[209] and my brother[210] those who would supplant him would have frequent oportunities of leading him into mistakes through his not knowing persons nor the affairs of this Country. They are just to him and never advise him but to the service of the King and Country, which appears plainly from hence that they cannot be taxed with the least corruption or gain: if it were true that they did more then their enemies pretend they doe, unlesse something be done amisse where is their fault. I think that is not pretended; the reports for granting away Lands or quitrents are not soe frequent as in other Governements, nor expedited as formerly which creates many enemies: In short the Irish and such as have shared in the spoil of this poor Country and fear to have their actions looked into, or at least are sure the same thing is not to be practiced again while Lord Capel hath the Sword,[211] are sworn enemies to him and all that come to the Castle and are not false to him: they are not to be frightned nor perswaded into a compliance. This is too long a letter, but depend on it our actions are very fair, and nothing can prejudice us but my fathers unalterable bent to throw away his money.

[204]Sir Francis Brewster, MP [I].

[205]Edward Wingfield, MP [I].

[206]Presumably at the assizes held there, as Edward Wingfield was also a barrister.

[207]Presumably a sister of Alan's first wife.

[208]Francis Brewster, jr, a son of Sir Francis Brewster, had been returned for Midleton in 1695 on the recommendation of Thomas Brodrick. Sir Francis himself had formerly been a staunch ally of the Brodricks, but was shifting his ground by autumn 1696 and declaring that he would 'have nothing to do with the government' (Hayton, *Ruling Ireland*, 68–9), a change of tack which was coincident with, and possibly a consequence of, the onset of personal financial difficulties (*DIB*, i, 829).

[209]Richard Aldworth, MP [I].

[210]Thomas.

[211]i.e. holds the position of chief governor (a reference to the sword of state).

21. *Alan I, Dublin, to St John II, Lamb Buildings, 20 May 1696*

(1248/1/284–5)

This will come to your hands by Mr Stone[212] that goes expresse from our new Lords Justices (Lord Blessinton[213] and Colonel Wolseley[214] who were sworn last Monday) to the Lords Justices of England: I am sensible that matters which are transacted on this side the water are very diligently represented and spread on the other much otherwise then they really are: Witnesse the expresse that went hence near three weeks agoe with an account of an impossibilitye of Lord Deputyes recoverye[215] and the certainty of his death in a very few dayes after its going away, notwithstanding which, they who sent it know he is yet living, and if he had not fallen into convulsions ten dayes after they sent away, might have been soe for many years. But to begin the matter: my Lord Deputies freinds, I mean my Lady,[216] his Nephew Lord Montrathe[217] and others advised him (and I am told his Physicians agreed in it) that nothing probably would so much contribute to the recoverye of his health as recesse from businesse; and after this was frequently repeated to him he ordered the Atturnye General and me, to view his patent and to give him our thoughts whether he were thereby authorized to make Justices; upon view and consideracion of it we found and certified he was: some dayes after he told us he would have a warrant drawn and signed, for our, or one of our preparing a fiant[218] accordingly; and then said, he had Lord Blessinton and Sir Christopher Wandesford[219] in his thoughts: and as I heard sent Lord Blessinton word to come to town, but not on what occasion: His Lordship also ordered us to attend him at a day which I forget at Chappel Izod;[220] and my apprehensions were that it was to give us the warrant for drawing a fiant accordingly to make them Justices: When I came thither I was told Mr Wolseley was pitched on instead of Wandesford, in my Lords intencions; at which I was surprized; but not being concerned in appointing, or liking either, I went into the chamber where my Lord lay, and there my Lord, in the Atturneys and my presence, ordered his secretarye to fill up a blank warrant with the names of Blessinton and Wolseley, which was signed; and required us or either of us to draw a fiant for their being Justices pursuant to my Lords power of constituting them soe: The Speaker took it, and drew the fiant and it was carried to my Lord Chancellor to sign the

[212] Richard Stone, MP [I].

[213] Murrough Boyle (c.1645–1718), 1st Viscount Blessington.

[214] William Wolseley, MP [I]: a political ally of the Brodricks (University of Kansas, Kenneth Spencer Research Library, MS 143 Cz: earl of Drogheda to Arthur Moore, 18 Aug. 1696).

[215] Capell died on 30 May 1696.

[216] Dorothy (*d.* c.1721), da. of Richard Bennet of Chancery Lane, London, and Kew, Surrey.

[217] Nephew by marriage: Charles Coote (c.1655–1709), 3rd earl of Mountrath, had married in 1691 Lady Isabella Dormer, daughter of Charles Dormer, 2nd earl of Carnarvon, by his wife Elizabeth, Henry Capel's sister. In addition, Mountrath's own sister was the wife of Lord Blessington.

[218] In Ireland a warrant to the court of chancery, constituting the authority for the issue of letters patents under the great seal.

[219] Sir Christopher Wandesford, MP [I].

[220] Chapelizod: a manor on the edge of the Phoenix Park, acquired for the crown in 1665, whose mansion house served as a country residence for the chief governor. Lord Capell endured his last illness and died there.

recepi,[221] which he declined the doing till he attended my Lord Deputye, which was done the day following; when Lord Chancellor made several objections to the draught:[222] I said whatever faults it might have, I was not answerable for them, never having seen it: soe Lord Deputye ordered the three Cheif Judges,[223] the Atturney and me to attend Lord Chancellor that afternoon to consider my Lords Commission and the draught of that fiant; and in the main we came to this general opinion that it was not proper that fiant should stand; but agreed on what might be received and passe the seal when his Excellencye should think fit; that is, we all agreed his Excellencye might create Justices, and passe a Commission with powers and in such maner as was then discoursed on. The Lord Deputye hereupon sent a joint warrant to the Attornye and me, to prepare a fiant pursuant to his Lordships power by his Commission, and we were pressed by repeated messages to dispatch it: I must observe to you that there was no objection at this time or ever before made, that passing a patent pursuant to the Commission given by the King to the Lord Deputye, would tend any way to the disturbance of the peace of the Kingdome, by making it a doubtfull matter whether the Justices Commission determined by the death of the Deputye or not; for if it doth, writs are to issue by 33 H.8 in this Kingdome to summon the Councel to chuse a Cheif Governor till the King appoints one: Upon this warrant the Atturnye and I drew and signed a fiant, warranted by my Lord Deputies Commission and warrant (as we conceive and that I think is not doubted) which was given the Secretarye[224] and hath been out of our hands about three weeks: Just before my Lords signing this last warrant he was much worse then he had formerly been, and mending afterward declined passing a Commission pursuant to it: In the mean time great applicacion was made to get Col. Wolseley out, and my Lord Deputye was so far wrought on, as to send to him to make it his request that he might be excused, and then Lord Droghedah[225] was to be the man; but he insisted, that being once declared in Councel and his name sent over to the King, he never could wave it, but must submit to his Lordships pleasure. My Lord Deputye upon this, desired the Atturnye and me to advise him in this exigence,[226] declaring he never had given Lord Droghedah any promise: we declined answering it, but, finding him to be in the greatest anxietye of mind, did with Secretarye Aldworth propose to him to make no Justices (being confined by his patent to two, soe as he must distast one of the three) but to recommend all three to be made soe by order from England: What was done hereon I know not; but my Lord falling into convulsion fits, soe as it was apprehended he could not probably live till he might receive an answer from England, on this motive (as I hear) his Lordship immediately ordered the passing the patent on the fiant drawn by the Attorney and me, which received some delayes not necessarye to be here mentioned: at length Lord Chancellor last Thursday the 14th of

[221] Literally 'I have received', the endorsement made by the lord chancellor (or keeper of the great seal) on a fiant before letters patents were issued.

[222] Porter's objection was to the clause appointing Wolseley and Blessington during the king's pleasure or until Capell was restored to health, which, he argued, would mean that they could stay in power after the lord deputy died and until the king's pleasure was known; this would take away the right of the Irish privy council (under the Irish statute of 1541 (33 Hen. VIII, sess. 2, c. 2)) to elect lord justices in the event of the death of the chief governor. (PRONI, D/638/18/66: Porter to Lord Coningsby, 29, 30 Apr. 1696; HMC, *Buccleuch MSS*, ii, 332).

[223] The chief justices of common pleas and king's bench, and the chief baron of the exchequer.

[224] Chief secretary Richard Aldworth.

[225] Henry Moore (*d.* 1714), 3rd earl of Drogheda.

[226] Exigency.

May gave his Excellencye some reasons against the signing the recepi, and passing the patent; told him it determined his Commission, took away his salarye and perquisites etc. and also said, it determined upon his death: Lord Cheif Justice Hely[227] said it was his opinion too; tho that was not the question; but, whether Lord Deputye (not being able to administer the Governement, and intending to put in Justices according to the power in his Commission) could order that Commission to passe, or in otherwords, whether his Lordship having given us his warrant to draw a fiant, we had exceeded or pursued the warrant. Lord Deputye considered of it, and afterward sent Mr Stone to know his Lordships answer as to signing the recepi; my Lord Chancellor said he would first speak with my Lord Deputye about it and went to him, but was for a time denied by my Lord Deputye to see till he had obeyed him; but upon Lord Droghedah's speaking with my Lord Deputye, his Excellencye sent for and heard Lord Chancellors farther reasons; and afterward sent him word he appointed him to attend with the Seal at three in the afternoon; Lord Chancellor said that could not be for he had just come from my Lord, and he said he should hear farther from him: the messenger Mr Dawson[228] told his Lordship, that was the farther hearing from my Lord Deputye and all that he must expect: his Lordship omitted to come and made my Lord wait till after eight, when my Lord Deputye sent him a positive message to sign the recepi and passe the patent out of hand: and the messenger had other orders in case of refusal to have called for the Great Seal; but his Lordship signed the recepi, and so that matter ended. You must note that after Mr Stones message Lord Montrath the Speaker and I were sent by Lord Deputye with an absolute order to sign the recepi, and that the answer he would not doe it til he saw Lord Deputye was given to us not to Stone. The circumstances, when where and with what difficulty we found Lord Chancellor may be subject of another Letter. In short my Lord Deputye had reasons which prevailed with him not to put Lord Chancellor into greater power, and his Lordship was I beleive unwilling any Justices should be constituted, hoping the choice of the Councel (considering the restrictions in the Statute) might fall on him. This for your own satisfaction.

22. *Alan I, Dublin, to St John II, Lamb Buildings, 9 Dec. 1697*

(1248/1/296–7)

I own my self much indebted to you for Letters and my self to blame in not answering; nor will I now tell you all the reasons for not answering them immediately; businesse (and that beyond what you can think tho not in the way of my profession only, but in Parliament the Castle, Councel board, the Inns on the Irish Claims[229] the Custom house etc. added to some businesses out of Munster) was a great part but not all the cause: I must write on

[227] Sir John Hely (*d.* 1701), appointed lord chief justice of common pleas in 1695 (Ball, *Judges*, ii, 57–8).

[228] Presumably Joshua Dawson, MP [I], at this time a clerk in the chief secretary's office (*Hist. Ir. Parl.*, iv, 25).

[229] In Aug. 1697 the Irish lords justices and privy council had appointed a commission, comprising the judges in king's bench, common pleas and exchequer, to hear any remaining claims under the Articles of Galway and Limerick, which had brought to an end hostilities between Williamite and jacobite armies in 1691. This commission met at the King's Inns in Dublin. (Crawford and Balcarres, *Tudor and Stuart Proclamations*, ii, 164–6).

subjects I abominate the thought of; therefore expect not to hear from me about what is in agitacion at Middletown;[230] the accounts thence almost distract me …

23. *St John II to St John I, Midleton, 1 Feb. 1698*

(1248/1/293–4)

My Cozen Hatton's L[*ett*]re will have acquainted y[*o*]u with the death and Burial of my Aunt Hatton;[231] I am afraid you'l stay to hear the News of Sir Walter St John's too,[232] And if you should, unless some strange, unheard off, advantages and satisfactions spring up in Ireland, twill never make you, or your Family, the tenth part of Amends for what both have suffered by your unaccountable stay there. Notwithstanding my Resolutions to the contrary every time I write, I cannot forbear the giving my disregarded Opinion: But I think I have a double right to doe it. For duty obliges a Child, (whether it have any Effect or not,) to warn, and be instant with, a Parent that is throwing himself into a certain Ruine; and tis not disobedience, to persist in the neglected Advice; And I am sure, if losers ought to be allowed a Liberty of speaking, my tongue ought not to be tied up from this subject … I have your L[*ett*]re with an Account of the Frize etc. sent by Mr Poole: He sent the things up by the Carrier, but not any Certificate of the Duty beeing paid; so they were seised at the Inne; and before the Certificate could be gott, they were opened: The shalloons and Ratteen[233] will be forfeited, and must be overbought if had at all; And the t'other will give abundance of trouble and some charge. I mention this onely to caution you not to put yourself to the trouble of any thing of the kind when you come yourself: Tis a vain thing for Ireland to attempt to withstand it: A party in the house are resolved to ruine all the Western parts of it, and the rest are willing enough to see it done, [234] And this in plain English is all the return your vast Expences will make you: Of which, if you look over my L[*ett*]res, you must doe me the right to own, I have given you notice for 3 or 4 years together, tho I could not be hearkned unto.

Another part of my Advice has been, that you would sell some part of your Estate, and put yourself once before hand in the world; Every day confirms me more and more in the Opinion that tis the most advisable thing you can do: I can have no design in pressing it, but only your reputation and advantage: I assure you, from the time that I found all my Entreaties that y[*o*]u wou'd have some pitty on yourself and Family, and not ruine both under the Notion of Improvements, were so slighted, I never counted upon any share of your Fortune. I sent the L[*ett*]re you wrote to me about Lady O[*rkney*]'s Affair to my Brother

[230] Midleton.

[231] Lucy, a sister of Sir Allen and Sir St John Brodrick, had married Sir Roger Hatton (1622–66), an alderman of London. They had at least one son, Francis.

[232] Sir Walter St John (1622–1708), 3rd Bt, of Lydiard Tregoze, Wilts., a first cousin once removed of Sir St John Brodrick, through Sir St John's mother Katherine (née Nicholas).

[233] Two types of woollen cloth, the latter more thickly woven.

[234] A reference to the efforts of west-country woollen interests in the English house of commons to introduce legislation restricting exports of Irish woollen yarn and cloth (see Patrick Kelly, 'The Irish Woollen Export Prohibition Act of 1699: Kearney Re-visited', *Irish Economic and Social History*, vii (1980), 22–44).

Tho[*mas*].[235] You may be sure that he will not meddle in that matter, and tis not at all fitting or reasonable that he should. The Dean of St Pauls[236] has been dangerously ill, but I thank God, he is well again.

24. *Alan I, to St John II*[237], *'to be left at Mr Wilkinson's, at the Black Boy', 13 Aug. [1698]*

(1248/1/292–3)

This Dear St John I write at Shaftsbury[238] fearing I may not overtake the post at Sherborn where I design to lye. I need not tell you how nearly it will concern me to have what I left in charge with you concerning the letters you were to deliver brought to a good and speedy end: it will certainly prove of considerable trouble and with pains may be brought to passe as I could wish; and your best endeavours I need not doubt: On my faith I will readily doe a thing of greater difficulty for you when you ask it: If you can possibly pray by no means send into Ireland; if the other way do not take, that must be done; but be cautious how far you goe. I write thus dark for fear of eyes tho under a fictitious superscription.

You know all men ought to take notice of what occurs remarkable in their travails; and soe have I done. First then, Let men take what measures they will of Ireland, if they find a more barren ill favoured peice of ground then for Egham to Hartleroe[239] (15 miles in length and I guesse twice as broad for I could never reach the skirts of it on either side with my eye) I am mistaken. At Hartleroe I met the hole of an house of office a foot and three quarters diameter; and saw two of the fattest bucks that I beleive were ever killed in England; they came from Wilton[240] … The vale from Salisbury to Shaftbury seems the pleasantest I ever saw; but I beleive the heaths I had seen before, and the downs I was then on sett it much of. My Lord Pembroke was a fortnight agone at Hartlerow and the Judges having taken up his lodgings he resolved they should not sleep in them; pull them out he dared not; but prevented the old mens rest by roaring. Justin MacCarty[241] was with him. Wilton is one of pleasantest seats I have seen, where I am told my Lord of Pembroke hath lately been much beaten[242] …

[235] In relation to Irish forfeited estates, in which Thomas acted as agent for Lady Orkney.

[236] William Sherlock (1639/40–1707), for whom see *Oxf. DNB*.

[237] Under the cover-name of 'Charles Shute'.

[238] In Dorset.

[239] In Hampshire.

[240] Wilton House, in Wiltshire, the estate of Thomas Herbert (c.1656–1733), 8th earl of Pembroke.

[241] Hon., Justin MacCarthy, second son of Donough MacCarthy, 4th earl of Clancarty, by the former Lady Elizabeth Spencer, daughter of the 2nd earl of Sunderland.

[242] Presumably a reference to the general election of July 1698, which saw the return for Wilton of the London merchant Sir Henry Ashurst, 1st Bt, alongside the tory John Gauntlett. While Gauntlett may well have been Pembroke's nominee, Ashurst had probably been returned through his own efforts (and money) and with the assistance of the substantial Dissenting interest in the town. (*HC 1690–1715*, ii, 696–7).

25. *Alan I, Dublin, to Thomas, Whitehall coffee-house, King's Street, Westminster, 28 Dec. 1699*

(1248/1/316–17)

I am in some pain till I hear again from you notwithstanding yours of the 15th in which you own the receit of mine by Captain Stafford,[243] and promise to answer it at large soon afterward, but then you were not at leisure to doe it: The fifteenth was on a Fryday which is no post day from London; and it is plain by the Close of it that your letter was wrote in the morning; for I suppose the votes of that day have altered your opinion from what it seemed to be when you wrote that letter; I wish you had taken the trouble to have added two words at the end of your letter when you knew what the Commons had done that day. [244] In the letter which Mr Stafford delivered I very sollicitously enquired after a former letter I wrote to you in which I gave you an account who were forming an interest against our familye in the County of Cork[245] and proposed some methods which I thought we ought in prudence to take; since my writing that, Arthur St Leger[246] hath been in town and hath discoursed me at large on that subject and owns that many in our Countrey have endeavoured to represent us as men that in the last Session of Parliament had been entire Courtiers, and in opposicion to the true interest of our countrey: the persons he desired to be excused for not naming, but assured me he beleived it all to be meer calumnye and to arise from our being against the addresse to break the five French Regiments:[247] this confirms me in the necessitye I think lyes on us to be as careful as possible to hinder these rascals from proceeding, or at least from succeeding in their malicious designs against us, and this is now the more necessarye, since neither your affairs nor mine permit either of us to reside in the County of Corke which is almost indispensably necessarye to keep up a firm constant interest: and I fear ones being there as he now is, rather hinders then advances it. Beside this mortificacion this morning assoon as I came to town from Radenstowne[248] Colonel Conygham told me that the party here have it buzzed abroad that the next pacquets will certainly bring in an account of the house of Commons[249] having taken notice of you by name as concerned in interest in the forfeitures, whereas (as they say) you were not to be concerned in interest but to do some thing in trust or by direction from Lord Capel: and farther that you might have set the private estate[250] at £25000 per annum and was offered that rent and a years rent in hand to secure the paiment till the end of the term. In the main

[243]Edmond Francis Stafford, MP [I].

[244]The commissioners of inquiry into Irish forfeitures appointed by the English house of commons submitted their report at Westminster on 15 Dec. 1699, upon which a committee was appointed to prepare and bring in a bill of resumption (Henry Horwitz, *Parliament, Policy and Politics in the Reign of William III* (Manchester, 1977), 262–3).

[245]In the expectation of a general election (the Irish parliament having been dissolved on 14 June 1699).

[246]Arthur St Leger, MP [I].

[247]At the beginning of 1698–9 Irish parliamentary session the 'country party' in the house of commons, exploiting popular opposition to a standing army, and popular resentment of foreigners, had sought to secure the disbandment of the Huguenot regiments on the Irish establishment, but in the committee of supply on 8 Oct., and again in the House on the 10th when the committee reported, the court party had secured their continuance (McGrath, *Constitution*, 142).

[248]In Co. Meath.

[249]In England.

[250]Of King James II.

I am well assured that you never acted any way disingeniously or unfairly in either of those two or in any other matter; and therefore am in no farther concern about you then I must be for the innocentest freind in the world that hath by his integritye disobliged men who will make no sort of scruple of taking any methods to blacken your reputacion to make it of colour with their own: And if they can but get you named in the house of Commons they will beleive they have done a great thing. This with many other things convinces me that I told you right all along that acting an invidious part for great people was not the most prudent course to steer in my opinion: I am sure my Uncle and father have both suffered by it in their fortunes, and found cold returns of their services: I wish you may not be the third of the familye able to tell the same story. Let us now make a farther use of our having soe many enemies abroad, and become for that reason more united among ourselves: I do not speak to you as if I had ever found you averse to any reasonable thing for preserving a right understanding; for you have often and particularly just before we parted last expressed your self very desirous of peace, but indeed my head is so bad that I cannot retain all the condicions and terms; therefore I beg you to sit down and at large let me know what the particulars of difference between my father and you are, and what it is you expect: that I may either settle the matter intirely between you (which I do not despair being able to doe) or at least attempt it and goe as far as possible. You write the matter of Cogan so darkly that I really do not apprehend your meaning, therefore state that matter also to me at large, tho I fear it will come too late.[251] In a letter to Conollye[252] you seem to apprehend that Sir R[*ichard*] L[*evinge*] had dealt by you like a Gentleman and that you would take a time to own it: do not deceive your self, you have not a more bitter enemye in the world, and no man endeavoured your particular prejudice so much as he: Let me too beg you not too far to trust the Gentleman of whom Lucy[253] can hardly ever speak with patience; that you may know who I mean, it is he that was once to be in a project with L. C.[254] He is too much a freind with all our enemies to have much concern for any of us; or (to come nearer the mark) we act like freinds and honest men with a man that values freindships no farther then they are subservient to his immediate interest and purpose. Let me know if it be true that the three Commoners that did not subscribe[255] were in danger: so we say here.

[251] *A List of the Claims as They are Entred with the Trustees at Chichester House on College Green Dublin, on or before the 10th of August 1700* (Dublin, 1701), 233, listed a Richard Cogan as claiming a mortgage interest in three properties in the barony of Barrymore, Co. Cork, formerly the property of Thomas Barry. He was also recorded on the same document as a forfeiting proprietor in the same barony (220).

[252] William Conolly, MP [I].

[253] His second wife.

[254] Presumably Laurence Clayton. Sir Francis Brewster may be the subject of this circuitous reference.

[255] Sir Richard Levinge and two other members of the commission of inquiry into the Irish forfeitures, Lord Drogheda and Sir Francis Brewster, had dissented from the decision to include King James II's personal estate with the rest of the forfeited estates and had refused to sign the report, for which they were denied their remuneration. Levinge also fell foul of the English house of commons for having allegedly accused his fellow commissioners of using 'disrespectful expressions' of King William, and was sent to the Tower, where he remained for four months. (*HC 1690–1715*, iv, 625).

26. *Alan I, Dublin, to St John II, Lamb Buildings, 29 Jan. 1699[/1700]*

(1248/1/309–10)

The pacquett boat which came in last night brought me yours of the 11th, 12th, 13th, 16 and 18th and tho every thing from you is welcome to me you may easily imagine that the news was not very pleasing:[256] but in one thing I take comfort that neither you, nor the votes taking notice of my brothers having offered any thing in his own vindicacion to the house with reference to that part of the report which relates to him,[257] I have cause to beleive you had some regard to my opinion in that matter; who by hearing with what firm assurance of being supported[258] the Commissioners acted here had reason to beleive it would be difficult to stem the current that would be on their side in the house, but that which weighed most with me was least he might lay imputacions on this side as he seems to doe in the rough draught you sent me over: However why did not you mencion the receit of my letter; for since things are carried on with so much warmth I know not how far any expression may be stretched to my prejudice. Sir R[*ichard*] L[*evinge'*]s commitment put me in mind of what lately hapned in the County of Corke, where a Gentlewoman thought she saw a parson in bed with another mans wife and said all that she thought; the parson libelled in the Court Spiritual for defamacion, and she insisted on the truth of what she had said; but by the Canon Law no fewer witnesses then two shal be credited against a Clergyman[259] and the woman was forced to stand in a white sheet.[260] He that pities him or Sir F[*rancis*] B[*rewster*] know little of their behavior in this whole affair; we are much misinformed if the later was not one of the great contrivers of the first scheme on which the bill was framed for Commissioners; in the valuacion and other most material things they all joined, to that part of the Judges acting favourably etc. I think they subscribed; in few words I doe not see that any thing they differed in from the other Commissioners had other meaning then not to disoblige and consequently to ingratiate themselves with a few particular people who they beleived have good footing at Kensington:[261] In your next let me know whether Sir F[*rancis*] B[*rewster*] be yet satisfied whether it was his freinds act or done by his enemies that he was kept out of the Tower: for the story here is that he was excused as an old infirm

[256] A reference to the progress in the English house of commons of the bill to resume the Irish forfeited estates. On 18 Jan. an attempt by ministerialists to reserve one third of the lands to the king's disposal was defeated on a division, and resolutions were passed condemning the grants and those who had been instrumental in passing them (Horwitz, *Parliament, Policy and Politics*, 263, 264).

[257] There were two explicit references to Thomas: one, that he had received £3,000 from a grant made to Lord Romney in trust for the earl of Albemarle; the other, that he and William Conolly had secured lands at a cheap rate by rigging the cants (auctions) in which they were sold, and had then rented them out again at a profit, an impropriety exacerbated by the fact that Lord Deputy Capell had appointed him to investigate complaints about the conduct of the cants (*The Report Made to the Honourable House of Commons, Decemb. 15 1699. By the Commissioners Appointed to Enquire into the Forfeited Estates of Ireland* (1700), 11, 14).

[258] By the 'country party' in England (Hayton, *Ruling Ireland*, 72–4).

[259] Ecclesiastical courts required proof from two witnesses for any allegation, whereas 'in the temporal court one witness, in many cases, is judged sufficient' (Edward Bullingbrooke, *Ecclesiastical Law; or, The Statutes, Constitutions, Canons, Rubrics and Articles, of the Church of Ireland* … (2 vols, Dublin, 1770), ii, 1318).

[260] To purge her sin in public.

[261] At Kensington Palace, i.e. at court.

doting fool.[262] Now he that beleives him self the wisest man in Europe will probably do as his predecessor Achitophel did when matters would not goe his way.[263] The warmth of the house I beleive was in great measure owing to their resolucion that by some publick Act they would shew the bill must passe;[264] and that there being now no possibilitye of opposicion sure they will hearken to reason in putting in Clauses that are equitable and yet will not obstruct the main design of raising the money intended out of the forfeitures: I have often told my brother how thanklesse and unhappy an emploiment he had taken on him in undertaking the management of Lord Albermarles[265] and Lady Orkneys affairs;[266] but as the draught of the bill now is he is undone to all intents and purposes if it passe: as indeed are all that have acted for grantees residing in England who have set Leases on fines or sold Land as Commissioners: for by words of the Act whoever hath received money on any bargain, sale etc. is made liable to answer it to the purchaser, without distinguishing whether he received it on his own account or as employed by another; and he hath received much more for that Lord and Lady then he is worth: In the next place the Lessees and improving undertenants (who are the great body of Protestants) are all undone if no care be taken of them. But there is one Clause of most prodigious consequence in the bill as I understand it out of the short abstract you send me; for if I take it right all most pretensions and titles to any Lands seised or in the Kings hands as forfeited whether their claim be to the Land itself or incumbrances on it are to be unappealably heard before the Commissioners[267] and by them to be determined: now methinks it is hard that my right that I had to Land before the rebellion should be made worse by the Irish going into rebellion, and that I must be concluded without the benefit of a trial by my neighbours: The Commissioners I hope will be men out of England, and men of great worth and understanding: but he is in unhappy circumstances whose cause is to be finally decided upon a summary hearing on the testimony of Irish witnesses by Judges who know not the men nor how ready they are [to] forswear themselves on a very slight occasion. When the bill is [be]fore the Lords why may not something be offered in justification of particular persons that are mentioned in the report? As to the businesse of Cogan I will act the best way I can, and am wholly of opinion with you about Nuttley[268] and have told Mr C.[269] as much who seems to be convinced and of the same mind. Continue while this matter is in agitacion to give me farther accounts of it, especially let me have the alteracions and amendments made and offered to the bill. If it were not for fear of being in danger for doing it I could entertain

[262] Brewster's date of birth is unknown, but he had served as lord mayor of Dublin as far back as 1674–5 (*DIB*, i, 828).

[263] The biblical character Achitophel, King David's counsellor, was famous for his sagacity, but deserted his king at the time of Absalom's revolt. In Dryden's poem 'Absalom and Achitophel' (1681) the story was adapted as an allegory of the events of the Exclusion Crisis, with the first earl of Shaftesbury cast as 'the false Achitophel'.

[264] By 'some publick act' Alan presumably meant the resolutions passed on 18 Jan.

[265] Arnold Joost van Keppel (1670–1718), 1st earl of Albemarle, William's Dutch favourite.

[266] In relation to Irish forfeited estates, Thomas having acted as agent for both Lord Albemarle and Lady Orkney.

[267] The trustees to be appointed under the provisions of the bill, who were to receive the resumed property and sell it to raise money for the English public purse.

[268] Richard Nutley, MP [I], an English lawyer with powerful tory connections, who would be one of the standing counsel for the trustees (Ball, *Judges*, ii, 39, 72; Hayton, *Ruling Ireland*, 7).

[269] William Conolly, MP [I].

you with some freedomes Gentlemen have taken with the King, but will confine my self to an expression Mr Richard Goodenough[270] used last Saturday night in the company of a great many Gentlemen who met upon a Law affair: he said in his opinion England was already a Commonwealth, for that they could turn out the King when they pleased and being taken up for his expression justifyed it by asking this question, By what means else did King James lose the Crown? I do not care to inform but told him people had suffered enough by hearing things spoken by him and in his company. I have wrote to my father but he is infatuated.

27. *Alan I, Dublin, to Thomas, Whitehall coffee-house, King's Street, Westminster, 25 Feb. 1699[/1700]*

(1248/1/311–12)

I have yours of the 15th and am heartily troubled at what I foresee is like to be the event of the misunderstanding between my Father and you; my part is to the last degree difficult, who must act wholly without the advice of others for fear of making your resentments publick which ought if possible to be kept from the knowledge of a malicious world, that will triumph at soe great a misfortune of our unhappy familye. And you must know how hard a task it is for me to behave my self so equally between my nearest relations as not to disoblige both: instead of writing to my father directly you bid me to let him know your purposes, which if I should expresse in as few and plain words as you doe, or should send him your letter, it might be hereafter said that I took that way to create or continue animosityes in hopes to be a gainer by them my self in the end: on the other hand, if I should not let my father know what your purposes and resolucions are; people may say if I had fully represented what you insisted on my father might have been brought to a compliance to prevent an open rupture. Upon the whole matter I resolve by next post to let my father know (but in the softest words that will expresse it) what you expect and have concluded on, and will desire his full and plain answer to it: But I cannot but find fault with your never writing to me an answer I formerly wrote to you for to my letter what particular demands you had to my father and what the terms were on which you were inclined to close: It is true you discoursed me in your own chamber on that subject and I thought I pretty well apprehended what you meant, but do find that it will be impossible for me to mediate this matter with prospect of successe (especially considering the hast your last letter expresseth you to be now in) unlesse the particular demands you have against my father and he had or may now have to you be mentioned and a way proposed to adjust them. I cant charge my memorye with the pretensions on either side; but think yours to be that you may have the English estate put into your possession, together with an account of the profits of it; that likewise the account of the Lands my father held from my Uncle, and the

[270] An active whig in England during and after the Exclusion Crisis, and implicated in the Rye House Plot of 1683, Goodenough was later paymaster-general in the army raised by the duke of Monmouth in 1685. He was captured after the battle of Sedgemoor and pardoned, after which he came to Ireland, was admitted to the Bar in Dublin, and practised law in the city until his death in 1708 (K.H.D. Haley, *The First Earl of Shaftesbury* (Oxford, 1968), 717–18; Peter Earle, *Monmouth's Rebels* (1977), 30–1, 154, 165, 177; *King's Inns Adm.*, 192; *The Register of St Nicholas Without, Dublin*, ed. James Mills (Exeter, 1912), 206*).

Leases he hath purchased from your tenants may be stated: if there be any thing else pray expresse it in particular. I think my fathers demands to you are, an account of his rents and money by him paid for you; and what is payable to him or chargeable by him on your estate by vertue of your marriage settlement: There may be more on each side, do you let me know yours as I hope from him to have his demands: My brother St John seems to think you estrange your self much from him; perhaps it is your indisposicion or businesse or his melancholy that moves him to think soe; but surely you have no reason for doing so; and if the English estates having been in his management since my fathers being here occasion any jealousye you deal very severely by him who must know how great a sufferer in all respects he hath been and is by ever having undertaken the management of my fathers affairs at Wandsworth. It is seldome that I have wrote to my father of late, for I have so often given him my thoughts of the methods he hath engaged in and given him so many promises not to be again troublesome to him on the occasion that I think it as idle as I am convinced it will be fruitlesse to say more of that kind to him: but I hear from Mr Luther[271] he is building an house somewhere and goes on with inclosing a Park at Cahirmone,[272] tho he hath no patent for it, nor money to pay for it: How far these things agree with my wishes I can appeal to you and him to both of whom I have often spoke my sense at Large. For Gods sake be well advised how far the bill as framed may touch you as having received money for others; Blith[273] and that Club[274] talk of falling on you to rights: Beside this Conellye[275] tells me you have given D.D.[276] a note for £3000 if some things did not proceed; do you remember your having given such a note; he speaks of one, and I beleive it to be so; take care of yourself and advise with St John in this affair and that of my father …

28. *Alan I, Dublin, to Thomas, 17 Mar. 1699[/1700]*

(1248/1/313–14)

Notwithstanding my writing to my father by the very first post I could after receiving yours and my brother St Johns letters and pressing for an answer with all possible importunitye yet have I not yet heard from him; whether it proceed from resentment at my way of writing (which indeed was most extraordinary close, but not more soe then I thought the nature of the thing required) or that he is in confusion in his thoughts and so can come to no resolucion or that the letters lye in the post office, or that through melancholy and despondencye he lets things run adrift, or that he be ill (which I mightily fear, tho I have heard no thing to that purpose) I cannot guesse: but the minute after Lucyes lying down

[271] Probably Henry Luther, MP [I], and himself also a barrister (*Hist. Ir. Parl.*, v, 140).

[272] Cahermone, Co. Cork, the neighbouring estate to Ballyannan.

[273] Thomas Bligh, MP [I].

[274] Presumably a gathering of Irish tories, even jacobite sympathisers, since Bligh was known as a 'high-flyer' (HMC, *Ormonde MSS*, n.s. viii, 271–2).

[275] William Conolly, MP [I].

[276] Possibly Denis Daly (c.1638–1721), a justice of common pleas in Ireland under James II, and after 1691 a spokesman for a group of catholic lawyers claiming the benefit of the articles of Galway (*DIB*, iii, 16–18). For a connection with Thomas Brodrick in negotiations over forfeitures, see Eoin Kinsella, 'In Search of a Positive Construction: Irish Catholics and the Williamite Articles of Surrender, 1690–1701', *EC I*, xxiv (2009), 33.

and being in a fair way of doing well I resolve for Munster; and will prevail on him to give his last result in that and all other affairs; and therefore as I have begged my brother in a letter I wrote to him yesterday, I likewise intreat you not to do or order any thing new till you hear from me thence; and if I can not prevail with my father to doe what may answer your and my brother St Johns reasonable expectacions, I will interpose no farther but give all over as an irretreivably lost game … Looking over some letters of yours I find by them that Sir R[*ichard*] L[*evinge*] hath for some time past, particularly by a discourse he had with you in England in 1697 about Lord Romneys Parliament[277] endeavoured to create in you good thoughts of him: but let not the viper into your bosom, for he will sting you to death: retain alway in your thoughts his management during the Last Session, his personal hatred to you and endeavours to expose you in the matter of the Bophin bill:[278] Remember how he treated Lord A[*lbemarle*] in that affair, and I think you have not been just to him if you have not endeavoured to let him have a true character of the man: his usage of Lady O[*rkney*] was of the same kind: but the truth is, his quarrel to both was more on your account then theirs: And if you think his last behavior hath any way attoned, my opinion is that it hath only added fool to his former character: Did he not join in the false value, unfair examinacions, unjust representacions etc. Be not deceived nor ever trust him or recommend him as fit to be employed with honest men. I formerly pressed you, and again advise that as far as without meannesse you can doe it you endeavour to establish a good understanding with the Burlington familye.[279] Will Conelye is at Newtown;[280] Colonel Cuningham is now in my house and well: Pray use all possible arguments against my brother St Johns retiring; and particularly discourse with him and let him [*know*] that there neither is nor shal be any strangenesse or misunderstanding between him and you …

[*PS.*] If there be any talk of a Parliament here meddle not in it, at least never give any hopes what people will be disposed to doe for assure your self they think themselves hardly used, and are not yet so crushed but they retain the spirits of men.

29. *Alan I, Dublin, to Thomas, 6 June 1700*

(1248/2/4)

I am impatient till I receive your answer, and the opinion of those on your side the water who are fit to be consulted, whether the Commissioners[281] not employing the Atturney[282]

[277] The Irish parliament of 1692–3.

[278] John Bourke (1642–1722), brother of Richard Bourke (*d.* 1704), 8th earl of Clanricarde, and styled Lord Bophin from the jacobite barony he had been granted in 1689, had commanded a regiment in James II's army until captured at the Battle of Aughrim in 1691. A significant obstacle to his pursuit of his claim to the benefit of the articles of Galway was the fact that his estate had been granted to Lord Albemarle. In 1698 the Irish privy council prepared a bill to reverse his outlawry and allow him to raise £9,000 on his estate, £7,500 of which was to go to Albemarle as compensation for his loss and the remaining £1,500 to those who had been intermediaries in the affair (including, presumably, Thomas Brodrick). Unfortunately for Bophin, the bill was lost in the Irish house of commons in Jan.1699 (Simms, *Williamite Confiscation*, 70–1).

[279] The Boyles, earls of Cork and Burlington.

[280] Limavady, Co. Londonderry.

[281] The trustees for Irish forfeitures.

[282] The Irish attorney-general, Robert Rochfort.

and me as Councel for them we be not at liberty to take fees against them. I own there seems to me to be no difficultye in the Case, since the lands are devested out of the Crown and vested in the trustees and since no part of the produce of them is to go to the King: but our Case now is like to be worse if what is here talked privately be true, that they have resolved not to let any of the Kings Councel plead before them for the claimants yet think fit to use other Councel for themselves. If this be soe, I think nothing can be so great a reflection on us that we are not to be entrusted with the Kings affairs if soe they will allow them; or if not how have we forfeited our right of defending our Clients Causes. This matter is but whispered as yet, and perhaps may be only discourse; however I wish we may have the thoughts of our freinds in things of this nature, and not go upon our judgements which on your side the water of late have found very little countenance … Pray answer this assoon as you possibly can …

30. *Alan I, Dublin, to Thomas, Whitehall coffee-house, King's Street, Westminster, 5 Sept. 1700*

(1248/2/5–6)

Tho I am very sensible that you and my brother St John both expect to hear from me upon my return out of the County of Corke and that I ought to inform you how things are there, yet it is almost as great a violence to me to bring my self to write on that subject as it would to cut my own throat, since I either must lye or give you a very unpleasing and unsatisfactory account of matters there; but I have brought my self to resolve writing, and now my pen is in my hand I will let you know how matters stand.

What time we spent in the Countrey was at Corke, Mallow and Ballyanan … Mr Spence and his wife[283] were very civil to us and ready to doe any thing to oblige us; we had freedome of your park and according to the liberty you gave we killed fowre brace of deer; you bid me kill what number I pleased, and tho I confesse it be a very great one yet I hope it will not dissatisfye you since I can assure you we have left very good deer and killed no young ones: In my opinion that little spot of ground will be soon over stocked unlesse you turn out or dispose of some of the rascally deer. Spence I beleive keeps a strict correspondence with you by letter … I doe not know what number of Cows you allow him to graze in the Parke, but I at one time saw nine of his in that part of the Parke which lies Northward of the wall that divides the greatest division from the furzy part, I mean in that part which is coursest in which the gate to Middleton road stands. I do not understand countrey affairs, if I did I might be able to give you a farther light into things, but this I know that people shake their heads, as if you were preyed upon by him: Pray look on this as no more then an hint for you to endeavour being farther informed. My father hath very good opinion both of him and his wife … And now as to my father; With reluctancy I dined at Dick Bettesworths[284] because it necessarily brought me by the wall he hath built; It is I beleive eight foot high, lime and sand; and is built up either almost or wholly, as

[283] Possibly William Spence (*d.* c.1719) and Elizabeth (*d.* c.1729), both of Midleton (Phillimore, *Indexes*, ii, 150).

[284] Richard Bettesworth, of White Rock, Co. Cork (see Appendix 1).

far as it runs between Middleton and Inchinabackye Church:[285] It not only takes in part of your Land Westward, but comes into the high way, being built without the great ditch that runs along Youghal road; It runs almost as far Eastward as to the new house he hath built … and then runs down Northward toward the Land of Inchinabacky, but thereabout there is little built as yet: After dining at Dick Bettesworths I resolved to go setting toward Broomfeild and Knocknegriffin[286] and went over by Cahirmone Castle; but at my coming over against the Lane that leads out of the road to Tallough[287] to Mrs Downings house I became almost distracted; for there I mett the wall again running along in the very high way from Middleton to Killeagh[288] and it hath so straitned it that tho people are shy of saying as much to me, yet Dick Bettesworth assured me the Countrey muttered mightily and I must own with very good reason: I begged him with all the earnestnesse in the world to give off there whatever he did in other places for that when he had finished it, the Country would present it and have it pulled down as a nusance: I have wrote to him to the same purpose since I came up, but I fear to no purpose: for he told Lucy one day after he had carried Mr Justice Tracy[289] and her to see this wall, and she had declared her opinion freely against it, that he had rather she or I would take a board and cover him with it alive (that was his expression) then disswade him from proceeding in what he had begun. Hitherto Brother I have spoke with reference to the publick, but as to you I doe not know what to say: I know not the names of Lands nor can so describe the meares to let you know exactly how much of your ground he hath taken in, but I am sure it is a great deal: God, my father, and my own conscience are my witnesses how often and earnestly I have protested and exclaimed against this design of his, and entreated him not to proceed in it, but since Cahirmoane is to be mine or my childrens lott I know not how far I may be hardly thought of by strangers, as if I either promoted or was at least passive in the carrying it on. If this should take place in peoples thoughts it would trouble me; but I hope you cannot be soe unjust to think I ever consented or by my silence gave way to this vast expence which will never turn to any account; much lesse to the inclosing your ground, which may create jealousies now and endlesse contests in our familye for ought I know hereafter: I asked my father why he would inclose your Land without your permission, at which he was so started as to be able to give no other answer then that it was done and that he would give you what you your self should judge an equivalent … I put him in mind of the settlement, and that perhaps you would not accept any equivalent to which he said that he hoped you would not take up that resolucion, but that if you did, that after the Leases he had of the inclosed Lands were out the wall would be of service and use to you. For Gods sake brother let not this prove a bone of dissension among us; do not think I forward or am pleased with these things: I wish I could prevent them but I cannot. I spoke to him again of the difference between him and you, and his last result was this, that he was not able to provide for my sister if you insisted on remitting the £550 payable by you after his death: I can neither say nor doe more then I have said and done to bring your differences to an end; I hope you have taken

[285] Inchinabacky, Co. Cork.

[286] Knocknagriffin, Co. Cork.

[287] Tallow, Co. Waterford, just over twenty miles north-west of Midleton.

[288] In Co. Cork, eight miles east of Midleton.

[289] Hon. Robert Tracy (1675–1735), judge of king's bench [I] 1699–1700, later a baron of exchequer [E] and judge of common pleas [E].

possession of what little you have right to by my Uncles will in England[290] according to what he consented to when I was with him in the Spring, and will be ready to doe what else he consented to, that is to call on him for the rents that shal become due from the times I formerly told you he expressed himself willing to begin ... Doing thus much will be a means of preventing the breach from widening ... Let me hear from you soon, and try if possible to bring things to an end with him; before God the longer they run the worse it will be for you and for all of us. As to my own particular I have brought matters to this passe, I have a general discharge under his hand and seal for all debts duties and demands and of all accounts from the beginning of the world: I have also gott him to perfect a settlement of what he obliged himself often to settle; first by letters on my first marriage, next by articles on my second, and afterward by agreement to which you were a witnesse in consideracion of £1000. When I say I gott him I would not be understood that he did it with difficultye, on the contrarye he expressed great readinesse in it and that he would doe the like for my brother St John, I wish he would give me leave to have deeds perfected for his use: but by this settlement I am not to receive a penny during his Life: I was sensible the draught was imperfect being drawn in hast, therefore left a power of revocacion if both consented to the end a firmer conveyance might be made which shal be done out of hand. You will not find fault with me for endeavouring to secure something for my little ones, considering I acquainted you and St John with this whole matter long beforehand, and had both your consents to and approbacion of it. Remember me to St John, and for Gods sake visit him, you will comfort one another in very great misfortunes; for so I take both your Cases, and that of our whole familye now to be; we are from a promising, and thriving number of people dwindled almost to nothing in estate, and interest; but our discontents are truly the most deplorable part of our Case ... After all I think in my conscience my father will be over before All hallowtide ... The packett went not out till I received yours of 31 Aug. 1700 and in it that which distracts me; prevent it brother, or he is undone and so is our whole family; Where is he going, what will become of him? if he ever leaves England; my eyes never will behold him more: Unhappy father indeed, whose management robbs us of another in addicion to the losse of my poor Mother. I can say nothing about the house, but will write what will carry my father over, if he yet remain in his senses: Do not proceed to extremityes, till I have your answer. Farewell unhappy Brother. Conceal my fathers weaknesses and faults if you can; but how can they be concealed? after my brothers discontent hath ruined him, the cause will be enquired, and laid open.

31. *Alan I, Dublin, to Thomas, Whitehall coffee-house, King's Street, Westminster, 1 Oct. 1700*

(1248/2/7–9)

I have your letter from the Bath, in which I am sorry to find you so very full of resentment as you expresse your self against my father: it is to no purpose for me to doe more then I have done to prevent a publick scandalous and unchristian breach between you: I have

[290] By Sir Allen Brodrick's will, dated 19 Apr. 1680 and proved the following Nov., Thomas Brodrick inherited his property in Wandsworth, although Sir St John was given a life interest in Wandsworth House (TNA, PROB 11/364, ff 132–3).

endeavoured all I could to hinder it and if it must fall out, you give the finishing stroke to render us the most contemptible, as we already are the most unhappy familye in the Kingdome. There remains now but one thing to be done which is that I send down to my father your own original letter in which you lay down the terms to which you expect he shal comply or else an open war must ensue: I wish he may doe that or any thing rather then let our misery be publick and the scorn of all that hate us: the inconvenience that will ensue is not yet fully seen but in a little time will be heavily felt, and I fancy the event will hardly answer your expectacion. If I had not all along disswaded my father from all those methods that he hath taken of laying out his Money, or had received any part of it my self I should be lesse ready to speak my mind thus freely to you; but I am one of his sons who have spent my life in his service, and can boldly say that beside the money he hath laid out in my educacion at school, Oxford, and the Temple (in all which places he knows I was far from being expensive) I never had one shilling settled on me, tho twice married; you know I have to support the credit of our familye lived like a Gentleman and I am sure have been out a great deal of money that way: I have given my father just paiment of any money I ever received for him, and paid him down one thousand pounds as the consideracion of his settling an estate on me and mine after his death which I might modestly have expected a part of in possession during his life: this I doe not say to upbraid him, but to remind you that if his unhappy management hath put him into such circumstances as that he hath made use of some thing which is yours, that yet you have had some thing from him which no other of his children yet hath had: and tho you have two things to offer that they have not, your being elder and having a Legal settlement made on marriage, yet stil it is your father hath done this and not given it to your younger brothers, but unhappily misemployed it otherwise. Now give me leave to remind you that in my opinion you vary from what your former sentiments were: for I never do remember that you named that you positively expected the £550 should be discharged; I am sure you did not expresse that so before I went to Munster in March last: perhaps you might intend it under the general words of quitting scores, and giving general releases for what was past: and I will endeavour to find your letters on that subject, if they are yet in being. If you have kept my letters you will see by one I wrote soon after the second day of April when I was at Middleton that my father thought you never intended to discharge your estate of that power of charging it, being a great part of the provision by him designed I think for Katy or some other of his younger children … I am far from finding fault with you (considering the unhappy misunderstandings that rage so furiously between you as not to admit of correspondence by letter or indeed discoursing together) for not renewing Leases to my father of those Lands where he hath purchased your tenants interest; you allow he ought to hold them during the residue of the terms that are in being and he can expect no more: whether they are for thirteen years or for one or more Lives makes no difference; when they are out the Lands are yours, and till then he like other tenants must pay you his rent. You cannot but know that I all along opposed his buying in Leases, turning farmer, buying stock and building: and more then any other was furiously averse to the Park he now hath almost inclosed; I urged the expence, the no advantage or satisfaction to any body hereafter, the grounds of dissension which enclosing any of your Land might lay to the ruine of peace and perhaps the fortunes of our familye: the odium I should very probably incur as done in favor to me, and to the prejudice of his other younger children: These things I repeated by letter, by word of mouth without ceasing, but all to no purpose: now as I told you formerly I know not the bounds of your Lands, and hope none of yours is within the wall but what is now in Lease to my father; so as by inclosing it, he hath done a most unadvisable or inconsiderate action yet it is no wrong: a tenant may build on his farm, but can expect no benefit of it after his Lease is expired; this is your Case I hope with my father, because then there can be no immediate cause of complaint as having come on your Land and built there without your permission: and at the end of the term you are at your discretion to act as you shal think fit. You know that I was so far averse to the building this wall, that in hopes that might prevent, I concurred in opinion with you not to give your consent to the inclosing any of your Land within it; but that you see hath not taken place: Before those Leases are determined it is possible some temper may be found to make these matters easier; at least in all probabilitye my father will not live to see, what his heart was so fondly (I may add extravagantly) sett on, pulled down: but there needs no resolucion be declared in that matter at present, since it cannot prevent what is past; I mean no publick one, for as to my father I have all along told him it would be a bone of contention and cause of animositye among us. If there be any Land taken in that is not in my fathers tenancy I know not what to say being resolved never to propose any thing about an equivalent to you being in some measure in my own behalf … Pray write to me tho you should tell me you resent what I have wrote and will not regard it, that I may prepare my self to be a publick mark to be pointed at as one of the unhappiest name on earth.

32. *Alan I, Dublin, to Thomas, 8 Oct. 1700*

(1248/2/10)

You will justly think me troublesome in writing soe often to you, but I cannot refrain … My head is almost turned with the misfortunes that have crowded on the neck of one another of late: This difference between my father and you sticks close to me; his conduct (by which he hath mightily straitned himself and incumbred his little fortune to the prejudice of his own credit and the ruine almost of his younger sons) is an heavy load, and will continue soe till he alters it, which God incline him to: but the consequence of most fatal concern is what my poor brother St John suffers through the resentment and melancholy these matters have thrown him into: the cheif credit and support of our familye is gone, and I fear irretreivably lost: else sure I should have heard from him or you where he is, and how to write to him: My child[291] is got into a vicious world and under no freinds guidance: What shal I doe with him? In addicion to all this I am grown very sickly, and likely to be more soe daily. Advise how I shal act in relacion to Senny; to whom I shal remit money and with what directions; for I know not who his tutor is, nor to whom else to write unlesse to Dr Sherlock:[292] Unlesse St John[293] had been discomposed very much in his mind he would have said something on these points. Other little disadvantages as the losse of my practice by my not being permitted to appear for Claimants before the trustees[294] where

[291]St John III, who had just gone up from Eton to King's College, Cambridge.

[292]Thomas Sherlock (1677–1761), then a fellow of St Catherine's, later bishop of London.

[293]Their brother.

[294]For forfeited estates.

only money is stirring, I passe by: Pray brother write to me and advise and while you are in England have an eye after Senny from whom I never hear one word …

33. *Alan I, Dublin, to Thomas, Whitehall coffee-house, King's Street, Westminster, 11 Oct. 1700*

(1248/2/11–12)

There arrived six English pacquets last night, and one of them brought your letter from Bath of 28th September, with my brother St Johns of the 17th from the Hague; which almost distracts me; for beside that he in it expresseth an intent of going farther then Aix le Chapelle and conceals whither he designs till he arrives at his journeys end; methinks his way of mentioning Lucy and me and never writing to me upon leaving England, nor saying with whom or how he left Senny nor what methods I should take with him for the future, argue that he takes something ill of me: how unkindly and unjustly God knows. If I have given him general answers about my fathers return, it was because I could not with truth make other: If I have told him that I beleived my father would give over his building etc. and return for England, it proceeded from being over credulous and hoping better then I ought of his purposes and resolutions: If at other times I have been silent it was because I hated to be the messenger of the most unwelcome tidings in the world; but I have beyond duty or modestye pressed my father to return and give off what hath brought all these miseryes upon us. Pray superscribe and forward the enclosed to him, which I leave open that you may add to it what you think proper. I can add nothing to my last unlesse it be to desire you not to take ill my earnestnesse in pressing you to do any thing to prevent a rupture between my father and you: to shew you I am in earnest, altho I can at this time very ill spare it, I will rather deprive my children of so much of my little fortune as may remain in difference between you then have the last degree of miserye and publick shame befall us. Perhaps you may wonder at my saying I am not very well able to spare money; but if you consider my two English journeys and the losse of practice by means of them added to the expence, and that no money is now stirring but before the trustees where the Kings Counsel are not admitted to appear for the Claimants, nor called on by the Trustees but in matters wherein they care not to be concerned; and in addicion to this if you remember that we could not be for the Claimants that were to have the benefit of the Limrick articles (from whom the money was to be gott) and that our allowance from the King on those claims is hardly any of it paid, and my great charge and expence you will find my condicion not soe plentiful as it is thought … Let me know whether I may hope to see you here or not this winter; on many accounts methinks it were necessarye, yet considering that thereby you put your self in the power of people that hate you because they know they have wronged you, I know not how to advise your coming. But let me tell you one thing, I am confirmed in my opinion that my neighbour after all his professions is no more a freind to you then to the rest of the world that is no farther then interest leads him.[295] People here are thinking how to act to get some redresse next Sessions of Parliament, particularly Lord Albemarles purchasors[296] and I think since you were concerned for him in selling his

[295]Possibly a reference to Sir Richard Levinge, MP [I].

[296]Those who had purchased forfeited estates in Ireland granted to the earl of Albemarle.

granted estate you should endeavour to perswade him to reimburse the purchasers upon moderate terms which they may be brought to; this I know you have formerly pressed in vain, but perhaps he may lend a better ear to it, when he is told it will else end in an applicacion to the house of Commons; and how fond a favourite will be of being named there his Lordship will consider. I know not whether you have any hint of it, I am kept perfectly in the dark I mean nothing hath been spoken to me on the subject but just on Lord Chancellors Landing,[297] and then he talked of a Parliament here; but I am morally certain the thing is in agitacion; and conclude it from three observacions among others: One, that my neighbour expressed great dread of what would become of Sir John Meade in the Case of the Earle of Meath and Lord Ward;[298] another that Lord Galwey[299] was mighty pressing to have the quo warranto against the Brewers decided one way or other, being begun at the request of the Commons and to prevent complaint:[300] the third that Lord Chancellor is very nice in disobliging the Lords by expecting that a Peer ought on a contempt to be examined on interrogatories on oath.[301] To feel Lord Chancellors pulse about a Parliament I spoke to him, as if I understood from you that some people in England discoursed as if such a thing were in thought, but he seemed perfectly a stranger to any such intentions …

34. *Alan I, Dublin, to Thomas, Whitehall coffee-house, King's Street, Westminster, 2 Nov. 1700*

(1248/2/13–14)

…Pray be as often with my brother St John as you can; and let me know what you can observe is most likely to restore him to a little content, that if it be possible it may be attained. Our people of Corke are all sett together in partyes and factions by Mr Sealy our

[297]John Methuen (c.1649–1706), lord chancellor [I] 1697–1703.

[298]The legal case between on the one side Edward Brabazon (1638–1707), 4th earl of Meath and his countess, and on the other Edward Ward (1683–1704), 3rd Baron Ward, together with various English associates) originated in a suit successfully brought by Ward and others over lands in Co. Tipperary to the palatine court of Tipperary in 1686. Meath persuaded the Irish house of lords to grant a petition in 1695 to have this judgment set aside and was put into possession of the property. In response, Ward, having failed in an initial appeal to the Irish house of lords, took his case to Westminster, where the upper house, exercising its claim to an appellate jurisdiction over Ireland, found in his favour and ordered the chancellor of the Tipperary palatinate, Sir John Meade, to restore Ward to his property. Alan Brodrick was speculating (one must assume with relish) that acting in obedience to the decree of the English house of lords, and thus endorsing its claim to an appellate jurisdiction, would involve Meade in difficulties in Ireland, though when the Irish parliament eventually took cognisance of the case, in 1703, Meade's role was ignored. (*LJI*, i, 548–9; ii, 35; F.G. James, *Lords of the Ascendancy: The Irish House of Lords and Its Members, 1600–1800* (Blackrock, Co. Dublin, 1995), 69.)

[299]Henri de Massue (1648 –1720), 2nd marquis de Ruvigny, and 1st earl of Galway, lord justice [I] 1697–1700.

[300]In Jan. 1699 the Irish house of commons, on foot of an inquiry into the scarcity and high price of bread, had passed resolutions condemning the bakers', brewers' and butchers' guilds, whom they blamed for cornering the market and driving up prices in a time of dearth. Messages were sent to the lord justices and privy council calling for writs of quo warranto to be issued to recall their charters, and in the case of the brewers' charter, the process was quickly set in motion. (*CJI*, ii, 878–9; *CSP Dom.*, 1699–1700, 82–3).

[301]Methuen must be the person intended, there being at this time no lord chancellor in England (Lord Somers having been replaced in the spring of 1700 by a lord keeper, Sir Nathan Wright). The incident presumably took place during the 1699–1700 session of the English parliament, in which Methuen sat in the house of commons (for Devizes) but has not been identified.

present Mayor[302] … Pray let me hear what people say and think of our trustees and their proceedings, and whether there be any prospect of things going easyer next Sessions …

35. *Alan I, Dublin, to Thomas, Whitehall coffee-house, King's Street, Westminster, 29 Jan. 1700/1*

(1248/2/1–2)

Before I trouble you with my own affairs let me tell you what I beleive you already in part know that the tenants of the private estate[303] are upon a project and are come to a resolucion of making a purse and sending Dick Wolseley[304] and Jack Rotton[305] agents for England to sollicite the Parliament for a clause to preserve the tenants leases; this I know by the Copy of a letter George Rogers[306] wrote to me this post out of their original signed Charles Alcock,[307] Marmaduke Coghil,[308] Edward May,[309] John White,[310] Michael Tempest,[311] Jeremy Rosco,[312] Thomas Moore,[313] John Marshal,[314] Richard Wolseley; in it they demand half a quarters rent to be advanced by him at present for defraying the expence of Rotton and Wolseley etc. As to the thing intended, tho I do not see any prospect of their succeeding yet everybody that thinks their Case as hard as I doe must wish they may find some releif against the severityes lately imposed on them, if they mean no more then that: but since the thing is carryed soe privately that I never heard of it here in town, tho very well acquainted with most of the subscribers till I received this letter out of the Countrey which I beleive they did not expect would have come to my sight, I think I ought to acquaint you of it, and at the same time caution you that as on the one hand noebody can blame you for opposing any attempt they may make against your self, soe on the other you doe not embark your self in behalf of Lord or Lady Orkney[315] or any body else in opposicion to their finding releif somewhere: beside the Justice of the thing that they should not be wholly losers, as they are like to be (not being purchasers of Inheritance) for any thing in the late Act, what equivalent have you received or can you expect for getting the ill

[302]John Sealy (*d.* c.1720?) (*Cork Council Bk*, 285; Vicars, *Index*, 418).

[303]James II's private estate, which had been included in the forfeited estates to be resumed and sold by act of the English parliament.

[304]Probably Richard Wolseley, MP [I].

[305]John Rotton (*d.* 1713), attorney, of Dublin (*King's Inn Adm.*, 430).

[306]George Rogers, MP [I].

[307]Charles Alcock (*d.* after 1719) of Powerstown, Co. Tipperary (Lodge, *Peerage*, ii, 256; Reg. Deeds, 24/398/14164).

[308]Marmaduke Coghill, MP [I].

[309]Edward May, MP [I].

[310]John White (*d.* by 1719), of Cappagh, Co. Tipperary (Maurice Lenihan, *Limerick: Its History and Antiquities, …* (Dublin, 1866), 302; Vicars, *Index*, 487).

[311]Michael Tempest (*d.* c.1701), of Dublin, barrister (*King's Inns Adm.*, 476; Vicars, *Index*, 452).

[312]Jeremiah Rosco (*d.* c.1718), of Dublin (Vicars, *Index*, 406).

[313]Thomas Moore (*d.* c.1702) of Chandlerstown, Co. Tipperary (Vicars, *Index*, 335).

[314]John Marshall (*d.* 1717) of Clonmel, Co. Tipperary (Burke, *Hist. Clonmel*, 487).

[315]George Hamilton (1666 –1737), 1st earl of Orkney. For his wife, the former Elizabeth Villiers, see above, p. 60.

will of soe many suffering honest English Gentlemen of your own Countrey, with whom you are to live and whose interest stands on the same bottom with yours? Nay you having acted in setting those Lands and receiving those fines (as far as fairly you can) ought to be assisting to them in helping them to some ease or redresse: but pray create your self no more enemies by acting for them; for resentments are durable, but services are immediately forgotten. George Rogers will not go in to the thing I beleive till he hears from you, to whom he will write on the subject.

What follows very materially concerns me: The inclosed letter to the Lords of the Treasury is to the effect of the endorsement on this; to which I refer you. By it you will see the money came due to us for our attending the claims and can not be paid now out of the produce of the forfeitures, that fund being applyed to other purposes: If the Lords of the Treasury think how hardly we earned that money, and that it is but performing the word of the Lords Justices and Councel, and how great losers we have been by being hindred from practicing before the trustees for claimants, because we are the Kings servants they will not scruple signing an order in our favor for paiment out of the Treasury here, where by the admirable management of Lord Gallway there is money enough to answer much greater summes after clearing the civil and military list to the first day of this month inclusive.[316] I doe not know whether the Duke of Bolton[317] be in town or not; if he be, he will befreind us in speaking to Mr Smith of the Treasury[318] and his other freinds there; and the rather because his Grace was the very person who commanded our attendance and promised us paiment. Lord Gallway and Lord Chancellor[319] will both doe the same, and the later assured me he would manage the whole matter himself; but I am against that for more reasons then one …

36. *Alan I, Dublin, to Thomas, Whitehall coffee-house, King's Street, Westminster, 13 May 1701*

(1248/2/20–1)

I have your letter of the third and should have been pleased if the Westerly winds would have permitted the letters of the sixth from London to have come in before I answered it; for by them we may expect to be able to form some judgement what we are to feel farther from our Governors the trustees; it is not unlikely that the matter of taking one of the seven

[316]Copied at the foot of this letter, in a different hand, is an undated petition of Robert Rochfort, Alan Brodrick and William Neave, MP (serjeant-at-law), to the lords justices of Ireland for the money due to them 'for attending the Court of Claimes on behalf of his Majestie for prosecuting those who had no title to the Articles of Limrick and Galway'; a referral to the Irish revenue commissioners, 20 Jan. 1700/01; the commissioners' report, in favour, 20 Jan. 1700/01; and a request sent by the lords justices to the treasury commissioners in England, Jan. 1700/01, asking them to identify an appropriate source of funding out of which the petitioners might be paid. The three men were finally reimbursed by the English treasury in July 1701, each receiving £701 (*Cal. Treas. Bks*, xvi, 88, 310, 318).

[317]Charles Powlett (1661–1722), formerly marquess of Winchester, who had succeeded his father as 2nd duke of Bolton in Feb. 1699. He had served as a lord justice in Ireland 1697–1700.

[318]John Smith (c.1655–1723), MP [E], a lord of the treasury.

[319]John Methuen.

hundred thousand pounds a year from the King may soe employ the fifth of this month[320] as to put off the hearing the trustees to a longer day; but when ever they are heard, I own that I do expect what ever representacion they make will take place, and that they will make one as much to their own benefit and our prejudice as it is possible: If they are sent over again among us without encrease of powers, we must be used with more insolence and arbitrarinesse then we have mett hitherto: If their powers are encreased, no honest man in the Kingdome can say he is Master of a foot of estate or of his reputacion: Knaves that will be supple, and flatter them may passe their times as easily as such slaves deserve or desire to doe; but whoever shews an aversion to their tyranny shal one way or other smart bitterly under them. This letter tells me you now think in good earnest that the purchasers will have relief, and that the lessees seem to stand on a pretty good foot; your former hinted that the purchasers would have some clause but clogged with a more beneficial provision for others; for my part I begin to think it is with us (as with people in a fire) very happy to save any thing any way: I cannot understand what you intend by bidding me keep my self in reserve in a matter where people of this Kingdome (insignificant as it is) are intended to be made use of: If there be any thoughts of summoning a Parliament we shal never agree with those that at present employ Chichester House;[321] and depend on it, their jurisdiction and ours in Parliament are so incompatible that no body will let us be at once in esse that doth not intend to knock one against the other. Whoever wrote the dialogue[322] and jus regium[323] have omitted many very material instances of the pressures this Kingdome lies under from the trustees and the vipers employed by them in the Countrey who are ten times worse in the execucion of their orders then even their orders seem to require or expect, I do not say warrant. Pray let me know who are said to be the Authors of those pamphlets: Nothing but the terror people lye under hinders men from giving such instances of oppression and wrong as are not to be paralleled, and will hardly obtain credit. My Lord Chancellors being in England is soe great a mischeif to the Kingdome that his best freinds cannot open their mouthes in his defence: to have causes hang undecided, great part of the businesse remain unheard and all suits of equitye to run into the Exchequer is what men must take notice of and resent: for my own particular by not being permitted to gett any money at the trustees and having the Chancery shut up, my gown is hardly worth the wearing. And now I mencion not being permitted to practice before the trustees, perhaps it might not be amisse if notice were taken by some members of the house how the Kings Councel are used in this matter; but I would not have it made my own particular Case nor stirred at all unlesse we might reasonably hope to be permitted to use our professions in a Court that takes up all the Councel of the Kingdome. I have often wrote to you about the money due to the Attorney and me and Serjeant Neave: there is now a great deal of money in the treasury beforehand, and a little sollicitacion might obtain an order in our

[320]The vote in the English house of commons to reduce the civil list to £600,000 (Horwitz, *Parliament, Policy and Politics*, 289). Another Irish observer, Thomas Keightley, who was himself in Westminster observing parliamentary proceedings, took the same view (NLI, MS 45304/7: Keightley to Sir Donough O'Brien, 3 May 1701).

[321]For their accommodation the trustees had commandeered Chichester House, on College Green, Dublin, the meeting place of the Irish parliament.

[322]*A Short View of Both Reports, in Relation to the Irish Forfeitures, in a Familiar Dialogue between A. and B. Most Humbly Offer'd to the Consideration of Both Houses of Parliament* (1701).

[323][Lord Somers], *Jus Regium* ….

favor I should think: pray let me know whether any and what steps have been made in it: Lord Galwey, and Lord Chancellor are on the spot and will do us justice …

37. *Alan I, Dublin, to Thomas, Whitehall coffee-house, King's Street, Westminster, 15 June 1701*

(1248/2/24–5)

I delayed answering your last letter till I could get a duplicate of the Lords Justices letter to the Lords of the Treasury[324] and Mr Palmers[325] being out of town on Saturday made it impossible to have it till this night; and now what I send is not strictly a duplicate, which it seems is another letter of the same tenor and date with the former signed by the Lords Justices own hand; but the new Lords Justices will not sign such, being wrote in the time of another Governement; soe that a Copy under the Secretaryes hand of the Entry in the former Lords Justices booke is all that can be had now, and will I hope be sufficient; else sure Mr Lowndes[326] mislaying the letter is not only a grosse neglect but may prove an irreparable injurye: especially if matters bear as ill a face with you as they are represented with here. For Gods sake give me some light or hint that I may by it understand whether we have reasons to beleive the worst of evils is ready immediately to fall on us: If what I mean should happen, tho England may escape better for a little time, the English here are the most undone wretches on earth.[327] The Attorney General[328] is now in London, and sure will bestir himself in what touches him soe nearly in his profit: If this money be not gott out of hand I shal almost despair ever getting it.

38. *Alan I, Dublin, to Thomas, Whitehall coffee-house, King's Street, Westminster, 28 June 1701*

(1248/2/22–3)

Your letter which you mencion to be sent by Mr Spring[329] I have not received, nor is he landed tho you say he left London on Thursday fortnight: We are in great expectacion what the heats between the houses will come to;[330] I hope resentments run not soe between people without doors: the Irish are very much up on the occasion. It will be impertinent to remind you about our money, since the King will be in Holland before this can come

[324] See above, p. 91.

[325] William Palmer, MP [I], deputy clerk of the privy council [I] and reappointed secretary to the lords justices in Ireland in Apr. 1701 (*Clarendon Correspondence*, ed. Singer, ii, 358).

[326] William Lowndes (1652–1724), secretary of the treasury [E].

[327] Presumably a reference either to the debates in parliament and press over the desirability of a war against France, or more specifically to the ongoing attempt by tories in the English house of commons to impeach the three junto lords, Halifax, Orford and Somers, and the duke of Portland (Horwitz, *Parliament, Policy and Politics*, 286–92). Despite the passage of the Act of Settlement (given the Royal Assent on 12 June) Alan seems to have interpreted English tories' reluctance to commit to another European war, and determination to bring whig ministers to book, as tending ultimately towards a jacobite restoration.

[328] The Irish attorney-general, Robert Rochfort, MP [I].

[329] Francis Spring, MP [I].

[330] The dispute between the house of lords and house of commons at Westminster over the impeachments.

to your hands and then I fear it will be too late to hope for any thing to be done in it, which is not passed before his going; tho I know no reason why the Lords Justices[331] may not doe it in his absence: If soe just a demand (when the Treasury is far from being empty here) cannot find successe without such difficulty and delay, men have little encouragement to doe their dutyes on such uncertain hopes; but the Attorney General being in England ought to stir in it, therefore remind him of it and tell him you discharge your self of it and lay it wholly on him; but if you doe soe he will goe near to gett his own share, and sacrifice us; there is no relying on him only in it … I wish I could make a guesse how matters are like to be; Mr Attorneys freinds here are all very uppish on accounts from your side that he will be Lord Chancellor;[332] I think nothing so improbable; he is mad if he accepts it if offered; and they know little of Ireland that propose doing any thing here by his promotion.

39. *Alan I, Dublin, to [Thomas], 4 July 1701*

(1248/2/26)

Yesterdayes post brought me yours of the 26th of June and in it the account of what is done about the money due to the Attorney General, me, and the Serjeant: which fully assured me that the matter was at length brought to an issue, but at the same time Mr Keightley[333] read to me a part of a letter to him from another hand, which ordered him to acquaint the Atturney and me that he had expedited that matter: Pray let me know how far I stand obliged to him in it that I may not omit returning thanks if due; but I thence collect two things, that Mr Attorney had not expresse directions from him to come to London as his freinds here give out he had, and next that some body is willing to be thought ready to oblige on this side the water; and I had a long discourse of how great service his representacions would be to this Kingdome in England, being known to be in the interest of England by all people[334] tho Lord Galway might not be soe much relied on tho never soe just in his representacions, since he might have an interest separate from that of England; I think the Gentleman meant, people in England beleived he loved this Countrey and perhaps – too well.[335] This morning I spoke to Serjeant Neave about the five Guineas and he gave me a sort of confused, insignificant answer; and at last said he would write to you about it. By the Justice,[336] the Commissioners of the Privy Seal[337] and

[331] Narcissus Marsh (1638–1713), archbishop of Dublin, Hugh Montgomery (1651–1717), 2nd earl of Mountalexander, and the earl of Drogheda were sworn as lords justices in Apr. 1701, replacing the duke of Bolton, the earl of Galway, and Charles Berkeley (1649–1710), 2nd earl of Berkeley.

[332] In fact the whig John Methuen retained the office until 1703, despite the presence as viceroy, 1700–3, of the tory Lord Rochester (Laurence Hyde (1642–1711), 1st earl).

[333] Thomas Keightley, MP [I]; first commissioner of the revenue [I].

[334] If Keightley is meant, more weight should probably have been attached to the fact that, having married a younger daughter of the 1st earl of Clarendon, he was brother-in-law to the lord lieutenant, Rochester (and also to Princess Anne, and, through the deceased Queen Mary, to King William).

[335] An alternative explanation might have focused on Galway's national origin as a French Huguenot.

[336] William had made three judicial appointments in Ireland in May 1701: two were tories, Sir Richard Cox, 1st Bt, and the Englishman Gilbert Dolben (c.1659–1722) in common pleas; while at the same time the whig James Macartney was advanced to become a justice of king's bench.

[337] On 30 June 1701, following the death of the whig Lord Tankerville, the lord privy seal [E], the King had placed that office in commission, appointing Edward Southwell, Christopher Musgrave (1664–1718) and James

indeed every thing the King hath done of late methinks he is very well pleased with the measures the present ministry have advised him to; and if his speech be not a perfect Ironye, resolves to meet the same parliament again.[338] Our trustees are mightily at a stand to know how they shal employ their time since the clause in the late Act, which indeed hath given them time to breath fresh air now and then:[339] the discoveries are so unsuccessefull that they are now going to take in hand the preys taken from the Irish in time of war if what I hear prove true: nothing but being infatuated can put them upon doing things of that sort and therefore I suspend my beleif till I hear it confirmed, tho our freind of Dunmanway[340] (who is no great enemy of theirs) is my author …

40. *Alan I, Dublin, to St John II, at his chambers in Lamb Buildings, Middle Temple, 28 Sept. 1701*

(1248/2/27–8)

I write this before our going to Ballygaule[341] or the coming in of any English packett with an account of your safe arrival at the Head;[342] but considering the fairnesse of the weather and steddinesse of the wind I can have no doubt of your having landed by fowre yesterday morning. I give you my hearty thanks for the kind visit you made us, and am sensible that it hath firmly determined my father out of hand to leave Ireland and put a stop to his unhappy management of affairs here. You may depend on my doing all you left with me in charge with all expedicion … But you must resolve for one month after you receive this to continue your care of the house at Wandsworth; you see what my father writes but I fear you took not much notice of it being in an hurry at parting … Really when I consider Sennyes expence it seems to me to be very extravagant unlesse the Universitye way of living be much altered from what it was among the most profuse in our time; what will he expect when at the Inns of Court, who being a boy hath cost me above £200 in one year at the Universitye. Pray let not my fathers earnest desire about the house be neglected; really I beleive he is to the bottom of his heart greived at his past ill conduct and will endeavour

337 *(continued)* Vernon (1677–1756) as commissioners (*CTB*, 1700–1, p. 258). Southwell and Musgrave were from tory families, Musgrave a younger son of the tory party chieftain Sir Christopher, 4th Bt, but each had a strong background of court service (*HC 1690–1715*, iv, 993–5; v, 528–31), while Vernon, the son of Secretary Vernon, and already a clerk of the privy council, had more solidly whig credentials and was besides a protégé of Lord Albemarle (*HC 1690–1715*, iv, 993–5; v, 745–7).

338 In his closing speech to both Houses on 24 June, William thanked the Commons for their 'despatch' in granting supplies and for their 'encouragement' to him to enter into alliances 'for the preservation of the liberty of Europe, and the support of the confederacy', adding, 'so I make no doubt, that whatsoever shall be done, during your recess, for the advantage of the common cause, in this matter, will have your approbation at our meeting again in the winter' (*London Gazette*, 23–26 June 1701). For the studied improvement in relations between William and his tory ministers in the latter stages of the session, see Horwitz, *Parliament, Policy and Politics*, 290–2.

339 The English act granting duties on wines and spirits and continuing various other duties (12 and 13 Will. III, c. 9), which included a proviso (sect. 30) that the trustees were not to take action until after the end of the next parliamentary session in cases where claimants to property had petitioned the house of commons, except those in which they had pronounced judgment.

340 Sir Richard Cox, 1st Bt.

341 Ballynagaul, Co. Cork (about eight miles north-east of Cork).

342 Holyhead.

to retreive as far as he is able … My Lord Lieutenant enquires heartily after you[343] and soe doe your other freinds. My services to the Baron[344] and the few other acquaintance I have in London …

[*PS*.] Remember to give me constant accounts of things that relate to this Kingdome and early ones and I will not fail to doe the like to you; let us resolve hence forth to write to one another every Tuesday and take no notice of the wind and weather.

41. *Alan I, Dublin, to St John II, at his chambers in Lamb Buildings, Middle Temple, 4 Oct. 1701*

(1248/2/29–30)

Tho I find that you landed early on Monday morning yet we had not your letter that you sent by the ship till this morning; but George Rogers who was at the head when your vessel arrived told us of her being safe, but knew nothing of your being there till you left the place. By all my fathers letters I am now fully perswaded he hath overcome his habitual fondnesse to building and projects and will be in England out of hand; let me therefore for Gods sake intreat you to give your self the same trouble and care about the house as formerly; a denial in this now he expresseth himself ready to comply with any thing that shal be proposed to him for the good of his familye will really sink soe deep into him that I fear it will overwhelm him and break his heart … The trustees act now more exorbitantly then ever as I hear from others, for you know I never goe near them: My Lord R[*ochester*] was extremely alarmed at an intended publick applicacion to be made to him (as some people designed) about the mischeifs the English here lye under by means of the Act of resumption and the execucion of the Act by the trustees: That method seems not to be now intended to be taken,[345] but every body is astonished at the consequences they see and daily feel arising from that Act and the benign exposicion given it at Chichester House and at the proceedings there many of which seem to most but those concerned to have no sort of foundacion on the Act of Parliament.[346] I wish [*Lord Rochester*] could or would doe any thing to remove out of peoples minds the opinion they have taken up of his having been a well wisher to the getting the Act passed,[347] and not being yet sufficiently sensible of the slavish pressures and injustice the Protestants lye under by such an Act so executed: If there be no redresse found I think we must expect other difficulties to be put on us; for it seems to me that the matter hath been carried too far, unlesse the design be to carry matters farther …

[343]The earl of Rochester. For the long association between the Hyde and Brodrick families, see above, p. 3, 9–10.

[344]Hon. Robert Tracy, who must have been known to the Brodricks since their days at the Middle Temple (to which Tracy had been admitted in 1673, a year after St John). In 1700 Tracy had been removed to the English court of exchequer.

[345]Instead, those opposed to the act organised a campaign of county addresses to the King, the so-called 'national remonstrance'. See below, p. 103.

[346]The English Forfeitures Resumption Act, which established the trust (11 Will. III, c. 2).

[347]For the extent to which the Resumption Act was 'a Tory undertaking', see Hayton, *Ruling Ireland*, 75–9.

42. *Alan I, Dublin, to [St John II], 11 Oct. 1701*

(1248/2/31–2)

… I was yesterday of Councel with the Archbishop of Dublin[348] upon a peticion of his to the house of Commons which is referred to be reported by the trustees;[349] and in the argument of the Case one of the trustees saying something as if a sale made by them would be conclusive to all persons, I (as the nature of my Clients case lead me) did argue that a sale by them of nothing but of Lands vested by the Act in them was binding; and that (if they should take on them to sell other Lands which I supposed they would not doe) a sale of any other Lands by them would not bind the title of the right owner: the occasion of the discourse was; The Bishop gott a patent of the Lands of Seatown[350] in 1693 as forfeited by one Russel in the rebellion of 1641; and he claimed by vertue of this patent, and also petitioned the house of Commons, least if his patent should be void his claim might be dismissed by the trustees and so the See might loose the Land which was granted to it as an augmentacion:[351] the trustees title was this: that the forfeiting person in 1641 was only tenant for Life, with a Remainder in tail to his grandson who was innocent of the rebellion in 1641 and guilty of the late rebellion; which if true lodged an estate for life only in the Crown on the rebellion of 1641, which was all the Bishops title and then (the grand father being dead) the estate vested in the trust by the attainder of the grandson: The Bishop insisted that the Grand father was seised in fee: But on the debate of the Case this point came to be insisted on, or rather indeed touched or mentioned; that admitting the Grand father was seised in fee and so the Crown intitled to the Inheritance in 1641 that yet that estate was vested in and disposeable by the trust; and one of the trustees said that he apprehended a sale made by them would bind every body; I said, I thought not, unlesse it was of Lands vested in them which were only Lands forfeited by the last rebellion; Mr Trenchard[352] said that point would be debated time enough when they were gone: Some time after other businesse came on and Mr Anesley[353] and several of the trustees went off the Bench and returned and when the Court was rising Mr Fellows[354] said he could not but take notice of what had been said about their sales being controverted; that the Clause in the Act was full in their favor and that the Kings Sollicitor[355] declaring his opinion soe might much prejudice their sales; and it was muttered among them that it was fit to

[348]Narcissus Marsh.

[349]One of a large number presented to the English house of commons in the preceding session, on which the trustees had been asked to report (*CJ*, xiii, 554, 588–9, 628).

[350]Near Malahide, Co. Dublin.

[351]The Seatown Castle estate, forfeited by Christopher Russell (*d*. 1682) after the 1641 rebellion, had been restored to his son Bartholomew in 1688 but forfeited again and granted by William III to the archbishop of Dublin, a grant eventually confirmed by an English act of parliament in 1705 (4 Anne, c. 26) (*CSP Dom.*, 1693, 168–9; Simms, *Williamite Confiscation*, 154–5).

[352]John Trenchard (c.1689–1723), a trustee.

[353]Francis Annesley, MP [I], a trustee.

[354]William Fellows or Fellowes (1661–1724), a trustee (Richard Polwhele. *The History of Devonshire* (3 vols, London, 1793–1806), iii, 388; John and J.A. Venn, *Alumni Cantabrigienses* … (10 vols, Cambridge, 1922–34), pt 1, ii, 129; Hayton, *Ruling Ireland*, 76).

[355]Alan was still Irish solicitor-general.

be represented: I told them that what I had said was in argument for my Client and was my opinion; that I might be mistaken but hoped I was not: Sir Cyril Wyche[356] then said that he had observed I alway took occasion to obstruct their proceedings or to that effect: I told him I supposed that might be his single opinion. By this I plainly see that if they can they will make matter of complaint of this against me; but if being of a reasonable opinion or declaring or pressing a Court in argument on a matter that tends to the event of the Cause be a crime I am under a mistake: but this I am sure of that if ever their sales and consequently their surveys (for they intend to sell by the metes and bounds[357] their Surveyors have measured Land) be made conclusive, no more propertye remains here to a person then they please to allow him. You know I resolved to appear no more for claimants before them; but they not being Judges but barely to examine and report a fact in this Case; I (before I spoke in the Cause) told them that I was to be Councel for the Archbishop if they thought it proper and not interfering with the rule they had made of not hearing me in claims; and they told me I might proceed and ought to be heard. Pray shew this to Mr Baron Tracy, and give him my service.

43. *Alan I, Dublin, to St John II, at his chambers in Lamb Buildings, Middle Temple, 16–18 Oct. 1701*[358]

(1248/2/33–4)

You find that I am better then my word if writing oftner then once a week will be thought soe … I have just received yours of the seventh, and have nothing to say in answer to it but to desire you to give my services to Mr Attorney[359] and Mr Pooley[360] who are so kind to enquire after an old acquaintance, removed into a land toward which almost all kindnesse is forgotten and therefore theirs the more obliging …

44. *Alan I, Dublin, to St John II, at his chambers in Lamb Buildings, Middle Temple, 8 Nov. 1701*

(1248/2/35–6)

As you had cause to think I wrote oftner then there was occasion after your leaving Ireland first, I am sensible I have given you too just cause of complaint for my breaking my resolucion of writing once a week; but I have to say in excuse that I was exceeding ill one of the dayes I was to write being in danger of being suffocated by a squinzey[361] the night before, which forced me to bleed exceedingly and purge and this brought me very low and weak:

[356]Sir Cyril Wyche (c.1632–1707), MP [I], a trustee.

[357]The required method of producing a 'legal description' of land by defining boundaries.

[358]Begun on the 16th and completed (possibly after the sentence beginning 'I have just received yours of the seventh …') on the 18th.

[359]Sir Edward Northey (1652–1723), who had been appointed attorney-general for England in June 1701; a fellow Middle Templar.

[360]Henry Poley.

[361]A quinsy, i.e. an inflammation of the throat.

and to say truth I am not in perfect good health tho I make a shift to hold up and bustle about in the Courts … My father is in his bed with the gout and assoon as he can gett out of it I am morally certain will begin his voyage for England: I hope my brother Will may succeed here at the bar; he speaks sensibly and well, but is wholly a stranger to businesse, which puts me under a necessitye of directing him and spending more time therein then I can well spare; but I cannot employ it better, if it may be a means to make him in love with businesse by getting him money, and bringing him into good esteem at the bar. By one thing that passed at the bar this day I fancy some people begin to look on him as likely to doe well: for he having moved once, my Lord Chancellor[362] soon after called to him to move again, and Mr Foster asked whether my Lord Chancellor had called to that Gentleman again; I overheard him and told him he had: I look on it as envious enough, and very base in Foster considering he succeeded him in the revenue.[363] As to our trustees they proceed triumphantly, but I have reason to mencion nothing about them or any other thing here till I can write by a safe hand: but I apprehend we are like eternally to groan under the pressures of their act and the execucion of it, and could be very willing to conceive hopes that those to whom you and I wish well, were willing to releive us; but I conceive I daily see lesse reason to believe it.

There was the Case of one Moore reheard last Tuesday that makes a base noise about town,[364] and were worth knowing if it could be gett fully reported and be sent safe: If an oportunitye of sending it or any thing else offer I will endeavour to let you have it truly; but really some men are named in it little to their honour …

45. *Alan I, Dublin, to St John II, at his chambers in Lamb Buildings, Middle Temple, 19 Nov. 1701*

(1248/2/39–40)

Tho the beneficial businesse of this term is not enough to excuse my not writing as often as I ought, yet I doe assure you my time is soe taken up with matters of several kinds that I can hardly say I am Master of half an hour in a week … You may remember what you and I have talked of together here; but we are so perverse a generation of people that it is impossible to doe us any good: There is not the least tendencye to doe any thing toward what may be of publick use; some are so great fools as not to see the way of coming at having

[362]John Methuen.

[363]John Forster, MP [I], was appointed counsel to the revenue commissioners [I] on 30 June 1699, when the commissioners withdrew their previous recommendation of William Brodrick because of information received concerning his 'bad character' (*Calendar of Treasury Papers*, 1697–1702, 314).

[364]Lewis Moore of Ballina House, Co. Kildare, who although a lieutenant in Lord Mountcashell's regiment in the jacobite army in 1689 (John D'Alton, *Illustrations, Historical and Genealogical, of King James's Irish Army List, 1689* (Dublin, 1855), 486) had not suffered outlawry, claimed the estate of his cousin Colonel Charles Moore of Ballina House, a colonel in the jacobite army, who had been outlawed and was killed at the Battle of Aughrim. It was later alleged, in the anti-trustee pamphlet (*The Secret History of the Trust, with Some Reflections upon the Letter from a Soldier* … (1702), 7–8) that the former Irish MP Maurice Annesley, a cousin of the trustee Francis Anneseley and himself employed by the trustees as a receiver (Hayton, *Ruling Ireland*, 78), had asked Moore for a bribe of a hundred guineas to secure Francis's favour, a story Moore himself strenuously denied (*Mr Moore of Ballyna's Deposition, Relating to the Paragraph in the Sixpenny Secret History of the Trust* ([?Dublin, 1702]). The case is discussed in Simms, *Williamite Confiscation*, 146.

right done; some so cowardly as rather to submit to any imposicion then venture to incur the censure or displeasure of Colledge Green:[365] some beleive it a lost game; others will not venture to lay out one penny to preserve themselves and their posteritye: but indeed it proceeds cheifly from the dread every body lyes under of being crushed and ruined by their adversaries if they should stir. Soe that if I write any thing farther to you on this Subject it shal not be by post. There hath lately hapned an odd affair at Chichester house, of which you shal have a full and true account (when I am able to send it) by some safe hand. The trustees have been applied to by the Lessees of the private estate and of other Lands who petitioned the Parliament and whose peticions are to be considered next Session,[366] that they would order their receivers to demand no more rent then they were to have paid by their Leases made to them by the Lady Orkney and their other Landlords if the Act for vesting the Lands in trustees had not passed; but before the passing of that act they have been forced to take the Lands from the trustees at much higher rents, and most of them say dearer then they can make of the Lands from undertenants: The reason they give for their making this request is that there is a Clause in the Last Act, that they shal not be prejudiced or disturbed in their possessions or interests etc. and they doe not see any other intent that clause can have but to leave them in possession subject to the rent they were to pay by their former leases (which they petitioned to have made good to them) till the Parliaments mind was known: Now the trustees could not disturb them against their own Leases if they paid the rent reserved thereon: But as I hear they have declared they expect the full rent, and look on so doing to be no way against the intent of the Act: The true reasons of their opinion I know not, but what follows (tho confidently talked of) I beleive may be a story; that if they should respite so much money, there would not be enough to pay their own and servants salaryes: But this you know is mighty incredible. I heard it the other day very boldly asserted by one who carried a long letter last year from me to you, that the private estate, as now sett by them, will yeild this year half of what Sir H.S. last year told the house of Commons they did not despair to make of it:[367] for it is racked[368] to £17500 this year as he saith, and pretends to be certain it does not exceed that summe. Really it is not their fault if it yeilds no more; for never were more extraordinary diligence, care and means used to make things hold out; and if it will not be who can help it? No doubt considering there is full two years rent due att All Saints last and that all care is taken to prevent mens running in arrear, which will bring in all last half years rent before Christmas, they will have a good part of the rents in bank; but the fees of offices which poor claimants and sutors have paid (if they are called on for an account of it) must needs be a considerable addicion. Your acquaintance and mine of All Souls[369] hath shewn himself a little too plainly in favor of the

[365] Where the trustees had their headquarters, in Chichester House.

[366] Among the petitions to the English house of commons in May 1701 was one from Captain Richard Wolseley, MP [I], Captain Charles Meredith (probably Charles Meredyth, MP [I]), Captain St John Webb, and Morgan Bernard (b. 1670, a son-in-law of the planter Sir Vincent Gookin), who had petitioned on behalf of themselves and other 'lessees and tenants' of King James II's 'private estate' (*CJ*, xiii, 556, 628).

[367] Sir Henry Sheres (1641–1710), who together with his fellow trustees Francis Annesley and John Trenchard had attended the English parliament in May 1701 (*Cocks Diary*, ed. Hayton, 136).

[368] Raised to the highest possible level.

[369] The barrister Anthony Upton (1656–1718), who had graduated from Oxford University as a member of All Souls'. A tory in his politics, Upton was to be appointed justice of common pleas [I] the following year. (Ball, *Judges*, ii, 66–78).

Irish lately, and his and other mens behavior who came over lately give enemies occasion to speak to the disadvantage of one we wish well to: you know I told you how surprised he was upon any thoughts of applicacion by numbers or in writing against the trustees act, or the execucion: but particular Gentlemen for the Leassees, others for purchasers etc. have spoke and laid open their particular pressures; but the ruinous consequences to the whole Kingdome particular persons doe not meddle with: it is a deplorable thing that it is impossible to have the pressures of the Kingdome made known; for a few mens going over will not doe, and the sense of the people cannot be known for want of their meeting in a body as a representative of the whole. Men are dispirited and strangely impoverished since the beginning of this project, and as the gain will be very inconsiderable to the people of England should they proceed farther in the matter, I am morally certain the Kingdome hath already spent more in attending the trustees Court then ever the forfeitures will amount to: this is as true, as that it is an horrid shame it should be soe: never Ireland felt such a tax ... This packett brings surprising news of the dissolucion of the Parliament;[370] my Country men[371] hang the head greivously; God send it be for the best, but assuredly their discontent is a sign that in their opinion the next will be worse for them, and if they judge right for their great support the French King. We are sure their interests and ours are perfectly opposite. I am told that Mr Bags[372] lately took occasion to say on the bench that if it was other peoples design to unsettle the Protestant interest of Ireland, he came not over on that errand, nor would go into such measures: Doe not report this till you hear again from me, because I am not certain of it, at least in the maner, but I beleive in the main it is true: They are civiller I am told, but I have received too many slights from them to put it in their power to affront me farther, or by civilityes attone for past rudenesses.

46. *Alan I, Dublin, to St John II, at his chambers in Lamb Buildings, Middle Temple, 29 Nov. 1701*

(1248/2/41–2)

Our term is now over which gives me more leisure to write to you then I of late have been Master of: There goes as good an hogshead of Pontack[373] by long Sea from hence as this Kingdome affords; directed and consigned as that which the Baron had, of which I wish to hear some account: I mean as to the goodnesse: I am sure it is admirable good if Cairnes sent that hogshead I pitched on which very nice palats tasted and approved: and since I gave him his own price he ought to deal very fairly with me and let my friend have the

[370]The English parliament had been dissolved on 11 Nov.

[371]Irish catholics.

[372]John Baggs (1661–1706), a barrister of Gray's Inn, and a trustee (*Allegations for Marriage Licences Issued by the Bishop of London* ... ed. G. J. Armytage (2 vols, Harleian Society, 1887), ii, 305; Joseph Foster, *The Register of Admissions to Gray's Inn* ... (2 vols, 1889) i, 325; *The Pension Book of Gray's Inn* ... ed. R. J. Fletcher (2 vols, 1901–10), i, 83, 136; *K. Inns Adm.*, 15).

[373]Most commonly the high status Bordeaux wine of Château Haut-Brion, though other wines also carried the Pontac name. See Tim Unwin, 'The Viticultural Georgraphy of France in the Seventeenth Century According to John Locke', *Annales de Géographie*, cix (2000), 401, 404–5, 412; Charles Ludington, *The Politics of Wine in Britain: A New Cultural History* (Basingstoke, 2013), 83–91.

top wine of his Cellar. Give me a just account how that, and what I now send you, proves; that I may shew him the letter …

47. *Alan I, Dublin, to St John II, at his chambers in Lamb Buildings, Middle Temple, 15 Dec. 1701*

(1248/2/43–4)

It hath been impossible for me to keep my resolucions of writing constantly or giving you a weekly account of the weather as I intended; but in the main we have had a wet season till within these last ten dayes which have proved very fair and open. The resentments of the Kingdome of the miserye it lies under by means of the trustee Act and the maner of its execucion and the excessive expence it puts all sorts of people to on Wednesday last shewed it self in our privy Council, when my Lord Blessinton[374] moved my Lord Lieutenant that he would represent the condicion of the Kingdome to be very miserable by means of that Act;[375] that the Cost the Kingdome was put in attending the trustees and defending or claiming their estates far exceeded the Land tax granted to the Crown; that the burthen falls generally on the English Protestants, the Act being rather an Act of Settlement to the Irish then otherwise.[376] His Lordship, and others gave it as their own and the sense of the Kingdome in their opinion that the English interest here suffered more under that Commission then by the late rebellion:[377] and some Lords that spoke desired if any Lord present at the Councel or other Privy Councellor was not of the same mind, that they would declare it: upon which many said it was the general sense of the people and their own, and the rest consented to it by acquiescing and silence. My Lord Lieuten[*an*]t declared that as he found that to be the sense of the board, soe he had been informed to the same effect by several other Gentlemen of figure and fortune from several parts of the Kingdome, and gave great satisfaction to the Councel by assuring them that he would truly and fully represent the matter to his Majestye.

The trustees they say are wondrous angry at this proceeding, and talk big among freinds what farther severities this will bring on us from England: but for my part till I find other men beside them, Sir Robert Hamilton[378] and a few more of that Kidney dislike the proceeding I cannot but think it is very fit the King and people of England should be informed of our Condicion by men whose representacion carries as much weight as the trustees denials which particular men know not how to controvert or take on them to disprove, for fear of being crushed for daring to say they are injured. The Kingdome I am confident will follow this example and set forth the ruine of their fortunes to make particular men great estates: Probably the way may be by an addresse or peticion from each County, City, and

[374]Viscount Blessington.

[375]The Forfeitures Resumption Act.

[376]In other words an equivalent to the Restoration Act of Settlement, but this time benefiting catholics rather than protestants.

[377]Presumably a reference to the Irish rebellion of 1641.

[378]Sir Robert Hamilton, 1st Bt (*d.* 1703) of Mount Hamilton, Co. Armagh (Lodge, *Peerage*, i, 270; *Complete Baronetage*, iv, 219). For Hamilton's high church proclivities and connections, see TCD, MS 1995–2008/972: Hamilton to Bishop King of Derry, 26 Dec. 1702.

borough in the Kingdome directly to his Majestye; which seems to some the most likely to speak the sense of the Kingdome, since it will be the Act of those who have right to send representatives to Parliament to speak the mind of the aggregate body of the people.[379] I wish some rules or measures could be chalked out, what and in what way might be done that would give least offence and attain the end desired, to be rid of our taskmasters: and you will not wonder at it when Mr Upton[380] lately in their Court said he did not doubt but that they would sit seven years yet to come. I would not write what passed at Councel but that I find the whole town full of the discourse and no doubt letters have carried it both into the Countrey and England: Vouch not me, but what passed was much to the purpose above; in the debate the Chancellor[381] and Lord Cheif Justice P[*yne*][382] spoke warmly to the effect that Lord Blessinton moved; and only one seemed to differ, but after expressed himself that he owned all that had been said was true, but doubted whether the method proposed was the way to attain the end, without forming some scheme of an equivalent. Let me assure you, that I fear your freind Mr J. D.[383] is very far from a freind to us in this affair tho he promises his assistance in the house in any thing that can be reasonably offered toward our releif. He went hence on Saturday with Dr H[*ickman*][384] and Mr Secretary Gwyn[385] goes in the boat which carries this. Let me hear from you soon, and particularly how we may best frame a representacion of our real miseries …

[*PS.*] Tell my brother he may depend on Mr Ogle[386] and apply to him as to a most hearty enemy to this hellish design for our ruine.

48. *Alan I, Dublin, to St John II, at his chambers in the Middle Temple, 18 Dec. 1701*

(1248/2/45–6)

I have very little to trouble you now with farther to … assure you not only from my fathers letters, but the accounts I have by letters from others and by word of mouth from one who very lately saw him that he is very weak in his bed where he hath been confined for a great many weeks past, and a numnesse and swelling having seised his legs I am apprehensive of his falling into a palsey or dropsye either of which must prove fatal to a man of his age.

[379] The method that was adopted early the following year, in the form of the so-called 'national remonstrance', a collection of county addresses organised by William Conolly, Marmaduke Coghill and others (Simms, *Williamite Confiscation*, 125–7; Walsh, *Making of the Irish Protestant Ascendancy*, 56–7).

[380] Anthony Upton.

[381] Presumably the lord chief baron of the exchequer [I], Robert Doyne (1651–1733) (Ball, *Judges*, ii, 62), rather than the recently appointed lord chief justice of common pleas [I], Sir Richard Cox, whose political associations were tory.

[382] Richard Pyne (1644–1709), lord chief justice of king's bench [I] (Ball, *Judges*, ii, 59–60).

[383] Probably Joshua Dawson, MP [I]. Although he was not himself a member of the house of commons at Westminster, Dawson's administrative connections might well have enabled him to assist.

[384] Charles Hickman (1648–1713), one of the lord lieutenant's chaplains, and gratified with appointment as bishop of Derry in 1703 (*Oxf. DNB*; Bodl., MS Ballard 36, f. 19: William Perceval to Arthur Charlett, 10 Dec. 1701).

[385] Francis Gwyn (c.1648–1734), Rochester's chief secretary.

[386] Samuel Ogle, MP [I]. At this time a revenue commissioner in Ireland and member of the English house of commons.

Really I think his greif for past mismanagements hath sunk deep into him, and nothing so sensibly afflicts him as what you have suffered by it in particular; a line from you would more comfort him then any other cordial. Pray send to my brother Tho[*mas*] and caution him not to embark at all in any project of giving a summe of money in nature of an equivalent for the forfeitures; the difficulties will be innumerable, it will ruine the interest he hath yet left here; but what is most considerable is that the Kingdome is not in condicion to give any thing that England will hearken to and considering the favours the Irish have mett with, what remains (beside the private estate) will be very inconsiderable. Underneath comes an addresse from the County of Corke which is to morrow to be presented to my Lord Lieutenant by my Lord Insiquin[387] and me …

49. *Alan I, Dublin, to St John II, at his chamber in Lamb Buildings, Middle Temple, 7 Jan. 1701/2*

(1248/2/49–50)

We are in an amaze at not having packets in tho the wind hath been as fair as it can blow out of the sky these three dayes; I have for two dayes last past forbore to write to you in hopes of letters every hour; and from the time my Lord Lieutenant went hence till Monday morning Lucyes very great indisposicion gave me neither leisure nor inclinacion to mind any thing but her: her pain in the head was excessive, and being advised to drink waters, neither they nor any thing else passed with her for fowre or five dayes, which put her into violent burnings, and me into apprehensions of making her come before her time; but she is now better, yet in great pain, her skin being stretched and ready to burst; which the Physicians attribute to her waters not passing but say there is nothing of a dropsical humor in it, she not having any great droughth on her: God send her a safe deliverye; she is strangely big tho I dare not tell her soe, and she apprehends herself to have two children. My Lord Lieutenant went away soe early in the morning and without timely notice that not one fifth part of the town could take their leaves of him: I could not overtake him before he left the Castle but hoped to have done it at Rings end;[388] but he went into a boat at Lazy Hill[389] and I was not able to come out of my Coach before the boat was putt off: Pray fail not to make an excuse for me; an omission I cannot call it, but it was a misfortune not to be able to wait on him: and he may perhaps resent it as a slight, if he be willing to beleive me opposite to his interests for being very forward against the trustees: I formerly told you that I apprehended he was unwilling to have publick representacions against them come through his hands as Cheif Governor; I alway expressed my self with utter abhorrence of the Act and the maner of executing it to his Lordship and never pretended that the Protestant interest of this Kingdome could thrive without giving it another turn; and before his Excellencye went away I told him I would go in to the methods then in hand to represent the fatal consequences of that Act by publick addresses: his Lordship was for having a little time over

[387] William O'Brien (1662–1719), 3rd earl of Inchiquin.

[388] Ringsend, near Dublin; the usual point of embarkation of the packet-boat.

[389] Lazy Hill, or Lazars Hill, was a street to the north of Trinity College running parallel to the River Liffey; the term was also used for the entire area of land lying between Trinity and the river at Burgh Quay.

before any thing was done and more then hinted it to me to be his mind to have the thing delayed; but that was the very night the addresse was signed in town, and letters wrote into the countrey;[390] soe as if it had been advisable, it was too late to think of giving it any delay then: and the next morning I waited on him and told him soe, and said also that I would sign the addresse which I have done.[391] They who will not openly appear against it say it ought to be to the Parliament as well as the King, and blame applying to him for releif against an Act of Parliament as if that implyed his being able to dispence with or repeal it: Others say the addresse treats the Act too roughly in saying the scheme of it is prejudicial to the Protestants and for the advantage of the Papists: If it hath its faults it is our misfortune not to know the forms, which the newnesse of the Case may something excuse. P[ray] write constantly to me while this matter is on the a[?nvil] and tho my brother Tho[*mas*] should not call on you, doe send to him when any thing for the good of this unh[appy] Kingdome occurs to you: the rough draught of the addresse as signed went to him on Christmas day, tho I did not see it till several dayes after; I hope he let you see it, and expect the next packets will bring the sense of our freinds in England how it supposed it will take there. The talk here is privately that the Irish one while were for making a counter addresse; but that they beleive will do more harm then good: and in hopes to establish what hath been done pretend now to complain of the trustees too: but this may be only prate; and if begun would go on so awkwardly and with so ill a grace as soon to be soon [*sic*] through …

50. *Alan I, Dublin, to St John II, at his chambers in Lamb Buildings, Middle Temple, 20 Jan. 1701/2*

(1248/2/51–2)

This must be a letter of course as many more of this post, to let you know that Lucy on Sunday morning last about ten brought me a very lusty boy;[392] and tho her reckoning was not full out, soe as by that she must come before her time, yet she either must be mistaken (as it is very easy for a woman that hath not a very moderate husband) or else the boy was soe well gott that he thought he might venture into open air before the ordinary time: the truth is, I wonder she had room for him so long, much more then that she could find him lodging no longer: for he is so long and large a child that it is an amazing thing to me how it is possible for her to goe out her time with him; They tell me and he seems to promise as much, that he is very likely to live and make her amends for the losse of her other boy. I write this post to my brother Tho[*mas*]. The addresses are gone generally through the Kingdome about the trustees, and what is very remarkable the Clergy have as I hear in many places opposed them: What their motives are I doe not know; whether their fondnesse of the persons who promoted that honest act, or the little benefit they gett

[390] A circular letter, signed by the earl of Meath and 39 others, and dated 13 Dec. 1701 accompanied a draft address to the king sent out into the country (BL, Eg. MS 917, f. 179; *CJ*, xiii, 718).

[391] A 'general address', rather than a county or city address: this was not presented to the English parliament, see below, p. 122.

[392] Alan II.

by it by the grant to them of the forfeited impropriate tythes,[393] or that they have a mind to convince people that they have no regard to the Protestant interest of the Kingdome I know not: but I am not surprised at any proceedings of theirs that relate to the benefit of any persons but themselves. The votes that came over by the last packets about the trustees[394] are now made use of by them and their little emissaries and rascally flatterers to this purpose, that now there is no need of farther applicacion since the matter is in a way of being done to our hands; and addresses (especially which say that the scope of the Act is favourable to the Papists and very prejudicial to the Protestant interest of the land) may provoke people otherwise well disposed in our favor and especially because no applicacion is by them made to the Parliament, but only to the King. By these and a thousand other instances all considering men must see we are a very extraordinary composicion, made up of a great deal of folly, and something else with a very little honestye or honour here and there thrown in: Our Clergy, some of our Judges and Mr Attorney will have the honor of baffling these applicacions if they should fail, but I am sure they cannot doe soe unlesse in very few Countyes of the Kingdome. In Limrick the thing is stopt, and I hear in Westmeath and Louth by means of one I have just now named:[395] whether he thinks to make his Court this way I know not, but hope the Countrey will know and distinguish him. In short I would not have you overconcerned for people that are born to destruction and cant be preserved; that never fail to contribute to their own ruine and malign all that would serve them …[396]

51. *Alan I, Dublin, to Thomas, at the Whitehall coffee-house, King's Street, Westminster, 28 Jan. 1701/2*[397]

(1248/2/59–60)

I now have yours of the 13th before me for answer, and must tell you that you put me by it on a task that I am neither willing to undertake, nor able to goe through with: What method can I propose of repealing that Law,[398] or of substituting one in the place of it? If the injustice of it be not yet perceived, I think the same people will never apprehend any

[393]The Forfeitures Resumption Act included a provision requiring the trustees to convey all impropriate rectories and tithes to nominees of the bishops of the established church, to be used for the repairing and rebuilding of churches and the augmentation of small livings (Simms, *Williamite Confiscation*, 116, 128).

[394]On 7 Jan. the English house of commons had ordered the attendance of two of the trustees and had required the delivery of documents from the trust stating the value of all claims allowed, and what remained to be adjudicated; an account of all sums of money received and what was outstanding; an account of expenditure; and a table of the fees the trustees had allowed their officers to levy (*CJ*, xiii, 656). The *Votes* of both houses of parliament (a cursory record of proceedings, comprising no more than orders and resolutions), were printed and issued on a daily basis (Betty Kemp, *Votes and Standing Orders of the House of Commons: The Beginning* (House of Commons Library Document, no. 8, 1971)).

[395]Robert Rochfort, the Irish attorney-general, whose principal country estate was in Westmeath, was governor of the county (the Irish equivalent of the English lord lieutenant) and had represented the county constituency in parliament. For his influence in Co. Louth, see below, p. 108.

[396]Added at top of last page: 'Talk not about Clergy Judges or Attorney'.

[397]The letter is dated by Alan as 20 Mar. 1702 but has been amended, possibly by Thomas, as January and endorsed in another hand as 28 Jan., which from the contents seems to be the correct date.

[398]The Forfeitures Resumption Act.

thing that is said against it, nor credit it: But suppose you or any body of this Kingdome should offer a reasonable scheme that might answer the publick as effectually what they can ever gett by that Act and in as good a maner, as if the Act continued: and that this scheme were as reasonable with relacion to Ireland as it is to England; and that it should be complied with: I must tell you that we have among us soe many knaves, and soe very many more blockheads that either we should not goe into fit measures to make good what must be at least probably made appear to be the event of the repealing that Law, or else it will draw with it soe many difficultyes by opposicion of persons and parties, that it will be an heart breaking to the well meaning people that endeavour to sett it on foot and carry it on for the publick service, to bring it to any perfection; and if they should be fortunate enough to quit themselves with honor of the engagements they must lye under, it can no otherwise be done then by disobliging almost every body: and the errantest temporizing rascal in the Kingdome will reap an equal advantage with the honest slave that works like a horse to bring it about. But after all I doubt whether ever we can be of a mind to make such a Law or lay such a tax as will be expected in lieu of our trustee Act: every body will be concerned in interest, consequently we shall fall into factions and partyes and do nothing right. This I mencion not to discourage others, and therefore desire you to keep this secret: do not engage your self in reputacion for the peoples doing any thing that is honourable or honest: We are such a medley as is not to be found again on the face of Gods earth: for my part I will not for the value of the forfeitures inslave myself to be obliged to carry on the fittest thing in the world in a Parliament here: I have been a slave in such an assembly so far formerly, tho I never did or promoted any one thing but for the publick good, that I will not be tyed so much as to constant attendance, much lesse have the task and calumnye of being a manager: I can bear the ruine of Ireland and live in England better than those rascalls who will be sure to traduce all that is done for the good of the Protestant interest here as proceedings from private designs and self ends and will therefore be no farther concerned in the event of affairs then other people: In short I think he is a madman that is either an undertaker or framer of a scheme; for every scoundrel that never puts his hand toward lifting the burden, will over his Ale find faults with what is done; whereas tho it should be true that something more perfect might be framed, yet they ought to be encouraged not traduced and exposed who finding others not to stir in so necessary a work first took it in hand and managed it according to the best of their judgements. For example, Suppose I should fancy that it were not difficult now to see that the forfeitures of Ireland will not answer a summe certain neat money, doing all the hardships to Protestants, Lessees, purchasers etc. which the Act as it now stands hath done them: and that the Parliament of England were inclined to remit somewhat in favor of those Lessees purchasers etc. and would therefore expect a lesse summe then their real value out of the forfeitures: suppose they should be content wholly to repeal the Act (which seems also to be very unlikely) and leave the settlement of those matters to a Parliament here, and should give the King funds as much short as they expected Ireland should make good in lieu of the forfeitures: what a struggle would there be between the purchasers, Lessees, incumbrancers etc. As to the Grantees they can expect little favor here: the Irish will be sure to oppose this to their utmost and we shal have a fine task to frame a reasonable bill in our own house, but when it comes before the Councel board here, it will meet difficulties in abundance and I beleive not be free from such in England: but for the house of Lords I am of opinion if the bill be a reasonable one for the Protestant interest here it will have the usual fate bills of that sort find there:[399] The more I think of these things the more I am confirmed that I never will concern my self in any thing that layeth me under any obligacion to wish earnestly or zealously prosecute any thing in Parliament upon the peril of mine or my friends Credit: for interest I can as easily suffer in it and bear the losse as any body; but my peace of mind is lost to fail in credit so as to be thought trickish in not going through with a matter any way undertaken on the credit of promises made by me or freinds. It is very strange if you had a Copy of the Addresse signed by the Lords and Gentlemen in and about Dublin and sent into the Countrey (as I am told you had inclosed in a letter dated on Christmas day) that you take no notice of it to me or in yours to my neighbour; if there were any thing in it soe offensive as we are here told (by saying the whole scheme of the Act is for the benefit of the Papists and prejudicial to the Protestants) methinks we should before this time have had hints from your side the water: The Cant now is, that it is unnecessary to proceed; for matters are going on of themselves and our addresses may give offence; others say that neither the Bishops nor Judges have signed any addresse (which I beleive to be true) and they also add Mr Attorney. It is plain the addresse is rejected in the County of Limrick by means of the Clergy; and hitherto the addresses from Westmeath and Lowth are not returned: some words give either offence or create fears; but you know who pretends to influence one of those Countyes by himself and the other by his brother B[*ellingham*].[400] Beside Mr Barton[401] is very eager against it. At Kildare Sessions you may beleive the Anesleys[402] were against it; Mr Bourke their brother in Law[403] and Mr Keating[404] would not sign; nor Mr Jones (the Bishop of Kildares son in Law)[405] but a majoritye of the Bench signed; the grand Jury were returned by the Sherif Mr John Anesley and such a parcel of fellows that young Mr Ecchlin[406] assured me the worst of 21 grand Jurors for the County of Dublin would have purchased them all: and then they must be sad rogues, for really some of Dublin were very indifferent. The two

[399]The process of legislating in Ireland required that bills should originate in the Irish privy council and be transmitted for scrutiny and possible amendment to the privy council in England, which might or might not return them to Ireland, where they were presented to parliament for acceptance or rejection without the opportunity of further amendment. In practice most legislation originated in either the Irish house of lords or commons, as draft bills ('heads of bills'), which were then sent to the Irish privy council to be turned into form.

[400]Robert Rochfort's brother-in-law Thomas Bellingham, MP [I]. They had married sisters (*Diary of Thomas Bellingham, an Officer under William III*, ed. Anthony Hewitson (Preston, 1908), 2, 128–9).

[401]William Barton, MP [I].

[402]Presumably the four surviving sons of John Annesley (1616–95) of Ballysonan, Co. Kildare: Francis, MP [I] New Ross 1695–9; Maurice, MP [I]; John of Ballysax, Co. Kildare (*d.* 1720); and George (Lodge, *Peerage*, iv, 118; 'Fitzgeralds of Ballyshannon (Kildare)', *Journal of the County Kildare Archaeological Society*, iii (1899–1903), 448–9).

[403]Walter Bourke of Moneycrower, Co. Mayo, and Kill, Co. Kildare, had married Anne Annesley, a daughter of John Annesley of Ballysonan (Lodge, *Peerage*, iv, 118). He was the uncle of John Bourke, 1st earl of Mayo.

[404]Maurice Keating, MP [I].

[405]Thomas Jones, MP [I], stepson of William Moreton (c.1641–1715), bishop of Kildare, who had married as his second wife Mary (née Harman), the widow of Sir Arthur Jones (John Burke, *A Genealogical and Heraldic History of the Commoners of Great Britain and Ireland* … (4 vols, 1833–8), i, 346).

[406]Robert Echlin, MP [I] for Newry, who had married a daughter of Sir Maurice Eustace (c. 1637–1703), MP [I], of Harristown, Co. Kildare (*Hist. Ir. Parl.*, iv, 117).

Sanders[407] would needs have me write in favor of Robin Sanders son[408] to recommend him to Lord Galwey in whom they pretend an interest: I told them I had not that intimacye to write to him; they then desired I would mencion the young man to you to speak for him, which I said I would; but you know how far I lye under obligacions to them Gentlemen: but indeed I would have you doe all you can for Robin Foulke.[409] I differ with you as to your being chosen if there be a Parliament, but would have you serve for your own borough[410] and then you may come over at your own time: Upon Mr Ogles[411] saying he would be very ready to serve Ireland in Parliament here or in England I told him rather then want so good a man we would secure him an election in the County of Corke; pray when you see him make him the complement of Middleton; he will doe us signal service in England and is a most freindly Gentleman.

52. *Alan I, Dublin, to St John II, at his chamber in Lamb Buildings, Middle Temple, 7 Feb. 1701/2*

(1248/2/55–6)

We want fowre packets through the storminesse of the weather and crosse winds, which makes us uneasy who have our eyes fixed on the proceedings of the Parliament of England; our happinesse or ruine depending thereon as I think. You may be very sure the trustees are thoroughly nettled at the addresses against their Act and proceedings;[412] but I beleive you could not expect that Mr Conollyes[413] acting in forwarding those addresses and discovering the printer of a libel (here set forth to ridicule them and represent those concerned therein as disaffected to the English Governement)[414] should cause such rage in the trustees as again to stir in the matter of Parker[415] of which you have formerly heard; but his freinds assure me that they have sent over a representacion of that matter, and you may be sure a very full one on their own side, in order to bring him under their lash if possible, or which

[407] Possibly the Irish MPs Anderson Saunders and Morley, both of whom were lawyers, though of a different political complexion to the Brodricks.

[408] Robert Saunders, MP [I], Morley's father, another of whose sons, Robert, was an army captain (*Hist. Ir. Parl.*, vi, 244).

[409] Robert Foulke, MP [I].

[410] Midleton.

[411] Samuel Ogle, MP [I].

[412] Eleven addresses were presented to the house of commons on 14 Feb. 1702 (from the cities of Dublin and Galway, and Counties Cavan, Clare, Cork, Dublin, Kilkenny, Meath, Queen's County, Roscommon and Tipperary). In addition a further twelve manuscript addresses survive, as BL Add. Chs 19526–38 (from Waterford city and Counties Antrim, Armagh, Carlow, Donegal, Down, Galway, Kerry, Londonderry, Longford, Tyrone, and Waterford).

[413] William Conolly, MP [I].

[414] [John Trenchard,] *The Several Addresses of Some Irish Folkes to the King and the House of Commons* ([1702]).

[415] At a hearing before the trustees in Jan. 1701 in respect of a claim on the earl of Tyrconnell's estate, allegations had been levelled against the claimant, John Parker, which implicated Conolly in the forgery of deeds and other nefarious practices. Parker appealed the dismissal of his claim, and at a further, public, hearing before the trustees, on 3–14 Feb. the allegations were elaborated. Alan Brodrick, who had given Conolly legal advice on the case, testified on his behalf. The appeal was dismissed, and, although no further action was taken against Conolly, the possibility hung over his head for some time. (Walsh, *Making of the Irish Protestant Ascendancy*, 51–5, 59.)

is worse under the censure of a vote of the house of Commons; worse I call it, because I think reputacion much preferable to fortune, and no censure of the trustees can injure the former. Sure it will be considered whence such proceedings arise, and be asked why this was not last year laid before the house if at all fit to be brought into it; but thus it must fare with men that will not fall down to and worship them; especially that have traced Mr Trenchards brother[416] to be one and his Clerk the other who brought that libel to the presse. Your memorye is not soe bad as not to remember his Case, and it may be refreshed by letters now lying by you; It were to be wished that some Gentlemen may be prepared to speak to this matter at its first being moved in the house; and I think the Baron will shew so much freindship for a Gentleman he knows as to befreind him by giving such a character of him to his acquaintance as he thinks he deserves. I doe assure you they are full of fury, and I hope their reason is the same with that given for anothers being soe, because they know their time is short. The methods they use to discourage men from making publick applicacion against them are without number; but the cheif are the giving out what interest and assurance of successe they have against all opposers; tho most claims are heard very few are so determined as not to be stil in their power, for hardly one adjudicacion is signed; nay I am truly informed that they having signed one for Mr McDonnel recalled the same and gott it again into their hands, and they only know when or in what maner it will be returned; so as claimants whose claims are heard remain stil at their mercy: and much more those who are yet to come on. But the threats they give out of what the house of Commons will doe terrifyes men to the last degree. As for my part I am told that they hint at me as one to whom they purpose to doe ill offices in the Parliament: I have tasted of their goodnesse already, and expect the utmost effects of their displeasure: but I thank God I have never done any one Act in the course of my life that can render me obnoxious and therefore I defye malice, provided it keep within the bounds of truth: If they mean that I did in open Court say that their sale of Lands not vested in them would not be conclusive to the title of the right owners I confesse it: and am of opinion the Act never intended to confirm any sales that should be by them made but what were pursuant to the Act; and that the Act only empowred them to sell Lands of forfeiting persons which were vested in them: and if I mistake herein the Kingdome is much in their power. Whether these threats are only given out to terrifye me or have ground I know not: but desire that you will not fail to speak to some sensible men whom you know that no design of Hell or Mr A[*nnesley*][417] may prejudice me in my reputacion by having my name in publick votes, or being sent for over to the detriment of my credit as well as fortune. If my brother T[*homas*] had not been so basely traduced in the first report I could have sate down as easily with my losses by the Act and bore its consequences as well as others; and when ever this matter is over I will let publick affairs goe as they may without burning my fingers by meddling in them. Pray let me hear from you …

[416]William Trenchard (1678–bef. 1710), a younger son of William Trenchard of Cutteridge, Wilts., and brother of the trustee John Trenchard, had been appointed (through his brother's influence) as secretary to the trust (HMC, *Portland MSS*, iv, 1; *London Post*, 19–22 Apr. 1700).

[417]Francis Annesley, MP [I], the trustee.

53. *Alan I, Dublin, to St John II, at his chamber in Lamb Buildings, Middle Temple, 22 Feb. 1701/2*

(1248/2/56a–56b)

We are here very uneasy for want of packets out of England, and what adds to our troubles is that we have not one boat on this side the water; so that here are now in the Post office the English letters which the six last posts brought to Dublin. Captain Stafford[418] will send or deliver this to you, who hath at long run procured licence from our Lords Justices to goe over into England;[419] and is able to give you a fuller account of our matters here then I can by letter: The trustees are in high rage and threaten mightily those who have addressed against them; and some of them are to the last degree incensed at the preferring and finding a bill of indictment against one Camell their printer[420] and against a Clerk of one of the trustees and Mr Trenchard their Secretarye for printing and publishing a libel made to ridicule the addresse: Of which having made mencion I think it fit to answer the objections you say people on your side make to the letter that went with it into the Countrey: I do assure you I never saw any one of those letters before they were signed and sealed up, nor read them: but doe beleive that there is such an expression in them as you hint at That our freinds in England approve etc. and that care shal be taken they be presented to the King by proper hands: [421] On discourse with some Gentlemen who subscribed and were at the penning the letter I find them to explain those expressions in this maner: That several Gentlemen now in London who have estates here have held correspondence by letter with some Gentlemen in Dublin or elsewhere in Ireland, which was very necessarye to be done before hand if it was expected they should undertake to forward the thing in England, and that some thing of the nature of the addresse then sent down was what they in England as well as in Dublin thought proper: This was thought very necessary to be told the Gentlemen in the Countrey to prevent the trustees story and that of their emissaryes being beleived that it was the Act only of a few self interested persons. As to the matter of presenting them by proper hands no more they say was intended thereby then that they should be laid before the King in the most respectful way, that is be first given to the Lords Justices here to be transmitted to the Lord Lieutenant and to be by him offered to the King: and that this was the intent of the words proper hands appears by the instructions

[418] Edmond Francis Stafford, MP [I].

[419] As an army officer, Stafford needed to procure a leave of absence from the lords justices. One of the purchasers of the forfeited estates granted to Lord Albemarle, Stafford had interests to pursue in England (*A List of the Claims* …, 88; HMC, *Portland MSS*, viii, 88). He and Samuel Dopping, MP [I], had presented a petition to the house of commons at Westminster, on which the trustees reported, and the Commons debated on 18 Apr. 1702 (*CJ*, xiii, 855–6; Simms, *Williamite Confiscation*, 101–2, 140–1; *Cocks Diary*, ed. Hayton, 271).

[420] Patrick Campbell (*d.* 1720), for whom see Robert Munter, *A Dictionary of the Print Trade in Ireland 1550–1775* (New York, NY, 1988), 48–9; M. Pollard, *A Dictionary of Members of the Dublin Book Trade 1550–1800* … (2000), 82–4). Campbell had been appointed in June 1700 as 'stationer to the trustees' (PRONI, D/1854/2/2: trustees' minute books, ii, 2).

[421] The circular letter sent on 13 Dec. 1701 with the draft address was printed, and commented upon, in John Trenchard's second contribution to the pamphlet controversy, *A Letter from a Souldier to the Commons of England, Occasioned by an Address Now Carrying on by the Protestants in Ireland* … (1702). The original letter contained neither of the phrases Alan mentions, although it did cite 'the opinion of or friends in England' advising this course of action (22), and in a postscript promised that the various addresses would be collated and transmitted to 'proper persons' in England (23), a phrase Trenchard's scornful commentary transformed into 'proper hands' (24).

signed and given to Mr Dopping and Captain Stafford whereby they are required first to wait on my Lord Lieutenant with the addresses (supposing the Lords Justices would have sent them by their hands) and their farther directions are not to make any farther applicacion on those addresses to either house of Parliament if it may any way obstruct his Majestyes or the publick affairs of the Kingdome in Parliament: The instructions are something to this purpose but I have not the copy of them, so cannot be very particular. They say farther that it was needful to assure Gentlemen in the Country that proper hands would be found out to present them, to contradict the trustees boasting that no persons so hardy would be found out to deliver them in England. As to a particular addresse being recommended, they say that they sent down a Copy of one agreed on between them here, but no way pressed all Countyes to adhere to that form but left them at liberty to expresse themselves in their own words. I find there are among the other things on this side the water for want of a packett boat fifteen addresses stil in the Lords Justices hands … Lucy and my sister, the boy and girle are very lusty and well. God send us good news when we hear from you. You know I went with you to Mr Isham and Mr Baggs[422] lodgings just before your leaving Ireland, but I never had a return of my visit from either; and I thought the impertinence of Dr King[423] was a little incouraged by the former; and since they returned not visit for visit I have not seen them since, but when we meet we talk freindly and both enquire for you: but since our addressing they have never been at our end of the town, nor I at theirs; and my Lord Lieutenants leaving the Castle hath taken away the occasion of meeting at the Castle: but by all I can hear Mr Bags continues to be moderate in Court, more then the other. My services to my freinds; to the Baron alway in particular.

54. *Alan I, Dublin, to St John II, 23 Feb. 1701/2*

(1248/2/56c–56d)

Yesterday arrived here six packets in which I had one from my brother[424] dated the 3d; and two from you of the seventh and fourteenth instant: and am in no sort surprised at the good offices Mr Anesley[425] and Mr Hooper[426] have alway endeavoured to doe me:

[422] John Isham (*d.* 1746), the younger brother of Sir Justinian Isham, 4th Bt (Betham, *Baronetage*, i, 303), and a trustee. John Baggs was his 'cousin' (Northamptonshire Archives, I.C., 2192: John Isham to Sir Justinian Isham, 20 Sept. 1701).

[423] The English civil lawyer and writer William King (1663–1712), who had secured appointment as a judge of the Admiralty court in Dublin in 1701, through an association with Rochester, but had been unable to take up his post because of objections lodged by Dublin city corporation. He was a friend of Anthony Upton. (*Oxf. DNB*).

[424] Thomas.

[425] Francis Annesley the trustee.

[426] James Hooper (*d.* 1709), formerly secretary to the commissioners of inquiry and now a trustee. Annesley and Hooper attended the English house of commons on 3 Feb. 1702 in response to a request of the house, although they had already set off for England before the request was made, on the instructions of the trustees the previous Dec. (*CJ*, xiii, 717–19; PRONI, D/1854/2/5: trustees' min. bks, v, 61).

but find it to be very true that innocence gives a man courage and unmoved assurance: Be not you troubled on my account, for most assuredly if that matter be farther stirred in, it will end in their shame and confusion and not mine, who said nothing before the trustees which I would decline owning to have said in any place on earth, if called on to own or deny it. By the boat which carries this letter there goe such testimonials of what passed at Chichester house as will stop the mouth of calumnye and silence malice; but I dare not venture them but by a safe hand who I doubt not will deliver them assoon as he comes to town: the Case of the Archbishop of Dublin (as the trustees have reported the fact to be and I own I beleive it to be with good reason) I send you on the back of this; but we that were of Councel with the Archbishop endeavoured to lodge an estate in fee in Christopher Russel the Grand father notwithstanding the claim and decree of innocencye of Bartholomew Russel the son, and notwithstanding the deed sett forth in that claim and decree; and offered that the decree it self only removed the incapacitye of the Claimants recovering if he had a title, but was not sufficient proof of the deed of settlement, which ought to be proved: we also insisted that the deed of settlement was not produced, the judgement in the Exchequer was given on the Attorney Generals confession only and not on any trial and that the Lands being in the Kings hands the same were by patent in September 1694 granted to the See of Dublin: and inferred thence that if the Grand father Christopher was seised in fee in forty one, the lands were vested in the Crown by the Acts of Settlement and explanacion and consequently the grant made to the Archbishop not within the act lately made for resuming grants of forfeitures since His Majestyes reign: Some thing was then offered against the Archbishops grant being good; in answer to which I said that would not avail the trust, because if the estate did not passe by that patent, yet it remained in the King and was not disposable by the trustees: whereupon one of them (I think it was Mr Isham) said if they sold the Land, the sale would be good: I said softly looking toward him that if the Lands were not forfeited by this rebellion their sale would not bind, noe Lands being disposable by them but such as the Act vested in them which by the whole tenor of the Act extended only to forfeitures since his Majestyes accession to the Crown: Mr Anesley then called to me and asked me what I said: at that time I saw it was a trap laid for me by that honest man, but thought it not prudent to be frightned by him from speaking truth; especially when what I said plainly tended to the benefit of my Client, supposing Christopher Russel to have been seised in fee in the year 1641; which the trustees had not then declared their opinion against. This shews it was not officiously brought in by me, but that the thing arose from an affirmacion of one of themselves; then the matter was stirred a new by Mr Anesley, and the thing was pertinent to my Clients cause: and after all what I said was most unfairly represented in the house by Mr Hooper. The whole auditory apprehended that the trustees then openly declared (I mean Mr Fellows and Sir Cyril Wyche for the rest were silent) that their sale of any mans Land (tho not forfeited) would be conclusive, and that was the only point between us; as may appear by their asking me whether I apprehended they would sell any Lands that were not forfeited: in answer I told them that I beleived they would not, but hoped we had more to relye on, then their not doing so, before we lost our titles to our estates: I also then told them that what I said was in argument only and that I might be mistaken, but that I did argue with my opinion. After having said thus much I must own that I think other peoples condicion very miserable whose all may depend on some mens bare affirmacion, when a matter transacted in the face of the Sun can be thus misrepresented. Lord Abercorne[427] and Mr Delamere[428] who are now in England, and I think Mr Dopping[429] were in Court when this matter hapned; and I think spoke to the former to mind it, and gave Lord Chancellor[430] an immediate account of what passed and so I beleive did many other Gentlemen: soe as this cannot be a story now framed; beside you know I wrote to you immediately after the thing hapned, tho in a shorter maner then now. The truth is, they have all along been endeavouring to make way for a clause that their sales shal be a good title against all mankind: which if they compasse, then the words following (as lately surveyed by the Surveyors appointed by the Trustees etc.) added to any denominacion of land sold by them will take in a great part of the Lands of this Kingdome that were never forfeited, they having surveyed many parcels of other mens estates: beside that tho they should not design to doe it yet they may sell other mens estates by particular denominacions of small parcels of Land, every feild almost having a particular name among the Irish whereas the English know only the names of the town Lands[431] or grand denominacions; but this I hope needs not be argued. The Souldiers letter[432] tells you that the Commissioners of the Court of Claims had as great a power as this:[433] that is a mistake, for they had only a right to grant certificates of Lands long before that time seised and sequestred and known to be soe by being in Charge and paying rent to the Commonwealth,[434] soe as it was known what Lands they could grant certificates of and all persons that pretended titles to such Lands were obliged to claim and make out their right: but forfeitable interests can only be known by themselves; if the words of the Act were that their sales should be good against all persons (whose claims are not by them allowed) of Lands found to be in the Crown by inquisicion or sett or disposed of by the Commissioners of the revenue or of which the trustees themselves received the rents before

[427]James Hamilton (c.1661–1734), 6th earl of Abercorn, one of the moving spirits behind the 'national remonstrance', and a signatory to the circular letter promoting the addresses.

[428]Walter Delamare (or Delamere), of Ballynafid, Multyfarnham, Co. Westmeath (NLI, MS 5326, f. 6: Charles Lynegar, MS 'historical genealogy' of the Delamare family). Although from an Old English catholic family, Delamare received forfeited estates on account of his 'great services' to the Williamite cause (*CTB*, xi, 244–5; *CSP Dom.*, 1702–3, 665–7). He remained in close touch with surviving catholic landed families, assisting them on legal and business matters on both sides of the Irish Sea (NLI, MS 40901/5 (22): Gregory Nolan to John Browne, 31 Dec. 1698), but was numbered among the 'Protestant purchasers' who applied to the English parliament for relief from the effects of the Forfeitures Act (Simms, *Williamite Confiscation*, 125), submitting a petition on his own behalf to the English house of commons which was read on 31 Mar. 1702, when a bill for his relief was ordered (*CJ*, xiii, 833–4). He is also said to have been the author of *A Letter to a Member of Parliament Relating to the Irish Forfeitures* (1701).

[429]Samuel Dopping, MP [I].

[430]John Methuen.

[431]The smallest division of land in Ireland.

[432][Trenchard], *A Letter from a Souldier* ….

[433]In *A Letter to a Souldier* …, 13–15, Trenchard sought to dispose of the allegation that the activities of the trustees would bring all land title in Ireland into question, noting that this was a baseless insinuation first made by Alan Brodrick while speaking in the 'court of claims'. Trenchard stated that 'full as large powers were committed to the commissioners, who executed the Act of Settlement, and I believe it was never made a doubt whether they had power to judge what lands were vested' (15), but he went on to distinguish between the purpose of the Act of Settlement of 1662, which enabled the current addressers to 'enjoy the lands set out by the parliament of England to their ancestors' and the Forfeitures Resumption Act, by which 'other lands are taken from them, who either begged or bought them for an inconsiderable price, from those who had at best but a precarious title, and restored them to such who are to give the same valuable considerations for them, that the addressers' ancestors gave for theirs under the Act of Settlement'.

[434]The commonwealth of England, 1649–60.

the time for filing claims was elapsed men might have notice of their danger and defend themselves against it by claiming in time: but to say indefinitely that all their sales shal be confirmed must proceed from an extraordinary good opinion of those Gentlemen or a very little regard to our propertyes …

[*PS.*] For more clear proof that it could not be officious in me to say the sale of Lands by the trustees which were not forfeited would not bind I have sent the breif I had from Thomas Ash Esqr the Lord Archbishops Seneschal[435] yesterday, which is one of those his Graces Councel had on the hearing, by the whole tenor of which it appears that the Archbishop insists on Christophers being seised in fee in 1641, which whether true or false you see is the allegacion of the Bishops peticion who saith Bartholomew had no Legal title to forfeit by his rebellion, the Lands being forfeited by Christopher in 1641: and to the best of my memorye the Survey returns Christopher to be the proprietor and not tenant for Life, which is made a record by Act of Parliament and very strong evidence: and supposing this fact to be true (which when I spoke was not settled to be otherwise by the trustees, tho in their report made after the hearing they say Christopher was only tenant for Life) and the patent made to the Archbishop to have been good when granted, it was very material for my Client to say the trustees had no right to sell those Lands: But the truth is they had a fancy that whatever Lands were in the Crown by the former rebellion and not disposed of were vested in them; at least they were willing to have that thought to be their opinion; and if you consider the two and twentieth paragraph of the trustees report made the Last year and the Souldiers Letter etc. (Mr Ts[436] handywork) you will find their insisting to have all their sales indefinitely confirmed is what they all along pretended to and aimed at. I send two certificates by this hand, one under the Archbishops hand, but so great is the power of the trustees that he desires it may not be used unlesse there be great occasion for it: Another under the hands of Colonel Hamilton,[437] Captain Stafford[438] and Thomas Ashe Esqr the Archbishops Seneschal and Steward who were in Court the whole time: Tomorrow I will send one under the hands of some Gentlemen of the bar, but they either are favourites or under such awe of the Trustees that I make it almost a matter of conscience to ask them to certifye truth so much to their prejudice. God deliver us from the burthen of the insolence and calumnye we lye under from some people …

55. *Alan I, Dublin, to St John II, 7 Mar. 1701/2*

(1248/2/56l–56m)

The same boat brought in yours of the 17th, 20th, 24th, and 26th of last month, and the last packett that of the 28th with the inclosed print for which I thank you. So many letters coming in at once occasions your not having earlier accounts of the receit of those which lye long att the Head.[439] The very next packett boat shal bring you some thoughts on

[435] Probably Thomas Ashe, MP [I] for Swords 1695–9 and for Clogher in 1713, brother to St George Ashe, bishop of Clogher.

[436] John Trenchard.

[437] Gustavus Hamilton, MP [I].

[438] Edmond Francis Stafford, MP [I].

[439] Holyhead.

the reasonablenesse of the trustees expectacions in having their sales confirmed, whatever Lands they shal sell whether forfeited and vested in them by the Act or not: together with an account what powers the Commissioners of the Court of Claims had, and wherein those desired by the trustees exceed and differ from them. In the mean time let me tell you, that if Mr H[440] or any body else informed the house of Commons that many adjudications or certificates of Claims were delivered by the trustees and none were refused, that he grossly imposed on the house: unlesse he will shelter himself by saying that he meant the certificates to the purchasers of their proporcion of the £21000 allowed them by the Act,[441] most of which are I beleive given out: but having mentioned this I will transiently take notice that the trustees have not paid one penny to them. But as for other adjudicacions, if thereby be meant the certificate which the Act requires seven or more of the trustees to sign when they have heard and allowed any claim,[442] I am morally certain there are few, I beleive none in the Kingdome given out the minute I write this but only one (I mean Mr C[*onolly'*]s)[443] for MacDonels was for certain gotten back after it was signed: It may be possible that very lately some may have been privately given out to be able to say some are given out, therefore I will not be positive having no possibilitye of getting any informacion by certificate from the office: but this I doe positively aver that within five minutes of my beginning this letter I sent for Mr Thomas Richards, a person employed under them (but I know not by what title dignifyed)[444] and who is one of the two persons that take the minutes on the hearing of claims who assured me there were but two claims yet so passed as to have certificates signed by the trustees, one he said is McDonels; and remains yet in the office; the other he did not name, but I am pretty well assured it is Mr C[*onolly's*]. That the man may not suffer from the indignacion of his employers as a betrayer of their secrets I must tell you, that I gott this secret out of him in this maner: I told him my father and some other freinds had claims which were allowed by the trustees upon being heard, but had not their certificates or adjudicacions signed and asked him whether the trustees did not yet give out such certificates: He told me that they were very busy in hearing claims and would doe that after the 25th of March, whereas they could not after that time hear more claims:[445] I desired to see the form of an adjudicacion or certificate; he told me he had several draughts for their signature ready prepared and would shew me one: I answered that I knew how to draw the form of one but desired the sight of one that had passed and was signed by the trustees; upon this he said only two had been yet signed, and that McDonels was yet in the office and he would endeavour to gett me a Copy of it; but he

[440]James Hooper.

[441]Sect. 32 of the Forfeitures Resumption Act of 1700, provided that £21,000 could be allowed by the trustees to purchasers of forfeited estates, 'in equal proportion according to the respective sums of money actually paid by every such purchaser, who shall prove the actuall payment of such purchase-money, before the 10th day of August, 1700'.

[442]Sect. 16 of the act stipulated a minimum of seven trustees needed to certify any claim allowed.

[443]William Conolly, MP [I].

[444]Thomas Richards, one of the registers employed by the trustees, and identified as such in a subsequent letter (PRONI, D/1854/2/6: trustees' min. bks, vi, 138; see below, p. 117). A Thomas Richards was admitted as an attorney into the King's Inns in Dublin in 1664 (*K. Inn Adm.*, 421). He may be identical with the Thomas Richards described as an attorney of king's bench in Dublin in 1720 (*Reg. Deeds, Wills*, i, 108), and with the Thomas Richards, gent., of Dublin, whose name appears in a deed of 1710 (Reg. Deeds, 6/140/1590).

[445]Sect. 12 of the Act allowed the trustees until 25 Mar. 1701[/2] to hear and determine claims.

telling me that was an allowance of a claim of a Lease for Lives I pretended it would be of little use to me, and so we parted: only he declared he knew of no order from the trustees posted up for claimants to come and take out their adjudicacions. In short the truth is this; they have signifyed their intentions so publickly not to sign adjudicacions (tho claims have been heard and allowed) till toward the end of their power, that the Sollicitors and Agents have told their Clients it is in vain to apply for certificates till toward the expiracion of their Commission so that the Claimants have acquiesced and not generally spent money in vain in pressing for such adjudications till their Honors appointed time were come; and the rather because such applicacion would certainly have incensed them and probably have given occasion to rehear the Cause; which I take it they think to be within their power, after having allowed a claim, if there be any hope of benefiting the trust; tho I never heard of an instance where a claim once dismissed was admitted to be reheard. But Mr Ludlows Case[446] which I had this morning out of his own mouth is remarkable: His was one of the first claims that was heard and allowed; and he drew and sent to the Trustees or their officer a draught of a certificate or decree about fourteen months agoe: they kept it by them for some time, and then made some alteracions in it, which he agreed to more then ten months since and desired it so amended; but hath not yet gott the same; he added farther that this very morning he sent to Chichester house for it and received this answer that the trustees did not yet sign adjudicacions or certificates but that he should have his when other people had theirs. I told him after he had said thus that I would give an account of what he said into England, but he injoined me not to have his name used so as to oblige to take an English journey and I told him I would not do him that mischeif but I doubt not of his giving it under his hand or making oath of it before a Judge here or magistrate if required.

56. *Alan I, Dublin, to St John II, 10 Mar. 1701/2*

(1248/2/56r–56s)

In performance of the promise made you in my last letter I send you the enclosed papers,[447] which I presume will be proof amounting to demonstration that (whatever the two Gentlemen may pretend)[448] there are but few certificates given out by the trustees; I told you formerly that they had given certificates to the purchasers of their respective shares of the £21000 being the third of their purchase money allowed them by the first Act, and I beleive have denied no person who called for it his certificate on this behalf: but am convinced that what Mr Rickards one of their Registers[449] told me on the 7th instant, not only then was, but the day I write this is true, that no more then two certificates have been signed by the trustees to persons whose claims have been heard and allowed (except before excepted) one of which (McDonnels) was called back again and gott into the office, but I hear is since (very lately) delivered out again: and I affirm it to be their posicion that they can at

[446] Stephen Ludlow, MP [I].

[447] Letters to Alan I from Richard Fleming, 9 Mar. 1701/2 (SHC, 1248/2/56n–56o) and Stephen Ludlow, 8 Mar. 1701[/2] (SHC, 1248/2/56p–56q).

[448] Francis Annesley and James Hooper (the two trustees sent to give evidence to the English house of commons).

[449] Thomas Richards.

pleasure rehear any cause formerly determined by them, tho the Claim were allowed on the hearing, at any time before the expiracion of their time for hearing claims: and consequently noe body can be secure that he is out of their power, which keeps people in great awe and dependance on them: but they reap a yet greater convenience by this method of proceeding, since if the certificates were signed and claims finally allowed it must follow that the Claimants ought to be put into possession of their estates or receive the full profits of the Lands morgaged to them till their debts (allowed by the trustees) are satisfyed; but that would lessen the income, and there would not be enough stock remaining to carry on the trade: but in truth in Case of morgages the Master of references[450] and Mr White[451] ease them exceedingly, by delaying the account soe long that it cannot judicially appear to their Honors that the debt is unpaid and till they know there is something due to the Claimant you may be sure they pay him nothing. I will make oath that Rickards told me what I wrote last Saturday; and send you inclosed Mr Ludlows letter (he is a Six Clark[452] and a man of extraordinary repute and great estate) by which you may perceive he will make good what he told me which was just what I wrote to you; but you see his letter mencions an order for his receiving the ground rents in the mean time (which are very small) but his decree could not be got to be signed, and consequently is stil in their power. The inclosed case of Simon Carick and the daughters of Mr Borr was given me by Anderson Sanders one of the Six Clerks[453] on Sunday last; I went last night to Mr Richard Fleming (an Atturnye of the Kings Bench of a fair reputacion and fortune)[454] whose hand writing the original was (for what I send you is but a Copy, the original I keep) and desired to know whether he was able and willing to justifye the truth of it in every particular on oath, if occasion offered: he told me he had drawn it out of minutes kept by him of the whole proceeding, being agent in the Cause for the Claimants, and that he would depose that the whole was true: but said he hoped he should not be forced to goe for England on the errand: I said I would send over word what he said and do desire no use may be made of that or Mr Ludlows Case if an English journey be the consequence. But neither of them will refuse to make oath before a justice of peace, judge, or Master of Chancerye of the truth of the papers sent you. Mr Fleming moreover told me that the claimants the Mrs Borrs were befreinded by some of the trustees or else he apprehended he should have mett with more difficulties and delays; and then you may judge how claimants that are ill looked upon can dispatch their affairs. Probably when the trustees hear of this Case they will procure a significacion under the young Ladyes hands that they are satisfyed with the dispatch as well as justice of the proceedings, but if those steps have been taken which Mr Fleming mencions others may judge how far the trustees have acted in this matter conformable to what they give out to be the method of their proceedings, and the reasonable use to be made of such a certificate will be that the Ladyes think them selves very well used in respect of the treatment others meet with. For fear you should not well apprehend the Case as Fleming states it, I

[450]William Spring (PRONI, D/1854/2/2: trustees' min. bks, ii, 161).

[451]Abraham White, listed among the trustees' officers in 1700 as 'agent' (PRONI, D/1854/2/2: trustees' min. bks, ii, 161); and described as 'their clerk' in Brodrick, *Short Remarks upon the Late Act of Resumption*, 13.

[452]One of the six clerks in chancery [I] (since 1669).

[453]Anderson Saunders, MP [I], had been appointed one of the six clerks in 1682.

[454]Richard Fleming (*d.* c.1730) of Dublin (Vicars, *Index*, 174).

will abstract it. Sir John Eustace[455] in 1667 acknowledges a Statute Staple[456] to Carick in trust for Mr Borr, who by will devises that debt among his daughters the Claimants; the question before the trustees was whether the debt was satisfyed; but on the hearings of the Cause it appeared that interest was paid till 1686: One inducement to the trustees to beleive the money was paid was that the defeasance of this Statute was found in the hands of the Claimants or some freinds of theirs, but therein the Court received satisfaction: Another presumption was that the Comisor of the Statute had sold an estate to Sir Patrick Trant[457] subsequent to the acknowledging this Statute, which purchase was treated and carried on by Sir Stephen Rice[458] on Sir Patricks behalf and that a bill was filed in the name of Trant against Sir John Eustace to oblige him to discover what incumbrances the estate was subject to, and Sir John did not in his answer mencion this debt in particular; but the truth was he said he owed about £1200 and not above, to which that Land was liable (but did not remember to whom) and Sir Stephen Rice being examined for the trust declared he knew nothing of its being paid and that he was not concerned for Trant after 1685 whereas it plainly appeared the interest was paid in 1686. The Court at long run did the Ladyes right, but first, that a Claimant msut be at the charge of swearing their witnesses, nay summoning and bringing up at their own charge such as Mr White saith are to be examined in the Case, as will appear through this whole Cause; that a Cause should be put of one day by reason of Mr Fellows absence; another by Mr Daniel Gearyes[459] (for so his name is and not Geering as Mr Fleming calls him) being arrested at the suit of a stranger to the Claimants (which Geary appears not to know any thing of the matter, but to have told several lyes that others as Pinsent, Kent etc. could prove the debt paid) that so many hearings, mocions, orders, and attendances on the Master [*of References*] and White should be allowed of is what would seem strange to any body that is a stranger to the proceedings of Chichester House. One thing I would caution you of, that you doe not misapprehend the meaning of Mr Whites being spoke to: it is not that he had mony given him, but I send it in Flemings own expression that the Copy and original may agree to a title: Inclosed I also send you a letter from Mr Fleming to me, by which another extraordinary practice of the trustees Court is taken notice of, that their officer never will give any note on the depositing deeds; yet without doing so, no claim can be heard.[460] There are two reasons to be given why it is not soe easy as you imagine to send many instances of this kind; the terror claimants lye under if they should be named; but cheifly the Agents knowing it to be the settled rule not to sign certificates have all along told all their Clients it would be throwing money away to

[455] Sir John Eustace (*d.* 1704) of Brannockstown, Co. Kildare. He and his brother Sir Maurice (MP [I] Harristown 1692–5) were nephews of Sir Maurice Eustace, lord chancellor [I] 1660–5.

[456] A recognisance for debt. The Irish staple had been established in the 13th century to regulate trade in staple goods, but by the 17th century had become a mechanism for regulating debt (Ohlmeyer and Ó Ciardha, *Irish Statute Staple Bks*).

[457] Sir Patrick Trant (*d.* 1694), 1st Bt, a revenue commissioner [I] 1688 and a member of James II's Irish parliament in 1689 (S.M., 'The Trant family [part 1]', *Kerry Archaeological Magazine*, ii, no. 12 (1914), 241–4).

[458] Sir Stephen Rice (c.1637–1715), baron of the exchequer [I], 1686, chief baron 1687–91.

[459] On 8 Dec. 1698 the English secretary of state James Vernon wrote to Matthew Prior, secretary to the Irish lords justices, to let him know that Daniel Geary and an accomplice had gone to Ireland in order to attempt to discover concealed forfeitures but that he had already warned the lords justices that the two men were rascals (HMC, *Bath MSS*, iii, 302–3).

[460] Fleming reported that 'the Master of the References' had refused to give him a receipt for deeds he deposited (SHC, 1248/2/56n–56o: Fleming to Alan I, 9 Mar. 1701/2).

move for them; and this is the settled practice of all the Agents and hath hitherto been soe: but now all hands are at work in drawing up adjudicacions and decrees because the 25th of March is near they say, but I think because their freinds with you tell them how much dilatorinesse hitherto is censured. Perhaps they may denye that they conceive no person ought to replevy[461] any distresse taken by their order: that is otherwise; I have seen original letters under their Secretaryes hand to the contrarye and one at least of that kind is gone over and you may see it for sending to Mr Stafford: This day sennight is the date of a letter from Colonel Ponsonbye in the County of Kilkennye[462] intimating that he being a tenant formerly to Lady Orkney of some part of the private estate and since the Act of resumption having agreed with the trustees for a greater rent, the trustees receiver called on him for All Saints rent and he paid as much as he was to pay by the Lease from Lady Orkney but refused to pay the remainder of what he was by agreement with the trustees to pay above Lady Orkneys rent, being one of the Lessees who petitioned the Last Parliament and who by vertue of a clause in their favor in the Late Act are not to be disturbed or prejudiced in their possessions till their peticions are considered in Parliament:[463] He it seems thought distraining for more rent then he was to pay by his first Lease, which he petitioned to have preserved to him would be a disturbing him in his possession before etc. and indeed if it be not soe, I see not what benefit the peticioners can have by that Clause: for without it their possession could no otherwise be disturbed by the trustees then by distraining for the full rents reserved on their new Leases. However the trustees agent distrained, and he replevyed; and he informs me that the Sherif is summoned to appear before the trustees for granting a replevin and he for not paying his rent. I send you his original letter, but have been very cautious in advising him how far the Act of Parliament qualifieth him to retain his plus rent on his hand till the Parliament determine on the tenants peticions: but hence you may observe first, that the trustees by this method deprive the peticioners of all the benefit intended them by the Act, as far as I can judge: Secondly that they conceive a replevin lies not against them, and that the Sherifs granting one is a contempt for which he must appear before them in person: thirdly that he who will not or (which is now become too common a Case) cannot pay his rent, must appear in person before them. Sure their power of sending for persons etc. was not meant to be thus executed. Pray send to Mr Stafford[464] and he will let you see two Cases one of the Children of Mr Colvil,[465] the other of one McNaghten[466] which Mr Campbell sends him by this post which I think are very

[461] Replevin: a legal remedy for the recovery of personal property.

[462] William Ponsonby, MP [I], wrote to Alan I on 3 Mar. 1702 (SHC, 1248/2/56i–56k) that, despite the recent clause in favour of the lessees of the private estate who had petitioned the English house of commons, he had been summoned before the trustees for refusing to pay the surplus rent for the land he leased from Lady Orkney; and the county sheriff had also been summoned for granting him a replevin in case he was distressed for the surplus rent. 'If this be the methods of the law', he wrote, 'I am a great strainger to it it being very new but I rather beleeve its the act of ou[r] 12 Ap[*os*]t[*le*]s [*the trustees*] who are able to work miracles and will I supose in a little time … subvert the whole constitution of this Kingdom.'

[463] See above, p. 100.

[464] Edmond Francis Stafford, MP [I].

[465] No such printed case is recorded in the English Short Title Catalogue (ESTC): http://estc.bl.uk.

[466] Again, no such printed case appears in ESTC, but a claim had been entered on behalf of John McNaughten of Benvarden, Co Antrim, for a debt of £410 due on the forfeited estate of Sir Neil O'Neill (information from Charles Ivar McGrath and Frances Nolan, who are preparing an edition of the *List of the Claims as They Are Entred with the Trustees …* (Dublin, 1701) for the Irish Manuscripts Commission). McNaughten's will had been proved

odd ones. I wish you would let him, my brother and others who usually meet know what I here send you and that you would acquaint each other what materials you are respectively furnished with, and consult of common measures to shorten the time of this Countreys being insulted as it now is by some people. The Irish brag Dr Davenant[467] is writing some thing much to the service of the Trustees and them, and in our prejudice.[468] …

57. *Alan I, Dublin, to Thomas , at the Whitehall coffee-house, King's Street, Westminster, 11 Mar. 1701/2*

(1248/2/57–8)

When I consider how important matters relating to the English interest of this unhappy Kingdome are now in agitacion at London I should hope to hear from you now and then, and perhaps such a commerce might be of use as well as a satisfaction to both: but the constant accounts from the Temple[469] give me such a Light into affairs that I am the more easy under your silence: This however I cannot but observe, that you and my brother St John seldome meet, and as I apprehend never concert measures together in reference to the mortal enemies of the Protestant interest of this Countrey: pray let it be otherwise: his businesse confines him to his chamber, and there he is surely to be mett, and will allow all his spare time to attain releif against those who we beleive treat us very injuriously to give it noe worse a term: and to say truth what I think may be of use I constantly send to him as a person whom I can trust and who (in my opinion) can and doth make better use of what is put into his hands then any other whatsoever: Goe or send to him for what he hath lately received hence, and when you see Mr Palmer[470] inform your self from him whether he hath heard out of Ireland lately. The inclosed was given me by the Recorder[471] who desired me to send it to England as his justificacion if any attempt should be made to his prejudice by the Trustees on the account of their Secretarye;[472] for he you must know hath talked very big on the Subject, but no regard is to be had to some mens prate. And having this oportunitye of sending the letter, methinks there is an expression or two in it, that the Lords have no great reason to thank the writer for; and when the letter is shewn to secure the Recorder from being prejudiced the other expressions will be made publick of course and without breach of honour in exposing private Letters. Be sure you shew this letter to Mr Ogle,[473] who is the Recorders great freind, and expresse great concern for him, as far as

466 *(continued)* in 1700 (Vicars, *Index*, 307), a fact which may account for Alan's description of the case. Equally, this may have arisen from concern at McNaughten's own political credentials, since he had been one of the commissioners of supply for Co. Antrim appointed under the Supply Act passed by the jacobite parliament in Dublin in 1689 (*Acts of James II's Irish Parliament*, ed. Bergin and Lyell, 14).

467 The political and economic writer Charles Davenant (1656–1714).

468 Davenant's previous work, *A Discourse upon Grants and Resumptions* … (1700) had been a decisive intervention in the debate on the resumption of the Irish forfeitures.

469 From St John II.

470 William Palmer, MP [I].

471 John Forster, MP [I] had been chosen recorder of Dublin the previous year.

472 William Trenchard.

473 Samuel Ogle, MP [I].

can consist with his not thinking you a very weak man to dread any thing such a fellow can doe; but this will intitle you to make the matter more publick and to shew the letter to a great many people … For Gods sake, in what maner are we to be governed if a war happen.

58. *Alan I to St John II, [Mar. 1702]*

(1248/2/60i)

The insolencyes done by rascally pamphlets and villanous papers to those who have addressed against the trustees is beyond expression: no lye so foul that is not posted at their Chichester house door; particularly that some Lords a Lawyer Attorney and some other person razed their names out of the Addresse and inserted others and thereby escaped punishment: The meaning is to induce people to beleive that I struck my name out after I had signed it to the Addresse:[474] I would sooner have cutt off my hand then have done so base an action: but the truth is my name was to the General Addresse and I doe not find that was before the House of Commons at all: This I am credibly informed to be true, that it was given to the Lords Justices here, and where it stops I know not; but am proud to have signed an addresse complaining of the Act and its execucion, tho there was a clause in it that I never could approve of: but thought it reasonable not to pretend to more wisdome then so many others who had signed it before ever I saw it …

[*PS.*] Lord Massareene[475] writes this night about his being denied the minutes taken on the hearing of his Claim which was dismissed; he complains of their dealing with him in that matter, I know not how justly being a stranger to his Case: but sure since no releif lyes from their judgements but to the Parliaments, they ought to furnish persons who think themselves aggreived with the footsteps of the proceedings in the Cause: How else can the house know whether the Case deserves releif or not: He doth not say they positively now deny him those notes, but that he once was denied them and is now so putt off from time to time that if he gets them at all, it must be probably too late to be of use to him. If you see Mr Stafford[476] or send to him I beleive he will be able to give you Lord Massareenes case particularly, and I beleive he carried over eminent instances of their refusing to sign adjudicacions.

59. *Alan I, Dublin, to St John II, Lamb Buildings, Middle Temple, 5 May 1702*

(1248/2/61–2)

The pacquett came in this morning and brought me yours of the 28th, in which you tax me for being soe tardy in writing to Lord R[*ochester*] and for ought I know you are in the right of that matter; but this you may depend on, that a former letter which you fancy you wrote containing an account of what passed between his Lordship and you with reference to me never came to Lucyes hand or mine; yours of the 18th shews that you were in doubt (when

[474] See above, p. 105.

[475] Clotworthy Skeffington, 3rd Viscount Massereene (1660–1714).

[476] Edmond Francis Stafford, MP [I].

you were writing) that you were interrupted after you had sate down to give an account of that transaction, and I beleive really you were soe; for most certainly I never received nor heard of that letter. I would not fail to pay all duty and gratitude for the great favor my Lord hath done me and will never decline her Majestyes service while I am thought worthy to continue in it; but if such alteracions are worth making here, as with you,[477] I doe not think my self of long continuance; nor shal be surprised or displeased at being put out of an employ which I neither gott into nor can hold on any terms but what consist with the good of the English interest of this Kingdome. I mention not my brother W[*illia*]m because really I can say little to his advantage; he stil loves play, I cannot say he stil playes at dice but his fingers itch soe to be at cards, that when I am at Ombre[478] in my own house (which with respect to Clients is all one as if I were in my Closett) he chuseth to sit by a looker on rather then spend his time in his chamber, or in reading Law which he much needs to doe: but I have pretty well broke him of this Custom at my house, and I now find he is often at Lord Chancellors:[479] his acquaintance there are Mr Burridge[480] a Clergyman and Mr Lake my Lords Secretarye:[481] with the former his conversacion can only be news and politicks (in which he delights to smatter.) with the Later he may play at Cards being a great player at Picquett:[482] but whether he soe employes his time with him or not I have not yet learned: but in the main his businesse seems to decrease rather then mend, which yet perhaps proceeds from the ilnesse of the term and times in general: but this I assure you, that he stil continues to doe little disgracefull things, and that there is no relying on what he saith. As to my father I know not what to say: Be satisfyed that his weaknesse this winter was real, he being much in drink at Michael Golds[483] wedding and falling in a water coming home in a cold night where he had like to have been drowned and gott such a cold that his Limbs were benummed and the use of them almost wholly lost: He can dally no longer and must either goe over immediately or publish to the world he hath hitherto deceived and imposed on as many as beleived him in earnest when he said he would return. Before God I know no reason why he should not go over unlesse he owes more money then we know and is in fear of being clapt up. Doe not think that ever he will buy from the trustees; I think such a thing cannot enter into his heart, beside he hath no money; and I will caution him against it with all possible earnestnesse. Lucy is not well, but hath been

[477]The reconstruction of the English ministry, with Lord Godolphin as lord treasurer, and most leading places occupied by tories.

[478]A fashionable card-game, based on the taking of tricks, against which the English parliament had once proposed to legislate.

[479]John Methuen.

[480]Ezekiel Burridge (1661–1707), rector of St Paul's, Dublin (Brendan Twomey, *Smithfield and the Parish of St Paul, Dublin, 1698–1750* (*Maynooth Studies in Local History*, no. 63, Dublin, 2005), 47–8). In his will Burridge named Alan Brodrick and William Conolly as executors (ibid., 48).

[481]Francis Lake (*d.* 1721), a Dublin solicitor (Vicars, *Index*, 275; King's Inns, Dublin, MS N3/3/4/4: notebook of Francis Lake, 1684–1721). Lake was secretary to successive lord chancellors [I] until at least 1710 (Narcissus Luttrell, *A Brief Historical Relation of State Affairs* (6 vols, Oxford, 1857), vi, 537), and was reappointed when Alan I was raised to the lord chancellorship in 1714 (*Post Boy*, 9–11 Nov. 1714).

[482]Piquet: a fashionable card-game.

[483]Michael Goold (*d.* 1722), of Jamesbrook Hall, Ballinacurra, Co. Cork (Vicars, *Index*, 197; Richard Henchion, *The Gravestone Inscriptions of the Cathedral Cemetery of Cloyne, Co. Cork* (Cloyne, 1999), 137), land agent for the earl of Inchiquin (NLI, MS 453211/3, 45626/4, passim; *The Inchiquin Manuscripts*, ed. J.F. Ainsworth (Dublin, 1961), 88, 95, 102, 104, 107).

much worse then she now is; I have pressed her to goe for England and car[?ry] her little ones thither, but have not been able [to] perswade her, but hope to doe it soon: How far it will be possible for me to goe with her I cannot yet determine, till I know whether I am to hold or be superseded my emploiment; if I am turned out I shal be entirely at my own disposal and will God willing meet you at Bath at the time you mention and doubt not yet but that my father will be at Wandsworth before that time …

[*PS*] Ought not I to part with the land I lately bought here? I think I ought: Tell me.

60. *Alan I, Dublin, to St John II, Lamb Buildings, Middle Temple, 19 May 1702*

(1248/2/63–4)

This morning I received yours of the second and ninth together; so ill am I used in the Post Office here: Major Bellew[484] told me in the Coffee house and others talked publickly that Lord Pembroke is to succeed Lord Rochester in the Governement here, and that Lord Rochester is to be Master of the horse; soe that what you but hinted and my brother spoke more plainly but under a tye of not mentioning it is become town talk: By this means I doe beleive all my pretensions of continuing Sollicitor are at an end, resolving to keep my word with my Lord Rochester of applying to him only: beside I have no acquaintance with any body that is well with my Lord Pembroke; but I am not very sollicitous in this matter. I wish my mind were as much at ease in reference to Senny now his tutor is dead: what to doe on this occasion or how to dispose of him very much perplexes me; but as you hitherto have had the trouble, care, and direction of his educacion I must entreat the continuance of it in prescribing such rules for his future conduct as may contribute to his becoming a good and useful man if God spare him life: Let me know is the season so hot with you as here? It is mid July in Dublin: Nay we have whispers of the sicknesse or something near it with you. Lucy mends, the girle is very well and the boy fine and healthy to a wonder, all at Ballygaule;[485] My sister went yesterday to Munster, will return soon and at Bath (God willing) they and probably I with them will meet you in August. People here are highly sensible of your trouble, care, and kindnesse in the Irish affairs; and expresse it loudly and unanimously: My father continues really extremely weak in hands and feet; and if he be not able to rise very soon I fear the next Autumne will carry him off. My brother Will very unaccountable, seldome comes near us having been cautioned of some little things he has lately been faulty in, which perhaps distasts him; but if he will do mean things I cannot be wanting to my self and him in passing them by without notice. The releif the house of Commons have designed for the Protestant purchasors will be very much short of their intent by their making the rent of the year 1701 their measure; for you may depend on it that as things now stand, thirteen years purchase is a very fair and full value for Lands in most parts of the Kingdome[486] and more then they generally will yeild where Lands are sett at moderate rates as they now goe here by the means lately taken for utterly ruining

[484] Thomas Bellew, MP [I], a major in Col. Meredyth's regiment of foot.

[485] Ballynagaul.

[486] The 1702 English act for the relief of protestant purchasers of Irish forfeited estates (1 Anne, c. 32) permitted claimants to keep their estates at a cost of thirteen years' purchase for 'estates of inheritance' and six and a half years for 'estates for life', the annual rate being the rental charge for the year 1701 (sect. 1). The sum of £21,000

and impoverishing us; but the exorbitant rents people have contracted for with the trustees some in hopes of being in a better condicion by continuing in possession and others who little regarded whether the Land yeilded the rent or not, resolving to run away if they could not pay their rent, have made it an exorbitant price: and the remote parts from Dublin will never be able to pay that rate were it not for the allowance of the two thirds of their purchase money[487] … Give my humble services to Mr Baron Tracy, and Mr Ettrick[488] for the kind mencion he made of me: Is it true that he is to be our Lord Chancellor; we talk of Mr Justice Dolben:[489] they are very different men.

61. *Alan I, Dublin, to Thomas, Whitehall coffee-house, King's Street, Westminster, 30 May 1702*

(1248/2/65–6)

Yours of the 23d instant hath put us here in great confusion at the surprising and heavy account of my dearest brother lying sick of a feavor; God grant your next may remove the melancholy and dismal apprehensions your last hath raised. I doe not think it proper for me to enter on any businesse especially relating to my self when what is dearer to me then any thing that can concern my fortune lyes in danger: therefore I omit to give any answer to what he in his letter mencions to Lucy, whether I would continue in my emploiment if any one were put over my head. I confesse that seems to me a very foreign matter unlesse the Attorney is intended to be promoted; for I think he will fail in no sort to deserve well by being a most dutiful and condescending servant to what Superiors find advisable: and I am apt to think his compliances as well as applicacions will secure him much longer then I can expect to stand who am not skilful in either. But too much of this: write if it be but a line by every post till poor St John is well. Alderman Singleton I have not yet heard of.[490] The Country is miserable poor; no money at all stirring …

62. *Alan I, Dublin, to Thomas, Whitehall coffee-house, King's Street, Westminster, 11 July 1702*

(1248/2/67–8)

By your letter of the 25th of June I concluded to have seen Mr Palmer[491] and Sir John Dillon[492] long ere this; and have now reason to think the former hath left London before

486 *(continued)* granted by the Resumption Act to be distributed (in proportion) as compensation was to be deducted from this purchase price.

487 The previous allowance of £21,000 compensation, roughly one third of the £59,502 alleged to have been expended in the purchase of property from the grantees, was to be increased by a further third (sect. 4), the result of an intervention in the Commons at the second reading of the bill on 7 May (*CJ*, xiii, 884–5; *Cocks diary*, ed. Hayton, 282–3).

488 William Ettrick (1651–1726), MP [E] and a bencher of the Middle Temple (to which he had been admitted a year before Alan). Referred to by Alan in a subsequent letter as 'my cousin Ettrick' (below, p. 000).

489 Gilbert Dolben. Both men were tories, though Ettrick was less a party man and more attached to the Court interest.

490 Edward Singleton, MP [I] for Drogheda, and an alderman of that borough.

491 William Palmer, MP[I].

492 Sir John Dillon, MP [I].

this time, but none at all to expect the later in some months: for my Lord Blessinton[493] (with whom his converse by letter is) tells me that he beleives he intends to wait on Lady Blessinton[494] over, and her Ladyship goes to the Bath this Season, yet had not left London when she wrote to him by the last post which we have received. Soe that probably you will lose the next half years rent by depending on his bringing over the Act:[495] pray write to me if you find the Act is come over by any other hand who the person is that brings it. I hope you have taken care to have your deeds proved by witnesses sworn before some of the English Judges according to the Act of Parliament, or else you may depend on meeting all opposicion that a sett of honest Gentlemen (our particular freinds) can give:[496] and for fear of an afterclap I wish something were entred on soe that the trust were in some measure executed for fear of an entire disappointing or defeating the whole affair in the next Parliament. I doubt the Bishop of C[*loyne*] for the time being is to be one of the trustees or overseers; if soe, he that stil is so (notwithstanding his letter to be removed)[497] will doe us all the ill offices in his power; being of all mankind the most ——. I know not yet whether St John will presse our coming over this Summer; if soe, really it will almost ruine me …

63. *Alan I, Dublin, to Thomas, Whitehall coffee-house, King's Street, Westminster, 6 Aug. 1702*

(1248/2/69–70)

At my return hither from Munster I found Lucy in bed after having miscarryed on this day sennight; probably we may yet goe to the Bath this Autumne, but if we doe it must be directly from Chester and back again by the same way without seeing London. The Bishop of Clogher[498] hath brought over and left with Lucy the deed you sent by him, and Sir John Dillon is landed but went to Lismullin[499] before I came to town, soe as till I can hear from him I shal be in the dark about the act which he brought over: All possible care shal be taken to have the matter laid before the trustees time enough to intitle the persons to whom the conveyance is to be made to the next half years rents; but beside the sought

[493] Lord Blessington. Dillon had married Blessington's daughter Mary, but the marriage was dissolved by private act of the English parliament of 1701 (10 and 11 Will III, priv., c. 1), on the grounds of her adultery.

[494] Blessington's second wife, Anne (c.1654–1725), daughter of John Coote, 2nd earl of Mountrath.

[495] A portmanteau private act of the English parliament of 1702, for the relief of Francis Spring and other protestant tenants of the forfeited estates in Ireland, for confirming a protestant settlement at Portarlington and a charity (school) at Midleton, and for the relief of Alice, dowager countess of Drogheda and Sir John Dillon (13 and 14 Will. III, priv., c. 58). In Oct. 1696 Lady Orkney had conveyed part of her Irish estates (held for her in trust since the previous year by her brother Edward and Thomas Brodrick) to Alan Brodrick and Laurence Clayton for the endowment of a 'free school' at Midleton. This private act instructed the Irish forfeitures trustees to draw up an indenture conveying the lands once more to the designated trustees, which was done on 26 Mar. 1703. By Lady Orkney's original indenture, Alan Brodrick and Laurence Clayton were named as governors of the school (with others, including Thomas Brodrick, Lords Orkney and Inchiquin, and the bishop of Cork *ex officio*). (Michael Quane, 'Midleton School, Co. Cork', *Journal of the Royal Society of Antiquaries of Ireland*, lxxxii (1952), 4–5, 10, 13–14).

[496] The forfeitures trustees.

[497] The outgoing bishop of Cloyne, John Pooley (1646–1712), who was translated to Raphoe in Sept. 1702.

[498] St George Ashe (1658–1718.)

[499] Lismullen, Co. Meath, Dillon's country estate.

occasions of delay which they out of their abundant good will to you and those who wish well to the school will be sure to lay hold of, I fear the wording of the clause (as you sent it over to me in your letter) will give them too good an handle to take time to consider before they will execute conveyances: but the fault shal lye at their door not mine … I am sorry your taking an house at Newmarkett gives us cause to despair of seeing you soon …

64. *Alan I, Dublin, to Thomas, Whitehall coffee-house, King's Street, Westminster, 8 Sept. 1702*

(1248/2/71–2)

Sir John Dillon being in the Countrey I wrote to him for the Act in which the Clause relating to the school of Middleton is contained and at length gott it, but immediately after Mr Doppin[500] called on me for it being the Act which provides for the improving tenants on forfeited estates and I delivered it to a Gentleman who by his order called at my study for it, who gave me a promise of extracting the clause which concerns the school and sending it to me: I will put that matter into Mr Lambes[501] hands and order him to retain such Councel as will be most useful, but you know I goe not among them at all, beside I am now as trustee a party in interest: It is a jest to think they[502] will part with this half years rent, I am much in doubt whether they will not keep matters off so as to receive Lady day rent too; and if people presse them, it is ten to one they find out some pretence of doing them in particular an evil turn: at least I fear that the difference of the description of the deed you sent me and that in the Act will give them an handle; one is made by Mrs Villiers, the other by Lady Orkney; who tho in truth the same person yet they make what doubts they please.[503] Last Saturday they had it solemnly argued whether the purchasers who are to be allowed to purchase at thirteen years purchase might pay in tallies or must lay down ready money: It was warmly spoken to by Burgh[504] and Nuttley[505] the trustees Councel that it must be money: on Thursday their honors say they will declare themselves therein; but by this means they have kept people in suspence whether tallies will be taken and consequently have hindred people disposed to purchase from buying them and secured this half years rent … now considering that one Parliament hath done what hath been already done with relacion to the purchasers under a Legal grant, may not people hereafter mislike the applicacion of the forfeitures now made, and say they might be better applied? If the transport service etc. should hereafter not be thought so necessarye to be paid this way, another Act may again defeat me of my purchase. In short I give full

[500] Samuel Dopping, MP[I].

[501] William Lamb(e), an attorney in the court of exchequer (Reg. Deeds, 1/310/1096; 2/252/346). Possibly identical with William Lambe (c.1665–by 1724) of Willow Grove, Co. Wicklow (Reg. Deeds, 17/104/8306; TCD, MS 1995–2008/1965: William Lambe to Abp King, 29 Nov. 1720; Vicars, *Index*, 275).

[502] The forfeitures trustees.

[503] In the deed of 1696 Lady Orkney had evidently used her maiden name (SHC, 1248/2/90–1: copy release by trustees of forfeited estates to Alan Brodrick I and Laurence Clayton of lands to endow a charity school at Midleton, 26 Mar.1703).

[504] Either Thomas Burgh MP [I], or his namesake Thomas Burgh of Dublin (*d.* 1711) (Hayton, *Ruling Ireland*, 77–8).

[505] Richard Nutley, MP [I].

ten years purchase in ready money (the Land sett at rack[506]) for a title under the trustees; and I doubt (considering all things) whether it be advisable to purchase any Lands in the Kingdome on those terms. Pray let me have your advice soon, that I may resolve on my affairs. Last night the Lords Justices[507] and Mr Gwin[508] (who is go[ing] for England) told me there were thoughts of a Parliament here, next Spring or Summer; told me I stood well at the Castle, and had a credit in and knowledge of the Countrey, asked my thoughts etc. I was very cautious, said we were a miserable oppressed countrey, and that they must expect to hear we were so when we mett; that if they looked for money (as no doubt that is the occasion of our meeting) they must hope for no more then what was absolutely necessary, and what we could pay and in our own way, and that there was no prospect of granting it for any long time: that people so used should have some thing that might be of real good done to them after such treatment as we have mett; I mentioned our paying forces in the West Indies,[509] trustees, our unsafety on pretence of discoveryes etc. they seemed ready to promise all ease possible and compliance in every thing: Consider and write to me; and particularly about serving for our County, who is fit to be in the Chair[510] etc. …

65. *Alan I, Dublin, to St John II, Middle Temple, 29 Nov. 1702*

(1248/2/73–5)

This letter will be delivered you by my sister Courthope,[511] who leaves Ireland in a very inconvenient time for a Sea voyage and a tedious journey by land; and when Lucyes indisposicion and melancholy would have made her company very obliging if she could have allowed it us a little longer: but we ought to thank her for it hitherto and not repine at not enjoying it longer: I think I may venture to write plainly what my thoughts are in reference to our affairs, and what is now in agitacion here, since I see no danger of having letters that goe by a private hand searched or looked into. You may depend on it that our successes in Flanders and in Gallicia[512] have not soe mortifyed the Irish, as the prospect they apprehend they fairly have of seeing — return[513] hath exalted them; they are turned admirable good subjects and very fond of the Church, and never cease to extol the very good understanding that is between the Queen and Commons in comparison of the late King and Parliament; and are very well pleased to find the lower house of Parliament and convocacion to be on

[506] See above, p. 100.

[507] The earl of Mountalexander, Thomas Erle and Thomas Keightley had been appointed lords justices on the accession of Queen Anne (Keightley replacing Archbishop Marsh of Dublin).

[508] Francis Gwyn.

[509] In July 1701 two foot regiments in Ireland were sent to the West Indies but remained on the Irish military establishment. A further regiment was added in the summer of 1702. The government's Irish managers identified this as a grievance, and when the Irish parliament met in Sept. 1703 the lord lieutenant, Ormond, promised to do what he could to bring the troops back and to ensure that money raised in Ireland was spent there. (C. I. McGrath, *Ireland and Empire, 1692–1770* (2012), 150–2.)

[510] To be Speaker of the house of commons when the Irish parliament eventually met.

[511] Martha or Rachel Courthope.

[512] The military advances in Flanders at the end of the 1702 campaigning season, culminating in the taking of Liege, and Sir George Rooke's naval victory at Vigo Bay in Oct.

[513] The 2nd duke of Ormond as lord lieutenant.

soe extraordinary terms as their late messages or resolves import.[514] There is no money in this Country; beef is in Corke at 4s per hundred,[515] butter at 18s, and soe in proporcion as to other goods: this I mean is the price given by such as will buy at all; but it is not one fifth part of our goods that will sell at all for any thing. When Land Lords, nay the Queen, or (to goe yet one step farther) the trustees call for their rents in several parts of the Kingdome, they are forced to take the stock of a farm for the rent due already on it; judge then out of what the next half years rent will be produced. If you expect any account from me of the proceedings at Chichester house, you must be content with a very imperfect one: The Act for releiving Lessees as to their improvements[516] will be of little or no avail to them, as well by reason that the remote parts of the Kingdome hardly heard there was such an act till their time for making out what they had laid out was elapsed, as by reason of the charge of coming up hither with their witnesses and the delayes they find before they can go through with their matter, and then the allowances given are such as few are the better for. The purchasers clause (tho well meant) will not I think be of any avail except to some few particular men, who had the good fortune to make their way to an advantage by getting the Lands to be moderately sett in 1701: but assure your self in general they were then lett at very much more then the real value, and consequently thirteen years purchase will be very dear to give, where Lands sett at moderate rents are not worth more, take one part of the Kingdome with another. The trustees took care to keep the point whether the purchasers might pay in tallies[517] malt tickets[518] etc. so long in doubt that few provided themselves timely enough with them to tender them before All Saints rent became due, resolving not to buy any other Lands, what ever they did as to those they formerly had purchased: and by this means they gott the All Saints rent: they have been selling for some time past, and at first declared they would sell for ready money; but purchasers not coming in on those terms, they have altered and accept fowre fifths in talleys etc. and the rest in money. I am of opinion they will (if possible) not leave any of their own or Clerks, agents etc. salaryes or wages in arrear: and when they have done soe, noe body can truly say that (after so many have been ruined by this Act) no body hath been the better for it. I am

[514] On 10 Nov. the Commons had passed an address of congratulation to the queen which linked the achievements of the duke of Ormond and the tory admiral Sir George Rooke with those of the duke of Marlborough (W.A. Speck, *The Birth of Britain: A New Nation 1700–1710* (Oxford, 1994), 42–3). Previously the archbishops, bishops and lower clergy of the convocation of Canterbury had presented a loyal address thanking the queen for her 'unmoveable resolution to protect and support' the church of England, and alluding to the 'zealous affections' to the Church exemplified in the recent addresses of both Lords and Commons in parliament (*London Gazette*, 9–12 Nov. 1702; Luttrell, *Brief Historical Relation*, v, 232).

[515] Hundredweight.

[516] The private act for the relief of Francis Spring 'and other Protestant tenants' of forfeited estates, 'in respect of their real improvements', which had also confirmed Lady Orkney's settlement of forfeited estates to establish a charity school at Midleton.

[517] Tally-sticks: the wooden receipts traditionally issued by the exchequer, which could be used as a form of payment.

[518] Malt lottery tickets, issued under the English Malt Lottery Loan Act of 1697 (8 and 9 Will. III, c. 22). Of the 140,000 tickets printed (each valued at £10) only 1,763 were sold, the remainder being issued by the English exchequer as promissory notes (P.G.M. Dickson, *The Financial Revolution in England: A Study in the Development of Public Credit* (1967), 49).

told that after they had agreed with one Spread for a purchase all in ready money,[519] and after he had paid in his purchase money and had a receit for it, that they would not perfect conveyances to him till he made up a mistake committed; for it seems he had paid Guineys not at £1 3*s* as current here but at £1–1*s*–6*d* as they go in England: but they have found out that Guineys are to be received by them only at £1–1*s*–2¾*d* and so I hear he hath been obliged to passe them. One Wade (a very silly idle fellow)[520] brought an ejectment for Lands that it seems he had claimed before them, and his claim was dismissed; Mr Nuttley[521] came into the Kings Bench last Thursday or Fryday and told the Court there was such an ejectment[522] served, and that he came by order of the trustees to let them know there had been a claim by Wade and that his claim had been dismissed, which dismission he shewed under their hands, and then insisted or rather demanded that the Kings Bench should suffer noe farther proceedings on that ejectment: the Court said they would consider of it, but he (as I hear, for I was not present) was dissatisfyed with that answer, and seemed to expect an obedience and that the Kings Bench should not pretend to hold plea of any Lands that they had ever judged to be vested in them: by this it seems they are not content that their sales should convey a good title, but expect to be sole judges as to what Lands ever were in their opinion vested in them, even after they have passed their adjudication. Sure the Courts of Law are to determine what force their adjudicacions and sales will have when once they have given their judgements or made sales, unlesse they expect to be perpetual Dictators. But this blockhead hath given them an handle (and probably with the advice of some no enemyes to the trust) to apply to the Parliament for a clause to confirm all their sales, acts etc. whether pursuant to or warranted by the Act or not; and this they will say is no more then absolutely necessary, for the encouragement and securitye of purchasers: since while they are yet here, their judgements are called in question. There is this farther mischeif in the case, that all unbiassed sensible men beleive the trustees to be in this instance in the right, and the complainer in the wrong. I have formerly told you that closeting was with many other late fashions come again into practice: last night the Lords Justices summoned the three Cheif Judges,[523] Attorny general and me to the Castle:[524] the pretence was to advise what good could be done for Ireland in which the Major General[525] promised his endeavours, and Mr Keightley[526] gave large assurances of Lord Lieutenants[527] concurrence

[519] William Spread (*d.* by 1710) purchased the town and lands of Ballycannon, Co. Cork for £499 from the trustees in Mar. 1702 (Vicars, *Index*, 435; W. M. Brady, *Clerical and Parochial Records of Cork, Cloyne and Ross* … (3 vols, 1864), i, 196).

[520] John Wade of Herbertstown, Co. Meath (*A List of the Claims* …, 202; S.C. Wade, *The Wade Genealogy* … (New York. NY, 1900), 185–6).

[521] Richard Nutley, MP [I].

[522] A civil action to recover possession of, or title to, land.

[523] Sir Richard Cox, lord chief justice of common pleas; Robert Doyne, lord chief baron of the exchequer; and Richard Pyne, now Sir Richard, lord chief justice of queen's bench.

[524] This may be the meeting reported by Mountalexander and Erle to Rochester on 30 Jan. 1702 (*CSP Dom.*, 1702–3, 563–4).

[525] Thomas Erle, MP [I].

[526] Thomas Keightley, MP [I].

[527] Lord Rochester.

as far as his power and interest could goe: but it was added that our thoughts should also be employed on what methods could be taken to have a Parliament sit in the Summer or Autumne soe as to continue the addicional dutyes: The not paying three regiments beyond sea was named,[528] and we were told that was formed already by my Lord Lieutenant and found an easy reception in the house of commons:[529] this was moved by Lord Cheif Justice Cox: Pyne was for guard ships, and Laws against the Irish inheriting while they continued Papists, and for admitting no preists into the Kingdome:[530] Doyne said he thought good Laws would doe us little good, that we were ruined for want of trade, and had not money to go to the markets: The Attorney could not find a word to speak yet; I said guard ships would be of use when we had trade and not till then, that the matter of the regiments I supposed was already resolved that they should not be paid here while they continued out of the Kingdome, for indeed it was impossible: that our propertyes and constitucion had been so shaken of late by the trustee Act etc. and our trade so ruined by that of the woollen,[531] and the half penny act which we are to pay in England and also to enter there from the plantacions[532] that unlesse some care were taken to put new life into us we could not possibly subsist, and instead of giving additional dutyes should be obliged to pay our Army in beef, butter, corn and frize: I found it mightily uneasy to talk of the woollen or plantacion bill, and not lesse soe when that of the trustees was mencioned: not but that all the Justices owned them to be very severe and mischeivous laws to us, but as to the two former they seemed to say no body would adventure to move the repeal of them in an English house of commons; and as to the trustees, they seemed to say they were wearing out and would not be continued: My Lord Cheif Baron said boldly, that things would not be well till that act was laid aside. But it was impossible to gett Cox or the Atturnye to touch on that string. The Major General and Lord M[*ountalexander*] hinted at the reasonablenesse of our bearing a part of the charge in a publick war; and were answered (as the truth is) that we have born more than double nay treble our proporcion of what hath been spent since the revolucion by means of it and the war with France; regard being had to the trade and wealth and sufferings of both Kingdomes. It was then put on this foot by Mr Keightley; Supposing the revenue would not support the army, must it be disbanded or live on free quarter; which must be unlesse people were disposed to give mony. I answered that a Parliament was the best place to think of an expedient in, where the mischeif is so great and that it would ill become us to flatter them with an expectacion of supplies from a people neither able, nor

[528]The three regiments on the Irish establishment that had been sent to the West Indies. Erle subsequently wrote to Rochester to tell him of his fear that an Irish parliament would not wish to provide funds for fifteen regiments if they discovered that only seven were needed for the defence of Ireland (Churchill College, Cambridge, Churchill Archives Centre, Erle papers, 2/53/3: Erle to Rochester, 11 May 1703).

[529]Presumably the English house of commons.

[530]The Bishops' Banishment Act of 1697 (9 Will. III, c. 1 [I]) had already expelled bishops and regular clergy.

[531]The English Forfeitures Resumption Act of 1700, and Woollen Act of 1699 (11 Will. III, c. 13).

[532]The English Navigation Act of 1672 (22 and 23 Chas II, c. 26), continued in 1685 (1 Jas II, c. 17) and extended in 1697 (7 and 8 Will. III, c. 22), prevented the direct importation into Ireland of specific, 'enumerated', goods from the plantations and imposed an additional duty – a halfpenny on the pound on tobacco and a 'half-duty' on other goods (George O'Brien, *The Economic History of Ireland in the Eighteenth Century* (Dublin and London, 1918), 174–5: *Calendar of State Papers, Colonial* ..., 1685–8 and Addenda, 567).

(if they were) for ought was known soe well pleased with their late usage as to be willing to doe all that was expected: that the way to find them ready to answer her Majestyes occasions was by doing some Acts of grace, and putting us into a prospect of recovering from the languishing condicion we are now in, and when we were made sensible they intended not to ruine us utterly, but on the contrary to support us, we should be very ready to doe all in our power. We parted with taking notes of doing something toward opening some trade, to some place or other (which was Mr Attorneys share of the debate) and I suppose they are convinced something must be done for us, or else that we must not meet: but my freedome on this occasion no doubt will goe over, and I shal be represented to be (as I am) a person that will complain of our usage, and will never agree to give till I know a reason for it, and am convinced the Country can and ought to bear a tax.[533] It was often insisted that we should find out the particular things that would doe us good and were to be brought to passe; by which last words I looked on it that the woollen bill, trustee, and plantacion acts were meant to be excluded: I said, some had been named, and that the ministry and freinds of Ireland in England were the proper Judges what would passe there; and that it was very hard, that it lay soe easily in every bodyes power and knowledge how to hurt us and that they never wanted oportunityes to doe it, whereas all people there were strangers to what tended to our good or preservacion. Major General Erle said that the Crown was the proper preserver and protector of the Protestant interest of Ireland, and that we ought soe to act as to oblige the Crown and intitle our selves to its favor and protection; I ventured to say we had done soe, and that I apprehended our sufferings were not the lesse for having so affectionately adhered to the Late Kings interests;[534] and that we should bear the same duty to the Queen who we hope may be able to doe all for our preservacion which the King would have done if it had been within his power. Mr Keightley stil insisted that the Queen and ministry would doe all in their power for our releif, but that we ought not to be too querulous nor expect more from them then they can accomplish. It then came out that the Session of Parliament in England would be soon over[535] and they would not have time to meddle with any thing relating to us this Session, and that the woollen Act etc. were only to be considered in Parliament etc. but that is a plain banter, for before the Parliament met the Lords Justices were told the same things by other Gentlemen, and by me in particular at Mr Dawsons[536] house when Mr Gwyn[537] was by: we may therefore have the assurance of peoples best endeavours next meeting if we can find out money in the meantime, and give it for fowre or five years that there may be no occasion for bringing angry people together afterward, when nothing is altered for our ease, and perhaps new burthens laid on our shoulders …

[533]The report sent by Mountalexander and Keightley on 30 Jan. stated that all present were 'of opinion that in view of the poverty of the kingdom the meeting of parliament should be postponed as long as possible'. Where Alan Brodrick was said to differ from the rest was in reviving 'the former famous point of sole right', and insisting that no money bill should be offered by the privy council.

[534]William III.

[535]The parliament was prorogued on 25 May 1702 and dissolved on 2 July following.

[536]Joshua Dawson, MP [I].

[537]Francis Gwyn, Rochester's chief secretary.

66. *Alan I, Dublin, to Thomas, Whitehall coffee-house, King's Street, Westminster, 6 Jan. 1702/3*

(1248/2/78–9)

I received yours of the tenth of the last month by Mr Brewster[538] and doe assure you that I burnt both sheets with my own hand; but am strangely surprized at your trusting any thing of concern in that hand: by his way of addresse and calling you his freind I suppose the Gentleman hath forgot his behavior last Parliament to the English interest in general, and his particular ingratitude nay rancour toward you and all of us, or thinks me to have an exceeding ill memorye, or to be of a very relenting kidney. If any of that familye (and particularly the deliverer of your letter) can perswade you to look on them as men fit to be confided in or conversed with, I shal beleive you are a very good christian but not overprudent: pray give it me under your hand that you never can have freindship for or depend on any of the kindred. You doe know the injury the old fellow endeavoured to doe me in his scheme of politicks prepared for and laid before Lord Capel;[539] and the insulting way the young used in declaring tho he served for M[*idleton*] he would vote as he pleased; that is in direct opposicion to all he knew was for the good of the Countrey, and to what you and all of us designed; with this sting in the tail of it, as if you expected his voice should depend on him by whose interest he was elected: tho he well knew how free all people were from sollicitacion on the side we voted of. And now we talk of a Parliament, depend on it (notwithstanding what you seem to think) it is fully intended to hold one here the next Summer, and people are as busy as ever to make interest for getting men in, that will give and forgive everything.

This morning I have a letter from my father dated att Middleton on New years day which tells me the pinnace[540] was then come thither to carry him to the Cove[541] to goe on board the meremaid for Bristol: I hope you will have had news of his safe arrival long before you can receive this, but the weather hath been soe exceeding stormy that my heart akes to think of his being at sea these long nights in soe tempestuous a season. It will be very well worth your while, and his, and indeed concerns us all to consider that the animosityes which have been too long in our familye should be laid aside: Perhaps there have been faults on both sides, and I am sure I am most unfit to determine who is or are most to blame; but the matter of accounts and all money affairs being settled between him and you, ought not both to forget all resentment and strangenesse? What repute can a familye bear in the world, where father and son doe not meet like freinds but either keep a sullen silence or fall into revilings? For Gods sake brother pardon me for saying this to you, I am not backward in speaking my mind very freely to my father: but neither of you can either live innocently or dye happilye unlesse you heartily endeavour to lay asleep the animosityes that have too long boiled in your breasts. You see (no body better) to what affairs in England seem to

[538] Francis Brewster, MP [I].

[539] Sir Francis Brewster, MP [I].

[540] A small boat used as a tender to larger vessels.

[541] Modern-day Cobh, Co. Cork: a port on the south of the Great Island.

tend: yet sure you doe not lay up for a storm which probably is not far off: to say truth, I know not two men in the world of so little personal expence on themselves that are able to give so lame an account of the produce of two soe good estates as yours and his since the troubles:[542] I am only advising what is fitt to be done hereafter, not taking on me to call your conduct in question or finding fault with your disposing your own. I am sorry to hear what I doe of Sennys expensivenesse, but will not endure it …

67. *Alan I, Dublin, to Thomas, Whitehall coffee-house, King's Street, Westminster, 21 Jan. 1702/3*

(1248/2/80–1)

Methinks you are very remisse in taking no notice of the letter I wrote to you some time since about the deed to be executed by the trustees for conveying the Lands to support Middleton free school: I gave you my thoughts that it would be absolutely necessary to have some peticion claim or paper lodged before them praying the benefit of the Act, and that the original deeds should be sent over: but having never heard a word farther from you on that subject am much surprized, and cannot well tell what to attribute your silence to unlesse you have put it into some agents here (which I hope you have done) or else despair of doing any good. The conveyance is I think by the Act to be executed before the 25th of March which is now drawing nigh, and the trustees being now selling the private estate may out of particular kindnesse to you dispose of those Lands beforehand, and I have not the names of them soe as any way to prevent it. Pray advise with my brother and others in the matter, for as the clause is drawn I am very doubtful of successe considering how violent enemyes you have to deal with. I beleive you know what a turn they have given to the clause that gives Protestant purchasers their estates at 13 years purchase as the Lands were sett from May 1701: They say the rent is to be the measure where they sett Land for that year, but where the Land was under former Lease or the tenants were continued from year to year they say they are judges: and so consequently will have it in their power to give better or worse pennyworths, as the partyes have or shal deserve kind treatment. Depend on it from me that your judgement about a P[*arliament*] being to meet soon here is erroneous: you are as surely mistaken as you live, and I have irrefragable reasons for what I say: you take no sort of care while all other people are making interest; is this a time to let any matter of reputacion fail for want of diligence? You must appear, or else your withdrawing from the insolence and tyranny of our Bashaws will be construed guilt of your having done some unjustifiable act which makes you decline your Countrey. Doe not think to be able to support interest or credit here by a Newmarket Life. Things are miserably low in the country and no buyers to be had at the very lowest prices …

[542]The jacobite war, 1689–91.

68. *Alan I, Dublin, to Thomas, Whitehall coffee-house, King's Street, Westminster, 1 Mar. 1702/3*

(1248/2/82–3)

Before my Lord Cheif Justice Cox[543] went the Circuit he told me that Sir Edward Percival (I think his name is Edward)[544] would stand for Knight of our County, and that he could not assist Clayton[545] in opposicion to him tho he was very ready to doe it against Mr St Leger[546] or any body else,[547] and seemed to propose his quitting soe as Sir Edward Percival and you might be chosen without any difficultye. I wrote to Clayton about it who tells me (as the truth is) that he hath a very great interest in the Countrey, and gives me plainly yet modestly to understand that he thinks himself sure to carry it for one if he doe stand, but that he will intirely wave if Sir Edw[*ar*]d Percival will give assurances of coming over and sitting, and of joining interests with you; but he saith very truly that this must be known and declared soe as to be depended on in time: he saith that he knows you doe deserve it the best of any (notwithstanding I must tell you that your living in England, my living in Dublin, and another bodyes unhappy conduct in the County of Corke,[548] added to your having been concerned for my Lady Orkney have much lessened your interest here) and that he never will doe an act that may lessen you in the eye of the world or lose you one vote; and as for Sir Edward Percival, he is willing to give way to a Gentleman soe nearly related to him and of soe fair a fortune if he will come and join with you against all mankind: I write by tomorrows post to Cox and would have you goe to Sir Edw[*ard*] Percival or Mr Southwell[549] and adjust this matter; for I suppose none of the Boyle familye think of coming over. Let me intreat you not to delay this, for I would not on any account have a slight put now on you. Nuttley[550] is gone over to make interest to succeed Sir John Meade;[551] I wrote to Sir John, and to Mr Meddlycott[552] to let them know I did not apprehend it would be his Graces service[553] to be advised to promote any of the Chichester House gang.[554] Pray let me know fully what passed at your second waiting on him.

[543]Sir Richard Cox.

[544]Sir John Perceval, 5th Bt., MP [I]. Perceval was not yet twenty years old (and would not be so until July 1703) but this was evidently no obstacle to his candidature, for he was returned for the county later that year in advance of attaining his majority.

[545]Laurence Clayton, MP [I].

[546]Arthur St Leger, MP [I].

[547]Cox had informed Perceval that he would support Clayton for the county constituency against St Leger, or indeed anyone else except Perceval (BL, Add. MS 47025, ff 60–1: Perceval to Cox, 11 Mar. 1702/3).

[548]Presumably their father, Sir St John (see above, pp. 4–5).

[549]Edward Southwell, MP [I].

[550]Richard Nutley, MP [I].

[551]As knight of the shire for Tipperary.

[552]Thomas Medlycott, MP [I].

[553]The duke of Ormond, who could claim to possess the principal interest in Co. Tipperary.

[554]The forfeitures trustees, whom Nutley had served as counsel.

69. *Alan I, Dublin, to Thomas, Whitehall coffee-house, King's Street, Westminster, 10 Mar. 1702/3*

(1248/2/84–5)

The packets are come in and have brought me yours of the second instant, and one from Mr M.[555] You may depend on my having wrote two letters to him, one the day after term and the other about ten dayes after, which I conclude intercepted and probably on this side since the receit of them is not owned, which could never happen but from the subject being displeasing; and that I am sensible by your letter it cannot be, since you say my Lord resents the matter of Mr N[*utley*] and will never goe into it, and nothing else could be disagreeable but the contrary. I am wonderfully pleased at the accounts you give me, Col. Conyngham, and others; what fair reasons you have to beleive all will goe well: You are honest and uncapable of dissembling by nature, and thereby rendred apt to beleive well of other people: remember your thoughts of Sir Fr[*ancis*] B[*rewster*] and some others, and alway mind mens morals and characters in the world beyond their fair speeches when occasion requires their seeming to be very good: This caution I cheifly level against your too far trusting or unbosoming your self to one who I find hath created an intimacye with you, and proposes to doe it with me. But what can be the meaning that you never so much as mencion my Lord Chancellor,[556] for whom we have a Successor (one Jennings[557]) named in the publick letters and prints: but depend on it I saw Lord Nottinghams[558] letter to my Lord Cheif Justice Cox to let him know the Queen commanded him to repair forthwith for England about the affairs of this Kingdome;[559] the letter found him in his circuit at Roscommon and yesterday he came to town and goes by the boat which brings this packett: I have no difficultye but that it is with intent to put the Seal into his hands: Are you kept out of this secret, or can you be soe easy as your letter expresses you to be to have Mr Methuen turned out and not provided for? Or is it a turn to which my Lord Lieutenant is yet a stranger? If my Lord be perswaded it is necessary Mr Methuen be removed to prevent heats in the house of Lords,[560] I own I doe not see that argument is of any force: Will the Lords fall out with the Lords of England? I suppose that may put the Duke[561] under a necessitye of a suddain ending the dispute: if not, how can the Lords quarrel at the Chancellor and

[555] Presumably Thomas Medlycott.

[556] John Methuen.

[557] Edward Jennings (c.1647–1725), a Q.C. [E], and formerly attorney-general for several Welsh circuits; later a tory MP (*HC 1690–1715*, iv, 495).

[558] Daniel Finch (1647–1730), 2nd earl of Nottingham, secretary of state for the southern department [E] (which included Ireland within its responsibilities).

[559] *CSP Dom.*, 1702–3, 592: Nottingham to Cox, 16 Feb. 1703, requesting Cox's presence in England as the queen was 'considering many Irish matters in which he may be useful'. Cox was appointed lord chancellor [I] later that year.

[560] Over his conduct in the disputed question of the appellate jurisdiction which the English house of lords claimed over Ireland, and recently exercised in the cases of the *Society of London* v. *the bishop of Derry*, and *the earl and countess of Meath* v. *Lord Ward and others* (James, *Lords of the Ascendancy*, 68–70; Philip O'Regan, *Archbishop William King of Dublin (1650–1729) and the Constitution in Church and State* (Dublin, 2000), 97–111, 116–24), aggravated by Methuen's absence from Ireland since Feb. 1701, and recent acceptance of a posting as envoy extraordinary to Portugal (*HC 1690–1715*, iv, 806–7).

[561] Ormond.

passe by the house of Lords in England, whose order he executed? But as to the Commons, in my opinion no Chancellor can be so useful to the Queen and Lord Lieutenant with them as Mr Methuen. But if our private hints be true that he is to be succeeded in the Common Pleas by Justice Dolben,[562] whose cushion is to be filled up by some of the trust, people will beleive things go on in the old way. I hope my Lord Lieutenant will use his interest not to have any of the trustees, especially the reporters to be in the Commission about the forfeited estates after 24th of June:[563] I wish Mr A[*nnesley*][564] were in another service rather then his, he will be fallen upon whoever supports him:[565] and he is no friend to my Lord that endeavours to fix him in his service or esteem …

70. *Alan I, Dublin, to Thomas, Whitehall coffee-house, King's Street, Westminster, 11 Mar. 1702/3*

(1248/2/86–7)

Having put off our journey till to morrow gives me leisure to write once again to you before I leave town, and the occasion is my having forgott to say any thing to you in answer to that part of yours of the ninth of February which relates to Mr Ogle;[566] this is one of many instances of my memoryes beginning to fail, at which I am not much surprized considering the infinite multiplicitye of things my head is alway full of. You must understand what he means (by desiring if I am not engaged that I would think on him) by what I wrote to you in the late reign of his design to be in the Parliament supposed like to meet then; this you were acquainted with and I have your answer assuring him an election att M[*idleton*] but since that he on his going for England wholly declined it and said if the Governement inclined to chuse him they had boroughs enough to recommend him; if not, that he would not subject his freinds to answer for any sins but their own: In short, he hath a good employment[567] and expressed himself resolved not to hazard it by becoming a stickler for Ireland, and therefore you may very well say to him that on his soe expressing himself to me I acquainted you and that you are engaged elsewhere; but then this should be done soon, and you must add if you had understood him you would at first have told him soe: If the Governement be well he will be soe too: but let his being chosen or not be your act only, for an offer once declined is as if never made; and for ought I know the country may at this time resent bringing in

[562] Gilbert Dolben.

[563] By an English act of 1702 (1 Anne, c. 21), all property not sold by the trustees before 24 June 1703 was to be vested in the queen; the rents were to be collected in her name and deposited in the exchequer. Presumably Alan believed that commissioners would be appointed for this purpose.

[564] Francis Annesley, MP [I], the trustee, was employed in the management of Ormond's Irish estates (D.W. Hayton, 'Dependence, Clientage, and Affinity: The Political Following of the Second Duke of Ormonde' in *The Dukes of Ormonde, 1610–1745*, ed. T.C. Barnard and Jane Fenlon (Woodbridge, 2000), 217).

[565] On 27 and 28 Sept. 1703, shortly after the opening of the 1703 parliament in Ireland, Annesley was questioned by the Commons about a passage in the report of the forfeiture inquiry commissioners in 1700, which, it was resolved, had 'scandalously and maliciously misrepresented and traduced the Protestant freeholders of this kingdom'. He was then expelled from the House. (*CJI*, iii, 17, 19–21; NLI, MS 991, pp 135–6: Edward Southwell to the earl of Nottingham, 30 Sept. 1703; BL, Add. MS 28891, ff 104–5: same to John Ellis, 2 Oct. 1703.)

[566] Samuel Ogle, MP [I].

[567] As a revenue commissioner [I].

one unknown. I am amazed to hear nothing farther about the Lands that were intended to be settled on Middleton school; you know what I have formerly wrote, how the Act varyes from the words of the conveyance, mentions neither Lands in particular, nor truly recites by whom the deed was made nor saith to whom: the 25th of March is near[568] and I am of opinion this matter will at last miscarry: I gave you early notice of this, I am sure as long agoe as in October. You wrote there were some deeds in England that should be sent over, but I hear not of them. The thing is in Mr Lambes[569] hands with the best directions I can give him.

71. *Alan I, Cork, to Thomas, Whitehall coffee-house, King's Street, Westminster, 26 Mar. 1703*

(1248/2/88–9)

We came hither yesterday from Mallow, and found your two letters with the enclosed from you to my Lord Cheif Justice Cox, I mean the copy of that you wrote to him: but no doubt very soon after writing it you found he was gott to London, soe as your letter was unnecessarye. I have on my leaving town given you a true account of what passed between him and me on his suddain return from the Circuit, and before his going for England: He will not deny but that he gave all those assurances which I mencion in my letter, which I wonder he should give without being able to say they should be made good: and I conclude that he had not sufficient power to say soe by your mencioning Sir John Percival and Mr Southwell[570] not so ready to join with you, to prevent disobliging any other Gentlemen that might stand.[571] But what I am most surprised at is to find young George Crofts[572] write letters and sollicite the whole countrey for St Leger,[573] and the report here is that Sir Johns tenants have had a letter written to them in favor of St Leger: If this is true, Clayton[574] you and I are very ill used. When I was at Mallow I spoke to some of the freeholders there and engaged ym for you; Mr Chinerye[575] told me that Lord

568 A quarter day; also the beginning of the year according to the Julian calendar.

569 William Lamb(e).

570 Edward Southwell, MP [I].

571 Perceval had written to Cox on 11 Mar. reporting the state of play (BL, Add. MS 47025, ff 60–1): 'Mr Brodrick' had let it be known that the election would 'in all probability' lie between himself, Perceval and Laurence Clayton, other candidates being likely to drop out; also that Clayton's interest was the strongest but at Brodrick's request he would desist to ensure Brodrick's return. Perceval drew the following conclusion: 'Now, if Mr Brodrick's interest stands in need of Mr Clayton's desisting and my joining with him, how know I but by doing so he may prove a dead weight to me, if the other gentlemen should persist to stand? Not to mention the enemies I should create by siding with one person against another.' He therefore resolved to leave the decision to 'the gentlemen of the county'.

572 George Crofts (*d*. by 1741) of Churchtown, Co. Cork, son of George Crofts MP [I] for Charleville in 1692 (*Hist. Ir. Parl.*, iii, 542; Vicars, *Index*, 112).

573 Arthur St Leger, MP [I].

574 Laurence Clayton, MP [I].

575 George Chinnery (1653–1713) of Castle Cor, Cork (James Grove White, *Historical and Topographical Notes … on Buttevant, Castletownroche, Doneraile, Mallow, and Places in Their Vicinity* (4 vols, Cork, 1905–25), i, 64; Michael Henchion, *The Gravestone Inscriptions of St John the Baptist Cemetery Midleton, Co. Cork* (Cloyne, 2009), 56–7). His younger son, George, married Alan Brodrick's niece Eleanor Whitfield, and became master of Midleton school.

Insiquin[576] has said you should not be elected: I would not have you report this till I give you better reason to beleive it: for tho he may be ingaged in inclinacion and by word for his relacion Mr St Leger,[577] yet this goes beyond that and seems the result of resentment: perhaps making him pay his debt hath disgusted him, and my refusing to lend him money: But I think his interest and Lord Kingstons[578] will not much prejudice you. Mr St Leger hath also gott Lord Barrymores[579] recommendacion to his freeholders, and his emissaryes brag of having not only Lord Burlingtons[580] but my Lord Ormonds interest too. Your story of Jack Hayes[581] convinces me of how little credit the news is as far as it relates to Lord Burlington, and makes me beleive there is little faith to be given to any other part of their assertions: However they possesse people with an opinion that so matters stand, and I must assure you great industry is used to baffle you: The talk of Piercy Freake[582] is silly; but now we have a new account that Mr Henry Boyle[583] will come over, and doe assure you I saw a letter from Robin Oliver[584] to Laurance Clayton to this purpose and that he resolved to stand for Knight of our Shire: it passes my beleif that he can have thoughts of coming over and I think is calculated that under any pretence you may be put by. What date Mr Southwells letter to Mr Oliver bears I know not, but I saw it on Tuesday last I mean Robins letter. You best can judge (by weighing and considering the times you saw Mr Southwell) how far you are candidly dealt with by being told of Mr St Leger and Mr Freke, if at the same time they knew of Mr Boyles standing: But I beleive this to be an after game which they beleive cannot fail to give you the go by when the interest made for St Leger may be out ballanced. Speak to Sir Richard Cox with confidence of having all made good that was promised to me and send me such a letter as I may have shewn in the Countrey to disabuse Sir John Percivales tenants that Sir John doth not join with Mr St Leger, if the thing be really soe. I am sensible my letters to Mr M.[585] were cautious and soe I intended, and it is very fit to be on the reserve with men that are entirely dependant on a single person; beside if I may judge by past actions, he is not a man to be over much depended on. I am very glad to find that my father is employed in that kind of building which you say is of real use; it will divert him, and prevent spending his money another way. By a letter received this day from Mr Burridge[586] I conclude Lord Chancellor[587] is out[;] pray if possibly you can, interpose in favor of Frank Lake his Secretarye being continued in his emploiment under the succeeding Chancellor. I am pleased at my Lord Lieutenants[588] resolucion not to

[576]The 3rd earl of Inchiquin.

[577]They were cousins: Inchiquin's mother, née Elizabeth St Leger, was the sister of John St Leger, Arthur's father.

[578]John King (c.1664–1728), 3rd Baron Kingston.

[579]James Barry (1667–1747), 4th earl of Barrymore.

[580]Charles Boyle (1666–1704), 3rd earl of Cork and 2nd earl of Burlington.

[581]John Hayes, MP [I], St Leger's father-in-law. Once an office-holder in the Irish revenue, he had now returned to England and was domiciled in London (*HC 1690–1715*, iv, 306–8).

[582]Percy Freke, MP [I].

[583]Hon. Henry Boyle, MP [I] 1692–9.

[584]Robert Oliver, MP [I].

[585]Probably Thomas Medlycott, MP[I].

[586]Ezekiel Burridge.

[587]John Methuen.

[588]The 2nd duke of Ormond had been appointed lord lieutenant in Feb. 1703.

countenance the Chichester house worthies:[589] As to Baron W[*orth*] you should not forgett that I owe him personal service for doing me all the good offices in his power when I first came over; which I have alway owned and endeavoured to return by firmly adhering to his younger sons interest[590] against his adversary and have done him signal service in it:[591] I alway shal retain a sense of gratitude toward him that hath obliged me, and tho I am by no means of the same principles with him in all things, yet I never will act to his prejudice; and the lesse you do (notwithstanding the part he hath acted in relacion to the publick) the better in my opinion; considering the intimacye that was once between you. I neither have nor will give any promise about any election at Middleton; that of Ogle my last mentioned. The sooner you come over the better. Pray concert with a few prudent and honest men there what may be done by us at our meeting: the number of those who deserve both epithets here is very scanty. You cannot imagine what persons embottom themselves in the Trustee Act by purchasing under it: therefore we must not repose confidence etc. nor act a publick part to expose ourselves.

72. *Alan I, Dublin, to Thomas, Whitehall coffee-house, King's Street, Westminster, 14 Apr. 1703*

(1248/2/92–3)

I came to town on Sunday soe ill that I was not able to goe down stairs till this morning, by reason of an excessive cold I took in my way hither. Let me advise you to depend little on any promises of any people whatsoever on this side the water; when you know that Mr Ludlow,[592] the Recorder;[593] Colonel Cuningham[594] and a pretty many more of that kind are become purchasors under the trust, you may judge what event any vote proposed against them may find:[595] but what think you of some mens extravagance of offering at a bill here for confirming the purchases under the trust? Talk not of this to any living man, but make this use of it not to be foolishly carried on in endeavouring to doe good to a people that neither deserve it, nor ever did or will join with them that endeavour it. Your own nature will keep you from mean (and more from unjust) compliances; but I would not have you expresse any stifnesse in matters of meer punctilio,[596] wherein you will certainly be deserted by those who quit their former professions[597] in relacion to things wherein their true interests were concerned. If you have one of your proposals laid before the Parliament

[589] The forfeitures trustees.

[590] James Worth, later Tynte, MP [I].

[591] Possibly in the inheritance of the Tynte estates, against a counter-claim from Laurence Clayton, whose first wife Catherine had been the sister of William Worth's second wife, Mabel(l)a Tynte.

[592] Stephen Ludlow, MP [I].

[593] John Forster, MP [I].

[594] Henry Conyngham, MP [I].

[595] Archbishop King of Dublin wrote to Francis Annesley on 6 Apr.: 'I hear from several hands that the forfeitures go off at great rates and the addressers the great buyers, which will stop their mouths for ever' (TCD, MS 750/2, p. 188).

[596] A strict adherence to correct form.

[597] Those who renege on what they have formerly professed.

in 1692 send it me over;[598] I wish you had never done any thing of the kind: the freinds of the trust, the new purchasers and your enemyes lay the foundacion of the whole on that project of yours …

[*PS.*] Since being in the County of Corke I found by discourse one had with Colonel Taylor (Sir John Percivals receiver)[599] that Sir John had never so much as wrote to him about serving for our County, soe as I see it to be only a project of Sir R[*ichard*] C[*ox*]. however since matters have gone soe far, I would not have you break off from the offer made to Sir John; but your interest is secure in the County; and if you and Clayton joined, you would put any other two competitors so hard to it that they would find a difficult task to weather either[600] …

73. *Alan I, Dublin, to Thomas, Whitehall coffee-house, King's Street, Westminster, 19 Apr. 1703*

(1248/2/94–5)

Perhaps this letter may not overtake you in London which will oblige me to write more obscurely then otherwise I would, yet hope to make you understand what I mean, and the persons I hint at. Be not too ready to give faith to all fair professions made, while you see men continued nay advanced who neither are nor ever were or will be just to any thing but their own interest: Why is Mr A[*nnesley*][601] stil employed in all the particular affairs of —;[602] how comes so entire a confidence to be reposed in our countryman[603] as I find there is? People newly landed assure me he is an oracle; and you know what spirit he prophesyes by. I am sure if you doe not, I doe. I have had such [a] character of a Gentleman whose conversacion and sense you speak well of, and whom you recommend to me as worth being well with, that I can never have a value for him nor consequently desire any intimacye with him till I find whether he be injured in the character I heard given him: but it was by a man of so good sense and nice honour that it sinks deep with me: but what adds to it is that we hear he is become purchaser of a certain dwelling in trust for a certain person: If this be soe, his emploiment is of that nature that I cannot desire to be acquainted with him that acts in it. Your enemyes here make what use they can of your speaking hopefully of things, and coming over as you intend, to incline people to think you are ready to comply to any thing on good terms offered.

[598] On 1 Jan. 1693 the English house of commons had appointed a committee to receive proposals for raising money on the forfeited estates in Ireland (*CJ*, x, 605). The following year Thomas Brodrick published *Proposals for Raising a Million of Money out of the Forfeited Estates in Ireland Together, with the Answer of the Irish to the Same, and a Reply Thereto* (1694). In Nov. 1703, in response to attacks in the Irish house of commons on the English commissioners of inquiry into Irish forfeitures, based on supposedly derogatory comments made in their report in 1700, the tory Arthur Annesley drew attention to this publication (which he referred to as 'The million project'), in which, he said, Thomas Brodrick had included 'matters of as high reflection on the country' as anything in the commissioners' report (*CSP Dom.*, 1703–4, 198).

[599] William Taylor (*d.* 1712), who was Perceval's cousin as well as his estate agent. For his role in the management of the Perceval estates, see BL, Add.MS 46964A, passim.

[600] See above, pp. 135, 138, 141.

[601] Francis Annesley, MP [I], the trustee.

[602] The duke of Ormond, the newly appointed lord lieutenant.

[603] Sir Richard Cox.

74. *Alan I, Dublin, to St John II, 4 June 1703*

(1248/2/98–9)

Yours of the 29th of May came in last night, but before I come to answer it particularly let me acquaint you that my Lord Lieutenant landed this morning and was sworn about ten of the clock; he was received with all the marks of honour and respect this Kingdome can shew, and the people expressed the regard they had for his person and the honour they retain for the memorye of his grand father[604] by their acclamacions while he passed through the streets. My brother[605] is not yet come in, it being his fortune to take passage in one of the men of war who were ordered to convoy the transport ships who sailed out of Highlake[606] with the Duke but were not able to make as good way as the Yatch, so as that frigot was ordered to attend the heavy Ships; and the wind came about to the West soon after the Duke gott into the bay, and perhaps we may not see him this week. Your last letter gives me an account of one wrote from this side the water in which I was mentioned, as one who had given large reasons in writing to uphold the sole right etc. and of what a Gentleman (who was present at the letters being read) said on that occasion. I know how sensibly you are touched with any indiscreet act your freind is ever guilty of, and you cannot excuse me from being indiscreet at least (if not very faulty) if I have acted as is represented. What I am now about to write will goe no farther then your own breast, unlesse you trouble the person who was soe kind to inform you what was offered to my prejudice of the truth of the thing; and you may depend on it to be as followeth. Some time before any talk of Lord Rochesters not coming over, and when it was expected he would return and hold a Parliament here, the Lords Justices called the three cheif Judges, the Attorney and me to the Castle and there told us a Parliament was to be held,[607] that the state of the revenue (by the expiracion of the Act for the addicional dutyes)[608] required it; and asked our thoughts as to the time of the summoning a Parliament, and what we thought must [*sic*] proper to be offered to bring people into such a temper that matters might be reasonably expected to succeed to the Queens satisfaction and for the publick good: the first step was made in the Lords Justices declaring a Parliament must be soon held; and all agreed as to the time, that it was to be delayed as long as possible considering the great povertye of the country, and the resentment that people may be supposed to have for the severe treatment of several sorts they apprehend themselves to have for some time past lain under. We farther generally agreed (at least no body that I remember spoke to the contrary) that the expence which the pay of the regiments on our establishment being carried out of the Kingdome put the nation to, by having so much of our little running cash drawn off that way, must soon ruine us: I think my Lord Justice Erle seemed to think

[604] The 1st duke of Ormond.

[605] Thomas.

[606] Hoylake, on the Wirral, a port of embarkation for Ireland.

[607] Cf. the account of this meeting given above, pp. 130–2.

[608] 'Additional duties' were voted by the Irish parliament on a temporary basis to supplement the crown's hereditary revenues in Ireland: the duty on woollens granted in 1699 would expire in Mar. 1702; those levied on tobacco, beer, ale, wine, muslins and calicoes, granted in 1697, in Dec. 1702; and the additional tobacco impost granted in 1699, in June 1703 (McGrath, *Constitution*, 35–7, 39–40).

it bore no proporcion to what England payes toward the war, but beside him no body that I know or now remember said one word to the contrary of this. Some proposed that England having stopt up all the sources of mony that used to come hither, or at least most of them, we could not subsist unlesse some trade (not interfering with theirs, yet beneficial to us) were opened for us; but no body was happy enough to find that out: At length it came to be discoursed what bills were proper to be prepared in order to be offered to the Councel here for a transmission into England;[609] and a discourse arose about sending a money bill: I delivered my thoughts frankly, that it would be ill taken to have a mony bill sent by the Queen and Councel rejected; I added that perhaps it might soe fall out, either because the nature of the tax or the time of its continuance might be disliked: and since if the publick occasions were answered, it mattered not what way it was brought about, and that they who were to give, best knew where the tax might be laid soe as to doe least prejudice and inasmuch as I beleived the Parliament would not fail to give to the utmost of their power, when they were convinced of the necessity of giving a supply I thought it would be the safest way to attain the end if the bills of supply were left wholly to the house. The Attornye (who, by the by, was the person who first started the question about and in expresse words added the offensive word sole to the question,[610] for it originally run thus, that it was the right of the commons to frame money bills) harangued, that he was on his oath to preserve the prerogative, and that he could not with justice to the Crown or with faith to my Lord Lieutenant admit that soe essential a prerogative as sending a mony bill should be neglected; having been sent by all former governements since the revolucion: and Mr Keightley[611] harped much on this later part of the Attorneys discourse, which in truth was not begun by him with any regard to the Crown; but to incline my Lords freinds (Erle and Keightley) to beleive he was very sollicitous of my Lords well fare, and that I neglected it or rather laid a trap for him, as if it might be made matter of complaint hereafter in England against him that he had not sent such a bill: I knew my own intentions, and having real service for Lord Rochester and beleiving a Parliament would certainly have been held by him, was very sollicitous about the successe of it; I knew that his Lordship was not so acceptable to a great part of this Kingdome as I could wish, and that there were some here that would take any handle to disappoint him in holding a Parliament successefully, who would not appear barefaced by denying money, but by quarrelling at the maner and nature of the tax; which would as effectually answer their ends as a flat denial: for we have not funds of different kinds to pitch on as in England: our land in many parts hardly is able to pay the quitrent, and will bear no tax; our exports are very inconsiderable and our trade is at too low an ebb to give it a farther discouragement by laying addicional dutyes on the exports: soe as the continuing the addicional excise or addicional dutyes on wines and tobacco were the only funds left us, and if a bill should be offered us for continuing those dutyes and be rejected on any pretence whatsoever, we can not the same session bring in another bill to lay dutyes on them and then the supply could not be granted for want of a fund: I was not free to let every body then present know my reasons for remitting the whole matter of money to the house, but gave this in general that I thought it the best

[609] According to the provisions of Poynings' Law, which required that bills be prepared in the Irish privy council in order to the calling of a parliament.

[610] In the parliament of 1692 (see above, p. 54).

[611] Thomas Keightley, MP [I].

and most certain method to have aids granted according to the wants of the publick; that supposing the Crown might send money bills, there was no necessitye of alway doing it and that I beleived omitting it would neither be a betraying the prerogative, nor the sending one an incumbent duty on my Lord Lieutenant: but I found by Mr Keightley that he took it as done in prejudice to Lord R[*ochester*] and asked me if I had ever before advised former Governements not to send money bills; I told him I never had given advice one way or the other, and said that if the money bill they resolved to send should miscarry on any account I was free from that miscarriage having given my sense against sending any, which they would please to remember: he said resentingly, it should be remembred: Before this meeting the Judges and Queens Councel had met on the same occasion at the Councel chamber where I was of the same opinion, and differing from most if not all the rest about sending a money bill. Sir Richard Cox desired me to draw my sense in writing which I did (I think on a sheet of paper on which he had wrote some thing else) but it no way imported any asserting the sole right, nor I think mentioned it; at most it was to caution them least sending a money bill might draw the matter into debate at a season when people were (as I thought) too much irritated by the treatment they have mett: but that I delivered any paper of reasons to assert the sole right to the Lords Justices, or ever wrote any thing to that purpose (so much as in a letter) these seven years, I would say is an hellish falsitye if I were not informed who have wrote the contrarye: but on this trial I will put my self, to be exposed for the most profligate villain and falsest rascal on earth if any such paper can be shewn of my writing or signing: If I gave them such a paper, they can produce it. If any writing they have of mine about a money bill, I never gave it them but was desired by Sir R[*ichard*] C[*ox*] to reduce my sense into writing, and he perhaps may have officiously handed it to Mr K[*eightley*] and the other two have been perswaded it imports my asserting the sole right, which it doth not and for the truth of this I appeal to the paper. We are here now wholly under his[612] ministry (I mean in subordinacion to Lord O[*rmond*]) he visibly takes on him to be acting minister, expects to be soon declared Chancellor and I wish a notion, that nothing but making him the new Chancellor and laying aside the old can facilitate the Queens businesse in Parliament, may not imbarasse it: he neither is the valued nor beloved, nor Mr M[*ethuen*] the distastfull man he would perswade and great people apprehend: and assure your self people wonder how Mr M[*ethuen'*]s behavior in Portugal[613] hath intitled him to be disgraced when he could stand his ground against all efforts till he had brought that matter to passe. Burn this letter and shew it to no body … I grow sickly and weary of seeing matters go as they are like to doe with reference to this poor country. One thing I will remind you, that upon my word he misrepresents matters in saying I am the only Lawyer of opinion with the sole right; for I assure you if I am of that opinion, I am not alone: but as I never broached the notion much lesse (if I had) with intent to make an advantagious use of it, I never will pretend to be of another mind to curry favor: that and all other things that can call this a free country are over, and tho I will not flourish on its ruine I am too old to sacrifice my self for a senselesse sort of wretches, lead by a dish of meat, a flask of Burgundye, and above all by the caresses of great men … I … will not long be on this side the water, but while here will endeavour to act for the Queens service,

[612] Cox.

[613] As envoy-extraordinary 1701–2.

my Lord Lieutenants honour, and the good of this unhappy country, which are not the principles all steer by that pretend to doe soe …

[*PS.*] Part of this letter is wrote since my brother landed on the 6th. I should tell you my Lord[614] is civil and truly kind to me.

75. *Alan I, Dublin, to Thomas, Mallow, 7 July 1703*

(1248/2/100–1)

Yesterday morning early I gott to Ballygaule[615] where I mett my sister and children very well; God send that I may by next post have an account of your being soe. The little time I have been here hath given me so much light into matters that I have good reason to beleive Mr L[616] will not pretend farther; at least he hath very lately declared in publick he will not accept of it,[617] nor be in the house if any thing of the kind should be intended; but since he once swerved from what he promised, his declaracion is no farther to be regarded then as the words of a man that will not doe an ill thing without prospect of successe: and that I take to be his case, after all the efforts that have been made. I find too that the pretensions of — have endeavoured to be again sett on foot; nay Sir Sir J[*ohn*] M[*eade*] hath been named, and Sir R[*ichard*] L[*evinge'*]s name hath been thrown out to see what peoples sentiments might be; but I have reason to beleive all will end in an unanimous choice of the man that was last in some peoples intencions,[618] and that a vertue will be made of necessitye: doe not so much as speak of this, or indeed of the chair at all, otherwise then to declare my pretensions continue as formerly: I will soon either write you the whole series of this management, or tell you it by word of mouth if I may soon expect to see you. Let me caution and intreat you not too far to trust or unbosome your self to the Gentleman that praised your stud etc. or the person you wrote to about a man of figure that was endeavoured to be sett up etc. they are both men of intreague; I have demonstracion for it, but ask no questions …[619]

76. *Alan I, Dublin, to Thomas, Cork, 14 Aug. 1703*

(1248/2/105–6)

I can be particular with you but would not have you communicate it; the matter of Mr Ludlow is wholly declined, and I am secure of his, Mr Tenisons,[620] Mr Johnsons,[621]

[614] Ormond.

[615] Ballynagaul.

[616] Stephen Ludlow, MP [I].

[617] The Speakership of the Irish house of commons.

[618] i.e. himself.

[619] Added at top of page: 'Sir R[*ichard*] C[*ox*] was sworn yesterday [*as lord chancellor*].'

[620] Henry Tenison, MP [I].

[621] Robert Johnson, MP [I].

Mr Crows,[622] and Mr Blighs[623] interest; Lord Chancellor now tells me I may depend on Lord Lieutenants not interposing, so as the contest will be between the Atturnye and me; he stil is working all he can, but I beleive it will be without successe. However I have wrote to Hassett[624] into Kerry, Oliver[625] to Limrick, Stratford[626] for Kildare and Carloe, Sir John Dillon[627] for Meath and will to others in other Countyes, to send me a list of those I may depend on. I think you will doe well as you come up to call in at Kilkennye, and it will be of service to be in town with some freinds a little before the day. I take it Charles Oliver will be chose for the County of Limrick, and his son[628] at Kilmallock; if so, there will be a place void at Middleton, for I doe not foresee there can be any trick plaid either in the election of the County or City of Corke nor doe I think any thing like it is intended; however it will be fit for you to inform your self of the time and place of election, and to be on the spot with some freinds beforehand; but let it be done in concert with Sir John Percival and seem to have no diffidence, particularly not of the sherif; who I really take to be a very honest young Gentleman. But the Middleton election must not be appointed till that of the County and City are both over; tho from the later I have all assurance in the world to find no opposicion. I apprehend none unlesse a little cunning man with whom you formerly had more intimacye then you now have should put in some freind or son of his own;[629] I would not put such a thing into peoples heads, however you may endeavour to inform your self, and particularly about St Dominicks.[630] I have no reason to doubt but that the Lieutenant General will remember his promise to me, and must not doubt his being a man of honour; he told me to day he was assured when last in Corke of being elected without going down,[631] and that he spoke of leaving mony in some freinds hands to make the City drink successe to the Session of Parliament, but that he was told it was unfit or unnecessarye I know not which. For my part I neither need nor intend to buy votes with treating, but desire you will take care to have a brace of bucks (one at the Mayors,[632] the other at Mr Peningtons[633]) out of Cahirmone, and a chine and surloyne of beef at each place; and Clarett to make such drink as think fit. I leave this to your care and desire you to consult the Mayor and Tom Brown[634] in the management of it. I would not be profuse, nor mean

[622]William Crowe, MP [I].

[623]Thomas Bligh, MP [I].

[624]John Blenerhassett, sr, MP [I].

[625]Charles Oliver, MP [I].

[626]Edward Stratford, MP [I].

[627]Sir John Dillon, MP [I].

[628]Robert Oliver, MP [I].

[629]Possibly Sir Francis Brewster, MP [I].

[630]This may well be a reference to Glanworth, Co. Cork, the residence of Bartholomew Purdon, MP [I]; St Dominic's holy well was nearby.

[631]Robert Rogers, one of the outgoing MPs for Cork had already stepped aside for lieutenant-general Thomas Erle, having been informed that Erle wished to be returned for the city (Churchill Archives Centre, Erle papers 2/55/2: Rogers to Erle, 25 Oct. 1702).

[632]John Whiting of Mountrivers, Co. Cork (*Cork Council Bk*, 301; Charles Smith, *The Antient and Present State of the County and City of Cork …* (2 vols, Cork, 1815), i, 177).

[633]Ferdinando Pen(n)ington (*d*. by 1724), sheriff of Cork city in 1697 (*Cork Council Bk*, 259, 448).

[634]Thomas Brown(e) (*d*. by 1729), common councilman of Cork 1690, town clerk 1695, later sheriff and alderman (Vicars, *Index*, 58; *Cork Council Bk*, 207, 239, 242).

in the maner of doing it: remember Burrige; a proposal is made that his freinds and Mr Ashes shal be put in a roll, and the lesse number join with the greater to oppose any third man;[635] this I think very fair but Burrige is out of town and I have not had opportunitye to communicate it to him. I do[?e] write to Clayton,[636] but both you and he must put Sir John Percival in mind of me, and he must speak to Robin FitzGerald of Castledod.[637] My brother and Senny are both well and your servants. Make it your businesse to engage all people to be up the day before our meeting at the farthest; perhaps he whose interest lies cheifly in the nighest province may have a short adjournement given out, but depend on it we fall to businesse the first minute.

[*PS.*] If Lord Doneraile[638] be come over or when ever he does praye secure his two members for me[639] by his promise: and if you have thoughts of Arthur Hyde[640] at Middleton, make him assure me the vote of his father in Law George Evans.[641]

77. *Alan I, Dublin, to Thomas (or in his absence Richard Bettesworth, White Rock,[642] near Midleton), 19 Aug. 1703*

(1248/2/107–8)

Senny is gone this morning with my sister Martha Courthope[643] in my chariot to Camphire:[644] indeed one main reason of his going down was to oblige my sister to goe down in the chariot, who positively refused to take it and would not have been perswaded to use it but under the impossibilitye of sending him otherwise. It was a great doubt with me whether I should let him goe down or not; staying in town had its objections, and going down a great many: but considering the short time allotted him to stay, soe as it will be morally impossible in that space for pick thank people to insinuate themselves into him, especially as I have formed to my self the way of his spending his time in Munster I agreed in opinion with my brother to let him goe down.

They will be at my Lady Foulkes[645] on Sonday before which day this letter will reach you if Dick Langley forward it as I desire; pray let a servant (with an horse for him to ride) go

[635] Presumably a reference to the forthcoming general election, in which it seems that 'Burridge' and 'Ashe' were to stand together. One Thomas Ashe, was returned for the freeman borough of Cavan in 1703; his namesake, who had represented Swords in the preceding parliament, was not elected in 1703. 'Burridge' has not been identified, though he may be identical with Thomas Burrows or Burroughs, who was elected for Carysfort, Co. Wicklow in the general election of 1703 but unseated on petition on 15 Oct. 1703 (*CJI*, iii, 45).

[636] Laurence Clayton, MP [I].

[637] Robert Fitzgerald, MP [I], of Castle Dod, Co. Cork.

[638] Arthur St Leger, MP [I], 1st Viscount Doneraile [I].

[639] For the borough of Doneraile.

[640] Arthur Hyde, MP [I].

[641] George Evans, sr, MP [I].

[642] Part of the estate of Cahermone, leased by Sir St John Brodrick to Richard Bettesworth in 1700 (SHC, G145/box142/4, pp 16–17).

[643] Strictly speaking, his aunt by marriage.

[644] An estate in the north-west of Co. Waterford, lying across the Blackwater river from the Villiers property at Dromana.

[645] Probably the wife of Robert Foulke, MP [I].

thither early on Monday morning and bring him to White Rock on Monday night, where and about Middleton he may spend Tuesday and on Wednesday goe to Rathcormack and dine there and goe that night to Mallow, and spend Thursday there and goe on Fryday to Corke, thence to Middleton on Saturday and on Sunday to Youghal and see my sister Jephson[646] and early on Monday to Camphire soe as my sister and he may goe that night to Clonmel in their way and return hither. I am sensible how much trouble this must put either on you or in your absence on Dick Bettesworth, whom I must intreat to keep him company if you cannot: for tho I have noe great fear of any danger of peoples getting within him by insinuations, yet I will not trust him among some folke without guardians. His orders are to act by my brothers, or in his absence by Dick Bettesworths direction: and let me beg he may not have much time to spend with some people, especially at Youghal; and let him not fail to pay the greatest duty to my sister Clayton,[647] whose sister he is obliged to more then all the earth can tell except my self. He may hunt on Tuesday if he ask to doe soe, or be fond of it; but let it not be proposed to him. Bootes must be carried over for him, for I think he carried none down; Young Dick Bettesworth[648] is well. I am told the matter of Speaker is settled by the Attorneys waving all pretensions; yet my freinds must not depend too much on fair words. Pray let Dick Bettesworth[649] out of Popes money defray the expence of my election if received, if not I will remit it …

[*PS.*] I hope you will be able to come up with my sister; indeed it is of importance to the countrey and to me in particular to have you up early. I wish you would lye one night in Kilkennye and see the Duke;[650] but you need stay no longer. I gave him[651] twelve Guineys; let him be asked if he want money and if he doe supply him: for as I would not have him profuse I hate the thoughts of his being stinted so as to doe a mean thing. As I have laid it out he will lye one night at Youghal; my brother or Dick Bettesworth must keep him company there every minute, nay and lye with him.

78. *Alan I, Dublin, to Thomas, Cork, 26 Aug. 1703*

(1248/2/109–10)

I am not at all in pain about the election with reference to any thing intended by the Sherif:[652] but by a letter from Jemmy Barry[653] dated the two and twentieth I find he intends to make an harangue, and what the consequences of that may be I cannot foresee: the election was over assoon as I received it, so could not caution him in the matter, which

[646]Anne, née Barry, the sister of Alan's first wife. She had married William Jephson (*d.* c.1720), dean of Lismore.

[647]Anne, née Courthope, sister of Alan's second wife and husband of Laurence Clayton.

[648]Richard Bettesworth (1689–1741), of Dublin, son of Richard and elected MP [I] for Thomastown, Co. Kilkenny, in 1721.

[649]Richard, sr.

[650]Ormond: Kilkenny Castle was the Butler family's principal seat. Ormond had travelled there from Dublin the previous day (NLI, MS 991, p. 114: Edward Southwell to the earl of Nottingham, 19 Aug. 1703).

[651]St John III.

[652]William Supple (*d.* c.1715) of Aghadoe, Co. Cork (*Burke's Irish Family Records*, ed. Hugh Montgomery-Massingberd (1976), 174; Phillimore, *Indexes*, ii, 151).

[653]James Barry, MP [I], Alan's brother-in-law (from his first marriage).

considering all things may for ought I know have been very necessarye; for his haughtinesse may have carried him to doe or say some warm or indiscreet thing; if it did he was to blame: but if he managed himself with temper, he might well enough say that Sir John owed his election to the good will of the County and not to any one man that might pretend to have an interest in it to sett up a Knight of the Shire.[654] Now the time draws nigh and that the matter of being Speaker seems more then probable I am in great perplexity considering the difficultye of the Sessions and trouble of managing such a familye and keeping such an house as I am obliged to doe during the Sessions, considering the only stay and support of my life is taken away;[655] pray hasten up, that I may have your advice and assistance. You could not but guesse my Lord Lieutenant was at Kilkennye when I advised your coming that way, but now I see no occasion for it. I would have matters not run to any great expence at Corke. The boy is breeding more eye teeth and was hot last night, the girle is well; St John was out of order, but it is over. It will be of singular use if I can have a deer and some hare and partridge potted in small pots and sent up about the beginning of the Session; but the carriage and time of delivery must be expressely agreed for; some times they let things lye a month or six weeks. My Cousen Bettesworth is the only body I can trouble or depend on herein.

If you have not bought an hogshead of wine for Mr Mowlesworth[656] it will be too late to answer his end which is to spend at the election of this County[657] and then you must let it alone: if you have bought it, send it up by the first conveniencye.

79. *Alan I, Dublin, to Thomas, Cork, 31 Aug. 1703*

(1248/2/111–12)

I hope this will be the last letter you receive from me in the County of Corke; for really it is no more then necessary that people were in town a little beforehand, considering what is like to be in agitacion. By a letter from Jack Hassett[658] I find Arthur Hyde is elected or to be elected at Tralee, soe you are free from any promise there: and that makes room for what upon serious consideracion I think very advisable, that my brother St John be chosen and returned at Middleton. It is true he will not sit, at least this Session; but he is of opinion and soe am I that being of the house will be of some importance in more wayes then one, which are not fit to be committed to paper but you shal know when we meet. I doubt he will be gone before you come up, but by all means let him be chosen …

[*PS.*] His serving must silence all other pretenders and give no cause of distast to any body for his being preferred.

[654] Thomas Brodrick and Sir John Perceval were elected unopposed (BL, Add. MS 29589, f. 119: Edward Southwell to Nottingham, 29 Aug. 1703).

[655] A reference to the recent death of his second wife, Lucy.

[656] Robert Molesworth, MP [I].

[657] Co. Dublin.

[658] Either John Blenerhassett, sr, or his son and namesake: both MPs [I].

80. *Alan I, Dublin, to Thomas, at the Whitehall coffee-house, King's Street, Westminster, 25 Jan. 1703/4*

(1248/2/119–20)

Tho it be impossible that we should have any account of your having gott safe to Chester by the packetts boat which arrived this morning and brought six mailes, yet I make no doubt of your having made a good passage, the weather being very calm and the wind fair long enough to carry you over if we compute right. None of our bills are come, but Mr Southwell[659] shewed me a list of seven publick and fowre private bills that had been agreed to at Council: whether any alterations (which some have of late used to call by the name of amendments) are in any and which of them I cannot learn, I hope not in our bill of money. We are again adjourned in expectacion of their coming soon till Fryday the 28th of this month upon a message from the Lord Lieutenant.[660] Last Munster post brought you several letters which I open and send you the contents to save postage. … A letter from Sir F[*rancis*] B[*rewster*] is very pressing against the late Jury that passed their verdict on the estates of this Kingdome;[661] but beware of trusting him; it is true he hates them, but is not a whit honester then they. … Pray tell me, is not what I have too long been fearful of, making hast toward us …

81. *Alan I, Dublin, to Thomas, at the Whitehall coffee-house, King's Street, Westminster, 27*[662] *Jan. 1703/4*

(1248/2/121–2)

I have little doubt of your being in England safe tho we have not yet heard that you are soe; the weather was too fair to give us any apprehensions for you. Whatever you may think of your self I assure you in my opinion you came very well of in comparison of poor Mr N—tt,[663] who went to Wapping[664] and told a dismal and as he affirms a true tale of the Tories[665] in that part of the Countrey where his habitacion is; your never saw a fellow soe scared as he seemed to be (at my house) soon after at the reception he mett; to the best of

[659]Edward Southwell, MP [I], Ormond's chief secretary.

[660]Confirmed in *CJI*, iii, 164. The following day (26 Jan.) Southwell reported to Lord Treasurer Godolphin (NLI, MS 991, p. 229), 'Yesterday we received six packets together. The want of them had given great opportunities to several that wished it, to report the alteration of the money bill, that the calico clause was struck out, that the popery bill would not pass, and very few of the others which were industriously spread, so that cabals were forming to oppose the passing the money bill. I never saw an adjournment so well attended and in so bad a season but the extraordinary favour her Majesty and the Council have shown in despatching so many of our bills beyond all our expectation has made everything cheerful and easy, and I hope our session will be very short in the passing them after their arrival.' See also *CSP Dom.*, 1703–4, 509.

[661]The forfeiture trustees.

[662]Dated 27 Jan. and presumably begun on that day, but at least part of the letter must have been written on the 28th.

[663]Possibly Charles Norcott or Northcote, for whom see below, p. 166.

[664]Possibly a reference to Wapping Street in Dublin.

[665]Used here in the sense of an Irish rural brigand.

my memorye it was to this purpose, that the Gentleman to whom he made his moan asked him whether he could swear to the truth of all he had said; his answer was that to a great part of it he could, but not to all, but that it was the general complaint of the neighbourhood: he saith he was told that he deserved to be hanged for alarming or disturbing people as he did; I think those words import the reason given why he deserved to be hanged, but am certain I do not mistake the reward that Gentleman declared him intitled to for what he had done. I am well informed there is a presentment come up out of our countrey against several who have taken away Abbots daughter etc.[666] I will not trouble you with a long story of that matter, which will end in toryes being out for fear of sharing N—tts punishment as well as crime. The letter is come over for appointing Mr Everard[667] and Mr Tenison[668] two of our Commissioners in Carleton and Van Homrighs room;[669] and I am told it is with a blank for Tenisons Christian name, but I doubt not the man is too well known to have it doubted whether Harry Tenison be not the person that hath merited that station; soe as I presume such a matter will put no delay to the renewing the Commission. I received a letter yesterday dated the 11th from a Gentleman that I doubt hath been with you and hath prevailed with you to use more freedome toward him then I would have you. That you may know the man, he could be very well content to have made one in the Commission we last talked of, nay formerly to have been a trustee; I doe not mean a Knight, and now I think it very hard if you can mistake him. Keep free of him, for he doth not act upon principle, nay every act of his life in my opinion hath shewn him self ended. I will answer his letter which is a modest desire that I would write two or three sheets of paper containing an account of our proceedings, to be laid by him before great men for (as I guesse) to inform him how to represent things to them, who he saith know not what to beleive; I am perswaded that he will make private use of every thing and I will not doe an invidious act nor take a trouble on me to gratifye a man who loves himself only. The town is very full, and people begin to be uneasy at our being soe long in town to no purpose: we are again adjourned to Tuesday by message,[670] and how long farther God knows; for till our bills come I see we are not to doe businesse; so printing our representacion sleeps till the bills come over at least.[671] Gentlemen seem steddy to doe as becomes them, and I

[666]In this period the abduction and forced marriage of heiresses was a crime particularly associated with the province of Munster (James Kelly, 'The Abduction of Women of Fortune in Eighteenth-Centry Ireland', *ECI*, ix (1994), 25). The aggrieved father on this occasion may well have been Charles Abbott (*d.* c. 1706), of Derrysallagh, Co. Cork, who had married in 1689 and could thus have had a daughter of the appropriate age (Phillimore, *Indexes*, ii, 1; H. W. Gillman, *Index to the Marriage Licence Bonds of the Diocese of Cork and Ross …* (Cork, 1896–7), 1).

[667]Thomas Everard of Southampton (Southampton Archives Services, quarter sessions records, SC 9/5/283), formerly a gauger in that port and an excise commissioner [E] 1696–1700, with a reputation for zeal and ostentatious efficiency which did not always endear him to his colleagues. He was best known as the author of *Stereometrie Made Easy, or The Description and Use of a New Gauging-Rod or Sliding Rule …* (1684), which served as a manual for gauging and presented to the world a new slide-rule of Everard's invention. It went through eleven editions by 1750. See Edward Hughes, *Studies in Administration and Finance, 1558–1835* (Manchester, 1934), 186, 198, 208, 210, 230; W. J. Ashworth, *Customs and Excise: Trade, Production and Consumption in England, 1640–1845* (Oxford, 2003), 115.

[668]Henry Tenison, MP [I].

[669]Commissioners of the revenue in place of Bartholomew Vanhomrigh and Christopher Carleton, who died on 29 Dec. 1703 and 2 Jan. 1704 respectively.

[670]*CJI*, iii, 165, records the adjournment as being ordered on Thursday 28 Jan.

[671]The Commons had agreed on 20 Oct. 1703 a representation to the queen detailing 'the present distressed condition of this kingdom' (*CJI*, iii, 65–7): it denounced the forfeiture trustees, complained at the decline of trade

beleive men will be pretty much of the mind they were when we last parted. We talk here of Mr L[*udlow*']s[672] succeeding Lord Berkley in the mastership of the rolls;[673] he being an indigent man, if there be any part of the money wanting beyond what the disposal of his present emploiment yeilds[674] why should not a present of such a trivial summe be made to a person of so great merit? I hear there is a ballad made on some of our members in imitacion of that on the conformitye bill,[675] but I have not seen it; it is among those on whom it is made but I hear of no one whom I am acquainted with that hath it; whence I guesse it was made in England. George McCartney[676] tells me he saw it this evening in Jemmy Stopfords hands.[677] You cant imagine what an alteracion I observe in some mens faces: I have civilities, nay visits from some whom till very late I have not had the happinesse to be spoken to by in some months past; heats are desired to be avoided, and all things were intended for the best on all hands, and we shal and must be very good freinds again: nay (now we are told the money bill is not altered (which I will beleive when I see cause) they would not have given their vote for it, if it had been altered: Lady Dorchester I suppose they will think no alteracion.[678]

82. *Alan I, Dublin, to Thomas, at the Whitehall coffee-house, King's Street, Westminster, 10 Feb. 1703/4*

(1248/2/123–4)

If my predecessor prove my successor[679] I shal neither be surprized nor mortifyed, nor at all wonder at matters being carried with an high hand some where: Upon my word I took up my resolutions on good and mature deliberacion, and shal not lay them down for any of those motives which grand Jurors are sworn shal not influence them in their enquiries … Assoon as our Session is over I will endeavour to obtain leave to goe for England, which I find to be of absolute necessitye for my health; tho probably I may not have occasion to

671 (*continued*) and the 'want of holding frequent parliaments' in Ireland, and called for either a restoration of 'a full enjoyment of our constitution' or 'a more firm and strict union' with England. It is discussed in Hayton, 'Ideas of Union', 159–60, and (to the same purpose but in greater detail) in McGrath, '"Union" Representation of 1703', 11–35. On 20 Jan. 1704 the Commons resolved to print the representation 'the first day we come to business' (*CSP Dom.*, 1703–4, 506), but postponed this drastic step in expectation of receiving the queen's answer. When this arrived the decision of printing was put off for another month (Longleat House, Thynne MSS 25, f. 217: [——] to Lord Nottingham, 13 Feb.1703/4), with the result that eventually time ran out. Alan's papers contain three motions, in his own hand, relating to alternative dates for printing the representation (SHC, 1248/9/170).

672 Stephen Ludlow, MP [I].

673 William Berkeley (c.1664–1741), 4th baron Berkeley of Stratton, who had been appointed master of the rolls in Ireland in 1696 and retained that office until 1731.

674 Ludlow was one of the six clerks in chancery [I].

675 Probably Arthur Maynwaring, *The History and Fall of the Conformity Bill* … [1704].

676 George Macartney, MP [I].

677 James Stopford, MP [I].

678 The supply bill had included a clause imposing a tax on several pensions, including that granted by James II to his sometime mistress Catherine Sedley (1657–1717), *suo jure* countess of Dorchester (*CSP Dom.*, 1703–4, 194)).

679 As solicitor-general [I]. The previous incumbent was Sir Richard Levinge, MP [I].

seek the favor of being permitted to doe it.[680] Our Popery bill is cried up as the best in the world; Mr A. Sanders[681] and Mr Bernard[682] shewed me an extract of the heads of it and magnifye it extremely, as infinitely better then when we sent it over: Mr Attorney you know seldome commends or censures with overmuch moderacion, and runs out into high flights in its praise: People are to be possessed wonderfully in its favour, and it is done by them whom I never heard speak formerly in favor of it or concern themselves about it: We must see it and what the tacks to it are, the sacramental test is I find one of them:[683] A letter on this subject will be here before it passes.

11 Feb 1703/4

We have mett[684] and read the bill to make it treason to write etc. against the Succession,[685] and that of butchers being Graziers;[686] and Mr Stopfords and Mr Stephens private bills:[687] We have had the Queens answer to our representacion which if I can gett copied before I seal this shal be sent you,[688] and is worth considering. A mocion was made to print our representacion and that together, by Maxwell; and to be done forthwith: seconded by Mr St George[689] and others: Mr Attorney first opposed it; they who spoke are as follows and those who were against printing it then are dashed under; I put them in the order they spoke. Mr Maxwell Mr Attorney[690] Mr Ludlow Dopping Neve Ponsonby Blundell Conoly Mr Stewart[691] Mr A. Sanders[692] Clayton Dean[693] Ecchlin[694] Keightley Dopping again

[680] As an office-holder, Brodrick needed to obtain a licence from the crown in order to be absent from the kingdom without penalty.

[681] Anderson Saunders, MP [I].

[682] Francis Bernard, MP [I].

[683] The clause imposing on all holders of crown and municipal office the necessity of qualifying themselves by taking holy communion in the established church.

[684] On the 11 Feb..

[685] The bill to make it high treason in Ireland 'to impeach the succession to the crown, as limited by several acts of parliament' was presented and read for the first time on 11 Feb. (*CJI*, iii, 167).

[686] The bill to prevent butchers from being graziers and to redress several abuses in buying and selling of cattle and in the slaughtering and packing of beef, tallow and hides, which was also presented and read for the first time on 11 Feb. (*CJI*, iii, 167).

[687] Bills to enable the vesting in trustees property belonging to James Stopford, MP [I] in County Meath, to be sold for the payment of debts; and to confirm an exchequer judgment in the case of *Mary Poor* alias *Pennefather* v. *Walter Stephens*. Both were presented and read for the first time on 11 Feb. (*CJI*, iii, 167).

[688] Added at top of last page of letter: 'The Queens answer to our representacion. Anne R. Her Majesty having considered of the representacion made by the house of commons in Ireland has commanded this answer to be returned. That the first part of it seems to relate to matters past in Parliament, and the other part consisting only of things in general her Majestye can give no particular answer at present, but will take them into consideracion. [*Confirmed in* CJI, *iii,* 168.] Mr Attorney and others gave it the title of a gracious answer; but Conollye out did them all by stiling it a glorious one.'

[689] Henry, Oliver, or Richard St George: all were whigs.

[690] In this list an underlined name is clearly meant to indicate a tory, or at least a supporter of the administration, so that the remaining members must have been regarded as whigs, or opponents of administration.

[691] Hon. Richard Stewart.

[692] A teller in the division that followed against printing the representation 'forthwith' (*CJI*, iii, 168).

[693] Either Edward or Joseph Deane; both whigs.

[694] Either Robert Echlin, MP [I] Newry, or his namesake, a brigadier-general, who sat for Co. Monaghan. Both supported Ormond's administration.

(by leave)[695] Cuningham Johnson McCartney, Moore, Beachampe Whitshed, Tenison Leving Lord Moore,[696] Allen, Savage, Mr Attorney again Dr Sanders.[697] Do not think Mr Dopping changed his mind by the stroke on his name the second time, it was my mistake. The Question was put that our representacion be forthwith printed; Yeas 82 Noes 125:[698] second question That the printing it be put off for a month. Yeas 108. Noes 100.[699] It was after moved that these resolucions should not be printed but that fell by vote of adjournement.[700] We shal have a short and I think an easy Session, for many seem resolved to ask leave to goe into the Countrey and others will stay in town, enough to doe the businesse. Mr Richard Stewart made a sett speech[701] and (they say) a very fine on the subject; but Jack Allens was a very strange one. He said he was of opinion against printing, and had no sooner said so but had well moved roared out by our Judge that is to be[702] and a tall Gentleman that is famous for seconding all motions: but his reasons surprised them, which were; 1. because he had given his word it should be printed as soon as we mett, and was for swerving from it as well as others. 2. We had this very morning broken an order of the house in another ca[*se*] (he meant an order of 2 Nov. last about no serv[*ants*] being priviledged that were not entred with our Clerk as menial servants,[703] yet we sent for the Serjeants at the mace of Cork in custody for arresting one not soe entred:[704] 3. but his last was the worst, He said he expected an emploiment, and feared if our representacion should be printed now, he should loose it. Some people were in pain for him, but no body moved to call him in question; only Mr T[*eniso*]n went to him and in a freindly way asked him whether he could have so poor an opinion of any Gentleman within these walls as to think the expectacion of an emploiment could influence his vote; I hear he answered, that he did not think the expectacion of an emploiment influenced him. Others wondred that a Gentleman who spoke against printing the representacion should presently change his opinion and divide for it. But these were not very many.

[695] Presumably, as at Westminster, it was a rule of the House that no Member could speak twice to the same motion (unless by leave).

[696] Charles, Viscount Moore.

[697] Morley Saunders.

[698] Confirmed in *CJI*, iii, 168.

[699] Confirmed in *CJI*, iii, 168.

[700] *CJI* records that immediately following the second division the House adjourned to the following Monday 'on a question' (but without providing details of a division) (*CJI*, iii, 168)

[701] Prepared and written out in advance. See above, p.65.

[702] Robert Johnson, soon to be translated to the judicial bench as a baron of the exchequer [I], but still active in the House (*CJI*, iii, 173, 176). A writ for a by-election to his vacant seat was issued at the outset of the following session, on 10 Feb. 1705 (*CJI*, iii, 222).

[703] An order of the House on 2 Nov. 1703 that no individual could be regarded as the 'menial servant' of a Member and thus protected by parliamentary privilege unless registered as such in advance with the clerk of the House (*CJI*, iii, 93).

[704] On 11 Feb. one of the sheriffs of Cork city and the serjeants of the mace for the borough were ordered into custody for arresting a servant of 'Mr Freke' (*CJI*, iii, 167). This presumably Percy Freke, MP [I] for Baltimore, rather than his namesake George, MP [I] for Clonakilty, who held a military rank.

83. *Alan I, Dublin, to Thomas, at the Whitehall coffee-house, King's Street, Westminster, 17 Feb. 1703/4*

(1248/2/125–6)

I have yours of the tenth, and by it find that the same discourse is with you and here about Mr R[ochfor]t[705] being to be made a Lord, and Sir R[*ichard*] L[*evinge*] to come in play: by a former that I wrote you will find it to be no news, and that the scheme framed here is Sir R[*ichard*] L[*evinge*] to succeed him[706] and Mr B me:[707] We are in very great hast, in dispatching all affairs; we just read bills and ordered them generally another reading next day, and so committ them for the following etc. this will dispatch affairs, and all people seem willing the Session were over, either that my Lord Lieutenant may be at libertye to goe over assoon as he will, or for fear of matters being done which some neither wish nor are able to prevent. Our freind whom you are to sue for Lady O[*rkney'*]s money[708] seems to be very discontented, being for ought I can hear like not to succeed according to his either expectacion or merit: he broke out two dayes agoe in the house into this abrupt speech, Clayton sitting near him and no preceding words giving any rise to such a resolucion: By God I will goe into the Countrey next Monday, let the money go which way it will: there are more aking hearts then his: all will be done that is possible, but our Saviour could not without the expence of a miracle feed five thousand with so few loaves and fishes[709] as were then in store. I fancy it will be one part of — satisfaction to be free from the sollicitacions of so many mouths that he hath not wherewith to stop.[710]

Since writing the other side your letter of the twelfth is come in; I wonder at my good freinds the trustees making me a scribler: I saw the print which I beleive you mean,[711] for Ol St G[712] had one which came to him in a wrapper from an unknown hand, which he shewed me in the house and I brought home wiith me where I read it since. It is soe printed that in several places it is not intelligible, but since you say it gauls them I am very well content to have them beleive me the Author of it; not would I give them or any freind of theirs the satisfaction of disowning it being very much pleased any way to expresse the abhorrence and hatred I have to them and their proceedings. But really I cant devise what part of the pamphlet it is that makes them beleive it mine; there is one expression that the writer had formerly suffered by them for speaking truth, and perhaps they may found their conjecture on this, knowing that to be my case, but soe it was of many other Gentlemen. It seems to me not written by the same hand, at least that the writer was in hast when he had gone half through and had taken lesse care in the later end of it then in the beginning. In

[705] Robert Rochfort.

[706] As attorney-general [I].

[707] Francis Bernard, to succeed as solicitor-general [I].

[708] Possibly William Ponsonby, MP [I] (see above, p. 120).

[709] A reference to the two miracles of Christ recorded in Matthew, 14: 13–21; 15: 32–9; Mark, 6: 31–44; 8: 1–9; Luke, 9: 10–17; and John, 6: 5–15.

[710] The lord lieutenant, Ormond.

[711] Unidentified.

[712] Oliver St George, MP [I].

short Jack Hassett[713] tells me that about the town either you or my brother[714] is supposed the author, but I cant hear which; but they say it is the style of a Brodrick. I am sure the conjectures here are guided by those from your side the water: I fancy if you had any of them I might have received one as well as several other people here did this post.

84. *Thomas to Alan I, Dublin, 24 Feb. 1703/4*

(1248/2/129–30)

The time which yours of the 11th lay on your side, added to my being out of town on Munday when it came, will probably occasion this reaching you after your session ended,[715] for I doubt nott butt that the majority are as willing to bee rid of the others, as they are to goe home. The Duke of Bolton assures mee that when the bill against the growth of popery was by her Majesty in councill ordered to bee ingrosed the clause for the sacramental test was nott in, if by the extensivenesse of expression the militia officers should bee included, or even a latitude left for explaining whither they bee soe or not, the consequence in my opinion may bee very dangerous, for if the northern militia bee once rendred ineffectual,[716] I see noe other prospect then that the papists may uppon any favourable opertunity doe what I ever shall thinke them inclined to, though others may call these surmises such a crime as deserves hanging, I am out of their reach, and will keep soe, till I can foresee hopes of speaking my thoughts in order to the security of the protestant interest of Ireland, without running that hazard. Jack Allens[717] speech I find is in every bodyes mouth; a member of this house of Commons in the publique coffee house this morning began a discourse of a bill for creating a registry in a part of Yorksheer which was promoted and carryed on by the gentlemen of that country,[718] several whoe had neither estates there, or perhaps ever seen itt, seemed extremely carefull of the bill, least any inconvenience might arise to that country from it, those concernd declared themselves very fully satisfyd with the advantages of itt, thankt the others for their care, butt desired that they might bee allowd to judge for themselves. Hee turned to mee and askt whether I could apply what hee had sayd to a paralel case. The Lords Committees have agreed to their report on our Addresse touching the exporting linnen, which had been this day made had nott her Maj[es]tys coming to the

[713]John Blenerhassett, sr or jr, both MPs [I].

[714]St John II.

[715]The Irish parliament was prorogued on 4 Mar. 1704 (*CJI*, iii,210).

[716]The sacramental test imposed on office-holders by a clause added to the popery bill in the English privy council extended to commissions in the militia, thus technically excluding Ulster presbyterians, who would not indulge in 'occasional conformity' and qualify themselves (though in practice the restriction seems to have been ignored). The issue was debated in the Irish parliament during proceedings on the returned popery bill and eventually, in 1716, presbyterians were afforded some relief by an act which indemnified them against penalties incurred by taking and acting on commissions. (J. C. Beckett, *Protestant Dissent in Ireland 1687–1780* (1948), 49, 71–4, 83–4; Neal Garnham, *The Militia in Eighteenth-century Ireland: In Defence of the Protestant Interest* (Woodbridge, 2012), 20–7.)

[717]See above, p. 154.

[718]A bill to establish a public registry of deeds in the West Riding of Yorkshire, which had been passed by the house of commons at Westminster on 12 Jan. 1704, and agreed by the Lords on 26 Jan. (*CJ*, xvii, 278, 308).

house prevented:[719] The whole is very favourable to us, and concludes with their opinion that a bill bee brought in for allowing what wee desire, and giving all farther encouragement therein; tis very probable itt may bee done this session, att least I doubt nott its being ordered, the consequence whereof is, that by their rules they take itt up againe the beginning of the next, soe that I hope you have had this under consideration when your linnen bill was first read.

Their Honors (the Trustees)[720] seem in some paine that the report from the Commissioners uppon their accounts is not like to come in this session, for in such cases nothing can bee safer then a discharge in full, though they should one would thinke have little grounds for feare, since tis morally certaine this present parliament will continue another yeare, and to make all sure on their sides, I heare a great deale of paine is taking for making Mr Ar. Anesley one of the Commissioners of accounts.[721]

I will neither adventure to say what is commonly talkt in relation to the scotch plot,[722] or give you my own sentiments, farther then that I thinke a damnable one evident beyond contradiction: I believe wee shall know something more certaine herein, then what wee yett doe, before the parliament rises.

Affairs in Holland are extremely perplext, different partyes now avow their own, under the name of the countryes interest, the want of that great man (to whose memory (tis sayd here some with you as well as elsewhere can scarcely allow a good word)[723] appears every day more then other, and will I doubt continue to doe soe.

The usuall slownesse of the german princes bringing their quotas into the field, gives but too much reason to feare that the french will take itt in each place earlyer then there will bee any equall numbers to receive them: People are nott without concerne for the transport ships which saild on Tuesday night last with the residue of the men for Portugal; there is a whisper about town that the french have fourteen ships abroad, which being noe match

[719] A response to the address agreed by the Irish house of commons on 23 Nov. 1703, asking for encouragement for the linen industry in Ireland, and in particular for permission to export Irish linens directly to the plantations (*CJI*, iii, 109–10). This had been referred by the queen to the English house of lords on 4 Jan. 1705 (*LJ*, xvii, 360). A favourable report was eventually made (by the chairman of the committee, Lord Somers) on 17 Mar. (*LJ*, xvii, 485–7). 'Mr Brodrick' was reported to be active among an Irish lobby in London pushing for legislation to give effect to the Lords'recommendations (HMC, *House of Lords MSS*, n.s., v, 343–4).

[720] The trustees for forfeited estates in Ireland.

[721] Arthur Annesley, MP [I]. He was elected (albeit in last place) as a commissioner under the public accounts bill, then going through parliament, the result of the ballot being reported to the Commons on 25 Feb. (*CJ*, xiv, 357). The bill did not pass, however, and the commission never came into existence.

[722] The English government had received intelligence in the summer of 1703 of a supposed jacobite intrigue to raise a rebellion in the Scottish Highlands, and Nottingham, as secretary of state, had been working to uncover details. Simultaneously the duke of Queensberry, who headed the ministry in Scotland, reported a promise of information on a jacobite conspiracy, which in fact was no more than a concoction of an unscrupulous Scottish intriguer, Lord Lovat. The two episodes became conflated into the so-called 'Scotch Plot', which was brought to the attention of the English house of lords in Dec.1703, and exploited by the whig junto as a means of attacking Nottingham for allegedly concealing evidence of treason. The tory-dominated house of commons then reacted in defence of Nottingham by questioning the right of the Lords to conduct inquiries, as an infringement of their own and the crown's prerogatives. (Henry Horwitz, *Revolution Politicks: The Career of Daniel Finch Second Earl of Nottingham, 1647–1730* (Cambridge, 1968), 191–6; P. W. J. Riley, *The Union of England and Scotland: A Study in Anglo-Scottish Politics of the Eighteenth Century* (Manchester, 1978), 71–2).

[723] King William III.

for Sir George Rooke[724] may possibly wait for the others; I hope and believe this rumor groundlesse, however wee know they never want intelligence, and seldom misse making use of oportunityes. Things att home have this good propect, this that every where appears a noble spiritt in the people of adhering to the succession so happily by law established, and defending both religious and civill rights to the last extremity.

I have nott been able to see the children this morning, butt my wife tells mee they are very well.

I am glad to find you continue your resolution of coming soon over, whither in or out of employment, you will find freinds whoe vallue a steddy honesty beyond titles purchased att the expense of itt.

My humble service to all our freinds, Ile soon write to Clayton and Conelly from both whom I have received letters by last packett.

85. *Alan I, Epsom, to Thomas, Newmarket, 15 Apr. 1704*

(1248/2/131–2)

I have yours of the 13th to which I ought to return some answer, tho I am at a stand what it shal be: the horse you describe of my Lord Whartons must be an high prizd one, and I know not how our rough countrey and the usage I shal give him in buck season, considering how he hath been kept hitherto and the ill stables he must some times meet with when we hunt out lying deer at distance from home will suit with him: to say truth I am not fond of an horse that comes out of such hands, for I fear he will fall off with the best keeping we can give him in Ireland if I make the use of him I intend, I mean buck hunt him. It will be impossible for me to accept his Lordships invitacion to Berkshire,[725] but when I return to London will wait on him and thank his Lordship for the honour he hath done me in giving me such an invitacion. The Duke of Bolton hath been here and hath almost engaged me to spend some time with him in Hantshire.[726] There is a sort of a Lampoon come out in Ireland which came this day to St John[727] from an unknown hand; but I fancy the Doctor hath counterfeited his own fist, so as to disguise it from me, tho some letters are exactly cut as his ordinarye way of writing is: It hath more in it then the English catalogue which it is made in imitacion of;[728] and you will think soe, if you can recollect the several transactions it hints at. It is in the following words.

1. Decrees in Chancery for a two years tax and addicional dutyes; by Lord Chancellor.[729]

[724]Sir George Rooke (1650–1709), admiral of the fleet and vice-admiral of England, commanded the expedition which was to convey Charles III, king of Spain, to Lisbon (*The Journal of Sir George Rooke, Admiral of the Fleet, 1700–1702*, ed. Oscar Browning (Navy Records Soc., ix, 1897), 258–62).

[725]Wharton's country seat was at Upper Winchendon, near Aylesbury, in Buckinghamshire.

[726]Bolton's principal residence was at Hackwood Park, near Old Basing, Hampshire.

[727]St John II.

[728]*Poems on Affairs of State* … ed. G. de F. Lord *et al.* (3 vols, 1702–4) contains two squibs composed in this form, both dating from 1704: 'A Catalogue of Books To Be Sold by Auction near St James's' (iii, 432–4), and 'A Catalogue of Books to be sold by Auction at the City Godmother's in Mincing Lane, on the 29th of May Next, Being the Anniversary of the Restauration of Blessed Memory' (ibid., 434–7).

[729]Sir Richard Cox.

12o

2. The Art of Brewing by his wife.[730]
3. Tom Double returned to Ireland: a pamphlett by Sir Ri[*chard*] Levinge.[731]
4. An Essay upon mocion or well moving; by Lieutenant General St[*euar*]t.[732] 3 parts. fol.
5. The excise man turned Courtier: a Comedye: by Dr Bush.[733]
6. A new method of raising money by raising men: by Lieutenant General E[*rle*].[734]
7. The intrigues and amours of a fair Lady. By Col. G[*or*]ge.[735]
8. A treatise of hearth money; dedicated to the house of Commons. By J. South.[736]
9. A new method for the valuacion of funds. By Mr Keightley.[737]
10. The Irish worthies. By Mr Savage.[738] 12o.
11. A treatise upon burnt brandy and light houses: by Col. Hawley dedicated to the Admiraltye.[739]
12. Taxes the best remedye against povertye: argued in a letter to the Governement: by Mr Ludlow.[740]
13. The rise and fall of the sole right in Ireland: by Mr T[*eni*]son.[741]
14. An introduction to the history of James the third: dedicated to the universitye of Oxford. composed by A. Anesley.[742]

[730]Mary, the daughter of John Bourne of Carbery, Co. Cork, who has been described as 'a minor landowner' (*Oxf. DNB*, *s.v.* Cox). The reference to brewing remains mysterious, but could relate to her family background.

[731]A reference to 'the character of insincerity which he lies under' and his reputation as a man whose 'practice and endeavour is, if he can, to keep fair with both the parties of whig and tory' (BL, Add. MS 47087, f. 18: 'Character of Sr. Richd. Levinge', 1711). 'Tom Double', the archetype of the modern unprincipled whig politician, was the fictional creation of the English writer (and tory MP) Charles Davenant, in *The True Picture of a Modern Whig* … (1701).

[732]William Steuart, MP [I].

[733]Arthur Bushe, MP [I], formerly secretary to the revenue commissioners [I], had been appointed judge advocate-general [I] in 1702. He had been awarded the degree of LLD by Trinity College, Dublin in 1701.

[734]Thomas Erle, MP [I], commander-in-chief of the forces in Ireland.

[735]Richard Gorges, MP [I]. In 1704 he married Nichola Sophia, daughter of Hugh Hamilton, Baron Hamilton, and widow of Sir Tristram Beresford, 3rd Bt. Her supposed liaison with the 2nd earl of Tyrone (*d.* 1693) gave rise to a colourful tale, recounted and examined in H. F. Hore, 'Lord Tyrone's Ghost', *Ulster Journal of Archaeology*, vii (1859), 149–65.

[736]John South, MP [I] was a revenue commissioner [I].

[737]Thomas Keightley, MP [I], first commissioner of the revenue [I].

[738]Philip Savage, MP [I] The book title is possibly an ironic reference to Nahum Tate's poem of praise for the 'Kentish Petitioners' of 1701, *The Kentish Worthies* (1701).

[739]Henry Hawley, MP [I] for Kinsale. In a debate in the committee of supply on 19 Oct. 1703, when it was proposed to remove from the civil list the annuity given to Lord Abercorn for maintaining six lighthouses around the Irish coast, on the grounds that Abercorn had neglected their upkeep, Hawley intervened to observe that there was no functioning lighthouse in his constituency, where Abercorn was supposed to maintain two (D.W. Hayton, 'A Debate in the Irish House of Commons in 1703: A Whiff of Tory Grapeshot', *Parliamentary History*, x (1991),162).

[740]Elsewhere Alan I disparaged Ludlow as a man in need of money: see above, p. 152.

[741]Henry Tenison, MP [I], a tory who in Jan. 1704 had been recommended by Ormond for a vacant post on the revenue commission as one who 'has been very serviceable in the parliament here'(NLI, MS 991, p. 217: Ormond to Lord Treasurer Godolphin, 10 Jan.1703/4).

[742]During a debate in this session Arthur Annesley had supposedly noted that it was in the power of the the English parliament to alter the succession, a statement that was subsequently used by whigs in England to impugn his loyalty to the Act of Settlement (*HC 1690–1715*, iii, 28). He was a Cambridge rather than an Oxford man, and

15. A Panegyrick upon the Prince of Wales. By Mr Nuttley.[743]
16. A Satyr against drunkennesse. By Mr Crow.[744]
17. The compleat Cooke: by Mr Bligh.[745]
18. The shortest way with the dissenters: by Mr Ri[*chard*] Stewart; Oxford edicion.[746]

8o.

19. A perswasive to matrimonye: by Mr Philips. in 3 parts.[747]
20. The history of Geneva: by Mr Upton.[748] Large folio.
21. The true born Irishman by Mr Brownlow.[749] In sheets bound price 4½d.
22. Impudence and ignorance the way to preferment: proved by Mr Attorney General in a letter to the Chancellor of the Exchequer.
23. An answer thereto. by Mr Pollard.[750]
24. Jura populi Hiberniae: by Mr Sollicitor General. a very small 8o.[751]
25. The Courteous Knight a farce: by And[*erson*] Sanders.[752] printed for the author.
26. The useful ranger, or the amours of the deer Parker. By Sir T[*homas*] S[*outhwell*].[753]
27. A short way of raising troops of horse: by Sir Richard Vernon.[754]
28. Johnsons select orations in parliament; printed for the companye of Pastry Cookes.[755]

742 (*continued*) indeed represented Cambridge University in the English parliament, but for the purposes of the satirist Oxford was more immediately identified with high-flying principles.

743 Nutley's extreme toryism earned him a place in whig demonology as a member of the 'Swan-Tripe Club', for which see below, p. 204.

744 William Crowe, MP [I], a contemporary of Alan I, St John II and Thomas at the Middle Temple.

745 When Thomas Bligh was made a privy councillor [I] in 1706, Robert Johnson, baron of the exchequer [I] recalled some malicious verses that had circulated in Dublin in c.1698–9, in which several Irish MPs were satirised for supposed faults; in Bligh's case a lack of manners and polish (HMC, *Ormonde MSS*, n.s. viii, 272; *The Poems of Jonathan Swift*, ed. Harold Williams (2nd edn, 3 vols, Oxford, 1958), iii, 1071).

746 Richard Stewart, MP [I]. An obvious reference to Stewart's high church prejudices, and recalling Defoe's pamphlet *The Shortest-Way with the Dissenters …* (1702).

747 Chichester Philips, MP [I]. On 30 Sept. 1703 Henry Tenison had introduced into the Irish house of commons heads of a bill to secure Philips's title to property from the estate of the late Sir Simon Eaton. These lands had been bequeathed by Eaton in the first instance to his widowed daughter-in-law, Martha, with a remainder to Philips in default of Martha having children. She had since remarried, but her husband, George Mathew, was a catholic, and it was on these grounds that the measure was urged. The heads passed all stages in Ireland but the resulting bill was respited by the English privy council. See *Hist. Ir. Parl.*, vi, 63; ILD.

748 Clotworthy Upton, MP [I] was a prominent presbyterian and a parliamentary spokesman for the Dissenting interest.

749 Arthur Brownlow, MP [I], was a Gaelic scholar and collector of Gaelic manuscripts. He had also attended James II's parliament in Dublin in 1689, one of very few protestants to do so.

750 Walter Pollard, MP [I]. In opposition at this time and accounted a whig by 1713 (*Hist. Ir. Parl.*, vi, 85).

751 Presumably a reference to Alan's efforts in this session in defence of the 'rights of the people of Ireland' (a literal translation) with a sardonic hint at the way in which these had been limited or denied ('a very small 8o'). The title recalls Lord Somers' pamphlet, *Jura Populi Anglicani: or The Subject's Right of Petitioning Set Forth …* (1701).

752 Anderson Saunders, MP [I].

753 Sir Thomas Southwell, 2nd Bt MP[I].

754 Vernon was commissioned in 1702 as a lieutenant in the Coldstream regiment of foot guards and by Apr. 1704 was a captain in Ormond's regiment of horse. (Charles Dalton, *English Army Lists and Commission Registers, 1661–1714* (6 vols, 1892–1904), v, 47, 249; HMC, *Ormonde MSS*, n.s., viii, 68.

755 Robert Johnson, sr, MP [I].

a large folio.

29. Chichester house jests, bulls, quibbles and conumdrums; by Sir Francis Blundel: reviewed and augmented by Mr Ash.[756]
30. The art of paying visits and nothing else: by Mr The[*ophilus*] Butler.
31. The life of Themistocles suited to the present times: by Mr Parry.[757]
32. The renowned actions of the Knight of the sorrowful face. By Mr Maxwell.[758] A Romance in fol.
33. Truth is not to be spoken at all times: in a familiar letter to Sir Pierce Butler by Mr Ecchlin[759]
34. Gahans titles of honour.[760]
35. Instructions to the youth to face about in Parliament: By Muster Muster general Harrison.[761]
36. Of altering and lowering the coin: a familiar dialogue between B[*urton*] and H[*arrison*] sworn bankers to the D[*uke*] of O[*rmond*].[762]
37. Advice to the Frenchmen to wear shirts for the improvement of the linen manufacture: by Sir Tho[*mas*] Southwell.[763]
38. A new method of stating publick accounts: by Sir W. Robinson fol. in two parts. each volume imperfect, with errata, index waiting etc. [764]
39. Irish cry or representacion. A fair manuscript never printed.[765]

Catalogues may be had of several other books and manuscripts which will be exposed to sale at Chichester house 3d Oct. 1704.[766]

[756]Thomas Ashe, MP [I] Cavan.

[757]Benjamin Parry, MP [I].

[758]Henry Maxwell, MP [I]. In 1713 Lord Abercorn called him 'our Don Dismallo, or the knight of the sorrowful countenance' (PRONI, D/623/A/3/12: Abercorn to [Edward Southwell], 5 Jan. 1713/14). The nickname may already have been in use by 1704.

[759]Probably Robert Echlin, MP [I], for Newry, as his namesake in the House was an army officer and would have been known by his title.

[760]Daniel Gahan, MP [I], whose paternal ancestry, in the Gaelic Irish family of Ó Catháin or O'Cahan, furnished instances of rebellion against the English crown and the forfeiture of estates.

[761]Michael Harrison, MP [I].

[762]Benjamin Burton and Francis Harrison, both MPs [I], had established a banking business together in Dublin in 1700 (*Hist. Ir. Parl.*, iii, 316). The comment may have a political meaning, relating to their connection with Ormond's government, but for evidence that they also acted as the duke's bankers in a private capacity, see NLI, MS 2457, p.39: order signed by Ormond, 24 June 1701.

[763]Southwell was a keen promoter of the linen manufacture in Ireland (*DIB*, viii, 1084).

[764]Sir William Robinson, MP [I], had recently fallen foul of the Commons committee of public accounts in his capacity as deputy vice-treasurer and receiver-general. On 16 Oct. 1703 the chairman of the committee reported a resolution that Robinson had misrepresented the debt of the nation, upon which he was declared 'unfit for any public employment in this kingdom' and committed for a time to the custody of the constable of Dublin Castle (*CJI*, iii, 56, 162). Alan Brodrick had played a leading role in the Commons' pursuit of Robinson (*CSP Dom.*, 1703–4, 157).

[765]The representation to the queen on 'the present distressed condition of this kingdom' which the Commons agreed on 20 Oct. 1703, and on 20 Jan. 1704 resolved to print. See above, p. 000. It was never printed.

[766]The parliament met in Chichester House, Dublin. It had been prorogued in the first instance to 3 Oct. 1704 (*CJI*, iii, 210).

86. *Alan I, London, to Thomas, Exning, near Newmarket, 3 May 1704*

(1248/2/135–6)

I was yesterday to see my sister and endeavoured to inform my self when you would be in town, but she is altogether as much a stranger to that matter as I am, soe that I resolve to know it directly from yourself: I am now come to a resolucion of going over soe as to be in Dublin before the next term; the measures some people are taking and the rumors spread in Ireland as if I had entirely left it, make it advisable to appear soon there to support my own interest and prevent the designs of my enemies.

I should be glad your affairs would call you to town before I leave it, that we may talk some things which relate to the whole familye with my brother: I will not mention your fondnesse of horse racing to you, since your heart is unalterably fixed and bent on it; but methinks the complexion of affairs should a little incline you to good husbandry; and I am sure your own sense tells you, Newmarkett is not a place that much contributes to any thing of that nature.

87. *Alan I, Dublin, to Thomas, 8 June 1704*

(1248/2/137–8)

I intend to goe very soon into the Countrey, but resolve to write to you before I goe and to own your long letter, the news of which comforted those here that wish well to the Protestant interest; but upon my word I found matters represented on this side the water, as to the successes of the Duke of Anjou etc[767] much greater then in England, nay then the real truth; and the enemyes of France seemed to me to be very much dejected: but the last packett which brings account of the Portugueze having gotten some late advantages enlivens them again. It will be no news to you that Lord G[*alway'*]s being to goe over into Portugal is more acceptable tidings to some people then others; but one great comfort which some folks have in that matter is that he goes in a civil as well as in a military capacitye, and that Mr M[*ethuen*] is to be recalled: Nay a certain tall Gentleman gives out that he knew he would be recalled a fortnight before we had the news of Lord G[*alway'*]s being declared: but you know great Statesmen never mention things before they happen … We are here as secret as is possible in the matter of our parliament sitting in October, or being prorogued farther: for my part I am apt to think it is not yet resolved on, or that the ministry here are not yet let into the secret. Care must be taken to know in time what is resolved upon, on your side of the water; for there is no dependance on any informacion from hence. I hope you have not failed to wait on my Lord Treasurer[768] as you promised me … The new Judge[769] looks as kindly on a freind of yours as he used to doe when he was making select orations on the French; I suppose the indignation proceeds from not

[767] A reference to the progress of the war in Spain: Philip (1683–1746), duke of Anjou, the grandson of Louis XIV, was Bourbon claimant to the throne of Spain (he was later recognised as King Philip V).

[768] Sidney Godolphin (1645–1712), 1st Baron (and later 1st earl of) Godolphin, lord treasurer [E] since 1702.

[769] Robert Johnson, MP [I], now a baron of the exchequer [I].

being visited or complemented on his promocion: but you know the usual complements on such occasions are how overjoyed the visitant is of the others honour and how well he deserves it; and you may guesse whether the party in saying either of those things would have spoken his mind or not.

88. *Alan I, Dublin, to St John II, at his chamber in Lamb Buildings, Middle Temple, 11 July 1704*

(1248/2/141–2)

You may beleive we have been extremely rejoiced at the good news of my Lord Marleboroughs successe on the Danube;[770] The dejection some of the Irish (I mean such of them as I have seen) shew on this occasion is incredible. Pray let sister M[771] know I have received her letter of the fourth instant, and if my brother Tho[*mas*] be in town I wish he would not only mind what I wrote to him about by my last in relacion to Sir Jn P[772] but make use of this oportunitye of the misunderstanding that is between a fat Lady of your acquaintance and mine whom we visited one Sunday in the afternoon and found Mr Hamond[773] and other company with her son (If you should not understand who I mean my sister will be able to inform you, for she mencions her in her last letter) and a certain great man. If the matter be managed right, two good men may come into the room of two —— [*sic*]. I am forced to write soe as not to be liable to be torn in peices if my letter be pryed into, as I expect it will; for you must know we are mighty nice and curious, and having a great deal of guilt on us are wondrous suspicious and inquisitive … Your own good nature, and love for my brother Clayton, together with my sister Claytons[774] real worth will induce you to expresse great civilitye and kindnesse to her; but since there is no way left to pay what I owe to one that is gone but by kindnesse to those she loved, I must intreat you to be distinguishingly obliging to that remaining beloved sister of one that sincerely loved you.[775] Since my landing I have been visited and used with all the obliging respect imaginable by my freinds; but not received one visit from any one man of the other kidney, but several letters out of the countrey making large advances to the renewal of former, but lately discontinued, freindships: I act with coynesse, yet with great civilitye toward them, but resolve to have no obligation placed on me by being entertained, lying at houses etc. My businesse hath been soe great that the story now goes, that it was concerted by some meerly to keep up reputacion for a time, but that it will fall by next term: A tall Gentleman, one that lately scaped a scowring, and one concerned in the game of Leap frog seem all of a mind willing to give me interruption in my businesse, but I think it will not doe … My sister will tell

[770] John Churchill (1650–1722), 1st duke of Marlborough, at the Battle of Schellenberg, in Bavaria.

[771] Martha Courthope.

[772] Sir John Perceval, 5th Bt, MP [I].

[773] Possibly Anthony Hammond (1668–1738), a commissioner of the navy [E] and MP [E], for whom see *HC 1690–1715*, iv, 169–76. If, as seems likely, Alan is here considering electoral prospects in Co. Cork, the 'fat lady' is almost certainly Juliana, dowager countess of Cork and Burlington, whose son Richard (1694–1753) had recently succeeded to the earldom as a minor. For Juliana's political activities on the young earl's behalf, see Rachel Wilson, *Elite Women in Ascendancy Ireland, 1690–1745: Imitation and Innovation* (Woodbridge, 2015), 136–9.

[774] Anne (née Courthope), Alan's sister-in-law, who had married Laurence Clayton.

[775] Alan's second wife, Lucy (née Courthope).

you who said they would disclaim all interest and freindship with —— and join with the B[*rodrick*]s. The later part must be a damned mortification to a very proud and haughty spirit.

89. *Alan I, Cork, to Thomas, at the Whitehall coffee-house, King's Street, Westminster, 17 Aug. 1704*

(1248/2/143–4)

I shal goe out of town before the post comes in which we hope may bring some good news from beyond Sea; this poor Countrey wants encouragement to put a little life into trade which is at present at the lowest ebb imaginable. Yesterday Robin Meade[776] was with me on the old errand and in the old scurrilous railing humor; I bore him as long as I could, but when he told me that for ought he knew the trustees swallowed and converted the whole profits of the school lands to their own use[777] I was obliged to shew him the door of my chamber. You see what obloquy the not making one step toward that building yet, hath subjected us to; I mean not any progresse that is visible here: for I remember you told me you had contracted for a ship load of timber from Norway and insured it: for Gods sake doe not sleep on it for more reasons then one. Freinds enquire about it, having inclinacions to have a good school near them to put their children to, and others with intent to insinuate reflections …

90. *Alan I, Cork, to St John II, at his chamber in Lamb Buildings, Middle Temple, 27 Aug. 1704*

(1248/2/145–6)

… The account of the Duke of Marleboroughs successe against the French and Bavarians (I mean of the letter written by the Duke to the Dutchesse[778]) came hither no sooner then the 17th about twelve at night; but I doe affirm that the Irish had it among them on the Saturday before that is on the 12th of August; nay it was that day reported in Corke by the Irish who came out of Muskry[779] and other Western parts soe that they must have it some time before; they were thus far particular that it was not Prince Eugene[780] that had beaten Tallard,[781] but the Duke had beaten both the French and Bavarians. It is worth considering why the French should give them soe early an account of their own defeat, for people are seldome messengers of their own misfortunes: but considering what you write of an intent of destroying the Queen if the English had been beaten, perhaps it imported the

[776]Robert Meade of Kinsale (see Appendix I).

[777]The trustees of Lady Orkney's school at Midleton.

[778]The Battle of Blenheim. Marlborough's short note to his wife, which gave her the news of this 'glorious victory' is printed in *The Marlborough–Godolphin Correspondence*, ed. H.L. Snyder (3 vols, Oxford, 1975), i, 349.

[779]The barony of Muskerry, in the centre of Co. Cork.

[780]Eugène (1663–1736), prince of Savoy, field-marshal in the Austrian army and president of the Imperial War Council.

[781]Camille (1652–1728), comte de Tallard, marshal of France.

Monsieur to give some freinds here early notices that the English instead of being beaten had put the French General into my Lord Marleboroughs coach,[782] for fear of shewing themselves too early in confidence of the wished for successe of the French arms. Be it as it will they are most dismally dejected, but as to the plot against the Queen that they will by no means beleive; and which is pretty odd, Lieutenant General Erle who is one of our Lords Justices and is now here hath not one word of it in his letters as I heard him say last night at the Mayors[783] yet hath letters from the Castle[784] and from Mr Southwell[785]. If you have the deeds for settling Lands for building a school at Midleton pray gett me a close copy of them and send it over by a safe hand; I am a trustee in that matter and would discharge my trust, and people begin to be very inquisitive why the school goes not forward. For my part I own that I think it will not be fit to build a great house for the Master for reception of a great many boarders; for beside that it will retard opening the school and paying exhibitions, I know not how we can answer too great an expence of that sort if we be questioned why part of the money laid out in that building might not have been saved and applyed to maintaining scholars or sending them to the Colledge.[786] There is this more in the case: a great house for the master will wholly defeat one good designed by the foundacion, the bettering Midleton which can no otherwise happen then by boys boarding with the dwellers there … Mr Southwell writes the man of war and Yatch are to be at the Waterside for the Duke[787] on this day sevennight: our Portugal forces are here, but no transports or convoy yet arrived.[788] Give my humble services to my Cousin Ettrick and that whole familye, and take some little care of your infirm and crazy constitucion.

91. *Alan I, Cork, to Thomas, at the Whitehall coffee-house, King's Street, Westminster, 14 Sept. 1704*

(1248/2/150–1)

I write this the night before the post comes in designing to goe out of town to morrow morning early … I beleive you are entirely a stranger to the bounds of the estate my Uncle left you, which were worth your viewing: I make no doubt but that the estate suffers already and will do soe more and more daily by the bounds being betrayed, or encroached on. I have it from a good hand that some persons have it stil in their hearts to endeavour placing the last affront on — and why may they not attain their end? You may guesse what a defence

[782]Marlborough's note to his wife stated that 'Monsieur Tallard and two other generals are in my coach, and I am following the rest.'

[783]Edmond Knapp (1659–1747), mayor of Cork 1703–4 and MP [I] for the city 1715–27. Erle had been elected for Cork city to the parliament of 1703.

[784]Dublin Castle.

[785]Edward Southwell, MP [I], chief secretary.

[786]Trinity College, Dublin.

[787]Ormond.

[788]Three regiments from the Irish establishment which were being transferred to the Allied war effort in Portugal. They were to embark from Cork and Kinsale. (HMC, *Ormonde MSS*, n.s., viii, 78, 80, 81, 84, 88–90, 92–4, 109).

innocence is in many cases, and his freinds are either in other Kingdomes or stay quiet at home: he hath a fine time of it.

92. *Alan I, Nine Mile House,*[789] *to Thomas, at the Whitehall coffee-house, King's Street, Westminster, 21 Oct. 1704*

(1248/2/152–3)

I am come hither from Clonmel in ill weather and design to be in Dublin on Monday; in the mean time take the oportunitye while no body or thing interrupts me to write to you about some matters now fresh in my memorye, which perhaps I may forget by the time I come to town … You may think what you please, but I doe not foresee how it can in a little time be otherwise then that estates in Ireland will be of no other use to the owners but to eat drink and cloth themselves on the spot out of the produce of them; but to expect money hence and spend it in London on confidence of it is the last madnesse. I vow to God I cannot expresse the scarcitye of money, not a penny of silver is to be seen in most countrey peoples houses whatever their condicion is: I dined at Tallough[790] yesterday or the day before where among other meat there was a very fat fine rib of beef, it consisted of six ribs, and the Gentleman told me that he bought it in the market for seven pence; judge you what rent tenants can pay for Land at this rate. Let me know whether the rumors we heard about disturbances like to happen in Scotland be true; write as plain as you can for my informacion without giving handle to any body to find fault; for depend on it, more people then I, find their letters peeped into. We all take it for granted we are to sit,[791] and the doubt seems not to be what we will or can give,[792] but what will be expected. … I had almost forgott to have told you that at the quarter Sessions held the third instant at Rathcormack there was a representacion made by the Justices there (who as I heard were Mr Hyde chairman,[793] Capt Barry,[794] Will. Wakeham,[795] Peter Carey,[796] George Mansergh,[797] Mr Norcott,[798] and I think Dick Price[799]) with whom Major Wilkinson[800] joined in subscribing it, and put

[789] Nine Mile House, Grangemockler, Co. Tipperary, was situated on the post road from Clonmel to Dublin.

[790] Tallow, Co. Waterford, a parliamentary borough.

[791] The Irish parliament.

[792] In terms of a supply.

[793] Arthur Hyde, MP [I].

[794] Probably James Barry, MP [I] Naas 1695–9, 1711–13, Kildare 1715–*d.*

[795] William Wakeham (*d.* by 1718), of Little Island, Co. Cork (Vicars, *Index*, 470). A tenant of Alan I, in respect of property Alan had inherited from the Courthopes (SHC, G145/box102/4: rental, c.1712–28).

[796] Peter Carey (c.1681–c.1737) of Careysville, Co. Cork (*Al. Dub.*, 33; Vicars, *Index*, 76).

[797] George Mansergh of Macrony Castle, Kilworth, Co. Cork, son and heir of James Mansergh of Macrony Castle (NLI, Genealogical Office MS 142, p. 116).

[798] Charles Norcott or Northcote (c.1681–1730), prebendary of Cloyne 1709–19, dean of Kilmacduagh 1719–*d.* (*Al. Dub.*, 621; Cotton, *Fasti*, i, 299; iv, 203).

[799] Probably Richard Price (*d.* c.1712) of Ballyhooly, Co. Cork. A Richard Price of Ardmayle and Clonmore, Co. Tipperary, was the father-in-law of Hyde's eldest son.

[800] Cuthbert Wilkinson (*d.* by 1728), of Kilpatrick, Co. Cork and Sarsfield's Court, Glanmire, Co. Cork, collector of excise for Cork and Clonmel (*Acts of James II's Irish Parliament*, ed. Bergin and Lyall, 99; Phillimore, *Indexes*, ii, 115; Burke, *Hist. Clonmel*, 138–9).

into Capt Barryes hand to be sent to the Lords Justices;[801] it imports as I am told, that they find by good informacion from several parts of the County especially from Duhallow[802] and Muskry, that the Papists are become very insolent and seem to stand in contempt of the Laws and governement of the Kingdome: That they are the more induced to take notice of it, because one Keefe insulted and abused a Justice of peace (it was Mr Freeman[803]) in the execucion of his office, whom when the Justice would have gotten in secured and had granted a mittimus[804] etc. there appeared such a [rab]ble on his behalf that the constable was forced to let him goe, […][805] that he wears arms (Note he is a late pretended convert) and in all appearance will turn raporee,[806] having in all appearance held correspondence formerly with the Toryes that are out: It adds, that the Toryes are numerous and troublesome, and have so encouraged ill men that not only in Duhallow but several other parts of the County they stand in contempt of warrants and refuse to obey them. and submit all etc. I was also told that the Collector[807] made an oath that he was forced to have eight or nine armed men with him when he went to distrain in the mountainy parts for quitrent, and that his examinacion is also sent up. How welcome these matters may be I know not; I hope they will not expose the representers to censure or ill treatment for speaking their minds. I saw Longfeilds[808] examinacion about the matter of Keefe which shews it to have been an insolent and impudent barefaced riot: How Norcott came to put his name (after what he was once told which you cannot but remember) I cant guesse; unlesse he thinks the man that threatned him may the soonest of the two meet with the fate he was told he deserved

93. *Alan I, Dublin, to St John II, at his chambers in Lamb Buildings, Middle Temple, 21 Feb. 1704/5*

(1248/2/171–2)

This letter will be deliver'd by Mr Pierson,[809] soe as I may venture to write a little freer then by the post. Such hath been the applicacion of some people, such offers of emploiments, and caressing on the one hand; and such temptacions on the other through the miserable povertye of the countrey in general, and consequently of a great many — that nothing can fail of successe that is but wished. I am made more and more sensible that it is resolved

[801] The representation, dated 3 Oct. 1704, took notice of reports from across Co. Cork that 'the Irish papists are become very insolent', citing in particular the case of one Teige Keefe who had been arrested but released because the constables (possibly out of fear) would not act against him, and who was now openly bearing arms in defiance of the law. They also expressed their concern that 'the tories are very numerous and troublesome in the … county' and were openly contemptuous of the forces of the law. There is a copy in SHC, 1248/2/149.

[802] The barony of Duhallow, in the north-west of Co. Cork.

[803] William Freeman (*d.* by 1732) of Castle Cor, Co. Cork (Vicars, *Index*, 229; Dickson, *Old World Colony*, 180, 196, 202).

[804] An order directing an officer of the law to conduct an offender to prison.

[805] MS damaged.

[806] See above, p. 47.

[807] Of the revenue.

[808] John Longfield (1653–1730), of Castle Mary, Co. Cork (Dickson, *Old World Colony*, 88).

[809] An Edward Pearson wrote to Robert Harley in 1711 with information about public affairs in Ireland, claiming to be 'acquainted with the better sort in all parts of Ireland' (HMC, *Portland MSS*, v, 20–2).

by some people to place some affront on me before matters are over: you may depend on it that as I never did, I never will doe an action for which you or any freind of mine shal have just cause to blush; on the other hand I cannot promise you but that some method may not only be taken but brought to passe to put the last indignitye on me; either by saying I am faulty in matters of which I am no way guilty, or calling that a crime in me which in any other man alive would be none, nay perhaps an act in itself worthy: Of the first nature it is impossible for me or any living man to make a conjecture what may be broached; if there be people in nature to be found of invention and malice enough to cast an imputacion, there will be others who will (pretend (at least) to) beleive it, in order to gratifye —.[810] But I can hardly beleive any body can be soe villainous to invent an entire falsitye, for fear of detection: I more suspect the nature of things being altered by calling good evil, and evil good. We have a Statute declaring our priviledges of parliament continue 40 dayes after our parliament finished. When this Act was made in H[*enry*] 4. time the use was to dissolve and not continue parliaments by prorogacion: [811] In Lord Winchesters and Lord Galweys parliament notice was taken of the mischeifs occasioned by priviledge and my brother moved to wave it by vote of the house, and it was then soe done; but at the same time declared that nothing was meant by that vote farther then that the house would not take notice of proceeding after the forty dayes as an indignitye offered to the house, but every defendant was (and indeed must be) left at libertye to make his defence by pleading the Statute at Law, if the word finished was not meant of finishing all businesse depending, but dissolving the Parliament.[812] In another Session Sir W[*illia*]m Handcock[813] was very angry at that vote and expressed himself soe as to say my brother deserved to be impeached for his mocion, as tending to repeal a Statute by a vote: but all agreed his mocion had no such tendencye and many in the debate (and I particularly) said they thought there was no reason to expound the word finished in that Statute soe largely as that priviledge should continue during a prorogacion of six of twelve months. Last Trinitye term upon some case or other the Chancellor[814] and Judges agreed that by that Act priviledge was not continued more then 40 dayes after a prorogacion. I made a mocion in Chancerye in behalf of Lord Bellew[815] to allow his plea of priviledge etc. but was told the Judges had resolved it continued not after the 40 dayes in case of a prorogacion. When the rule was given I said that the Judges being unanimous in that exposicion confirmed me in my former opinion,

[810]Presumably the lord lieutenant, Ormond.

[811]The Irish Privilege Act, extending parliamentary privilege to 40 days after the end of the session was in fact 3 Edw. IV, c. 1 (Edward and Annie G. Porritt, *The Unreformed House of Commons: Parliamentary Representation Before 1832* (2 vols, Cambridge,1909), ii, 198).

[812]On 11 May 1697 the Irish house of commons resolved, on a division, and after 'a long debate', that, until 15 June following, no Member was to insist on parliamentary privilege to protect his goods or estate from the payment of debt or 'other legal and equitable demands'. Thomas Brodrick was a teller in favour of the motion (*CJI*, ii, 650–1). Sir Richard Cox observed that to use these numbers to calculate the strength of parties in the House would be a mistake, 'for the subject-matter of this vote did influence more than faction' (Bristol Archives, 12964/1, f. 57: Cox to Edward Southwell, [May 1697]).

[813]MP [I]. A Middle Templar. The occasion of this speech is most likely to have been a debate on 23 Jan. 1699 which issued in an unsuccessful motion for a resolution that no MP who had failed to attend since 25 Mar. 1697 could claim privilege during the forthcoming recess, in any matter 'between Commoner and Commoner' (*CJI*, ii, 882).

[814]The lord chancellor, Sir Richard Cox.

[815]Richard Bellew (*d*. 1715), 3rd Baron Bellew.

that my brother did not deserve to be impeached etc. and that the opinion I among many others had been of in expounding that Statute was not soe heterodox or faulty as some men were pleased to say they beleived. But I now hear that by way of postscript to a printed case that is to come out it is to be added That the Speaker officiously said in Chancerye upon the Lord Chancellors declaring the resolucion of the Judges in expounding that Statute, that he was glad they were come to that resoluction, and had alway been of that opinion. What if I had said soe? but I did not: yet if there occur not a more plausible handle, I beleive this may be made use of to put a question on me, and you may guesse of what nature it will be. Can I suffer in reputacion by a matter of this kind? I have been and am ill, took Physick yesterday and am this day confined to my chamber after bleeding, the air being very cold. Tell me will it be mean in me, being as I am indisposed, to chuse avoiding an insult from — who hath multitudes at his back, by going over before our next meeting (for I beleive it will not be attempted till our money bill come back and passe our house for fear of the worst) or stand the utmost malice of the powerful and revengeful. Write to me your thoughts: The fury and resentment of some is not to be expressed.

94. *Alan I, Dublin, to St John II,*[816] *24 Feb. 1704/5*

(1248/2/173)

What you propose as reasonable is not I think to be moved as we now stand disposed: it is impossible to describe how matters are managed. What I wrote by Mr Pierson will (if possibly to be attained) be attempted; but probably want of a prospect of successe may stop the design. Tho I hardly know what may not succeed, if people knew their own strength. This evening I hear an attempt is to be made on one whose son lay ill long of a feavor, whom my brother Tho[*mas*] often used to visit: the son is now at school near the place where Mr Carthy (formerly a servant to late Lord Orrerye)[817] now lives: you cant but know whom I mean. There is occasion for a vacancye. Our news is little; but in our profession we may give accounts of what happens. Mr Robert Sanders[818] is to be made prime Sergeant in Sir Tho[*mas*] Pagenhams[819] roome: he is a very deserving man, and soe are his brother, son, and Nephew; all members of our house, and very just to the interest of Ireland.[820] We were this day on the list of Protecting members and persons protected; but the number of offenders was too great to goe through with the matter; and all ended in a vote to rectifye matters for the future; that all offenders hereafter should incur the highest displeasure and censure of the house, which in the debates was declared to be meant expulsion. This past

[816] Addressed to 'Stephen Hervey esq to be left at the Fleur de Lys, near St Dunstan's, Fleet Street'. Stephen Hervey (1655–1707), of East Betchworth, Surrey, was MP [E] for Reigate and a bencher of the Middle Temple. For the privilege by which the correspondence of members of the Westminster parliament was carried free of charge with Britain and Ireland ('Members Franks') see Kenneth Ellis, *The Post Office in the Eighteenth Century* … (1958), 39. Fleur de Lis Court ran east from Fetter Lane, in the parish of St Dunstan's, London.

[817] Lionel Boyle (1671–1703), 3rd earl of Orrery [I].

[818] Robert Saunders, MP [I].

[819] Sir Thomas Pakenham, MP [I].

[820] Robert's brother Anderson Saunders, son Morley Saunders and nephew Richard Saunders, were all tory MPs in the Irish house of commons. Alan's statement is thus heavy with irony, and the word 'just' intentionally ambiguous.

unanimously; perhaps not for the same reason.[821] I hope all thought it fit to be soe: perhaps some were willing to compound for what was past for any thing in futuritye: but there might be a farther reason; for else continuing this Parliament will be impracticable.

95. *Alan I, Dublin, to St John II, at his chamber in Lamb Buildings, Middle Temple, 3 Mar. 1704/5*

(1248/2/174–5)

I know I am not punctual in my writing, but I cant help it: nor is it worth your while to know the many odd things we are doing. The vote for two years support of the Governement from Michaelmas next was carried 142; against 67.[822] The whole force on one side was in town, and increased or recruited by some that were once of another opinion: among the rest Gustavus Hamilton, Colonel Dean;[823] and my Lord Blessintons two neighbours Mr Spring and Mr Graydon.[824] There was an other whom I will not name, you know him: but his mortificacion is such that I think it ought to be forgotten that he transgressed. I think the reason was that such applicacion and industry had been used as not only to render the thing secure, soe as there could be noe possibilitye of carrying it for one year, but to possesse men that no body would venture to appear against it: thus some were induced to promise, others to give fair hopes of being passive in it at least, who formerly had been of an other opinion, and I beleive had no reason but sollicitacion and being of the greater number to alter till they came to the house: but when the matter came to be debated and Gentlemen thought it not unfit but their duty to give reasons against two years, some went out; a great many were not in town, and not above ten (to the best of my remembrance) of the 119 became converts. You cannot imagine the uneasinesse the managers were in when they saw a division demanded and peremptorilye insisted on: and soe you may be sure were those who left their former notions and embraced new ones. The galleryes were full during the debate, and if I hear matters truly the lesse number lost no credit in the opinion of the hearers. Several spoke well to it on our side: Mr Caulfeild,[825] Clayton, Parry, Conollye, Jo: Dean,[826] and others; but Mr Whitshead[827] spoke to a miracle. I beleive his discourse would have created attention, and the value of his hearers in the greatest assembly in the world, if that matter had been in debate before them. Assoon as you receive this, send to my brother Tho[*mas*] and let him know that if the house goe into issuing a new writ for the borough of Middleton I

[821] On 24 Feb. the Commons considered the number of personal 'protections' being issued under privilege, and resolved, nem. con., that if any Member for the future granted a protection to someone not employed by him as a 'menial servant' (in receipt of wages) he would 'incur the highest displeasure and censure of this House' (*CJI*, iii, 242).

[822] This was agreed on the report of the committee of supply on 28 Feb., but the *Journals* do not report a division (*CJI*, iii, 246). It is of course possible that the division occurred in the committee.

[823] Edward Deane.

[824] Blessington's seat was Blessington House, Co. Wicklow.

[825] Hon. John Caulfeild or, more likely, William Caulfeild, who was a prominent whig MP.

[826] Possibly 'Js: Deane' in the MS, but in either case this would refer to Joseph Deane.

[827] William Whitshed.

have promised young George Evans[828] an election there; he is a very good man, of a noble estate, and particularly a freind to Arthur Hyde who hath married his sister;[829] and Hyde hath been to me the most obliging man living. Loose no time least Sir John St Leger[830] should prevail with my brother; he hath a ready answer, that Lord Donerayle having sent by Mr George Eyre[831] to me that Sir John should be chosen at Donerayle, as he also told Mr Pennyfather,[832] I have passed Mr Evans my word. Beside I doubt whether my brother knows Sir John very well. There is one Mr Richard Meredyth heir at Law to Sir Charles Meredyth,[833] but Lord Montrath has a good part of Sir Charles estate settled on him[834] and I was of Councel with my Lord in recovering it from Mr Meredyth. Part of the estate not settled on my Lord but on Mr Meredyth in the Queens County (I think) being detained from him, he hath brought an ejectment for recoverye[835] of it, or else he is sued for some of that estate and needs the settlement made on the marriage of Sir W[*illia*]m Meredyth to defend himself or to recover by he is a very honest Gentleman, and hath intreated me to have my Lord spoken to that his agent (Mr Edwards) may either carry down the deed and let him make use of on the tryal, or put it into my hand with libertye to have it used on the trial by Mr Meredyth, and if it be lodged in my hand I will return it or forfeit the extream value of the estate. In equitye he hath a right to use this deed, but that will be dilatory and expensive. I hope Senny now and then sees my Lord Blessinton and my Lord Monjoy;[836] either of them will carry him to Lord Montrath, and doe Mr Meredyth a good office. The Assises are very near, soe as no time must be lost. We have ordered nobody shal hear our debates for the future;[837] you may guesse at the reason if you can. But indeed it is impertinent for people that are admitted to be hearers on curtesye to pretend to make judgements of things.

96. *Alan I, Dublin, to St John II, at his chamber in Lamb Buildings, Middle Temple,*[838] *6 Mar. 1704/5*

(1248/2/176–7)

I have … yours of the 28th now before me: and am surprised at your not having received the votes. I have constantly sent them under Mr Harveys cover; but perhaps have mistaken

[828] MP [I], and later 1st Baron Carbery.

[829] Hyde had married, as his second wife, George's eldest sister, Mary Evans (*Hist. Ir. Parl.*, iv, 119, 459).

[830] Sir John St Leger, elected MP [I] for Doneraile in 1713.

[831] George Eyre, jr, MP [I].

[832] Kingsmill Pennefather, MP [I].

[833] Richard Meredyth, MP [I], had succeeded to the estates, at Greenhills, Co. Kildare, of his uncle Sir Charles Meredyth (c.1627–1700), MP [I] Gowran 1692–3, who had died unmarried (John Burke, *A Genealogical and Heraldic Dictionary of the Peerage and Baronetage of the British Empire* (6th edn, 2 vols, 1839), ii, 706).

[834] Algernon Coote (1689–1744), 6th earl of Mountrath.

[835] A civil action to recover the possession of, or title to, land.

[836] William Stewart (1675 –1728), 2nd Viscount Mountjoy, Blessington's son-in-law.

[837] No such order is recorded in *CJI*.

[838] Redirected to Maidstone, Kent.

the direction, which I think was to be left at the Flower de Lis near St Dunstans etc. If that be a wrong direction, yet methinks member of Parliament should have carried the letter to the box in the Lobby of the house of Commons.[839] If my mistake in the direction hath not occasioned the miscarriage, let them who have had the curiositye to pry into what comes from me take the votes for their pains; for that is all they have mett with: I am as cautious of what I write as he that is to passe the Ordeal trial is where he places his steps … The heats between the houses are very uneasy to all who wish well to the publick; God send it may find a good issue.[840] Our Session cant be long;[841] we know what is to be done, and that what is resolved on will be carried: and are as willing to make a short Session as other people. Yesterday we voted that the summe to make up the deficiencye of the establishment for 2 years from Michaelmas next should be a summe not exceeding £150000:[842] All the yeas for the vote for 2 years were yeas here too I beleive; and I think most that were for one year neither said yea or noe. We were mightily applauded for paying the great respect we did to her Majestyes establishment by our Secretary of State:[843] for we past it all as necessarye:[844] and I fancy it is expected the two years addicional dutyes will passe nemine contradicente: but that is a future contingent, of which they have not any determinate certainty. It would be very acceptable to have it soe: but if some be of the same opinion and firmnesse they have hitherto shewn them selves, nem. con. will not be a part of the vote. We yesterday past through heads of a bill about qualifying future members of Parliaments:[845] and it being moved by Mr Maxwell, that having been unsuccessefull in this matter formerly,[846] the whole house should attend the Lord Lieutenant with these heads etc. it went smooth, tho I doubt whether with the good inclinacions of some Gentlemen: but it was too plausible to be opposed. I know not why some did not doe it; for according to those heads our next house will vary much from the present … Never man longed more to be out of the Gallyes then I doe to gett rid of what I am now engaged in …

[839] Boxes were kept by the door of the lobby of the house of commons for MPs' letters (*HC 1690–1715*, i, 367).

[840] Between the Lords and Commons at Westminster over the lawsuit of *Ashby* v. *White* over parliamentary elections for the borough of Aylesbury), for which see Eveline Cruickshanks, 'Ashby v. White: The Case of the Men of Aylesbury' in *Party and Management in Parliament, 1660–1784,* ed. Clyve Jones (Leicester, 1984), 87–106, esp. 97–102.

[841] After the mid-session break, on 22 Mar., the Irish parliament resumed work in earnest on 15 May, with the return of bills from England, and ended the session on 16 June.

[842] In the committee of supply (*CJI*, iii, 259), which reported the following day (*CJI*, iii, 260).

[843] Edward Southwell held this patent office as well as the chief secretaryship.

[844] On the report of the committee of supply on 6 Mar., which had recommended an additional supply of £150,000 for two years: *CJI*, iii, 260.

[845] Heads of a bill for regulating the election of Members, which were reported from committee and agreed (*CJI*, iii, 258).

[846] *CJI*, ii, 258, records a successful motion that the heads be recommended to the lord lieutenant 'with more than ordinary solemnity' and that the House attend in a body to desire that the bill be sent to England 'in due form'. For Maxwell's 'Country Whig' proclivities at this time, see Hayton, *Anglo-Irish Experience*, 105–9.

97. *Alan I, Dublin, to St John II, at his chamber in Lamb Buildings, Middle Temple, 14–19 Mar. 1704/5*

(1248/2/180–2)

This letter will wholly consist of an account of some misunderstandings that lately hapned between the house of Commons, and lower house of convocacion. On Saturday evening[847] one Mr Sale[848] came to my house and told me he was ordered by the convocacion to deliver me this memorial (and gave me a paper sealed up in form of a letter superscribed to the honourable Allen Brodrick Esqr Speaker to the house of Commons) I opened the paper, and found an enclosed sheet in the following words.[849] A memorial of the Deans, Archdeacons, and Proctors of the Clergie of the Church of Ireland assembled in convocacion. To the Speaker of the honourable house of Commons to be communicated to the said house. Whereas heads of a bill for the improvement of the hempen and flaxen manufactories of this Kingdome are brought into the honourable house of commons,[850] wherein there is a clause inserted to this purpose (viz) That no greater summe then (blank) per acre, and soe in proporcion for what shal be sown be paid for tythes of hemp and flax to such to whom the same of right belongeth. Which clause in the consequences thereof we apprehend may prove very prejudicial to the rights and properties of the Clergy of this Kingdome. And whereas we are here assembled to represent the said Clergy, and are entrusted by them with the care of their rights as well civil as Ecclesiastical. We doe therefore humbly represent unto the honourable house of Commons that the freehold and propertye of the whole Clergy are concerned in the said clause, and doe also humbly desire that the said clause may not passe in the said bill until our reasons, which we are ready to offer against it be first heard. Signed. S. Synge Prolocutor.[851] On Monday morning when the house had a little filled I acquainted the house with my having received such a paper, and delivered it in to the Clerk.[852] There was a perfect silence for about three minutes, and then Mr Anderson Sanders began the debate, and was followed by the Atturney and Chancellor of the Exchequer;[853] all agreed the paper imported an high violacion and invasion of our priviledges, but were for taking time to consider what was to be done in it: the Recorder[854] said we ought to come to immediate resolucions to assert our selves to be the representatives of the Clergy as well as Laiety. Mr Conollye and every body that spoke agreed that our

[847] 10 Mar.

[848] John Sale (bef. 1679–1732), 'actuary' of the lower house of convocation and later MP [I] for Carysfort, 1715–*d*. (*Hist. Ir. Parl*., vi, 230–1).

[849] Confirmed in *CJI*, iii, 271. For what follows, see *Records of Convocation*, ed. Gerald Bray (20 vols, Woodbridge, 2005–6), xvii, 11, 154–6, 169–70.

[850] These had been presented on 1 Mar. by Sir Thomas Southwell, referred to a committee of the whole house (*CJI*, iii, 271). According to orders, the committee should have discussed the heads on 10 Mar. but had been prevented by press of business and had postponed the committee sitting till the following Monday (12 Mar.) (*CJI*, iii, 270).

[851] Samuel Synge (c.1657–1708), dean of Kildare, for whom see J.B. Leslie, *Clergy of Dublin and Glendalough: Biographical Succession Lists*, rev. W. J. R. Wallace (Dublin, 2001), 1097.

[852] Confirmed in *CJI*, iii, 271.

[853] Philip Savage.

[854] John Forster, recorder of Dublin.

rights were violated, as well in the matter of the paper as in the maner of their addressing to us: but he was for giving the house time to consider etc Mr A[*nderson*] Sanders stood up and moved to take Sale into custodye: and was afterward (three or fowre having spoken between) seconded by Mr Ecchlin,[855] and Mr Attorney Mr Foulke, and Mr Silver went yet farther to take the Prolocutor into custodye. Clayton spoke after Conollye, very well, and shewed how very injurious a paper this was to the constitucion and being of the house but moved we should take time to come to vigorous yet wise resolucions. Serjeant Neve was also for time. Mr Ludlow said the paper could not be excused, they knew the import of words and meant what they said. Mr Singleton moved the house should come to a vote that they were the only representatives of the Commons of Ireland as well Clergy as Laietye. Nothing is more remarkable in this debate then that the mocion for committing Sale was made by Sanders, and seconded as I mentioned before and no one man of a certain kidney[856] spoke at all to it; That Mr Sanders the Attorney and Mr Ludlow spoke twice in this debate;[857] and that Conollye, Clayton, and Neve were for considering and taking time, and Clayton particularly.[858] But Sanders mocion for Sales being taken into custodye, seconded by Ecchlin, and Mr FitzGerald of Castledod, and others before named put the house on calling for that question; but precedent to it, they came to the resolutions following. 1. Resolved. That the commons in parliament assembled are the true and only representatives of and entrusted with the civil rights and propertyes of all the commons of Ireland as well Clergy as Laietye. 2. That no person, or body or men whatsoever within this realm hath or have a right to be heard against the passing any bill or heads of a bill under the consideracion of this house but by leave first obtained from this house upon the applicacion of such person or body of men by peticion to this house and not otherwise. 3. That the lower house of convocacion have invaded the rights and priviledges of this house by a memorial intitled, A memorial etc signed by their Prolocutor, and delivered to the Speaker of this house by their order, to be communicated to this House. I fancy (for I have it not by me) the third resolucion was in the following words. That the Lower house of convocacion by a paper signed by their Prolocutor, and delivered by John Sale to the Speaker of this house, intitled A memorial etc. and directed to the Speaker etc. have invaded the rights and priviledges of this house. 4. That John Sale by delivering the said memorial is guilty of a breach of the priviledges of this house. 5. That John Sale be taken into custodye etc.[859] Some little time after this Mr Tenison the Bishop of Meaths son[860] came into the house and told us that he had been discoursing this matter with some Bishops, and that they declared that they were no way consulted with about it or consenting to it. I should have told you that in the debate Dr Sanders[861] and Mr Nuttley moved against taking Sale

[855]More likely to have been the barrister Robert Echlin, MP [I] for Newry, than his namesake, MP [I] for Co. Monaghan, who was a serving army officer.

[856]i.e. tories.

[857]Each one a tory. Speaking twice in the same debate was in itself sufficiently unusual to be worthy of comment.

[858]Each one a whig.

[859]The third, fourth and fifth resolutions were later expunged from the journal and thus not printed in *CJI*, iii, 271.

[860]Henry Tenison was the son of Richard, bishop of Meath.

[861]Morley Saunders.

into custody, as acting by order, but never mentioned his being actuary to the convocacion: Sir Ri[*chard*] Leving moved to have him taken into custody and the question was called for. I delayed putting it for some time, and either twice or thrice asked whether it was insisted on to have me put it; for indeed I had in my head the priviledge of the servants of the members of the convocation, tho I had not lately read the 8 H[*enry*] 6.Cap.1[862] and the obstruction or hint I gave was as much as I could well justifye; but the question was loudly called for, and unanimously carried. On Tuesday we were told by Mr Tenison the convocacion had deputed persons to own they had done amisse in the humblest maner, that they were at the door, that he had a paper in his hand containing what they were willing to say;[863] but he mumbled it soe and the house was in such warmth at having this offered as reparacion that I could not understand fully the import of his paper, Mr Atturney indeed gave him a well moved, but Mr FitzGerald,[864] Sir Ri[*chard*] Leving, Sir Fr[*ancis*] Blundel and others said no satisfaction but under the prolocutors hand owning our priviledges particularly would doe. Mr Doppin said they would doe what we pleased, and desired we would say what would please us. But Mr Attorney had considered the 8 H[*enry*] 6. in England and 28 H[*enry*] 8. cap.12 in Ireland,[865] and gave us to understand we had broken the priviledges of the convocacion in taking Sale. You remember what share he and the Sollicitor[866] had in that vote. Mr Upton moved not to print our votes. Mr Stafford, Conollye, Maxwel, Dering, Silver, the recorder, and Mr Sandford were for delaying printing under an assurance we should have reparacion given us: Mr Wingfeild, Col. Eyre,[867] and Mr Pollard thought we ought not to goe out of our course of printing, but it was delayed by general consent till next day. Perhaps what I am going to say might have noe influence on Upton, Stafford, Maxwel, or Conollye, but the next morning a peticion was brought in by Ludlow in favor of the sacramental tests being repealed for benefit of the dissenters;[868] this I fancy was gone into by a certain party, to gett them to agree to the giving time: and afterward the bringing in this peticion was made use of as a reason to be easy with the convocacion, the enemies of the Church striking at her foundacion by that peticion as Mr Tenison expressed it. On Wednesday[869] Sale was discharged by our order,[870] as actuary of the lower house of convocacion, and for want of him (as they pretended) they could give

[862]The Privileges of the Clergy Act of 1429 [E].

[863]Not recorded in *CJI*.

[864]Probably Robert Fitzgerald, MP [I] Charleville (see above, p. 174).

[865]The English act regulating the privileges of the clergy, 8 Hen. VI, c.1; and the Irish act against proctors being Members of Parliament, 28 Hen. VIII, c. 12.

[866]Sir Richard Levinge.

[867]John Eyre.

[868]A petition of Arthur Upton (father of Clotworthy Upton MP [I]) and others, on behalf of 'the Protestant dissenting subjects of Ireland' (*CJI*, iii, 279). On the face of it, Alan's suggestion that this was introduced by the tory Stephen Ludlow looks decidedly odd, unless one accepts his suggestion that some devious tactical manoeuvre was afoot. However, it is worth noting that the *Journals*, while not identifying the MP who brought in the petition, do note that immediately afterwards Ludlow presented heads of a bill, to amend the recent act preventing butchers from being graziers, and it is possible that Alan may have misread the *Votes* and thus misrepresented what actually happened.

[869]14 Mar.

[870]Not recorded in *CJI*.

us noe answer till Fryday,[871] when we received a paper in the following words (delivered open to me by Mr Tenison in the chair).[872]

Sir, It is with great concern that the lower house of convocacion find themselves misunderstood in their late memorial, and that it hath unhappilye occasioned soe high resentments in the honourable house of commons. We never designed by any expression in our paper, to invade the rights of that honourable house, or to assume to our selves any part of that trust which by the constitution is vested in them: Therefore as the lower house of convocacion has and ever will have a due regard to all the rights and priviledges of the honourable house of commons, soe we humbly hope that that honourable house will have a just regard to ours, and that they will let fall those resentments which they have expressed against us. And having thus (we hope) given proper satisfaction to that honourable house, whose concern for the established Church in many instances we gratefully acknowledge, we humbly desire that they will be pleased to lett nothing remain on their journals which relates to that memorial; and give us leave to withdraw that paper, which we will likewise take care shal not appear on our books. This being the unanimous sense of the lower house of convocacion, I am commanded to lay it before you to be communicated to the honourable house of commons and am Sir your humble servant S. Synge. Prolocutor. From the lower house of convocacion March 16th. 1704. To A[*lan*] B[*rodrick*] etc. Sir Fr. Blundel, Mr Attorney, Tenison, Ecchlin, Chancellor of Exchequer, Ludlow, Stewart,[873] Nuttley, Mr Bingham, thought the paper satisfactorye, but the general sense of the house was otherwise, and to delay till this day under great expectacions of full reparacion. This being over, the next thing we did was in my sense the most extraordinarye I ever saw: Mr Tenison told us that this seeming misunderstanding will make people without doors beleive we are angry with the Church, to prevent which he proposed a vote that we would stand by and support the Church in all its just rights and priviledges: Mr St George,[874] Conollye, and Caulfeild[875] thought it very extraordinarye as timed; that we complained justlye that the convocacion had invaded our priviledges, and this vote looked as if theirs were in danger, which must be understood by us there being no complaint of any invasion or danger from any other place: It is plain this vote answers that part of their letter which desires us to have a just regard to their rights and priviledges. Mr Barry, Sir Ri[*chard*] Leving, Serjeant Neve, Mr Maxwel and Mr Anderson Sanders said it was a proper time, that this would induce and oblige them to give us reparacion: and this notion of Neves prevailed with St George to come off: soe it was unanimously voted.[876] Now you shal see what all this hath produced from them. On

[871] 16 Mar.

[872] The delivery and wording of the message (though not the identity of the messenger) is confirmed in *CJI*, iii, 282. The words underlined in Alan's transcription are not emphasised in the *Journals*. According to Henry Maxwell, MP [I], this communication followed discussions at Dublin Castle between bishops and representatives of the lower house of convocation on one side, and leading members of the government party in the house of commons on the other, at which the clergy had received an assurance that 'the memorial should be withdrawn, and all the votes made upon it should be razed out of our journals' (Centre for Kentish Studies, U1590/O141/11: Maxwell to James Stanhope, 25 Mar. 1705).

[873] Either Hon. Richard Stewart or lieut.-gen. William Steuart.

[874] Either Henry, Oliver, or Richard St George.

[875] Hon. John or William Caulfeild.

[876] Confirmed in *CJI*, iii, 283, where it is stated that Members voted nem.con. that they would 'upon all occasions, to the utmost of their power, support and defend the Church of Ireland as by law established, against all attempts and practices against it whatsoever'.

the 17th we were told by Mr Nuttley that the convocacion consisted of an upper and lower house; that the upper was adjourned before it was known whether the paper would be satisfactorye or not till Monday, and that the lower house could not act but in concert with them (tho the first day Tenison told us from the Bishops that they knew nothing of and disavowed their memorial) and moved for farther time;[877] the Chancellor of the Exchequer, Tenison, Peppard, the Attorney general, Baily, Bingham, Philips,[878] Stewart, Barry, Brigadier Hamilton,[879] the recorder, Ponsonbye, Singleton, Dr Sanders[880] and Harman, spoke to the same purpose: only some mentioned that the convocacion thought they had given us satisfaction, and Tenison said the Lords were conservators of their libertyes, and feared they might demand a conference if we printed our votes and what if we should be obliged to disclaim or recede? Mr Maxwel, Mr Moore,[881] Brigadier Sankey, Mr FitzGerald,[882] and Mr Foulke thought we were trifled with and were for no longer delay; Mr Spring said he was for giving them Monday, but then expected (as Mr St George[883] and Colonel Barry had done before) a ful reparacion by their disclaiming in the words of our vote, and into this Mr St George went. The Attorney, Chancellor of Exchequer, Stewart, and Nuttley thought we might keep it at large to give them time to give us satisfaction and reserve the judgement of what was soe to our selves: but the house would not let the matter fell [*sic*] without a question for printing unlesse gentlemen expressed their sense that they would accept no satisfaction but that proposed by Spring and on those terms it went off, tho I am sensible that we shal not have such satisfaction, but either no paper at all or one claiming a right to tax themselves and that Gentlemen will think themselves not obliged not to debate such a paper to be sufficient satisfaction. The fleece club[884] met last night on it.

19 March. 1704/5

I am now able to tell you what end this matter hath received: this morning Mr Tenison brought be a paper in the chair, directed and open as the last; a copy of which you shal have underneath.[885] Mr Corry and Bingham said it was satisfactorye, Conollye spoke against it, instanced the saving offered by the Lords to the bill of rights in favor of the prerogative (which see 1 Rushworth 564.)[886] but made not a just use of it, nor himself understood. But

[877] Not recorded in *CJI*.

[878] Chichester Philips or William Philips.

[879] Gustavus Hamilton.

[880] Morley Saunders.

[881] John Moore.

[882] Robert Fitzgerald, MP [I] Castlemartyr, or Robert Fitzgerald, MP [I] Charleville.

[883] Either Henry, Oliver, or Richard St George.

[884] Tories evidently met at the Fleece Tavern, in Fishamble Street, Dublin, in order to concert parliamentary tactics. Lists survive of those in attendance on two separate occasions: BL, Add. MS 9715, f. 34 (8 July 1707); Add. MS 34777, f. 70 (3 Oct. 1711).

[885] Confirmed in *CJI*, iii, 291.

[886] In May 1628, during proceedings over the Petition of Right: John Rushworth, *Historical Collections of Private Passages of State, Weighty Matters in Law, Remarkable Proceedings in Five Parliaments Beginning the Sixteenth Year of King James, Anno 1618 …* (2nd edn., 1680), i, 564.

presently it was voted satisfactorye.[887] Then long debates arose what farther to doe, for we had delayed printing our votes since 12 March. Some were for letting them withdraw their memorial, and at length we divided on this question. Yeas 66. Noes 88.[888] Then it was agreed that our two first resolucions should be entred on our fair journal under the memorial, the third fourth and fifth not be inserted in it (is not this extraordinarye, but Sir Ri[*chard*] Leving once a Speaker[889] moved it) that the two papers from the convocacion, and our resolucion of their being satisfactorye should be entred, and afterward we (forsooth) must vote we would stand by the lower house of convocacion in their just rights and priviledges; but this and the other proceedings relating to this affair are not to be printed. Ludlow, Stewart,[890] Tenison, Chancellor of Exchequer, Singleton, Attorney, Keightley, Corry, Nuttley, Ecchlin, Sir Fr[*ancis*] Blundel and Bingham spoke for withdrawing the memorial: Yet Keightley and Bingham divided the other way. Upton, St George,[891] Conollye, Neve, Moore, Maxwel, Doppin, Barry, Silver, Henry Edgeworth, Brigadier Hamilton, Parry, Sta[fford] and Foulke spoke against it: and Neve very well against not [lett]ing all stand in our journal as at that time entred? What may we not undoe after this? Their last paper was in these words.[892]

We the Deans Archdeacons and Proctors of the lower house of convocacion had hopes that the letter which this house sent to the honourable house of Commons on the 16th instant would have sufficiently explained the memorial sent to the speaker the 10th instant; but since we are informed that it has not had the effect for which it was designed, we therefore crave leave to explain our selves farther, that if possible all sort of misunderstanding may be wholly removed. We assure that honourable house that our meaning in the said memorial was to expresse that we in convocaction represent the inferior clergy of the Church of Ireland in matters Ecclesiastical, and that we are so far intrusted with the care of their civil rights as to be obliged by suitable applicacions to the legislative power to endeavour the preservacion of them; but we never meant thereby to draw in question the undoubted right of that honourable house to represent the Clergy as well as laietye in their civil rights and properties: And we humbly hope that that honourable house will preserve to the convocacion such rights and priviledges as all former convocacions in this Kingdome since the reformacion have enjoyed. If in our applicacion we have not pursued proper methods, it is hoped it will be attributed to the long interval of convocacions whereby we have been deprived of the benefit of presidents and experience upon these occasions.[893] And having thus as we hope given satisfaction to that honourable house (whose zeal for the preservacion of the established Church we have often experienced and doe gratefully acknowledge) we humbly desire that honourable house to lay aside their resentments, and that neither the occasion nor effects of them may any longer remain. By order of the house. S. Synge. Prolocutor. From the Lower house of convocacion March 19th 1704. To A[*lan*] B[*rodrick*] Esqr Speaker of the honourable house of commons to be communicated to the

[887] Confirmed in *CJI*, iii, 292 (voted nem. con.), which also record a second resolution, 'that this House will on all occasions, assert the just rights and privileges of the lower house of convocation' (*CJI*, iii, 292).

[888] Division not recorded in *CJI*.

[889] In the Irish parliament of 1692.

[890] Hon. Richard Stewart, or William Steuart.

[891] Henry, Oliver, or Richard St George.

[892] Wording confirmed in *CJI*, iii, 291.

[893] Before its recall in 1703, the convocation had not met since 1666.

said house. This paper if in nature of a letter to me hath neither the word Sir at top, nor the form of a letter in the conclusion, but is really rather an order from the convocacion requiring the Speaker to doe an act, viz to communicate it to the house, and signed as such; but we are high Church men and can swallow this and more.

98. *Alan I, Dublin, to St John II, 24 Mar 1704/5*

(1248/2/183–4)

This letter will be given you by Mr Haltridge who hath desired me to recommend him to your acquaintance as a Client: he is a man of a fair fortune, and very honest; his principles both in and out of Parliament have appeared to be worthy and generous[894] … We adjourned on Thursday[895] by the order of the Governement to the first of May.[896] You must know that the heads of our money bill were reported on Wednesday,[897] at which time Sir Ri[*chard*] Leving made an oily harangue that nothing was intended but to permit us to sit as long as we found necessarye for the dispatch of the businesse before us: and assoon as it was reported the same Gentleman told us that as we had been very happy in the quiet and unanimous temper of the house, so it would well become us to give his Grace thanks by addresse for his care of the safety of the Protestant interest; and to desire him to apply to her Majestye that she would order such summes to be disbursed as should be necessary to repair the fortificacions, and to provide arms and ammunicion and to build baracks in Dublin and to assure her Majestye that if the funds already given should fall short of these ends, we would make good the money in another Session[898] This motion was made when it was more then half an hour after fowre of the clock, and I am positive (for I reckoned them) the house did not then consist of more then three and fifty persons: and I was told last night by two men as likely to oppose the mocion as any two in the house that they were invited out to dinner just before by persons who seldome placed that complement on them: Upton and Maxwel were the men. One while there were but 47 in the house. I had before prayers in the morning observed Sir Ri[*chard*] Leving to carry A[*nderson*] Sanders behind the chair and shew him a paper, which he read in a low voice, yet soe as I heard the word next Session: when this was moved it immediately occurred to me that the paper was the addresse calculated to be brought in on that resolucion and I called Leving and desired him to gratifye me in letting the paper he shewed Sanders in the morning be the addresse: he smilingly told me it should: afterward I called to Sanders and gave him to understand that I had discovered the secret, he said that he had no hand in drawing it nor was advised with about it, nor saw or heard of it till Leving shewed it him. There was but one man named on

[894] John Haltridge, MP [I], described a few years later as 'a grandee of that party [the Whigs] of the first magnitude' (NLI, MS 41580/36: Dorothy Rawdon to Jane Bonnell, 28 Nov. [1711]).

[895] 22 Mar.

[896] Confirmed in *CJI*, iii, 300.

[897] For granting the queen an additional duty on beer, ale, strong waters, tobacco, calicoes, linen, muslins, and other goods.

[898] The passage of this order is recorded in *CJI*, iii, 297.

the committee to prepare it who was not of the same sentiments viz. Mr Conollye;[899] the Committee withdrew immediately and the secretarye[900] was gott into the chair,[901] and the first word he heard was the question put for reading the addresse paragraph by paragraph: he desired to see the order of the house appointing the Committee, but there was neither order, nor the names of the Committee nor any Clerk; soe he told them they might as well put the question on the whole addresse and left them and returned to the house; soon after the addresse was reported,[902] and he spoke handsomely against the maner of coming into it, and the timing it after we had given all we intended, and members were gone into the countrey: he observed there was nothing new had hapned since our committee of Supply was past (as in the case of the £8000 men in the last parliament in England[903]) but that the fortificacions, arms, ammunicion, baracques etc. were all mentioned in the Speech:[904] he called it a morgaging the Kingdome by a very few people; but it was carried on the question, hardly any body being in the house but well wishers to the secret. The intent you see is to assure the Queen of money when she pleases to let some body demand it. People talk freely of this procedure and some few blush at it, but the much greater part pride themselves in the ingenuitye of the Stratagem. Let my brother Tho[mas] see this; but I must not be vouched for scandalous news of this kind. Pray inform yourself in what maner the convocacion (I mean the Lower house) transact matters with the Commons when they have occasions of any sort to doe soe.[905] Is it a mighty solecism to give a person outlawed of treason a capacitye to purchase and inherit, yet let his outlawrye remain? One Nugent was outlawed on the Statute of foreign treasons by means of Mr Eyre when he was but eleven years old, he is become a Protestant and married to one;[906] we would not reverse his outlawry for fear of the precedent, the confirmacion of outlawries being the great securitye the purchasers under the trustees relye on; yet thought we should releive him and took this

[899]Besides William Conolly, the MPs named to the committee were Robert Rochfort, Edward Southwell, Stephen Ludlow, Anderson Saunders, Henry Tenison, Richard Stewart, John Forster, Sir Richard Levinge, Philip Savage, William Steuart, Sir Francis Blundell, Thomas Erle, 'Mr. Philips' (Chichester or William), and Charles Dering. Alan must have overlooked Forster, who was also a whig.

[900]Edward Southwell, Ormond's chief secretary.

[901]Of the committee. This election, and the fact of the 'immediate' withdrawal of the committee, are confirmed in *CJI*, iii, 297.

[902]The address of thanks to the lord lieutenant, reported by Southwell, who had also chaired the committee which prepared it (*CJI*, iii, 297).

[903]In her speech from the throne at the beginning of the English parliamentary session of 1704–5, Queen Anne had drawn attention to charges 'necessary next year which were not mentioned in the last sessions, and some extraordinary expenses incurred since, which were not then provided for' (*CJ*, xiv, 391).The Commons subsequently identified these as having arisen as a consequence of 'the Portugal treaty' (*CJ*, xiv, 408), the so-called 'Methuen treaty' between England and Portugal, signed in 1703.

[904]At his speech at the opening of the session, on 10 Feb. 1705, Ormond had recommended to the consideration of the house of commons 'that care be taken of the fortifications and of such a supply of arms and ammunition as may secure the public from the insults of pur enemies' (*CJI*, iii, 220).

[905]Meaning the lower house of convocation in England.

[906]Hyacinth Richard Nugent (1684–1737), 2nd son of the Irish catholic lawyer Thomas Nugent, 1st Baron Nugent of Riverston [I], had been outlawed in 1694 (Marquis de Ruvigny et Raineval , *The Jacobite Peerage* … (Edinburgh, 1904), 133), but had since conformed to the church of Ireland, and in 1703 married Susanna, da. of Sir Tristram Beresford, 3rd Bt. The outlawry had been declared in England. Given that his estates were in Co. Galway, it is reasonable to assume that 'Mr Eyre' was probably John Eyre, MP [I] 1692–1709.

way.[907] He hath no estate, nor was his father or any ancestor of his a forfeiting person.[908] I goe on Monday to Munster.

99. *Alan I, Cork, to St John II, at his chamber in Lamb Buildings, Middle Temple, 3 Apr. 1705*

(1248/2/187–8)

I can hardly write to you, soe hard have I been plyed since my arrival at Corke; from Dublin I went to see my brother and sister Clayton, he is in the gout but his fit as to pain is over but he continues confined to his bed; she and her boy are well. This morning many Aldermen Burgesses and Citizens of this place did me (what they meant) a respect to meet me at the bounds of the City which is fowre miles from this place, where the Sherifs had a very handsome entertainment, and at my coming to town the Mayor invited me to a very handsome dinner, and with me the people of the first rank that came to meet me. By my writing, you will see that we staid till very late together; upon my word as this proceeded from kindnesse to me, and an inclinacion to own my way of acting hitherto, the news we have of an expectacion of altering things in England had no hand in it: we begin to have our eyes open here.

100. *Alan I, Cork, to Thomas, at the Whitehall coffee-house, King's Street, Westminster, 5 Apr. 1705*

(1248/2/189–90)

… For Gods sake tell me what you intend to doe about the school[909] every body calls on me, and I know not what answer to give them: have you any thoughts of being here this Spring or Summer, or not. Let me also know whether the treatment a freind of yours and mine mett with be in the opinion of some people to be alway acquiesced under as

[907] Heads of a bill to reverse Nugent's outlawry, while ensuiring that he could not take possession again of any of his forfeited property, were introduced by John Eyre on 9 Mar. 1705, and after amendment by the English privy council were presented to the Commons again as a bill on 9 June, but progressed no further (ILD).

[908] Added, at the bottom of the letter;'The addresse. To his Grace etc. The humble etc. May it please etc. We her Majestyes most dutiful and Loyal subjects the commons in Parliament assembled doe with great satisfaction embrace this present occasion to return our humble and hearty thanks to your Grace for your signal care of the Protestant religion and securitye of the Kingdome. Her Majestyes faithful commons have agreed on the best and most proper funds for supporting her Majestyes establishment; and (had their present circumstances permitted) they would have made expresse provision for the repairing the necessary fortificacions and for arms and ammunicion for the publick safety. They beseech your Grace to apply to her sacred Majestye for her orders to issue such summes of money as may be necessarye for such fortificacions, and for a sufficient supply of arms and ammunicion, and for such other summes as her Majestye shal think fit for building barackes in Dublin for the better accomodacion of her Majestyes troops and the ease of the Inhabitants of that City. And we pray your Grace to assure her Majestye on our behalf that if the funds already given shal not be sufficient for these ends that this house will freely and cheerfully make them good to her Majestye in the next session of Parliament.' (Wording confirmed in *CJI*, iii, 298: the address was agreed on 21 Mar.).

[909] Lady Orkney's school in Midleton.

hitherto? Sir R[*ichard*] L[*evinge*] lately at the globe[910] expressed to Mr N[*utle*]y[911] and other company of the same stamp[912] that all was going wrong etc. Will a mans being ready to put on any form qualifye him for an honourable station in the opinion of all persons in authoritye, as it doth in the thoughts of some? Faith, people know when they are ill used, and by whom: and can worse bear it from those in one common interest with them then in an opposite one. Clayton[913] is in bed of the gout; this town did me the honour to meet me at the bounds of our City toward Mallow with the Sherifs, Aldermen, and a great number of freemen and gentlemen: the day was very rainye; there was very good meat and wine provided at the little house on the bounds, thence we came to Corke where they attended me to my Lodgings att Mr Hawkins house on the marsh: then I was invited to dinner by the Mayor[914] where I was kept till very late, and much made of, and all the expressions and signs of respect and kindnesse shewn me. I leave it to you whether you will let this be known or not since it will be a mortificacion to have it discoursed abroad as I am sensible it is a very great that I have been used with soe great tokens of esteem. Peoples eyes in this town are much opened, and I beleive we may (if ever we have another parliament in any reasonable time) have one member a merchant or Citizen; but whether the Souldier or Lawyer will make room for him[915] time must determine … I hope Lawry is soe true a son of high Church that he will vote for Aneslye at Cambridge[916] after all his candor and integritye toward you; If Senny or he have any freinds in the Universitye let them make use of them to oppose that Jac[*obite*].[917]

101. *Alan I, Cork, to St John II, at his chamber in Lamb Buildings, Middle Temple, 8 Apr. 1705*

(1248/2/191–2)

I have yours and Sennys dated yesterday sennight the last of March: the remark you make of the intercourse between the postman and penners of our addresses, and the use intended of soe early publishing and dispersing them[918] I have for some time taken notice of. No doubt when our last addresse was concerted (for I have already told you that it was brought into the house ready before we had voted to goe into one)[919] the managers looked on their affairs in a dangerous posture and all hands were sett on work to shew the strength

[910]The Globe Tavern, in Essex Street, Dublin (J. T. Gilbert, *A History of the City of Dublin* (3 vols, Dublin, 1854–9), ii, 161–2).

[911]Richard Nutley, MP [I].

[912]i.e. tories.

[913]Lawrence Clayton, MP [I].

[914]William Andrews.

[915]Thomas Erle is the soldier; Alan himself the lawyer.

[916]Lawrence Brodrick, Alan's brother, who had a vote in the university constituency by virtue of holding a Cambridge MA.

[917]Arthur Annesley, MP [I], was a candidate in the tory interest in the forthcoming parliamentary election for Cambridge University (*HC 1690–1715*, ii, 54–5).

[918]The tory newspaper the *Post Man* had published in London on 24 Feb. 1705 the loyal address from the Irish house of commons in response to Ormond's speech from the throne at the start of the parliamentary session.

[919]See above pp. 179–80.

of a certain party here. Upon my word if fearfulnesse continue to be soe predominant a qualitye in a certain great man, it may and I think will bring all the evils on him which he thinks to avoid by his great warinesse. You must know for some time (tho you seem to write otherwise) that I purpose immediately after Trinitye term to be over with you; sure you cannot imagine there will be any need in a prorogacion to mencion my thoughts of going at the Castle in nature of asking leave. If there be such a scarcitye of persons that will accept the G[*reat*] S[*eal*][920] I dare say there is a proper Gentleman in a certain part of the world that will not beleive himself unqualifyed for it if tendred to him: tho perhaps (considering his hand and able pen) a Secretaryeship might be as proper a post for him; or taking his skil in controversial divinitye in thought, why might not he succeed at Winchester? he had like once to have taken orders, and would (no doubt) have been a very instructing preacher. I could be very well pleased to hear the Duke of Shrewsburye were in England, and not the lesse soe if he brought a safe and honourable peace along with him[921] …

102. *Alan I, Nine Mile House, to Thomas, at the Whitehall coffee-house, King's Street, Westminster, 20 Apr. 1705*

(1248/2/193–4)

I am come hither on my way toward Dublin, and take the oportunitye of an ill Inne and want of company to write to you at large concerning what I have observed of your affairs since my being in the Countrey; which businesse and troublesome people would hardly have afforded me time to doe after my coming to town. Mr Atkins[922] came to me and told me of a thing to which I have hitherto been perfectly a stranger, tho by what he saith (if true) you are not soe. He saith that there lies a peice of glebe Land belonging to the parish of Moyeshy[923] in the little meadow lying on the right hand as you ride the lane from Ballyanan house to the Parke Gate … When I seemed surprized at this, he told me you knew it very well, and that you took the glebe and your own tithes at forty shillings a year, and appeals to all the acquittances taken from him whether they doe not mencion rent to be paid for glebe as well as tythes. He went farther and said that he proposed to you to have a ditch made to ascertain the glebe, but that you said that would spoil your meadow; and in lieu of it promised to plant trees as a boundarye. Upon discoursing him I doe not find that he can well ascertain how much it is or where it lies, but told me Dean Davies[924] informed him that part of it lay in that meadow and run acrosse the lane up

[920] Since the early months of 1705 there had been rumours of the imminent dismissal of the lord keeper [E], Sir Nathan Wright, but in the event he lasted until Oct. (*Oxf. DNB*).

[921] Charles Talbot (1660–1718), duke of Shrewsbury, had been living on the continent since 1700, for the benefit of his health. He set out from Rome in Apr. 1705, but did not reach England until Dec. (*HL 1660–1715*, iv, 647–8).

[922] Walter Atkin (1671–1741), vicar of Castrachore (the parish in which Midleton was situated) and Ballyspillane, and rector of Mogeesha (which included Ballyannan); later (1710) treasurer of Cloyne (Brady, *Clerical and Parochial Records*, ii, 50, 109–11, 389–90).

[923] Mogeesha.

[924] Rowland Davies (1649–1721), dean of Cork.

toward the hill; and that while he was minister there he enjoyed it. But the cheif tendencye of his discourse seemed to me to propose that an equivalent should be given in exchange somewhere near Middleton, pursuant to our intended act for exchanging glebes, if the case fall within the compasse of the Act.[925] I found by him that he had been discoursing the Bishop[926] on the subject, and that they had already pitched on the equivalent without consulting you or any body else. Pray let me know how this matter stands, and whether Dean Davies enjoyed any glebe there and in what maner and what quantitye of Land and how bounded: as also what passed between Mr Atkins and you about it. I will peruse my fathers patent, and see whether there be any right in the minister of that parish to challenge glebe there. It is very well to be weighed whether in prudence we ought to exchange any Land in Middleton for it, supposing the Church to have a right: for tho it be a desirable thing to have the minister live there, I doubt much whether it be soe to let him have an house and Land in it the fee of which shal belonge to the Church, which may encrease its interest in that corporacion by future acquisicions (if it once ever gett footing there) but can never be bought out if the neighbourhood should prove troublesome. How busy a sort of men are in other Countryes as well as ours in elections you know; and I am not fond of having one alway in the heart of the town to instil principles which perhaps may not be soe much for the safety of the Kingdome as the grandeur of a certain sett of men. You know the temper of the now minister;[927] but if it were perfectly otherwise that ought not to influence you; since God only knows who may be his Successors … You will laugh at what follows, but depend on it the thing is true: I have it from the mouth of a person concerned in the matter. The foreman of the Grand Jury (Mr Cox[928]) brought in an addresse ready cut and dried (following the late example of a greater assembly[929]) to thank the Queen for many things; but the burthen of the song was for sending us soe excellent a ——.[930] People could not well digest things being prepared before they were resolved on or so much as debated or proposed; it was asked who drew it? Mr Rose.[931] Was it not too late in the Assises? Gentlemen were gone out of town etc. but it was urged till one took heart of Grace[932] and spoke against the timing, maner, and in some measure against the addresse, as not mentioning Lord Marleboroughs successe which the County had never done:[933] At length it cooled and was modestly withdrawn, and all care is taken not to have a word spoken that such a thing was ever proposed. What doe you think if it should be done at the Quarter Sessions at Bandon? If soe this story told (but not from you) would be a cruel

[925] The 1704 Act for exchange of glebes (2 Anne, c.10 [I]).

[926] Charles Crowe (1654–1726), bishop of Cloyne.

[927] Walter Atkin.

[928] Richard Cox, MP [I], eldest son of the lord chancellor.

[929] The house of commons: see above, p. 182.

[930] Lord lieutenant.

[931] Almost certainly Henry Rose, MP [I], from the neighbouring county of Limerick, who at this point in his parliamentary career was supporting the administration (*Hist. Ir. Parl.*, vi, 189).

[932] Plucked up courage.

[933] The victory at Blenheim. Evidently this was the first time an address from Co. Cork had omitted mention of a battlefield triumph.

crosse bite. The Grand Jury were Cox, Mansergh,[934] Warham St Leger,[935] Hyde,[936] Mich. Gold,[937] Longfeild,[938] Will Wade,[939] Jo: Jervis,[940] Connor Callaghan,[941] Morison,[942] Tom Rigs,[943] Rob. Gookin,[944] Stawel Mills,[945] Tho: Purdon,[946] Frank Hodder,[947] Jonas Stawel[948] and Wakeham[949] who was absent. Can you guesse how such a Grand Jury should omit so material a thing. I fancy I have marked the naughty people with a dash under their names.

103. *Alan I, Dublin, to St John II, at his chamber in Lamb Buildings, Middle Temple, 26 Apr. 1705*

(1248/2/195–6)

Just now I received yours of the one and twentieth, and shal be pleased to see the other you promise me by next post: for tho my passions are not soe much exercised at present as those of some other people here, who look on alteracions on your side the water as forerunners of the like here, yet I shal be pleased to see matters soe settled that we may hope to see no more experiments of the same nature with that the Queens Speech hints at.[950] I shal be very well pleased at your not declining what you say is proposed, and approve of your not seeking it: it will be of reputacion on that side the water where people are endeavoured to be lead into a beleif that the being of the name is an irremoveable obstacle.[951] Hath not Mr

934 George Mansergh.

935 Warham St Leger (*d.* by 1766), of Heyward's Hill, Co. Cork (Burke, *Commoners*, iv, 486; Phillimore, *Indexes*, ii, 150).

936 Arthur Hyde, MP [I].

937 Michael Goold.

938 John Longfield.

939 William Wade (*d.* by 1734) of Feal, Co. Cork (Reg. Deeds, 92/223/64419).

940 Joseph Jervois (1653–1737), of Brade, Co.Cork, steward to Percy Freke, MP [I] (Reg. Deeds, 3/79/685; *The Remembrances of Elizabeth Freke 1671–1714*, ed. R.A. Anselment (Camden ser. 5, xviii, 2001), 92, 94, 256).

941 Connor Callaghan (*d.* aft.1709), of Co. Cork (Reg. Deeds, 2/232/428).

942 Possibly William Morrison (*d.* by 1737) of Midleton (Phillimore, *Indexes*, ii, 143).

943 Thomas Riggs (*d.* aft. 1725), of Riggsdale, Co. Cork (Reg. Deeds, 47/188/29747).

944 Either Robert Gookin (*d.* by 1710) of Courtmacsherry, Co. Cork (Phillimore, *Indexes*, ii, 47), or his son Robert (*d.* aft. 1735) of Courtmacsherry (University College Cork, Archives Service, IE BL/SC/CB/3, 8: deeds, 9 Apr.1712, 3 Sept.1735).

945 Stawell Mills (*d.* by 1726), of Ballybeg, Co. Cork (*Dublin Weekly Journal*, 22 Jan.1725/6).

946 Thomas Purdon (*d.* 1736) of Kilpatrick, Co. Cork (Reg. Deeds, 100/487–8/7135–60).

947 Francis Hodder (*d.* by 1725) of Cork (Phillimore, *Indexes*, ii, 56).

948 Jonas Stawell (*d.* by 1708) of Coolmain, Co. Cork (Phillimore, *Indexes*, ii, 103; Smith, *Antient and Present State of Cork*, i, 241).

949 William Wakeham, of Little Island, Co. Cork.

950 Queen Anne's speech at the close of the English parliamentary session on 14 Mar. 1705 (*LJ*, xvii, 720) included a pointed reference to the kingdom having 'narrowly escaped' from the 'fatal effects' of 'our own unreasonable humour and animosity', which should be 'a sufficient warning against any dangerous experiments for the future'. This was an obvious reference to the Tack, the attempt by tories in the English house of commons on 28 Nov. 1704 to attach (or 'tack') the Occasional Conformity Bill to the Land Tax Bill, and thus guarantee its passage through the whig-dominated upper house.

951 On 21 Apr. Narcissus Luttrell had reported that St John was to be one of the serjeants at law called up next term (*Brief Historical Relation*, v, 542). He was installed on 9 June (ibid., 561).

Haltridge delivered the long letter with an account of the difference between our house and the convocacion?[952] I am surprised that I hear nothing of that and some other letters I have written lately ….

104. *Alan I, Dublin, to St John II, at his chamber in Lamb Buildings, Middle Temple, 3 May 1705*

(1248/2/197–8)

This morning I received yours of the 26th and 28th of April; in answer to the former I must caution you of what consequence it may be to me (as a certain assembly stands constituted) to be vouched for any words that passed within that house, which may be made use of to the prejudice of any member of it in another place: nor doe I think it to be any way your businesse to make the thing personal as to your self, that you will justifye that he used any words in the house of commons that he is not willing now to be told he made use of. No letter that I wrote you (all which I have carefully inspected) touches at all on this matter; but as far as my memorye goes at this distance of time the matter hapned in this maner. When the debate or mocion was about an addresse, some moved to have it a part of the addresse to stand by the succession in the Protestant line, as by Acts of Parliament established in England: and Mr Anesley did say that he hoped we intended as it now was or should hereafter be settled by Acts of Parliament in England; or words to that effect.[953] I cannot say that he said these words as speaking to the Chair, for I beleive he spoke at the same time that some other person was also up and speaking; but he was standing, and spoke so loud that I am confident many Gentlemen heard him. That this is soe I have beside my own memorye these concurrent reasons to confirm me: I dined accidentally this day with Mr Whitshead[954] and Dr Burrige,[955] and asked the former what he knew or remembred of the discourse: he said he could not charge himself with particularly remembring the words used but beleived and alway took it that he spoke to that effect: the later affirmed that he heard the very day the addresse was voted that he spoke to that effect and that from several hands and never heard it contradicted or doubted. Jack Jephson[956] came to my study this afternoon on another occasion and on my desiring him to recollect himself what he remembred of that matter said, that he very well remembred that on that occasion it being moved that they would stand by the succession in the Protestant line as by Acts of Parliament settled, that Mr Anesley said or that should be made; or as it should be settled. I doe not remember precisely the words he used, but it was to this effect: as the succession was settled or should be settled, or else as by Acts of Parliament made or that should be made: but I refer you to his knowledge of the thing by getting sight of a postscript on that subject

[952]See above, p. 173–9.

[953]The address was voted, and a drafting committee appointed, on 24 Sept.1703 (*CJI*, iii, 14).

[954]William Whitshed, MP [I].

[955]Ezekiel Burridge.

[956]John Jephson, MP [I].

to a letter by him wrote to the Bishop of Ely.[957] Burrige will write this night to Mr Rigs,[958] and he will let you see his letter. Clayton[959] is in Munster and many other Gentlemen out of town who I beleive would readily tell their knowledge herein: but I fancy letters will goe from other people to other hands on the same subject. I should tell you that Jephson apprehends the thing passed in the maner I mentioned, he standing up and speaking soe loud as to be heard by a great many near him: but he cannot say the words were spoken to the chair; for indeed it is no new thing with us (not much to our credit, particularly to mine in the chair if I could prevent it) for two to stand up and speak at once: but his was not at that time a sett speech[960] he using to the best of my remembrance only those few words at that time of speaking. Whether he was chairman of the Committee that framed that addresse I cannot say, nor am able to inform my self, neither having the votes[961] by me (for I left mine with you in England) nor being able in the whole town to gett a sett of them: but you may by looking over the beginning of the Sessions inform your self who reported that addresse, for the chairman alway doth that; but if he was (as possibly he might be) the chairman, he ought to make no merit of naming the Princesse Sophia,[962] since by the debates of the house the Committee were sufficiently instructed, and heartily inclined to doe it without his being the mover; but what passed at the Committee I am not able to give you any account, never being at any committee but of the whole house. I hear that Mr Parry[963] and Maxwel[964] (both in town but I cannot speak with them before this goes to the post house) remember the thing very well.

105. *Alan I, Dublin, to St John II, at his chamber in Lamb Buildings, Middle Temple, 5 May 1705*

(1248/2/199–200)

Since my last I have gott a sett of our printed votes by which it will appear that on the 27th of September leave was given to bring in heads of a bill to make it high treason in this Kingdome by word or writing to impeach the succession of the Crown as limited by several Acts of Parliament in England; and that it was recommended to Clayton, Chancellor of the Exchequer, Attorney and recorder to bring them in.[965] Our method is alway to name him the first of the persons who are to bring in the heads, that first moved the thing; and Clayton was the man. These heads were brought in by Clayton the sixth of October, and he was chairman of the Committee of the whole house on the seventh when the bill was

[957] Simon Patrick (1626–1707).

[958] Edward Riggs (*d.* 1706), MP [I], for Bandon 1692–9, or more probably his son Edward, a Middle Templar, elected to the Irish parliament in 1707 at a by-election for Baltimore.

[959] Laurence Clayton, MP[I].

[960] See above, p. 65.

[961] The published daily *Votes* of the House.

[962] Sophia (1630–1714), formerly electress of Hanover: heir presumptive to the English and Irish thrones under the Act of Settlement [E] of 1701.

[963] Benjamin Parry, MP [I].

[964] Henry Maxwell, MP [I].

[965] Confirmed in *CJI*, iii, 19.

under their consideracion; and was the person who was sent up to the Lords for to desire their concurrence therein to have it transmitted into England;[966] and their Lordships on 14th Oct letting us know they did not think fit to proceed in that method he was ordered to carry it to my Lord Lieutenant.[967] In this whole matter Mr Anesley had no share, but Clayton was soe deep in it that he hath thence acquired the nickname of Hanover Clayton among his freinds. As to the addresse it was voted on the 27th of September, but after Claytons mocion to bring in the heads of the bill as you may see by the print; where it will also appear that a Committee was appointed to prepare the addresse on the debates of the house; soe as the subject matter and points to be touched on were pointed out to the committee and not left to their choice, the wording it was all their businesse. Mr Anesley was chosen chairman of that Committee,[968] but sure he forgets himself in saying he brought in the clause for the Princesse Sophia; for if you look on the addresse itself in the votes of the first of October, you will find her not soe much as named in the addresse;[969] but if he means the last clause which is in the following words (And we doe unanimously assure your Majestye that we will to the utmost of our power support and maintain your Majestyes rightful and lawful title to the Crown of this realm and the succession in the Protestant line as the same is settled by Acts of Parliament in England)[970] It is a great truth that it was one of the heads arising from the debates, and I am much mistaken if Claytons mocion did not in great measure give an handle to the mocion for addressing as well as making that part of the subject matter. Whether the penning the addresse was left to him by the Committee as Chairman I know not, perhaps it might, and if that was soe, it may in that sense be true that he brought in the clause; but he was not the mover in the house for mentioning the Succession, but when others spoke to that, used the words in my last, in the maner there contained, or words to the same effect. Mr Parry and Mr Maxwel told Dr Burrige they both remembred the thing, and he gave me hopes they would write to some freind by last post but I find they did not: The proceedings on your side are of such a sort, that people begin to despair of any good.

106. *Alan I, Dublin, to St John II, at his chambers in Lamb Buildings, Middle Temple, 8 May 1705*

(1248/2/201–2)

… You cannot imagine with what industry the matter of Green Madder etc. is represented here as the horridest of murthers,[971] and with an air as if they fared never the better for being

[966] Confirmed in *CJI*, iii, 37–8.

[967] Confirmed in *CJI*, iii, 50–1.

[968] Annesley reported from the committee on 29 Sept. (*CJI*, iii, 24).

[969] Confirmed in *CJI*, iii, 24.

[970] Confirmed in *CJI*, iii, 25.

[971] The execution of Thomas Green, captain of the *Worcester*, Thomas Madder, his first mate, and another crew member, John Simpson, at Leith, on 11 Apr. 1705, after being found guilty of piracy and murder. The case related to the alleged capture by Green of a Scottish merchant ship off the Malabar coast, the murder of the crew and theft of the cargo. The evidence was disputed, but the case raised patriotic passions in Scotland, where trading interests faced superior (and in their view unfair) competition from the English chartered companies. Despite

English or Church men: pray for my own private satifaction let me know how that matter stands, and the sentiments of judicious unbiassed men about it. Our people here would have the world beleive all is safe as to the danger some formerly apprehended themselves in on this side the water, when alteracions were making on the other: but after a storm the sea continues sometime disturbed and unquiet tho the wind be laid … Our fleet for Portugal that lay in Corke harbour weighed anchor last week but was put in again, and one of the transports run aground; but the fair winds for three dayes past make us conclude they are well on their way to Lisbon by this time. It is incredible how a certain principle spreads in this Kingdome; if it be not the wish of some people elsewhere to have it doe soe methinks some method should be taken to prevent it. We swarm with pamphlets, and your book woman utters not half soe many as a certain Gentleman of a certain coat, whose near relacion was in his life time married to a Gentlemans daughter who lives near the house where you and I spent most of our time in vacacions before we were called to the bar …

107. *Alan I, Dublin, to St John II, at his chamber in Lamb Buildings, Middle Temple, 16 May 1705*

(1248/2/203–4)

I have yours of the 10th; pray let me know whether Stephen was a tacker;[972] I find Wm Harvey (member for Rygate) in that List.[973] If you can gett leisure, make the Archbishop of Dublin[974] a visit; he is a man of very good sense, and spirit, and really a valuable man: he mencions you in letters with great regard. Our Court seems to be in great hast to have our parliament affairs soon over; I suppose my Lord Lieutenant would willingly be at this juncture on your side the water, but we have been soe often told how admirable a Cheif Governor he is that some people seem to desire his longer continuance among us, as beleiving no deputye or Justices he will leave can be of soe much use to the countrey; and that he will doe us as much service here as in England: you know, if my inclinacion to forward his wishes did not weigh with me as it doth, the advantage of the next term, would induce me to be for dispatch of all our affairs before that time. What will you say if our convocacion should stir the matter of their memorial again, and be soe successeful as to bring us to alter what we did the last Session and expunge our two votes?[975] Such a thing is in their thoughts and I have seen very odd things come to passe. Is my brother Tho[*mas*] buried at Exning? Sure his own affairs might make him answer some of my letters: Perhaps they lye uncalled for at his Coffee house in Westminster. For the future I will regard his

971 (*continued*) a request from the English ministry to postpone the execution the Scottish privy council, probably intimidated by the Edinburgh mob, ensured that the sentence was carried out, and Green and his crew were presented in England, especially by high church tories and others opposed to any union with Scotland, as martyrs to Scottish Anglophobia. See G.M. Trevelyan, *England under Queen Anne* (3 vols, 1930–4), ii, 249–56; *Oxf. DNB* (*s.v.* Green, Thomas).

972 Stephen Hervey, MP [E] for Reigate. A whig, Hervey appeared in other published lists as having voted *against* the Tack (for which see above, p. 185). These lists were published in the hope of influencing voters in the general election of 1705, in which the Tack was a significant issue (Speck, *Birth of Britain*, 76–8, 84–7).

973 William Harvey, tory MP [E] for Old Sarum, was a Tacker.

974 William King (1650–1729).

975 See above, p. 173–9.

affairs as little as he doth: but I cannot chuse but be in pain about a letter I sent by Mr Haltridge (containing a full narrative of our affair with the convocacion) before I went to Munster.[976] Sure he delivered it, and I hope you saw it; by an hint I observed lately I fancy some letter of mine hath been intercepted: I had rather it were any then that, tho I shal not be much concerned if they should have peeped into that; it contains much truth … I fully purpose to see you about the tenth of July. My services where due. Duty to my father and blessing to Senny and the little ones. Was Lawry at the Cambridge or Hertfordshire elections; if so hath his zeal carried him (as before) to vote for Mr Anesley at Cambridge,[977] or the highflyers elsewhere? Deal freely with me: I know not whether he hath a vote in Hertfordshire, but remember his inclinacions.

108. *Alan I, Dublin, to St John III, at his chamber in Lamb Buildings, Middle Temple, 21 May 1705*

(1248/2/205–6)

In my last to your Uncle[978] I owned yours of the tenth; his of the 15th and another from my sister Courthope[979] of the same date came in yesterday with the bills. I hope the regard Ally[980] and her company shewed my birth day this year will not create such resentment as Gentlemens meeting the last year in London on the same day on that occasion did in a great mans breast: to prevent it I will keep it a great secret that I had so much honour done me even by my own relations and children: for nothing can be a greater heart burning to some people then to have common respect paid me. Ask your Uncle whether it was he that alarmed me, by the last packet; if so, he will know what I mean by the question; if not, I shal not be very inquisitive after the name of my freind: but I fancy I know the hand that corrected the (ass:) in the word (compassed) in the eighth sheet of a certain pamphlet. Sure the publisher of that paper thinks him a mighty timerous man whom he sets up as a mark to be impeached for the common good (as he calls it) if he fancies such blustering can deter him from acting according to what he beleives he owes to his Queen and countrey. But the charm must be dissolved, and certain men must not be preserved in their greatnesse: I beleive it to be the publishers wish, but with an intent not [*to*] preserve the nation from but bring it to ruine by other hands. The second and third lines of the last paragraph shew of what coat the publisher is. I think I gave my brother to understand in my last that we knew of Lord Treasurers[981] recommending Sir Ja: Montague:[982] if soe, I added that the

976 See above, p. 173–9.

977 See above, p. 182. The Cambridge University election took place on 17 May; the Hertfordshire election on 10 May.

978 St John II.

979 Probably Martha.

980 His daughter Alice.

981 Sidney, earl of Godolphin.

982 Sir James Montagu (1666–1713), of the Middle Temple, MP [E] and a junto whig. Godolphin had recommended him for the post of deputy high steward of Westminster, which was in Ormond's gift as high steward. It was eventually given to the tory Thomas Medlycott, one of the duke's clients.

Duke[983] admitted not Sir Christopher Wandesford who came on the errand till his letters were sealed up, and then told him without staying till he made his businesse known that he knew what he came about, but that it was disposed of. It cannot but be observed that the maner of Serjeant Bonithans death[984] makes it unlikely it could be promised before hand, as that of poor Will Porter did who by a lingring distemper gave people time to apply and gett promises of his places:[985] Sir Ja: Montagues recommendacion came I beleive as early as the news of the Serjeants being dead: soe that it must be a more potent recommendacion that prevailed; I beleive none on this side of the water could have balanced that of Lord Treasurer. The observacion my brother makes on my Lords asking this is very just: yet it may proceed from another cause; for if my informacion be true there is more then this due, in return of recommendacions complied with from this side of the water. Desire your Uncle with the very first oportunitye to let me know whether if we should goe soe far in our house as to endeavour to ruine the little remains of a constitucion left us, by accepting and not rejecting an altered money bill[986] I ought not by some eminent instance shew my abhorrence of it; my dissent in a committee will not be I think enough; the hatred I have to the thing will I believe so affect me, as not to be able to be in the chair the day after to put the question of agreeing with our committee, if they shal act in such a maner as I apprehend utterly destructive of our little remaining freedome in parliament. I know the consequence will be a thing that will be very acceptable on any other occasion to put another in my room, and the losse of this Session money after the losse of a term and great part of the expence of it is over: but if I should be ill, this must be born. Talk not of these things. Let me injoin you to be very respectful to your Uncle, and to follow your study; you are too much inclined to lying long in bed in the morning: break your self of that unmanly custom, and act soe as may make you able to stand the designs of enemies; for such you will have if you tread in mine or any of your nearest relacions steps; and I hope you never will purchase a reconciliacion by going into the principles [?and] practices of those that malign us only for acting on motives of more honour and justice then they doe. You cannot imagine how much the eyes of the freinds and enemies of any familye are on a young man of your age that comes with the advantages you doe into the world. If by prudence and spirit you establish a just reputacion it will be a mighty joy to your freinds, and a great addicion of strength to the interest of the familye: if you fail, it will be cause of triumph to base people, cause your nearest relacions to blush for and detest you, and go a great way to fill the measure of the afflictions of your truly affectionate father …

[*PS*.] 22 May. 1704

We talk of two privateers on this Coast and fear our packet boat that went hence Saturday night is taken; none is come in this day tho the wind be fair and one due and a boat on the other side.

983 Ormond.

984 The vacancy arose when the previous deputy high steward, Charles Bonython (c.1653–1705), 'shot himself through the head with a pistol' (*HC 1660–89*, ii, 676–7; HMC, *Ormonde MSS*, n.s., viii, 152).

985 William Porter, commissioner of appeals in the revenue [I] 1691–*d*., and master in chancery [I] 1699–*d*. New patents were issued for both offices in Oct. 1706 (*Lib. Mun.*, pt 2, pp 22, 136).

986 Thereby infringing the claim of the Irish commons to be the sole arbiter of supply legislation. In the event, the money bill was not altered by the English privy council.

I am now credibly informed our money bill is not altered from what it went hence, at which I am rejoiced as removing the difficultye I was under. Why had not I any notice how our bills were cooked on your side the water?

109. *Alan I, Dublin, to St John II, at his chamber in Lamb Buildings, Middle Temple, 7 June 1705*

(1248/2/207–8)

I was in great hope that our Session might have been over this day but I find all things are to fall out crosse to my wishes: for by the pacquet which came in on Tuesday last we are told that our linen bill[987] of which we were wholly out of any expectacion is to be here in some time, and this will continue the Session long enough to disappoint me of this whole term or the greatest part of it: I wish it may be such as will turn to the publick benefit and I shal very easily submit to my own private losse; tho I own I wish it had come time enough to have passed with the rest of our bills and given me oportunitye to have gott some mony this term to have spent in the vacacion in England. There will be time enough to have your answer to this before I can have thoughts of leaving Ireland … If you tell me that I can be time enough before your circuit is over at London, and yet see Corke tho but for six dayes I will go down to prevent any body playing tricks in that corporacion on the election of a new magistracye, as perhaps may be attempted. When I was last there I opened mens eyes and convinced them of the tricks that were endeavoured to be put on them by the representacions of designing men … Yesterday we had an humble peticion of Sir Wm Robinson preferred owning his error and fault, and our justice; and expressing great concern for lying under the unsupportable load of our displeasure; [988] you must know it was put into the hand of a very honest Gentleman to move (Mr Moore[989]) It was long debated whether we should receive it or not: at length it was brought up to the table and read, and heartily spoken for by several; who insisted on the submissive maner of it, and that all crimes (on repentance) might be forgiven; and Mr Keightley proposed a question that his submission was accepted by the house: Mr Dering, Savage, Ludlow, Sir Francis Blundel, Mr Ecchlin,[990] Mr Bingham, and Mr Crow for taking his submission. Mr Conollye, Caulfeild,[991] St George,[992] Maxwel, Jemmy Barry,[993] all against that question: We had voted him uncapable of any emploiment for endeavouring to impose a debt of £103368 on the Kingdome: he owns his guilt, and now we are to own our selves satisfyed. Of what? Of his guilt we were convinced before we passed the vote; and his owning it

[987]The bill 'to repeal an act entitled an act for the advancement of the trade of linen manufactures', having been returned from England, had been sent to the Lords on 27 Feb. It eventually passed into law as 4 Anne, c. 3 [I].

[988]Not recorded in *CJI*. For Robinson's case, see above, p. 161.

[989]John Moore, MP [I], a strong whig.

[990]Probably Robert Echlin, MP [I] Newry.

[991]John or William Caulfeild.

[992]This could refer to any one of the five members of the St George family then sitting in the House, including Sir George, MP [I] Carrick-on-Shannon, and Sir George, 2nd Bt, MP [I] Co. Roscommon.

[993]James Barry, MP [I] Dungarvan.

cannot be reason to make way for him to come into the same or some other publick emploiment to serve us again in the same maner. There could be no other meaning in the displeasure he lay under of the house being soe greivous to him but the losse of emploiment: he was out of confinement, not voted unqualifyed to sit in the house nor expelled: At last Conollye offered if Gentlemen would goe in to laying the incapacitating vote before the Governement he was willing to let fall all other resentment. They that were against Keightleys question were for letting the peticion lye on the table; but that was quickly laid aside by an almost general consent: for some feared it would be resumed and a vote passe in his favor. Others doubted that would not be the consequence, and then the house being in possession of the peticion, that would be uncontroulable evidence of his owning that to be a crime which (you cannot but remember) hath been boldly said to be no fault at all in him: Mr Doppin was for a mighty pretty trimming way to adjourn the debate (the consequence of which would have been a consult at a certain place, a resolucion, and vote) But at length the peticion was allowed to be withdrawn. I should have named Mr Singleton and Jephson as speakers against him and Mr Parry; Mr Stewart[994] and Westgarth for the peticions being received. Such inclinacions checked as they were I never saw, but the majoritye detested the thing.

We have two extravagant matters depending before us in nature of complaints: one shews our twelve Apostles to be no Saints[995] and [*the other*] is against an Anesley:[996] What we can can doe in one or shal doe in the other time will shew.

This was written before our going to the house; we have expelled one Flood for acting much amisse as an officer and Justice of peace.[997]

110. *Alan I, Dublin, to Thomas, at the Whitehall coffee-house, King's Street, Westminster, 12 June 1705*

(1248/2/209–10)

Least I should forget it I will now mind you to inform your self (if possible) what will Jack Hayes made:[998] it is at Lord Downerayles[999] desire I doe this, who expresses great

[994] Richard Stewart or William Steuart.

[995] The subject of this comment is not obvious from the record in *CJI*, unless Alan is referring to the case of Francis Flood, MP [I].

[996] A petition from Eustace Sherlock, presented to the Commons on 25 May and reported on 9 June (*CJI*, iii, 311, 332–42), alleging 'undue practices' on the part of his guardian Maurice Annesley, formerly MP [I] and a cousin of Francis Annesley, MP [I]. Annesley's controversial guardianship of the Sherlock estates was to give rise to the notorious legal case of *Annesley* v. *Sherlock*, which ramified into a major constitutional conflict when in 1717 Annesley appealed a decision of the Irish house of lords to the upper house at Westminster.

[997] On 7 June the army officer Francis Flood, MP [I] was expelled the House and removed from the commission of the peace after numerous allegations had been proved of his having embezzled funds, and also abused his authority while stationed in Co. Kilkenny by wrongful billeting, and forced recruitment (*CJI*, iii, 328–31; James Kelly, *Henry Flood: Patriots and Politics in Eighteenth-century Ireland* (Dublin, 1998), 21–2). Two months earlier he had been cashiered by Ormond for 'false musters' (NLI, MS 992, p. 189: Edward Southwell to Sir Charles Hedges, 8 June 1705).

[998] John Hayes, MP [I] who had died in Mar. (*HC 1690–1715*, iv, 308).

[999] Viscount Doneraile.

confidence in your freindship:[1000] he is kept in the dark as far as is possible, and cannot gett a sight or copy of the will. Where to inquire for it unlesse in the Prerogative[1001] I know not. Why doe not you give me some hint about the probable event of what some time past you asked my opinion, and I approved your going into it: Doth it proceed from your being as ill treated now as formerly you were on a like occasion; upon which I wrote you a letter very much at large? My Lord Bellew and your freind Sir T[*homas*] S[*outhwell*] give it out here that your horses were most scandously beaten att Newmarkett, I mean all that ran, and the rest paid their forfeits: this I had from Lucius O'Bryen[1002] at Castlemartin,[1003] who told it me in a way seeming to bemoan your misfortune, and at the same time said he and Sir John Dillon were mightily troubled that the breed of the countrey would mightily suffer in the opinion of the world by this means. Can you think your breeding horses or following Newmarkett will ever turn to account? You must not take it ill that I tell you my thoughts, that your mind would be much easier if you took a firm resolucion against all maner of play (at which I assure you you are to the last degree unskilful) and would employ your Land in any thing rather then breeding of horses. This is against your inclinacion; yet a late quitting both is better then persevering, which keeps you in continual streights. I suppose Webber[1004] hath given you an account that the house have voted Piercy Smith and his men guilty of a breach of priviledge, and ordered them into the custody of the Serjeant at arms, and me to issue my warrant to the Sherif to give you possession:[1005] He little deserved favor if what Pritchard[1006] saith be true, that he would spend £100 of his own mony in that matter tho Mr Pen[1007] his Land Lord should decline it: but this he denied before me. But in my hearing he told the Committee in answer to a question asked by Mr Maxwel How it hapned that he suspected possession would be given up of the rest of the Land and not of that? That he beleived my father at the time of taking Pritchards Lease intended to hook in that Land to Copingerstowne. He afterward pretended to explain himself, and owned he did not beleive soe, but that my father alway looked on it as part of Copingerstowne: and indeed I had a letter under his hand that shewed he to his own knowledge abused my father in that matter. This is one of the suckers whom my father took into his bosome, and

[1000] Hayes's only child was Viscountess Doneraile. Hayes left her an annuity of £300, together with £1,000 to each of her children and the residue of his estates to her eldest son (TNA, PROB 11/489/277).

[1001] The prerogative court of Canterbury.

[1002] Lucius O'Brien, MP [I].

[1003] Castlemartin, Co. Kildare, an estate acquired from the forfeiture trustees by O'Brien's father-in-law Thomas Keightley, MP [I] (*Eighth Report of the Commissioners of Inquiry into the Collection and Management of the Revenue Arising in Ireland, Scotland, etc.*, H.L. 1824 (142), 72), and included as part of O'Brien's marriage settlement, 29 Dec. 1701 (NLI, MS 45290/4–5).The property was sold in 1717 to the banker Francis Harrison, MP [I] (NLI, MS 45295/3: Mrs Catherine O'Brien to Sir Donough O'Brien, 26 June 1717).

[1004] Probably Edward Webber (c.1672–1730), of Cork, town clerk of Cork and MP [I] Cork 1727–*d.* (*Hist. Ir. Parl.*, vi, 509–10).

[1005] Percy Smyth (*d.* by 1714) of Ightermurragh, Co. Cork (Vicars, *Index*, 433). The committee of privileges had reported in favour of Thomas's petition on 4 June, a decision to which the House agreed nem.com., ordering the Speaker to issue his warrant to restore Thomas into possession of the disputed property of Copingerstown or Coppingerstown (also known as Ballycop(p)inger) in Co. Cork, formerly the seat of a branch of the Cotter family. During the course of proceedings the committee had heard evidence from Alan on his brother's behalf. (*CJI*, iii, 324–5).

[1006] Peregrine Pritchard (c.1690–c.1743) of Midleton had given evidence before the house of commons on 1 June, after Thomas's petition had been presented but before it was committed (*CJ*, iii, 317).

[1007] William Penn (1644–1718), the Quaker, who had inherited his family's estates in Co. Cork.

this the return he makes: Beverley Usher[1008] and Frank Smith[1009] are two more of those he was fond of, and both have used him ill I mean in point of money, but not traduced him as this spark did … Let my father know of Smiths behavior, and goe now and then to Wandsworth for reputacion as well as conscience sake: He cannot live long and it will greive you to the minute you fall into your grave if any distance and misunderstandings between you be not removed in his and your life times. He can remember the matter longer then most people and can tell whether that Land doth of right belong to Copingerstowne: If it doth not, tho you have been and are now in possession, and that Mr Smith ought not to have entred as he did yet you ought not to detain his right, or put him to an ejectment to evict your possession; that I know to be for several years past with you, but I am not able to speak to the ancient right …

111. *Alan I, Dublin, to Thomas, at the Whitehall coffee-house, King's Street, Westminster, 18 June 1705*

(1248/2/211–12)

If you have a mind to see what attack was made on Saturday last upon me[1010] and the event of it goe to Bond street and you will find it: I thought a letter to a woman might more likely goe unsuspected and unopened then one from me addressed to you. Upon my word I have more then once had foul play of that nature shewn me. Whatever good opinion you formerly had of Mr M[*a*]nl[*ey*]'s principles in point of publick affairs you noe doubt had reason for; but as men alter in age and other respects soe they may in thoughts from those they once entertained.[1011] I can not think him of the sentiments you told me he was when he came over. Be very cautious whom you trust; you are too honest to be soe open as you are … When you doe see —— I wish you would apprise him of what past last Saturday; for no doubt the baffle some people received by being disappointed in their intencion will be endeavoured to be hid by pretending a great point was gained in refusing me thanks (for so they will call it, tho there was no question put). On my conscience I think if my freinds had insisted on the question they had carried it. I hear people think I said not enough at

[1008] Beverley Ussher (c.1668–aft. 1727) of Kilmeaden, Co. Waterford (W.B. Wright, *The Ussher Memoirs* … (Dublin and London, 1889), 205, 210–13). A first cousin of Percy Smyth.

[1009] Francis Smyth (*d.* 1727) of Rathcoursey, Co. Cork, Ussher's brother-in-law (Phillimore, *Indexes*, ii, 101; Wright, *Ussher Memoirs*, 205).

[1010] In a debate in the Irish house of commons on the vote of thanks to the Speaker, several MPs took the opportunity 'to speak against him' (*CSP Dom.*, 1704–5, 291).

[1011] Isaac Manley, MP [I] had participated in Monmouth's rising in 1685, escaping to Holland, and had been specifically excepted from James II's general pardon to the rebels in 1686 (George Roberts, *The Life, Progresses and Rebellion of James, Duke of Monmouth* (2 vols, 1844), i, 262; ii, 51, 260). After appointment as postmaster-general [I] in 1703 he seems to have supported the government, though Ormond's chief secretary did not trust him (NLI, MS 991, pp 206–7: Edward Southwell to Ormond, 30 Dec. 1703; *Hist. Ir. Parl.*, v, 190). His brother John, MP [E], was always a strong tory (*HC 1690–1715*, iv, 746–51). In 1710 Swift noted that Isaac was unpopular among Irish tories, though Edward Southwell was still well disposed towards him, and he remained in danger of dismissal and dependent on the assistance of friends like Southwell and Jonathan Swift (Swift, *Journal to Stella*, ed. Williams, 93, 213, 223, 385). However, by 1714 he had resumed his whig allegiance, to the extent that Swift would call him 'the most violent party man in Ireland' (*Swift Correspondence*, ed. Williams, ii, 11).

presenting the money bill in complement to the Duke, and by mentioning Spain hinted at Lord Galweys services:[1012] So I am guilty of Commissions and omissions.

112. *Alan I, Dublin, to St John II, at his chamber in Lamb Buildings, Middle Temple, 21 June 1705*

(1248/2/213–14)

I have yours of the 16th, in answer to mine which I wrote purely to be determined by you in what maner we might with most innocent satisfaction spend this vacacion, and resolved when I wrote to be wholly determined by you in it. Whatever your letter of last Tuesdayes date directs I will fully complye with: The money given by Mr Webber for Mr Haltridge was my brother Tho[*mas*]s wine licence money[1013] for last Christmas: he gave him the very peices which he received, which in so small a summe is the easyest and best way to send money for London: send it to him; As he manages, noe body ought to keep money of his longer in hand then is absolutely necessarye. I cannot be perswaded but that he plays; how else can he live as he doth, and yet be stil bare? His keeper once told me that Sir Tho[*mas*] Felton[1014] once in his hearing swore he never could keep one penny in his pocket while he kept Frampton[1015] company. I have very great inclinacions to goe (if possible with any sort of conveniencye) in a ship under the convoy of the men of war that carry the Duke:[1016] but his departure is soe soon (if our talk hold true) that I shal not be able to begin my journey as early as he: for Tuesday next (the 26th) is mentioned as his day of departure, and my leaving town then will probably cause me to leave two hundred pounds behind me which by staying a fortnight longer I may probably gett maugre[1017] the frowns of Courts etc. If going sooner would be of publick advantage I should despise that summe; but I am sensible of the contrarye; and to goe (as I am pressed) now just as the Duke is going, will be only to give cause of offence and jealousy without doing any service: if one were to be attained, I should much slight the other. I wrote either to my sister or to you about getting me clothes and a wig to wear; for you know that it would be a madnesse to bring good ones hence; if I had such as were fit to wear in London, travailing would spoil them. The heat of the Summer is a very good reason for my sisters and little ones to remove forthwith into the countrey: and I mightily like Epsom for the place: Why should they not go before hand and gett into an house? … Give my blessing to Senny, and tell him that I promise and assure my self he hath made a considerable progresse in the studye of the Law since I saw him: Indeed the difficulties he and every honest man must expect to find whose lot is

[1012] Galway was in command of the Allied troops in Portugal and directing operations on the Iberian Peninsula.

[1013] By the terms of a statute of 1569 (11 Eliz. I, sess. 4, c. 1 [I]), Irish privy councillors were allowed to import wine free of customs duty. By the 18th century this privilege seems to have been transmuted into a standard annual cash payment.

[1014] Sir Thomas Felton (1649–1709), of Whitehall, Westminster and Playford, Suff., master of the royal household and MP [E] (*HC 1690–1715*, iii, 1023–5).

[1015] The notorious sportsman and gambler Tregonwell Frampton (1641–1728), of Newmarket, Suff., who trained Queen Anne's horses (*Oxf. DNB*)

[1016] Ormond, going back to England after the end of the parliamentary session in Ireland.

[1017] In spite of.

fallen unfortunately in this countrey will be ground enough for him to know it will be of absolute necessitye for his own preservacion to make himself valued by his applicacion to businesse …

113. *Alan I, Dublin, to Thomas, at the Whitehall coffee-house, King's Street, Westminster, 24 June 1705*

(1248/2/215–16)

This will goe by Will Conollye, who goes off to morrow morning in Welsh[1018] under the convoy of the man of war which carries my Lord Lieutenant: the occasion of writing it is pretty odd. We the day before we rose agreed on two addresses one to the Queen, the other to my Lord Lieutenant: when the Clerk made out copyes of Saturdayes votes, he also made out in a distinct paper copyes of the two addresses for the presse: I usually read over the Clerks copy of the votes for fear of mistaking the sense of the house or his doing things informally: but the addresses you know I can neither add to nor any way alter and really did not read them. In copying the addresse to the Duke, which began thus: We her Majestyes loyal subjects, the Clerk (Mr Golborne[1019] as I now find) wrote it We your Majestyes loyal subjects; and soe it went to the presse. Before I goe any farther I should lett you know, that I never heard of the matter which is the subject of this letter till three this afternoon, so as what I mention in order of time which hapned before this day yet was a secret to me till then, as was that mistake of the Clerk. When the votes came out there was an alteracion made in the beginning of the addresse to the Duke; which in all probabilitye hapned thus: The man employed by the Printer to sett the presse observed that it would not be sense to begin an addresse to the Duke with the words We your Majestyes etc. (which indeed was true, for it ought to have been her Majestyes etc.) and to remove that blunder, and without considering the following word subjects, put the word Graces in the room of Majestyes; soe as the print runs (We your Graces loyal subjects). It is usual after printing one sheet to send it to me to peruse; and the votes of that day consist of three sheets: one of the three I certainly saw, for I find my hand writing in the margin: whether I saw the sheet in which this grosse mistake is or not I cannot tell: It is possible I might, for I find an addicion of a d in the margin somewhat like my d; but not very like: but this I am sure of, that I never had the votes of that day brought me to be viewed after the presse was corrected by a proof sheet as is usual; and which is the only allowance that I ever give of publishing the votes. This error was as I now find discovered on Fryday, but not one word was spoken of it to me either by the printer, or Mr Tilson the Clerke of the house,[1020] or any other body till the printers wife told me of it at Lord Blessintons this afternoon when her husband was in

[1018] Conolly had purchased a Welsh estate in c.1700, comprising lands in Cardiganshire and Carmarthenshire (Walsh, *Making of the Irish Protestant Ascendancy*, 69). He may have been intending to inspect his property.

[1019] Daniel Golborne (c.1651– by 1720) of Dublin (*Al. Dub.*, 329; Vicars, *Index*, 196; Glenn McKee, 'The Operation, Practices and Procedures of the Irish House of Commons from 1692 to 1730', King's College London PhD, 2017, pp. 43, 272).

[1020] Thomas Tilson (c.1640–1722) of Dublin, who held the patent for the office jointly with his son, also named Thomas (1672–1744) but drew a higher remuneration, indicating that he was the principal clerk (McKee, 'Irish House of Commons', 54, 270).

custody after examinacion. Now noe doubt some people will endeavour to make a great noise of it; for you must know that a great part of this afternoon hath been taken up in the examinacion of it, and it is not yet over (tho near ten at night) and altho the Cheif Justice[1021] and Atturnye said Lord Lieutenant made little of it, when Mr Southwel came he told plainly that he was concerned at it and would know the bottom or to that effect. I offered to give my oath of neither having directed, nor observed any alteracion in the print from the Copy, and the Secretarye seemed to say it would be reasonable: but I am sensible since my leaving them they have asked questions whether ever I gave any orders in it. What danger should I stand in if I had as many or such faults as some people whom you and I know? If this can amount to an inadvertencye in me it is all: but as to that, first I am not sure I ever saw the proof sheet where that alteracion is: nor is it pretended that I had any notice of the alteracion either by word or putting any mark in the print: beside any oversight of mine might and would have been corrected by me, if the votes when printed off had been brought to me before they were dispersed. But I find that the printer having been told of the error on Fryday dispersed but few of those prints, and altered those he had by him by expunging your Graces and printing her Majestyes in the margin; and this before any complaint or notice taken of the error. Pray lay this matter before your freind, and also let my brother St John know and be able to discourse the matter before it is spread about to my disadvantage. Indeed you cannot imagine what a bustle this makes in this town: but It will be a nine dayes wonder; yet the printer must be bound over, and no doubt this will make a very pretty subject of diversion in baiting me next Session. No doubt the freinds of somebody will be the officious spreaders of the prints in which the mistake is; and the care taken to rectifye the error (as is said) may possibly divulge it more then any other way it could be. I protest seriously I am weary of my life, and tho I will sooner dye then act against what is in my judgement for the service of my countrey yet I may honestly withdraw my self from being the but to be shot at by all that malign me on other accounts and take an oportunitye of reeking their spleen against me when ever any colour offers. I hope to be soon with you. Doe not write an answer to me, but you may direct a letter to me to Kenna's at the Golden falcon in Chester. You must order soe that I may know by whom I may depend on being introduced to kisse the Queens hand: I beleive somebody will endeavour to obstruct it …

[*PS.*] Doe not think this a slight matter; endeavours will be used to expose me in print on your side of the water.

114. *Alan I, Dublin, to St John II, at his chamber in Lamb Buildings, Middle Temple, 7 July 1705*

(1248/2/217–18)

This I intend, and hope will be, the last I write to you or any my freinds from this side of the water; for the minute I can be happy in a warrant for a man of war (without which I will not at this time venture over) I resolve to set sail. My very loving and worthy freind Sir Ri[*chard*] Leving I find is like to be my companion, for he intimated as much yesterday by saying if we went in the same ship he was sure neither would wish the other drowned:

[1021] Sir Richard Pyne, lord chief justice of queen's bench [I].

I told him I had more reverence for the decrees of providence, which I was perswaded had determined him a dry death. What you tell me is a meer banter of the promotion of a freind of mine, I doe assure you hath strangely alarmed some good people on this side the water. I wrote to my brother, and for fear of his not thinking it a thing of soe great consideracion as I think it to be, repeat it to you that I think it indispensably necessary to have things so prepared that I may not be to seek for some person to introduce me to kisse the Queens hand: You know by whom I will not seek to be introduced (unlesse I am overruled by my freinds) and probably he may endeavour to obstruct its being done by any other hand … Tell my sister our minister Mr Pountney[1022] is dead; and let my brother know that a very honest Gentleman of our house Mr Somervile[1023] dyed also last night: he is the only one of us that dyed since beginning of our sitting.

[*PS.*] I have now reason to beleive the man of war will go next Monday and then I may hope to be with you this day sennight. Last night I saw one who left Antegoa[1024] the first of May and saw my brother[1025] the night before: he is a sober fellow that tells me is and will do very well.

115. *Alan I, London, to St John II, 19 July 1705*

(1248/2/219)

… The Duke of Somersett[1026] is in town, the Queen at Kensington, and my brother Tho[*mas*] told me that Lord Hallyfax[1027] had on his speaking to him undertaken to have the matter of my being introduced by the Duke of Somersett to kisse the Queens hand settled by my Lord Sommers[1028] speaking to the Duke: and by his directions I have staid within the whole morning (it being now near one of the clock) in expectacion of being called on by Lord Hallyfax: but I hear nothing of or from him. I am under great disquiet in the matter; either there is nothing done in it, or some difficultye raised: the later I am sensible is too unreasonable to be likely. If I had spent soe much time and money at meetings among great company as my brother hath I should at least have known somebody of qualitye ready to doe soe smal a favor, or should have thought my money and time ill bestowed. I beleive I must at last throw my self on fortune, and try some other way. Till this is over I can say nothing of Epsom. We are all well here …

[1022] Thomas Pountney, rector of St Mary's, Dublin 1699–*d.* (Leslie, *Clergy of Dublin and Glendalough*, rev. Wallace, 983).

[1023] James Somerville, MP [I], *d.* 6 July (*Hist. Ir. Parl.*, vi, 302–3. Ormond's political supporter Robert Johnson described Somerville as 'ever perverse while he lived to vote' (HMC, *Ormonde MSS*, n.s., viii, 291).

[1024] Antigua.

[1025] William.

[1026] Charles Seymour (1662–1748), 6th duke of Somerset.

[1027] Charles Montagu (1661–1715), 1st Baron Halifax, one of the junto lords.

[1028] John, Lord Somers.

116. *Alan I, London, to St John II, Guildford, [20 July 1705]*

(1248/2/233)

Fryday 11 of Clock

I am extremely troubled at the disturbance my affair gives you, especially on receiving the third letter in which you propose going with Sir Richard Onslow[1029] to Windsor to morrow: but I think that will be unnecessarye; for I have this minute an assurance from my brother that my Lords Sommers and Hallyfax were both yesterday to have seen the Duke of Somersett, and missed him; that Lord Hallyfax told him just now the thing should be right done, and that at parting my Lord said he would see me, and both he and Lord Sommers would goe with me to the Dukes. I stay within to that purpose, and have some ground to beleive it is not with any regret to them that I am this way to be admitted to kisse the Queens hand: my reason is, I hearing Mr Smith[1030] was come to town and soon to go out again sent to know if he might be waited on; I was told I might see him: before I came (and for any thing I know before I sent) Lord Sommers and Lord Hallyfax were with him: I declined going to him having company: I was told their names and that they knew I was below and must come up; they were [*up*] two pair of stairs,[1031] received me very well, and spoke of my being gazetted[1032] with the last contempt to ——.[1033] Lord S[*omers*] said he had disclaimed us of Ireland being his Subjects. Till this matter is over I cant tell what to say as to our Epsom journey; if it be done this day and I can have time to morrow to see the Duke of Somersett and these two Lords I will be in the evening at Epsom …

[*PS*.] Give my humble services to my Lord Cheif Justice.[1034]

117. *Alan I, [London], to St John II, at Mr Denzil Onslow's*[1035] *house in Surrey, [20 July 1705]*

(1248/2/231–2)

Fryday eleven at night

After all I am I think at as great uncertaintyes as ever; no Lord hath come near me, and my brother now tells me he would have me goe and see Lords S[*omers*] and H[*alifax*] in the morning. The Queen is to goe to Windsor to morrow, soe that I must be forced to go thither of course, tho one of those Lords should introduce me to the Duke of S[*omerset*] soe as to make me known to him and by him to be carried to the Queen to kisse her hand: and whether that will be or no I protest I mightily doubt after the disappointments I have mett with. To morrow I will go to see them and will be at night at Windsor, where I desire I may meet you according to your first proposal: but I doubt my letter of this day will prevent

[1029] Sir Richard Onslow, 3rd Bt (1654–1717), of West Clandon, Surrey, MP [E] and later 1st Baron Onslow.

[1030] John Smith (c.1655–1723), MP Andover [E] and a lord of the treasury [E].

[1031] Two flights of stairs.

[1032] In the sense of being given an appointment under the crown. Whatever preferment Somers and Halifax thought had been intended for Alan, he did not receive anything at this time.

[1033] Presumably the duke of Ormond.

[1034] Sir Richard Pyne.

[1035] Denzil Onslow (c. 1642–1721), of Purford, Surrey, MP [E] Guildford, uncle of Sir Ricjard Onslow.

Sir R[*ichard*] O[*nslow*] coming with you. I am concerned for my brother, because I see him to the last degree uneasy at this matter, and I am convinced he hath done his utmost; but either there is some difficultye in the thing, or he is very little regarded by them. How much impertinent trouble and confinement hath this matter occasioned me …

118. *Alan I, Chester, to St John II, at his chamber in Lamb Buildings, Middle Temple, 20 Oct. 1705*

(1248/2/223–4)

Mine to my sister from Coventry gave you an account of our proceedings soe far; we are now gott safe hither and to morrow design for the Head,[1036] tho it be Sunday; this is occasioned by a letter I found here from the Captain of the Seafort man of war[1037] who came into Hyle lake[1038] late on Sunday and went off thence on Wednesday for Ireland, but assures me will not fail being back at Holyhead next Wednesday and bids me be ready to put my foot into his boat which he will send off for me; soe as that being a place into which a man of war cannot come in, but must stand too again I must be there before him: Mr Conollye[1039] and his crew went with him. Yet after all I am in some doubt whether I may not be disappointed; for a ship that carries a library of books for the Primate[1040] was to have been conveyed from this river to Dublin by that frigott when she sailed last, but she did not fall down tho the man of war fired; but another did, and took the oportunitye of convoy, and the Captain of the Seafort beleived her all along to be the librarye carrier till she came into Dublin: perhaps she may be sent back to Chester water for this ship, if soe I shal be obliged to goe in the packet boat: Cairnes tells me there is no danger of privateers and I fear not any rogue that may have followed St Paul out of Dunkirke.[1041] It went to my heart to have you come out the morning we left London; my sister would willingly have excused the complement, God send it doe not put you back again into your rheumatism. The account you give me of what passed when you waited on my Lord Keeper[1042] is exceedingly pleasing to me, because if it happen you will be at ease and be able to spare your self which your condicion of health requires, and you lye under no kind of obligacion to trespasse on your impaired constitucion, as I doe that have children to provide for. But let me remind you of one thing, that you may yet be disappointed without having reason to make the remark you doe, that then there is some hidden decree against you which is not to be surmounted. I should be sorry for any thing of that kind: the indiscretions of some

[1036] Holyhead.

[1037] Aletter from William Cairnes, MP [I], from Dublin to Alan I, 9 Oct. 1705 (SHC, 1248/2/ 221A–B), telling him that arrangements had been made for the captain of the *Seaforth*, who was carrying various Irish passengers to Chester, to wait there to bring Alan back to Dublin or to pick him up at Holyhead.

[1038] On the Wirral.

[1039] William Conolly, MP [I].

[1040] Narcissus Marsh, archbishop of Dublin. This was the library of Edward Stillingfleet (1635–99), bishop of Worcester, which Marsh had recently purchased (W.N. Osborough, '6 Anne, Chapter 19: "Settling and Preserving a Public Library for Ever"' in *Marsh's Library: A Mirror on the World. Law, Learning and Libraries, 1650–1750,* ed. Muriel McCarthy and Ann Simmons (Dublin, 2009), 44).

[1041] Marc-Antoine de St-Pol (1665–1705), commander of the Dunkirk squadron of the French fleet.

[1042] Sir Nathan Wright (1654–1721).

of our relacions cannot have such an influence; soe as any thing of that nature must have its rise from my conduct: I have acted honestly, and shal never repent of my having taken the methods I have used till I can reasonably think they affect you: and then I shal beleive my Lord O[*rmon*]d hath too great a power and uses it much too far. God send us some good news from Barcelona and that our print about Bajadox prove true;[1043] but I take it for granted my Lord Galway would not sit before it (as you expressely say he hath) without a moral certainty of successe. I understand Mrs Haynes letter[1044] very well: she hath been an humble servant to a great many, and an obliged one; but never more by me then by taking her fee as Councel and endeavouring to deserve it as such. That of Lady Kingsland is about a suit in Chancery wherein her Lord is plaintif;[1045] he hath been wronged and I think cheated by one employed by him as his Councel, and drawn in to an unreasonable disposal of part of his estate by scurvy methods; to be releived against the fraud he sues in equity: You know how difficult his case must be and how plain the imposicion must appear to intitle a man to be releived against his own act, especially against those who derive (but not as purchasers for valuable consideracion) under the person charged with the fraud: there is really great proof of ill practice etc. but how far a Court of equitye will releive I am not a Judge: but I shal be careful how I advise my Lord to appeal because I remember something was read in the defendants deposicions toward the end of the cause as if either my Lord or Lady had said if they could not carry the cause in Ireland they would apply where they had sufficient interest etc. this layes an imputacion where I shal be very unwilling to be the means of having room given to read such a deposicion: When she saith she will appeal according to my advice, if she means she will be guided by it she saith well; but if she hints that I should have encouraged her to appeal I really never did; nor was there room for it, since the Court never gave any opinion in the cause before my leaving Ireland. If after what I shal say to her when ever the Court gives judgement she be for appealing I will transmit you the best state of the case and proofs I am able … This afternoon I have seen some of this town by whom I find Lord Peterboroughs expedicion[1046] is much jested at by some here, who would be as glad, as you and I shal be mortifyed, if it fail of successe. My most worthy freind whom we saw at Hockeril[1047] came late into this town over night and left

[1043]Badajoz in Extramadura, Spain, then under siege by Allied troops under Lord Galway.

[1044]SHC, 1248/2/220A–B: Jane Haynes to Alan, 26 Sept. 1705, expressing her wish to retain him as a counsel. Jane (née Borrowes) (*d.* bef. 1732), married first Gilbert Rawson of Donoghmore, Queen's County, then Rev. Marcus Ussher (1644–98) of Balsoon, Co. Meath, and finally Capt. John Haynes (*d.* 1736), of Cannycourt, Co. Kildare. Ussher left her his estates for life. In Easter term 1706 her eldest son Henry Ussher (1684–1744), who had recently come of age, commenced a chancery suit against his stepfather, alleging that the will was invalid, that the estates were rightfully entailed on him, and that Haynes and his mother had illegally possessed themselves of his father's real and extensive personal estate, on which they had 'committed great waste and destruction'. (Wright, *Ussher Memoirs*, 64–6.)

[1045]Nicholas Barnewall (1668–1725), 3rd Viscount Kingsland [I] and his wife Mary (née Hamilton), the stepdaughter of Richard Talbot, earl of Tyrconnell [I]. *Kingsland* v. *Nicholas Barnewall and others* was heard in chancery in Dublin on 11 Dec. 1705, after which Kingsland appealed the ruling to the English house of lords (Josiah Brown, *Reports of Cases upon Appeals and Writs of Error in the High Court of Parliament* … (7 vols, Dublin, 1784), i, 164–6; HMC, *House of Lords MSS.*, n.s., vii, 7–8; Parliamentary Archives, HL/PO/JO/10/6/105/2291).

[1046]Charles Mordaunt (c.1658–1735), 3rd earl of Peterborough, had been appointed in Mar. 1705 as commander-in-chief of the forces sent to Portugal. At the beginning of Oct. Peterborough and his troops had been heavily involved in the taking of Barcelona.

[1047]Hockerill, nr Bishop's Stortford, Herts.

it next day, without receiving the honours due to his character and what he as once their recorder might expect[1048] …

119. *Alan I, Dublin, to St John II, at his chamber in Lamb Buildings, Middle Temple, 31 Oct. 1705*

(1248/2/225–6)

… I sent a very impertinent print under Mr Herveys cover;[1049] it was preached (as I am told) in a much more warm maner but rectifyed (as they term it) before made publick; as it is, you see the hereditarye monarchy, the tender bowels for the late King James, the much greater danger from Presbyterians then Papists, the weaknesse of King William, the false representing the State of the nation, and the odious moderacion soe much now dreaded, sett of in a sort of rhetorick peculiar to the Author;[1050] but if you remember, Higgen hath been an Orator ever since the Beggars bush was written.[1051] Pray let Senny order Tim Goodwin[1052] to send me by the first safe hand the memorial,[1053] and Sacheverels[1054] and Tillyes sermons;[1055] and if that mentioned by Sir Joseph Jekyl[1056] is to be had let that bear them company. What will Mercurius politicus[1057] doe for a new subject, now Mr Smiths election to the chair hath rendred his old one uselesse;[1058] perhaps my Lord Keeper[1059] may be chosen as a proper subject for that villanous pen. The last was a very warm night in several taverns and houses in this town on the news of the Speaker; a certain sett begin to

[1048] Sir Richard Levinge had served as recorder of Chester 1685–8.

[1049] Presumably Stephen Hervey, MP [E].

[1050] Francis Higgins, *A Sermon Preach'd Before Their Excellencies the Lord Justices, at Christ-Church, Dublin; on Tuesday the 28th of August* … (Dublin, 1705). The emphasis on 'hereditary monarchy' is to be found on p. 6. For Francis Higgins (1669–1728), the 'Irish Sacheverell' see *DIB*, iv, 681–2; and *Oxf. DNB*.

[1051] In the jacobean comedy 'The Beggar's Bush', by Beaumont and Fletcher, with Philip Massinger, first performed in 1622, 'Higgen' was one of the beggars, referred to as 'Orator Higgen' (Act II, sc.i).

[1052] Timothy Godwin (c.1670–1729), formerly domestic chaplain to the duke of Shrewsbury and currently archdeacon of Oxford. He was made bishop of Kilmore in 1715 and archbishop of Cashel in 1727.

[1053] *The Memorial of the Church of England* … (1705).

[1054] Henry Sacheverell (c.1674–1724), of Magdalen College, Oxford, the most notorious of high church preachers. Sacheverell had not published a sermon since his *A Sermon Preach'd Before the University of Oxford on the Tenth day of June 1702* … (1702) but had assisted John Perks in producing *The Rights of the Church of England Asserted and Prov'd: In an Answer to a Late Pamphlet, Intitl'd The Rights of the Protestant Dissenters* … (1705).

[1055] William Tilly (c.1675–1740) was a fellow of Corpus Christi College, Oxford. He had preached a sermon at Oxford assizes on 10 June 1705, which was published on 20 Sept. as *The Nature and Necessity of Religious Resolution, in the Defence and Support of a Good Cause, in Times of Danger and Trial* … (1705) (*Daily Courant*, 20 Sept.1705). For whig outrage at Tilly's comments on occasional conformity, see *The London Diaries of William Nicolson Bishop of Carlisle 1702–1718*, ed. Clyve Jones and Geoffrey Holmes (Oxford, 1985), 321.

[1056] Sir Joseph Jekyll (1662–1738), of Westminster, MP [E], and a bencher of the Middle Temple.

[1057] The periodical *Mercurius Politicus, or, An Antidote to Popular Mis-representations, Containing Reflections on the Present State of Affairs* had first appeared in June 1705.

[1058] John Smith had been elected to the chair of the house of commons at Westminster on 25 Oct. The previous incumbent was Robert Harley (1661–1724), later 1st earl of Oxford.

[1059] The whig William Cowper (1665–1712), of Hertford, later 1st Earl Cowper, had recently succeeded Sir Nathan Wright as lord keeper.

sneak;[1060] the Oxford Swan Club[1061] are not now willing to appear as formerly; many of them are out of town, the place of meeting altered, but their meeting continues tho I cannot yet tell at what place … Sir Ri[*chard*] Leving (I was told by Mr Wilkins) much blamed his freind Dean Frances[1062] for running out pretty freely last Sunday against the Presbyterians, and comparing the enthusiasm of the dissenters with that of the Papists: he shook his head, said it was all wrong, we were to be all of a peice, to join against the common enemye, he was for moderacion etc. the Dean should hear of it, they must for the future be two if such things were persisted in: that he must not expect preferment on such terms etc. Sure we shal be very good in time, provided we have the right Cue given us. My services to my sister and at Bolt Court,[1063] Lord Chief Justice,[1064] Justice Tracy, the Attorney,[1065] Sir Jo[*seph*] Jekyl, Mr Hervey etc …

120. *Alan I, Dublin, to St John II, at his chamber in Lamb Buildings, Middle Temple, 3 Nov. 1705*

(1248/2/227–8)

Soon after I landed I heard from several freinds, of my Lord Rochesters letter, about which you and I spoke to Mr Knight,[1066] and found that inferences had been made from it much to my disadvantage; I went to Mr Keightley[1067] and told him I must see the letter; this was on the first of this month in the morning. It will be unnecessarye to relate what passed farther then that my reputacion was concerned which I would vindicate, by seeing whether the letter contained any thing to my prejudice, and if soe by asking Mr Keightley why he made any thing of that sort to my prejudice publick as well as expostulating the thing in a proper maner with the writer. He told me no more was contained in it then that my Lord should goe the next day to Cornburye[1068] where he would drink his health, as he had done the day before with the Speaker[1069] who dined with him at Newparke;[1070] but said his servant who had the Key of the Escritoire was abroad and he could not then come at it: I said next day would serve as well. He came next morning to my house where I had desired

[1060] Those moderate tories in England who had voted with the court and the whigs (or had abstained) in the division of 28 Nov. 1704 over the 'Tack' had been stigmatised as 'Sneakers'.

[1061] A dining- and drinking-club of high-flying tories, a number of them clergymen, and some with Oxford connections, which met at the Swan Tavern in Dublin. The club and its members had been satirised in *The Swan-Tripe Club in Dublin: A Satyr* …, first published in Dublin in Jan. 1706. See Gilbert, *Hist. City of Dublin*, i, 42; ii, 12–13; F. E. Ball, *Swift's Verse* … (1929), 58–9; *Poems of Swift*, ed. Williams, iii, 1077–8.

[1062] John Francis (c.1661–1724), dean of Christ Church, Dublin.

[1063] Off Fleet Street.

[1064] Sir John Holt (1642–1710), chief justice of queen's bench [E].

[1065] Sir Edward Northey (1652–1723), MP [E] and another of Alan's contemporaries at the Middle Temple (*HC 1690–1715*, iv, 1047).

[1066] Rochester's brother Clarendon had employed a John Knight as his secretary ('my drudge') in 1686–8 (*Clarendon Correspondence*, ed. Singer, i, 350; ii, 121, 225).

[1067] Thomas Keightley, MP [I].

[1068] Cornbury Park in Oxfordshire, the seat of Henry Hyde (1638–1709), 2nd earl of Clarendon.

[1069] Alan I himself.

[1070] New Park, Petersham, Surrey, the seat of Clarendon's brother, Lord Rochester.

two honest Gentlemen, Dick St George,[1071] and Mr Moore of the Kings County[1072] to be witnesses of what past: I asked him if he had gott the letter, he said yes but would not shew it to every body but would let me see it; I told him it was not reasonable to make it publick provided I had right done me in knowing what was in it which related to me; he pointed to a paragraph in the middle of it and gave it into my hand, and I took it to the window, and cast my eye on it; but recollecting that I ought not to read those parts of it in which I was not concerned gave it again to him and desired to know whether when he received and first read it he thought any thing in it tended or was meant to lessen or prejudice me or could give ground for any thing of the kind: he said, he thought not: I asked him what induced him to shew it, he said, he thought he received it at Wexford at dinner, and that some company seeing him open letters enquired after my Lord Rochester, upon which he read the letter, but with no other intent then to let them know where he was and that he was well: I asked him whether he apprehended at the time he shewed the letter that any body at the table thought any thing in it tended to lessen me, or that I had done any mean thing toward my Lord: he said no body seemed to have any such apprehension; and then read the words of the letter to this purpose to the best of my memorye. I goe to morrow to Cornburye, where I will drink your health as I did yesterday with your Speaker who dined with me, [1073] and said a great many kind things. I then said, it was true we had drank his and a great many other healths; that upon discoursing my Lord O[*rmond'*]s treatment of me, particularly in relacion to my Sollicitorship and gazetting,[1074] I had expressed very different sentiments toward his Grace and my Lord Rochester who had on all occasions treated me very well and particularly sent me a warrant to renew my patent of Sollicitor on the Queens accession to the throne without my soe much as applying to his Lordship by letter; and tho I did not tell Keightley soe, the truth is his Lordship did at New Park expresse himself noe way to approve what was done in the Gazette. I told Mr Keightley it was between my Lord and him that he shewed my Lords letters, that since neither he nor any body at hearing it read thought me slighted or reflected on that I would say no more on the occasion then that I had been ill treated of late, and that I apprehended some men made their court by making free with my reputacion, which if I should find any body doe hereafter I would cut his throat. I had been disgraced, as far as turning me out of an emploiment upon certain motives and suggestions could doe it but I would not be trampled on. He expressed trouble at the letters giving occasion of discourse and threw it into the fire; and then the company rose, and the two Gentlemen going into their coach he returned and told me he thought there was no need of taking any notice of it to Lord Rochester. I gave no positive answer, but am now of an opinion you should goe to him and expostulate the matter, and have his sense of it; for after all (tho when he denies it I can go no farther) I am inclined to think the publick shewing it could have no tendencye but to incline people to think or give out I either sought his Lordships protection, or a reconciliacion with the Duke by his means; one I doe not need, nor ever will desire the other. He knows my Lords hints, and if he thought he meant it not to lessen me he would not have made that use of it; I shal not

[1071]Richard St George, MP [I]

[1072]John Moore, MP [I].

[1073]Robert Harley, Speaker of the house of commons [E] 1701–5.

[1074]See above, p. 200.

be fully satisfyed of the writers intencion till he expresseth himself plainly to you on the subject …

121. *Alan I, Dublin, to St John II, at his chamber in Lamb Buildings, Middle Temple, 9 Nov. 1705*

(1248/2/229–30)

I thank you for yours of the third; our home news is good, but our foreign scurvy … I have nakedly laid open my circumstances to you who know my charge: It is above £500 per annum certain without my own, and that of housekeeping, servants etc. viz. £100 per annum to Senny, and £20 per annum in books for him, £215 per annum for the children, £100 per annum Coach, £45 per annum house rent; and I am at the charge of keeping Dick Bettesworths son at school; being (beside our freindship and relacion) one at whose house I reside eat and drink when in Munster, and who takes the care and trouble of my affairs. I have three children, who may (if my sister dye, as is likely) be far from enjoying my brothers estate. Pray know his thoughts and let me have yours whether it will not be advisable to have the whole money put out at interest here at £8 per Cent: at least he may do soe, or rather we for him but by his consent, till that season of the year when exchange is easyer. The risque of ill securityes here is not more in my judgement then in England, unlesse the whole English interest be hereafter unsecure; the interest when remitted must pay exchange, but will that way yeild a pretty deal more then that summe will afford in England …

122. *Alan I, Dublin, to St John II, at his chamber in Lamb Buildings, Middle Temple, 1 Dec. 1705*

(1248/2/234–5)

I thank you for your late letters, in particular those which gave an account of what passed in the house of Lords on the dayes when they were in a committee on the State of the nation, and the heads of the bill for preserving her Majestyes person and the Succession:[1075] let me give you an hint that as we were beforehand with her Majestyes speech in our votes of the 25th of May last, so have we been earlier then the house of Lords in making it treason here by writing or advised speaking to maintain the right of the pretended prince of Wales, or denye that of the Successors as the succession is settled in the Protestant Line;[1076] nor was the following addresse the result of the resolves of the house of Lords, for beside that the presentment was actually given in before the packett arrived which brought in the Lords resolves, or the heads and directions given the Judges to draw that bill, you may I beleive

[1075] 15, 19, 20, 21, 30 Nov. 1705 (*LJ*, xviii, 18–23, 36–7)

[1076] The Irish house of commons agreed on 25 May with resolutions proposed by the committee on the state of nation to denounce those who sought to create misunderstandings between protestants in Ireland, or published pamphlets insinuating that the Hanoverian succession posed a threat to the established church (*CJI*, iii, 234). In 1704 the Irish parliament had passed an act making it high treason to impeach 'by word or writing' the succession in the crown, as established by acts of parliament in England (2 Anne, c. 5).

depend on it that a freind of yours saw a draught of this addresse about the beginning of term. It is in the following words.[1077]

We do present that whereas the unanimitye of Protestants of all sorts in this Kingdome against our common enemy the Papists hath hitherto under God greatly contributed toward the preservacion of our religion, Laws, and Libertyes; insomuch that it was our peculiar happinesse to have scarce any distinction known among us but that of a Protestant in opposicion to a Popish interest, till of late a seditious and unlawful assembly or club was set up and continued at the swan tavern, and other places in this City with an intent to create misunderstandings between Protestants by groundless suggestions of danger to the established Church;[1078] for prevention of which pernicious practices the honourable house of Commons of this Kingdome on the 25th of May 1705 resolved nem. con. 1. (That endeavouring to create or promote misunderstandings betwixt Protestants of this Kingdome tends to the advantage of the Papists, and weakning the Protestant interest, is seditious and of dangerous consequence to her Majestyes governement and the succession in the Protestant line as by Law established. 2. That by writing dispersing of pamphlets or otherwise to insinuate danger to the established Church from the succession as by Law established, tends to promote Popery and the interest of the pretended Prince of Wales. 3. That it is the indispensable duty of all magistrates in this Kingdome to put the Laws strictly in execucion against all persons who shal be guilty of such pernicious practices). And whereas notwithstanding these seasonable resolucions several persons have since continued and frequently assembled at the aforesaid seditious meetings on purpose to instil dangerous principles into the youth of this Kingdome, to widen the breaches among protestants, and to promote new ones even among those of our established Church by aspersing the prudence and moderacion of persons of known and steddy affections to the Church with the imputacion of insinceritye and want of zeal for her defence, and to distract the minds of unwary persons with groundlesse jealousies and apprehensions of danger to the Church, which (if at all) is to be feared from the designs of those who give the false alarm: We do therefore present the aforesaid meeting to be an unlawful and seditious assembly, as tending to forment animosityes among Protestants, and to give great advantage to the enemyes of our establishment both in Church and State: and that it is a duty incumbent on the magistrates of this City to use their utmost endeavours in suppressing such meetings, and in bringing to condigne punishment all such persons as shal presume by word writing or otherwise to insinuate unreasonable mistrusts among Protestants, or jealousies of danger to the established Church under the glorious reign of her present Majestye, or from the succession as by Law established.

The Cheif Justice[1079] told the Jury they would have done well to have named some of the persons, and that the Court would then have taken care to punish them according to Law: The Attorney and Sollicitor were in Court and harangued largely on the goodnesse and seasonablenesse of the presentment, and I am told the later expressed himself soe far of King Williams sentiments that there ought to be no distinction among us but Protestant and Papist, and moved that no body might print it but her Majestyes printer:[1080] what thanks

[1077] A presentment by the grand jury of Dublin city, made in the court of queen's bench, 28 Nov. 1705, printed in *Post Man*, 11 Dec. 1705.

[1078] The so-called 'Swan-Tripe Club'.

[1079] Sir Richard Pyne, lord chief justice of queen's bench [I].

[1080] Andrew Crooke (c.1659–1732) of Cork Hill, Dublin (Pollard, *Dublin Book Trade*, 129–31).

he hath had or will have for it from some of his dear freinds I know [*not*], but I have not yet heard the print cryed about by the hawkers, soe as I fancy the Queens printer hath not yet received directions for setting the presse at work. I cannot tell what persons the grand Jury mean by this Club; but the town saith, Mr Percival[1081] and Mr Higgins[1082] (two of our warm high divines) Mr Nuttley,[1083] Mr Lock,[1084] Mr Hinton,[1085] and some others whom I forbear to name used to drink an evenings bottle at that tavern now and then: and they talk too that at the Club (but of whom it consisted then I cannot say) an health to number 22 and confusion to Philo-sophy have been drunk; the numbers 14, 5, and 3 make 22:[1086] and the Princesse Sophia hath freinds. I saw a letter dated from the inner temple and subscribed S.Leving[1087] giving an account to our Sollicitor here of his brother Sollicitors[1088] and your argument in Dixon and Anesleys case,[1089] and a fair representacion it seemed to be; but in it were these words that you should have used, that you doubted if the people of Ireland should by the reversal of that judgement know there had a sett of men been sent among them with power to dispose of the most innocent mans estate, such a knowledge of their vassalage might cause such rancor and sowrnesse in their disposicions as may indeed be of very bad consequence: He concludes in saying Anesley will bring a writ of error before the Lords, and if worsted there it may cause an applicacion to the Legislature to add to or expound the Act; else there will be more ejectments of the sort. You may be sure all use possible will be made of your words to your prejudice; but it will be no losse to you to wear a bar gown and stand, instead of a more easy and lesse gainful Cushion.[1090] I was mistaken in saying the Sollicitor was for having the presentment printed by the State printer, I am now told it was another; who hath not much thanks from some freinds for his pains. I beleive it will be printed with our representacion[1091] if it wait till the State printer hath orders to doe it …

[1081] William Perceval (c.1675–1734), archdeacon of Cashel.

[1082] Francis Higgins (see above, p. 213).

[1083] Richard Nutley, MP [I].

[1084] Richard Locke, MP [I]. For his reaction to the presentment see *Hist. Ir. Parl.*, v,102.

[1085] John Hinton (c.1671–1743), archdeacon of Ossory.

[1086] A reference to the combined regnal numbers of Louis XIV of France, his grandson Philip V of Spain, and the jacobite pretender, 'James III'. Philo-sophy' is an obvious pun on the name of Sophia of Hanover.

[1087] Sir Richard Levinge's cousin, Samuel Levinge (c.1666–1748), of the Inner Temple (*Calendar of Inner Temple Records*, ed. Inderwick et al., iii, 265; iv, 541; West Sussex RO, SAS–S/262; http://www.kentarchaeology.org.uk/Research/Libr/Mls/HIG/01/htm (accessed 19 Nov. 2017).

[1088] Simon Harcourt (1661–1727), MP [E] and later 1st Viscount Harcourt.

[1089] The case of *Henry Dixon* v. *Francis Annesley*, over the possession of land at Tippenham, Co. Kildare, turned on a controversial decision of the forfeiture trustees in favour of Annesley (himself, of course, a trustee). It had originally been decided, in Dixon's favour, in the court of queen's bench in Ireland, but was then appealed to the queen's bench in England, which upheld the original judgment, and finally to the house of lords at Westminster, which on 10 Mar. 1706 finally confirmed Dixon's claim. St John Brodrick appeared for Dixon (with Sir Joseph Jekyll), and argued that the lands in question were outside the jurisdiction of the trustees (HMC, *House of Lords MSS*, n.s.,vii, 43; Brown, *Reports of Cases* …, i, 171–8)

[1090] The seat of a judge or senior legal officer.

[1091] The representation on 'the present distressed condition of this kingdom', agreed by the Irish house of commons on 20 Oct. 1703 and never printed despite a parliamentary order to that effect. See above, pp.151–2.

123. *Alan I, Dublin, to Thomas, at the Whitehall coffee-house, King's Street, Westminster, 9 Dec. 1705*

(1248/2/236–7)

This letter probably will not come to your hands in some time after I write it, for I hear you have been of late and perhaps may stil be in Wiltshire: however before I leave town (which I hope to doe to morrow) I resolve to write to you. I neither can add any thing to my two last in relacion to your own affairs nor doe I belong [*recte* believe] the subject is pleasing to you out of my mouth, considering you took no notice of either to me: but upon my word by all I can understand, your affairs in the countrey run to ruine apace … We want three packets. You may have heard of the measures taken in settling the magistracye in the City of Galwey, town of Clonmel, and borough of Athenree;[1092] if not, Oliver St George[1093] and Ned Rigs[1094] will be able to inform you: no doubt no more is in prospect but the good governement of the towns, but they all send members to parliament, and a tall Gentleman told Sir G. St G.[1095] my Lord ——[1096] interest must be supported, or that he must have an interest in Galwey. I hear Mr L[*udlow*] instead of the Rolls will accept being Chancellor of the Exchequer,[1097] if so a new parliament is intended.

124. *Alan I, Dublin, to St John II, at his chamber in Lamb Buildings, Middle Temple, 9 Dec. 1705*

(1248/2/238–9)

Do not beleive I have been remisse in writing; letters are stopped in the post office if some of you have not heard from me almost every post. Justice McCartney came in this evening, and three packets the same tide; which brought yours of the first and fourth instant; I wish I knew how Lord R[*ochester*] maintained his ground last Thursday, since he was for bringing the matter to a tryal:[1098] I saw a proper Gentleman this evening, by whose way of telling it I find a party here looks on the carrying the question that it should be an instruction to the committee to receive a clause to hinder the repealing the Act of uniformitye, as a mighty

[1092] The disputed mayoral election for Galway in Aug. 1705 was prolonged by the refusal of the whig town clerk to release the corporation books to the victorious tory faction (National University of Ireland, Galway, Hardiman Library, Galway corporation MSS, book E, 17–32). Conflict persisted into 1707, with proceedings by *quo warranto* and a petition to the Irish house of commons (BL, Add. MS 38155, f. 47: Sir Richard Cox to Edward Southwell, 22 May 1707; *CJI*, iii, 423–4; BL, Add. MS 9712, f. 82: Richard Stewart to Edward Southwell, 18 Nov. 1707). For the disputes in Clonmel corporation, see Marsh's Library, Dublin, MS Z. 2. 1. 7 (82): case of Alderman Hollington, 1708; and for those in Athenry, *CJI*, iii, 388, 451–3.

[1093] Oliver St George, MP [I].

[1094] Probably Edward Riggs, jr, chosen MP [I] Baltimore in 1707.

[1095] Sir George St George, MP [I] for Carrick-on-Shannon, whose estate was in Co. Galway.

[1096] Ormond.

[1097] Stephen Ludlow, MP [I], received neither appointment, though he was eventually made a revenue commissioner [I] in 1711 during Ormond's second viceroyalty.

[1098] In the debate in the English house of lords on 'the Church in danger', on Thursday, 6 Dec. 1705, for which see Clyve Jones, 'Debates in the House of Lords on "The Church in Danger", 1705, and on Dr Sacheverell's impeachment 1710', *Historical Journal*, xix (1976), 764–9; *Nicolson Diary*, ed. Jones and Holmes, 320–5.

point gained:[1099] and by what another gentleman tells me, a certain Secretarye spoke of it as a great blow given to the whigs;[1100] I think there is no thing in it, but much is endeavoured to be made of it.

Pray let me know whether Mr Harveys[1101] cover brought you Mr Higgins sermon;[1102] and whether you had my letter with the City grand Juryes addresse. … I go to morrow toward Corke …

125. *Alan I, Dublin, to St John II, at his chambers in the Middle Temple, 23 Feb. 1705/6*

(1248/2/240–1)

I shal not write to you again till I leave this town; I received yours of the fourteenth and fifteenth: pray let my brother know that last night Robin Oliver[1103] did assure me Sir Tho[*mas*] Southwel in his cups declared that the next Session of our parliament they would fall on him[1104] about not proceeding on the school of Middleton: This with what I have said before shews the necessitye of going on with that work out of hand, and that his scheme of good husbandry … is not for reputacion at least. Our talk here is, that Lord Keeper and Lord Cheif Justice Holt proposed you for Cheif Baron.[1105] When I heard it I ventured in a publick Coffee house to say I would lay £100 they did nothing of the kind, on this supposicion first that they would not put a difficultye on you to refuse it if complyed with, if accepted at Court: for I beleived you would not goe into a thing of that kind and keep me a stranger to it; next, because I beleived you not fond of breathing this air at present: but in my opinion the secret is to possesse people that tho some body hath not an interest to name one, he hath to oppose at least one of our name. Write to me on the subject. The Attorney[1106] too is named as a recommender of yours: We are highly dejected at the disappointment of our recommendation.

126. *Alan I, Dublin, to Thomas, at the Whitehall coffee-house, King's Street, Westminster, 25 Feb. 1705/6*

(1248/2/242–3)

I have stayed longer in town then I proposed to my self, and resolve God willing to goe by the dawn of day to morrow toward Munster: this morning since I left Court I had an

[1099] The resolution on 30 Nov. to instruct the committee of the whole house on the Regency Bill to insert a provision to prevent the lords justices who were to govern the country between Queen Anne's death and the arrival of the designated protestant successor from repealing the Act of Uniformity of 1662 (*LJ*, xviii, 36–7).

[1100] Robert Harley, now a secretary of state [E].

[1101] Stephen Harvey, MP [E].

[1102] Francis Higgins, *A Sermon Preach'd Before their Excellencies the Lord Justices, at Christ-Church, Dublin; on Tuesday the 28th of August* … (Dublin, 1705).

[1103] Robert Oliver, MP [I].

[1104] Thomas.

[1105] Of the Irish court of exchequer. Holt thought of St John II as 'my most special friend' (SHC, 1248/2/308–9: Holt to Alan I, 14 July 1707).

[1106] Sir Edward Northey, attorney-general [E].

account that Captain Breholt[1107] brought a box to the Custom House from Chester directed to me, and take it for granted that it contains the draught or model of the school house which your former mentions. My last to you acquainted you how very much Laur[*ence*] Clayton and I and all your other freinds differ in opinion with you as to the beginning on the school, with our reasons: and since that I have told my brother St John that Robin Oliver heard a certain freind of yours when he was flustred declare that the next Session of Parliament your name should be brought on the Carpett on this score. I am without hesitancy perfectly convinced of the necessitye in point of reputacion to make a progresse in it, and I will goe a great way in advancing money out of my own pockett rather then have oportunitye given malicious knaves to rail and prate in a place where they will be heard with pleasure against you. For Gods sake come to some resolucion as to your attendance and expectacions etc. How much money have you spent and with how little satisfaction and successe you best know: I think unlesse you have fair and probable prospect of soon attaining your aim, you should come over and make yourself easy here, as you may with great facilitye by a little good husbandry: provided you goe not on with your stud.

127. *Alan I, Dublin, to Thomas, at the Whitehall coffee-house, King's Street, Westminster, 11 Apr. 1706*

(1248/2/246–7)

What I have to say is not worth postage, yet we ought now and then to converse by letter, since our distance will not allow it otherwise. I am stil of the same opinion as formerly about immediately going on with the school; reputacion is deeply concerned in it, and you know that I neither have skil to oversee or direct in it, nor will my affairs allow my being on the spot. When I was in the countrey I found that a certain person, finding it had taken wind that subscriptions were procured to remove it to Cl[*oy*]n,[1108] gave the matter this turn: that truly he heard the D[*uke*] of O[*rmond*] had intentions of getting it removed to Carick;[1109] and that he being unwilling to have it removed out of the Province[1110] had wrote to the Archbishop of Cashel[1111] to join with him in endeavouring to have it fixed in Cloyne. Nay a certain Peer in my hearing, who owed you money, and cannot easily forgive your calling for it, was very inquisitive what progresse was made in it. Need I repeat my advice to you of looking after your own affairs, and bringing matters to an upshot? Sure good husbandry, looking after your estate and the school, and appearing a little in the countrey to support an interest will induce you to come over, unlesse you have very prevailing reasons to the

[1107] George Breholt (*d.* 1741), captain of the yacht *Charlotte*, which was retained on the Dublin station at the disposal of the lord lieutenant (John Charnock, *Biographia Navalis* … (4 vols, 1794–6), iii, 6).

[1108] Cloyne, Co. Cork. The 'certain person' may have been the bishop of Cloyne, Charles Crowe.

[1109] Carrick-on-Suir, Co. Tipperary, where Ormond was ground landlord (until he disposed of his holdings there in 1711).

[1110] Although Co. Tipperary was in the province of Munster, Carrick-on-Suir belonged to the diocese of Ossory, and thus the ecclesiastical province of Dublin.

[1111] William Palliser (1646–1727).

contrary. But I will trouble you no farther on this subject then to tell you, if you had lived here you might be as happy and have more money in your pocket.

128. *Alan I, Dublin, to Thomas, at the Whitehall coffee-house, King's Street, Westminster, 30 Jan. 1706/7*

(1248/2/252–3)

When this letter gets to London I suppose Lord Cutts affair will not have so disordered the great men of our countrey that they will only have leisure to see that nothing be done to the detriment of a great mans commission,[1112] and not mind such a concern as the Barnstaple peticion against bringing yarn out of this Kingdome into England.[1113] Upon my word if that act passe into a Law, the ruine of the English of our part of the countrey is effectually compleated. Will not England allow us to be day labourers in the poorest and most slavish part of the woollen trade, as spinning is? It will in consequence prejudice England; spinners for want of employ here will goe into other countreys where they are allowed to earn their bread, as our weavers have done into France, Holland, Scotland etc. to the no small damage of the woollen trade in England. Men may pretend to have some remorse at the difficultyes this Kingdome hath of late been put under,[1114] and that some thing will be done for its releif: but if such an act as this take place to the utter ruine of a Kingdome at the instigacion of a little borough or two, I must think the ease designed us is like that given criminals in France to give them a death stroke to put them out of their lingring pain.[1115] Mr Boyle[1116] is as much concerned in this as any one man I know; his tenants about Bandon and indeed our whole country will be utterly ruined, and in consequence wool will at any risque be exported into other countreys. Others I suppose have wrote on this subject; our Cheif Governor and Secretarye[1117] will no doubt act as usually for the benefit and preservacion of the Country.

[1112]John Cutts (c.1661–1707), 1st Baron Cutts, lieutenant-general of the forces in Ireland and one of the lords justices, died in Dublin on 25 Jan. 1707 (*HC 1690–1715*, iii, 815–21). The question having arisen of whether his replacement should be elected by the Irish privy council, the English law officers confirmed that this could be instead done by royal warrant under the signet: since the chief governorship was not vacant, the Irish statute of 1533 providing for the election of a lord justice would not apply (TNA, SP 63/366, f. 74: Sir Edward Northey to the queen, 5 Feb.1706/7). Sir Richard Cox, the surviving lord justice, described this episode as 'the most critical juncture of my life, for my judgment, my courage and my integrity were all at stake': at one point he was threatened with impeachment for refusing to issue writs for the election of Cutts's successor (*The Autobiography of Sir Richard Cox,* ed. Richard Caulfield (1860), 20). Those pushing hardest for replacement by election were said (by a high church clergyman) to be 'the nasty faction of the Brodricks' (BL, Add. MS 47025, f. 71: William Perceval to Sir John Perceval, 14 Feb.1706/7).

[1113]A petition from clothiers and those employed in the woollen manufacture in and around Barnstaple in Devon, drawing attention to the damaging effects produced by the importation of cheap Irish yarn; presented to the English house of commons on 21 Jan. 1707 and referred to a committee (*CJ*, xv, 244).

[1114]A reference to the provisions of the English Woollen Act of 1699 (11 Will. III, c.13).

[1115]The *coup de grace* which could be administered during the method of execution known as 'breaking on the wheel'.

[1116]Hon. Henry Boyle, MP [I], bro. of the 2nd earl of Burlington and whig MP [E], later 1st Baron Carleton.

[1117]Chief Secretary Edward Southwell.

129. *Alan I, Dublin, to Thomas, at the Whitehall coffee-house, King's Street, Westminster, 8 Feb. 1706/7*[1118]

(1248/2/254–5)

My writing very lately to you on this subject cannot prevent my again laying before you the inevitable ruine of the whole Province of Munster (at least) if the peticion for prohibiting our exporting bay and woollen yarn into England succeed. A letter I received yesterday from Corke shews that part of the countrey to be under the same confusion and terror, as if an incensed and powerful Army were at their gates ready to reduce them into the last degree of beggary and servitude: Let reasons be urged against this procedure; their past severityes on us be layd before them, that they have all fallen on the English Protestant part of Ireland: Let them be made sensible that we are in this trade no more then poor day labourers to prepare materials for their manufactures: that the most any one spinner gets is but a very scanty and poor subsistance, and if they be hindred to get their livings by that trade here, they will probably follow several concerned here in the woollen trade when they were hindred from using it as formerly, into parts where they have encouragement, and where they will doe England more mischeif really, then is now pretended we doe it in Ireland. Let the person whose letter you enclosed to me know, that as nothing can make him so welcome here as heartily and successefully appearing for us in this matter;[1119] that we shal be much out of humor and with great ground full of resentment and complaints if this matter take place. If any freind of ours doe heartily interpose in our favor, let them be named in letters, that may be shewn; for it is most sedulously given out that Lord S[*tamford*] is one great enemy to our little remaining woollen trade, and soe foolish are they as to say that he (being one of the Commissioners of Trade)[1120] was the person that obstructed a continuance of the money granted by the Crown for some time past to carry on the linen trade for more years to be added by a new grant: Doth not this matter affect Lord O[*rmond*]? Hath he no body about him to put him in mind that Ireland deserves to have some little of his care? Gett St John (to whom I have wrote) to speak to Will Ettrick, Mr Eyre,[1121] Mr Harvey[1122] etc. We are undone if the act passe, and for my part let men tell us what they please I shal never be lulled asleep after this with promises and fair words. I dare not trust my thoughts to paper, they are so disordered on this occasion. Take pains in this; and write to me.

[1118] On the outside of letter is a note to Thomas from St John II: 'Pray see the Gentleman whom you lately visited, and Lord S[*omers*] too on this occasion, and let 'em see the Lettre and the disorder in which tis written – Loose no time – I have no Letter as mentioned within.'

[1119] Presumably, Thomas, Lord Wharton, who was expected to be named as the next lord lieutenant (BL, Add. MS 38155, f. 23: Sir Richard Cox to Edward Southwell, 26 Apr. 1707).

[1120] Thomas Grey (c.1654–1720), 2nd earl of Stamford, president of the board of trade 1699–1702, 1707–11.

[1121] Either John Eyre (1665–1715), MP [E] for Downton, or, more likely, Robert Eyre (c. 1667–1715), MP [E] for Salisbury, who was more prominent in the house of commons (*HC 1690–1715*, iii, 1003–7).

[1122] Presumably Stephen Harvey, MP (E).

130. *Alan I, Dublin, to Thomas, at the Whitehall coffee-house, King's Street, Westminster, 20 Feb. 1706/7*

(1248/2/244–5)

The above coming open to me under a cover on the same subject, I to save postage write under it: The Colonel is grown sickly and weak and turning his employment into money will be a great support to his familye; You know by whom he is crushed and why maligned: therefore try to gett him a Chapman.[1123] Last week I had another letter from the Bishop of C[*loyne*] about the school;[1124] that he was wrote to that in conscience he ought not to let it remain neglected as it does, and about removing it to England or Kilkennye: I suppose his correspondent may be his mad predecessor:[1125] however pray think of forwarding it: When will you be over? What directions doe you give in the mean time? For I beleive it is wholly now at a stand till you are on the spot, tho the Season of the year draws on. If the Duke comes[1126] I am certain this will be moved in Parliament to disgrace and mortifye us at least: Indeed it is hard to answer all that hath or may be objected on that head: the best way is so to forward it now as to make it past removing, or causing obloquy.

131. *Alan I, Cork, to Thomas, at the Whitehall coffee-house, King's Street, Westminster, 13 Apr. 1707*

(1248/2/258–9)

… I am glad you seem now resolutely determined to come over; your own affairs require it, soe doth the supporting your interest in the Country, and indeed your credit in relacion to the going on with Middleton school; and notwithstanding the fair smooth words of a certain person you know, he is a more dangerous enemye then an open professed one; I have ground sufficient for what I say. This City will not with any patience hear of my standing for the County, nor will I ever put a slight on it: on the other hand I must not pretend to stand for the County without giving assurances to the electors of serving if I be elected: soe as I resolve to decline it and Clayton and I have spoken and will continue to speak and to make interest for him and you. I have wrote about Mr R[*oger*]s to some that have interest in B[*ando*]n:[1127] and will doe what is proper in that and other affairs of the kind.[1128] Fail not to write to my Lord D[*oneraile*] and to have Senny write such a letter as is proper on the occasion, full of acknowledgements for his favor and expressing an entire dependence

[1123]Usually a merchant or dealer, but could also be used to mean an agent, or a purchaser (*OED*).

[1124]At Midleton.

[1125]John Pooley.

[1126]As late as the end of Apr. Ormond was expecting to travel to Ireland to preside over the next parliamentary session and was making preparations when the queen suddenly dismissed him in favour of the earl of Pembroke (HMC, *Ormonde MSS*, n.s., viii, 299; BL, Add. MS 47025, f. 74: Edward Southwell to Sir John Perceval, 3 June 1707).

[1127]Either George Rogers MP [I] Lismore 1692–9 (and returned for Midleton as well in 1692), or his elder brother Robert, MP [I] Cork 1692–9.

[1128]Parliamentary elections.

on his promise and great satisfaction in appearing first in the world under his countenance; you know the man, and that applicacions of this nature will be well received. By the death of Peter Bettesworth[1129] I suppose one of the trustees for the school of Middleton is to be new chosen; for I take him to have been one of them: Let me know who the trustees or overseers were, and who have power of electing a new one that it may be done out of hand: for you cannot but consider of what consequence it is never to let a certain person have too good an interest among the trustees. My brother Clayton and I think Dick Bettesworth a fit man to be chosen in his fathers room: What say you to him? The money you formerly drew over to buy timber with, will now be suddenly wanted: if you can not well spare it now, give me timely notice and I will provide it.

132. *Alan I, Dublin, to St John II, at his chamber in Lamb Buildings, Middle Temple, 28 Apr. 1707*[1130]

(1248/2/260–1)

(1) Qu. Whether old or new?[1131]

A new will answer all reasonable expectacions at least as well as the old: not depend on any single person, not lye under any tye to follow directions from E[*nglan*]d: will speak the true sense of their principals, who are most affectionately and dutifully devoted to her Majestys service: will shew the falsitye of that position that a certain person was and alway would be necessarye: The successe of a new will be owing to the wisdome and prudence of the Cheif,[1132] without being shared with another: animosityes which may otherwise continue will be removed, and no danger of disappointment from resentment, if any be retained.

(2) Qu. Bill where to arise?[1133]

This matter (I think) ought rather to be resolved on hereafter, when ——[1134] knows people better: if of necessitye to be now stirred in, will come better from the other side: will meet great difficultyes at more places then one.

[1129] Peter Bettesworth (*d.* 1707) of Ballydullea, Co. Cork (a copy of whose will is at PRONI, T/633/11), the father of Richard Bettesworth, sr, of Whiterock.

[1130] Written on the outside of this letter is a note from St John II to his nephew, St John III: 'I have a Letter which bids me tell you, A certain blank is to be filled with the name of Whitshed. The same Letter directs the immediate writing to my Brother [*Thomas*] to caution him positively to insist upon the promise relating to you. It adds, I suppose he and Senny wrote formerly to him on that Subject, as I advised in [*a*] former Letter? Did You? bee sure to write to my Brother Tho[*mas*]'

[1131] Parliament.

[1132] The lord lieutenant.

[1133] Whether a supply bill should be drawn up by the privy council in Dublin or arise from heads presented and discussed in the Irish house of commons; the issue at stake in the controversy over the supposed 'sole right' of the Commons to prepare supply legislation which had festered since the abortive Irish parliament of 1692 (see McGrath, *Constitution*, chs 3–6; McGrath, 'English Ministers, Irish Politicians and the Parliamentary Settlement in Ireland 1692–5', *EHR*, cxix (2004), 585–613.

[1134] Presumably this is a reference to the incoming viceroy, Pembroke, whose appointment was officially dated on 30 Apr. but was clearly expected. Cf. McGrath, *Constitution*, 194.

(3) Qu. Is there time enough for an new?[1135]

There is if proper methods are taken to dispatch businesse: directions may come to summon all persons concerned, as soon as the writings are perfected: and without this, another method lately used here and elsewhere will doe.

(4) Qu. Whether advisable to pay off old incumbrances?

The incumbrancers benefit hath been soe considerable, that they will be unwilling to assign: but their being obliged to doe soe will be uneasy to very few beside themselves: their continuing on the estate will be of no advantage to it or to the owner, and they will be careful of shewing uneasinesse for fear of being called to account for wast and destruction formerly committed, supposing they could shew any to purpose, which they cannot.

(5) Qu. What are the characters of — and —?

The former hath a great share of sense, courage, integritye and Law: the later is equal to him in two of those qualityes, and hath more of the first and last then some in higher stations.

(6) Qu. Who is fit for —?[1136]

The former is; but if it be impossible for him (as I hope it will) call on the Gooke[1137] and he will tell you the Gentlemans name; I will not sett it down at large here.

(7) Qu. Is it necessarye to reform the — ?

There is no one thing of more indispensable necessitye in my opinion: reasons would plainly shew what I mean ought to be reformed, since they only can be applyed to that place, therefore I forbear least this come not unopened to your hands.

133. *Alan I, Dublin, to St John II, at his chamber in Lamb Buildings, Middle Temple, 29 Apr. 1707*

(1248/2/262–3)

I have yours dated on Easter Eve:[1138] whatever accounts I had of likelyhood of a new Governor came from you only out of England, and some hints now and then from Dr Burrige; the letter from the D[*uke*] of — related only to getting informacion whether any and what persons encouraged making opposition to the Union in the North.[1139] Whether

[1135] In other words, would there be sufficient time for a newly elected parliament to enact an extension of supply before the current additional duties expired in Sept. 1707?

[1136] Alan was presumably thinking of a possible nominee at Midleton in the event of a new parliament.

[1137] Possibly Robert Gookin (see above, p. 185).

[1138] 23 Apr.

[1139] Opposition to the Anglo-Scottish Union among the presbyterians in the north of Ireland, who were all of Scottish descent and many of them recent immigrants from Scotland.

we shal have a new Parliament or not here is much doubted among us; some people dread it knowing the consequence of a new election; but I beleive the old will meet, considering how strict a scrutinye the actions of some relacions of a Lord now in England who hath a great stroke in our affairs may undergoe in a new.[1140] The City of Corke will not on any account hear of my standing for any place but that, soe as I declined all thoughts of the County and Clayton and I spoke to some freeholders for him and my brother just before his going toward Dublin; soon after which and since my leaving Corke the news came of Lord Pembrokes being declared, and that the night before I began my journey hither: Their absence and mine hath given Jemmy Barry[1141] oportunitye of setting up for himself, and soe indefatigably industrious hath he been as to have secured most of the freeholders I beleive: for Lords Donerayle, Barrymore, Insiquin,[1142] Mr Southwell[1143] and others join with him out of envy: I may thank my self for ever putting it in his power to be able to do this. I wrote to Lord Donerayle about his promise that Senny should serve in his borough;[1144] his answer is that if the promise be insisted on by my brother he will make it good: but he seems desirous to be acquitted of it, and perhaps Sir John St Leger[1145] will urge him to doe soe. Assoon as you receive this write a line to caution him, and bid him positively insist on that promise: I suppose he and Senny have wrote formerly to my Lord on that subject as I advised in a former letter. Lord Donerayle said to a Gentleman, We must be for Barry who lives generously and hospitably among us: My brother will hardly beleive this. Tell Senny a certain blank is to be filled with the name Whitshed.[1146]

134. *Alan I, Dublin, to Thomas, at the Whitehall coffee-house, King's Street, Westminster, 30 Apr. 1707*

(1248/2/264–5)

I am perfectly surfeted with writing letters about our parliament affairs, supposing a new one should be called: it is time to speak on another subject …

[*PS*] … It is hardly worth while to say that yesterday there mett a great number att the Bowling Green to dine together, it being the Duke of Ormonds birthday:[1147] it amounted I

[1140] Presumably Ormond.

[1141] James Barry of Rathcormac, Alan's brother-in-law by his first marriage, and currently MP [I] for Dungarvan, told the tory MP Anderson Saunders in Oct. that he was confident of being elected for Co. Cork instead of Thomas Brodrick whenever the parliament should be dissolved (BL, Add. MS 9715, f. 203: Saunders to Edward Southwell, 18 Oct. 1707). Saunders observed that Barry was 'very fair to us in the general, but where the Speaker's interest comes into play, he owes too many oblighations to him, to be against him' (ibid.). After Ormond's reappointment as lord lieutenant in 1710 Barry promised not to work against Ormond's interest should there be a new election (BL, Add. MS 21553, f. 71: Barry to Ormond, 2 Jan. 1710/11).

[1142] The 3rd earl of Inchiquin.

[1143] Edward Southwell, MP [I], the former chief secretary.

[1144] Doneraile, Co. Cork.

[1145] Lord Doneraile's much younger half-brother, aged about 13 in 1707, who was himself elected as a whig for Doneraile in 1713.

[1146] See above, p. 215. William Whitshed, MP [I] is meant; he was not in fact given any appointment at this time.

[1147] Sir Richard Cox was told that about eighty guests attended a celebration at 'Ashbury's' on 29 Apr., of whom 57 were MPs (BL, Add. MS 38155, f. 27: Cox to Edward Southwell, 29 Apr. 1707). Fifty-six MPs had been

am told to sixty one. I know Lord Cheif Justice Pyne, the Cheif Baron,[1148] Lord Mayor[1149] and Recorder,[1150] Mr St George[1151] Mr Conollye[1152] and others were invited but refused to goe; nay I had an invitacion, who was never thought worthy before. Is not this to lett somebody know that a sett of men will shew his Grace more respect now he is out of the Governement then they ever shewed any man but him in it; or him till in the Governement? I hear his speedy return was drunk, no doubt it was meant in his private capacitye. The Sollicitor general was one, but the Attorney and Baron Johnson himself missed this meeting. Doe not read this letter publickly.

135. *Alan I, Dublin, to St John II, at his chambers in Lamb Buildings, Middle Temple, 20 May 1707*

(1248/2/267–8)

I have yours of the 13th, and upon the encouragement you give me by it have wrote the enclosed, which you will take care to deliver. As I am fearful somebody hath gone too far in his sentiments, soe it is plain they have been told to others; which I hope hath been a sufficient caution to him not to shew my letter to any one alive: but to render him unexcusable I did in expresse terms enjoyn the contrary considering the different sentiments of people on that subject; soe as he can never answer it if he hath done it, and I know and will take one certain way to be served soe noe more. But my thoughts in that and all other letters were and will alway be that new will doe much better then old,[1153] that there are several inconveniences which must attend one that will be entirely removed by the other; that the true service of the Crown and Kingdome will be as well done by a new, without many difficultyes that unavoidably must attend the old. If a letter I wrote to Senny came to his hand (of which advise me) you will see my naked thoughts:[1154] but if there be a formed design to bring in a certain bill the first meeting,[1155] I should be unwilling to give too great hopes of its not meeting with difficultye in a new, which they who are fond of the old will industriously raise in a new, and then lay the blame on not keeping the former

1147 *(continued)* present at 'the Bowling Green banqueting house' the year before on the same occasion (BL, Eg. MS 917, f. 234). The bowling green in Dublin was situated at Oxmantown; according to John Rocque's map of 1756, at the end of Hendrick Street and next to the Pipe Office Yard (*The A to Z of Georgian Dublin: John Rocque's Maps of the City in 1756 and the County in 1760,* ed. Paul Ferguson (Lympne Castle, Kent, 1998), opening 6).

1148 The lord chief baron of the exchequer, Richard Freeman (1646–1710); promoted to lord chancellor [I] later in 1707.

1149 Benjamin Burton, MP [I].

1150 John Forster, MP [I].

1151 Either Henry, Oliver, or Richard St George, all of whom were sitting in the Irish house of commons in 1707. Henry was the only one of the three without a military rank, and thus likely to have been referred to as 'Mr'. Moreover, he had been recorded as attending Ormond's birthday celebrations the previous year (BL, Eg. MS 917, f. 234).

1152 William Conolly, MP [I].

1153 A new parliament.

1154 His letter of 28 Apr.

1155 Presumably a supply bill, drawn up by the Irish privy council in violation of the Commons supposed 'sole right'.

on foot, which they will then pretend would certainly have done it, tho perhaps it would have mett as much opposicion in the old. Unlesse some things be done (one particularly) complaints and loud ones will be made: Consider on what diffcultyes the one years men will be put if the old remain:[1156] they have formerly acted according to their sentiments and not out of picque; they see no great reason to alter their minds and would not be put on a necessitye of doing a disobliging thing or rendring themselves obnoxious to the scurrilous reproaches of those who would object their altering their sentiments. If we must be so held to it that the same P[*arliament*] must meet and two years must be insisted on give me your advice how to act soe as not to disoblige when I do what I think is fittest; and how far the alteracions of circumstances may give reasonable ground for doing that now which was not fit to be done before. I think there is a great deal of reason for a man to be against making ill precedents, but when made against ones will and when there is no prospect of preventing them from being followed I doe not see that a man is always bound to make himself obnoxious by a fruitlesse opposicion in behalf of a C[*ountr*]y that deserves not the care some people have had of it to the exposing their persons and prejudice of their fortunes …

136. *Alan I, Dublin, to St John II, at his chambers in Lamb Buildings, Middle Temple, 22 May 1707*

(1248/2/269–70)

By letters from England by this pacquet and hints in former accounts I am convinced we are to have all matters just as they please who were the tools of a late —:[1157] what difficultyes that will necessarily put on honest Gentlemen here will be easy to foresee; especially if it be determined to insist on the damned precedents that have been lately made.[1158] Men will unwillingly disoblige where reasonable things are expected, but never will be brought to doe things inconsistent with their honors and judgements: I doe hope care will be taken not to put them under such difficultyes; I am sure if unanimitye among us be desired or valued, and it be thought for the good of the Kingdome to compose animosityes, the way will be not to insist on what was the first occasion of them. But this is not the only cause of dissension that is like to arise, if what I hear be true, that great endeavours are used to continue ——:[1159] As sure as his head is on his shoulders he will be the subject of warm debates (if things goe no farther, but I think they necessarilye must) if it be insisted on that he act the part and keep the Station —. Doe people think it was the person, or the actions and creatures of somebody that were obnoxious? There will be lesse satisfaction then were to be wished if the Chariot keep the same track, and only changes the Driver. I wish from my heart a method may be found to keep us from breaking in peices and being as warm

[1156]Those, like the Brodricks, who had supported a grant of supply for one year only in the previous two sessions (McGrath, *Constitution*, 167–9, 185). Sir Richard Cox interpreted the situation in a somewhat different light: 'It mortified the faction, that this parliament continue, for they know their party will moulder now, and they will not have the government in their power' (BL, Add. MS 38155, f. 31: Cox to Edward Southwell, 1 May 1707).

[1157]Lord lieutenant.

[1158]In relation to bills of supply.

[1159]Sir Richard Cox.

against and opposite to one another as ever. Things and not persons only gave the offence. If any thing can be done in this matter it must be before resolucions are unalterably fixed. Give me your thoughts.

137. *Alan I, Dublin, to his 'sister' [Martha Courthope], 5 Aug. 1707*

(1248/2/316)

By a former I told you that Dr Burrige was ill of a distemper which I beleived would prove mortal, and my conjecture was too well grounded: he died on Sunday night about twelve of clock, his wife being about fowre and twenty hours before brought to bed of a son, and you may be sure she is in a very dangerous condicion. You may be satisfyed he leaves a good character behind him since you knew him to be a man of very great integritye; none but high flyers rejoice at his death, and they have prudence enough to suppress all expressions of their malice hitherto. I resolve to tell you what I have lately observed, tho I am not very superstitious: I dreamt several dayes before I had the account of my dearest brothers death[1160] that I saw him fall into a deep water and sink down; that I dived to the bottom to find him but could not, but at length found something else which I brought to the shore and discovered it was not him: I waked in great disorder, and running back from the day when I heard of his death I compute it was the very night he dyed; yet at that time I had no reason to apprehend his death near. The next day I called by accident for black clothes which I wore till I made new ones to mourn for him, and having occasion on the Sunday after his death and five dayes before I heard of it to goe out of town to dinner in my Coach I took a book with me, and accidentally lighted on Dr Patricks book to prevent immoderate greif on the death of freinds:[1161] A book I find I needed not to read that can so easily bear soe great a losse as I doe that of soe deserving soe dear a freind. The night after Dr Burrige fell sick I dreamt I saw him pale and ghastly coming toward me; I shunned him and he followed me and seemed very desirous to speak to me, but I declined it under an apprehension of infection: I told Mr Conollye[1162] this he said it was an ill dream, and told me he beleived he would dye. His feaver was a very malignant one, and he expressed a great desire to see my brother Justice McCartney Mr Conollye and me: Oliver St George[1163] disswaded me from going for fear of infection, and indeed considering my dream I was not very desirous to see him: but I think I should have gone if he had not in lesse then an hour fallen speechlesse: What good offices I can doe his disconsolate wife I will not fail to doe while I stay behind him: How long that may be God only knows. Our matters goe pretty easily; we have had many difficultyes and rubs laid in our way; but with great pains, resolucion, and temper we have gott through them all, with good conscience I am sure, and I think with very great reputacion: notwithstanding they who would have had us miscarry and lye under ill thoughts in England have no game to play but to say we have altered our

[1160] St John II.

[1161] Simon Patrick, *A Consolatory Discourse to Prevent Immoderate Grief For the Death of Our Friends* (1671).

[1162] William Conolly, MP [I].

[1163] Oliver St George, MP [I].

principles in giving more then a year:[1164] but in truth it is not altering our principles but our measures. Our principle was and alway will be to doe what was most for the service of our countrey; and it was soe to doe as little as possible for one Cheif Governor, and not to be equally close handed to another; not to lengthen this letter with twenty other reasons that induced us to act as we have to the confusion of our enemyes and satisfaction of our countrey … Poor Dr Burrige hath appointed Mr Conollye and me his Executors in trust for his wife and child, which confidence we shal very faithfully discharge …

138. *Alan I, Dublin, to Thomas, at the Whitehall coffee-house, King's Street, Westminster, 4 May 1708*

(1248/2/326–7)

I apprehended when I was in London that you had thoughts of seeing Munster this Spring, but I doubt that is impossible considering that no thing but the unseasonablenesse of the weather hinders us from calling the time of the year when I am writing Summer. If the school be not finished this Summer we shal be exposed to calumnye, nay to just censure … Your tenants will suffer extreamly now the Countrey is arraying for want of somebody to serve under;[1165] they will be I doubt arrayed under Lord Barrymore or Jemmy Barry.

139. *Alan I, Dublin, to Thomas, at the Whitehall coffee-house, King's Street, Westminster, 1 June 1708*

(1248/2/328–9)

When I saw the emploiment you were put into in the Gazette I concluded it would not be possible for you to think of seeing Ireland this year[1166] … I beleive … the charge of passing your patent, and putting yourself into a dwelling proper for the emploiment will (falling on you at once) create you some uneasinesse. If my sister Martha can gett in as much money of mine among my English debtors, you may if you please call on her for one or two hundred pounds, and pay it in three or six months as money comes in. I have prepared her for it by telling her that I shal give you the trouble of disbursing money for me; soe as you need only give her a note to be accountable to me for soe much. Beleive it, things grow worse here daily; and in a short time this countrey will not yeild a penny of ready money. Our freinds in England complain extremely of the Court; particularly of a freind of yours: with what reason they or you may know, but I doe not … Give me some dark hint

[1164] Having previously insisted on the necessity of granting additional taxes for one year only, in order to guarantee annual sessions of the Irish parliament, Brodrick had compromised his principles under Lord Pembroke in 1707 and consented to a vote of a year and three-quarters (McGrath, *Constitution*, 197–203).

[1165] In the Irish militia.

[1166] At the end of Apr. 1708 Thomas had been advanced from the post of comptroller of the salt to joint comptroller of accounts for the army (*London Gazette*, 29 Apr.–3 May 1708).

what we may expect. We say here there will be a good Parliament,[1167] I mean our freinds think soe; but that all goes up hill elsewhere …

140. *Alan I, Cork, to Thomas, to be left at the Whitehall coffee-house, King's Street, Westminster, 18 July 1708*

(1248/2/336–7)

I am very much and very truly concerned at a letter I received by last pacquet from my sister Martha Courthope in which she tells me that you were a few dayes before her writing it seised in a very violent maner; and continued of your former opinion not inclined to consult with a Physitian. Indeed you will find that letting such things goe as far as you doe before you take the directions of some good Physician will turn to your great hazard if not losse of life: your constitution is weak naturally and much impaired, and needs all helps and supports: I am younger then you tho not much, and I think of a constitucion as strong as yours; yet I find mine extreamly impaired and that I must take more then ordinary care to keep my self in any tolerable condicion of health …

141. *Alan I, Cork, to Thomas, to be left at the Whitehall coffee-house, King's Street, Westminster, 16 Aug. 1708*

(1248/2/338–9)

Before I forgett it let me desire you to give me directions how to apply to you at your office, and by your name of office, that your letters may not only come safe but free from postage. Sir John Percival hath been very busy in this County not only in his own part, but made a late progresse to the West to secure votes,[1168] and hath made a visit to Mr Freake,[1169] soe as I presume he hath joined his interest to the others by the intervention of Sir Richard Cox: pray have you any thoughts of a new Parliament? You have not hinted any thing of the kind, nor doe I hear from any other freind that this parliament is to be dissolved. It seems to me improbable unlesse Sir Johns intelligence foresees another alteration, of which I confesse I doe not find the least probabilitye. If there should be a new Parliament I shal lye under great difficultyes: I am pressed to declare that I will stand for the County, yet resolve never to doe any Act to disoblige the City to which I owe a great deal; and in my opinion my enemyes cannot have a fairer handle given them then my standing for the County, the consequence of which must be that I will serve it too if chosen and neglect the City: which may be improved to the prejudice of Senny whom I intend forthwith to put into my place here, but with all privacye.[1170] I have wrote to Clayton on this subject and desire your thoughts on it. To declare for the County immediately till the other matter is effected will not be

[1167] A reference to the British parliament elected in May 1708, which met on 16 Nov. following.

[1168] Confirmed in BL, Add. MS 47025, f. 93: Perceval to Ld Orrery, 4 Aug. 1708; BL, Add. MS 47025, f. 94: Daniel Dering to Perceval, 10 Aug. 1708; and HMC, *Egmont MSS*, ii, 228–9.

[1169] George Freke, MP [I] (HMC, *Egmont MSS*, ii, 228).

[1170] In other words, keep this confidential.

advisable, and delayes will give people reason to say they have not been applyed to in time and that they are for that reason engaged …

[*PS*] I suppose it was Mr Burgh that P[*erceval*] spoke for, to oblige Lord Cheif Justice Holt.

142. *Alan I, Dublin, to Thomas, to be left at the Whitehall coffee-house, King's Street, Westminster, 30 Oct. 1708*

(1248/2/344–5)

Such hath been the neglect or misfortune of Peter Bettesworth and Mr Ward that they may for ought I know loose the Commissions you got for them unlesse you take a farther trouble on you. It is a good while since to my knowledge you wrote them word that they had Commissions, but you knew not in which of the regiments, at least at first, to the best of my memorye. [1171] But I think you said the Commission for Robin Bettesworth was for being a Lieutenant, and I doe assure you I have Peters by me which is only to be an Ensign. You know the agreement between Dick and Peter about Peters succeeding in Robins place: I told Dick how necessary it was for them to enquire about their Commissions, and I suppose he wrote soe to them: but to be short they either did it heedlessely or not at all, but I fancy expected to be wrote or sent to by the Captain, Colonel, or Agent:[1172] When I came to town I enquired at Dawsons[1173] about their Commissions, who could give a very imperfect account, but referred me to the Agent one Captain David Dunbar.[1174] To his house I went and neither of us knew the other by face; I told him I came to enquire about those Commissions; he said he heard they were two boyes: I assured him the contrary and found by him Pet[*er*] Bettesworth was and had been all along in his hands: but that Wards was gone into England and was in the hand of the Major one Sewel[1175] who is now in Chester. He added that he had commands from the Colonel to let his Officers know that they must repair for England, and that he had sent word to all to whom he knew how to direct to that effect: and that Colonel Jones had an assurance from Lord Pembroke that new Commissions should be granted in room of such as should not be in England by 10 November. I expressed concern at their misfortune as my relacions and said I knew Captain Gore[1176] and would write to him to Chester (which I have done) and would gett somebody

[1171] Peter Bettesworth and Cromwell Ward were commissioned as ensigns in the newly formed regiment of Colonel Edward Jones on the Irish establishment, 28 Aug. 1708 (Dalton, *Eng. Army Lists*, vi, 254). Cromwell Ward, from the Ward family of Bangor, Co. Down, was a career soldier who was eventually appointed lieutenant-governor of Carlisle in 1749, and died in office there, by 1755 (TNA, PROB 11/814/141). Edward Jones (1674–1735), of Wexford, was MP [I] 1713–*d*.

[1172] Regimental agents were assistants to the commanding officer, generally civilians, responsible for various elements of administration, including pay and provisions.

[1173] The office of the under-secretary, Joshua Dawson (MP [I])

[1174] David Dunbar (c.1687–1752), a captain in the Inniskillings, Jones's former regiment (Dalton, *Eng. Army Lists*, v, 91; vi, 233), and later MP [I] 1719–27.

[1175] Jonathan Sewell (*d.* by 1714) (Dalton, *Eng. Army Lists*, vi, 255; TNA, PROB 11/540/136).

[1176] Arthur Gore (bef. 1685–1730), of Clonroad, Co. Clare, later MP [I] (Dalton, *Eng. Army Lists*, vi, 254; *Hist. Ir. Parl.*, iv, 272–3).

to write to Captain Senhouse[1177] who is Wards Captain and is now at Cockermouth in Cumberland. He assured me the Captains could doe nothing in it. By the whole I thought the Colonel would be glad to have such an oportunitye of disposing two Commissions of men not brought in by himself. Before we parted Sir John Dillons daughter came in, and then I discovered Mr Dunbar was the Gentleman that was married to her, [1178] and by this means I came to know him and he to be informed who I was. Since that he hath acted as if he would do all acts of freindship for them: tells me he beleives applying to Colonel Jones will dispense with their going over; and assured me they should not suffer by their absence hitherto. That Wexford Duncanon[1179] and Waterford are appointed for their quarters; that fifty recruits of that regiment are now on their march to Waterford, and more daily expected; that they may in a little time be ordered to take care of those men as they arrive. Pray order matters so as to find Colonel Jones (he is to be mett with at old Mans Coffee house[1180]) and settle this matter with him; and if he be not in town, Robin Pooley[1181] (his great acquaintance) can tell how to write to him: And for fear of the worst it were not amisse if my Lord Pembroke or Mr Dodington[1182] be in town to speak to them too. This matter hath tired me with running to and fro, and writing to both of them and to Dick Bettesworth; and I must now again go to Captain Dunbar this night to know whether he can order them to take care of the men at Waterford, or those orders must come from the Colonel. I know how uneasy this must be to you, but without it all you have done hitherto is lost and Ward is the helplessest creature on earth. It is very hard that Pyne or our freind at the Colledge[1183] should soe put in as to have Ralph (that lives at Rathbarry)[1184] returned one of the three and pricked for our Sherif in prejudice of Arthur Hyde. I know this to be so and that directions are come to this purpose from the other side; but be cautious in mentioning it plainly, for then my Author will be known, which must not be on any account. I wish you could doe Mr Hyde any good in it; but I doubt it is too late …

143. *Alan I, Dublin, to Thomas, to be left at the Whitehall coffee-house, King's Street, Westminster, 5 Dec. 1708*

(1248/2/346–7)

… You will hardly imagine what an alteration appears in the hearts and countenances of people here of late:[1185] A letter from Mr D[*odington*] assures the juncto[1186] that he hath

[1177] William Senhouse (Dalton, *Eng. Army Lists*, vi, 254).

[1178] Dunbar had married, in about 1708, Mary, the daughter of Sir John Dillon, MP [I].

[1179] The fort at Duncannon, Co. Wexford, commanded the entrance to Waterford harbour.

[1180] Old Man's coffee-house in Scotland Yard (*Survey of London*, xvi, 215).

[1181] Probably Robert Pooley (b.c.1644) of Dublin, MP [I] Castlemartyr 1692–9, and brother of the painter Thomas Pooley (*Hist. Ir. Parl.*, vi, 106).

[1182] George Dodington, MP [I], Pembroke's chief secretary.

[1183] Trinity College.

[1184] Ralph Freke (later 1st Bt) of Rathbarry (later Castle Freke), Co. Cork, MP [I].

[1185] The announcement of the appointment of Thomas Wharton, now 1st earl of Wharton, as lord lieutenant in place of Pembroke.

[1186] Presumably a reference to the leaders of the tory interest in Ireland (despite the use of the term 'juncto').

liberty to tell them all things will goe on as formerly, every body be as well looked on etc. He is an happy Gamester who having once gott a good hand, is sure never to alter for the worse, let him goe never soe often to stock, whatever card turn up trump: and every body who knows any thing of Ireland knows that there is a sett of men somewhere who have expressed their hatred as well as fear of one suit. I think the sense of all considering men is that Europe can never be safe if we should patch up such a peace now as formerly we used to doe, by stopping the French Kings carreer for the present, but leaving him in possession of his unjust acquisitions since 1667; and that he must be reduced to the condition France was in before that; else he will have it in his power to devour the little that is left on some future favourable oportunitye. Hath not a party had oportunityes of engrossing almost every thing that is desireable into their own hands, and hath that party neglected to make use of any of those oportunityes? Is it not by this means only that they are become formidable? It is not to the riches, or sense of their people that they owe their being considerable, but to a fixed principle among them to prefer and support all of their kidney, and depresse and trample on those who differ in sentiments from them. You know what influence a certain sett of men have in the Executive nay legislative power; you know how much greater autoritye a fewer number here hath, then all Westminster hall: and of what consequence in preferring men and influencing elections a certain board is.[1187] You know how a great part of these bodyes is inclined. If it be the policye of England to suppresse one thing there, and when they know that the clear contrary prevails here to let it run on in that chanel, to sit unconcerned, people will be convinced it is a stream too strong to be stemmed; and for ought I know this may be a means to encrease that party more then will be found convenient in the end. I have formerly wrote my sense as to a new ——[1188] or continuing the present: it is hard we cannot be made masters of what is intended: if nothing that is unfit for men of honour and principle to goe in with, all that are of that kind may be depended on, and I doe not see but that if cards should be shuffled, in all probabilitye there would not be the fewer of that sort (to speak very modestly). I am perswaded a knot here have empowred the Committee in London to promise to go into all measures provided the company may be kept up and no liberty given for an interloping trade.[1189] How far those assurances may be depended on, will be worth considering: we seldome trust reconciled enemies, and whether a certain person hath not or had not lately many such among that fraternity can be a secret only to those who are perfect strangers to our affairs. I will now tell you some news: we have a new test sett up here: Will you give your word not to repeal the test Act[1190] is the condicion imposed by many Gentlemen of a certain coat[1191] on those who desire their suffrage in an election: and the doctrine is, such a man must not be chosen he will be for repealing that Act, and a great deal of industry is used to confirm Gentlemen that religion is ruined if that should happen. How the old company[1192] stands affected this way is well known;

[1187] By the 'new rules' for boroughs issued in 1672 the election of a chief magistrate in Dublin and 19 other named boroughs required formal approval by the Irish privy council.

[1188] Irish parliament.

[1189] An arch reference to tories in Ireland and their friends in England, by analogy with the Old East India Company (a tory-dominated corporation which had been challenged in the 1690s by the whiggish New East India Company).

[1190] Strictly speaking the test clause in the 1704 Popery Act [I].

[1191] The clergy (often referred to as black coats on account of clerical dress).

[1192] The tories.

and as to any thing relating to what may be wanted I think there can be little hazard at any time. If mens hopes are now disappointed of some redresse, it will be as great folly as impudence in any one to endeavour to support them in an expectacion of seeing things run in any other channel then what was cutt out about the year 1700.[1193] You forgett to write to your freinds, which you ought not to doe; but I conclude the reason is that you are not yet Master of schemes laid down. I beleive it will be found there will be a good summe in the Treasury beside what is due to the Civil and military list: Of this I am very glad as well on account of the publick as because by it (if we should not meet in Spring) I may see England. I really am ill, and must think of going off businesse.

144. *Alan I, Dublin, to Thomas, to be left at Mrs Courthope's house in Bond Street or at his lodgings, Whitehall, 12 Dec. 1708*

(1248/2/348–9)

Dr Owen Loyde[1194] will give this to you; his character and deserts are too well known to every body who is not a stranger to the men of principles here to need my saying any thing of him to you. I wish the person recommended by his Grace were of the same stamp;[1195] but he is not and on trial will be found soe; it is become a matter of triumph among the party here that he is so recommended and regarded as I find him to be: consider who probably recommended him to his Grace (the namesake)[1196] and that may be one measure by which he may be estimated. If the bearer be not provided for as his learning, standing, and steddy adherence to the constitution, and revolution; and bold owning truth in any assembly where may things of that kind are entertained with resentment enough, well deserve; one sort of men will be extremely mortifyed and another rejoice and insult. Doth Lord Sommers take care to recommend good men to Lord Burlingtons boroughs[1197] if there be a new Parliament? What answers have Mr S— Mr T— Mr D— etc. given;[1198] for sure they have discoursed and been discoursed with. What saith Lord C—[1199] for his freinds? I hope care is taken not wholly to sink us with the bill for regulating the woollen

[1193] A reference to the appointment of Lord Rochester as lord lieutenant in 1700, and (as Alan would now have seen it) the consequent establishment of a tory ascendancy in Irish government.

[1194] Owen Lloyd (c.1664–1738), fellow of TCD, and dean of Connor 1710–*d.* (*Al. Dub.*, 506; Cotton, *Fasti*, iii, 254). Alleged by Swift to have been 'the only clergyman [in Ireland] that declared for taking off the sacramental test', and to have been appointed chaplain to Lord Wharton on the recommendation of Thomas Brodrick (*The Prose Writings of Jonathan Swift*, ed. Herbert Davis et al. (16 vols, Oxford, 1939–74), iii, 182–4).

[1195] Thomas Milles (1671–1740), an Oxonian (once of Christ Church) and a high churchman, whom Pembroke had recommended to the vacant bishopric of Waterford and Lismore earlier in the year.

[1196] Alan probably intended a reference to Thomas Lindsay, bishop of Killaloe, one of the leading lights in the high church party in Ireland, but in fact Milles's family and personal connection with Pembroke was long established (*Letters from Abroad: The Grand Tour Correspondence of Richard Pococke and Jeremiah Milles*, ed. Rachel Finnegan (3 vols, Piltown, Co. Kilkenny, 2011–13), i, 30–1).

[1197] Four Irish parliamentary boroughs in Counties Cork and Waterford – Dungarvan, Lismore, Tallow and Youghal – in which the principal interest lay with the Burlington family, now headed by a minor, Richard, the 3rd earl, whose affairs were managed by his mother, the dowager countess.

[1198] Probably the prominent Irish tory MPs Philip Savage, Henry Tenison and Samuel Dopping.

[1199] Probably Thomas, Baron Coningsby.

Linen and Iron manufactures:[1200] pray let me know the import of it as it relates to the woollen. I beleive the last industry is used to prevent attaining an end which (if in Lord W[*harton'*]s instructions)[1201] will be extremely difficult if at all to be attained.

145. *Alan I, Dublin, to Thomas, at his lodgings in Whitehall, 13 Jan. 1708/9*

(1248/2/350–1)

I find by a letter wrote by Lord Cheif Justice P[*yne*] to Will Conollye that there is a pamphlet printed in England relating to the repealing the test clause in which you are named[1202] and I am certain in a most false maner if the matter be in the print as he writes it; because I know you are not capable of being guilty of such behavior as is there laid to your charge toward the Bishop of Kilaloo.[1203] He is not in town but I will endeavour to gett him to doe you the right to certifye the falsitye of the story, which is the motive that induced him to mencion it in his letter. This pamphlett is in town, and I hear Borachio[1204] hath one but I have not had a sight of it yet; but hear I am also named by the title of Speaker as having made great efforts to have this clause repealed:[1205] Why doth not some body send over one of them, with their thoughts to whom the world is indebted for soe ingenious and candid a narrative? But methinks we lye under a very hard fate to be made the cheif marks of all the rancour and malice of a party on every occasion. We neither are dissenters, nor are our relations or acquaintance of that sort: Presbyterye is planted in the North and is hardly known among us; soe as it is very hard we must be made the butts to be alway shot att on every ferment of contending parties. For Gods sake doe not give cause to them who revile us to doe it with any reason; by speaking severely of one side or too favourably of the other; for altho they may complain of hard usage in having the clause inserted into

[1200] A bill to encourage the woollen, linen and iron manufactures in Great Britain had been introduced into the house of commons on 29 Nov. 1708 and committed at its second reading on 13 Dec. (*CJ*, xvi, 24, 46). It did not reach the statute book.

[1201] The official set of instructions (often separated into public and private sections) issued by the monarch to a newly appointed lord lieutenant.

[1202] Swift's *A Letter from a Member of the House of Commons in Ireland to a Member of the House of Commons in England, Concerning the Sacramental Test* (1709). It was reprinted in Dublin (TCD, MS 2531, p. 44: Archbishop King to Francis Annesley, 27 Jan. 1708[/9]). Thomas was not named in the pamphlet, but strong hints were given as to the identity of the MP who was supposedly the author of the letter.

[1203] On p. 14, Swift wrote, in the character of a member of the Irish house of commons: 'I must let you know that an honest bell-wether of our house (you have him now in England, I wish you could keep him there) had the impudence in parliament-time (I think it was last year) to take my lord bishop of Killaloe by his lawn sleeve, and tell him in a threatening manner, that he hoped to live to see the day when there should not be one of his order in the kingdom.' The bishop of Killaloe was the future tory primate Thomas Lindsay.

[1204] The Irish clergyman Francis Higgins, who had been satirised as 'Borachio' (the drunken follower of Don John in Shakespeare's *Much Ado about Nothing*) in *The Swan-Tripe Club in Dublin: A Satyr* … (Dublin, [1706]): see above, p. 208.

[1205] *A Letter from a Member of the House of Commons in Ireland* …, p. 5: 'it is manifest that our S[*peake*]r, when he was last year in England, solicited in person several members of both houses to have it repealed by an act there, though it be a matter purely national, that cannot possibly interfere with the trade and interest of England, and tho' he appeared formerly the most zealous of all men against the injustice of binding a nation by laws to which they do not consent.' See also *Swift Correspondence*, ed. Williams, i, 77,79.

the bill when and in the maner it was,[1206] yet I am satisfyed their behaviour since hath not made them objects of compassion, on the contrary hath altered many mens judgements to their prejudice: and I cannot but say their acting in the matter of Droghedah[1207] savours of a temper that affects more then liberty of serving God in such maner as their conscience allows of, and that aims at dominion and power. No doubt every body that wishes well to the Governement and succession in the Protestant line as by Law established had their fears on the invasion how far such treatment of the dissenters might influence them to be sullen on such an occasion;[1208] but really I should be extreamly uneasy to have that matter brought to a question, and must own that I see no likelyhood of their succeeding. Mr Boyses sermon against Episcopacye lately printed,[1209] and sending preachers to form (instead of preaching to) a congregation already formed (as it is alledged the case of Droghedah is) are acts not to be accounted for, unlesse they will own their design is to destroy one and substitute presbytery in the room of it. Some people I find both on your side the water, and here turn the whole good and welfare of Ireland on repealing this clause and enlarging the term for the linen:[1210] For my part I wish these Gentlemen had some little regard for other parts of the Kingdome as well as the North: when our woollen was taking away, the North was at least passive in the matter, and the linen is only a benefit to them; as to the other it affects the North only;[1211] and altho I was of opinion (and continue soe) that the adding that clause to the bill against Poperye was intended to loose that bill or disunite Protestants, yet now it is passed I foresee such difficultyes in the consequence of attempting to repeal it that I shal not be an adviser of the experiment; and see no cause why the dissenters soe warmly last Sessions were against an Act to tolerate them to serve God their own way,

[1206]The 'test clause' had been added to the 1704 Popery Act by the English privy council, who, according to their powers under Poynings' Law, could amend or respite engrossed Irish bills before they were presented to the Irish parliament, which could only accept or reject the bills as they stood.

[1207]In 1708 the presbytery of Armagh responded to a call from the presbyterian community in Drogheda, which had not worshipped as an established congregation since 1688, and sent a minister to preach there. However, the local rector, strongly supported by the borough corporation and by the archbishop of Armagh, instigated a prosecution against the minister in question for breaching the Act of Uniformity by preaching in a place where he was not licensed. The view of the local clergy, and of members of the established church more generally, was that this was proof of the expansionist intentions of the General Synod of Ulster. See Reid, *Hist. Presbyterian Church in Ireland*, iii, 3–5; PRONI, DIO/4/29/2/1/2/15: presentation by grand jury of Drogheda, 7 Oct. 1708; *A Sample of True-Blew Presbyterian Loyalty, in All Changes and Turns of Government* ... (Dublin, 1709), 12; Connolly, *Religion, Law and Power*, 163.

[1208]The abortive jacobite landing in Scotland in Mar. 1708.

[1209]Joseph Boyse (1660–1728), an English presbyterian minister based in Dublin, and a frequent controversialist, published in 1708 a two-volume edition of his sermons, one of which denied any scriptural basis for episcopacy, provoking angry responses from Church of Ireland clergymen. Boyse republished the offending sermon, with a rejoinder, in *The Office of a Scriptural Bishop Describ'd and Recommended, From 1 Tim. Chap. III. Vers. 1. An Ordination Sermon, with an Appendix to It: and a Postscript Containing an Apology for the Publication of It* (Dublin, 1709). In 1711 the Irish house of lords ordered this work to be burned by the common hangman (*Oxf. DNB*, *s.v.* Boyse). Archbishop King cited the same two episodes – the Drogheda controversy and the publication of Boyse's sermon – as examples of recent events which had given 'a great shock to many that seemed great friends to the dissenters' (TCD, MS 2531, p. 45: King to Francis Annesley, 27 Jan. 1708[/9]). He subsequently commented that the 'insolency and impudence' of the dissenters had alienated a great many former sympathisers (TCD, MS 2531, p. 62: King to Edward Southwell, 16 Feb. 1708[/9]).

[1210]On 24 June 1709 the Irish house of commons agreed to ask the queen to interpose to extend the period during which Irish linen cloth could be exported to the plantations (*CJI*, iii, 472).

[1211]The English Woollen Act of 1699 hit hardest the wool-producing counties of Munster, whereas the nascent linen industry was concentrated in Ulster.

as I understand they were.[1212] They persist in sending ministers to Droghedah, and I find the town and minister there will put it to a trial whether the soe doing be justifiable or punishable by Law. I cannot with patience bear the thought that the whole Kingdome must be put into a ferment upon such an affair soe unnecessarilye (not to say unjustifiably) sett on foot. Your prudence will tell you how dangerous it is to intermeddle soe much as by being in company with their Agent Mr Stevens:[1213] he is as hot as any of them, for soe in discourse with me he plainly shewed him self. I am farther of opinion that instead of anything of this kind being intended on your side the water, a weight is laid on it from thence; and soe you will find when you come to observe matters nearer. This letter does not bespeak me sick, yet I am not well: I goe out sometimes in the evening and play at Cards with Lord Blessinton, and now and then to the Strand[1214] about noon; but my ague hangs about me, yet Il to shake it off if the term doe not rivett it upon me.

I am told they of Droghedah are advised and intend to proceed against the dissenters as rioters: Where will this end? It will be an horrid shame to have publick Masses said over the Kingdome, after such a proceeding;[1215] and the precedent will reach the whole body of dissenters. This only to yourself; but let me know what people say with you on this subject. No letters since 1 Jan.

146. *Alan I, Dublin, to Alan II, at Mrs Courthope's house, Bond Street, 18 Jan. 1708/9*

(1248/2/352–3)

This being your birthday some of your freinds drunk your health with me, but no body did it in a worse maner then myself: for I dare drink but very little wine. Last Wednesday Justice McCartney perswaded me to goe out with him to the Strand: the day was colder then either he or I apprehended; and I am apt to think I took cold, for from that time I have had a return of my feavor, constant fits but not very violent. I have your Aunts letter

[1212] Presbyterians' indifference towards the enactment of an official toleration has been explained with reference to their overriding concern after 1704 with obtaining a repeal of the sacramental test clause and a belief that 'the establishment of legal toleration would weaken the case for removal of the test' (Beckett, *Protestant Dissent*, 49, 78–9)

[1213] 'Counsellor Stephens' or Stevens had been employed by the General Synod of Ulster since 1705 'to negotiate some things relating to this church' (*Records of the General Synod of Ulster* … (3 vols, Belfast, 1890–8), i, 157, 186, 214). He was evidently an Irish lawyer (*Swift Prose Writings*, ed. Davis et al., iii, 238). Of the likely candidates, Walter Stephens, later a master in chancery [I], was a beneficiary of the will of the presbyterian Sir Arthur Langford, 2nd Bt. (*Reg. Deeds, Wills*, i, 44). It is worth noting that in 1704/5 Alan Brodrick I had given legal advice to the General Synod, through a third party, as to the advisability of their continuing to accept the *regium donum* (the royal pension granted originally by Charles II and renewed after the Revolution) given the passage of resolutions in the Irish house of commons declaring it to be a grievance (*General Synod Records*, i, 89–90, 101–2, 138).

[1214] Either the 'North Strand' towards Clontarf, or the 'Strand of Merrion' on the south side of Dublin Bay, beyond Donnybrook. (*The A to Z of Georgian Dublin*, ed. Ferguson, opening 26).

[1215] Under the law, those registered catholic priests who took the oath of abjuration were permitted to say mass in chapels that were open to the public. Government action against unregistered priests, regular clergy and bishops varied in intensity and there is some evidence of a relaxation in vigilance on the part of the authorities in the period c.1708–11 (*Catholic Ireland in the Eighteenth Century: Collected Essays of Maureen Wall,* ed. Gerard O'Brien (Dublin, 1989), 4; Hugh Fenning, *The Irish Dominican Province 1698–1797* (Dublin, 1990), 50).

with Dr Ratclifs[1216] prescriptions which I will stick close to, and endeavour to shake off that which has shaken me and will doe more soe unlesse I can soon gett rid of it. In my fits I have little sicknesses at my stomach, and sometimes inclinations to vomit; I usually take the cordial Julep[1217] when I find my self soe, and find it helps me for the time. Dr Ratclif never prescribed any vomit on those occasions: desire your Aunt to ask him whether he will allow my taking one? If my illnesse continue I will doe little (if any businesse) this term …

147. *Alan I, Dublin, to Thomas, at his lodgings in Whitehall, 22 Jan. 1708/9*

(1248/2/354–5)

I find my letter wrote to you last Saturday about the time of Lord Lieutenants coming and our sitting was soe much paper and time thrown away, the Governement having received orders to prorogue the parliament to the 28th of April: how meeting then will answer the occasions of the publick I know not: one great reason of peoples going into a year and three quarters formerly was to obviate our sitting in Summer again, which was thought could be no way soe well provided against as by making it the interest of the Crown to have us meet in Spring, before the funds expired: I am sure it will be with an ill grace (if at all) that Gentlemen will passe the bill with a retrospect or that the duty shall commence from a day before the Royal assent given. [1218] As to my own particular, Easter and Trinitye terms are intirely lost to me,[1219] and my allowance[1220] will make me a sorry recompence for them (supposing no expence attended the Session) nay not half answer my losse: but what is yet more vexatious is that I foresee the inevitable destruction of my health which must be the consequence of sitting in a close house in the heighth of Summer … I wonder you never sent over the pamphlet which I hear names you and me in most vile abusive terms, but I cannot yet gett a sight of it. Pray who is supposed to be the Author? By my own observations, and letters which I see other Gentlemen have I find my self confirmed in the opinion I was of when I wrote two lines to you or to be told you in a letter to one of my little ones. There is a villanous pamphlet come over hither (the Harwich dream etc.)[1221] and that with the account of the ridiculous paper about repealing the test in England being burnt etc.[1222] hath caused some people to give themselves great airs. Pray be not too free

[1216]John Radcliffe (1653–1714), the well-known English physician.

[1217]A sweet, syrupy drink to which medication might be added.

[1218]The additional duties granted in 1707 were due to expire in June 1709 and would have to be renewed by a further supply act passed by that date (McGrath, *Constitution*, 211).

[1219]The legal terms.

[1220]As Speaker, amounting to £500 per session (*Lib. Mun.*, pt.7, p.70).

[1221]*An Account of a Dream at Harwich. In a Letter to a Member of Parliament about the Camisars* (1708). *A sequel, An Account of a Second Dream at Harwich, Supplying All the Omissions and Defects in the First Dream. In a Letter to the Same Member of Parliament, about the Camisars*, was published in London in 1709.

[1222]*Of the Sacramental Test: To a Member of Parliament Who Was for the Occasional Bill in the Former, When That Bill Was on Foot* … (1709). On 10 Jan. 1709 the English house of commons voted it 'a scandalous and seditious libel', and ordered it to be burned by the common hangman (Abel Boyer, *The History of the Reign of Queen Anne, Digested into Annals … Year the Seventh* (1709), 275).

with somebody; Lovet[1223] protests he never said one word of what you write, never saw you at Lord Whartons, never heard you had such discourse there as your letter imports: This in presence of Justice Coote.[1224]

148. *Alan I, Dublin, to Thomas, at his lodgings in Whitehall, 9 Feb. 1708/9*

(1248/2/356–7)

I wish this very cold snowy weather may agree with you and my other freinds in London, but really I am hardly able to keep my house warm with all the fires I can make and shutters I can use: in my conscience I think this North East wind finds the way through the very walls. Your letter by Mr Shaw[1225] and two lately I have received, and desire if possible you will give me a certain account when my Lord Lieutenant leaves London, that I may know whether it will be possible for me to goe to Munster: without air and retiring out of this town before the Session to avoid businesse I shal not be able to hold up my head during the Parliament. Doth not my Lord intend to order our Justices to prepare some bills to sett us on work;[1226] if we are not employed we shal employ ourselves you know: methinks the bill which we last Session rejected for the alterations made in it in England might be a very proper one:[1227] Hath my Lord any body near him that reminds him of these matters? Beleive me some who (I beleive) make great professions would not be mortifyed at any miscarriage or disappointment during his administration. Make your own use of it, but take it from me as what may be depended on and is most certainly true, Lord C—[1228] hath a very great interest in him: it is not your businesse to shew any shinesse toward him, tho I shal not be an adviser to you to goe into all his measures … You know poor Jack Hassett is dead.[1229] Will Lord Lieutenant recommend to the Deanery of Down; it is a very good one, about £700 per annum:[1230] The Justices have sent me a case for my opinion whether they have a right to give that living: this to yourself: but a word from my Lord for Dr L[*loy*]d[1231]

[1223] John Lovett (*d.* 1710) of Liscombe, Bucks, and Dublin, builder and proprietor of the Eddystone lighthouse, who had recently arrived in Ireland (*Verney Letters of the Eighteenth Century from the MSS at Claydon House*, ed. Lady Verney (2 vols, 1930), i, 192–213).

[1224] Thomas Coote, justice of queen's bench [I].

[1225] Possibly Robert Shaw (c.1684–1727), of Newgrove, Co. Galway, subsequently elected MP [I] in 1715, who was a Middle Templar (*Hist. Ir. Parl.*, vi, 263).

[1226] It was an accepted practice that the Irish privy council could begin the legislative work of a session in advance by preparing and engrossing bills and despatching them to the privy council in Whitehall for approval, without waiting for 'heads of bills' to be produced by the Lords or Commons in Dublin. In this case the preliminary drafting would be done by the judges.

[1227] As explained in the postscript, this was the previously unsuccessful bill to explain and amend the Popery Act of 1704.

[1228] Probably Thomas, Lord Coningsby.

[1229] John Blenerhassett, sr, MP [I].

[1230] A list of church of Ireland dignities and their annual values, dating from the mid-18th century, estimated the annual income of the deanery of Down at £1,000 (Lambeth Palace Library, MS 2168, f.128).

[1231] Owen Lloyd, who became dean of Connor in 1710.

would doe the worke. I gave Captain Howard (Lord Effinghams brother)[1232] five broad peices for my children, but he is not sailed yet …

[*PS*] The bill I mean is that for the amendment of some defects in the Act to prevent the farther growth of Poperye.

149. *Alan I, Dublin, to Thomas, at his lodgings in Whitehall, 28 Feb. 1708/9*

(1248/2/358–9)

It is necessary for my health and my affairs that I see Munster soon, which I cannot propose to doe unlesse I make use of the little time I shal have before my Lord Lieutenant lands, and therefore resolve to take horse to morrow: Pray give me notice by a line directed to me at Whiterock near Middleton by the post of Tallough[1233] when his day is fixed for leaving London and in what time he expects to be here. You cannot imagine what a ferment the bill for reversing Lord Slanes outlawry hath occasioned, [1234] and it is very carefully remembred that Lord Wharton was the man who brought it into the house of Lords, and that he was seconded by Lord Pembroke;[1235] you see whose freinds they are that fail not to mention those names on this ungrateful occasion. The purchasers under Lord Slanes forfeiture you may be sure are justly alarmed least any thing in the bill may weaken their title or securitye, but of that I am very well satisfyed care hath been taken: however they have by last pacquet sent over a peticion and directions to oppose the bills passing the house of commons.[1236] Indeed it is surprizing to see a man who to the last adhered to the French and Irish here[1237] have a pencion of £500 per annum on our establishment, and a regiment in our pay, and now to be restored to his bloud, and consequently capable of sitting in our house of Peers:[1238] but a neighbour of ours (who once owed you money and

[1232] Francis Howard (1683–1743), who in 1725 succeeded his brother as 7th Baron Howard of Effingham, and in 1731 was created 1st earl of Effingham.

[1233] Tallow, Co. Waterford.

[1234] The former jacobite Christopher Fleming (1676–1726), 17th Baron Slane, had been outlawed and attainted after 1691, and his Irish estates forfeited. After a period in the French service he joined the Allied forces in Portugal in 1704, rising to the rank of major-general. Queen Anne granted him a pension in 1707 in recognition of his services and made him colonel of a foot regiment in 1708. He now professed great loyalty to the queen and 'zeal' for the protestant religion (HMC, *Portland MSS*, viii, 242). A bill to reverse the outlawry and attainder, but not the forfeiture of his estates, was introduced into the British parliament in the 1708–9 session, and eventually received the Royal Assent in Apr. 1709. During its passage it had been published in London as *An Act to Reverse the Outlawry and Attainder of Christopher Lord Baron of Slane, in Ireland*. Lord Wharton wrote from Dublin that the bill had 'made a great clamour here' (BL, Add. MS 61634, f. 73: Wharton to [Sunderland], 3 June 1709).

[1235] Whether or not Wharton made the original motion, the bill was in fact presented by Slane's cousin Lord Sunderland (*LJ*, xviii, 633). Sir John Perceval was informed that it was through Sunderland's intercession that Slane 'did … obtain the queen's favour for bringing in his bill' (BL, Add. MS 47025, f. 116: Edward Southwell to Perceval, 5 Mar. 1708/9).

[1236] The fears of Irish protestants focused on the potential subversion of the land settlement, despite the specific wording of the bill (*Addison Letters*, ed. Graham, 140–2). It had been read for the first time in the Commons on 24 Feb. 1709, and before the second reading a petition was received on 4 Mar. from a number of those who had purchased Slane's former property following the resumption of forfeited estates in 1700. In response, the committee on the bill inserted a clause to protect their interests. (*CJ*, xvi, 122, 136, 148, 175, 196.)

[1237] In other words, the jacobite cause during the Williamite war.

[1238] On 7 June 1709 Slane petitioned the Irish house of lords for his writ, but no order was made (*LJI*, ii, 266).

whom you have eternally disobliged by making him pay you) said it ought to be considered how nearly related he was to my Lord Sunderland, and added the bill was recommended to Lord Wharton by the Queen. This was said at my Lord Chancellors before his Lordship,[1239] Mr Conollye,[1240] and me; and a certain person who is talked of to marry his daughter[1241] said lately the Lord Slane did well to apply to the Parliament of England since he could not have justice here: and wished he were to be restored to his estate too, with which being upbraided by one who sate by he expressed himself to mean that the purchasers should be repaid their money. All care is used to render Lord Wharton obnoxious on this as well as every other occasion, and upon my word many well meaning Gentlemen are strangely shocked at the procedure, and others very artfully insinuate they suppose this to be a forerunner of the reversal of Lord Clancarthy's outlawry; whose nearer relacion to Lord S[*underland*] entitles him to more of his favor and interest.[1242] Thus careful are some to sowre and poison others, and I am told by one to whom the words were spoken that a young Gentleman whom we very well know publickly said in the Coffee house he was going to drink Lord Rochesters health; for what had he done more directly and openly prejudicial to the Protestant interest then the bringing in this bill. There needed not any help to be given those who intend to render his administracion uneasy; the concionazimur[1243] is beaten furiously, and no longer agoe then yesterday in the afternoon we were told thence that the wickednesse of this present age proceeded from the little regard had to the Clergy and its power and authoritye; that Atheists, Deists,[1244] Erastians[1245] Independants[1246] and others were pulling down the hedge; that it was the duty of every man to sett themselves against many things which he said were in agitacion and design by such as Hickernigil[1247] Tindal[1248] Toland[1249] etc. and the words Now is the time were very often used. I doe assure you this discourse outdid Dr Hicks Regale and Pontificale[1250] in my judgement: the preacher was one Scott a schoolmaster.[1251] Doe not you render yourself obnoxious to

[1239]The Irish lord chancellor, Richard Freeman.

[1240]William Conolly, MP [I].

[1241]Slane's only child, Helen, never married.

[1242]Donough Maccarty (1668–1734), 4th earl of Clancarty, was Sunderland's brother-in-law. He and his wife were living in exile in northern Germany.

[1243]From the Latin concionor, meaning to preach or harangue. A concionator was one who preached or harangued his audience (*OED*).

[1244]In essence, a denial of revelation (through scripture or miracles) as a basis for religious belief: Deism proposed that human beings could only come to a knowledge of the Creator through understanding the laws of nature (by the observation of natural phenomena and the application of reason), since God does not intervene in the functioning of the natural world.

[1245]Those who followed the teachings of the Swiss theologian Thomas Erastus (1524–83), that the state should have supreme authority in matters ecclesiastical.

[1246]Calvinistic separatists opposed to a state church or any over-arching ecclesiastical structure and requiring the independence of individual congregations: identified with the radical puritans of the Civil War and interregnum.

[1247]Edmund Hickeringill (1643–1708), Church of England clergyman and religious controversialist.

[1248]Matthew Tindal (1657–1733), freethinker.

[1249]John Toland (1670–1722), radical 'commonwealthman' and anti-clerical writer.

[1250]Edmund Hickeringill, *Essays Concerning* … ([1706]), of which the sixth was on the subject of 'Absolutions and excommunications, as meer politick tools, and belonging to the regale, not pontificale.'

[1251]Possibly John Scott (b.c.1677), curate of St Michan's, Dublin (Leslie, *Clergy of Dublin*, rev. Wallace, 1038).

be insulted as I hear my Lord Cheif Justice Pyne was the other day in the Smirna Coffee house[1252] by Savage[1253] and Tenison,[1254] by talking about this Sermon, yet I think you should give Lord W[*harton*] hints what is doing to render his administration uneasy and prepare people to do soe by representing to them that hellish designs are on foot. Pray wait on Lord Pembroke and mencion Frounce to be continued Gunner of the new built Yatcht which is to be on this Station and not to remove him with the old Yatcht to another; he desired me to write to you on this subject. You know his name is Richard …

[*PS*] Let me have a full account of Lord Cheif Justice Pynes matter.

150. *Alan I, Dublin, to Thomas, at his lodgings in Whitehall, 4 Feb. 1709/10*

(1248/2/374–5)

You have on the other side what is on our books relating to the addresse for enlarging the term for exporting linen to the West Indies;[1255] by it I find it was no addresse to the Queen in writing, but my Lord Pembroke was attended by the members of the house who were of the Councel with the desire of the house: what he did in it I cannot tell but we never received any answer. Tho this trade was brought in to the ruine of the woollen, and probably a great means of it, yet since it is what a great part of the Kingdome depends on pray doe what you can in it; and the rather because I foresee great difficultyes are intended to be laid in my Lords way the next Session and all prudent precautions should be taken to remove them. And tho perhaps you may not think yourself or Laur[*enc*]e Clayton to have been well treated yet that ought not to induce either to permit the enemyes of our common interest as well as of my Lord Lieutenant to gett any advantage; and by the by the Toryes have it among them that you are piqued and resolve not to come over. I chuse to

[1252] Presumably the Smyrna coffee-house in Pall Mall, there being no establishment of this name in Dublin.

[1253] Philip Savage, MP [I].

[1254] Henry Tenison, MP [I].

[1255] On the first page of the letter, in a different hand, is the following:

'Jovis 14o die Augusti 1707

Sir Thomas Southwell according to Order Reported from the Committee of the whole House to whom Heads of a Bill for the further Encouragement and improvement of the Hempen and Flaxen Manufacture were Committed, That they had gone through the Same and Agreed thereto with some Amendments which he read in his Place and after delivered at the Table where the same were again read and agreed to by the house with some further Amendments.

Ordered that Sir Thomas Southwell do attend his Excellencie the Lord Lieutenant with the Said heads of a Bill and desire the Same may be transmitted into Great Brittain in due form.

Sir Thomas Southwell Reported also that they had come to the Resolutions following

Resolved That it is the Opinion of this Committee that Mr Lucas by setting up a linnen Manufacture in the County of Monaghan And the information by him given deserves to be Encouraged and rewarded.

Resolved that it is the Opinion of this Committee that an humble Addresse be presented to her Majesty that the time limitted for Exportation of the linnen Manufacture of this Kingdom may be Enlarged.

To which Resolutions the Question being Severally putt the house did agree.

Ordered that Such Members of this house as are of her Majesties most honourable Privy Councill do attend his Excellency the Lord Lieutenant with the Humble desires of this house That her Majestie will be pleased Graciously to Interpose their favour That for the Encouragement of the Linnen Manufacture in this Kingdom the Term for Exporting Linnen Cloath to the Plantations be Enlarged.'

Confirmed in *CJI*, iii, 467–8.

write this to you rather then directly to my Lord Lieutenant but desire you to tell him that it is the sense of Justice McCartney, the Attorney and Sollicitor, Mr Conelye and others that Mr Bligh will for the future not only be with my Lord Lieutenant in all respects[1256] but influence his freinds to be soe if he may be received: he by Baron Johnson gives the Attorney assurance he will settle the affair of Trim to my Lords wishes,[1257] will alway act with the last respect to my Lord, and never fail him where he can be of use. What he means by not lying under his displeasure I conceive to be that he apprehends an interest is not only making but actually formed against him in the County of Meath that will throw him out from being chosen for that County the next Parliament, and that he may be removed from the Councel: now Mr Conelye and all the rest think it will be an heart breaking to Sir Ri[*chard*] Leving and that party to have their dear freind Bligh forsake them, and the competitor is rather set up then stands of his own accord in opposition to him: so as if it be my Lords pleasure, I should think he should be assured of not being ill looked on if he shal give reason to depend on these terms being performed and actually execute his part out of hand in relation to Trim which indeed I wish were quietly settled for more reasons then one. The warm people endeavour to make a mighty stir about that. I go Munster Circuit.

151. *Alan I, Ballyannan, to Thomas, at his lodgings in Whitehall, 16 Mar. 1709[/10]*

(1248/2/380–1)

My last was from Mallow to my sister of the seventh as I take it … The weather hath been excessively stormy and wett of late, and I riding in a pair of thin hunting bootes took cold; which seised me in the reins and small of the back soe that I verily beleived my ailing was the gravel; for I was not able to rise without help, or almost to sit my horse: I was told riding was very good for it, and gott on horseback on Tuesday; but was forced to come hither that night in Mr Boyles coach. The day was bad and deceitful, the finest you ever saw in the morning and a deluge of rain soon after: this increased my cold and consequently my pain; but I took some Venice treacle[1258] (I think it is) I mean the electuary[1259] Dr Ratclif prescribed me when any way feavorish, and that sweated me and hath done me a great deal of good; my pain is not soe great as it hath been, but continues very sharp: and tho possibly I may have taken cold and that may contribute much to my uneasinesse, yet by the vast deal of slime and sand in my water it is most plain to me that the gravel is my cheif ailment. The weather being very ill I keep within doors to avoid taking cold; else I would make a shift to gett on horseback in hopes that gentle riding might contribute to my ease and recoverye before this day sennight: for as I am I really cannot go the Circuit, but my pain

[1256] Thomas Bligh, MP [I] Co. Meath, who died at Bath 28 Aug. 1710 (*Hist. Ir. Parl.*, iii, 213). He opposed Wharton's administration in the 1709 session (*Addison Letters*, ed. Graham, 176, 178).

[1257] A disputed election for port-reeve (chief magistrate) of Trim in Sept. 1709 had provoked violent conflict when the losing party, headed by Bligh, the defeated candidate, nonetheless claimed legitimate authority. The Irish privy council, which had jurisdiction according to the 'new rules' of 1672, decided in the following Nov. in favour of Bligh's election (NLI, MS 2993: Trim assembly book; BL, Add.MS 47025, f. 140, William Perceval to Sir John Perceval, 12 Nov. 1709; *Swift Prose Writings*, ed. Davis et al., iii, 240).

[1258] Theriac, or sometimes 'theriaca Andromachi', a homeopathic panacea supposedly dating back to the ancient Greeks.

[1259] A medicinal paste including some sweetening agent to hide the taste.

lessens removes and falls lower as the gravel comes away. I am sure I have formerly owned either directly to you or to one of my sisters the receit of all letters from you which came to hand, which are dated, the 11th, 14, and 16th of February, and now the second and fourth of this month: I have all these before me and no one of them contains (what your last hints at) any desire of my thoughts to what uses supplyes that may be demanded next Session will be best applyed: If before my leaving town I received any letter from you on that subject (which I doe not remember, and therefore beleive the contrary) I am certain I answered it: and can only now say that the question seems to me of an extraordinary nature since if there be occasion for money that occasion will be the ground on which to found a demand, and the supplyes given will be applyed to those uses. Perhaps this question might arise from an expression in a letter I wrote that it should be very well considered on what foot a demand should be made if any was intended, as I suppose there is. The difference between England and Ireland is this; there funds are the difficult matter to be found out, here the way to employ them. In truth there is not that man in the Kingdome lesse capable to advise in this thing then I; yet I stil must think it of the last consequence to my Lord Lieutenants honour and the credit of his freinds that the demand be on such a foot as Gentlemen may with reputation goe into it: Every body knows there will be opposition, but it will come to nothing if there be reason to demand and consequently to grant a supply: but if this should fail, nothing will incline men to act against what they beleive is fit for them to doe. I thank you for the account of the Dr and his Mob:[1260] I hope before this, the one, and some of the other are in a fair way of having their deserts: pray name persons especially of one Bench[1261] who were for punishing the Doctor. Captain Corker[1262] told me on Tuesday last at Castlemarter[1263] that the Gentleman who now dwells at Roxborough[1264] upon a discourse what would become of Sacheverel said he beleived he would not be punished or would do well enough or to that purpose for that the Mob were for him: Now this discourse was on Fryday 10 March … at which time the letters of the second and 4 March were not come in: soe as the Gentleman had a shrewd guesse at what would happen, unlesse he might have heard the news by shipping from the West, and I am told a Bristol ship arrived in Corke harbour that possibly might bring it. It is incredible how sollicitous a sett of men are for the Doctors good delivery; and if that fail, least the character should suffer as if they were antirevolutioners:[1265] There are not many of one sort whom I have heard go farther then to call it an hot, indiscreet or injudicious discourse … Do not estrange yourself at Dover Street.[1266]

[1260]Dr Henry Sacheverell, whose trial was in progress in Westminster Hall. On 1 Mar. 1710 riots had broken out in London in support of Sacheverell, for which see Geoffrey Holmes, 'The Sacheverell Riots: The Crowd and the Church in Early Eighteenth-century London', *Past and Present*, no. 72 (1976), 55–85.

[1261]The bench of bishops in the British house of lords.

[1262]Edward Corker, MP [I].

[1263]Castlemartyr, Co. Cork.

[1264]Most probably Robert Price (*d.* c.1725) of Roxborough, Co. Cork, an estate lying close to Midleton (Phillimore, *Indexes*, ii, 146).

[1265]Sacheverell had been impeached for 'high crimes and misdemeanours' on the basis of a sermon in which he had allegedly impugned the principles of the Glorious Revolution by denying that it had embodied resistance to James II.

[1266]The site of Lord Wharton's town house.

152. *Alan I, Dublin, to Thomas, at Whiterock near Midleton, 8 July 1710*

(1248/3/3–4)

I find by Tom, who gott hither this morning, that you reached Middleton pretty early on Tuesday: I wish there were any good news to send you, but in my opinion every thing looks very cloudy, and I am sure the Toryes have all maner of assurances of successe given them by their freinds: this their behavior shews to a demonstration, tho they could be masters of their tongues, which also are very lavish on the occasion. Lord Blessintons answer to my letter came this day sennight, in as obliging a maner as I can possibly expresse: and Lady Blessintons came to Mrs Hills hand yesterday; soe that the writings are now drawing, and I doe not foresee there can be any reasonable cause to doubt the successe of this matter;[1267] but till all is settled and over, the lesse is said of it I think is the better: however we publickly own on both sides that such a matter is in agitation. I find there will be occasion for ready money, more then I foresaw, for presents, wedding clothes etc and I shal be put under difficultyes about it: for really the money I have paid the trustees of the hollow blades[1268] for Elfordstowne,[1269] and the difference between a Lawyers gains and Judges salary make it more difficult to find ready money then heretofore. Pray tell Dick Bettesworth this, and let him assure my tenants that I have a real and most pressing occasion for money at this time, and that I shal take it very ill to be disappointed on such an emergencye … Lord Lieutenant is at Chappel Izod,[1270] and either melancholy and out of humor, or at least soe to me …[1271] God send us a merry meeting. You will not take it ill of me to remind you how necessary it was to lay up a little ready money against an ill time: All we can expect to enjoy hereafter is our estates, and while that is allowed us we are well enough: but I remember a time when they yeilded us nothing …

153. *Alan I, Dublin, to Thomas, at his lodgings in Whitehall, 12 Aug. 1710*

(1248/3/11–12)

By the proceedings in England as we see them in publick papers, and the accounts we have from those who come thence matters seem to be determined that way which suits with the wishes and expectations of one sort of people:[1272] It will be of great use to me to

[1267]The marriage of St John II to Anne, da. of Michael Hill, Lord Blessington's nephew.

[1268]The Company for Making Hollow Sword Blades in England, an English finance company which had acquired considerable tracts of land in Ireland through speculation in the forfeitures resumption.

[1269]About five miles north of Midleton.

[1270]Chapelizod.

[1271]Wharton was concerned at the delay in returning bills from the British privy council, suspecting that 'the intention were to keep him' in Ireland 'till the heat of the elections is over' in England (TNA, SP 63/366, f. 195: Edward Southwell to Lord Dartmouth, 13 July 1710). In his correspondence with ministers in England he made clear his anxiety to leave Ireland as soon as possible (TNA, SP 63/366, ff. 225–6: Wharton to Dartmouth, 3 Aug. 1710).

[1272]Principally the dismissal of Lord Treasurer Godolphin on 8 Aug. and his replacement at the treasury by a commission comprising Robert Harley (who also became chancellor of the exchequer) and several of Harley's close associates, a change which would have been gratifying to tories in Ireland.

know from you (who are on the spot) whether what you and I have more then once talked of as being in agitation, be not ready to come on us out of hand. Mr Leslyes Good old cause speaks plain English, and tells us what the wishes and expectations of people of his principles are:[1273] but pray doe other men think the game soe sure, as he would possesse and perswade the world? We hear he is taken up;[1274] and tho it should happen soe that he could be proved to be the Author of that treasonable paper, his freinds here beleive his censure may be more mild then others think his crime deserves; or that it may fall out that he may have the happinesse of not having it put in immediate execution: for they say such things have been, and give late instances. You know how much it imports me to have the earliest account you can give of what is likely to happen: if the nett be drawing, I resolve not to stay to be covered. In short I can see nothing drawing on, but what we have for more then twenty years past been (in all appearance) endeavouring to prevent; and the consequences of such an event, which I need not name, and in which I am sure to bear a full proporcion.

154. *Alan I, Dublin, to Thomas, at his lodgings in Whitehall, 15 Aug. 1710*

(1248/3/13–14)

On Sunday night I received yours of the seventh from Bath, and the same maile brought us the astonishing news of Lord Treasurers being out: I need not tell you how different the effects were of such tidings; both partyes looked just as in the beginning of eighty eight, before any news of the Prince of Oranges expedition. I am glad to find the waters have done you soe much good, but I make no doubt as new Lords occasion new Laws, soe your stay at Bath is over and that this will find you in London making up matters soe as to be ready for a removal. As that will be no surprise, soe neither will it be one penny losse to you, if you please to make that prudent use of it that you may and I hope will make. I fear that out of your plentiful estate, and employment you neither laid money by, nor ever will while you continue in the same course of living as hitherto: This gives you the fairest oportunitye in the world to withdraw from England, to give off breeding horses, and to lay up a great deal of money yearly, yet live better and much more to satisfaction and with more credit then you doe now: Is not all that I say true, and are not the things which I propose very desirable and easily attainable? If Ireland be a place for honest men to live quietly in, let you and I live privately together in the County of Corke: but if it be not easy to live here while matters keep that course they seem to be now taking, retire into the country, and by giving over all maner of expence which consists in chance enable yourself to live and appear handsomely without a place. What I write is done in freindship and will I am sure be taken soe: pray tell me how far off doe you think is ——?

[1273] Charles Leslie (1650–1722), a nonjuring church of Ireland clergyman and jacobite pamphleteer: the pamphlet was *The Good Old Cause, or, Lying in Truth, Being a Second Defence of the Lord Bishop of Sarum, from a Second Speech. And Also, the Dissection of a Sermon It Is Said His Lord*[s]*hip Preached in the Cathedral Church of Salisbury Last 29th of May* … (1710).

[1274] Leslie's arrest had been ordered in July 1710. When he did not surrender himself by 8 Aug. he was declared an outlaw and went into hiding for a time before fleeing to St Germain in the following Apr.

155. *Alan I, Dublin, to Thomas, Whitehall, 22 Aug. 1710*

(1248/3/29–30)

I take it for granted that this letter will meet you in London, where I doubt you will not long have the same pleasant lodgings in which I left you: but I depend on your giving timely notice how to direct when you are on removing thence. For fear I should forgett it I will begin with telling you My Lord Lieutenant read part of a letter from Lord Sommers, in which he takes notice of your having a vote at Ryegate by what my brother St John left you there, and desires it for his freind:[1275] I hope you have not disposed of that little thing, and that you will wait on him and let him know how desirous you are to doe what in you lyes to have a good man chosen in that borough. Captain Camock[1276] is not come in; you must be sure I wait his arrival with great impatience: Unriddle Lord G[*odolphin'*]s doing what he hath done lately since being removed: the Toryes mutter that he is in the secret.[1277] Pray let my sister know Lord Lieutenant leaves this place soon: I beleive some time next week … If I be not mistaken our freind in Smithfeild aims at succeeding me by Lord Angleseys interest;[1278] my sister will tell whom I mean: this to your self.

156. *Alan I, Dublin, to Thomas, 23 Sept. 1710*

(1248/3/19–20)

I can now tell you that Thursday night your Nephew marryed Misse Hill, and hath the greatest reason in the world to own the happinesse, of being as well disposed of as his own

[1275] For Somers's interest at Reigate, where in 1710 he unsuccessfully put up his nephew James Cocks, and a local gentleman, William Jordan, see *HC 1690–1715*, ii, 584–6.

[1276] George Cammock or Camocke was a naval captain, supposedly Irish-born, and serving on the Irish station in 1709, based in Kinsale, Co. Cork, when he was ordered to take his warship the *Speedwell* to search for two French privateers which had entered Bantry Bay and captured a London merchant ship, the *Ruth* of London, returned from Jamaica with a cargo allegedly worth £20,000. Cammock captured both privateers and recovered the prize. The crew of one privateer turned out to be mainly Irish sailors, who were sent to Cork to be tried for high treason. (*The Supplement*, 23–26 Dec. 1709). Early in Sept. 1710 Cammock was granted salvage money for the recapture of the *Ruth* (*CTB*, xxiv, c. 436). In 1714 he was cashiered as a jacobite sympathiser, and after spending some time at St Germain (TNA, SP 78/160/108: Thomas Crawfurd to John Pringle, 22 Jan. 1716 N.S.) entered the Spanish service and commanded as an admiral at the battle of Cape Passaro in 1718. In 1725, 'upon some information given against him' he was imprisoned in Spain and subsequently exiled for six years, after which he was permitted to return to England and may have resumed a command in the Royal Navy, dying in about 1733 (*British Journal*, 18 Dec. 1725; *Read's Weekly Journal, or British Gazetteer*, 28 Aug. 1731; TNA, PROB 11/658/191; Vicars, *Index*, 74).

[1277] For a time after his dismissal Godolphin continued to assist the queen's government, by reassuring City financiers and foreign allies (*HL 1660–1715*, iii, 111), which raised tory suspicions that the ministerial changes would not produce the results they desired.

[1278] John Annesley (1676–1710), 6th earl of Anglesey [I]. He died on 18 Sept. 1710 and was succeeded by his brother Arthur, MP [I]. Given the Annesley connection, 'our friend in Smithfield' may have been Anglesey's cousin, the former MP [I] for Downpatrick and forfeitures trustee Francis Annesley, though his London address is recorded as Lincoln's Inn Fields (*HC 1690–1715*, iii, 34). In the next letter Alan refers to rumours that Francis Annesley was to have the lord chancellorship of Ireland, with Sir Richard Levinge taking his own place as chief justice of queen's bench. It is possible that Alan was referring here to Smithfield in Dublin, the area in which he himself kept his town house and where he was a member of the parish vestry (Twomey, *Smithfield*, 29).

heart could wish, due as much to your kindnesse as to that of any freind he hath. She will (if I have any judgement) make an admirable wife, and I hope he will prove a good husband to her; and see no cause to suspect the contrary … On Monday morning I sett out for Munster where I shal have but one months time to spend before term, if our removes doe not reach this place before that time: If they doe, and I am thought soe obnoxious as to be turned out of the service of the Crown a third time, my next consideration must be whether I will ever put on my gown again: It is no lessening of me to doe it: I remember Sir Ri[*chard*] Reynell[1279] (when superseded) at the bar; and Sir Francis Pemberton[1280] did the same after being turned out of his Cheif Justices place. The great losse it will be to me to quit businesse entirely, and the strange course of life which I must take up, from a great deal of emploiment to become perfectly sedentary and idle, will and justly ought to have weight with me: beside my enemyes may insult and apprehend they have gotten a great advantage over me in making me discontinue my profession in a pique or resentment as they will term it; And it will be a pleasure to them not to have me a witnesse and observer of what steps are taken in the Courts and elsewhere: But all these considerations shal give place and have no weight with me, if (as we are told) Anesley came to be our Chancellor, and Leving Cheif Justice. Nothing is soe strange to one party, but may seem highly reasonable to another: Why may not one mans being expelled one house be sufficient merit to recommend him to be Speaker of another?[1281] Or giving her Majestyes affairs the utmost opposition during two Sessions of Parliament intitle a second to promotion? For my part if a third time I fall into disgrace, it must be a great oversight in me again to subject my self to a like misfortune hereafter: nor had I been now in the power of a certain person to procure the getting me slighted a second time, if her Majestye had not in Lord Pembrokes governement without any application of mine, or any freind of mine, honoured me with an employ of greater value then that she was pleased to turn me out of in Lord O[*rmond'*]s Governement.[1282] It is true indeed when I was made Atturney, and had in the chair of the house of Commons almost sacrificed my life in the service of the Crown and countrey, I then made application for the Post I am now in, as what would allow me some ease, and would be a creditable way of retiring from fatigue and businesse: but this I should not have been soe hardy to have sought, without the encouragement I had given me by being of her Majestyes free Grace taken into her service before, which perswaded me I should not fall under her displeasure till I failed in my duty, which I cannot upbraid my self with having ever been guilty of. Pray let me know with as much speed as you can whether we are to have those persons put over us in all Stations that are most disagreeable to us; and forgive me for putting you often in mind how much it is in your power to triumph over the malice of your enemyes, if you please. And sure it would be an unspeakable satisfaction to me to give them the mortification of seeing me live better, in more order and plenty and grow more rich and

[1279] Sir Richard Reynell, 1st Bt (c.1626–99), justice of king's bench [I] 1674–86, and chief justice 1690–5.

[1280] Sir Francis Pemberton (1624–97), lord chief justice of king's bench [E] 1681–2 and of common pleas [E] 1682–3.

[1281] Annesley had been expelled from the Irish house of commons on 28 Sept. 1703 for having 'scandalously and maliciously misrepresented the Protestant freeholders of this kingdom' in his capacity as a commissioner of inquiry into Irish forfeitures. The lord chancellor was *ex officio* speaker of the house of lords.

[1282] Having been dismissed as solicitor-general [I] in 1704, Alan had been appointed attorney-general [I] in 1707.

considerable after being turned out then before, and this you know is so much in your power, that to will it brings it to passe … Must I stil direct to White Hall?

157. *Alan I, Dublin, to Thomas, at his lodgings in Whitehall, 7 Nov. 1710*

(1248/3/21–2)

I will not let the pacquet goe off without a letter, tho I have no other accounts to give you hence then what are usual, that we take our measures from England, and our pulses beat here just as yours doe in London; some with great chearfulnesse and vivacitye, others with lesse spirit and strength. Let me desire you to be particular in describing the behavior of the two Doctors in the election for Surrey;[1283] if one of them did not to the utmost of his power endeavour to serve Sir Richard Onslow[1284] he is the last and worst of mankind; and I would no more trust him then I would a Pirate or highwayman: I must impute the mismanagement of another person to infirmitye and being overperswaded by some who never fail to make use of oportunityes when men decay in their facultyes.[1285] Depend on it there is a complaint gone over against Sir John Whitronges[1286] officers or some of them, for a very foolish action (not to say worse) done by them at Limrick: the particulars I am a stranger to, but I hear from every hand that they acted very extravagantly more then once, and once at least gave just cause of offence to the Bishop: which it seems is to be carryed soe far as to endeavour to break the regiment.[1287] That this is true I know, for I had it out of the mouth of a person much confided in by the party complaining: It will be a matter of triumph to break that regiment in particular, considering what the Colonel is, and how far befreinded by Lord W[*harton*].[1288] This you may hint as you think fit. Let me know

[1283] For the Surrey election of 1710 (which took place on 11 Oct.), and the involvement of the clergy in support of the tory candidates, see *HC 1690–1715*, ii, 572–3.

[1284] Onslow was one of the defeated candidates.

[1285] This may have been Katherine Brodrick's husband William Whitfield, who in Jan. 1711 sent a long letter to his brother-in-law Alan in an effort to explain himself (SHC, 1248/3/33–4: Whitfield to Alan I, 11 Jan. 1710[/11]).

[1286] Sir John Wittewronge, 3rd Bt (1673–1722), of Stantonbury, Bucks., MP [GB] 1705–10, colonel of a regiment of foot on the Irish establishment, and a whig in his politics.

[1287] For this incident, in which officers of the regiment, stationed in Limerick, had been heard carousing under the window of the high church bishop of Limerick, Thomas Smyth, and drinking 'confusion, damnation, plague, pestilence and famine, battle, murder and sudden death to Dr Sacheverell and his adherents', see Maurice Lenihan, *Limerick, Its History and Antiquities* … (Dublin, 1867), 310–12; T. C. Barnard, 'Athlone 1685; Limerick 1710: Religious Riots or Charivaris', *Studia Hibernica*, xxvii (1993), 72–3. Archdeacon William Perceval reported to a friend in Oxford on 4 Nov. that 'a complaint has been made to the government and affidavits have been sent up … and Lieutenant-General [Richard] Ingoldsby, who commands here … has suspended the major and six more officers of the regiment, and has also sent the affidavits over to England so that we are in hopes that these officers at least, if not the whole regiment … will be broke' (Bodl., MS Ballard 36, f. 63: Perceval to Arthur Charlett, 4 [Nov.] 1710). See also copy of resolution of mayor and common council of Limerick, 17 Nov. 1710 (TCD, MS 1995–2008/1389). The regiment was not in fact disbanded until the autumn of 1712 (*HC 1690–1715*, v, 910–11). Richard Ingoldsby MP [I], was commander-in-chief of the forces in Ireland from 1706 and a lord justice [I] 1710–11.

[1288] For Wittewronge's connection with Wharton (through whose patronage he had secured his colonelcy) see Bodl., MS Ballard 36, f. 63: Perceval to Charlett, 4 [Nov.] 1710; N. Yorks. R.O., Chaytor of Croft papers, ZQH; draft account by Sir William Chaytor of the military career of Henry Chaytor; *HC 1690–1715*, v, 910–11.

(if you see Harry Owens[1289] or Harry Beecher[1290]) whether they are going forward with their bill in Parliament[1291] … I know how careful people ought to be how they write, but a general hint may be given and I shal understand it: I own I am convinced things will goe as I formerly thought. Lord Chancellor is not well.[1292] Breaking this regiment will make room for raising another new one, and for some men of merit to gett Commissions.

158. *Alan I, Dublin, to Thomas, at his lodgings in Whitehall, 14 Nov. 1710*

(1248/3/31–2)

I have a letter from you and another from Lord Montjoy of the seventh, both to the same purpose; and write to him this night and assure him that I will act as you and he advise; and never intended to doe otherwise unlesse it were the opinion of those with whom I alway have concurred that I ought to act otherwise. Great interest is making for Sir W[*illia*]m Fownes and Phil Savage in Dublin[1293] to turn out the Attorney[1294] and Ben Burton;[1295] and the Sherifs are all to be named on your side the water; which makes people conclude a new parliament is intended here. I beleive if there were a certainty or probabilitye of having as good an one for their purpose some men would advise dissolving the present, if it were only to have another Speaker: but they are not wise nor my Lord O[*rmond'*]s friends who put things to an hazard one way, when there is none (in my opinion) the other: and the men of sense among them will see this, and put a stop to a dissolucion. My thoughts are a new one cannot doe their businesse better and probably will be lesse to their mind then that in being. I wish you be not too sanguine in the matter I wrote about: it is your temper to hope against hope. Senny tells me he hath wrote to you about taking Ballyanan: indeed all things goe strangely to ruine there. If he and I could compasse money enough, we would purchase the Duke of Richmonds estate in the County of Limrick,[1296] about which I intend soon to write more at large; you may hint to him you beleive you shal gett him a Chapman[1297] for it or part of it, but name nott us; yet gett a promise of the preference if you can …

[1289] Presumably Henry Owen (*d.* c.1738) of Mooghna, Co. Cork (Phillimore, *Indexes*, ii, 85). A Henry Owens married Cecilia Coningsby in Dublin in 1691 (George Coningsby, *A Pedigree of Coningsby of Hampton Court* … (n.d.)).

[1290] Henry Becher (c.1665–aft.1726) of Creagh, Co. Cork (*Al. Dub.*, 54; *Reg. Deeds, Wills*, i, 171).

[1291] In 1698 leave had been given for a private bill to enable 'Henry Owen' to sell his estate in Ireland to pay debts and legacies (ILD).The fact that Francis Bernard, MP [I] was ordered to prepare the bill would suggest a Co. Cork connection. No further private bill to benefit either Owen or Becher is recorded in ILD.

[1292] The Irish under-secretary, Joshua Dawson, MP [I], reported visiting Lord Chancellor Freeman on 11 Nov. and finding him 'distracted'. That evening, after consulting Dawson and Freeman's fellow lord justice, General Richard Ingoldsby, MP [I], Mrs Freeman took medical advice and had her husband confined to bed. The opinion of the physicians was that his condition showed no prospect of improvement (TNA, SP 63/366, f. 278: Dawson to Edward Southwell, 11 Nov. 1710). Freeman died 20 Nov. 1710, as a result of a 'brain disorder' (Ball, *Judges*, ii, 33–4).

[1293] The Dublin city parliamentary constituency.

[1294] John Forster, MP [I].

[1295] Benjamin Burton, MP [I].

[1296] Charles Lennox (1701–50), 2nd duke of Richmond. The estate, which Richmond did eventually sell, was at Croom, Co. Limerick (Lenihan, *Limerick*, 729).

[1297] A purchaser.

159. *Alan I, Dublin, to Thomas, at his lodgings in Whitehall, 2 Dec. 1710*

(1248/3/23–4)

I have sate three dayes in the Court of Chancerye with another of my brethren to hear causes there pursuant to our new Commission constituting the Judges and Masters commissioners to that purpose, which is more then my proporcion of that businesse: for I am sure there is not enough between this and next term to take up nine dayes more: soe as I resolve on Monday to begin my journey toward Munster. This I doe on more reasons then one: you know I alway was fond of the countrey, and my inclinations continue the same in that particular: beside really matters have received such a turn here, that I had rather live retired and where you shal see none but freinds, then be subject to be in promiscuous company, where every word is watched and turned to the worse sense; and where you are liable to hear many things which a man can not easily passe by in silence, nor yet take notice of without doing himself a prejudice, and irritating the rage and malice of those who need no spurs to put them on saying or doing very hot and extravagant things: but really I propose a benefit to my self in point of health by my journey: for I plainly find the return of my distemper just in the maner I was this time twelve month in London: I wake at a certain hour in the night in disorder, and find a little quicknesse in my pulse and ferment in my bloud, with a stretching which continues about an hour and then I fall asleep and when I wake again my head akes a little and the fit goes off; while the fit (if I may soe call it) is on me I have a little sicknesse in my stomach; and tho I have a tolerable appetite this little ailing plainly weakens me, soe as my legs fall away and on the least quick motion or taking any pains in Court by speaking much my legs tremble: and I am very chilly and extreme fond of being near a good fire. Pray desire my sister as soon as she can to send to Mr Beale and gett him to send me word what the medicine was which Dr Ratclif prescribed me to take every night just when the fit was coming on me: It was some liquid in a very little bottle, which the Dr said would prevent any necessitye of using the bark.[1298] This I would have sent to me directed to Middleton near Tallough by the first oportunitye: for I doubt I shal have occasion for it in the countrey. At the same time I would know how I am to take the bark, if there should be need of my doing it: I think an ounce should be divided into twelve doses, to be taken each dose at the distance of fowre hours one after the other. It is a melancholy thing to have this creeping distemper perpetually hang on and attend me; but so it is, and I now beleive I shal never be free from returns of it. We have a letter in town which (as I am told) tells the answer made by the Elector of H[*anover*] to Lord R[*iver*]s:[1299] but I doe not beleive it was just as that letter is said to import: nor doe I beleive

[1298] 'Jesuit's Bark' or 'Peruvian Bark', a remedy against fever made from the bark of the cinchona.

[1299] Richard Savage (c.1654–1712), 4th Earl Rivers, had been despatched in Aug. 1710 as an envoy to Hanover. The elector's written response to Rivers' 'propositions' about peace negotiations, delivered as a memorial to the British ministry, was printed as *A Memorial Deliver'd to One of Her Majesty's Principal Secretaries of State, by His Excellency the Baron de Bothmar, Envoy Extraordinary from His Electoral Highness of Hanover* ([1711]).

that matter is soe publick: if it be let me hear what it really was. Our politicians deny a new Parliament is intended, but they are all making what interest they can: we say here that some body did what was in his power for a certain person having our great Seal:[1300] but without successe: If so, upon my word they did him service who disappointed him in his desires. None of you give us any hint who is to be the man: the men who are supposed to know most of private affairs now name Mr Ward[1301] for the man: I am well satisfyed that some who call themselves freinds of —— join'd in a letter or representation to shew how inconvenient it would be to have our country man succeed … Things go here as some men wish.

160. *Alan I, Ballyannan, to Thomas, at his lodgings in Whitehall, 19 Dec. 1710*

(1248/3/25–6)

I have been here since Wednesday hardly able to put my nose out of doors; so tempestuous cold and wet is our weather; and to my great satisfaction a messenger from Corke brought me in a pacquet with your three letters of the 19th and 30th of November, and of the 7th of this month: It also brought my sisters of Nov. 28th and Allyes of the 5 December: none of which I can this post answer at large, for the messenger is just going: but I desire you will tell my sisters of their letters and Allyes being come to hand The behavior of the D[*octo*]rs in behalf of Sir R[*ichard*] O[*nslow*] is just as I expected; ingratitude is as natural to some men as pride. As our sentiments are entirely the same in reference to that matter as well as others depend on it I had formed to my self the same resolutions on that occasion which I find you have taken, and I will keep them living and dying. Very much was due to the freindships of our deceased Uncle,[1302] very much personally to Sir R[*ichard*] O[*nslow*] on account of one of them tho the kindnesse was not designed meerly personal to him but I think in general to the familye, and particularly in testimony of love to one now in his grave: the personal worth of Sir R[*ichard*] O[*nslow*] ought to have been of great weight: But as to me, when ever any freind of mine avowedly espouses what in my thoughts is inconsistent with all I think valuable I think it high time to forgett that freindship which he by his actions hath soe violated. Brigadier Gore[1303] is a very worthy man, hath a good estate, but I cant say how far it answers the proposal but will soon inform you. I have not heard of Mr Evelyn.[1304]

[1300] Almost certainly Sir Richard Cox, the former lord chancellor [I], as Cox was also from Co. Cork and is referred to by Alan as 'our countryman'. Cox became lord chief justice of queen's bench [I] instead.

[1301] The English tory lawyer John Ward (1670–1749) of Capesthorne, Cheshire, MP [GB]. This rumour was widely current in Ireland (NLI, MS 13242: James Coughlan to Richard Musgrave, 5 Dec. 1710).

[1302] St John II.

[1303] Francis Gore, MP [I].

[1304] Certainly a member of the noted Surrey family; and most likely John Evelyn (1682–1763) of Wotton, son and namesake of the diarist, and later created baronet, who had lost his parliamentary seat at the 1710 election.

161. *Alan I, Ballyannan, to Thomas, at his lodgings in Whitehall, 24 Dec. 1710*

(1248/3/27–8)

In my last to Ally I owned among other letters the receit of three from you; the long one that came by Mr Jenkins, that of Nov. 30th and 7 December; but I had not leisure then to read them over, much lesse to give them answers at large. None of your news surprises me; only I fancy Commissioners places here are too valuable for soe many of them to fall at once into the mouthes of men of this Kingdome[1305] … I blush at the ungentlemanlike treatment Sir R[*ichard*] O[*nslow*] hath mett from some people but am no way surprised at their acting as they have done: for I have long known that when the word is given among a sort of men; honour, gratitude, freindship, tyes of bloud, every thing is to give place to the resolutions of the directors: Let me intreat you to doe me this signal act of freindship, in my name to wait on Sir R[*ichard*] O[*nslow*] and tell him how deep a sense I have of a treatment he hath mett with from some of our familye soe different from what he was a thousand wayes intitled to; tell him that there are some living and one in his grave who would have scorned to have been guilty of such basenesse; for I can give it no other term. And methinks the part which both of us probably shal have in this matter ought to be considered: both the Gentlemen were as sensible as we can be, how far their designs succeeding in the main, would in all probabilitye influence your affairs and mine: the use I resolve to make of it shal be, to have an equal regard and concern for them and theirs as they have shewn for us. But the basest part remains yet unmentioned: to make use of oportunityes to induce one man to act soe, as whoever shal mention it must at the same time lay a blemish on him living and in his grave, unlesse charitye impute it to proceed from Misinformacion and imposition on the frailtyes of old age: Nothing else could have effected it. I think I told you in my letter to Ally that I had not seen nor heard from Mr Evelyn, nor have I received the letter you mencion to have wrote in his behalf: when I see him you may be sure I will act to the best of my power to serve him; but as matters now stand on this as well as your side the water I doe not see how it will be in my power to help him to any thing worth his acceptance: This I mencion not as declining to doe all I can to shew my regard for your recommendation and for a familye whose freindship our most valuable Uncle had a true regard for, but out of concern that it will not be in my reach to act toward the young Gentleman as I would. I once mentioned the matter which Mr Bertie[1306] spoke to me about to Sir P.C.[1307] but it was entertained then in such a maner, that I thought it advisable to let it goe off without making any particular offer; but now I will doe that in the best way I am able, and if it succeed will acquaint you of it, if it be rejected shal be sorry not to have had it in my power to serve Mr Bertie …

[1305] The commissionerships of the revenue.

[1306] The most likely candidate among the many members of the Bertie family is Peregrine Bertie (c.1663–1711), MP [GB] and formerly vice-chamberlain of the royal household, who had been a contemporary of Alan II and St John II at the Middle Temple.

[1307] Sir Peter Courthope, the father of Alan's second wife.

162. *Alan I, Dublin, to Thomas, at his lodgings in Whitehall, 23 Jan. 1710[/11]*

(1248/3/37–8)

I have yours of the sixteenth and my sister Martha's of the same date … I have also received that from Mr W.[1308] and send it such an answer as I think it deserves this night. Pray tell me doe you stil continue of the same mind? Can you remain as sanguine as formerly? I own that all which you and other freinds on your side the water have said is not sufficient to remove my jealousies: on the contrary I think the grounds for my judgement of matters evidently encrease: God Almighty send that I may be mistaken; I shal gladly own my error. I am you know alone; Senny is yet att Mrs Hill, and upon my word I think it neither convenient nor safe to converse with many: To bear what must be born in company is next to impossible: to discourse on the subjects started is dangerous. It is not in my power to describe the insolence of some mens behavior. Are my freinds stil of the same mind as to me? Are they determined in their judgement that I should continue the but of some mens malice rather then by giving up what I am maligned for purchase quiet for the rest of my dayes? This is hard: but I will shew them I neither want courage or constancy to doe the part of an honest man; and will submit my sense to theirs; tho God knows my desires to retire; for I hate being alway in a storm, and would dye in quiet if I might. Yesterday Sir Constantine Phips[1309] (who landed Saturday night[1310]) was sworn at the Councel board Lord Chancellor, and afterward Lord Justice with Lieutenant General Indgolsbye, the Primate being left out of this Commission.[1311] He received me with great humanitye and freindship when I waited on him: you may be sure that a sett of men are very assiduous in making their Court; we act as formerly with great respect toward him as Lord Chancellor; and the character he justly bears of being a man of probitye and maners as well as good nature gives just reason to beleive he will not know W[*hi*]g from T[*or*]y in matters of justice, and that is all that reasonably can be wished. They seem fond of him,[1312] and in my opinion others are pleased with him: and promise themselves equal justice and fair treatment. Ask my sister what religion a certain Lady is of. The question hath been put to me, and I have answered that I never heard one word of her being of any other then that of the Church of England: She will guesse who I mean if there be any reason for the question, as I hope and beleive there is not …

[1308] Possibly William Whitshed, MP [I].

[1309] Sir Constantine Phipps (1656–1723), lord chancellor [I] 1710–14.

[1310] On the government yacht from Holyhead (*Daily Courant*, 27, 29 Jan.1711).

[1311] Since 1707 Narcissus Marsh, archbishop of Armagh, had been a member of every commission of lords justices deputising for an absent chief governor. He had been appointed with Ingoldsby in Nov. 1710 but requested to resign in anticipation of Phipps's arrival from England, because of ill health (*Daily Courant*, 29 Jan. 1711; *Scholar Bishop: The Recollections and Diary of Narcissus Marsh, 1638–1696,* ed. Raymond Gillespie (Cork, 2003), 7).

[1312] The tories.

163. *Alan I, Dublin, to Thomas, at his lodgings in Whitehall, 6 Feb. 1710[/11]*

(1248/3/39–40)

I write this on no occasion but to remove any apprehensions you may receive of the plague being in Kerry by means of a Dantzick ships being cast away in Kerry lately:[1313] last night a Councel was summoned on a letter which came to the Commissioners[1314] from that country: as far as I can find the matter stands thus. One of the Custom house officers there writes that several people who came from on board (or to say more truly were shipwrackt out of) a ship that was lost on that coast dyed suddenly there to the number of six, and that several of the country people have since dyed in few dayes of the same distemper; but the officers letter is founded on one written by a very idle man, a younger son of Mr Anthony Raymond of Mitchelstowne,[1315] and that letter is dated the thirteenth of last month: We have several letters in town dated in Tralee, Dingle, Castlemain[1316] from men of sense on the 27th of January that mention not one word of the matter; the ship in which it is supposed the infection was brought suffered shipwrack in December, and before I left Cork which was the thirteenth of January we heard of the losse of this ship from Dantzick and it was then the discourse of people that coming thence she might bring the infection. I write this as well for the ease of the minds of those who have any concern for us here, as to prevent such a rumor doing us prejudice in trade. You shal next mail hear again from me; for if tomorrw post bring no ill news, it must be as I am perswaded it is an idle false report. I will then too give you a full account of a tryal which was yesterday in our Court.

164. *Alan I, Dublin, to Thomas, at his lodgings in Whitehall, 13 Feb. 1710[/11]*

(1248/3/41–2)

Our term is now over and I have time to write to my freinds, which I hardly had while it continued … There is not the least ground for the rumor of the plague being in Kerry; a ship from Sweden came some time since into this harbour: he pretends to have come from Colmar;[1317] the Councel ordered him to perform his Quarantaine, but he neglected to fall down[1318] according to direction, which caused the councel to meet again to reinforce their

[1313]Plague had been reported at Danzig in 1709 and had spread around the Baltic by early 1711. Edward Lloyd, the Dublin bookseller, was informed that a ship from the Baltic found 'floating' in the bay at Kenmare had been inspected by revenue officers, who had then shown symptoms of the disease (BL, Add. MS 9712, ff 108–9: Lloyd to Edward Southwell, 6 Feb. 1710[/11]). The Irish government had enforced quarantine on Baltic shipping by reason of the plague on 28 Nov. 1710, and renewed this in Aug. and Oct. 1711 (*The Proclamations of Ireland, 1660–1820,* ed. James Kelly and Mary Ann Lyons (5 vols, Dublin, 2014), ii, 634, 641–3).

[1314]The commissioners of the revenue.

[1315]Anthony Raymond (*d.* 1695) of Mitchelstown, Co. Cork, had six sons, one of whom, also called Anthony, was a clergyman, a fellow of TCD, a Gaelic scholar, and a friend of Jonathan Swift (M.A. Hickson, *Selections from Old Kerry Records* (1872), 302; *DIB* (*s.v.* Raymond, Anthony)).

[1316]Castlemaine, Co. Kerry.

[1317]Kalmar, in the province of Småland in the south-east of Sweden, over two hundred and fifty miles from Stockholm, the centre of the most recent outbreak of plague in that country (Karl-Erik Frandsen, *The Last Plague in the Baltic Region, 1709–1713* (Copenhagen, 2010), 66–8).

[1318]Anchor.

orders: and now he is fallen down to the bottom of the bay: This I mention to you, least their meeting a second time may give you in London the same jealousies it caused here that she was infected; the contrary of which I am fully convinced of, but we resolve to make every ship from those parts to perform a quarantaine, whatever reasons are offered of being healthy. On Monday sennight one Patrick Campbel a bookseller[1319] was tryed in the Queens Bench on an indictment for uttering and publishing a seditious libel intitled Quaeries to the new hereditary right men. The book you either have seen or may see in London, if what was given in evidence on the tryal was true; that it is sold publickly in London. It appeared on the trial that the pamphlett was printed in England[1320] and some of that edition came into this Kingdome, and Campbel (a bookseller by trade) sent one of them to one Francis Dickson a printer[1321] as a copy by which he should print off another edition, which he did to the number of 300: which were brought to Campbel and sold by him in his shop all except twenty odd which were seised in his shop. When the warrant to apprehend him and search for the libel came to be executed he did not deny having sold the book, but said he knew no harm in it, and that it was sold publickly in London. It was insisted strongly by those who prosecuted Campbel that the Quaeries were a seditious libel, and that the causing it to be printed and selling it was full evidence of his maliciously and knowingly publishing it: the Councel for Campbel were very large in endeavouring to shew it not to be wrote with any seditious intent, and tho it should be a libel yet that there was not sufficient evidence to induce the Jury to find him guilty of having knowingly and maliciously published a seditious libel: that publishing it unlesse done knowingly and maliciously was not indictable, and that there being no other proof of either but his causing a book to be printed and sold, which was acting in the way of his trade, without any expresse proof of his being acquainted with the contents of it was not such evidence on which the Jury could find him guilty: one of my brethren was clear of opinion and soe directed the Jury that they ought to find him guilty; tho he owned at the same time that to make it criminal in Campbel it must be done knowingly and maliciously: the other said he did not apprehend the quaeries to be seditious, and tho they were yet that they were published knowingly and maliciously was a matter of fact which he must leave to the Jury on the evidence: that it was no necessary consequence of his sending it to be printed and selling it that he knew the import of the book, or published it knowingly and maliciously. I thought it would be time enough to give my opinion of it being or not being a seditious libel after verdict, since the whole book being sett forth at large in haec verba[1322] in the indictment, its not being seditious would be saved to the traverser in arrest of judgement[1323] if the verdict should be against him: but did not apprehend it to be the duty of the Court to say the Jury ought to find one way or the other, but to lay the evidence fairly before them (which I did) and to tell them that causing it to be printed and selling it was strong evidence; yet

[1319]Patrick Campbell (for whom see above, p. 111), sold books at Blind Quay, Dublin. He was tried and acquitted on 5 Feb., a verdict attributed by tories to whiggish bias (Pollard, *Dublin Book Trade*, 82–3).

[1320]*Queries. To the New Hereditary Right-Men* (London and Edinburgh, 1710). It is usually attributed to Daniel Defoe.

[1321]Francis Dickson (*d.* 1713), whose workshop was at Cork Hill, Dublin (Pollard, *Dublin Book Trade*, 152–3).

[1322]Literally 'in these words', a phrase used to denote the incorporation of text verbatim into a legal document.

[1323]In law a traverse was a pleading which denied an allegation made by an adversary; arrest of judgment was a refusal by a court to enforce a verdict because of some defect or error in proceedings or because the verdict was not supported by the evidence.

that it was but presumptive evidence of his acting knowingly and maliciously: for that many booksellers have books printed for them and sell them yet are not acquainted with their contents; and many witnesses gave Campbel the character of being very well affected to her Majestyes governement and an enemy to the Pretender; for the indictment laid that he published the book with intent to draw her Majestyes right to the Crown in question; and it appeared that he was not contriver of the book, there being an English edition before. The Jury first found he published it but not knowingly or maliciously and afterward found him not guilty; at which some here are extremely incensed.

165. *Alan I, Dublin, to Thomas, at his lodgings in Whitehall, 27 Feb. 1710[/11]*

(1248/3/43–4)

The pacquett hath brought me yours of the 22th … When I observed how many lying stories were raised in town by a sett of men immediately after the acquittal of Campbel I thought it reasonable to sett that matter in a true light; and soe I did in the fairest maner possible to you: but by what I can guesse from some hints contained in yours to me I suppose my part in it may have been represented to my prejudice and then I am certain it was done unfairly: for I acted with great circumspection and to the best of my understanding; without apprehending the resentments of one side, or valuing the good word of the other. If I were to be happy or miserable to eternitye according to my equal behavior, and that cause were to be tryed again before me under those circumstances, I should not doe more or lesse then I did when that cause was tryed before us in the Queens Bench: for in the presence of God I acted without favor or affection to the traverser or his cause and according to what I thought to be the duty of my place and of my oath. The Bishop of Cloyne gives out he will have it enquired into the next Parliament why the school att Middleton is not yet open, and why so little care is taken of the Palatines;[1324] you know how far some mens malice will carry them, and how far popular assemblies are to be depended on where the complaint is against people not well att Court; you should and I will take all care to ward against the blow.

166. *Alan I, Limerick, to Thomas, at his lodgings in Whitehall, 10 Mar. 1710[/11]*

(1248/3/45–6)

You can not expect much businesse from me while I am on the circuit, yet I will not omit writing to some one of you every week: My last was from Waterford to my sister of the fifth, and after my return from Ennis to which place I am ready to take horse I intend again

[1324] Protestant refugees from persecution in the Rhenish Palatinate, who had come to England in 1709. At least three thousand of these Palatines had subsequently been brought to Ireland, primarily to Counties Limerick and Kerry, but for various reasons the scheme proved only a limited success, fewer than two hundred families making their permanent residence in Ireland (Connolly, *Religion, Law and Power*, 125, 302). Some had been settled among Thomas's tenants; others on Alan's property at Elfordstown, Co. Cork (SHC, 1248/2/368–9: —— to Thomas Brodrick, 31 Oct.1709; ibid., G145/Box 102/5: rental).

to write. I have now settled it with my brother Coote[1325] not to go to Tralee, soe as the businesse of Kerry will fall most of it to his share, as that of Corke will to mine. Yesterday att Mr Olivers[1326] I mett Mr Evelyn[1327] who delivered me your letter of 12th January: I had seen this Gentleman before att Ballyanan last Christmas and yesterday discoursed him in what maner I could serve him acceptably: he with all the modesty in the world declared him self willing to embrace any thing, and named being one of my Clerks. You know how little interest I have in recommending him to any publick emploiment as matters now stand at the Castle, and in all probabilitye I shal soon be out of my Cheif Justiceship, soe as his offer will in that case be only an argument of his humility, without any fruit to him by it. Beside Mr Webber[1328] is now my Clerk; but if I continue I see no reason why I may not put him into Mr Webbers place: but first will this be agreeable to his freinds? In the next place I shal be in some confusion and difficultye how at the same time to treat one as good a man as my self in such maner as not to give offence to my brethren in the treating of their Clerks. But of this I will write more at large from Corke …

167. *Alan I, Dublin, to Thomas, at his lodgings in Whitehall, redirected to Newmarket, 20 Apr. 1711*

(1248/3/47–8)

In mine of Tuesday I owned the receit of yours of 31 March: and cannot but approve of the resolucion you have taken in relation to being or not being here next Session of Parliament: the returns you have mett hitherto for the services you have endeavoured to doe are of the same nature you and every man that acts on your principles will not fail to find; therefore neither putt yourself to the expence of the trouble of a journey, much lesse endanger your health to serve those who deserve little from you. By what passes daily I am more and more confirmed in what I have for some time apprehended to be in agitation, not withstanding the sense of my freinds on your side the water that there is no danger of any thing of the kind: Things are carryed here in that maner which pleases a certain sort of men extremely, and I make no doubt what is expected by the party here[1329] will in a great measure succeed to their wishes when a certain person arrives.[1330] Webber tells me that his place of being Crown Sollicitor in criminal causes is disposed of last night to Mr Schuldham:[1331] I doe not hear any fault laid to his charge: it seems his brother the Doctor[1332] bought the emploiment

[1325]Thomas Coote, his fellow assize judge.

[1326]Robert Oliver, MP [I].

[1327]See above, p. 244.

[1328]Edward Webber.

[1329]The tories.

[1330]Ormond (as lord lieutenant).

[1331]Edmond Shuldham or Schuldham (*d.* c.1723) of Dublin, an attorney of the king's bench [I], and subsequently solicitor for the crown in criminal cases (Burke, *Commoners*, i, 653; Vicars, *Index*, 417; *Reg. Deeds, Wills*, 26; *K. Inns Adm.*, 440; *CJI*, iii, 23).

[1332]Probably Edmond's brother Lemuel (c.1667–1719), a clergyman who did not have a doctorate but was prebendary of Blackrath in the diocese of Ossory (J. B. Leslie, *Ossory Clergy and Parishes* … (Enniskillen, 1933), 114).

for about £300 from Trench and he officiates for him: it hath not been usual to remove people that buy without some fault or compensacion as I am informed, but no doubt it may be justly done. I told you formerly what I intended to doe for Mr Evelyn, but I make no doubt that matter will be soon out of my power … Upon my word I wish my self with you.

168. *Alan I, Dublin, to Thomas, at his lodgings in Whitehall, 19 May 1711*

(1248/3/49–50)

I have already owned in one to my sister or the little boy the receit of yours which was written on your return from Newmarkett: but could have been pleased that what I proposed of having a licence of absence gotten for me while he was in England had been moved; for by that means I should probably have found out what is determined in reference to being removed or continued on the Bench, which I must now despair of till our Lord Lieutenant lands; and yet I cannot but think it would have been of use to me to be informed before his arrival, for reasons not fit to be committed to a letter: but now I must despair of knowing it, unlesse it could be soe contrived that one who once resided for some time in my house and is now in a great station with you (and who used to call Ally his Mistresse, and (that my sister may certainly know whom I mean) that desired my poor Lucy to propose a match between him and Lady Colvil)[1333] could gett the secret out of him that certainly knows it; him you cannot but guesse, and he is the others Patron. But how to sett this matter a foot I must leave among you to manage. What makes me more then ordinarily desirous of knowing it now is that I have received such an account of my poor fathers weaknesse from my sister Whitfeld yesterday that I am in the greatest perplexitye till I see him: and let me intreat you (Dear Brother) to go over to him and by kind deportment to give him the comfort of knowing that (if any past misunderstandings have been between you) they are forgotten. You cannot imagine the true content of mind this will create you, when you consider the comfort it will minister to a weak, broken spirited, old, father; nor how many anxious thoughts the omitting so good soe pious an action may create, when it is impossible to doe it, be your inclinations to it and your convictions of the reasonablenesse and religion of the Act never so great. I am sure brother you will doe this, and make his parting with the world as comfortable as you can: His misfortunes his age (not to add his temper) require all assistances and how worthy and blessed an act will it be to minister them. As soon as you receive this pray send to my sister that it is my earnest desire my children may immediately goe to him; their innocent kindnesse will be some comfort to him. I goe this afternoon to Mr Conelyes[1334] where I propose to spend five or six dayes privately: and have not leisure to give you a large narrative how matters stand with relation to the not approving Alderman Barlow who was chosen Mayor of Dublin for the ensuing year.[1335] Assure yourself things seem to me not to grow cooler here, whatever they do with you.

[1333] Olivia (*d.* 1724), née St George, the widow of Sir Robert Colvill, had married as her second husband in 1703 the 4th Viscount Ikerrin, but he too had died at the end of 1710 (HMC, *Ormonde MSS*, n.s., viii, 325).

[1334] William Conolly, MP [I].

[1335] In Apr. 1711 James Barlow (later Sir James, *d.* 1716: *Weekly Journal*, 30 June 1716), had been elected lord mayor of Dublin to serve for the year beginning at the following Michaelmas, but his election been disapproved

169. *Alan I, London, to Thomas, Newmarket, 9 Oct. 1711*

(1248/3/56–7)

I gott safe to town yesterday about eleven, and soon after my brother Laurance came into my sisters house where I then was: I took an oportunitye of acquitting my self of the promise I made the Duke of Kent[1336] in your hearing; reminded him how he owed his prebend to the Whigs,[1337] and that the Duke had his part in helping him to that promotion; and that it was pretty unaccountable to find his father in Law sett himself in opposition to my Lord Dukes interest. He said he never did it but in one instance when his Grace would have had him vote for Lord Edward Russel,[1338] to which the other answered that his Grace had formerly given him too good reasons to the contrary ever to vote for him. In short I find Humphryes[1339] to be what the Duke describes him, and if I were on my oath could not say I beleived the other differs from him in principle. The dissatisfaction he gave me of his sentiments and inclinations yesterday exceeds my fears which I formerly had of his being of other notions then consist with the revolution and our safety: and I look on him as one of those to whom in time all of our principles may owe the ruine of their fortunes, libertyes, and lives, and as such shal consider him hereafter: so much for him. I now passe to another subject: As soon as I gott home I found Irish letters and among them two of equal date viz 29th September. one wrote by Col. Berry,[1340] the other by Mrs Richardson (whom you know, but perhaps not by that name, but you cannot forgett Nancy Beckett[1341]) to the same purport; that Mr Robert King, receiver in Ireland to Lord Wharton, being dead,[1342] one desired in his own behalf, the other for her husband that I would recommend them to my Lord for the place: I would have given my promise to the first of them which had

1335 *(continued)* by the Irish privy council, upholding a claim by one of the defeated candidates, the tory Robert Constantine (*d.* c.1724), to a right of election by seniority. Barlow was elected a second time, and again disapproved, and after a series of further disapproved elections and a petition from the city to the queen the dispute was eventually settled early in Oct. by a compromise choice. See *Calendar of the Ancient Records of Dublin,* ed. J.T. Gilbert and R.M. Gilbert (17 vols, Dublin, 1889–1921), vii, 531–2, 542–4; *The Case of the City of Dublin, in Relation to the Election of the Lord Mayor and Sheriffs of the Said City* ([Dublin, 1711]); TNA, SP 63/367, ff. 110, 186, 206–7: Ormond to Lord Dartmouth, 20 July, 7 Sept., 3 Oct. 1711; TNA, SP 63/367, ff. 204–5, petition of lord mayor and aldermen of Dublin to the queen, Sept. 1711; BL, Add. MS 47087, ff 4–8: Sir John Perceval's journal, 3 Oct. [1711]; *Appendix to the 26th Report of the Deputy Keeper of the Records of Ireland* (Dublin, 1893), 181. Swift disparaged Barlow as 'a tailor' (*Swift Correspondence*, ed. Williams, i, 232).

1336 Henry Grey (1671–1740), 1st duke of Kent.

1337 Laurence had been preferred to a prebend of Westminster in July 1710 after serving as a chaplain to the British house of commons.

1338 Lord Edward Russell (c.1642–1714), 4th s. of the 1st duke of Bedford and MP [GB]. Presumably Kent, whose principal seat was Wrest Park, Beds., had requested a vote in one of the polls for Bedfordshire, which Russell had contested in 1705, 1708 and 1710 (*HC 1690–1715*, ii, 5).

1339 Laurence Brodrick had married Anne Humphreys at Gray's Inn on 27 Apr. 1710, the marriage being performed by 'Mr Humphreys' (Joseph Foster, *The Register of Admissions of Gray's Inn, 1521–1889 …* (1889), Marriage Register, p. xxi). The identity of Anne's father is unknown, but an Arthur Humphreys (*d.* 1718) whose first wife (*d.* 1700) had been called Anne, was at this time rector of Barton-le-Clay, Bedfordshire (Venn and Venn, *Alumni Cantabrigienses*, pt 1, ii, 430).

1340 William Berry, MP [I].

1341 Anne, wife of John Richardson of Rich Hill, Co. Armagh. She was the daughter of William Beckett, prime serjeant [I].

1342 Robert King, MP [I].

desired my interposing in their favor (and that had been a fair answer to the party which came later) because I think very well of both of them; and resolve to give that answer to Mr Riley from whom I had a letter on his own behalf and to Mr Forster,[1343] who also wrote on behalf of Mr Sale both which came by the pacquet that came in yesterday after I had received my former letters, and consequently was bespoke beforehand. But the method I have taken between the two first is this, I have laid their pretensions and applicacions before my Lord, with my request that one of them may be employed, without giving preference to either of them. Colonel Berry tells me he hath sold at an under rate,[1344] having mett very bad treatment of late; I supose you cannot but guesse the reason, for he alway hath acted the part of an honest man; and hath expressed great regard for my Lord Wharton very often in the most publick maner, and no doubt fares not the better now for soe doing. Mrs Richardsons husband I beleive you know, he is brother to Major Richardson of the house of commons,[1345] a very good man, well principled and deserves encouragement: they are both qualifyed for the emploiment and will I make no doubt discharge it with faithfulnesse and sufficiencye; soe I make no request for one in [preference[1346]] to the other; but if it consist with his Lordships pleasure I wish one of them may succeed, and desire you to speak to his Lordship on the subject. The Dublin affair is over, Alderman Gore is elected and two whig Sherifs,[1347] and the Recorder[1348] assures me they will be confirmed. I suppose some intimacion was given from this side on the peticion of the City to her Majestye; Gore is not the man that was intended but Stoyte,[1349] and the Lord Mayor[1350] played a trick in not putting him on election; but Gore gives all assurances of doing good things, and is really an honest man, tho a little too high: but methinks the City have carryed their point that the magistracye is elective and not successive, and that Constantine shall not be Mayor by help of his N[*ame*]sake,[1351] whatever assurances have been given to the contrary. His Grace[1352] hath expressed great resentment at the recorder; and said he was told by several Gentlemen that heard the speech made to him by the Recorder at his Landing, that it was a banter upon him:[1353] and that the City addresse resembled his Governement to Lord Tirconels.[1354]

[1343] Unlikely to be John Forster, whom Alan would have almost certainly called by one of his official titles. It may be a reference to John's brother Nicholas (c.1673–1743), later bishop of Killaloe and Raphoe, given that 'Mr Sale' could well have been John Sale, sometime 'actuary' of the lower house of convocation in Ireland (see above, p. 173).

[1344] Disposed of his regimental commission.

[1345] William Richardson, MP [I].

[1346] MS damaged.

[1347] Ralph Gore (*d.* 1716) of Dublin (*Cal. Ancient Recs Dublin*, ed. Gilbert and Gilbert, vii, 572). See above, pp. 251–2.

[1348] John Forster, MP [I].

[1349] John Stoyte (c.1663–1729), of Dublin and Eccles Grove, Co. Wicklow, alderman of Dublin, and elected MP for the city in 1728 (*Hist. Ir. Parl.*, vi, 359–60).

[1350] Sir John Eccles (1664–1727) of Dublin and Eccles Grove, Co. Wicklow, the outgoing lord mayor (PRONI, T/1128/11).

[1351] Sir Constantine Phipps.

[1352] The duke of Ormond.

[1353] Given at Dublin Castle on 4 July 1711, when the corporation of Dublin attended the newly arrived lord lieutenant, and printed in the *Post Man*, 12–14 July 1711. Having been parodied by a tory sympathiser in verse form in *The R*[ecorde]*r's S*[pee]*ch Explain'd* (Dublin, [1711]), it was defended by a whig in *The Recorder's Speech: With the Principles of the Whigs Defended. By a Lover of His Country* ([Dublin,] 1711).

[1354] The jacobite administration in Dublin, 1687–9.

In short he is now as unhappy in being the mark of his Graces displeasure as I have been for some years past. Mr Walker asked me yesterday att St James Coffee house[1355] if your good luck continued: when I seemed not to understand him he told me you had the only luck he saw att Newmarkett, having won one hundred pounds from Lord Harvey[1356] at the Chocolate house[1357] in a very short time. Dear Brother you can live handsomly without play, but while you indulge your inclination to it I doe assure you, you never will be able to keep a penny in your pockett. Do not take this ill of me.

170. *Alan I, Dublin, to Thomas, at his lodgings in Whitehall, 25 Oct. 1711*

(1248/3/58–9)

I know you expect some account from me how I apprehend matters to stand here; and beleive you will be more pleased with the earliest notices tho very imperfect, then with waiting in hopes of being better informed. If I am not mistaken, an acquaintance of my sisters hath more power and interest at a certain place, then all those who were in favour formerly put together; to the great mortification of those who have been forced to make way for him: nay I hear it is gone such lengths that a countreyman of ours hath complained among freinds that people would not be easy while he was in possession, and now had gott little by the exchange:[1358] The story put me in mind of the fable of the frogs, who not being satisfyed with King Logg, had a stork sent in the room.[1359] This person however I doe not doubt is much advised (I will not call it directed) by a certain person, who was reported to be setting up on his own account: how far that may be in view I cannot say; but it must be at distance, and is not apprehended by those whom it most concerns. When I landed I found another face of things then I expected; great spirit in people who according to honest Abels phrase[1360] are of the ruined party, and others under disorder. I am apt to think the disapproving magistrates elected for so many corporations may have alarmed people;[1361] the house is extreme full; and you know the publick businesse is alway best done then: One Taylor had formerly upon an applicacion of the house of Commons been

[1355] A coffee-house near St James's Palace, frequented by whigs.

[1356] John Hervey (1665–1751), 1st Baron Hervey, formerly whig MP [E].

[1357] White's Chocolate House, in St James's: another whig haunt.

[1358] Probably a reference to Sir Richard Cox, who must have observed with some bitter gratification that those Irish whigs who had opposed his own reappointment as lord chancellor now had much more to complain about.

[1359] From Aesop's fable of the frogs who asked Jove to send them a king. He threw down a great log, of which they were at first afraid but then began to treat with impunity. When they begged for a replacement the enraged god sent a great stork, which ate them up.

[1360] Abel Roper (1665–1726), the London publisher, whose *Post Boy* was the most prominent newspaper on the tory side.

[1361] By the 'new rules' for boroughs issued in 1672 (see above, pp. 30, 225). There had been several instances earlier in Anne's reign where the council had disapproved elections on what appeared to be partisan grounds, notably the case of Trim in 1709 (for which see above, pp. 30, 235). But the tory administration in 1711 seemed to have elevated this tactic into a systematic policy to 'garble' corporations, which, to politically unsympathetic observers recalled the attempt by Lord Tyrconnell in 1687–9 to 'pack' municipal government and by extension parliament. (PRONI, T/3416/A: certificates of election of magistrates, 1711–1816 (*s.v.* Carrickfergus, Clonmel, Coleraine, Dublin, Trim and Youghal); BL, Add. MS 47087, ff. 2–4: Sir John Perceval's journal, Aug.1711). The issue was raised in the Irish house of commons on 29 Oct.1711 (*Perceval Diary*, 116).

turned out of the Commission of peace for the County of Galwey having turned Papist in King James time:[1362] he was lately put into Commission by my now Lord Chancellor (on the recommendacion as I hear of a certain Archbishop,[1363] Lieutenant General St[*euar*]t,[1364] and Sir D[*onough*] O'Br[*ien*][1365]). This matter was intended to be moved in the house, and for ought I know something might have been intended or stirred in the debate as to my Lord Chancellor. But three or fowre Conaght men went it seems that morning or the night before and gave him notice of it:[1366] Upon which as soon as the house sate the next day Mr D[*awso*]n informed the house that Taylor had been put into Commission on the recommendacion of two Gentlemen of the house; that since that, his Lordship came by the notice of the house having applyed to have one of that name struck out of Commission; to which vote he was intirely a stranger till very lately, as he stil was whether the person meant was the same whom he had put into Commission. That he was most ready to comply with the sense of the house if he could but know it, and what was proper on that occasion to soften people was not omitted: The Conaght Gentlemen then stood up and said his Lordship had expressed himself in the same maner to them and spoke much to his advantage as to the deference he said he would alway pay to the house of Commons. I doe not see but that the house might reasonably beleive his Lordship knew nothing of the vote, being some years before he came into the Kingdome; probably some things were spoken sharply enough against any one that should knowingly have done this; but the matter ended in turning Taylor out. Senny said whatever excuse my Lords not knowing the vote might be as to him, there was no pretence for justifying the two members of the Councel and also of the house who had recommended him and desired they might be named, but it could not be come. This morning I went to my Lord Chancellors, who told me my son had in a particular maner spoke slightingly of him in the house and in debating had used the words This Chancellor more then once. I have not seen Senny since, so cannot tell what he saith to it: I told my Lord as I never did interpose with my son but left him to follow his own sentiments, soe I should be sorry he should treat him in any maner amisse or unhandsomely; and indeed I shal be concerned if on enquiry I find my Lord had ground for expostulating as he did; that he was the only man in the house who had not treated him generously; for beside that it is commendable in all instances to doe every thing in a gentlemanlike way, I should be sorry he should be the man that should distinguish himself on this occasion, considering that my brother had a freindship for my Lord, tho they differed in principles. I told my Lord I could not answer for a young mans warmth, nor ought he too much

[1362]On 18 Oct. 1711 the Commons, recalling that on 14 Aug. 1707 they had requested the then lord lieutenant to remove from the commission of the peace all those who had become catholics under James II, even though they might since have conformed again to the established church, identified John Taylor of Co. Galway and William Dobbin of Co. Waterford as j.p.s appointed since 1707 who also fell into this category and requested their removal. (*CJI*, iii, 346, 658). For Taylor, of Castle Taylor, Co. Galway, see Patrick Melvin, *Estates and Landed Society in Galway* (Dublin, 2012), 72–3.

[1363]John Vesey (1638–1716), archbishop of Tuam and a strong tory, who subsequently served with Phipps on the commission of lords justices appointed after Ormond's return to England (TNA, SP 63/367, f. 230: account of parliamentary debates enclosed in Edward Southwell to [Lord Dartmouth], 19 Oct. 1711).

[1364]William Steuart, MP [I]. According to a report transmitted to the secretary of state, Lord Dartmouth, only Vesey and O'Brien had recommended Taylor (TNA, SP 63/367, f. 230).

[1365]Sir Donough O'Brien, MP [I].

[1366]In fact they gave notice to Samuel Dopping, MP [I], who then reported the matter to Phipps (TNA, SP 63/367, f. 230).

rely on peoples informacions which are often malicious; and really by all I can yet learn from several Gentlemen I doe not find he gave just ground of being taxed with acting in an unbecoming way. And now I will tell you a foolish story; while Taylors matter was in agitacion, Lieutenant General St[*euar*]t gave an account of the attacque of Athlone, that he commanded it, how they advanced, what men made the first assault, the orders he gave, how many were killed etc[1367] and at length said Taylor was upon the bridge on his right hand at that attacque, that an Irishman was going to shoot him, and Taylor killed the Irishman and then drew that conclusion which naturally followed from the premises, that therefore he did not deserve to be turned out of Commission.[1368] Jos[*hua*] Allen in his stuttering way[1369] said he had a great value for him for preserving the life of the honourable Gentleman, and was going on with a but etc. The Lieutenant General stood up and said that Allen had mistaken him, for that Taylor did not save his life; Allen told him that if the matter was soe he had not half soe much value for him as he had before, and thought he ought to be turned out of Commission. Poor Ned Synge hath been complained of by the Lower house of convocacion to the upper, for reading a different lesson from that appointed by the rubrick:[1370] He to prevent punishment told them how the matter was, that the chapter in the apocryphal book of Tobit appointed by the rubrick to be read was that which among other things mentions Tobits dogs following and that he had chosen another;[1371] the upper house did not concur with the lower in thinking it such a crime as they need censure. This is an odd story, but I am assured a true one.

Ch[*arles*] Dering in a committee used some words to this effect, that people who spoke about the privy Council as some then had reflected on my Lord O[*rmon*]d: this put them into a terrible heat, and it was owing (as I hear) to the interposicion of honest Jack Moore his brother in Law[1372] that it was passed by on his explaining himself; or possibly he might have been called to the bar.[1373]

[1367]The Williamite success in taking Athlone and crossing the Shannon in June 1691. Steuart had been present as colonel of the 9th Foot.

[1368]Steuart's speech is confirmed in TNA, SP 63/367, f. 230: account of parliamentary debates enclosed in Edward Southwell to [Lord Dartmouth], 19 Oct. 1711, which adds that Taylor had left King James's army to fight for King William, and that 'several other gentlemen' testified to the house on his behalf.

[1369]Swift's cruel nickname for Allen, 'Traulus', from the Greek *traulos*, can be translated as 'stutterer'.

[1370]Edward Synge (1659–1741), for whom see *DIB*, ix, 209–10, was a low churchman, and protégé of Archbishop King. He represented the chapter of Cork in the lower house of convocation. For this episode, see *Records of Convocation*, ed. Bray, xvii, 366–70. Such stories persisted, and in 1714, after Synge's elevation to the see of Raphoe, Sir Richard Cox reported that the new bishop was reported to have 'spoke slightly of the ring in marriage, cross in baptism, surplice, and kneeling at the sacrament', though Cox soon changed his mind about Synge and pronounced him perfectly orthodox (BL, Add. MS 381567, ff. 133, 134: Cox to Edward Southwell, 9, 12 Oct. 1714).

[1371]Tobit, xi: 2.

[1372]John Moore, MP. Dering had married (as her second husband) Moore's sister Margaret.

[1373]According to Sir John Perceval, Dering took offence at a particular comment made by James Peppard, MP, town clerk of Dublin. Dering's response raised a 'hubbub' during which there were angry calls for Dering to be brought to the bar. Perceval does not mention Moore's role in calming the situation. *Perceval Diary*, 113–14.

The Cheif Baron[1374] who at Corke Assizes put the presentment for having Loyde prosecuted for reprinting the memorial of the Church of England into his pocket,[1375] would have had Ned Hoare[1376] taken it here in town and sent it down to the Clerk of the Assizes: Hoare said he would not meddle with it: I fancy he feared to hear of it somewhere.

171. *Alan I, Cork, to Thomas, at his lodging in Whitehall, 4 Jan. 1711/12*

(1248/2/47–8)

… Tell my sister I have hers of 18 Dec. with my boyes scrawle at the top of it: By all the guesses I can make something is resolved upon and not to be prevented let people say or think what they please. God help us. We are sensible of the consequences of such a peace as some people apprehend, and hardly know how to think the French will be brought to a safe and honourable one. I thank you for yours of 22 Dec.

172. *St John III, Dublin, to Thomas, 12 Jan. 1711[/12]*

(1248/3/60–1)

I gave you the trouble of a letter very lately, and am sorry I am oblig'd now to repeat it. You will probably hear, from a pretty many hands of an affair in which I am concern'd, and which, for fear of its being represented to my disadvantage, or otherwise then the truth is, I beg leave to acquaint you with. On Tuesday noon last, when I came into Lucasses Coffee house[1377] I heard young Mr Ludlow[1378] and young Mr Burton[1379] very warme in an Argument, which I found afterward was about admitting the 12 new peers into the house of Lords.[1380] Ludlow in great warmth told me, who by this time was engaged in the dispute, that denying new peers sitting in the house, had not been practis'd since 41, and that he hop'd those times were now over: I told him in answer that what was done then

[1374]Robert Rochfort, MP [I] had been promoted from attorney-general [I] to lord chief baron of the exchequer [I] in June 1707.

[1375]In 1711 Edward Lloyd, the Dublin newswriter, printer and bookseller had reprinted the notorious English tory pamphlet *The Memorial of the Church of England …* (1705), with various additions, as *The Memorial of the Church of England: With An Impartial Account of What Pass'd Most Remarkable at the Tryal of Dr. Sacheverell. to Which Is Added, the Defence of the Church and Doctor, Made by His Excellency, Sir Constantine Phipps, Now One of the Lords-Justices, and Lord-Chancellor of Ireland* …. Lloyd had gone down to Cork to sell copies. On 12 Sept. the grand jury of the city of Cork presented the pamphlet as a 'false, scandalous and traitorous libel' and called for Lloyd's apprehension and punishment. The presentment was subsequently published unofficially. (*The Presentment of the Grand Jury of the City of Cork Septemb. 12, 1711. Against Edward Lloyd, for Publishing Several Libels in and about That City* (Dublin, 1711)).

[1376]Edward Hoare, MP [I].

[1377]On Cork Hill, Dublin (Gilbert, *Hist. City of Dublin*, ii, 9).

[1378]Peter Ludlow, MP [I].

[1379]Samuel Burton, MP [I].

[1380]The twelve new peers created by Queen Anne in Dec.1711, at the behest of Lord Treasurer Oxford (the former Robert Harley) to secure a ministerial majority in the British house of lords. They had been introduced into the House together on 2 Jan. 1712.

was in Lord Straffords case, and done upon better reason then he or I could answer;[1381] that the Commons who impeacht Lord Strafford were his accusers, and therefore twas not fit that, those new peers who were then in the other house, should be his judges too. This was what introduc'd the discourse of 41. We fell then to talke of other things and particularly a Paragraph in Roper that if the Duch did not agree to a Cessation of Arms he hop'd Mr. Villars at the head of 100000 men would prevail with them.[1382] This Mr Ludlow justified as very reasonable, and upon my speaking warmly against the French, said he thought now and hop'd that all animositys against them ought to cease and a good correspondence ought for the future to be cultivated. This I confess made me very hot, and probably indiscreet; so that upon resuming the debate of creating the 12 new peers, and justifying it, and constantly mentioning 41 as an argument against me, I did I beleive say, I thought there was not a more extraordinary Step taken in 41 then this, and immediately left the company. Mr Burton came the next minute to me and ask't me whither I had said that K Charles the 1st never did a more Arbitrary Act then this of calling up the New Peers, and told me withal Mr Ludlow was telling every one in the Coffee house I had said so. Upon this I immediately tax'd Ludlow with misreporting my words, for that I never us'd the name of K Charles. He then own'd to me he had said them, but upon my explaining myselfe and denying them, he seem'd satisfyed. However this Story took air, and came at last to the ears of one Thomas a Clergyman, who immediately carryed it to the Government. Upon this Mr Ludlow was on Thursday morning sent for by them, and being examin'd, as he pretends much against his will, swore that I said either that this was a more arbitrary thing, or a higher straining the prerogative then any thing in 41, but could not be positive which one. Captain Manser,[1383] who says he listned and overheard all our discourse, was examin'd, and swore I said, talking of the new peers, that this was a more arbitrary proceeding then any thing that was done, either in 41, or since 41, but cant be positive which Accounts were immediately sent of this into England, as I hear, to Lord Treasurer and Duke of Ormond and the examination too. I was at this time at Castlemarten, and did not hear a word of all these transactions till yesterday morning and the moment I did, came to towne, and gave in Baile for my appearance the 1st of next Terme, to Lord Cheif Justice Cox and waited upon the Government to know their pleasure. Mr Ingoldsby told me the matter had been transmitted into England but without the least aggravation, and that he would do all in his power not to have matters carryed to extremity and beleiv'd Lord Chancellor was of the same opinion.[1384] For my part, tho I do not apprehend any danger tho the words should be prov'd against me, which considering the difference of the witnesses in their Testimony I beleive they cannot, yet I cannot but be concern'd that my Indiscretion, for so I must own it to be, should have brought me into

[1381] At the trial of Thomas Wentworth, earl of Strafford in 1641, when the House excluded the bishops and those temporal lords giving evidence in the case (Paul Christianson, 'The Peers, the People and Parliamentary Management in the First Six Months of the Long Parliament', repr. in *Peers, Politics and Power: The House of Lords, 1603–1911,* ed. Clyve Jones and D.L. Jones (1986), 66).

[1382] One of several issues of the *Post Boy* in Nov. 1711 in which Abel Roper gave offence to the Allies by his outspoken support for a peace. After diplomatic complaints Roper was arrested and bound over to appear at queen's bench, though he subsequently recanted and escaped punishment (*Oxf. DNB*).

[1383] Captain Daniel Mansergh (c.1664–c.1725) of Ballybur, Co. Kilkenny, cousin and heir of George Mansergh of Macrony Castle (for whom see above, p. 166) (NLI, Genealogical Office MS 142, p. 116; 813/14; Vicars, *Index*, 314).

[1384] Richard Ingoldsby, MP [I] had again been appointed a lord justice on Ormond's departure for England, this time in commission with Lord Chancellor Phipps. However, Ingoldsby died on 29 Jan. 1712.

the trouble it may now possibly do. I do not write out of any opinion of your interest with our Cheif Governour, but only to desire that if you can think of any expedient likely to prevent this coming to a publick Tryal I should be extremely oblig'd to you if you would do it for tho I have not the least apprehension of clearing my selfe in that case, and defy all the world to prove either a malitious or seditious intent, yet I fancy t'will not be much for my reputation to have my name brought in question on that account, and hope you will use your endeavours to prevent it. Mrs Hill[1385] tells me she did, in my absence, write to Mr Southwell,[1386] on this subject, so did Mr Keightley[1387] and to the Duke of Ormond too. If you think fit you may when you see Mr Sancky mention this matter to him and desire him to use his Interest with him[1388] to prevent it, and I beleive on mine as well as on other accounts he will not scruple doing it. I beg you likewise to use all proper applications to Mr Southwell, and to give me the earliest account from him what resolutions are like to be taken in this affair. This is a true account of the matter wch I depend upon your making use of to the best advantage of …

173. *Alan I, Dublin, to Thomas, at his lodgings in Whitehall, 18 Jan. 1711/12*

(1248/3/62–3)

I came to town but last night, soe have seen very few not having been yet abroad: nor will I stir out of my own doors but when necessitye requires; for if what I hear be true it is the safest way to be secure from being insnared in your discourse and informed against. On the road on this side Castle Dermod[1389] I was mett by an Irish man[1390] (one Tirwhit of the County of Kilkenny) who asked me if I had heard of any examinations being given in against Senny for some words; he could give me but an imperfect relation of them, but by what he said I find the report (as is usual) hath far exceeded the truth, I mean that the examinations doe not make the words soe exceptionable as the mans story did: and I suppose he telling it to me did not make it worse then he heard it. You may be sure I was in pain sufficient till I gott to Castlemartin; where I heard, that Senny coming into the Coffee house some time after the pacquet came in which brought an account of the making the twelve last peers found young Mr Ludlow (a brother barrister, his contemporary and acquaintance, and son to honest Stephen[1391]) in discourse with young Mr Burton; that it seems was the subject they were on; and after some things offered by Ludlow Senny used an expression, which every body will allow was an unguarded and imprudent one, but others think it of a much deeper dye: I say an imprudent one supposing him to have spoken the words sworn against him either by Mr Ludlow or by Capt Daniel Mansergh. You may be sure the examinations have not been yet seen, but have been thought of weight enough

1385 His mother-in-law (and later also stepmother) Anne Hill.

1386 Edward Southwell, MP [I], the chief secretary.

1387 Thomas Keightley, MP [I].

1388 Ormond.

1389 Castledermot, Co. Kildare.

1390 An Irish catholic.

1391 Stephen Ludlow, MP [I]. As Ludlow was a tory, the use of 'honest' was ironical. Peter Ludlow was a Middle Templar who had been called to the Irish bar in 1711 (*Hist. Ir. Parl.*, v, 138).

to be sent over into England. I hear Mr Mansergh saith the words were that making the twelve peers was as arbitrary a proceeding as any either before (or since) 1641: but whether he said before or whether since 1641 it seems he cannot charge his memorye: I hear that Mr Ludlows deposition is thus: that the words were, calling the twelve peers etc was an higher strain of power, (or a strain of power more arbitrary) than any in 1641. These, both have (before two) declared to have been the words. Ludlow declares he never mentioned any thing of since 1641. Soon after the words which he did use (what ever they were) he went into another room; and Ludlow said aloud, Good God! what will passion betray men into? Mr Brodrick said etc Which he being told, Senny came back, told him he had misrepresented the words, and dealt unfairly by him in repeating publickly what had passed in effect in private conversation (between him Ludlow and Burton) for tho it was in the Coffee house, the discourse was between them; but it seems Captain Mansergh was near and pretends to have heard it. There was a minister in the Coffee house one Thomas who hearing what Ludlow repeated said he would give 5 Guineas he had heard the words: It is yet a secret who carryed informacion to the Governement, for I hear the Doctor, the Lawyer and the Captain all deny it: but examinations were taken before one or more Judges of the Queens Bench, after Mansergh had been sent for by the Lords Justices and interrogated by I[*ngoldsby*] the other not asking one question, and seemingly passive in the matter. Senny hath given bayle to appear in the Queens Bench, and I am verily perswaded the letters wrote to a great man and to his Secretary[1392] will be of no avail; and I think he must expect and prepare to defend himself against all that can be done: his being your Nephew, my son, and his behavior in Parliament last Session will for ought I know subject him to a strict examinacion then perhaps such an indiscretion in so young a fellow would possibly have brought on another man: since this and what hath been done in relation to Sir Thomas Southwell[1393] and Mr Manlye[1394] people will be careful with whom they converse. I have those matters very imperfectly; but the story goes that Sir Thomas being at a christning, a young divine related to and invited by the Gentleman whose child was christned hath (as I hear) been prevailed on by a certain Lawyer to give an examinacion and if I hear true perfectly different from what the rest of the company remember Sir Thomas words to have been:[1395] they talk that this will be smothered, and so perhaps it may if Sir Tho: will allow its being soe, after an account gone into England, which may possibly ease him of his emploiment.[1396] Manly too is I hear represented over as having much interested himself in opposing etc. I could wish for the sake of both gowns that it had fallen lesse to the share of both to be concerned in promoting the trade of informing; the necessity of which as no body will dispute at some times, soe few would give five Guineas to be the persons concerned in doi[ng] it, but a person of great zeal. Do not read this public[kly] for you may

[1392] Ormond and his chief secretary, Edward Southwell, MP [I].

[1393] Sir Thomas Southwell, MP [I].

[1394] Isaac Manley, MP [I].

[1395] Thomas Lindsay, bishop of Raphoe, was told that Southwell 'rashly expressed himself to this effect, that it was now as high time to send over for the elector of Hanover as it was for the prince of Orange in '88' (Bodl., MS Ballard 8, f. 98: Lindsay to [Arthur Charlett], 25 Jan. 1711/12).

[1396] As a revenue commissioner [I].

depend on having your words and actions [?ob]served as well as Sennyes and mine: nay a Lady of great quality here hath reported that you were committed for words of the same nature in England; tho I think you were not in London when the last letters came away. I protest it seems to me that in a little time there will be a necessity for some people, if they desire quiet, to seek it elsewhere, if such care be taken of enquiring into mens most secret conversation as I hear is sometimes taken. This is my boyes birthday[1397] and I shal have some good company at dinner to drink his health; but silence is the thing most practiced now: I am sure it shal be by me among men of two professions; of both which however I know there are many very worthy men: but so I thought formerly some whom I now can hardly rank under that character …

174. *Alan I, Dublin, to Thomas, at his lodgings in Whitehall, 31 Jan. 1711/12*

(1248/3/64–5)

Tho I have very little inclination to write yet since yours of the fifteenth with my sisters of the same date and of the 22th inform me of the death of my poor dear father, and since you urge me to write to you out of hand on the occasion of his death I will say as much as I can to answer your expectations. By his ever declining to make a will of late years when I soe often pressed him to doe it I did apprehend he would not make any new one, but put it off from time to time till it would be too late: soe as unlesse some former will remain in being uncancelled I doubt he dyed intestate. I suppose you have taken care that his papers should be searched and viewed in the presence of such of his children as are on the spot, and other persons of character and credit; to see if any will appears among them. I will write into the County of Corke to enquire whether there be any will there, and if there be I will give you the earliest notice of it; to be communicated by you to my brother and sister in England … Tho I can ill afford to take a journey, either in respect of the trouble or expence of it, yet considering all things I doe not know but that it will be advisable for me to goe over; I shal see my freinds and children, I shal have an oportunitye of doing what may be necessary in Sennyes affair in England if I find any occasion to apply there: But really I beleive as well as hope that matter will not need assistance thence. Senny and my daughter will I think goe over with Mrs Hill, and I cannot goe in more agreeable company. I will soon write more fully to you on this subject, in the mean time I would not have administration taken out till I come over or you hear farther from me; as I will not think of taking or letting any body else take out administration here till you my brother and sister agree about it. My sister tells me you have been indisposed; God preserve you, and send us an happy meeting in these melancholy times.

I doubt some of my letters miscarry: Have you received one relating to Lady Burl[*ingto*]ns corporacions.[1398]

[1397] His son, Alan II (now ten years old).

[1398] See above, p. 226.

175. *Alan I, Dublin, to Thomas, at his lodgings in Whitehall, 2 Feb. 1711/12*

(1248/3/66–7)

Tho the great age my father was of and his weaknesse and infirmityes,[1399] added to the notices you and my sister gave me of his approaching end by the last letters you wrote before his decease might have prepared me for it, yet when the account came I must own it struck me in a more sensible maner then I thought what so reasonably might be expected could have done: and I doubt not my letter to you shews how much confusion and disorder I was in when I wrote it. It is a satisfaction to my mind to hear from my sister Martha Courthope both before his death and since that no care was wanting while he was, and that all was done that was possible for his preservation … I protest I am weary of being here; a man is hardly safe in common conversation: of which I had a vile instance this day. Sure care will be taken to discharge the servants, and to call in for those demands which people may have to my father, which alway swell as there is a longer time allowed to dresse up the account. You have I make no doubt taken possession of the house and done all necessary to prevent the plundering of it. I am not much sollicitous about the personal estate of my father; but it should not be at the discretion of servants or hangers on. Pray inform my brother and sister of what I write …

176. *Alan I, London, to Thomas, Newmarket, 19 Apr. 1712*

(1248/3/72–3)

If Lord Ryalton[1400] shal think it worth while to come to town by the first of May in expectation of what will probably be then communicated yet by that time I shal be near Chester, soe that I despair seeing you before I goe for Ireland. Abel hath told you the occasional prayers are ordered to be discontinued, that is those for her Majestyes forces and those of her Allyes engaged in war: the reason sure must be there is no further occasion for them.[1401] It doth not become me to be over sollicitous about the house att Wandsworth; but methinks your estate and the reputation of your familye should incline you to reside there rather than live in lodgings that are but precarious; especially now you are in no emploiment that requires constant attendance in town. That dwelling will answer all the ends you can have of being in town, and put you out of the way of some oportunityes which I beleive are of no advantage to you. Indeed it is worth your while to consider whether the unsettled way of living you are now in be either for your credit or satisfaction: nothing could reconcile it to your tast, but custom, and a too long use of it. I hope you will not take what I say ill, because it is meant with the truest kindnesse. Among my fathers papers there is an old one found which makes me his sole Executor: The benefit will be little, and

[1399] Sir St John had very recently passed his eighty-fifth birthday.

[1400] Francis Godolphin (1678–1766), only s. of the former lord treasurer [E], Sidney, 1st earl of Godolphin, was styled Viscount Rialton during the lifetime of his father.

[1401] Abel Roper, in the *Post Boy*.

I shal have some trouble; what remains after debts paid I will employ in the maner I think I ought …

177. *Alan I, Dublin, to Thomas, at his lodgings in Whitehall, 29 May 1712*

(1248/3/74–5)

I cannot but be concerned to see how you are abused and your estate incroached on by your tenants and others and you injured in another maner then any body else would bear; or then any body would offer to doe if they were not incouraged to it by the little care they see taken in opposing and preventing such treatment … If it were not losse of reputation as well as money I should be the lesse concerned; but really permitting things of this nature must lessen you in the eyes of those who see things of this sort soe little taken notice of. My profession obligeth me to attend my Law and not countrey affairs; nor would it look well in me to intermeddle in your estate: but ought you to sit by unconcerned? … Pray doe some thing in the matter of Sir Henry St John.[1402] My services to Lord Godolphin, Lord Ryalton and the few freinds I have with you …

178. *Alan I, to Thomas, at his lodgings in Whitehall, [9 June] 1712*

(1248/3/76–7)

In an hour I shal take horse with Charles Campbel,[1403] to spend this week with him at his house near Droghedah, but will not omit answering your last letter before I leave town. I am very sensible how desirable it is to have a stake in England especially at this time; but in the first place I never will touch what I design for Ally by using it in purchase; for tho I should make the Land bought her securitye that would not answer an offer of marriage like ready money: but there is another and a better reason: Money hath no earmark. The little I have else will not goe far in purchase of Lands, but I intend soon to draw in what is due to me here and make as good a summe as I can in England (apart from Allyes fortune) and with that to buy what can be compassed with it … The loyal Irish[1404] are transported with some late accounts; some of the English seem very well pleased too, but as far as I can read mens minds in their faces their joy swells not to soe high a degree as that of the others. In some people no signs of pleasure (equal to the occasion) appear, or I am not able to discern them: on the contrary they look (to my apprehension) not unlike what they appeared a pretty many years agoe. But we are assured from those who know best (I mean the people in power) we shal have a most glorious peace and all the desirable consequences of it: but what those terms or consequences are like to be (except the establishing the

[1402] Sir Henry St John, 4th Bt (1652–1742), father of Henry St John, 1st Viscount Bolingbroke, but, unlike his son, a whig in his politics. Among Sir Henry's properties was a manor house at Battersea, Surrey, not far from Wandsworth (Daniel Lysons, *The Environs of London* (4 vols, 1792–6), i, 30).

[1403] Charles Campbell, MP [I].

[1404] Catholics loyal to James II.

present ministry) I doe not find any of them pretend to say. Time will make us see or – the consequences as well terms …

179. *Alan I, Dublin, to Thomas, at his lodgings in Whitehall, 19 July 1712*

(1248/3/78–9)

… You send us no maner of news from London and I suppose are very little concerned at what passeth here; however I fancy by the great care people take about magistrates of corporacions, Sherifs, Justices of peace etc. it is not prudent to be entirely negligent. The most indefatigable industry is used every where to have magistrates of a certain kind, no doubt out of a prospect of an approaching P[*arliamen*]t: and they have gott some ground. Pray doe not think it not worth while some way or other to apprise a person, whose garden lyes very near that of a freind of mine, of what follows. A freind of ours at your house at W[*andsworth*] will presently tell you who I mean: she had a very handsome daughter which fell sick of the small pox the Saturday just before I left London, which hindred me from being admitted to take my leave of her tho I atttempted it; and if I had been able to have waited on her then, I resolved to have said what I now write. My constant correspondent at W[*andsworth*][1405] hath a very near relacion who lives with the person I mean. Under pretence of supporting the interest of that Lady and her familye in a certain place (where the young mans father that I mean liveth) an interest perfectly opposite to that which that Lady and familye is of is carryed on: the people awed and threatned with arrests, being distrained etc. if they vote for such a person to be magistrate;[1406] and this with a view to have elections of another kind[1407] influenced and carryed into the hands of those who mean and wish otherwise then those whose interest they pretend to espouse. To shew you this to a demonstration, the great promoters of this matter are two neighbours who live about two miles each of them from our part of the countrey, one Southward the other South East of M[*idleton*] and a third who lives about eight miles Northward from the place concerned, when he is at home: he is marryed to the Lady whose former husband was to pay you £200 for horses on his fathers death, whose bond you assigned me for £100 and I am out of my money to this day and am like to be so for ever. I am sure the people who are opposed and born hard on under pretence of opposing the Ladyes interest wish it as well as they who appear such sticklers for it: and there is another interest then that of her familye driving on under that pretence. Do not think it not worth while to stir in this, nor neglect doing it in time; you know the power <u>of a certain place</u> about magistrates: opposicion is already given to men chosen, whom I hear a very good character of:[1408] and if there be a new election, it will be of vast consequence if the Lady would write but a line to the man who lay in the court near the house where Mrs James lives, that her name should not be used to influence etc. My correspondent will recollect who I mean: he and I left London together.

[1405] Martha Courthope.

[1406] Youghal (see below, pp. 265–6.).

[1407] Parliamentary elections.

[1408] The Irish privy council, meeting in Dublin Castle. Since Oct. 1711 there had been six mayoral elections for Youghal, before the privy council had given its approval (*Council Book of Youghal*, ed. Caulfield, 401–4; PRONI, T/3416/A, *s.v.* Youghal).

I am to my heart sorry at the young Ladyes sicknesse which prevented my discoursing the matter at Large as I intended: but if some care be not taken of this and other places, our great folks expect to meet people near Colledge green[1409] very agreeable to what is now in prospect. Mrs Hill and her company are stil on the other side the water. Some people are much merrier and better pleased then others, and I suppose it is the same thing with you. Yesterday I heard a pamphlet cryed in the Courts by the title of The Queens peace or, A new war:[1410] Whether this be a paper in fashion or a Seditious one I know not: for you must know, those seem to me to be the terms of distinction, whatever suits not exactly with the humor that prevails at present becomes immediately seditious. My sister will be able to tell you whether Lady Juliana[1411] be recovered, and how far the smallpox hath injured her fine face …

180. *Alan I, Dublin, to Thomas, at his lodgings in Whitehall, 23 July 1712*

(1248/3/80–1)

This letter will be delivered into your own hands by Mr Warberton,[1412] soe that I may venture to expresse that in plain words which I was forced to cover in dark and ambiguous terms in my former letter. You can not imagine the indefatigable industry that hath been used to model corporations soe here, that when the time shal come of summoning a new parliament, it may answer the expectations of our great ones here. And truly considering the power of the Councel board in approving or disapproving magistrates, and their exercise of it, together with the means taken to have men of a certain stampe chosen into corporacions for the magistracy, and that the naming Sherifs will put the returns for Countyes into the hands of those who will doe every thing to please;[1413] I say considering all these things, and the restlesse pains the black coates[1414] take to have a Tory Parliament, together with our remissenesse in obviating these endeavours of theirs, I doe not know but that by calling a new Parliament they may alter their hands for what they call the better. Under pretence of serving Lord or Lady Burlingtons interest in Youghal a Tory faction is carryed on and supported mightily:[1415] Lord In[*chiqui*]n, the B[*isho*]p of Cl[*oyne*], Lieutenant General St[*euart*][1416] Rob. FitzG[*eral*]d[1417] and others are at the head of this affair: the design is to model the corporacion soe as it may return two Tory members instead of Mr Luther and Mr Hayman. There hath been an election of magistrates lately certifyed against which

[1409] The Irish parliament.

[1410] *The Queen's Peace; or, A New War* (Dublin, 1712), printed by the tory publisher Edward Waters and arguing strongly in favour of the ministry's peace policy.

[1411] The dowager countess of Burlington.

[1412] Richard Warburton, MP [I], a Middle Templar.

[1413] County sheriffs acted as returning officers in elections for knights of the shire.

[1414] The clergy of the established church.

[1415] For the disputes within the corporation in 1711–12 see T. C. Barnard, 'Considering the Inconsiderable: Electors, Patrons and Irish Elections 1659–1761', *Parliamentary History*, xx (2001), 117; NLI, MS 13254: Joseph Waite to J. Walker, 21 Aug. 1712; MS 13242: Jeremy Coughlan to Richard Musgrave, 13, 15, 22 Nov., 7 Dec. 1712.

[1416] William Steuart, MP [I].

[1417] Robert Fitzgerald, MP [I] Castlemartyr, who was recorder of Youghal.

there is a peticion lodged and I make no doubt they will be disapproved: and so by new elections a trial is to be made whether it will not in time fall on confiding men. I am told several of the Councel or freemen are threatned by Lady B[*urlingto*]ns agent to be distrained or arrested for their rent immediately after the election, if they do not act as directed. Sure if my Lady were made sensible what is driving on under colour of serving her Ladyships interest or that of my Lord, she gladly would give other directions. The way to continue and encrease her interest in Youghal seems to me to be rather to goe into the bent of the people then to thwart it in every instance of elections, as is done if I hear what is true: I am confident Badham[1418] is very instrumental in formenting this difference, in hopes of being chosen for that town by my Ladyes interest. If her Ladyship consider his emploiment,[1419] and knew him at all, she will readily judge how good a representative he is like to make. Grice Smith[1420] also proposes to be the other by the same interest; he is as high as the Doctor,[1421] in so much that honest Dick Smith his father[1422] hath no sort of power over him; the Preists have possessed him. My Lady by withdrawing her directions of opposing the magistrates by a line to Digby Foulkes[1423] or Mr Coghlan,[1424] and by recommending men grateful to the town to serve in Parliament as Mr Henry Luther and Mr Hyde[1425] will create and fix an interest much more (in my opinion) then by the measures taken by her present Commissioners and servants. I would not interpose in this thing if I did not apprehend it to be of mighty concern how the buroughs and interest of soe great a familye goe: and I hope I shal not be blamed for writing that which I apprehend may prove of publick use, and no disservice to a familye for which I have the greatest honour and alway pay my best services. Senny is not yet landed, soe that I shal not see them before I leave town, which I intend to do to morrow …

181. *Alan I, Cork, to Thomas, 5 Sept. 1712*

(1248/3/83–4)

You doe not mention whether you did any thing about the affair I wrote to you on; if what I hear be true that we soon shal have a new P[*arliamen*]t; it will be of importance something were done in that affair. Indeed very good people lye under great pressures by the means of misrepresentations made of them to Lady B[*urlingto*]n, who is a woman of good sense and on having the thing truly stated will presently see the drift of those

[1418]Brettridge Badham, MP [I].

[1419]Badham was a collector of customs and excise for Youghal and Dungarvan.

[1420]Grice Smyth (*d.* 1724), of Ballynatray, Co. Waterford (NLI, Genealogical Office MS 93, p. 137). In 1710 Lady Burlington had promised Smyth her family's interest at Youghal in the event of a new election (NLI, MS 13254/3: Joseph Waite to Digby Foulke, 27 Feb. 1710[/11]).

[1421]Sacheverell.

[1422]Richard Smyth (*d.* c.1712) of Ballynatray (NLI, Genealogical Office MS 93, p. 137; Vicars, *Index*, 433)

[1423]Digby Foulke (*d.* c.1710) of Youghal (Phillimore, *Indexes*, ii, 132), one of Lady Burlington's longest-serving Irish agents (Barnard, *A New Anatomy*, 218–19).

[1424]Jeremiah or Jeremy Coughlan (*d.* 1735), of Lismore, an attorney employed by the Burlington estate and since 1707 seneschal of the manor of Dungarvan (Vicars, *Index*, 107; Barnard, *A New Anatomy*, 222–3; Wilson, *Elite Women in Ascendancy Ireland*, 92),

[1425]Arthur Hyde, MP [I].

who carry on self ends and private designs upon pretence of serving her family. Pray let the matter be some way or other laid before her Ladyship, at least say nothing hath been done in it, that another way may be thought of how to give her true informacion. Our County grand Jury have made a very loyal addresse as it is called: no doubt your Gazette will give it the publick as soon as transmitted;[1426] perhaps there will not be the same honour done our poor City, whose thoughts and wishes may be content to appear to the world in some other paper of lesse notice. Neither the rhetorick nor complement of it come near our County, but is in the words on the back of this letter.[1427] Our Sherif (George Crofts) returned Lord Kingstons son[1428] Sir Em[*anuel*] Moor,[1429] Dick Cox,[1430] Arthur Bernard (the Sollicitors brother)[1431] Mr Hedges his tenant att Macrompe,[1432] our neighbour Mr Longfeild[1433] whom you know, Mr Badham[1434] and Mr Walker[1435] who are two of our Collectors, and one of them no freeholder as I hear; Grice Smith (who lives in the County of Waterford, seldome appears here, and hath been much affected with a deep melancholy, soe as not to speak for several dayes, of which distemper he went ill out of town before the Assizes were over) and Redmond Barry,[1436] both of which are marryed to two daughters of Colonel Taylor who is Sir John Percivals receiver, Hugh Hutchinson formerly employed in the fort of Kinsale[1437] and some others as our grand Jury. It was observed that pretty many

[1426]Both the county and city addresses were noticed briefly in the *London Gazette*, 21–24 Feb.1712[/13], without any recitation of the text.

[1427]An address from the grand jury, gentlemen, freeholders and inhabitants of the city of Cork at the assizes, 26 Aug. 1712. The most significant passage came near the end: 'We adore the divine Goodness that has put it in the power of your Majestye and your Allies to give a safe, honourable and lasting peace to Europe and Enable your Majestye to Exercise that great perogative of making peace with which the Crown is by the Laws Intrusted, for the good of the Kingdoms, Assuredly promising our selves from your Majestyes great Goodness and repeated Declarations all the Security that human Wisdom Can Contrive in the Enjoyment of our holy Religion Libertyes and propertyes by Continuing and Securing the Succession of the Crown as now Settled by Act of Parliament upon failure of Issue of your Majestyes body in the Illustrious house of Hannover' (SHC, 1248/3/82.)

[1428]James King (1693–1761), of Mitchelstown, Co. Cork, later 4th Baron Kingston, whose father John (c.1664–1728), had converted to Roman catholicism before the Revolution, served King James II in Ireland and followed the exiled king to France, suffering outlawry in consequence. In 1694 John was pardoned, and in 1715 he would take the oaths and resume his seat in the Irish house of lords. James, though born in France, had also by this time returned to his ancestral protestantism.

[1429]Sir Emanuel Moore, MP [I].

[1430]Richard Cox, MP [I].

[1431]Arthur Bernard, MP [I] brother to Francis.

[1432]Richard Hedges (c.1670–aft.1728) of Macroom Castle, Co. Cork (*The Kenmare Manuscripts,* ed. Edward MacLysaght (Dublin, 1941), 135; Marc Caball, *Kerry, 1600–1730: The Emergence of a British Atlantic County* (Dublin, 2017), 36–9).

[1433]John Longfield.

[1434]Brettridge Badham, MP [I].

[1435]Joseph Walker, collector of Mallow.

[1436]Redmond Barry (*d.* c.1739) of Ballyclogh, Co. Cork (Vicars, *Index*, 24). He married Catherine Taylor in 1700 (T.G.H. Green, *Index to the Marriage Licence Bonds of the Diocese of Cloyne* (Cork, 1899–1900), 91); and in the same year Gertrude, the daughter of William Taylor of Ballynort, Co. Limerick, married Grice Smyth (NLI, Genealogical Office MS 93, p.137; Green, *Cloyne Marriage Licence Bonds*, 91).

[1437]Hugh Hutchinson (*d.* by 1728) of Bantry, Co. Cork (Vicars, *Index*, 244). His name was included in a list sent to Sir John Perceval in Dec. 1711 of freeholders in Co. Cork who had pledged to support Perceval at the next parliamentary election (BL, Add. MS 46964B, ff. 142–3).

Gentlemen, and I beleive some of these were in town before the Judge; that there was hardly any talk but of an addresse and one of an extraordinary nature was expected; people say the Jury was not summoned beforehand as usual, but the panel brought to be approved or altered: What follows was new here, tho they say not unprecedented elsewhere; that the grand Jury was first empanelled sworn and charged before the grand panel of the County was called over. An addresse ready drawn and ingrossed was brought in by the foreman, alterations proposed and agreed to, and the amended addresse to be ingrossed; this would take time till next day: It was soe ordered that the ingrossement of the amended addresse was blotted soe as to need being fair written over, and during these transactions no doubt there was oportunitye to shew the amendments to a certain person. When the addresse came to be signed and the blottings of the amended addresse were observed rather then delay the thing so long as writing it over again would take up, the former addresse without alteracion was carryed. All due care was taken by the Judge by handing it about in Court and offering it in his chamber to be signed; and some hands were to it when I saw it on Tuesday night; but not many; whether the number might not be much increased by Wednesday when he went out of town or on the rode since (if any well affected persons came in his way) I cannot tell: but some refused to sign it both in open Court and in the chamber. I was not honoured with an offer to doe it, tho it passed twice by my nose; and once was in the hands of one Callaghan a new convert Lawyer,[1438] who said it was a most admirable one. Some people say the words import more then the Jury themselves meant, and if (as is given out) it imply any reflection on the late ministry I am of their minds: and doe beleive it will be an hard matter to perswade the protestants of this County in prejudice of them or the great Duke of Marleborough. There hapned lately a dispute between two freinds about the import of an expression in Tully which created a wager, and if Mr A[*ddiso*]n[1439] would give himself the trouble of rendring it into English and you send me what he translates those words by, you will oblige me. The passage is in one of Tullyes Epistles to Lepidus, in the 27th Epistle of his tenth book and runs thus. Pacis inter cives conciliandae te cupidum esse laetor: Eam si a servitute sejungis, consules et reipublicae et dignitati tuae: Sui ista pax perditum hominem in possessionem impotentissimi dominatus restitura est, hoc animo scito omnes sanos ut mortem servituti anteponant: Itaque etc.[1440] The words which seem difficult to be rendred into significant and expressive english are impotentissimi dominatus: But he is such a master of both languages as to be able to expresse in one the full import of them in the other. From Middleton I will write to you of your own affairs, where I propose to be to morrow …

[1438]Cornelius Callaghan, MP [I].

[1439]Joseph Addison (1672–1719), MP [GB] and [I]; formerly chief secretary [I] to Lord Wharton, 1708–10; his literary talents included a facility for translating from and composing in Latin. (*Oxf. DNB*; *HC 1690–1715*, iii, 11–14.)

[1440]Cicero, *Epistulae ad familiares*, x: 27: to Marcus Aemilius Lepidus, 28 Mar. 43 BC: 'I rejoice that you have set your heart on arranging a peace between the parties in the state; provided you dissociate that peace from any form of servitude, you will be doing the best you can both for the republic and for your own position; but if the peace you propose means the reinstatement of an unprincipled man in a long lease of absolutely uncontrollable tyranny, I would have you know that all men of sound views have made up their minds to accept death rather than servitude. Therefore …'

182. *Alan I, Mallow, to Thomas, at his lodgings in Whitehall, 23 Sept. 1712*

(1248/3/87–8)

Yours of the 13th came to Middleton on Sunday, but my being here prevented its coming to my hand till last night, soe that I could not answer it by last post. The postscript of Lord Godolphins death (for that I take to be the case)[1441] sensibly affects me: with him England lost an able, wise, and I think honest man: he had enemyes enough, of power and disposition to have laid him open if he had been capable of being exposed: soe that when I cannot find a want of will, I must beleive he acted soe that his enemyes could not lay hold on him. Will not his death wean you from Newmarkett, horses etc. Pray Dear Brother give yourself time to think how much an easier man you will be (then now) if you think fit to discontinue what hath at all times kept you under the last difficultyes. Our ayr is as certainly infected as yours; Every place is full of sick people of this new feaver; but only children and infirm old people dye of it: but a story I heard lately affects me a little. The crew of a Scotch bark arrived lately from Norway say that the people there told them the late pestilence in that countrey was preceded by just such a distemper as now reigns among us … My brother Clayton and I design to go about the end of this week to Middleton where I expect all the difficuyltyes that hypocrisye pride and envy can lay in our way in an affair you cannot but call to mind: I hope you will on occasion apply (successefully) to the party first concerned in setting this affair on foot, in which I apprehend some power stil remain … Everyone here looks melancholy except a certain party, who are soe much transported that I beleive in a little time they will think it out of the power (almost) of providence to disappoint their designs. We are not yet come to transpose the words, but James Kings health was begun by a papist in a publick company; a Protestant (by) said if the proposer meant James King of Mitchelstown (Lord Kingstons son) he would drink it: but I doe not hear there was any such exposition made.

183. *Alan I, Midleton, to Thomas, at his lodgings in Whitehall, 23 Oct. 1712*

(1248/3/89–90)

I am returned from Ballydullea where I spent three or fowre dayes with poor Dick Bettesworth, whom I parted with this morning and never expect to see him again; he is fallen away to nothing, hath an high, hectick feavor on him, hath lost all appetite to any kind of flesh meat, and cannot keep any thing in his stomach that is hot; broth is all he now lives on. Tho he hath formerly made too free with his constitution, of late it hath been much otherwise: he is troubled with a dry cough, which puts him to excessive pain, but when he is able to bring any thing up, it is only a little thin watery stuff; his cough hardly admits him to take any maner of rest. It is certain his feavor remits very much, if it doth not entirely intermitt, and Dr Rogers[1442] hopes the bark may be of use to him; I confesse I doe

[1441]Sidney, earl of Godolphin *d.* 15 Sept. 1712.

[1442]Joseph Rogers (1677–1753), MD, of Cork, author of *An Essay on Epidemic Diseases; and More Particularly on the Endemial Epidemics of the City of Cork* … (Dublin, 1734).

not expect it. However pray as soon as possible let Dr Ratclif know his case as far as I have described it, and without the losse of any time desire my sister to send me his directions; tell her I pray she will place the Doctors fee to my account. His ilnesse prevented his being here last Saturday, when Lord Insiquin and the Bishop of Corke[1443] gave Major Clayton,[1444] the Soveraign of Middleton[1445] and me (who are the only surviving Governors of the school now residing in Ireland) a meeting; what passed at it will be too long for a letter that will contain a deal of other stuff; and indeed it deserves a paper wholly on that subject. Only this I will say, that tho I expected a pretty deal of management I could not beleive I should have seen all that I observed passe that day. His ilnesse hath also hindred me from making those advances I otherwise might in giving you an account what Leases and on what terms may reasonably be sett for the benefit of this town, and to make it come to something. In this I depended on and wanted his help, but that I am not like to have and shal doe very little by my self: however I will give you the best account I can of your affairs here: But this also you must expect from Dublin … We grow very sickly here, I mean people now dye pretty much of this new feaver, especially the meaner sort and old people. The tame fowle are seised with a stoppage in their heads that kills them apace, as the good women say; indeed I have heard them make a strange noise much like the crying of a young child, when their heads are seised and stopped with the distemper. This is a very trivial observacion, yet it argues that there is in[fe]ction in the air when so many creatures of different kinds are affected at the same time …

184. *Alan I, Dublin, to Thomas, at his lodgings in Whitehall, 1 Nov. 1712*

(1248/3/91–2)

I am to answer my Dear Brothers of the eighteenth … My freinds sentiments differ entirely from mine in that which is the subject of your letter; not that the expence of an English journey and losse of businesse shal weigh with me; for those are things I can despise, if they stand in the way of my doing the least service to the publick at a very nice and critical juncture. But I am sensible it never can lye in my power in the maner you mention. If it hath been my fortune to influence any one debate or publick affair here, you know that hath proceeded from a good opinion that Gentlemen have conceived of me, as meaning the good of the Countrey, and knowing something of the constitution of it and what would be for its service or to its prejudice. And this opinion arose from a long knowledge of me, and a narrow observation of my actions; and to that alone I attribute Gentlemens sometimes going into my sentiments, not to any skil in parliamentary affairs; much lesse any abilityes above the common rate of other men. Now the case will be perfectly different in an assembly where I am altogether unknown, in a countrey whose constitucion I am much a stranger to (for under that word I comprehend trade when I am speaking about Parliament businesse) in an house whose orders I am not master of, and among men of that kind (I speak of the majoritye) from whom I may reasonably expect a continuance of the

[1443] Peter Browne (c.1665–1735), bishop of Cork since 1710.

[1444] Laurence Clayton, MP [I].

[1445] The chief magistrate of the corporation; currently John Sharpe (see below, p. 276).

favors they have shown me for several years past: Nay I shal be thought and perhaps told that I am (what of all things I would last chuse to be) an Irishman. Judge now Dear Brother whether under these circumstances I shal be more then a single vote, and how much I shal blush for my freinds sake as well as my own to be brought soe far to soe little purpose: there are Cyphers nearer hand that will supply the place as well as I shal; and many men of merit and character that will doe it to advantage and with repututacion to themselves, which I confesse I have not opinion good enough of my self to beleive I shal be able to doe. Beside if I should by the interest of my freinds be chosen, I shal lye under the obligacion of a longer attendance then you mencion: which will be considerably to my prejudice; for I cannot propose to make a sinecure of my practice as Sir G[*ilbert*] D[*olben*] doth of his Cushion.[1446] Let me therefore desire you, after making my acknowledgements to my freinds in the best maner for the good opinion they have conceived of me and the handsome offer they have made, to assure them I know my own defects too well not to be certain I shal not be able to answer their expectations; and I chuse to give this under my hand rather then convince them and my enemyes too in a more publick maner that what I say is too well grounded …

[*PS*] … I had no countrey letters yesterday, soe cannot say whether my poor cousen Bettesworth be dead or not; but verily beleive he is: God preserve all you.

185. *St John III, Dublin, to Thomas, at his lodgings in Whitehall, 6 Nov. 1712*

(1248/3/93–4)

… This towne is almost in an uproar. The occasion this. Tuesday last a vast number of Gentlemen to the number of 225 din'd at the Tholsel[1447] to remember our Glorious deliverer King William and bespoke the Tragedy of Tamerlane, with Dr Garths Prologue, at night. The G[*overnmen*]t sent positive orders to the Playhouse to forbid the latter and some few, as I hear, came thither to hiss it if spoken.[1448] The Gentlemen were intent upon it, and when twas forbid, young Moore, honest Jacks Brother,[1449] just before the play begun, got

[1446] His place as a justice of common pleas [I]: for the use of the word 'cushion' to refer to a seat of authority, especially judicial or legal, see above, pp. 137, 208.

[1447] Literally the 'toll-house': it stood in Skinner Row, near Christ Church cathedral, and housed the offices of Dublin corporation, the Royal Exchange and the Trinity Guild of Merchants. The medieval original had been rebuilt in the 1670s. (Maurice Craig, *Dublin 1660–1860* (Dublin, 1952), 47.)

[1448] On 3 Nov., the eve of King William's birthday, the city corporation held an 'entertainment' at the Tholsel, at which those present requested a performance the following day at the Theatre Royal in Smock Alley of Nicholas Rowe's *Tamerlane* (1701), a play which had become a favourite with whigs because of its contemporary resonances and was often performed in honour of William III's birthday. They also insisted on hearing the prologue written by Sir Samuel Garth for the first performance in the winter of 1701/2, which had among other things called for Britons to unite to prevent a Bourbon succession to the Spanish crown. A copy was sent to Joseph Ashbury, the theatre manager, who brought it to the lords justices. They 'thought it next to sounding an alarm to rebellion and commanded him not to allow it to be spoken'. (*CJI*, ii, 991; *Dublin Intelligence*, 8 Nov. 1712; NAI, M 3036, f. 38: Sir Constantine Phipps to Edward Southwell, 3 Nov. 1711). On this episode see H.M. Burke, *Riotous Performances: The Struggle for Hegemony in the Irish Theater, 1712–1784* (Notre Dame, IN, 2003), ch.1.

[1449] Dudley, the younger brother of John Moore, MP [I]. He was to suffer a fatal wound in a politically-motivated duel in a London coffee-house in Aug. 1714, having been 'taken up very sharply for speaking against Sir Constantine Phipps', and died a month later (NLI, MS 41587/3: Robert French to William Smyth, 31 Aug. 1714; John Lodge, *The Peerage of Ireland* …, rev. Mervyn Archdall (7 vols, 1789), ii, 89).

on the Stage, and begun to speak the prologue. There was a vast Hubbab and clapping in the House, and some very few Hisses, which, tis said, came from the Collegians,[1450] one of whom, the only one that was observ'd, met with pretty scurvy treatment, and some blows in the Play house. At last, a Gentleman whose name I know not, and if I did twould not be proper to mention it, got upon the stage, and standing very near Mr Moore, said aloud that all who hist that prologue were Papists, and jacobite Rascals, and desir'd all that were for having it spoken would put on their Hats. Upon this there was a prodigious a Clap, and so vastly the greater Number of Hats put on, that the Prologue was suffer'd to be spoken quietly, and very handsomly by the young Gentleman. Word was sent to the G[*overnmen*]t, who immediately order'd the Guards at the Playhouse to be doubled, and some of them came in with their Bayonets drawn, but were turn'd out by the commanding officer. We have had 4 or 5 quarrels to day on this subject, of which I dont know the event, and expect every hour more, so that Gentlemen go to the Coffee house with a full expectation of having a quarell [?fix't] on them, and I really expect a general one very soon, unless some care be taken to prevent it. For Gentlemen will not bear to be insulted, especially on such an account, either by Jacobites or Papists. The Drs,[1451] as in all other good works of Peace, have been the most active in blowing the Coals, and some of them either have, or narrowly escap'd being soundly drubb'd for some handsome language they were pleas'd to use to Gentlemen.

186. *Alan I, Dublin, to Thomas, at his lodgings in Whitehall, 15 Nov. 1712*

(1248/3/95–6)

The sicknesse of my Cousen Bettesworth rendred him incapable to give me that help he could have given and I very much wanted in the putting your affairs …in such a light that you might have given your last orders in it. He was stil living last Tuesday, but so weak that I despair of ever seeing him again in this world; so that I must not delay in expectacion of his help any longer …

187. *Alan I, Dublin, to Thomas, at his lodgings in Whitehall, 18 Nov. 1712*

(1248/3/97–8)

… [*PS*] Methinks some of you might give an hint about the main concern of this Kingdome; a word will be understood. Is what we hear true that the Scotch Clergy both Episcopal and Presbyterian have refused to take a certain oath?[1452]

[1450] Undergraduates at Trinity College.

[1451] The clergy of the established church.

[1452] The oath of abjuration (C.A. Whatley, *The Scots and the Union* (Edinburgh, 2006), 323). For the scruples entertained by some Ulster presbyterian ministers over the abjuration, see Beckett, *Protestant Dissent*, ch.6.

188. *Alan I, Dublin, to Thomas, at his lodgings in Whitehall, 29 Nov. 1712*

(1248/3/101–2)

I resolved to have wrote to you upon another subject, but this being the first after term brought company to my house that kept me too long with them to allow me to think of businesse by this post; however to keep my promise in my last that you should hear from me by this post I will make a silly mistake that hapned yesterday the subject of a letter …You must have heard of the speaking the Prologue to Tamerlane at the Playhouse here on the fourth of this month, and how that matter was resented by the Governement here. Yesterday being the last day of term the Grand Jury of the City had several bills of indictment sent up to them and among the rest one against Dudley Moore (brother to Jack Moor whom you know) and others: he it seems spoke the prologue and the rest were I suppose aiding abetting and assisting him in so doing, and (I think they say) guilty of a great riot: and for this I beleive they were to be indicted; but I having not seen either the examinacions or indictment can speak only what is common discourse. The Grand Jury consisted of three and twenty: five were for finding the bill against Mr Moore and for returning ignoramus against all the rest, two for finding the bill against all the persons in the bill of indictment, and eighteen for not finding the bill against any one of the persons named in the bill: however the bill was among a great many others returned with an indorsement under the foremans hand (Alderman Gore the last Lord Mayor) with a billa vera.[1453] The Jury was discharged by the Court before the mistake was discovered: for there is not the least ground for suspecting any thing like trick in the foreman, and I beleive there is not in this Kingdome so melancholy a man and heartbroken as he is for his inadvertency. When the mistake was known, before the Court was up he and several others of the Grand Jury came into Court and Mr Dean[1454] moved the Judges on the foremans affidavit that the indorsement was a mistake and against the sense and finding of the Jury; nay I hear and beleive it to be true that the five who were for finding the bill (as I mentioned before) were ready to declare the truth of what Mr Gore swore; and I hear and beleive it to be true that a great many more (I think the eighteen) have made a like affidavit. You will rally our Irish understandings;[1455] but perhaps some of you may pity the difficultyes they were put under to have so much and so important businesse (as this you know is) delayed and not laid before them till about one of Clock that day; and that the hurry should subject them to a mistake.

189. *Alan I, Dublin, to Thomas, at his lodgings in Whitehall, 23 Dec. 1712*

(1248/3/103–4)

… Let me beg you well to weigh with your self whether it will not be worth your while, if not of absolute necessitye, to come over this Spring into this Kingdome: really you will

[1453] A 'true bill'. A manuscript 'Lampoon of the 17 Aldermen of Dublin' [c.1713/14], written by a tory sympathiser, described Gore as 'A country boor with two blunderbusses. Charged at the head of an ignoramus jury writing billa vera on an indictment containing eight skins of parchment' (BL, Add. MS 21138, ff 23–4).

[1454] Joseph Deane, MP [I].

[1455] A derogatory phrase in common use in England at this time: see above, pp. 20, 63.

sett your estate much better then any servant you have or I shal be able to doe: you will see how things are, and (having more interest that your stud should be sold then they in whose management it is) may reasonably expect to do it tho other people have not succeeded in the attempt. And what seems to me to carry great weight with it as well in point of interest as reputation, now my brother Clayton is gone and Dick Bettesworth on his death bed, and irrecoverably ill if not actually dead[1456] is that I apprehend your presence to be indispensably necessary in order to stating the accounts of, as well as finishing and opening the school. What can be of weight enough to oppose what I offer except the difficultye of the journey; but the Spring will in a great measure remove that objection. For Gods sake think of this; and resolve once to undertake such a journey for the sake of credit and interest who have taken so many for the service of other people. I have not had time to inform you fully of the proceedings of the Earle and two B[*ishop*]s when we mett att Middleton:[1457] when I doe that will be another motive to you to resolve on taking this journey … God send you a better new year than we expect.

190. *Alan I, Dublin, to Thomas, at his lodgings in Whitehall, 28 Feb. 1712[/13]*

(1248/3/105–6)

… Lord C— hath been ill and out of town but is to be with me presently; he intends soon for England, and I hope the matter you know may in long vacacion be brought to a good end, when I propose to be over with you … My heart is near broken with losse of many freinds, absence from others, cloudy weather, ill usage, and multiplicity of businesse; but I trust in God I shal be able to bear up while I may be serviceable to my freinds, and till I have extricated my self from debt, which would be a terrible thing to my poor boy to discharge, if I should leave him incumbred …

191. *Alan I, Midleton, to Thomas, at his lodgings in Whitehall, 10 Mar. 1712[/13]*

(1248/3/107–8)

I am gott safe hither, and the first news I find is that Mr Pyne[1458] is killed in a duel; he left no son and by his fathers will his English estate comes to Robin Wakeham, my Lords sisters son:[1459] he is now with me and saith his Uncle told him not long before his death that his whole estate for want of issue male of his sons body was so settled as to come to him.[1460] Jack Freak[1461] and Dick Turner[1462] are the two freinds Sir Richard Pyne hath chose to leave

[1456] Richard Bettesworth, sr. His will was proved in 1713 (Phillimore, *Indexes*, ii, 122).

[1457] The earl of Inchiquin, and the bishops of Cloyne and Cork, on the business of the Midleton school.

[1458] Henry Pyne, MP [I].

[1459] Sir Richard Pyne's sister Jane was Robert Wakeham's mother: Robert duly inherited and took the additional surname Pyne.

[1460] As confirmed in Sir Richard Pyne's will (dated 15 Oct.1709: TNA, PROB 11/513/36), and in a note from Wakeham to Thomas Brodrick, 10 Mar. 1712[/13], included with this letter.

[1461] John Freke (1652–1717), barrister, of the Middle Temple.

[1462] Richard Turner (1653–1725), barrister, of the Inner Temple.

his estate in England to by his will,[1463] subject to the trusts and uses therein contained; and probably Dick Turner may have the original will, and a part of the settlement made on Mr Pynes marrying Mrs Edgecombe.[1464] It will be very freindly to Mr Wakeham and an obligacion to me if you will take the trouble to call at Mr Turners lodgings at a druggists near the bolt and tun in Fleetstreet to gett the best light and informacion you are able how the estate is settled … No doubt he, Mr Freake, or Sir James Montague[1465] can give a great light into this affair; and if you can without too much trouble assist Robin Wakeham it will be one of many acts of good nature and freindship you have done for people who have not had intimacy enough with you to ask the favor …

192. *Alan I, Mallow, to Thomas, at his lodgings in Whitehall, 20 Mar. 1712[/13]*

(1248/3/109–10)

I am at a very melancholy house; my sisters greif and sicknesse hath greatly impaired her health: and beside the losse of her husband, which she truly laments,[1466] I doe apprehend the condition he hath left his affairs in sticks very close to her; which I fear will appear much worse then either you or I or any of his freinds could have apprehended. … Pray excuse my not writing to my sisters, really my eyes are almost out by tumbling writings over …

193. *Alan I, Dublin, to Thomas, at his lodgings in Whitehall, 20 Apr. 1713*

(1248/3/111–12)

… This letter will be soe long that it will not be possible for me to write to my sister by this packet, but you will see her and let her know that I had a very handsome letter from one who lately made a visit in Bond Street; I cannot well expresse what it contains without transcribing it: but it is wrote with an air of sinceritye, and saith a great deal in favor of one you know; indeed more then I ought in discretion to repeat even to you, and is very pressing for my speedy going for England. This post I answer it with that respect which is due to the Gentleman I write to, and that caution which ought to be used in an affair of this nature. I am extreamly troubled to find you repeat and continue your complaints of pains which give you ground to apprehend the stone in the Kidneys; God forbid you should fall into that most terrible as well as dangerous distemper, and I trust in his mercy that I shal not be soe unfortunate to be deprived of almost the last male relation whom I have reason entirely to love: The losses I have already suffered have almost sunk my spirits … It is of mighty consequence to have a Sovereign of Middleton in whom we can alway

[1463] As trustees.

[1464] Henry Pyne had married, in 1705, Margaret, daughter of Sir Richard Edgcumbe (1640–88) of Mount Edgcumbe, Cornwall (*Hist. Ir. Parl.*, vi, 135).

[1465] Sir James Montagu, MP [GB].

[1466] Alan's sister-in-law Anne (née Courthope), the recently widowed spouse of Laurence Clayton.

confide; for he of course is one of the Governors of etc[1467] and all methods will be taken by people whom you will readily guesse to get him to be under their direction. I told you formerly, that in October last we chose Mr Boyle and Senny in the room of Peter Bettesworth and Mr Maynard;[1468] On the death of poor L[*aurence*] C[*layton*] I came to be informed that a neighbour of ours of a very smooth tongue designed to apply to be elected: I confesse the first thing in my opinion to be guarded against is not to let him or any who may make the same pretensions hereafter have any thing to doe in it: You remember who were in the Cabal to have the building erected a little Southward from the place it now stands:[1469] If there were no more in the matter, that is a sufficient obstacle in my opinion: but there is much more in it: A deeper and more designing man I know not, and if this should once take place the thing will for so much instead of being elective become (in effect) successive: Others will truly say after him they have an equal right to be chosen there as he had. And by the observations I have already made, one of a certain sort will give as much trouble and create all the difficultyes in his power. Beside it will not be prudent to let the corporacion (as a Parliament borough) come too much into the hands of people linked together by marriage. For tho now they are all full of respect and depending enough, they may not continue soe at all times hereafter. You know that Brownes son is marryed to Spences daughter,[1470] as is Harold to another of them:[1471] these are two of the burgesses and he himself is a third. By the death of D[*ick*] B[*ettesworth*] there is a burgesses place vacant, which Spence proposed filling up by electing Mr Pritchard;[1472] but tho he be an honest man, Will Smith[1473] is a Gentleman and one who will never goe into any party measures in the corporacion, or join with the commoner sort of them if they should be spirited up by any of our well wishers. Pray let me have your sense in this affair: As also who you think the fittest person to be the next Sovereign. You know a reason why neither you Senny nor I must ever think of it; which I will not mention: John Sharpe[1474] hath been Sovereign for two years and it is of some advantage. Mr Hutchins spoke to me for his brother in Law Browne, and used as a motive that he was in low condition, and might by that means be enabled to clear an arrear of rent which otherwise he was in no likelyhood of discharging. The latter part hath no weight with me, but the place being a support to his poor family would be an inducement if I did not apprehend some danger that his mean circumstances might tempt him to be influenced to act as others would have him in a matter which by being Sovereign he becomes interested in. I doe not think any body who is inclined to work on him would part with money on the occasion, and am satisfyed nothing else can prevail on him to doe amisse: but poverty is a snare and a very great temptacion. Write to me soon on this subject: Spence spoke to me about a Soveraign and I beleive hath it in

[1467] Of the school.

[1468] Samuel Maynard, MP [I]. Bettesworth and Maynard were named as governors in the original indenture of 1696 establishing the school (Trevor West, *Midleton College 1696–1996: A Tercentenary History* (Midleton, 1996), 9).

[1469] The school.

[1470] Probably William Spence: see, p. 83.

[1471] Edward Harrold married Elizabeth Spence in 1702 (Green, *Cloyne Marriage Licence Bonds*, 49).

[1472] Peregrine Pritchard.

[1473] Possibly William Smith of Ballymore, Co. Cork (Phillimore, *Indexes*, ii, 150).

[1474] Formerly employed by Sir St John Brodrick as receiver of his rents.

his eye for himself or his son in Law Harold ...We also chose Arthur Hyde a Governor in L[*aurence*] C[*layton'*]s room; the Earle of Insiquin was in the County of Limrick, the Bishop of Cork could not attend. Pray out of hand send your account about the lead money ...

[*PS*] I have just now received my sisters of 14 April. 1713 for which I thank her: Mr Arthur Hill[1475] is pretty well, as are all our other freinds here ...

194. *Alan I, Dublin, to Thomas, at his lodgings in Whitehall, 28 Apr. 1713*

(1248/3/113–14)

This letter shal be wholly written on the subject of the school; you know how much maligned Middleton is for the having that foundation in it; and how desirous some people were, if there could have been room for it to have had it removed to another place instead of being built there: but that not being practicable and disappointed the design now is to represent that the work hath not been duly taken care of ... By the deed the Governors are to purchase ground etc the conveynce is not settled and you know the difficultyes I mentioned in my last about doing it: but one way or other those must be surmounted, and there is one certain way (tho an expensive one) which you will readily think of. My thoughts are that there be but a small parcel of ground added as a play feild and garden: While the Governors of it stand on good terms with the owners of the town, there will not fail to be a convenience allowed on reasonable terms; and if by power, art, or indiscretion of those to whom the town shal belong the direction and Governement of the school fall into hands that would make use of that power to render the others uneasy and to encrease their interest in the borough; it will not be amisse to have it in the power of the owners of the town to make the Governors know it will not be for the good of the school to set up in opposicion to the reasonable aimes and views of the owners of the town for its benefit. I doe not find that there are any rules yet made for the Governement of it, which by the Copy of the deed Lady Orkney hath reserved to her self power to make, and in default of her doing it the Governors may doe it: The original deed I have not nor know I where it is. These rules should be now thought on and formed, and it will be worth your while to think of it and at leisure gett Copyes of the rules and foundacions of other freeschools, out of which may be chosen such as seem proper for this Countrey and that foundation, with the addition of such others as shal seem necessary. Whether you will think proper to settle this wholly till I come over, I leave to your consideration; but it must be done soon, and things should be in some preparacion. I think too that it will be proper then to lay before Lady Orkney the steps taken, the nature of the building, the accounts and expence, and the new Governors elected in the room of those already dead; for her consideration and approbation. The Governors at their last meeting on my moving it went into my proposing

[1475] Arthur Hill (c.1694–1771), MP [I] 1715–1766, later Viscount Dungannon; Alan's stepson.

to Mr Philip Chamberlaine to be school Master; and John Sharpes son to be writing Master when the school shal be opened. I have not yet spoken to Mr Chamberlaine; he is a Clergy man, very learned, virtous and of good principles:[1476] I doe not find any rule yet to oblige the Governors not to fix on a Clergyman for Master; to which there are some objections, tho I own there is one very great convenience attends it: the not being in danger of being removed on getting better preferment in the Church, which a deserving Clergyman cant well misse of …

[*PS*] The matter of the prologue spoken by Dudley Moore on 4 November is revived and an informacion filed by the Attorney General as of last term and he is to plead to it to morrow: but I suppose it will not be brought very soon to a tryal. He resolves he must be tryed for it to presse to come to his trial as soon as possible.

195. *Alan I, Dublin, to Thomas, at his lodgings in Whitehall, 20 June 1713*

(1248/3/121–2)

I am to thank my dear Brother for his of the thirteenth which I received yesterday; I goe immediately into my coach to take leave of Mrs Hill and my daughter att Castlemarten this leisure evening, that I may not lye under a necessitye of doing it when I can worse afford time or delay my journey on that score when my other affairs will allow me to begin it: but I beleive I shal once more that is on this day sennight in the afternoon see them again, and come to town the monday morning after; and about the middle of that week sett sail toward England … Possibly you may have heard of a mocion made by the Attorney General[1477] in the Queens Bench in the cause between the Queen and Dudley Moore. The point is shortly this. After what hapned in Michaelmas term about the mistake of Alderman Gore in signing the bill of indictment against Moore and seven others for repeating the Prologue to Tamerlane on 4 Nov. Billa vera instead of ignoramus,[1478] and the nolle prosequi in the next term against seven of them, and then quashing the indictment, or declaring it to be no indictment (in truth I know not what to call it nor say what the Court did in that matter tho I was present and heard what they said) the Attorney filed an informacion against Moore, and he pleaded to it and moved to be tryed last term; but the trial was appointed this term; that is on Fryday 12th June. But on Saturday the 6th, the Atturney moved on some English precedents that the Sherif should bring in the Grand panel and the Clerk of the Crown strike a Jury. This is what never was in any one instance practiced in this Kingdome on the Crown side and it was opposed as of the last

[1476]Philip Chamberlain (c.1675–1751), the son of a Dublin lawyer, became in Feb. 1714 a prebendary of St Patrick's cathedral, Dublin (*Al. Dub.*, 144; Cotton, *Fasti*, ii, 172; Leslie, *Clergy of Dublin*, 475).

[1477]Sir Richard Levinge.

[1478]See above, p. 273.

consequence, by Forster,[1479] Dean,[1480] Whitshed,[1481] Gore,[1482] Witherington[1483] Rogerson[1484] and me for Moore:[1485] Sanders,[1486] Cliffe[1487] and others spoke in it for the Crown;[1488] the consequences is poor Mr Moore is to be put till next term; whether the officer or better Sherifs are to return the Jury time will shew. Whatever notion people on your side may have that there is no harm in introducing this usage here, if they knew what will be the consequence of such an innovation here they would consider very well before they would desire to have things goe out of the constant course without any pretence why the Sherifs should not return the Jury. Not the least objection was made against the Sheriff returning the Jury.

196. *Alan I, London, to Thomas, Newmarket, 3 Oct. 1713*

(1248/3/123–4)

… Robin FitzGerald of Castledod[1489] writes to me to recommend him to you for Middleton, being not able to gett in elsewhere; he is an honest man, went against the Castle[1490] tho recorder of Clonmel and brother in Law to the Recorder of Kilkenny:[1491] I will give no promise, but if the County and City elections goe as I wish,[1492] think he and Mr Hyde will be two good men. My humble services to the Duke of Devon[1493] Lord Godolphin and Lord Wharton ….

[1479]John Forster, MP [I].

[1480]Joseph Deane, MP [I].

[1481]William Whitshed, MP [I].

[1482]George Gore, MP [I].

[1483]John Witherington (*d.* 1718) of Dublin, 3rd serjeant [I] 1714–17, 2nd serjeant [I] 1717–*d.* (*K. Inns. Adm.*, 517; *Reg. Deeds, Wills*, i, 70). Described by Jonathan Swift as a 'little nasty lawyer' (Swift, *Journal to Stella*, ed. Williams, 206).

[1484]John Rogerson, MP [I].

[1485]The legal notebook kept by Sr Richard Cox, the presiding judge in queen's bench, records that Levinge offered precedents from English legal practice, presenting a certificate from the English lord chancellor, Lord Harcourt, which Forster, and then Alan Brodrick, vehemently disputed. Both Forster and Brodrick presented themselves as taking up a constitutional cause 'for the good of the country'. Alan's contribution was prolonged and, as recorded by the unsympathetic Cox, high-flown, at one point dragging in the case of the Seven Bishops. (NLI, MS 4245, pp 64–8; TCD, MS 1995–2008/1457: John Parnell to Archbishop King, 18 June 1713.)

[1486]Morley Saunders, MP [I].

[1487]John Cliffe, MP [I].

[1488]Cox's notebook adds the names of other counsel on behalf of the crown: Garrett Bourke, Roscarrick Dunkin, John Staunton, Charles Stewart and William Swiney (NLI, MS 4245, pp. 53–68 and subsequent, unnumbered pages).

[1489]Robert Fitzgerald, MP [I] Charleville 1703–13.

[1490]Dublin Castle, i.e. against government. Fitzgerald had in fact been listed as a tory in 1711 but did not sit in the 1713 parliament and was appointed 2nd serjeant [I] in Dec. 1714 (*Hist. Ir. Parl.*, iv, 157).

[1491]Joseph Kelly, MP [I]. Fitzgerald was married to Kelly's sister. Kelly himself died on 21 May 1713 (*Hist. Ir. Parl.*, v, 14).

[1492]In Cork.

[1493]William Cavendish (1672–1729), 2nd duke of Devonshire.

197. *Alan I, London, to Thomas, Newmarket, 11 Oct. 1713, 'five in the morning'*

(1248/3/125–6)

Before setting out for Ireland (which I purpose to doe soe early this day as to reach Feny Stratford[1494] this night) I must own yours of the ninth from Newmarkett: The person who said neither of the brothers would come to spoke what will be found in the event most true: what makes it not altogether improbable that what you heard of one of them might have something in it is this; One of them one Tuesday last took leave etc. That night a letter was left att his Lodging that the great man[1495] desired to see him the next morning; it was left with a man servant att the Lodging and not delivered: about eleven next morning Sir J[*ohn*] S[*tanley*][1496] came to him, asked if he had been with the D[*uke*] according to appointment: He answered he knew of none, nor had seen or heard of any letter and sending for the letter to his Lodging it was brought to him unopened. By this time Sir J[*ohn*] S[*tanley*] knew the D[*uke*] was gone to W[*hitehall*] and began to discourse matters, and seemed pretty much sollicitous about the event of affairs: the other spoke his mind plainly and said people that had been injured would complain, especially since they saw the person whom they looked on as the cheif cause of their uneasinesse was stil to remain and be supported;[1497] and perhaps by too plain declaring himself early saved himself the trouble of hearing what was intended to be said if he had overtaken the D[*uke*] …

198. *Alan I, Dublin, to Martha Courthope, Bond Street, 7 Nov. 1713*

(1248/3/129–30)

Having formerly told you that I had overcome the difficultyes of my English and Welsh journeyes, and my sea voyage; and my late ramble to Munster and back again, you may expect to know how matters stand with me since my return to this town of confusion and bloud; for soe it is become. I thank God some businesse detained me longer in my house yesterday then I expected, soe that I passed through Skinner row and went by the Tholsel after the people were wounded there, and the man killed:[1498] I observed all along that Street a parcel of fellows of the lowest sort standing in clusters and muttering, but knew not the occasion till I had gott through Skinner Row and gott to the fowre Courts;[1499] where I was told a man or two were killed at the Tholsel. I then found in what danger I should have been if I had come a little earlier, and indeed was as I passed through that mob: for I heard one of them call out A Whig A whig, and soon after the late Cheif Justice Brodrick

[1494] Fenny Stratford, Bucks. A recognised staging post on the road to Holyhead. Another letter of Alan's survives, written from Fenny Stratford two years earlier (NLI, MS 41580/2: Alan to Jane Bonnell, 15 Oct.1711).

[1495] The lord lieutenant, Charles Talbot, duke of Shrewsbury, appointed on 22 Sept. 1713.

[1496] Identified in the text in a different hand. Sir John Stanley, 1st Bt, MP [I] had been named as Shrewsbury's chief secretary.

[1497] Lord Chancellor Phipps.

[1498] As a consequence of the riot at the Dublin city election, for which see below, pp. 281–3.

[1499] The courts of queen's bench, common pleas, chancery and excehequer, situated in Christ Church Yard (Edward McParland, *Public Architecture in Ireland 1680–1760* (New Haven, CT, and London, 2001), 116).

was named: I was not ashamed of the character, nor moved at what was said but did not apprehend it was meant (as I now do) to irritate an incensed mob to fall on me: but I thank God, who restrains the rage of the people as well as sets bounds to the Sea. In my conscience I think there never was more industry used to put us into confusion then hath been of late: the Cheif Justice[1500] and General Stewart[1501] are taking examinations: I intend as far as I can find out the truth to transmit an account to our freind who will not fail to shew it to you. If the single election of one man (the recorder)[1502] creates this fury, what will be the debate when the chair comes to be filled:[1503] but there the mob cannot come in for any part. I am sensible by what I see, the Session is like to be uneasy and shal not be sollicitous if I misse the chair, but I will not decline it, if chosen, tho I dye in it. Let not these things trouble you; on the contrary, it becomes people to expect the worst, and then what ever happens better then expectation will be the more acceptable …

199. *Alan I, Dublin, to Thomas, at his lodgings in Whitehall, 7 Nov. 1713*

(1248/3/131–2)

I should be to blame not to give you some account of what no doubt will make a great deal of noise in London, as it doth here; I mean the riot yesterday at the Tholsel.[1504] I have not seen the examinations, which I am told our Cheif Justice (assisted by some of the Councel, particularly Lieutenant General Stewart) hath been taking the greatest part of this day, so will not be positive that all I write is the truth of the fact, or that nothing material is omitted: but you may take as I doe for truth till you can be better informed. The elecion for this City came on last Tuesday, when the Recorder and Alderman Burton appeared on foot, Fownes and Tucker on horseback: the poll was adjourned to the Tholsel on Fryday. Forster and Burton sent word to their competitors that to prevent disturbance they resolved to go privately with a few freinds on foot to the Tholsel and desired the others to doe the like which was refused: Yesterday morning the recorder and Burton accompanyed with several Gentlemen on foot went two and two from the recorders house to the Tholsel, where the Sherifs[1505] were: some time after Fownes and Tucker came on horse back from Colledge Green through Castle Street and Skinner row, with Trumpets and hautboyes;[1506] vast crowds of dissolute fellows, many of them Irish Papists; as they were coming toward the

[1500] Sir Richard Cox, lord chief justice of queen's bench [I].

[1501] William Steuart, MP [I], commander-in-chief of the armed forces in Ireland.

[1502] John Forster, recorder of Dublin.

[1503] The Speakership of the Irish house of commons.

[1504] At the parliamentary election for Dublin city, at which the whigs John Forster and Benjamin Burton had been returned, defeating their tory opponents, Sir William Fownes (MP [I]) and Martin Tucker (*d.* c.1719) of Dublin (Vicars, *Index*, 462), the customs collector for Dublin. See, inter alia, *CJI*, iii, 698, 708–14; *A True Account of the Riot Committed at the Tholsel* … (Dublin, 1713); *An Answer to the Tholsel Account* … (Dublin, 1713); *Sir Will Fownes's and Tucker's Vindication* (Dublin, 1713).

[1505] The sheriffs of the city, Thomas Bradshaw (1660–1715) and Edward Surdeville (*d.* c.1723), who acted as returning officers (Richard Lee Bradshaw, *Thomas Bradshaw (1733–1774), A Georgian Politician in the Time of the American Revolution* (Bloomington, IND, 2011), 20; *Appendix to 26th Report of Dep. Keeper of the Records*, 823).

[1506] Hautboy: an oboe. Their use was justified in the tory broadsheet *An Answer to the Tholsel Account* … as being common practice at elections in England.

Tholsel some of them were heard to say, Knock downs the Whiggish dogs, Pull down the Scaffold (meaning some boards erected at the Tholsel for the voters to come upon in order to be polled) Their musick and people made such a noise that the Sherifs took notice to the Competitors that it was impossible to proceed on the poll while it continued and desired them to silence or send away their musick but that was refused. The Sherifs then proceeded to poll and polled seven, all for Forster and Burton; then the work began by pulling down the scaffolds, noise and blows and weapons drawn to prevent the poll proceeding there (for they would have had it at some of the extreme parts of the town) the Sherifs commanded the peace, and afterwards the assistance of the posse[1507] appprehending themselves and those who came to poll in danger of the mob and being murdered. Thereupon several Gentlemen drew their swords in defence of the Sherifs, and one of them (but I hear against the advice and desire of the Recorder) sent to the main guard for some Souldiers to secure themselves and the electors: Some Souldiers came, were beaten and many of them greivously wounded; at length after several blows given them one fired his muskett and killed a man and several others are wounded.[1508] I was going to Court just after this unhappy affray was over, and saw Skinner row full of very scurvy ordinary fellows: Fownes and Tucker passed by me on foot through the mob in the Street very much disordered as I apprehended, tho I knew not the reason, and Sir Samuel Cooke (the late Lord Mayor)[1509] in his Coach; they passed unmolested, but the Sherifs recorder and Alderman Burton were forced to have a Guard to convey them safe to the Lord Lieutenant at the Castle, whither they went to apprise him of the matter. I think no body justifyes the two horsemen for coming to the Tholsel in that maner, and so attended, but it is endeavoured to cast an odium on the Recorder by saying Souldiers should not have been sent for; tho for ought I can find the Sherifs, Aldermen, Recorder etc would have been mobbed and for ought I can see some of them murthered if the Guard had not come; for there was a prodigious mob all of one side, the others bringing only people of the first figure to poll at first. One of Lord Chancellors servants was very busy in demolishing etc[1510] The secret of not liking the Tholsel for a place to poll in was (as I hear) that people might be deterred passing the Keyes[1511] to the

[1507] The posse comitatus, a body of men whom a sheriff was enabled summon to preserve public order; the call for the posse was made at the scene by John Allen, MP [I] and other whigs (BL, Add. MS 38157, f.23: Sir Richard Cox to Edward Southwell, 17 Nov. 1713).

[1508] According to Sir Richard Cox, the whig sheriffs, together with Burton and Forster 'and their party' had 'possessed themselves of the court' and were bent on excluding their opponents, which so enraged tory supporters that they attempted 'to break down the steps of the stage, to make room'. The alarmed sheriffs then sent a message to the guard, which Lieutenant-General William Steuart, forewarned of possible trouble, had appointed to be ready to intervene when called in by the lord mayor and sheriffs. The first guards to arrive had failed to force their way into the Tholsel with drawn bayonets, but reinforced by the rest of the detachment of thirty soldiers, had fired into the building to clear the mob. (BL, Add. MS 38157, f.23: Cox to Edward Southwell, 17 Nov. 1713; see also *CJI*, iii, 711–12; 24–9; *A Long History of a Certain Session of a Certain Parliament, in a Certain Kingdom* ([Dublin], 1714).

[1509] Sir Samuel Cooke (*d.* 1726), a brewer, and lord mayor of Dublin 1712–14 (*Hist. Ir. Parl.* iii, 488), politically aligned with the tories.

[1510] Thomas Harvey, who was subsequently identified by the Irish house of commons (in a resolution directed against Phipps himself) as 'a chief fomentor of, and instrument in carrying on and putting in execution the riotous design and force used to obstruct the poll at the Tholsel' (*CJI*, iii, 712; *Perceval Diary*, 132–3). According to a report in the *Flying Post*, 21–23 Jan. 1714, he was Phipps's 'domestic gentleman' and a 'cryer' in the court of chancery.

[1511] Quays.

Hospital near Oxmantown Green[1512] by the insolence of the mob and rabble that very obsequiously attend one party; but the pretence is that it hath more convenient passages, the Tholsel being so near the Courts and in a narrow Street. I remember eighty eight,[1513] but remember nothing then like what I have observed since I came to town on Thursday. Be not too free in letting it be known I write this. The poll is adjourned till Monday, and I make no doubt the prudence of our Lord Lieutenant will be such as will (as far as is possible) prevent like mischeifs from happening.

200. *Alan I, Dublin, to Thomas, at his lodgings in Whitehall, 10 Nov. 1713*

(1248/3/133–4)

My sister sent me by last post the letter which Mr Sm[*edle*]y[1514] wrote to you to Newmarkett; and the pacquett before I had one directly from him to the same purpose, of the same date with that to you. I thought him a man of more judgement then to take up uncertain coffee house rumors for truth: especially when the subject matter is so altogether improbable in its nature as that which he hints att. This I am sensible you were convinced of before, and probably the discourse ariseth from the persons my sister means, to create jealousies between freinds, but that will take no place: in the mean time take this for a certain truth, that our Lord Lieutenant did publickly at the Castle last Sunday declare that he had it in commands from the Queen to recommend Sir Richard Levinge for Speaker.[1515] That persons who know the inclinations of the Court have used means with their freinds to bring the choice to devolve on the person desired is I beelive practiced very often; but whether it hath gone soe far as to name a person by the Queens order I cannot tell; but doe not remember it in practice before this time. I should think the Station and personal merit of Mr Attorney might goe a great way, especially if backed by the assistance of those who might have known the views of the Court tho so publick a declaration had not been made; but after such a declaration what can withstand his pretensions; unlesse people should beleive this a new thing and be averse to making a precedent. Several Gentlemen told me they had their eye on me, and I passed my word long since to them that I would serve in the best maner I could if the choice fell on me: What turn the affair will now take I cannot tell: but in this I am determined, not to doe any thing that shal give any Gentleman reason to say I have broke my word with him. It would be vain in me to think there needed all the weight of such recommendations to be put into Sir Richard Levinges scale if I only were to be weighed in the other: but it seems to me that whatever competitor he is apprehensive of, he doth him great honour not entirely to depend on his own personal qualifications. I fear my Lord Lieutenant doth not find soe much ease in the Governement as he expected and I wish him: this is but my conjecture; yet I cannot but think he hath difficultyes which he did

[1512]The King's Hospital, or Blue-Coat School. The tories' preferred place of polling (*A Long History of a Certain Session*, 39).

[1513]1688.

[1514]Jonathan Smedley (1671–1729), rector of Rincurran, Co. Cork, and later dean of Clogher.

[1515]Shrewsbury's private secretary, Charles Delafaye, noted that soon after arriving in Dublin the lord lieutenant 'took care to have it signified the q[*ueen*] recommended Sir R. Levinge for Speaker' (BL, Add. MS 61637B, f. 3: Delafaye's diary, 1713–14).

not expect to meet, especially from that quarter whence they seem to come. The matter of the Lord Mayor is not at all settled,[1516] tho I hear all people I converse with own that he hath done a great deal toward it; but I hear no one will please other people but one of the three. Time will shew the truth of these matters; in the mean while the confusion we are in is very great, and so is the resentment of people toward one another: God knows when or where these fewds will end. In time the whole proceedings of the City election[1517] will be more fully understood, then they yet seem to be by some. The Irish[1518] laugh in their sleeves, but are pretty busy in making part of Fownes and Tuckers Cavalcades.

201. *Alan I, Dublin, to Thomas, 26 Nov. 1713*

(1248/3/135)

I have been silent of late to you partly on account of your being out of town, and partly for want of being able to tell you any thing with certainty: but the cheif cause hath been that my time hath been so employed in the matter of the chair that I have not had a moment to spare, being taken up endeavouring to countermine those who left no means unattempted to prevent me of the honour of the chair. We were to have mett on Fryday last, but we were prorogued by proclamation on Thursday to the five and twentieth:[1519] We say here this was done as well by the approbation or desire of the Whigs as Toryes, but what foundation that hath I am yet to learn: nor can I tell what effect or influence that prorogation might have on the election of a Speaker; for in fowre or five dayes time, so many persons as sollicited that matter might have great oportunityes of making impressions, and very probably made use of their time. This I am sure of, that if we did not much miscompute on this day sennight, several Gentlemen altered their minds between that time and yesterday; when the house proceeded to the choice of a Speaker. Sir John Standley was first up in the Clerks eye and proposed Sir Richard Levinge as a person every way qualifyed etc but did not mention his being recommended by or acceptable to the Crown as is groundlessely reported here:[1520] his mocion was seconded: Mr Conelye proposed me, and soon after the house fell into a loud repetition of our several names as every man stood affected: but without violence or great warmth;[1521] both sides agreeing it should be decided by a question to be put first on

[1516]The dispute over elections to the Dublin lord mayoralty had continued into 1713. After the aldermen had again chosen a whig for 1713–14, and the privy council had disapproved the election, the incumbent lord mayor, Cooke, whose duty it was to nominate three candidates from among whom the aldermen made their choice, put forward an all-tory slate. A majority of aldermen (17 in all) refused to accept this nomination and proceeded to make an election of their own, without Cooke, which was also disapproved. Neither side would back down, and the stalemate remained unresolved when the Irish parliament met, despite Shrewsbury's best efforts. (*CJI*, iii, 731–8; Hayton, *Ruling Ireland*, 165, 170–1.)

[1517]The parliamentary election for Dublin city.

[1518]Catholics.

[1519]By a proclamation issued by the lord lieutenant on 19 Nov., the day before the session had been scheduled to begin (*LJI*, ii, 418).

[1520]Sir John Perceval reported that Stanley 'acquainted us that his grace had been pleased to direct the choice of a speaker, and therefore he offered Sir Richard Levinge … as a very well qualified person to fill the chair' (*Perceval Diary*, 125).

[1521]Confirmed in *Perceval Diary*, 125.

Sir Richard Levinge: some time was taken to clear the galleryes.[1522] Mr Anderson Sanders was appointed teller for the yeas, Mr John Moore for the noes. They reported the Yeas to be 127 and the Noes 131.[1523] Thus he had the mortificacion to have a negative putt upon him after such a recommendation as seemed to me to be very new in this Kingdome, and the greatest sollicitation imaginable by people of almost every sort and condition. The question then was putt on me, and some negatives were given to it; but it was not found advisable to divide the house, soe I was putt into the chair, being led up by Mr Molesworth and Lord Brabazon.[1524] Great endeavours (I hear) were used to prevent my being approved, and several of great figure and Station sollicited the matter if my intelligence be good; in so much that my Lord Lieutenant (being very ill) could not admit of being seen after eight last night:[1525] and this day I was approved. I send you the Lord Lieutenants speech to the houses and what I said to his Grace when the house presented me as their Speaker on the back of this letter.[1526]

[1522]Confirmed in *Perceval Diary*, 125; omitted in *CJI*.

[1523]Confirmed in *CJI*, iii, 689.

[1524]Chaworth Brabazon, 1st s. of the 5th earl of Meath, and styled Lord Brabazon.

[1525]Shrewsbury's condition had worsened sufficiently by 10 Dec. for his physicians to recommend that he leave Dublin for the healthier air of the viceregal lodge at Chapelizod (TCD, MS 2021, p. 34: Sir John Stanley to Ld Bolingbroke, 10 Dec. 1713), where he remained for much of the remainder of the parliamentary session (NAI, M 3036, f. 84: Anderson Saunders to Edward Southwell, 19 Dec.1713).

[1526]Overleaf is written:

The Lord Lieutenants Speech

My Lords and Gentlemen

Her Majestye having by Gods blessing upon her pious endeavours procured a safe and honourable peace, has nothing now to wish but that her subjects may enjoy the benefits and advantages of it.

For this purpose she has called you together that you may consider of and provide such Laws as you shal judge necessary, for the farther securitye of the Church of Ireland as by Law established and the advancement of the trade and welfare of this Kingdome.

Her Majesty has nothing more at heart then the preservation of the rights and liberties of her people; and the settling them upon a lasting foundation by securing the Protestant Succession in the house of Hanover.

Gentlemen of the house of Commons

By the several estimates and accounts which I have directed to be laid before you by the proper Officers you will see what supplyes are wanting to support the civil establishment and maintain a sufficient number of forces for your securitye against any danger that may be apprehended from the great number of Papists in this country.

Her Majestye does not doubt of your contributing chearfully such summes as may be effectual to answer these purposes; and has commanded me to assure you that there shal be no misapplication of them, and that what you grant shal (as much as possible) be spent among yourselves. To this end she has ordered the two regiments of foote which being upon the Irish establishment are yet in Great Britain to be sent over as soon as thier accounts can be made up and their English arrears satisfied.

The money given last Sessions to rebuild the publick Offices destroyed by fire has been applyed to that service as far as could be done in soe little a time; and I will take care that those buildings shal be finisht with all convenient speed. As the several additional dutyes will expire att Christmas, her Majestye (to prevent their lapsing) has sent over a bill to be offered to your consideration, to continue them for three months whereby you will stil have an oportunitye farther to provide for the credit of her Governement and your own safety by such wayes and means as you shal think proper. My Lords and Gentlemen, I am very sensible of the great honor her Majesty has done me in placing me in so eminent a Station, and of my own inability sufficiently to discharge so great a trust. But this I will beg leave to assure you that no one endeavoured it with more zeal for her Majestyes service and for your interest (which I take to be inseparable) then I am firmly resolved to do. I must therefore earnestly recommend it to you that as the Protestants in this Kingdom are united in one common interest you may all agree in the same means of promoting it, and shew by a dutifull comportment toward her Majesty and by laying all aside all warmth and resentment that every one of you is equally concerned for her Majestyes service and the good of this Kingdome. This will appear by the unanimity of your proceedings and you may depend upon it that I shal make a faithful representation of them [*remainder missing*].

202. *Alan I, Dublin, to Thomas, at his lodgings in Whitehall, 1 Dec. 1713*

(1248/3/136–7)

Tho what hath passed hitherto is hardly worth your notice, yet since you desire it, I who ought to deny you nothing, resolve as leisure will allow to transmit some account of the proceedings in our house. Mine of Thursday gave you some light into the maner used to bring Sir R[*ichard*] L[*evinge*] into the chair, and the event of that affair. On the eight and twentieth I gave my sister to understood that we had voted an addresse to her Majesty (with the words of the vote) and another to the Lord Lieutenant. Sir John Standley was chosen chairman of the committee for drawing the addresse to her Majesty, and Sir John Percival for that to my Lord Lieutenant. Yesterday they were both reported, and for your better information I have sent you a Copy of each addresse, as drawn in, and agreed to, by the Committees; and another of the addresses, as they were agreed to by the house.[1527] By comparing them you will easily see the temper of the house, when the amendments were proposed: and how cautious we were not to give any engagement to be entirely guided by any sentiments but our own. Indeed hardly any body relished that high complement in the later end of the addresse to the Duke, tho every body spoke with great respect toward him: but the strain was thought a little of the highest. I make no doubt but that Criticks will easily observe some inaccuracy in wording the clause that is added after the first paragraph of the addresse to the Queen: and the repetition of the mention of the house of Hanover.[1528] I am sure I did tho no Critick: but the Gentleman who brought in the clause in the house had hardly time enough to word it well, soe as to make it come aptly in; and people were resolved to passe it as it is, rather then recommit the addresse for reasons you will not be long to seek. They thought the addresse as drawn was very full in giving the terms of safe and honourable to the peace, and were willing to expresse some of those things which made them goe into that matter, beleiving the peace not more safe or honourable on any other account then that by it the Hanover succession is acknowledged, and such care taken as is taken to disappoint the hopes of the Pretender: and therefore were desirous to mention those things as instances for which they thought they might goe into the addresse of congratulation for a safe and honourable peace. This I beleive was the sense of several Gentlemen. That paragraph, and the following relating to her Majestyes care to have the Pretender removed etc was offered by Will Caulfeild, who had it in his hand ready written:[1529] whether he drew it in the house or that it was concerted before I must leave you to guesse: but I am apt to beleive it was ready prepared out of an apprehension the house might not have the patience to wait for the penning a thing of that length, but might be inclined to recommit the addresse. And if this was the case, you will easily account for

Shrewsbury's speech is printed in *LJI*, ii, 421–2; *CJI*, iii, 690–1.

[1527] Confirmed in *CJI*, iii, 691, 695–6.

[1528] The addition ran as follows: 'We humbly beg leave to express the deep sense we have of all your Majesty's graces and favour to this kingdom, in preserving to your people their religious and civil rights, and in the care you have taken to transmit those blessings to posterity by securing the Protestant succession in the house of Hanover.' (*CJI*, iii, 695).

[1529] Confirmed, as are other details in this letter, in NLI, MS 50545/2/18: Henry Rose to David Crosbie, 2 Dec. 1713.

the connexion not being soe just as otherwise it might have been. A relation of yours[1530] brought in that addition to the addresse to the Lord Lieutenant of his being in an eminent maner instrumental in bringing about the glorious revolution in 1688 to which under God we owe the preservation of our religion, libertyes and propertyes, in defence of which we are resolved to venture all that is most dear to us. On his proposing this addition Mr Dopping stood up and said, since we were drawing his Graces character we ought to make it compleat and proposed the addition of the following remarkable words, and hath since shewn as sincere a concern for the interests of the Church and Prerogatives of the Crown as he did then, for the liberty of the subject. The Gentleman who proposed the former amendment of his Graces appearing in the revolution stood up and said he apprehended (tho it was not so meant by him that proposed it) that those words strongly implyed what was done by his Grace in the part he had in the revolution in 1688 did not shew as sincere a regard for the interests of the Church as what he had done since, the contrary of which he apprehended to be true; and that the Church as well as state was saved by that revolution. Mr Dopping disowned any such view, and the clause was afterward worded by the chair as you have it entire in the addresse agreed to. And now I hope all people are pleased; we have called the peace safe and honourable, we have shewn our satisfaction in what hath been done to secure the succession in the house of Hanover and to disappoint the hopes of the pretender, and the true value we retain for the revolution in eighty eight: We have told two great truths, that there is a vast number who have hopes to defeat that succession and that we will venture our lives in the support of it. You can not but observe the soft term used in the addresse to the Duke, which mentions the Irish[1531] to be the greater number, and indeed we shal be alway cautious of letting it obtain, that tho they are more then we, yet that the disproportion is not very considerable. I cannot beleive any thing of that kind was intended to be insinuated by the framer of the addresse; but the words were capable of such an exposition, and I know it is very industriously insinuated that the Papists are fewer in number, and the dissenters more then we have hitherto apprehended: the meaning of this and who cultivate this notion is no difficult task to discover. Tho I date this letter as wrote on Tuesday, it is indeed written on Monday night, altho the pacquet goes not off till to morrow in the evening; but perhaps I may not then have leisure to write at large as I now doe: but I hope to be able by a postscript to tell you that the Recorder hath carryed the chair of elections against Mr Anderson Sanders, on the successe of which almost as great stresse is layd as was on the chair of the house: they made indeed the struggle there not to be between me and Sir R[*ichard*] L[*evinge*] but (to create envy) between —— and me: and now they say that the re[corder] is endeavoured to be put in in opposition to my Lord Chancel[lor]. But the truth I beleive is, there are some very ticklish elections like to come before the Committee, and it may be of consequence to have so able and deserving a man in the chair as Mr Sanders. The Lords I hear have taken notice of the people that delight in war, but whether they have mentioned the Pretender I cannot hear, nor have I been able to gett a sight of their addresse.[1532] As far as I am able to form a judgement of the

[1530]St John III (NLI, MS 50545/2/18: Henry Rose to David Crosbie, 2 Dec. 1713).

[1531]Catholics.

[1532]The Lords' address, agreed on 27 Nov. 1713, thanked the queen for concluding a peace 'notwithstanding the artifices used to prevent it, by those who delight in war'. There was no specific reference to the Pretender, though the Hanoverian succession received mention (*LJI*, ii, 424).

event of things I apprehend a great many Gentlemen are desirous to doe some good, and a great many to prevent any harm being done: soe that I hope if we doe no good we shal doe no harm. The matter of the City and of Dudley Moore stands just as it did for ought I can hear. You know I (being Speaker) doe not care to inform myself of matters before they come into the house: but they whisper that after voting a supply (which will be now very soon, our freinds intending to morrow to move to take my Lord Lieutenants speech into consideration) something will be done in relation to the pressures some Gentlemen think the countrey lyes under, either in a Committee of the whole house to take into consideration the state of the Nation or some other way: but this is only slight hearsay and not to be depended upon … Be cautious of shewing this hasty account of things, and the rather considering from whom it comes …

[*PS*]

Tuesday night

I can now tell you the Recorder carryed the chair of elections 127 against 121.[1533]

203. *Alan I, Dublin, to Thomas, 9 Dec. 1713*

(1248/3/138–9)

I know you are soe good to call often att Bond Street, and therefore conclude whatever I write to either of my sisters is as much within your notice, as if my letters were addressed directly to you; and you know that my time will hardly allow me to write to either of you as often as I ought, and am inclined to doe; so that you will be content with the summary accounts of our proceedings which I am able to send to any of you. Last night the Committee of elections sate, and had before them the double return for the borough of Maryborough: He that was the true burgomaster returned Mr Robert Pigott, son of Mr Pigott of Disert,[1534] my sisters near relacion; and one Mr William Wall: Mr St Leger Gilbert who is a member of our house and took on himself to be Burgomaster[1535] returned Mr Garrett Bourke (one of her Majestyes Councell at Law a new convert)[1536] and Mr Dodsworth a collector of the revenue:[1537] the Sherif affixed both indentures to the writ, so all fowre voted for the Speaker, the two former for me, the two later for Sir Richard Levinge. The Committee sate till six this morning, and at length came to a resolution

[1533]Figures confirmed in an anonymous report to the secretary's office in Whitehall, 1 Dec. 1713 (TNA, SP 63/369/15), and *Perceval Diary*, 128.

[1534]Thomas Pigott (*d.* 1702), of Dysart, Queen's Co.

[1535]The original election for burgomaster, on 29 Sept., had been disputed: Gilbert claimed that he was the rightful burgomaster even though William Wall was declared elected. Wall subsequently resigned the office to George Boyd, in order to stand at the parliamentary election, at which Boyd attempted to preside. Although Gilbert did not possess the burgomaster's mace, he appeared alongside Boyd, carrying a 'rod' of some kind, carried out his own election at the same time as Boyd, and made his own return (*CJI*, iii, 968–72). Gilbert, one of the commissioners of appeals in the revenue, was described by a pro-government source after the Hanoverian succession as 'a tory and corrupt in his office' (BL, Add. MS 61637C, ff. 12–13: list of the civil establishment [I] [1714/15]).

[1536]Garrett Bourke (c.1681–1740), of Dysert, Co. Galway (*Hist. Ir. Parl.*, iii, 226).

[1537]Edward Dodsworth (bef.1691–1730), of Maryborough, Queen's Co., collector of customs and excise at Maryborough (*Hist. Ir. Parl.*, iv, 69–70).

that Pigott and Wall were duly elected and duly returned; and the report is to be made to the house to morrow at one of the clock, when I think the house will agree with the Committee:[1538] tho I beleive by the mighty industry used for Bourke and Dodsworth in the Committee endeavours will be used to gett the house to disagree with the Committee, but if I can make any judgement, it will be in vain; considering the clearnesse of the case and the complexion of the house. This day was in a great measure taken up in hearing the case of Brigadier Francis Gore and Mr David Bindon[1539] at the bar of the house on a double return;[1540] it held till six in the evening, when Mr Gore was voted duly elected and returned and the Indenture which returned Bindon was ordered to be taken off from the writ to which it was affixed. Both of these Gentlemen voted for me, but I beleive Mr Gore is as good a man at least as his competitor, who tho a well meaning man is very much under the direction of a great man in the County of Clare, and hath too great a deference (some people think) to a son of his that is fellow of the Colledge.[1541] The truth is, there was nothing in the case. Young Mr Bindon the Provost of Ennis, son of Mr David Bindon,[1542] was taken into custody for misbehavior in the election and return. I own I could have wished Mr Upton[1543] had not moved it, but when it was moved, tho the previous question was put not to put that question then, and tho a great many good natured men were against putting the question then, yet it could not be stemmed; and the question was ordered to be put, 82 against 73:[1544] And when it was put there were not five negatives to his being taken into custody. So much I write on Wednesday. Thus the house is beginning to redresse the injuryes done by returning officers, and I think will not stop till they have done right to those who have been injuriously treated; yet I doe assure you they seem to me to act with strict regard to the right, without considering the inclinations of those who are petitioners or sitting members. We have not the same uneasinesse as I think would have been if things had gone in another maner then hitherto they have done.

[*12 Dec. 1713*] I begin this part of my paper on Saturday morning, no pacquet gone off on Thursday night: that day we being informed that several regulars and preists transported had returned into Ireland, contrary to the Statute which makes such returning high treason,[1545] and tho in gaol at Galwey could not be tryed; there being not Protestant freeholders in the County of that town sufficient to make a Jury allowing the prisoners their peremptory challenges, and the Papists never finding them guilty on the fullest evidence, ordered heads of a bill to enable Protestant freeholders [of] the County of Galwey to be Jurors in criminal

[1538]The House agreed without a division (*CJI*, iii, 972).

[1539]David Bindon (c.1650–1733), of Cloney, Co. Clare, returned as MP [I] for Ennis in 1715.

[1540]Ostensibly, the decision that this case should be heard at the Bar of the House was because of the 'extraordinary irregularities committed', but according to Sir John Perceval the real reasons were, first, to set a precedent of hearing cases in this way in order to enable John Forster to stand for the chair of the committee of privileges and elections, which otherwise he would have been prevented from doing by the existence of a petition against his own return; and second, because the whigs, 'thinking themselves a majority at this time, were willing that causes for elections should be tried in the whole house, where they were secure of their numbers, whereas committees for elections might frequently be ill attended' (*Perceval Diary*, 127).

[1541]Thomas Bindon (c.1685–1740), fellow of TCD and later dean of Limerick (*Al. Dub.*, 66).

[1542]Samuel Bindon (1680–1760), 1st s. of David Bindon, and elected MP [I] for Ennis with his father in 1715.

[1543]Either Clotworthy or Thomas Upton.

[1544]Not recorded in *CJI*.

[1545]The Bishops' Banishment Act of 1697 (9 Will., c. 1 [I]).

causes in the County of the town of Galwey. And being informed one Jacob Twisleton who went into France during the late wars and was a menial servant of the Pretenders in France was returned into this Kingdome,[1546] appeared in publick, gave out tickets in October last of performing a part in a musick meeting at the Inns[1547] (as the paper imported by order of the late Lords Justices) of which Mr Dawson[1548] had notice from Colonel Southwel,[1549] yet the man was not apprehended but remained stil in town; we ordered our Serjeant at arms to seise and secure him,[1550] which he did tho Dawson could not, who very narrowly after shedding some tears and very humble and moving intercession in his behalf escaped a severe vote of acting unfaithfully in his office of Secretary to the Lords Justices.[1551] These and other matters arising in the debate occasioned a mocion to bring in heads of a bill to attaint the Pretender and all subjects of this Kingdome his adherents, which was ordered accordingly.[1552] We were informed several had petitioned for licence to return out of France, and that their peticions were referred; and ordered a Committee to prepare an addresse that her Majestye would not grant such licences.[1553] Indeed everybody thought them of the last consequence.

The house sate till eight at night, yet would not adjourn the Committee of elections, tho a question was put for it: the house divided 149 against ninety five:[1554] the Committee voted Mr Dickson[1555] the petitioner duly elected for Randalstowne, and that Jones[1556] and Warren[1557] two whom the seneschal returned to have equal voices not to be duly elected or returned. The borough belongs in some measure to Charles O'Neile[1558] who was unanimously chosen and he would needs have another of his naming: but 45 of 52

[1546] Twisleton, formerly one of the state-trumpeters employed at Dublin Castle, had left Ireland in about 1707 to enter the service of the Pretender. His return in Sept. was in violation of the Irish act of 1697 (9 Will. III, c.5) 'to hinder the reversal of several outlawries and attainders …' (*Post Boy*, 17–19 Dec. 1713).

[1547] The King's Inns.

[1548] Joshua Dawson, the under-secretary, and MP [I].

[1549] William Southwell, MP [I]. Confirmed in BL, Add. MS 60583, ff 1–4: Dawson to Edward Southwell, 15 Dec. 1713. A warrant for Twisleton's arrest had been issued on 21 Oct. but he had not been taken up (*CJI*, iii, 966–7). It was Southwell who brought the issue to ther attention of the Commons (*Perceval Diary*, 130).

[1550] Confirmed in *CJI*, iii, 966–7. This time Twisleton was arrested (*CJI*, iii, 972).

[1551] Sir John Perceval reported a debate lasting some time 'whether there should not a vote pass upon Mr Dawson that he had not done his duty, and some were so fierce that they would have it run that he was a betrayer of his queen and country', but at last 'the debate dropped' (*Perceval Diary*, 131). The motion is not recorded in *CJI*. Dawson's account named Henry Maxwell as the proposer, Robert Molesworth as the seconder, and John Moore and George Macartney (MP Donegal) as speaking in favour, 'but the rest of the party, who are not so violent, were of another opinion'. He also believed that the whigs' original intention had been to use this incident as another means to attack Lord Chancellor Phipps, and that only when Dawson's own testimony exonerated Phipps did he himself become their prey. (BL, Add. MS 60583, ff 1–4: Dawson to Edward Southwell, 15 Dec. 1713.)

[1552] Confirmed in *CJI*, iii, 967–8: St John Brodrick was a member of the drafting committee.

[1553] According to *CJI*, iii, 967, this resolution preceded the order for heads of a bill to attaint the Pretender. St John was again a member of the committee appointed to prepare the address.

[1554] Division not recorded in *CJI* (because it took place in the committee).

[1555] Robert Dixon, MP [I].

[1556] Richard Jones, MP [I].

[1557] Westenra Waring (1677–aft.1716) (*Hist. Ir. Parl.*, vi, 502; Raymond Gillespie, *Early Belfast: The Origins and Growth of an Ulster Town to 1750* (Belfast, 2007), 151).

[1558] Charles O'Neill, MP [I]. A contemporary analysis of constituencies, prepared in advance of the 1713 election, confirmed that O'Neill 'has the interest' in the borough (BL, Add. MS 34777, f. 24).

electors were for Dickson; soe he, the Sherif, and one Felix O'Neile[1559] gott seven of the electors into a chamber with a dozen others who had nothing to doe in the borough, shut the door, indented for Charles O'Neile as chosen unanimously and Jones and Warren to have each 4 voices; thus they two gave their votes against my being chosen Speaker.[1560] At the hearing Warren waved his pretensions to Jones. The house ordered the Sherif and Seneschal into the custody of the Serjeant att arms: Mr O'Neile was sick in the countrey (some say of the same distemper of which my Lord Ikirryn[1561] labours) so he is ordered to attend in his place on 20 January, which possibly the right honourable may be sent home and discharged his attendance on the house, if the temper it now is of continues. We sate yesterday till eleven on the City election[1562] and heard all Tuckers and Fownes evidence; it appeared a sad affair of their own shewing; we go on it again this day and I think it will disclose a scene to the world of very dark and wicked proceedings.

We have ordered the report from the Committee of elections of the case of Randalstown to be printed[1563] and so we shal order this case heard at the bar (as I think) which will give a tast what methods were taken to pack a Parliament.

204. *Alan I, Dublin, to Thomas, at his lodgings in Whitehall, 19 Dec. 1713*

(1248/3/142–3)

The freinds of the Chancellor and Lord A[nglesey[1564]] were much imposed on by their emissaryes in the calculations they made of sure men (as they termed them) in this parliament, who in my opinion ought to be punished with utmost severitye the Law allows for false musters, considering the mischeifs their misrepresentations have occasioned.

The unexpected choice of a Speaker was in some measure attributed to a personal regard Gentlemen were supposed to have for one of the candidates beyond the other; and in my hearing after I was in the chair one who voted against me said that should be the single question which the Whigs should carry this Session. The several amendments made to the addresses as brought in by the chairmen of the Committees shewed the temper of the house not to be wholly conformable to what had been given assurance of: the proceedings on the hearing the City election (in which not only great men interested themselves but most of the privy Councel, all the Judges, Commissioners of revenue, Custom house officers and all other dependants on the Treasury or military list who had votes and would dispose them as directed, voted for Fownes and Tucker) were a farther confirmation that the house would not doe what was expected by those who have used to carry every thing before them beyond controul and with out possibilitye of resistance. This indeed alarmed our Great man,[1565] but when he found that his servant Hervey being accused as a principal

1559 Felix O'Neill of Neillsbrook, Co. Antrim (*Al. Dub.*, 639).

1560 That Jones and Waring both voted for Levinge in the election for the Speakership is confirmed in BL, Add. MS 34777, ff 90–1: 'List of votes for Sir R. Leving and A. Saunders'.

1561 Thomas Butler (1683–1719), 6th Lord Ikerrin.

1562 Confirmed in *Perceval Diary*, 131.

1563 Confirmed in *CJI*, iii, 708.

1564 Name completed in text in a different hand. Arthur Annesley, 7th earl of Anglesey.

1565 Phipps.

actor in pulling down the stage at the Tholsel to prevent the election there was proceeded against, and that on a division whether Hervey should in the question be named his servant, it was carryed on a question in an adjourned debate that the words should stand part of the question, he as well as his freinds were much agast. It is true, the division was a very near one, 122 against 120:[1566] But we plainly saw by that division that when matters of importance were shewn and proved to the house against the Great man (which we knew we were able to doe to a demonstration) he never could make so many freinds as to skreen him in a matter of that nature, who had not interest enough to keep his name out of a vote where there was no necessitye of inserting it: and it was resolved to loose no time. He on the other side with his freinds took all necessary precautions: On some pretence of scurrilous words spoken against him by one Nuttal (as I hear) the Lords have either in a vote, or by an addresse given him a very high character on Thursday last:[1567] We were under an absolute necessity of having the books of the Tholsel before us to make out some proceedings which we thought very extraordinary in the election of magistrates for this City, and immediately sent for them and had them brought before us; and I hear the Lords made an order the same day to have them laid before them, but whether their Lordships or our order were first made I did not much enquire, but we are in possession of them.[1568] The books of the Privy Councel would also have been of great service to us in the proceedings of yesterday, but the Lords had sent for them and gotten them into their possession.[1569] This put us under great streights however it was found advisable to proceed without delay even without the councel books, which probably the Lords might have occasion for too long for us to delay our enquiry. The order of the day was to take into consideration the Case of the City of Dublin, and the whole army was drawn up on both sides; but I think my Lord Chancellor's back freinds[1570] thought it would be more advisable to come at him another way, by bringing in two reports from the same committee one about the remisse prosecution of Edward Loyde for a treasonable and seditious libel,[1571] the other about the violent prosecution and unusual methods taken against Dudley Moore Senny was chairman

[1566] Division not recorded in *CJI* but figures confirmed in *Perceval Diary*, 133.

[1567] On 18 Dec. 1713 the Lords examined Joseph Cooper and his wife concerning words spoken in their presence in Aug. of that year by Richard Nuttall (*d.* c.1740) a Dublin attorney and exchequer official (who was to be rewarded for his party zeal by appointment in Dec. 1714 as solicitor to the Irish revenue commissioners). Nuttall, it was alleged, had called Lord Chancellor Phipps 'a canary bird, a villain … [*who*] had set this kingdom together by the ears and ought to be hanged'. After passing a resolution that these words were 'false, scandalous and malicious, tending to stir up sedition and highly reflecting on the government', and ordering the attorney-general to prosecute Nuttall, the House moved on to vote an address supporting the chancellor. (*LJI*, ii, 436–8; R.W. Smith, 'The Nuttalls of County Kildare', *Journal of the County Kildare Archaeological Society*, viii (1915–17), 181; *CTB*, xxix, 190; A.M. Taylor, 'Swift's Use of the Term "Canary Bird"', *Modern Language Notes*, lxxi (1956), 175–7).

[1568] On 16 Dec. the Commons ordered the town clerk of Dublin to bring in papers relevant to their inquiry into the proceedings over the Dublin lord mayoralty, which were delivered later that afternoon (*CJI*, iii, 713–14). The Lords made a similar order on the same day that produced no response (*LJI*, ii, 434–5).

[1569] The Lords had made their request for materials from the privy council office on the 17th (*LJI*, ii, 434–5), while the Commons waited two more days before sending a delegation to the lord lieutenant for the same purpose (*CJI*, iii, 723).

[1570] Pretended or false friends (*OED*).

[1571] In Sept. 1712 Edward Lloyd, the Dublin bookseller, had published proposals for a reprinting the *Abridgment of the Life of James II* from a London edition. His books and papers were seized and a prosecution was begun for treasonable libel, whereupon he fled to England and petitioned the lord lieutenant for mercy. When the petition was endorsed by the lords justices, Phipps and Archbishop Vesey, together with nine other privy councillors,

of both Committees, our time had been so taken up with the elections of Maryborough and Randalstown and the City of Dublin that we had hardly time to take necessary rest or refreshment, so the reports were not in readinesse yesterday morning. Our late sitting the night before on the election of Belfast (in which the house out of complement to a Lady kept a bad member and refused a good one duly elected I think[1572]) made me not come to the house till after twelve; prayers were soon called for and then I was called to the chair; and none of one side calling for the order of the day, I was interrupted in reading my postletters by a loud cry for the order of the day. The order was read and nothing said on it, and it was looked on that it would have gone over to a far day; but Mr Conelye hapned to move a matter, which might have been decided in two minutes, but held two hours; the truth is neither side was in hast; one was for giving time to Senny to finish the report, the other to gett the order of the City businesse passed over: I was complaisant and let them debate much at large. At length Senny came in and soon after Conelyes question came to a decision. He was ordered to make his report,[1573] and tho in hast had drawn it up very accurately, and we immediately entring on it we were moved to adjourn and dine and to sit in the afternoon and did soe;[1574] as I will the writing any more of this letter till I drink my tea. He[1575] was charged by the report among other lesse matters of recommending Loyde who was indicted for having the book called the memoires of the Chevalier de St George in his custody and publishing an advertisement to induce subscriptions in order to print it; the book was voted a seditious and treasonable libel: it appeared Lord Chancellor (but indeed it was with the Archbishop of Tuam) had recommended Loyde to Lord Ormond as a person having no ill design in that, and an object of the Queens mercy: it appeared by the testimony of three Alderman he had summoned the Aldermen before the Councel, and there told them that Dudley Moore (who was to be tryed soon after, and probably some of them would be on the Jury) was guilty of a riot, that the prologue was seditious etc we voted that in the first he had acted contrary to his duty and the Protestant interest; and on the second that for a Cheif Governor to prejudice etc was of dangerous consequence etc and voted addresse to the Queen to remove him for the safety and peace of her Protestant subjects and this afternoon agreed on an addresse to that purpose.[1576] I can not hold up

1571 *(continued)* Ormond stopped the prosecution. (Robert Munter, *The History of the Irish Newspaper, 1685–1760* (Cambridge, 1967), 126–9; Hayton, *Ruling Ireland*, 163; Pollard, *Dublin Book Trade*, 368).

1572 The tory Anthony Atkinson retained his seat against a petition by James Stevenson, who had also been returned for Killyleagh. The 'lady' in question was Catherine (*d.* 1743), née Forbes, the dowager countess of Donegall, who was currently managing her family's estates and electoral interest during the minority of her son, the 4th earl, and was described by one contemporary as both rich and a violent tory (BL, Add. MS 38157, f. 34: Sir Richard Cox to Edward Southwell, 17 Dec. 1713; BL, Add. MS 61637D, ff. 4–5: list of pensions on the civil establishment, [1714/15]; Hayton, *Ruling Ireland*, 197–8).

1573 The motion resulted in a resolution that chief magistrates of corporations should not vote in parliamentary elections other than to give a casting vote in the event of a tie, unless specifically sanctioned by the terms of a borough charter or, in the case of boroughs by prescription, by customary usage, 'time out of mind'. The *Journals* do not record the name of the proposer. (*CJI*, iii, 716). According to Sir John Perceval, this debate occupied the morning. St John Brodrick then made his report at 12 noon (*Perceval Diary*, 134).

1574 The House adjourned until 4 p.m. and then resumed debate on the report (*CJI*, iii, 721).

1575 Phipps.

1576 The address was voted on 18 Dec. and its preparation entrusted to a committee, after a debate lasting until at least 2 a.m. The following day William Conolly reported from the committee and the address was agreed. (*CJI*, iii, 721, 723; *Perceval Diary*, 134–6, 140–3.)

my head longer, soe must give off. If they come time enough from the Clerk Jack See will send you the resolves.

205. *Alan I to Thomas, at his lodgings in Whitehall, 22 Dec. 1713*

(1248/3/144–5)

I cannot write more then three lines; we sitt morning and afternoon: the above is the greatest part of our mornings work. I would send you over what I said at carrying up the money bill (I mean for a quarter of a years additional dutyes)[1577] if I had leisure to transcribe it and thought it worth reading; nothing gives me soe good thoughts of it as being told the Toryes and particularly Lord A[*nglesey*] is much nettled at it.[1578] The above votes are to be carryed by the whole house (I mean all but the last two) to my Lord Lieutenant to be transmitted and laid before the Queen.[1579] This afternoon we sate till ten hearing a cause on the petition of Sir George St George[1580] against James Donelan (Lord Straffords brother in Law)[1581] for the County of Roscommon: we turned out the Tory and voted in jolly Sir George, and tomorrow he makes his election for the County of Roscommon to make room for a good man att Carrick.[1582]

Our Toryes threatned us with prorogation or dissolution this morning; but when the assent was given to the money bill, we went down to our own house again to finish what was unfinished of our affairs before Christmas …

206. *Alan I, Dublin, to Thomas, at his lodgings in Whitehall, 24 Dec. 1713*

(1248/3/146)

The inclosed came from the presse since I sent my other letter of this dayes date to the post office; nor doe I think it worth postage, if you paid any: but my saying what I have said, and printing it by the order of the house will let the world see some of the proceedings in

[1577] An emergency supply bill prepared by the Irish privy council in advance of the session, and intended solely to prevent the additional duties from lapsing during the course of the session. It passed the Commons and was sent to the Lords on 19 Dec., receiving the royal assent on the 22nd. (ILD; McGrath, *Connstitution*, 267–8, 270, 274–5.)

[1578] Delivered on 22 Dec. and printed in *CJI*, iii, 729–30.

[1579] The letter begins with a copy of resolutions of house of commons, 22 Dec. 1713, that there 'has been a design … to subvert the constitution and alter the government of the city of Dublin'; that while Sir Constantine Phipps, the chancellor, and Lieut. General Ingoldsby were lords justices there was an attempt to bribe the lord mayor, Ralph Gore, to nominate common councillors from a list submitted by Martin Tucker, sub-collector of the port of Dublin; that Phipps had been responsible for 'great disorder' by 'frequent disapprobation' of persons elected as mayor and sheriffs of Dublin, unprecedented since 1672; that the council board had not the power to regulate city elections and the aldermen and mayor had the right to elect a new mayor.

[1580] Sir George St George, 2nd Bt., MP [I], and later 1st Baron St George.

[1581] James Donnellan of Cloghan, Co. Roscommon, a relation of Robert Rochfort, had married in 1704 Anne Wentworth, sister of Thomas Wentworth (1672–1739), 1st earl of Strafford (BL, Add. MS 31134, f. 24: Rochfort to Strafford, 31 Mar. 1704; 22228, f. 40: Lady Bellew to [Strafford], 12 Oct. 1713; *The Wentworth Papers, 1705–39*, ed. J.J. Cartwright (1883), 4, 16, 59, 386). The entry for Donnellan in *Hist. Ir. Parl.*, iv, 73–4, is incorrect.

[1582] Carrick-on-Shannon, where St George had also been returned.

order to have gott a good parliament: I am sensible we are not come at the bottom of the management, but have discovered more then was expected would have been laid open.

The Lords resolves on 23 Dec. 1713 are these.[1583]

(1) That it appears by the depositions of Alderman Ralph Gore that the Lord Chancellor did not by himself or any other person whatever directly or indirectly offer any summe of money to the said Alderman Ralph Gore when Lord Mayor to choose a common councel.

(2) That it appears by the depositions of Alderman R[*alph*] G[*ore*] that the Lord Chancellor did not send him the said Alderman R[*alph*] G[*ore*] any list or lists of common councel men to be chosen.

(3) That it appears by the depositions of Alderman R[*alph*] G[*ore*] that he had not any conversation with the Lord Chancellor or any person or persons deputed by him relating to that matter.

(4) That it appears to this house by the depositions of Martin Tucker that the Lord Chancellor did not by himself or any other either directly or indirectly speak to the said M[*artin*] T[*ucker*] to give any list or offer any summe of money to influence the election of a common councel when Alderman Gore served as Lord Mayor of the City of Dublin and that the Lord Chancellor had not any privity of any conversation the said M[*artin*] T[*ucker*] had with the said Alderman G[*ore*] on that subject.

You see how innocent a man the Chancellor is, and what pains are taken to vindicate him from any imputacion that faction, and malice may endeavour to load him with. But stil the money was offered, it is not likely it was to come out of a private pocket; nor could it out of the publick without the privity of the then Governement when it came to be paid. Mr Indgolsbye[1584] may be loaded, nay so may another brother Justice to protect Sir Con[*stantine'*]s innocence.[1585] I will get the deposicions of Alderman Gore; they must be strongly worded to warrant the above negative resolutions.

207. *Alan I, Dublin, to Thomas, at his lodgings in Whitehall, 24 Dec. 1713*[1586]

(1248/3/147–8)

Our house is now adjourned to Thursday 14 January:[1587] I think with a view that by that time they may see what effect this addresse will have; not that they have any great doubt of the event, notwithstanding the Lords and convocation not being able to find out any fault in his administration;[1588] if they had enquired where the C[*ommon*]s did they might

[1583] Confirmed in *LJI*, ii, 448. The Lords also agreed the same day (23 Dec.) to make a representation to the queen exculpating Phipps from the charges laid against him by the Commons (*LJI*, ii, 448).

[1584] Richard Ingoldsby, MP [I], lord justice [I] 1710–11 and 1711–12.

[1585] Archbishop John Vesey, lord justice [I] 1712–13.

[1586] Written upon a copy of 'The Humble Address' of the Commons to the queen requesting Phipps's removal from office, agreed on 19 Dec. (*CJI*, iii, 723–4).

[1587] The adjournment was ordered on 24 Dec. (*CJI*, iii, 743).

[1588] For the Lords' address in support of Phipps (18 Dec.), and representation to the queen (24 Dec.), see *LJI*, ii, 438, 447–9. For the joint address of both houses of convocation in favour of Phipps, see *Post Boy*, 26–9 Dec.1713;

have mett with a great many. This day the Committee to whom it was referred to draw an addresse of thanks to the Queen for her gracious answer to the addresse to her at the beginning of the Session did me the honour in some measure to follow my thoughts in what I spoke in the house of Lords on Tuesday when the money bill was presented. If the printer send me one of my speeches in time I will enclose it: I think in my last I sent you our resolves on the case of the City of Dublin.

When our freinds were going into the countrey they gave solemn assurances to one another to be in town as one man at the day to which the house adjourned, and to come up with a resolution that our ancestors used to bring … having greivances redressed when they gav[e] … [I] beleive none of the 136 will think of re … will be reinforced by six new men at nex[t meeting]. As inconsiderable as we are represented … done good things: We have shewn the weigh[t of the] nation is against the Pretender; that ne[ither] … of a Chancellor, nor the good opinion of … can skreen a man whom the Commons find … part prejudicial to the welfare of the N[ation] …[1589] [treat]ment the City of Dublin hath mett at the C[*ounci*]l, nor the severityes used to the Recorder and Aldermen, have prevented us from strictly examining the matter, and asserting the rights of the City, and doing justice to the characters of the Recorder and Aldermen who appeared in justification of the City Libertyes. The Recorder had from me by order the thanks of the house; and Alderman Gore a vote approving his integrity in refusing the £500 bribe offered him to pack a Common Council. The twenty Aldermen had also a vote of having acted with vertue and courage in defending the City Libertyes.[1590] The Lords have been very inquisitive after these matters, and have come to resolutions that Sir C[*onstantine*] P[*hipps*] knew nothing of the bribe offered etc[1591] but offered it was Tucker owned that, and said it was by General Indgolsbyes order (you know he is dead[1592]) Alderman Gore being since examined on oath before the Lords hath named the Archbishop of T[*uam*] as having spoken to him about settling the common Council I do not hear he goes farther as to him, much lesse charges him with knowing any thing of the bribe which Tucker offered some few dayes after … The Lords desired a conference yesterday for Molesworth saying of the Clergy (as they pretend) when the convocacion delivered their addresse yesterday That they who turned the world upside down are come hither also: This is the last profanacion of scripture;[1593] he is put

Patrick Delany, *A Vindication of the Convocation and the Lord Chancellor of Ireland* … (Dublin, 1714); *Lord Chancellor Phipps Vindicated* … (1714), [1].

[1589]Ellipses in this letter represent gaps in the MS.

[1590]The resolutions, voted on 23 Dec., are printed in *CJI*, iii, 739–40.

[1591]In their representation (*LJI*, ii, 447–9).

[1592]Ingoldsby died in January 1712.

[1593]Robert Molesworth, MP [I], made this comment – loud enough to be heard by a number of people in his vicinity – in Dublin Castle on 21 Dec., when representatives of convocation waited on Shrewsbury to present their loyal address. The following day Archbishop Vesey conveyed to the house of lords a letter of complaint from the prolocutor of the lower house of convocation, William Perceval, describing Molesworth's words as 'an intolerable profanation of the Holy Scriptures'. The Lords asked the Commons for a conference, which was promptly agreed. The committee appointed by the Commons to manage the conference included Molesworth himself, and St John Brodrick, who had earlier been one of the messengers sent to answer the Lords' request (*LJI*, ii, 441–3; *CJI*, iii, 1001–2; TNA, SP 63/369/123–4: Sir John Stanley to Lord Bolingbroke, 26 Dec. 1713). There was, however, no time for the conference to meet before the adjournment on 24 Dec. Molesworth's words were a direct quotation from Acts, 17: 6, where the Jews of Thessalonica applied them to St Paul.

into Toland[1594] and Asgils[1595] form etc.[1596] We shal consider of it at our next meeting. Pray what is the method[1597] when a commoner is charged with a breach of privilege of the upper house or of convocation.

We shal as much avoid quarreling with the Lords as possible, but will do nothing unfit. I hear Mr Haltridge is to be complained of for daring to appeal to the Lords of England against a decree of the Lords here:[1598] nay I am told I am to be roasted for behavior on the Bench, but I am innocent and am in no maner of pain; my freinds shal never blush for me.

208. *Alan I, Dublin, to Alan II, at Mrs Courthope's*[1599] *house in Bond Street, 26 Dec. 1713*

(1248/3/149–50)

Tho I love you very well, yet I cannot help almost envying you for the many advantages you have which I want: you broke up almost a fortnight since, I was forced to stay at school till late on Christmas Eve; you are in London, I must content my self with poor Ireland: you goe to bed and rise at regular hours, I have been kept fasting in the chair almost whole nights together; you may doe little wanton mischeivous tricks, and not be found much fault with: I am maligned for serving my countrey at the risque of my health and expence of my fortune: you are with your Aunts and sister, I am at a long distance from them and you. But I comfort my self with the thought that the time is near when I may hope to set my face toward your side the water.

I reckon you are as unsuspected a person to keep a correspondence worth being pryed into at the post Office as any body in Bond Street; for which reason and to prevent the charge of double postage I will write that to you which might otherwise be as well applyed elsewhere.

By the bent of the house of Commons I am perswaded nothing can carry another bill for granting the additional dutyes beyond the 25th of March but the removal of that person at whom the Commons have taken soe great, soe just offence: and I am confident my Lord Lieutenant is too wise a man not to be convinced of this truth beyond room for doubting, whatever representations others may have endeavoured to make in England of our being an easy pliant people, especially in giving money; but the miscomputation they have made of their freinds numbers and their interest in this house of commons shews their accounts

[1594]John Toland. He had been denounced in the Irish house of commons in 1697 for publishing *Christianity Not Mysterious*: The House had then ordered the book to be burned by the common hangman (*Oxf. DNB.*; *DIB*, ix, 397).

[1595]John Asgill (1659–1738), had been expelled from the Irish house of commons in 1703 after a pamphlet of his, arguing that true believers in Christ could be translated directly to Heaven without the necessity of dying first, had been voted 'wicked and blasphemous' by the Commons and ordered to be burned by the common hangman (*HC 1690–1715*, iii, 61–3; *Hist. Ir. Parl.*, iii, 111–12).

[1596]In their debate MPs had cited the cases of Toland and Asgill as precedents (TCD, MS 2021, pp. 67–8: Sir John Stanley to Lord Bolingbroke, 22 Dec. 1713).

[1597]In England.

[1598]John Haltridge, MP [I], together with his wife Grace, had appealed to the British house of lords in Feb. 1712 against an order made in the Irish court of exchequer in Nov. 1711 in the case of *Haltridge* v. *Sands* (HMC, *House of Lords MSS*, n.s., ix, 195).

[1599]Martha.

are not to be much depended upon. The Commons adjourned for three weeks with intent to see what answer their addresses and resolutions would meet: and I think he must be a madman that beleives any one of the men that voted against the Chancellor can think himself or the Kingdome in safety while he remains in his Station. If he be removed all things will be easy I think. If he be so far befreinded at Court, or it be thought necessary not to remove a minister, for fear of giving encouragement to like attempts hereafter, and for that reason it be determined to continue him, the natural consequence of those counsels must be the dissolution of this parliament and the calling another before 25th March. They are bold men who undertake to mend matters in a new one; there will indeed be alterations, but such as they who advise a dissolution will call for the worse. We have met to consder this matter, I mean a number of Gentlemen from the several parts of the Kingdome who very well know the several interests that can be made in Countyes and boroughs, and compute there will be at least twenty altered for what we think the better; and sure we are best able to know the power and interests in our respective countryes. All seem resolved to go into the measures which the majority of Gentlemen agree on, as to the persons who shal serve for Countyes and boroughs; and to make interest for them against their nearest neighbours or relations, if it be found the publick will be better served by others: this shews vertue and a sense we have how necessary it is for every one to exert himself, after such vile practices have been used to bring in people into this parliament to serve particular purposes. It is a melancholy case that in the boroughs where one of the noblest, as well as wealthiest and most English familyes hath interest,[1600] the weight is on the other side: there is one recommended who makes no scruple to tell his freinds he wishes he might act otherwise; but in every question of importance where the Court and countrey interest come in competition, he is a sure dead vote against the countrey. What reason is there that a man who by an employment at pleasure lies under the temptation of acting otherwise then perhaps he otherwise would, should be sollicitous to be chosen; or if he must be fond of a seat in the house, why should he be stil recommended after ten years proof how far he hath the interest of the countrey at heart, when his command may be supposed by him to be the sacrifice for going according to his judgement.[1601] His having been pitched on by a late Lord[1602] is no reason to continue him: Would that Lord if now living have continued his favor to him when he had seen the measures he took, and what regard he hath to the publick when his private interest comes in ballance? There is another person recommended of late for a town Eastward of Middleton;[1603] a more zealous T[*or*]y is not in the Kingdome, nor more warm in party, to my observation. Another recommended to another borough farther Eastward, tho disappointed there, hath sufficiently shewn in the house, and indeed every where, his regards to the interests of his countrey, and how much difference he makes between it and the orders of the revenue board.[1604] Is it not pretty odd

[1600] The Boyles, earls of Cork and Burlington.

[1601] Sir James Jeffreys, MP [I], an army general and governor of Cork: he had represented the Burlington borough of Lismore since 1703, and had the strong support of Juliana, dowager countess of Burlington, who was managing the family interest on behalf of her young son (NLI, MS13242: Joseph Waite to Richard Musgrave, [1711]; Barnard, 'Considering the Inconsiderable', 115).

[1602] Charles Boyle (1660–1704), 2nd earl of Burlington.

[1603] Youghal.

[1604] Brettridge Badham, collector of customs and excise for Youghal and Dungarvan and MP [I] for Charleville in 1713, had stood unsuccessfully in 1713 for the Boyle borough of Dungarvan, Co. Waterford (BL, Add. MS 34777,

too, that the son of a man must be chosen, who looks on himself bound to doe as he is directed at the peril of his easy seat.[1605] The secretary of the Person under whose direction these matters are at present is in the interest these people drive, and sollicites for them:[1606] and so I beleive doth a Lady that once lodged att Mrs Clerkes and often playes there. If the party concerned cannot be moved, another whose interest it will soon be should be spoken to; a line from him would put all things easy att L[ismore], Y[oughal] D[ungarvan] and T[allow]. [1607] There is indeed another place where the family once had an interest, but those whom that family have had great confidence in have destroyed it, and fixed one of their own:[1608] and if it be ever retreived, it must be done with great pains and will take up a good deal of time, and require prudent management. Your Aunt and Uncle know who is one of the persons intrusted by the will of the late Lord;[1609] if he would think it worth while to interpose it would be of vast consequence to settle these boroughs: which if once well done, would be enough to give a turn to a whole Session, if any ill thing should be attempted. If A[*rthur*] H[*yde*] could be promised to come in at L[*ismore*] which is entirely in the disposal of —[1610] and some good man at T[*allow*] in the room of the two I hinted at before,[1611] it would be of great importance, and this should be fixed in time. I think too that a neighbour of ours nearly related to the family might well be recommended in the stead of a late Gentleman at Y[*oughal*][1612] Desire your Uncle to stir in this matter. Mr Wallop[1613] also hath interest in the County of Wexford, which never fails to send members from its boroughs directly opposite to his principles. There remains a third thing, which for ought I know may be gone into, that is the scheme of striking off some pensions and half pay officers, and resting content with the hereditary revenue till people can be brought

1604 (*continued*) ff 42–4: analysis of election prospects, June 1713; NLI, MS 13242: Joseph Waite to Richard Musgrave and Thomas Baker, 9 Jan. 1713/14).

1605 Probably a reference to the election of James Barry, jr, at Dungarvan in 1713 on the Boyle interest (NLI, MS 13242: Digby Foulke to Richard Musgrave, 26 Dec. 1710). Barry (1689–1743), of Lisnegar, Co. Cork, was the eldest son and namesake of Alan's brother-in-law (by his first marriage), Colonel 'Jemmy' Barry, who had previously represented the borough, and had been returned for his own borough of Rathcormac in 1713. For 'Jemmy's' equivocal political loyalties, see above, p. 217.

1606 Joseph Waite, secretary to Lady Burlington.

1607 Identified in text in another hand. All boroughs controlled by the Boyle earls of Burlington.

1608 Bandon, which the Bernards of Castle Bernard now controlled. In 1713 Francis Bernard and his son Arthur were returned together. Arthur's father-in-law, who died in 1707, was Roger Power, an agent for the Burlington estates and himself MP [I] for Dungarvan. For the 2nd earl's difficult relationship with Power, who had grown rich in Burlington's employ, see Barnard, *A New Anatomy*, 220–1.

1609 In his will the 2nd earl of Burlington had appointed his wife as guardian to their son and heir, and had requested that she be advised in his education by the duke of Somerset, Lord Rochester, and Lord Somers (TNA, PROB 11/475, f. 331). Somers was presumably the person Alan had in mind.

1610 Lady Burlington.

1611 Richard Cox and William Maynard. While Cox was a strong tory, Maynard had been marked as a whig in a pre-sessional list of the 1713 parliament (BL Add. MS 34777, ff 46–7), and was not afterwards included in a list of those who had voted for Sir Richard Levinge as Speaker and for the tory Anderson Saunders to be chair of the committee of privileges and elections (BL Add. MS 34777, ff 90–1). Lady Burlington had recommended Cox to the Tallow voters in 1713 (TCD, MS 1180, p. 277: Sir Richard Cox to Edward Southwell, 22 Oct. 1713).

1612 Henry Boyle had been chosen MP [I] at a by-election for Midleton in 1707 but was returned for Kilmallock, Co. Limerick, in the 1713 parliament.

1613 John Wallop (1690–1762), of Farleigh Wallop, Hants, whig MP [GB] in 1715 and later 1st earl of Portsmouth (for whom see Sedgwick, *House of Commons 1715–1754*, ii, 507). His ancestor, the Elizabethan courtier Sir Henry Wallop, had been granted in 1585 the lands of the abbey and castle of Enniscorthy, Co. Wexford.

to what will be termed a better temper: but this I cannot think will take place; for beside that £80000 this year is a thing a Court will be unwilling to part with rather then Sir C[*onstantine*] P[*hipps*] it is well worth considering whether they will ever hereafter be able to gett a bill to passe for the same additional dutys which being now continued from time to time, will by being constantly continued become a thing of course and almost as good as an hereditary revenue. Wise men I say will consider this, and not let them fall in hopes of taking them up again at pleasure. But that which I think the most forcible argument used by some for a dissolution is, the certain expectation of our speaking English in respect to the Pretender and the Hanover succession before we part: and I must confesse I beleive we shal be very large in shewing the apprehensions we have of the P[*retender'*]s freinds making hasty steps to forward his interests and to weaken that of the house of H[*anover*]. This is a very long letter for so young a Politician as you: so I will close it with wishing you and all in Bond Street a merry Christmas, an happy new year, and a merry meeting with your friends …

209. *Alan I, Dublin, to Thomas, at his lodgings in Whitehall, 5 Jan. 1713[/14]*

(1248/3/151–2)

I received yours of 26 Dec. at Castlemartin, where I spent my Christmas, and should have been stil there but for a very suddain and unexpected summons by letter from Sir John Stanley dated 2 Jan. in which he intimated it to be my Lord Lieutenants desire that I should attend his Grace at seven that night if possible: Senny had a letter in the same terms.[1614] It was past two of clock before the messenger delivered the letters, however we galloped to town, and found Mr Conelye,[1615] Whitshed,[1616] Dean,[1617] Gore,[1618] Maxwel[1619] and the Recorder[1620] had the like summons; but my Lords indisposition made it impracticable to doe any thing that night. But we were appointed to be with him yesterday at six in the evening; I was one of the first that came, and found Lord Abercorne,[1621] Mr Dopping[1622] and Sir John Stanley there before me: When all the company was come his Grace after excusing his not seeing us the night before told us, he thought it would be easily beleived

[1614]Shrewsbury, having received on 2 Jan. the queen's order to prorogue the Irish parliament, consulted Phipps and Anglesey, who advised that he should 'send for some of the chief managers of the Commons that voted against lord chancellor, to acquaint them that Her Majesty being dissatisfied with their heats had ordered them to be prorogued, and to know whether they could give me any encouragement to hope they would come to such temper, as to induce Her Majesty to let them sit again to carry on her service and give the supply' (TNA, SP 63/370/247: Shrewsbury to Bolingbroke, 5 Jan. 1713/14).

[1615]William Conolly, MP [I].

[1616]William Whitshed, MP [I].

[1617]Joseph Deane, MP [I].

[1618]George Gore, MP [I].

[1619]Henry Maxwell, MP [I].

[1620]John Forster, MP [I]. Sir John Perceval's informant added the name of another whig MP, Gustavus Hamilton (BL, Add. MS 47087, f. 54: Perceval to Edward Southwell, 7 Jan. 1713/14).

[1621]James Hamilton (c.1661–1734), 6th earl of Abercorn.

[1622]Samuel Dopping, MP [I]. Abercorn and Dopping were invited as 'two of lord chancellor's friends' (TNA, SP 63/370/247: Shrewsbury to Bolingbroke, 5 Jan. 1713/14).

that some late proceedings had been displeasing, and that he had that day done that by the Queens order (viz. proroguing the parliament by proclamacion to Monday 17th January) which sufficiently shewed it: He said what he was going to say he had not orders for, but proposed that meeting with us as men of fortune and understanding, to know whether he might be encouraged to give the Queen assurances that if she suffered us to meet again, we would doe the Queens businesse, and lay aside heats that were among us and proceed with temper; that he had nothing to propose but was willing to hear what Gentlemen would propose; That if we did not proceed with such temper (or rather I think did not give assurances of our doing soe) it might be attended with very ill consequences to this Kingdome, he would not take on him to say what, but that it would not be difficult to guesse what they would be. There was a deep silence for more then a quarter of an hour; when his Grace said he did not know whether the silence proceeded from Gentlemens not being prepared to speak, or that they desired time to consider of it. Lord Abercorne thought his presence (being a peer) might occasion it, and offered to withdraw: but was told that was no reason of the silence. Mr Dopping told us how necessary it was for this Kingdome to have the Queens protection, that his all lay here, he wished Ireland well and was very fond of hearing something proposed that might make things easy. After this no body spoke in full a quarter of an hour; till Maxwel broke silence by saying he beleived his Grace meant the proceedings against the Chancellor:[1623] that he apprehended by what his Grace had mentioned of the Queens answer to the Lords addresse (for he mentioned it tho I omitted it) the Chancellor was not like to be removed; that he thought it hard to give money and stil lye under that greivance. I said I had not an oportunitye of giving my vote in the Lord Chancellors affair, but thought I should not act as a Lover of my countrey, if I did not now doe all in my power to remove one from so eminent a Station and a place of that power, who hath been censured by the commons in the maner he hath been, altho I had been originally against the votes or addresse for his removal: that the votes of the house as well as the proof made determined my judgement that he is guilty; and to have him continued must proceed either from a disbeleif of the truth of what the commons voted him guilty of, or from an opinion that a man guilty of those facts is stil fit to be continued Chancellor: that no body would undertake for other men,[1624] but I could not say that I beleived any one man who voted against him either had or would alter his opinion. The Duke said nothing of the nature of a retractation was expected, only let things lye as they are without resuming them at next meeting. I apprehended that

[1623]The account given by Lord Abercorn, who was sitting next to Alan Brodrick, confirms these and other details (PRONI, D/623/A/3/12: Abercorn to [Edward Southwell], 5 Jan.1713/14): 'to my great admiration there ensued such a very long silence, that it look'd like one of the sorts of Quaker meetings, whence they depart without uttering any parts of their meaning than what may be conjectur'd from sighs;and that sort of spirit moved the father and son then present [*Alan and St John*] to act each of them a considerable part, in this dumb show: at about a quarter of a hour's end, our Don Dismallo, or knight of the sorrowful countenance [*Henry Maxwell*], adventur'd, not indeed to dissolve the charm, but to disclose how indissoluble it was'. According to Abercorn, his own offer to withdraw, made because he was not himself a member of the Commons, was whispered into Alan's ear.

[1624]Although the word 'undertaker' was often used of parliamentary managers, in Ireland as in England, it retained its traditional pejorative connotations, and was highly resented by backbench MPs, for whom it was important that conventional notions of their independence be maintained. (Clayton Roberts, *Schemes and Undertakings: A Study of English Politics in the Seventeenth Century* (Columbus, OH, 1985), 25–8, 59–60,188; Hayton, *Ruling Ireland*, 115–16.)

would be altering our opinion indeed, which was that for the peace and preservation of the Protestant interest in Ireland we thought it necessary to addresse for his removal; which when we let fall we should fix on ourselves the brand of infamy that some people have endeavoured to place somewhere, by saying that what is spoken in prejudice of him is the voice of calumny and faction. I should have told you after Maxwel had mentioned the proceedings against Lord Chancellor to be the heats intended his Grace said, That among other matters. Gore said he could not answer for himself, much lesse for others, since he was alway influenced by debates; that he knew not how to distinguish between the good of the Queen and her people; and that if any great man misbehaved, he thought himself obliged to enquire into it. Dean said our misfortune was never to be able to complain of greivances but in parliament, the complaints necessarily passing through the hands that doe the injury. Mentioned the extraordinary proceedings in the case of Mr Moore and was going to give farther instances but was told by Lord Lieutenant that this was not a Court to try the Lord Chancellor in. Dean then said I will give no farther instances but this is the first time we have mett in parliament since the matters complained of hapned, and it will be unfaithfulnesse to our countrey not to represent them. Forster. That what was done in reference to the Chancellor was not the effect of personal resentment, but from a sense of his being the great cause of the dissension among Protestants, and other disorders in the Kingdome; that the redresse of greivances and money ought to go hand in hand. That the strength of the Protestant consisted in their unanimitye. Lord Lieutenant said he thought the Protestant interest here stronger now then ever; but if not ought we to deny the necessary supplyes for our preservation, and oblige her Majesty to lessen her forces? That the Queen would certainly remove Lord Chancellor if she beleived him an enemy to the Protestant interest here; tho we should addresse to continue him: that he beleived no one of those that voted for him would have done so, if they had thought him soe. Lord Abercorne either here or some time before mentioned that things had not been proved against him nor had he been impeached etc I expressed my self surprised that an impeachment should be expected to be laid before the Lords, who had before any accusation against him (only taking occasion from some loose words said to be spoken of him by one Nuttal) addressed in his favor, called him an excellent minister and declared beforehand they found no fault with him. Senny said he thought him guilty of what the Commons laid to his charge, that he had acted contrary to his duty and the Protestant interest of Ireland; that he knew not what greater misfortune could befal the Kingdome then to have a person so censured by a majoritye of the Commons continued in his employment after an effort in Parliament to remove him: that he had been and possibly might when his Graces back is turned be again in the Governement; that the Commons had passed by other delinquents to avoid the imputation of being querulous; that the last resentment must be expected from a man of his temper after the Parliament is up; and he beleived the Kingdome would be too hot for those who appeared against him if not removed. Lord Lieutenant said he did not think the businesse of that meeting was to enquire into Lord Chancellors behavior and was not easy to hear him ill spoken of, as being one of her Majestyes ministers; that he beleived we understood one another very well. Whitshed began to speak, but was told the matter was fully understood, and that we needed not proceed farther, so the meeting broke up. We went together to Mr Whitshed and left Lord Abercorne Mr Dopping and Sir John Stanley with Lord Lieutenant. This is to the best of my memory the substance of what passed; I cannot answer for particular expressions, and am sensible much of what was said is omitted. I told my Lord when I spoke first, that as his calling us together to advise with was a great honor done us, so it created us great difficultyes and might create misunderstandings in others, and might minister occasion of envy and jealousyes. To prevent this we resolve every where to publish what passed: but I would no[t] have you put this letter out of your own hands. My thoughts are that we shal meet on the 17th, that we shal be tryed whether we c[an] bring ourselves to give money and not open our mouthes if we think ourselves aggreived: I think too, we shal doe both, and find redresse if we convince the world we expect and deserve to have our greivances redressed. I should have mentioned that on my Lord Lieutenants saying by the Queens answer to the Lords addresse he beleived the Chancellor would not be removed that Conely said the resolves relating to the City of Dublin had not at that time been laid before her Majestye …

210. *Alan I, Dublin, to Thomas, at his lodgings in Whitehall, 7 Jan. 1713[/14]*

(1248/3/153–4)

I hope you will at the same time this comes to your hand receive a long one which I wrote last post about what passed at a certain place last Monday night; for I hear there are now on this side of the water five pacquets If fame speaks truth since Gentlemen declared their sentiments so resolutely, he, whose businesse it seems more particularly to be to desire to have it soe, hath made pressing instances to have the P[*arliament*] dissolved and a new one called; but we hear that it is thought a matter of such a nature as deserves particular orders from your side before any thing is done pursuant to the powers already come over what ever those powers are.

One of these two things I beleive will take place; either that things will be made easy by removing the cause of our uneasinesse, when at our next meeting the house appears to be of the same sentiments as they were of when they parted (which I beleive they will be, and doe apprehend other people think so too) or else an immediate dissolution will be to make way for a new parliament timely enough to passe a money bill before the 25th of March:[1625] and tho the town talk much of the later I incline to beleive the former method will be taken; and if it be found people are not to be wrought off any way, then what they think a greivance will I think be removed. One reason of talking so much of a dissolucion may be, to amuse members who live at a distance and by their nonattendance to be able to carry that in a thin house, that would not passe in a full. Yet after all perhaps we may be dissolved; and I hope you already have taken some care about the person[1626] whose gardens lye so near the dwelling of my nearest freinds: indeed it is of absolute necessitye, and will be of mighty consequence that something be done in it without delay. No longer since then this morning one of the representatives of the borough in which the mansion house stands[1627] told me on expostulating with him why he should make it his businesse to be chosen in Parliament, when he knew he had expressed himself under the last difficultyes by

[1625] When the additional duties granted by the recent Supply Act would lapse.

[1626] Identified in text as Lord Burlington, in a different hand.

[1627] Identified in text as Lismore, in a different hand. 'The mansion house' was Lismore Castle; the MP Sir James Jeffreys.

being obliged to vote as directed for fear of his employ: he owned he did so, and particularly in the choice of a Speaker:[1628] and added that before the calling this parliament he had by letter signifyed (I think he meant to the Secretary,[1629] but he did not say to whom) that he intended not to stand; and was told he had sate in the house many years, might secure an election and that it was expected he should doe soe; and in effect owned his being in the house was no more an effect of free choice, then his way of voting in the house. Is it not reasonable to deny such a man under such circumstances an election, tho in compliance with the commands of his superiors he should again apply to the person who recommended him now. Lord Sommers hath an interest in that familye by the trust reposed in him by the deceased;[1630] Mr Paul Methuen hath great influence over and power with the heir;[1631] I am not for creating misunderstandings between him and ——[1632] but something should be done in time to prevent the boroughs in which that familye hath an interest from sending so many T[*ories*] as they have done the last and this Parliament. I formerly told you Mr Wallop or Mrs Wallop ha[ve] interest in one or more boroughs in the County of Wexford, I think at Eniscorthy:[1633] I wish they would weigh and consider what kind of people they desire their borough should be represented by, and then examine how far those, who lately have, now do, or may hope hereafter to be elected by their interest, have answered or will answer their wishes in the house of commons. If Wallop himself should gett himself chosen, when he comes a very good man will be in the house a representative of that borough: and when he is absent, the borough will not in his room be represented by one of principles different from him …

211. *Alan I, Dublin, to Thomas, at his lodgings in Whitehall, 18 Jan. 1713[/14]*

(1248/3/157–8)

… I just now received a letter of the ninth from the Bath, which is the second since I left England, and I am sure will be the last till I return thither; for I resolve to be soe employed as not to find time to answer it. Most of the countrey Gentlemen are come to town in expectacion of doing businesse this day, and will shew the world they are in earnest by staying till the 27th if not dissolved before; for I think a farther prorogation impracticable.[1634] I doe not find the least relenting in any one man I discourse with, on the contrary they come full of the thanks of those they represent for what they have done and some of them charged with new matter to be laid before the house at its next meeting:

[1628] Jeffreys was a brigadier-general and governor of Cork. He had voted for Sir Richard Levinge in the Speakership election. (*Hist. Ir. Parl.*, iv, 476–7).

[1629] Chief Secretary Sir John Stanley.

[1630] See above, p. 299.

[1631] Paul Methuen (1672–1757), MP [GB] and the son of the former lord chancellor of Ireland, John Methuen.

[1632] Presumably the 3rd earl of Burlington.

[1633] See above, p. 299.

[1634] The Irish parliament had originally been prorogued until 14 Jan., but on 4 Jan. was further prorogued to the 18th, and before then, on the 14th, was prorogued once more until the 27th of the month (*CJI*, iii, 743; Kelly and Lyons, *Proclamations*, ii, 680).

which by the behavior of some of the other party they think not likely to be the Case: else our proceedings would not be treated in print as they are.[1635] I doe not think the preserving Lord C[*hancellor*] would be of weight enough to dissolve us; but if you consider the businesse we were to proceed upon immediately on our first meeting after Christmas, the treatment we have mett from two bodyes of men[1636] and the prospect of our having spirit enough to resent and return any thing we may think not fit to be born I doe not see how we can expect to be permitted to meet: no doubt some indignityes lately placed on us tended to render it impracticable to have us come again together without apparent probabilitye of expressing our resentment. Alderman Quin[1637] a City Justice took the examination of one Henry Murphy on the fifteenth of January 1713, of which the following is a true copy.[1638] The Examinant being duly sworn saith that he this Examinant on or about the nineteenth of December last past was inlisted by one James Roch merchant of this City (to serve the French King (as he pretended) in the regiment of foot commanded by Sir Andrew Lee,[1639] and that this Examinant was to land at Havre de Grace,[1640] and assured by the said Roch that he this Examinant should march from thence to Lorain, where he should see the young King; That one Mrs Catherine Lucas, who for several years past dwelt in France, and lately came into this Kingdome, is assistant to the said Captain Roch in listing persons to serve under the said Sir Andrew Lee, and promises them that they shal have fowre shillings six pence per week for subsistance, and a rout when they land in France.[1641] That the said Mrs Lucas to encourage this Examinant and the other inlisted persons, assured them that they should immediately march to Lorain and see the young King;[1642] and if they behaved themselves well, should soon return with preferment: That there are now two ships in the harbour ready to sail with the first fair wind with several of the said listed persons; which ships are called the John and Mary, and the John: and that this Examinant was on board the John and Mary five dayes, and that this Examinant was yesterday informed by a person inlisted that they beleived they had gott about fifty persons inlisted. The Justice bound Murphy over to prosecute in the Queens Bench and carryed the examination to Sir John Stanley who told him if it were delivered to my Lord Lieutenant his Grace could do no more then send the examination to the Lord Cheif Justice[1643] to examine the matter and

[1635] In both Ireland and England: in particular the Irish house of commons' attacks on Phipps had been debated at length in the London press, between the tory *Examiner*, and the whig *Englishman* (Abel Boyer, *The Political State of Great Britain* (60 vols,1711–40), vii, 33–8).

[1636] The Irish house of lords and convocation, in addressing on Phipps's behalf.

[1637] Thomas Quin (*d.* 1722), an apothecary of Skinner Row, Dublin, lord mayor 1698–9 (Gilbert, *Hist. City of Dublin*, i, 178; *Cal. Ancient Recs. Dublin*, ed. Gilbert and Gilbert, viii, 406).

[1638] It was printed in *Daily Courant*, 29 Jan. 1714.

[1639] Colonel-proprietor of a regiment in the French service from 1694 to 1704, when he was succeeded by his son Francis. On Francis's death in 1720 Andrew returned to the command until eventually replaced in 1733 (D'Alton, *King James's Irish Army List*, 494; David Murphy, *The Irish Brigades 1685–2006: A Gazetteer of Irish Military Service, Past and Present* (Dublin, 2007), 16–17).

[1640] Le Havre.

[1641] A Catherine Lucas was arrested in England in 1722 on suspicion of recruiting for the Pretender (P.K. Monod, *Jacobitism and the English People 1688–1788* (Cambridge, 1989), 109–10).

[1642] James Francis Edward Stuart, the 'old pretender'.

[1643] Sir Richard Cox, lord chief justice of queen's bench [I].

act in it according to Law;[1644] Mr Dawson[1645] being by said there was no Law against raising men to serve a Prince in alliance with us as the French King now is. The Alderman thought this to be no great encouragement and went away. The Recorder told me this later part, and what I have wrote above is to the best of my memory the substance of what he said, but I cannot be very certain of it, much lesse of the words in which it was delivered. Sure a little time will put us out of the suspence we are now in: I think in my conscience people are in as much apprehension now as they were in a year I am unwilling to name; God deliver us from seeing the hopes and expectations of the Irish come to passée …

212. *Alan I, Dublin, to Thomas, at his lodgings in Whitehall, [c.24 Jan. 1714]*[1646]

(1248/3/155–6)

To the Queens most Excellent Majestye.

The humble addresse of the high Sherif, the Justices of the peace, Clergy, Grand Jury and Gentlemen of the County of Corke att a general quarter sessions of the Peace held for the said County att Bandon bridge on Thursday the 12th day of January 1713/14.

Dread Sovereign

We your Majestyes most dutiful and loyal subjects of this County most humbly beg leave to approach your royal person and to congratulate you on the safe and honourable peace which your Majestyes unwearyed endeavours have obtained for the releif and comfort of your people.

We cannot but with greif and great concern take notice that the unhappy and fatal divisions which reigned and were fomented some years past doe yet continue in this Kingdome; notwithstanding the indefatigable zeal and application of the right honourable Sir Constantine Phipps Lord High Chancellor of Ireland and your other Excellent ministers to the contrary.

We cannot therefore but join with great pleasure and satisfaction your Majestyes most loyal Lords in Parliament, and your faithful Clergy in convocation assembled in their dutiful and humble request to continue your royal countenance and favor to that great minister; whose impartial justice, consummate abilityes, and unbiassed affection to the constitucion in Church and State are equal to those great trusts with which your Majestyes unerring wisdom, for the safety and honor of your Majestyes interests and the common good of your people has placed him. As we are thankful to God for the great blessings of the late happy revolution, and firmly resolved to stand by the succession in the illustrious house of

[1644] Chief secretary Sir John Stanley reported on 22 Jan. that Shrewsbury had received a presentment from the grand jury of Dublin, to the effect that 'great numbers of men' were being enlisted for the Pretender's service and transported to France, at which he instigated a search by 'the proper officers', who found twenty suspicious passengers on board ship for France. These were detained and sent to Lord Chief Justice Cox for examination. (TNA, SP 63/370/263: Stanley to Lord Bolingbroke, 22 Jan. 1713/14).

[1645] Joshua Dawson, under-secretary and MP [I].

[1646] Dated principally by reference to the forthcoming privy council meeting on 25 Jan. This letter was previously published in D.W. Hayton, 'Tories and Whigs in County Cork, 1714', *Journal of the Cork Historical and Archaeological Society*, lxxx (1975), 84–8. The address had been printed in the *Post Boy*, 28–30 Jan. 1714, and a copy, with a list of signatories, was included in TCD, MS 2022, pp. 151–3: Sir John Stanley to Thomas Hare,16 Feb. 1713/14.

Hanover, so we do not think the remembrance of the one, of the prospect of the other any motives to abate of our duty and allegeance; which at present is onely due to your Majestye; and are sorry that any thing or practice in this Kingdome should be observed, which might have any other views: and we hope that neither Popery nor schism can prevail with any of your Majestyes subjects to abett or assist any Pretender to the Crown and Kingdomes; or to disturb or elude your royal Successors.

May your Majestyes long and flourishing reign outlive all faction and sedition; and may the people of these nations forever gratefully and unanimously own them selves happy under the conduct and administration of the best of Princes.

Jemmy Barry[1647] gave me a paper which he assured me was a true Copy of the addresse, and I assure you the above is a true Copy of his Copy.

You see by the style of it that it is the addresse of the high Sherif (Mr Cox the Cheif Justices son, and a member of the house of Commons[1648]) Justices of peace, Clergy, Grand Jury and Gentlemen etc I doe not find any body (att least of our freinds) hath gott the names of those who signed; but I am informed Sir Mathew Dean and Mr Arthur Bernard (the Sollicitor Generals brother) who are also two members of our house have thought fitt to sign it: Mr King (son to the Late Lord Kingston who turned Papist in the reign of King James, but is now as good a Protestant as ever) Mr Hedges (the Sollicitors head tenant att Macroom) Mr Davis (another of his tenants and a new Justice, but I beleive not master of an acre of Land in which he hath an Inheritance[1649]) and some other Justices signed it whose names I cannot yet find out: but there were a good many of the Clergy who were in Commission that signed it: and particularly our parson Mr Atkins, Mr Stawel the minister,[1650] Mr Webber (another minister, brother to Dr Webber)[1651] and I hear Mr Michael Bustead,[1652] but I am not certain of it: Mr Atkins you know is a late Justice, as for Stawel and Webber I never heard till now that they are in Commission. George Rye[1653] was perswaded or as I hear rather frightned into it, with being threatned that all Whigs should be turned out of every Commission and employment; this account I have from Mr Herrick[1654] who with Mr Jonas Stawel, Mr Gibbins the Clergyman,[1655] Mr Longfeild and

[1647]James Barry, MP [I] Rathcormac.

[1648]Richard Cox.

[1649]John Davis (*d.* c.1721), of Bandon, Co. Cork (Phillimore, *Indexes*, ii, 32).

[1650]A John Webber (b. c.1688) was a deacon at Cloyne in 1712 (Al. *Dub.*, 777; Brady, *Clerical and Parochial Records*, iii, 251).

[1651]Samuel Webber (1675–1742), vicar of Killaconenagh, Co. Cork in 1715 and later a prebendary of St Patrick's, Dublin; brother of Edward Webber (for whom see above, pp. 194, 250). (*Al. Dub.*, 866; C.A. Webster, *The Diocese of Ross: Its Bishops, Clergy and Parishes* (Cork, 1936), 91; Leslie, *Clergy of Dublin*, 1161). He was not in fact appointed as a justice of the peace in Co. Cork until 1716 (H.F. Berry, 'Justices of the Peace for the County of Cork', *Journal of the Cork Historical and Archaeological Society*, ser. 2, iii (1897), 62).

[1652]Michael Busteed or Bustead (c.1677–1752), vicar of Ballyfeard, Co. Cork (G.F. Russell Barker and A.H. Stenning, *The Record of Old Westminsters* … (2 vols, 1928), i, 145; Brady, *Clerical and Parochial Records*, i, 344).

[1653]George Rye (1685–1735) of Ryecourt, Co. Cork (J.F. Collins, 'George Rye (1685–1735): His Family and an Appreciation of His Book "Considerations on Agriculture"', *Bandon Historical Journal*, xvii (2001), 39–55).

[1654]Gershom Herrick (c.1665–c.1731), of Shippool, Innishannon, Co. Cork (Burke, *Commoners*, iii, 641; Phillimore, *Indexes*, ii, 55; Rosemary ffolliott, 'The Herricks of Co. Cork', *Irish Genealogist*, iii (1956–67), 291–8).

[1655]Simon Gibbings (c.1662–1721), who had become rector of Mallow by the time of his death (*Al. Dub.* 322; Brady, *Clerical and Parochial Records*, ii, 324).

Mr Hugh Hutchinson refused to join in a thing of that nature. You know the County of Corke is very large, and that two Sessions are kept yearly for the Southside of the Lee and two for the Northside of the Lee; that no body ever is fined of the Northside for not being att Bandon Sessions, as none on the South are fined for not being att the Sessions held for the North att Mallow or Rathcormack. What interest the Cheif Justice, and Sollicitor, the Sherif or Arthur Bernard have lyes wholly near Bandon: The Sessions were held on 12th of January, when most Gentlemen that served for the boroughs in the County of Corke (except such who had the hint to attend the Sessions for a particular purpose) were either in town or on the road going toward Dublin, or preparing for their journey, the parliament being to sitt on the 18th of January. There were but five Justices from the North or East side the Lee att Bandon; Mr King who I am told by Mr Herrick was in the secret at Corke of contriving this addresse beforehand; Sir Mat Dean (who was in the same secret) and Mr Atkins of whom I will say nothing: these three were for the addresse. Mr Longfeild and Mr Gibbins were the other two and against it. I cannot be positive not having lately seen the Commission or numbred the Justices, but am told and beleive it to be true that there are 150 in Commission of peace for our County:[1656] and no doubt most of those who could be confided in were applyed to and desired to be present. It was managed with the greatest secrecy and brought ready ingrossed the last day of the Sessions. If the parliament meets again I apprehend they will think it worth their while to consider how far their own members have acted consistent with their duty in what they have done;[1657] if not and there be a new election, the sense of the freeholders will be known by the new representatives whom they will chuse. For my part I have resolved to join interest with honest Harry Boyle;[1658] and I hear the Sollicitor General is to join with Mr King: his name is James, and by a transposition people in the Countrey often call him King James. In the mean time I hope this addresse will not be thought to speak the sense of that large and honest County; indeed it doth not; and it may not be amisse that some hints of this kind were given to those who inform the world of the truth of things, and endeavour to undeceive them and not suffer them to be abused by appearances. The epithet loyal given to the Lords, and faithful to the Clergy, and the words faction etc point pretty plainly somewhere; and I think the things and practices which the addressers are sorry for, mean the dining together on King Williams birthday, and drinking the Succession in the house of Hanover, tho I am convinced several who signed it had no such intentions; and the general conclusion of eluding her Majestyes Royal Successors is large enough to comprehend the wishes of those who hope the Crown may after her Majestyes decease be worn by one who now doth, or

[1656]Berry, 'Justices of the Peace', 61–2, published details of appointments to the commission: according to his list, a total of 120 appointments were made between 1690 and Jan. 1714. A list of Co. Cork jps dating from about 1715 names 100 individuals, plus the mayors of Cork, Youghal, Kinsale and Bandon, and the revenue commissioners, ex officio (BL, Add. MS 46966, ff 161–2). The report in the *Post Boy*, 28–30 Jan. 1714, stated that 29 out of the 30 justices present signed this address. The copy sent to Whitehall by Sir John Stanley listed 83 signatories altogether (TCD, MS 2022, pp 152–3: Sir John Stanley to Thomas Hare, 16 Feb.1713/14).

[1657]Sir Richard Cox reported that 'The whigs are very angry at the County Cork address and swear they will expel Dick, Capt. Bernard, and Sir Mathew Deane who signed it' (BL, Add. MS 38157, f.61: Cox to Edward Southwell, 30 Jan. 1713/14).

[1658]Henry Boyle, MP [I]. This joining of forces was reported in BL, Add. MS 47027, f. 72: Sir John Perceval to Edward Southwell, 9 Feb. 1713/14.

lately did reside att Bar Le Duc:[1659] but this too I am convinced the subscribers had not in view, whatever the framers of it might have: The flying post they tell me (for I seldome read papers) puts the matter of Mr Molesworth in such a light as makes it better understood in London now, then it seemed at first to be.[1660]

We are stil in the dark as to our sitting on Wednesday: they who have treated the Commons as they have been treated since they endeavoured to ease the nation of what they apprehended a fatal greivance to it, had (no doubt) strong hopes, not to say assurances they should never meet again: and at this time the Toryes are making interest for being newly elected. Monday our Council sits again, when no doubt a proclamation will issue for our prorogation if we are not to sit; but I fancy yet we shal sit. [1661] The Toryes, and especially the most knowing and considerable, are very chagrin: I am told the Lord Lieutenant seems more easy then formerly; the Queens Bench have twice this term taken farther time to advise about the rule moved for, that the Officer should strike a Jury between her Majestye and Dudley Moore; and we were told on Thursday last on Monday or Tuesday the Court would give their opinion:[1662] now tho I have that deference for Courts of justice to be convinced that the sitting or not sitting of a Parliament never influences them in the judgement they give, yet I perswade my self (if we are to sit) no such rule will be made on Monday or Tuesday: possibly it may be rendred impracticable by the Attorney Generals entring a nolle prosequi on the informacion: or retracting his mocion if there must be a trial: possibly the Court will be then advised of their judgement and of opinion against the mocion: but of this later part I have not very sanguine hopes. On Monday too the Recorder and Aldermen are to attend the Councel, having put in an answer to a peticion of Sir Sam. Cooke in which he informs the board that he had laid a paper he received from Mr Dawson by order of the Councel before them, signifying the sense of the Queens Council in England (all but one) concurring with the resolution of the Council board here, that the Lord Mayor hath a right to name three persons out of whom the Aldermen must chuse one for Lord Mayor unlesse there be just exception to the persons nominated and that he continues Lord Mayor till a new one is elected, which the Councel recommended them to proceed to make, and to hold their Sessions and Courts as formerly, and own Cooke as Lord Mayor; to which they had not paid due obedience. The Aldermen in their answer sett forth what they did, and why they acted as they had done; denyed Lord Mayor had such right etc.[1663] Thus things seem to me to be pretty near a crisis here, and till the event is known mens minds will be under the last uneasinesse, which suspence in matters of great consequence never fails to

[1659] The Pretender had removed from French territory to Bar-le-Duc in Lorraine at the conclusion of the Treaty of Utrecht.

[1660] The whig *Flying Post*, 21–3 Jan. 1714, printed a long account of recent events in Dublin, with a focus on the convocation's complaint against Robert Molesworth (for which see above, pp. 296–7).

[1661] At some point before the Parliament could sit on Wednesday 27 Jan. it was prorogued again to 3 Feb., and finally (on 1 Feb.) to 10 Aug. 1714 (Kelly and Lyons, *Proclamations*, ii, 680–1).

[1662] See above, pp. 271–3, 278–9.

[1663] The majority of the aldermen, now twenty strong, were refusing to co-operate with Sir Samuel Cooke, who had originally been elected lord mayor in1712 and was holding over in office until a new election could be made and approved. The English law officers and queen's counsel considered the case and reported in favour of the Irish privy council, an opinion which the refractory aldermen would not accept. (BL, Add. MS 47087, ff 54–6: Sir John Perceval's journal, 8–17 Jan. 1713/14; BL, Add. MS 38157, f. 49: Sir Richard Cox to Edward Southwell, 9 Jan. 1713/14; *Daily Courant*, 26 Jan. 1714; TNA, SP 63/370/267–8: Shrewsbury to Bolingbroke, 2 Feb. 1713/14).

create. The Attorney General told me the contest was now pro aris et focis:[1664] I told him I thought soe as much as he did.

213. *Alan I, Dublin, to Martha Courthope, Bond Street, 26 Jan. 1713[/14]*

(1248/3/160–1)

I have already owned yours of the sixteenth, but none of that date came to me from my brother; this afternoon the pacquet boat arrived and brought me his of the nineteenth, which pray own to him. I am sorry your neighbour[1665] is soe little affected with the effect her mistaken point of honour hath had on that interest here, which she seems desirous to be thought to espouse: or does Mrs Higgins[1666] conversation prevail soe far, to reconcile her even to her principles too? All our men of politicks expected orders for dissolving the parliament, but since the letters are come in we hear nothing of the kind: on the contrary by the dejection observable in the Toryes faces I take it for granted we shal sitt to morrow sennight, to which day we were farther prorogued by proclamation yesterday before the pacquett came in. Our confusion and disorder is visible in every mans face; and such signs of dissatisfaction and resentment appear in Protestants faces one toward the other as give me a great concern: God open the eyes of the deluded, and make us all once again a people at unity among our selves …

214. *Alan I, Dublin, to Thomas, at his lodgings in Whitehall, 9 Feb. 1713[/14]*

(1248/3/163)

We are very barren of news for want of fowre pacquets from your side: I told you formerly that the company on the Queens birth day at the Tholsel was greater then ever, tho the General[1667] ordered it soe as to have a dinner at the Hospital where the greatest part of the Toryes in town of any condition dined; but their number was made larger then otherwise it would have been by some Officers dining there who could have been contented to have eaten at another place in other company.[1668] There was a paper printed and given about (as Quacks bills are[1669]) some little time before, in these words: Notice is hereby given to the Lovers of our most Gracious Queen, and present constitution that they are to meet on Colledge Green at ten of the clock to morrow morning, each with his Laurel in his hat (being her Majestyes birth day) and from thence to march through the City, in order to celebrate the same. Dated Fryday the 5 instant. 1714. There was also another paper printed

[1664] Literally 'for altars and hearths'; colloquially translated as 'for hearth and home'.

[1665] Lady Burlington.

[1666] Francis Higgins, the so-called 'Irish Sacheverell' had married, as his second wife, a sister of the English tory MP Sir William Glynne (for whom see *HC 1690–1715*, iv, 22–3).

[1667] William Steuart, MP [I], commander-in-chief of the forces in Ireland in 1714.

[1668] The whigs held a banquet at the Tholsel, while tories organised their own evening event at the Royal Hospital, Kilmainham (Hayton, 'An Image War', 38).

[1669] Handbills advertising the services and wares of quack doctors.

and sold about intitled the True Toryes answer to the Whigs question what is intended by peoples distinguishing themselves by wearing Laurels. These are not the words of the title, nor have I the paper by me, tho I have read it: nor did I ever see the paper to which that is intended for an answer.[1670] But it is a most heavy senselesse parcel of stuff, and hath only this thing remarkable in it, that it makes a doubt whether bloud will not be shed the following day; and saith if bloud be shed it must lye att the Whigs doors; his reason for it I could not well apprehend, but it seems to me to be this, because they would not take on them that badge which would secure the wearers from insults. And if that was the meaning, methinks it strongly implyes that it was foreseen and consequently intended that the Laurel men or their mob would insult those who dared appear without that feild mark. Some went to the Castle with laurels, and I hear Mr Savage,[1671] Stone[1672] and Chetwood[1673] named to have had laurels in their hats; but finding that was not the mode there, very wisely sneaked their distinction into their pockets: for I hear and beleive my Lord Lieutenant had to prevent mischeif expressed him self against marks of distinguition. Major Reading[1674] saw a company of his regiment with laurels; the Captain a French men who had marryed Lord Granards daughter;[1675] but he ordered and made them pull out their green out of their hats, and appear in the same maner as the rest of the regiment did and without any distinction.

The two inclosed are, one for Lord Shanon,[1676] the other for Lord Donerayle: you will know that to be for Lord Donerayle which mentions a brother: seal them up in covers and send them to the Lords. For Gods sake apply for Mr Boyle and me to Lord and Lady Burlington, and gett Mr Paul Methuen to speak to my Lord[1677] about his boroughs. My services where due. I wish Lord Wh[*arto*]n would at leisure write two lines to Will Jephson[1678] at Mallow and mention how handsomly they behaved themselves in Parliament I mean Will and his brother:[1679] it will do good.

These lines were made here which perhaps you will think not worth writing or reading, but I like the thought

O Laurel, Laurel, once Apollo's pride

To what vile purposes art thou apply'd!

[1670] *The World in Uproar, or The Hue and Cry After the Laurels* [Dublin, 1714]; probably published in answer to *An Enquiry About the Wearing of Lawrels* ([Dublin, 1714] (dated 14 Jan. 1713/14).

[1671] Philip Savage, MP [I].

[1672] Richard Stone, MP [I].

[1673] Benjamin Chetwood, MP [I].

[1674] John Reading (*d.* 1725), major in Wade's regiment of foot (Dalton, *Eng. Army Lists*, vi, 198, 367), had married in 1713 one of the daughters of Henry Tonson (*d.* 1703), of Spanish Island, Co. Cork (John Debrett, *The Peerage of the United Kingdom* ...(14th edn., 2 vols, 1822), ii, 1224).

[1675] Josiah Champagné (*d.* 1737) had married Lady Jane Forbes, 2nd daughter of Arthur, 2nd earl of Granard (John Forbes, *Memoirs of the Earls of Granard*, ed. earl of Granard (1868), 80). For his tory allegiance, see NLI, MS 2476, p. 521: Champagné to [Ormond], 6 Oct. 1713.

[1676] Richard Boyle (c.1675–1740), 2nd Viscount Shannon.

[1677] Burlington.

[1678] William Jephson, MP [I].

[1679] Anthony Jephson, MP [I].

Those Leaves which Marlbroughs brows oug[ht] to a]dorn

By Rochfort, Percival, and Pitts are w[orn]

You know the Cheif Baron[1680] and Prolocutor:[1681] but the Poet hath put them in vile company with Pitts the informer.[1682]

215. *Alan I, Dublin, to Thomas, at his lodgings in Whitehall, 20 Feb. 1713[/14]*

(1248/3/164–5)

I formerly sent you Copyes of the examinations of two persons at Waterford who swore that one Butler was listing men for the service of the Pretender; to them I refer you for their import; but they seemed to my Lord Lieutenant and Councel to be of that weight that his Grace and their Lordships issued a proclamation on the second of this month, to which I refer you;[1683] and send you one of the original proclamations under another cover by this post. If you in London ever trouble yourselves with our little prints in Dublin you will see by a news paper of this week that there have been some men discovered near this place going to France very lately, which the news paper makes to be some of Butlers men; but I apprehend the examination of Stephen Williams (a Copy of which I send you under the same cover with the proclamation) will shew that to be impossible, whatever inducement the news writer may have to desire they should be thought to be the same men. But before I speak of that, let me inform you that I received a letter from young Mr Christmas[1684] dated the 8th instant in which he tells me, that his father had received a private hint that a great man supposed to be the B[*isho*]p of W[*aterfor*]d[1685] had said, That the villain Alderman Christmas, and Mr Cooke a Presbyterian Parson[1686] corrupted the informants with a bribe

[1680]Robert Rochfort, MP [I].

[1681]William Perceval (c.1675–1735), archdeacon of Cashel, had served as prolocutor of the lower house of convocation in Ireland in 1713–14.

[1682]Charles Pitts (*d.* c.1755), of Dublin, an 'Exchequer attorney', was one of the informants against Dudley Moore in 1712 (*Appendix to 26th Report of Dep. Keeper of the Records*, 690; *K. Inn. Adm.*, 403; *Flying Post*, 11–13 Dec. 1712), and the following year was ordered into custody by the Irish house of commons for his involvement in the Dublin election riot, where he had been 'one of the managers for' Fownes and Tucker (*CJI*, iii, 713).

[1683]Two informants, Michael Lehy of Killoteran, and William Lehy of Three Mile Bridge, both in Co. Waterford, had sworn statements on 29 Jan, before the mayor of Waterford, Francis Baker, the recorder, Maynard Christian, MP [I], and an alderman, Richard Christmas, MP [I]. These had been considered by the Irish privy council, and a proclamation immediately ordered for the arrest of the recruiting officer, Lieutenant Toby Butler, and all those who had enlisted. The draft proclamation was presented to the council on 1 Feb. but the matter was thought to be of such consequence that discussion became prolonged and the wording was not agreed until the 2nd (TCD, MS 2002, pp. 105–7: Shrewsbury to Bolingbroke, 2 Feb. 1713/14; BL, Add. MS 47087, f. 60: Sir John Perceval's journal, 29 Jan.–2 Feb. 1713/14; *London Gazette*, 20–23 Feb. 1714; *Proclamations*, ed. Kelly and Lyons, ii, 681–2; Éamonn Ó Ciardha, *Ireland and the Jacobite Cause, 1685–1766: A Fatal Attachment* (Dublin, 2002), 139).

[1684]Thomas Christmas, MP [I]; son of Richard Christmas and himself an alderman of Waterford.

[1685]Thomas Milles (1671–1740), church of Ireland bishop of Waterford since 1708.

[1686]Possibly John Cook(e), ordained in Tipperary in 1701 (Katherine P. Meyer, '"The Last Day I Sate at This Board …": Sermons Recorded at Youghal, Bandon, and Mallow,1676–1688' in *Propagating the Word of Irish Dissent, 1650–1800,* ed. Kevin Herlihy (Dublin, 1998), 69).

of £10, to swear what they have done. He advised with me, whether these words were actionable, and told me the men were sent for up by the Governement. Upon enquiry I find it to be true that the men were sent for up to Dublin and were examined; but certainly not with any beleif or opinion that they should be found inconsistent with themselves on their farther examination: and I have some reason to beleive that it appeared beyond doubt that their first examinations were true.

I hope there is no truth in the acccount given to Alderman Christmas of the words spoken to his prejudice; why should any body be soe willing to have a truth of this nature concealed, or an honest Magistrate traduced for bringing such wicked practices to light? You will ask perhaps, why our Dublin news paper should endeavour to represent men listed in Dublin by Jones, to be the men listed in and about Waterford by Butler? But everybody knows that paper is written in favor of a person beyond Sea,[1687] which is an imputacion that cannot be I hope be justly fixed on the man who is supposed to have spoke those words of Mr Christmas. But let that be as it will, it is apparent from these Examinations, and others; particularly from some taken lately before the Mayor of Corke[1688] and laid by the Recorder[1689] before the Secretary[1690] that the trade of listing for a certain foreign service goes on a main and it is plain by the examinacion of Stephen Williams on 16 Febr. that the very good proclamacion of the second hath not put a stop to the practice. What hath been or will be done with the men of whom Williams speaks I cannot tell, but hear there were warrants and men sent out to apprehend them. For my part I confesse I think these are very silly fellows, if what I hear was told Alderman Quin be true, that there is no Law against listing men in the service of a Prince at amity with us, even tho there be no permission from the Governement to beat for or list such men. I formerly told you whose opinion that was: What need the person employed doe more, then say he lists them for the French King, and carry them to any other person? But perhaps it will facilitate the levyes to tell them they are to serve under the Duke of Berwick[1691] and to bring home the person mentioned in Williams examinacion. I have now before me copyes of the Mayor of Corkes letter dated 5 Febr. to Senny, in which he saith that he and Alderman Chartres[1692] hearing several strange persons were come to that place with intent to go to France that he ordered Constables to search for them and apprehended seven of them: viz. Cornelius Begly, Robert Grace, Oliver Grace, Thomas Grace, Thomas Purcel, Laughlin FitzPatrick and Jeremy Bryan. They were of a gang, but being examined apart told different storyes; Begly appeared the ringleader, was lately come from France and owned he designed to return thither; They had several papers when apprehended, some they tore, others they put into their mouthes and chewed them. I will not now send you the Copyes of their examinacions, but will doe it very soon. I will not trouble you with more on this subject of listing men here for a certain service then by adding the words of the postscript of a letter I received very lately from Mr Richard

[1687] The Pretender.

[1688] John Allen, described in the tory *Post Boy* of 23–5 Feb. 1714 as 'an honest and loyal gentleman'.

[1689] John Forster, MP [I].

[1690] Sir John Stanley.

[1691] James Fitzjames (1670–1730), 1st duke of Berwick; James II's illegitimate son and a marshal of France.

[1692] William Chartres (*d.* c.1723), of Tuckey's Quay, Cork, alderman of Cork (*Reg. Deeds, Wills*, i, 124). Sworn a justice of the peace in Dec. 1712 (*Cork Council Bk*, 357).

Boyle minister of Dungarvan son of Ned Boyle whom you well knew.[1693] His letter bears date att Dungarvan the 16th instant, and the words of the postscript are as followeth. We are under dreadful apprehensions of a massacre; for there was a man within three or fowre miles of this place double armed, who enquiring for one of those men listed for the service of the Pretender, and who was sent to Waterford Gaol by a mittimus from Captain Hubbert,[1694] said that if he was not hanged in two months, it would be out of all our powers to hurt him. Now tho I hope there is not ground for the dreadful apprehensions Mr Boyle hath of a massacre, yet from his postscript I conclude two things, that the men sent to Waterford Gaol by Hubbert are another sett, distinct from those listed att Dublin, Corke, or Waterford: for Hubbert lives near Dromanah,[1695] five or six and twenty miles from Waterford. But what seems to me of more weight in this, that the double armed men seems to have almost certain expectations of the person for whom these men are listing in two months. We hope care is taking on both sides the waters for our preservation. I will not end this long letter till I give you a true account of what yesterday passed in the Exchequer chamber in relation to the Sherifs of Dublin that were. Bradshaw and Surdevile were chosen approved and sworn Sherifs for one year from Michaelmas 1712. They served their year, and the Council board not approving the persons the City chose for new Magistrates, nor the City chusing such as would have been approved no new Magistrates were sworn att Michaelmas last. The old Sherifs were threatned to be fined by the Judges or some of them, I mean the two cheif Justices[1696] if they did not continue to act till new Sherifs were chosen; or at least till the end of Hilary term: under these threats they acted in the fowre Courts to the great neglect of their own affairs and prejudice of their fortunes till 12 Febr. Some dayes before they advised with Mr Dean,[1697] Whitshed,[1698] Gore,[1699] Rogerson[1700] and me whether by Law they were compellable to act beyond 12 Febr. resolving not to doe it on any consideration unlesse obliged to it by Law. We considered the City Chartres, the new rules, the Statutes of 14.Ed. Cap.7. 42 Ed. 3. Cap.9. 1.Ric.2. Cap.11. 12.Ed.4 (2) and 17 Ed.4 (6) 23 H.6. Cap.8. and other Statutes and were unanimously of opinion they were not compellable to act. They waited on my Lord Lieutenant before term was out, told him how they had been informed by their Council and what they had resolved to doe, that they might not be blamed if the City were destitute of acting Sherifs: My Lord probably directed the Judges to consider how the Law stood, but this we knew nothing of farther then by conjecture from what we heard after. We were told probably they should be fined for not attending the sittings after term and feed to speak in their behalf that they were not compellable to

[1693]Richard Boyle (b. c.1681), vicar of Dungarvan 1710–16, son of Edward Boyle of Killoneglary, Co. Cork, who had been collector of poll tax for the Bere, Bandon and West Carbery baronies of Co. Cork in 1696 (*Al.Dub.* 88; W.H. Rennison, *Succession List of the Bishops, Cathedral and Parochial Clergy of the Dioceses of Waterford and Lismore* … ([Waterford, 1922]), 162; *Proclamations*, ed. Kelly and Lyons, ii, 351).

[1694]William Hubbert (Hubbart) (*d.* c.1742) of Ballycarnane, Co. Cork (Phillimore, *Indexes*, ii, 137). His captaincy was a militia rank (*Cork Council Bk*, 339).

[1695]Dromana, near Cappoquin, Co. Waterford.

[1696]Sir Richard Cox (queen's bench) and Sir Robert Doyne (common pleas).

[1697]Joseph Deane, MP [I].

[1698]William Whitshed, MP [I].

[1699]George Gore, MP [I].

[1700]John Rogerson, MP [I].

act longer as Sherifs: We were all in the Exchequer when the Cheif Justice[1701] first came into Court, and before we could go thence to the Queens Bench the Court was up, after fining the Sherifs £200 for nonattendance. We went into the chamber and told the Cheif Justice that we made all possible hast to have been in Court in time to have spoken for our Clients and hoped to have offered that which would have prevented their being fined, and stil hoped he would not estreat the fines if they had not been faulty in not acting. He told us the Judges had agreed in opinion that they must act, but that we should be heard before them all to that matter. A Case was drawn and carryed to the Cheif Justice of the Common Pleas on Tuesday morning: who said it would be dishonourable to hear Councel to a point in which all the Judges had agreed before; the Cheif Justice of Queens Bench afterward gave hopes he would that night settle it with the Judges to hear Councel soon after; they gave their Case to the Cheif Baron who gave them no reason to beleive their Councel would be heard. This was all done on Tuesday. On Wednesday a writ was delivered the Sherifs (I mean Bradshaw and Surdevile) to execute criminals the Saturday following. No news from the Cheif Justice that their Councel should be heard tho they waited till seven on Thursday night, when they gave one peticion to the Lord Lieutenant, another to be transmitted by him to her Majesty praying releif in this matter. That night after ten the Cheif Justice Cox writes to them to tell them the Judges would hear their Councel at fowre next day in the Exchequer chamber; we attended, told them we were prepared to have argued, but having no prospect of being heard our Clients had laid the Case before the Queen and thought it unfit after that to apply to their Lordships for which reason only we would not speak in the matter. This I write because I suppose it will be said we might have been heard as we desired but had nothing to say.

216. *Alan I, Dublin, to Thomas, at his lodgings in Whitehall, 23 Feb. 1713[/14]*

(1248/3/166–7)

I hope that you have received my letters to you, in which I enclosed one to Lord Shanon, and another to Lord Donerayle for their recommendacion of Mr Boyle[1702] and me to their tenants to be chosen for the County of Corke in a new Parliament: If you knew with what indefatigable industry the matter is sollicited on the behalf of Sir John Percival and the Sollicitor,[1703] and particularly by our good neighbour the Bishop of Cloyne,[1704] you would not loose one moment in your application to them. I know the former hath several freeholders, and the later about twenty who all wait to know their sentiments. Lord Barrymore, Kingston, most of the Clergy, and all the Toryes and men in employment, especially the revenue Officers are as a man our open enemyes. Mr Boyle hath wrote to Lord Orrery,[1705] but I can pretend to no interest there. Indeed if the great people of our sentiments sitt idle, they will be in more likelyhood of having a Parliament to their wish,

[1701] Cox.

[1702] Henry Boyle, MP [I].

[1703] Francis Bernard, MP [I].

[1704] Charles Crowe.

[1705] Charles Boyle (1674–1731), 4th earl of Orrery.

then perhaps is yet imagined. Sure Lord B[*urlingto*]n young as he is hath been spoken to: must his boroughs be a perpetual weight in the scale against what his family have alway taken to be the true interest of their countrey. Must Sir Ja: J[*effrey*]s,[1706] and Major Smith[1707] be again recommended. If we have an ill Parliament, there will be no living for us in Ireland.

217. *Alan I, Midleton, to Thomas, at his lodgings in Whitehall, 23 Mar. 1713[/14]*

(1248/3/170–1)

My last was from Corke and carryed you the Copy of our County addresse,[1708] and of that which was intended by the Grand Jury of the City;[1709] but after I wrote my letter, I beleive some few alterations were made in the later: but what is become of it I cannot tell, for I have spent the week past in a maner not agreeable to me, I mean in keeping more company and drinking more wine then consists either with my inclinations or health: I went this day sennight to Kinsale, and drank an hearty bottle with my freinds there; and must doe the same thing to morrow at Youghal, on Saturday att Castlelyons: and some dayes next week att Mallow and Donerayle. When I have undergone this fatigue, I intend to close att Corke, and to go thence toward Dublin. You will hardly beleive me when I tell you that in Kinsale, in and about which the greatest part of Mr Southwells estate lyes,[1710] of which one of my competitors (the Sollicitor General) now is Recorder,[1711] as the Cheif Justice heretofore was,[1712] I have all the freeholders but two for me: and I perswade my self that Coxes and Bernards going thither this day, with all their retinue, will not shake any one single vote. You must know Mr Southwell hath several tenants who think they have votes as freeholders, but really are none: I have seen one of their Leases, and they are all of one form, but no freeholds; this I keep as a secret, as I beleive it is to them. There is no great dispute but that Mr Boyle and I shal both carry it against Sir John Percival and the Sollicitor, if there happen to be a new Parliament …[1713]

218. *Alan I, Cork, to Martha Courthope, Bond Street, 6 Apr. 1714*

(1248/3/174)

I wrote to you on Sunday from Mallow, which place I left this morning and return to morrow early, to dispatch some businesse … By my brothers of the sixth which came safe

[1706] Sir James Jeffreys, MP [I] Lismore, 1703–14.

[1707] Boyle Smith, MP [I] Youghal, 1713.

[1708] The address agreed at Bandon on 12 Jan. (see above, pp. 306–9).

[1709] Like Dublin, Cork was a county borough.

[1710] Edward Southwell, MP [I].

[1711] Francis Bernard had been recorder of Kinsale since 1693 (*The Council Book of the Corporation of Kinsale* … ed. Richard Caulfield (Guildford, 1879), 434–5.

[1712] Sir Richard Cox was recorder 1682–7 (*Council Book of Kinsale*, ed. Caulfield, 434–5).

[1713] Perceval wrote smugly to his cousin Daniel Dering from London on 15 May 1714 that 'Brodrick … may happen to be sorry for spending five hundred pound to secure an election that may not happen at last, for some say we shall sit again' (BL, Add. MS 47087, f. 71).

under Mr Henrys cover I find one of his to me is miscarryed; and by your not mentioning any one of three which were wrote to him on a certain subject I beleive they are fallen into ill hands; else they must have been in London long before 16 March when your last bears date. If that should prove to be the case I fancy the person that wrote them must be very uneasy, considering the subject they were written on: I will not speak plainer, yet probably you may not apprehend me, if the letters are miscarryed. I really begin to grow weary of struggling in vain against a torrent which I find we are to be overborn by, and long for a few months retreat and quiet before I leave the world. I see such bare faced oppression etc that I am quite tired with looking on it …

219. *Alan I, Dublin, to Thomas, at his lodgings in Whitehall, 20 Apr. 1714*

(1248/3/175–6)

I have yours and my sisters of this day sennight, and hers of the fifteenth: I find you were too sanguine in expecting more from your house then they would come up to, but am extremely pleased to see that our expectations as well as those of our enemyes are disappointed in the house of Commons of Great Britain. When it comes soe near an equalitye as forty on soe important a question as that of last Thursday I cannot be very apprehensive of any thing ill taking place.[1714] Lady Newburgh[1715] by letter hath lett people here know how signally you served her and this countrey in Lord Athenrees[1716] matter against Lord Bellew, and I am very glad of it on the countreys account as well as that you had it in your power to doe her Ladyship a service. I am in great pain to hear that my poor sister is ill, and long to be over with you: but how can I doe it? Yet how great are my occasions of being in England … I find three letters are intercepted (that is the Case) and so have some of yours; particularly that which my sister mencions in which you told me as much before …

220. *Alan I, Dublin, to Thomas, at his lodgings in Whitehall, 16 May 1714*

(1248/3/177–8)

… Our Judges are att a mighty losse how to make a report in the Case of the City consistent with a former and with truth too. I suppose things cannot be carryed so private, but that it is known that fowre and forty men are now taken of a much greater number listed for and going to France (we call it) but I hear some of them own it was for another service.[1717]

[1714]The critical division in the British house of commons on 15 Apr. 1714 to adjourn debate in the committee of the whole House on the state of the nation before voting on the motion that the succession was not in danger under the queen's government ('Proceedings in the House of Commons, March–June 1714', *Bulletin of the Institute of Historical Research*, xxxiv, ed. A.N. Newman (1961), 214–15).

[1715]Frances, née Brudenell (bef. 1677–1736), wife of Richard Bellew, 2nd Baron Bellew [I]. Her first husband, from whom she derived her title, had been Charles Livingstone, 2nd earl of Newburgh [S].

[1716]Francis Bermingham (1692–1749), 2nd Lord Athenry.

[1717]Shrewsbury reported to Secretary Bolingbroke on 16 May that two days earlier, having received intelligence that a large number of men who had enlisted in the Pretender's service were to leave in fishing boats from the hill of Howth, to the north of Dublin, in order to rendezvous with French ships lying offshore, he had sent

There are partyes out to seise the rest; an Officer who listed them was taken, allowed to ride his own horse, and rode fairly off …

221. *Alan I, Dublin, to Thomas, at his lodgings in Whitehall, 5 June 1714*

(1248/3/181–2)

About one this afternoon my Lord Lieutenant went off from Ringsend and I no sooner came back but I was accosted with the inclosed which I bought and transmit to you as a testimony of the submission to Governement, the respect, Toryes bear to one who never was thought a Whig, when he will not go their lengths and concur in their violent measures.[1718] You will be surprised to be told the Toryes are the only joyful people at his going off, and yet others are not soe weak to think him of their minds. No one man in the Kingdome hath lesse reason then I to say I have received favors considering the post I have been and am in as Speaker of the house of Commons: but he hath with temper and steddinesse stemmed those measures which must have made us most miserable. Beside my wishes to see my freinds, and some particular affairs which relate particularly to my family I own I wish to be on your side the water; yet hope one letter from you will give me a guesse before I come away whether we are like to be under the Cheif Governor who must be most fatally mischeivous to us.[1719] Pray see my Lord early, and act respectfully toward him …

222. *Alan I to Thomas, at his lodgings in Whitehall, 15 June 1714*

(1248/3/185–6)

This day John Riley,[1720] one Bourke and Carol[1721] were tryed in the Queens Bench for high treason by a Jury of the County of Dublin: The Indictment was for conspiring the death of the Queen and to depose and deprive her of her Royal dignitye: the Clerk of the Crown[1722] did not open the indictment with which the Jury was to be charged, nor charged them with it at large; I was in the Court, and should have observed it (I think) if it had been done, but I doe not mention this as any imputacion any where, but rather as an omission: for indeed he is a very good Officer and a very honest one; but I think it proceeded from Mr Stewarts beginning to open the indictment too early; he is one of her

1717 (*continued*) a detachment of troops to intercept them. Of the purported three hundred recruits, some forty prisoners were brought back to Dublin (TNA, SP 63/370/94–5). The story was extensively reported 'in the public papers' in England (BL, Add. MS 47087, f. 73: Sir John Perceval to Daniel Dering, June 1714).

1718 Patrick Delany's satirical pamphlet *The Life of Aristides, the Athenian* …, written to vindicate Phipps, was less than complimentary about Shrewsbury (who appeared in the guise of Themistocles) and his duchess.

1719 Lord Anglesey.

1720 Described by the duke of Shrewsbury as the organiser of the entire operation of recruiting Irish catholics for the Pretender (TNA, SP 63/370/94–5: Shrewsbury to Bolingbroke, 16 May 1714). Shrewsbury identified him as an Englishman, but Sir John Perceval was told that he was John Reilly, a catholic Dublin merchant and an alderman of the city under King James II's charter (Ó Ciardha, *Ireland and the Jacobite Cause*, 142–3).

1721 John Bourke and Martin Carroll (*Daily Courant*, 26 June 1714).

1722 Sir Thomas Domvile, 1st Bt (c.1650–1721).

Majestyes Councel,[1723] and to tell you the truth of it I did not observe it at the time, but think it was as I say on recollecting what passed.

That which makes me say this is that my notes mention the treason laid in the indictment very summarily and yet I think I took a succinct account of all that passed which seemed to me material, and they import that the indictment charged Riley with treason in inlisting Bourke and Carol for the Pretenders service and it charged them with being inlisted for that service and afterward meeting att Hoath in the County of Dublin with intent to transport themselves to France for that service. I have not seen the Copy of the Indictment but am sensible it must be more particular and that it contains more then I observed on its being opened. Mr Stewart opened it to be for conspiring to deprive her Majesty of her Crown and to kill and destroy her, and for inlisting men to cause insurrections, and put the Pretender on the throne contrary to her Majestyes will. I asked Mr Attorney if the five last words under which I have drawn a stroke were in the indictment, and he told me in Court that they were. Mr Attorney said the treason layd was conspiring her Majestyes death; the overt acts against Riley were Rileys inlisting Bourke and Carol and others for the Pretenders service, and against them their being inlisted: and after such inlisting assembling themselves at Hoath in the County of Dublin to transport themselves to go for France etc. That it would appear in evidence they knew and declared they were inlisted to serve the Pretender, whom they called King James the third; that they were listed to go to Lorain and that they were told they were soon to return thence into Ireland in his service, and were to have 9d per diem while in Ireland, £5 or 5 Guineas a man on landing in France; that they should come back soon and be rewarded with estates here for their service. That there were rolls kept of the names of persons listed, written by one McNally by order of Riley: That they went to Hoath to transport themselves from the rocks there on board a ship which was to wait for them and take them of in boats: that great numbers mett there on that occasion, some of them armed, and when a Constable and guard came to apprehend them fired at the Guard etc the Sollicitor said their intent was to bring the Pretender back again which would cause the last confusion etc the witnesses were 1. Thomas Purcel. He swore that he and Dillon (another witnesse) went on a Sunday morning (not asked what) to the house of one Hallyon or Hallon at the pyed horse in Dublin,[1724] called for ale, for the man of the house, and for John Riley (by that it seems he knew there was such a man there but nothing was asked as to their former acquaintance) one of the prisoners; that Riley said they were welcome asked them to go and dine with him and the other Gentlemen there which they did; that there were about twenty others, of whom Bourke and Carol were two; that he found by all their discourse they were mett for the service of the Pretender: that after dinner he swore them not to discover what passed, told them they should be rewarded if they would go to the Pretender and into his service; should have 9d per diem in meat and drink while here, and £5 or 5 Guineas a man when they landed in France, and swore it should be made good to them: said they were to be viewed in France by the

[1723] Charles Stewart (*d.* 1740), appointed a queen's counsel in Feb. 1713 (*K. Inns Adm.*, 464; *Lib. Mun.*, pt 2, p. 77).

[1724] A large brick-built house standing on the east side of Wine Tavern Street, opposite Cooke Street, and containing rented rooms on the first floor and an inn ('The Pyed Horse') on the third) Gilbert, *Hist. City of Dublin*, i, 160).

Queen (meaning King James his Queen[1725]) thence to Lorain and there to be received by the Pretenders Officers under whom they were to serve, and that they were to serve King James the third: that they only wanted a fair wind for France, that they should soon come back again and have Lands here for their service. That they and others to the number of 26 eat and drunk at Hallyons from Sunday till Fryday at the finding of Riley and on his account, fared very well; generally in a cellar to avoid being seen: that Hallyon had encouragement from the heads of them, particularly from one in Kilmainham Gaol now who was looked on to be their Captain. That Riley told them they should have 8d a day in money or 9d in meat and drink; That they were inlisted in this maner; McNally had a book and wrote their names by Rileys direction, some were to be common Souldiers, some horsemen, and five were to be of King James the thirds life Guard; that the persons who were to be of the Life Guard had an O sett before their names. Bourke was one of these, Carol was only to be a common Souldier; Riley shewed them a Commission he had at the Seige of Limrick from the late King James.[1726] There were ten inlisted as to be of the Life Guard. That Carol said they should have very good encouragement from the Pretender, and owned he was listed for him: but said Carol was known by the name of the Cobler and not called Carol. That Riley came on Fryday morning told them the wind was fair for France, that they must that night to Hoath either one by one, or by two and two at most; that the Guard was bribed and no notice would be taken of them, that there would guides be placed to shew them the way to the Hill of Hoath; that he went thither, mett above 200 there, the three prisoners of that number; that they discoursed one with the other and all their discourse was to the same effect that they were going to France to serve the Pretender; that Carol and Bourke owned they went in order to serve the Pretender, that Riley owned in his hearing he had maintained fifteen men three weeks at his own expence who were listed for the same service: That several of the men at the Hill of Hoath had arms, some had swords, some had fire arms, some none at all. That he saw no money distributed except for washing and Lodging, and that he saw Hallyon give Bourke money for that purpose at several times. I ventured to ask privately where Hallyon was, and was told it was true he had been taken, owned all, was designed to be made use of as a witnesse and was sett at large on his own recognisance, and now kept out of the way; but Mr Attorney whispered me that if they caught him they would hang him: I told him, he deserved it etc.

The second witnesse was Anthony Dillon, who swore to the same effect with Purcel, as to going to pyed horse, being carryed to dinner by Riley, his swearing them conceal his name etc inlisting them, declaring it was for the Pretenders service whom Riley called King James the third, their names wrote by McNally by Rileys order, Bourke and Carol two of them, that their subsistence in Ireland was 9d a day in meat and drink, staying from Sunday to Fryday at pyed horse, going thence on Fryday night by Rileys order to Hill of Hoath to be transported to France for Pretenders service, Carols Rileys and Bourkes being att Hoath that night, declaring their intent there to go into France to serve the Pretender, to have £5 a man on landing in France; talked with five who had listed and had formerly been in Lord Monjoyes regiment, who said they were to be in the King life Guard, meaning the Pretender, of whom Bourke the prisoner was one. He agreed with Purcel as to swearing

[1725] Mary of Modena, widow of James II.

[1726] The siege of Limerick in 1691.

them, eating usually in a cellar not to be observed, being directed by Riley to go to Hoath, the three prisoners meeting them there, declaring their intentions to imbark for France in the service of the Pretender when they were mett at Hoath: beleived there 100 men at the Hill of Hoath on that account, but it being night is not precise in the numbers. Said the person in Kilmainham gaol used to come to Hallyans, was looked on to be their Captain, used to welcome them: and that when the Constable and Guard came to seise them the prisoners were with the Captain, who drew a pistol against them and witnesse made off, and was mett and taken by Mr St Laurence:[1727] That he lay with Carol, who owned he was inlisted for the Pretenders service.

The third witnesse was Wm McGwyre swore he was inlisted for the Pretenders service by Riley, had 9d a day, went to Hoath on Fryday by his direction, who promised £5 on Landing in France and that they should have good estates when they came back. That he and many others, among them Bourke was dieted at the pyed horse by Rilyes direction, saw Carol at Hoath on the Fryday night etc

The fourth was Hawkins the Constable,[1728] who was sent with 12 men by the Governement to seise the men at Hill of Hoath, that there were above 400 there, among them that Carol, and the witnesse Dillon were there; and Riley at a part of the Hill near the sea called the Green baily, who said he was taking a walk, but that [...] Constable might take some of the men in cliffs before him, said his name [was][1729] Ryan: but Hawkins seised him and found powder in his pockett. That several boats were coming from ships to carry the men off, but observing that there were people to seise them made back to the ships; but one boat came from a ship and carryed off eight. That the man in Kilmainham (whose name the constable afterward told me privately was Callaghan) shot at him (I am not positive it was he that shot but one in his company did) called to the Constable told him they were there, standing behind a dry stone wall and bid him come and take them, and he made off to save his life: That he and the Guard took several, but did not say how many.

The prisoners said nothing for themselves; only Riley said he having a brother in France designed thither for employment: Bourke said Lord Dunbarton[1730] had promised to carry him for England, but left him behind; produced his discharge out of Lord Monjoyes regiment[1731] and said he was caught in a trap; I suppose he meant he was surprised to inlist. Carol said nothing, but only gave the witnesses ill words, as that they were not to be beleived. The Atturnye said the evidence was clear, so he would not summe it up; none else of the Queens Councel said a word to the Jury, the Judges summed up the evidence; the second Judge began: I reminded them it was the course for the Cheif Justice to doe it in treason: there was a very substantial and honest jury who immediately found them guilty. What follows I have only by hearsay, that after being condemned (for so they were instantly, which is not the course of the Court, but on another day) I am told they cocked their hats and in

[1727] William St Lawrence (1688–1748), of Howth, Co. Dublin, MP [I] 1716–27 and later 14th Baron Howth (*Hist. Ir. Parl.*, vi, 223–4).

[1728] John Hawkins (*d.* ?1758), later to acquire great notoriety as the corrupt keeper of Newgate prison in Dublin (T.D. Watt, 'The Corruption of the Law and Popular Violence: The Crisis of Order in Dublin, 1729', *Irish Historical Studies*, xxxix (2014–15), 1–23).

[1729] MS damaged.

[1730] George Douglas (1687–1749), 2nd earl of Dumbarton, had been brought up in exile at the jacobite court, but returned to England in 1710, became a protestant, and was commissioned in a regiment of foot.

[1731] Lord Mountjoy's regiment of foot had been disbanded in 1711 (Dalton, *Eng. Army Lists*, v, 240).

effect defyed the Court: this I heard from two or three but what follows I know to be true. One Pace a Cowper[1732] made oath in Court that one Kelly after they were found guilty asked whether they would be hanged: Pace answered they would: Kelly replyed with an oath, if they were hanged, he would be hanged for them. This I heard Pace swear: and am told Kelly either now is or was servant to Judge Nuttley.[1733] This is a rough account but a just one; make not use of my name tho you should communicate the substance, if it may be of service.

223. *Alan I, Dublin, to Thomas, at his lodgings in Whitehall, 24 June 1714*

(1248/3/187–8)

Next to the satisfaction I propose to myself in seeing you and my few other relations and freinds in England, the hope I have of finding people in better and more charitable dispositions in England then they are here makes me wish to be there; at least I shal be out of a place where a man that is honest and prudent too will be very shy of going into the company of those he doth not very well know.

The resentments, apprehensions, and fears which may be observed among people are not to be expressed: I doe not take on me to say how well grounded they are, but am convinced the hopes of the Papists and apprehensions of most of the Protestants with whom I converse were never greater in my memory. Hardly a night passes in which there is not something done either to alarm or disquiet the minds of men; I wrote formerly that at one end of the town in one night there were great numbers of Protestants doors marked with letter H: which some fancy was intended as if they deserved hanging, others that the dwellers were for the house of Hanover. Last night Sir John King[1734] and Mr Gores[1735] house in Capel Street had these words wrote on their doors, King James the third in spight of the Whigs: Others had a gallows painted on them with these words A fart for all Whigs; and indeed the haughty air the Papists give themselves, and their more then ordinary numbers in town give considering people very anxious thoughts:[1736] And yet in the country the Irish lye out of their houses in the fields by night, on pretence of being afraid of the Protestants: the same thing I remember practiced in the first year of King James, and soon after several English were committed and tryed for their lives as meeting together in arms which went then by the term of night walking. There hapned an odd affair lately in this town: Colonel Carrs regiment had pistols, which being bought by the Colonel or Officers for the men

[1732] Alan is either misspelling the word cooper, or is using the Scottish term cowper or couper, meaning a dealer.

[1733] Richard Nutley, MP [I]

[1734] Sir John King, MP [I].

[1735] Probably George Gore, MP [I].

[1736] The *Post Boy*, 26–29 June 1714, printed a report from Dublin, dated 19 June, that 'some of our Whigs have employed some of their own creatures, to go about these two or three nights past, marking their own doors with colours and words written,as if those doors that were marked the people within were to be massacred by the Tories and papists; but some of those sparks are seized and committed to prison; so it's hoped they will be forced to discover their employers'.

and not by the Crown, were not taken away when the Regiment was broken. [1737] Those belonging to five troops were laid up att Athlone, and by order of one Campbel who was an Officer[1738] and took care of them by order of Col. Carre they were brought up to town; and he being marryed to the daughter of one Martin an Attorney (who is a Presbyterian)[1739] to save the charge of hiring a place for them, they were put into Martins house: they had not been there above a night or two, but Martin was sent for before the Governement and asked what arms he had if any; he owned the thing; being asked about ammunicion he said he had none, told how they came there etc the Arms were seised and sent to the stores, but I had forgott to tell you that he was examined whether they came to his house by night, he said the contrary, as the truth was: But it hapned they came to town by some Irish Carrs and were for some time in the Carriers custody, during which time no informacion was given of such arms being in town. Col. Campbel was sent for and told by the General that some arms were brought to the stores which were now known to belong to him or to be under his care, which was not understood when they were taken from Mr Martins: I hear he said it was known whose the Arms were at that time, and that he had more arms under his command and care formerly and that he had made good use of them, that he would not take them back but expected to be paid for them. The weather is excessively hot, and hath the same effect on some people here that the like formerly had on Sir John Boles who was chosen by the City of Lincoln not foreseeing the house would sit till Midsummer.[1740] Lord A[*nglesey*] this day said in Lucas Coffee house that there was no difference as to goodnesse between Papists and Presbyterians; that being jumbled and mixed together they would make an excellent sallad for the Devil; and that he wished all Dissenters (or Presbyterians I think) hanged, to which Mr Stenhouse[1741] said that indeed that was a short way with them.[1742] Col. Brasier[1743] received a letter without a name in which he was told Lord A[*nglesey*] would be our Cheif Governor,[1744] and his Cousin and namesake[1745] Lord Chancellor in room of Sir Con. and that all things looked with an ill aspect on the Protestants. This letter he left in his coat pocket and after going to bed his servant took out his clothes, transcribed the letter and intended to send the copy as certain news to his father, telling him it was the copy of his Masters letter: this copy he brought to the bowling green, to which place he waited on his master the next day, and was going to seal it up in presence of one of the doorkeepers: but being overcautious for fear of being observed the doorkeeper snatched

[1737] Hon. William Kerr (bef. 1682–1741), whose regiment of dragoons, having been unmounted and placed on the Irish establishment in June 1713, was broken in Apr. 1714 (*HC 1690–1715*, iv, 552–3; TNA, SP 63/370/116: Shrewsbury to Bolingbroke, 4 May 1714).

[1738] John Campbell (Dalton, *Eng. Army Lists*, vi, 210).

[1739] Samuel Martin (*d.* by 1720), of Capel Street, Dublin. originally from Belfast (Vicars, *Index*, 317; Barnard, *A New Anatomy*, 124; Robert Whan, *The Presbyterians of Ulster, 1680–1730* (Woodbridge, 2013), 136).

[1740] Sir John Bolles (1669–1714), 4th Bt, elected for Lincoln in Dec. 1701, was arrested in June 1702 for speaking 'scandalous and treasonable words of the queen'. While in custody he was visited by a doctor, and although released on that occasion, was not elected again and was eventually declared a lunatic (*HC 1690–1715*, iii, 261).

[1741] A John Stenhouse was granted a lease of property in the suburbs of Dublin in 1712 (NLI, MS 36513/1).

[1742] MS damaged.

[1743] Kilner Brasier, MP [I].

[1744] For Anglesey's intrigues to obtain the viceroyalty, see Hayton, *Ruling Ireland*, 181–3.

[1745] Francis Annesley, MP [I] 1695–1703, 1713–14.

it out of his hand, said it was to a wench and that he must read it: the others being very unwilling increased the curiosity and three or fowre fellows read it, and it was of too black a nature not to be laid before the Governement. The fellow owned all to his master in the utmost confusion, and asked what he should doe, who bid him if sent for to tell the truth, which he did; then the Colonel was sent for and examined whether the Copy made out by the man was the Copy of a letter he had received and from whom: he said he had received a letter without a name, that he beleived it might contain much of what the copy imported, particularly that of Sir Cons being to be out; but as to that he had a much more particular letter by the following maile which assured him he might depend on it; he was asked who his correspondent was or whether he had the letter about him, he said he did not much care if he shewed it, only he would not doe any thing that looked like disclosing freindly correspondent, but that he verily beleived the intelligence was true, and soe he was dismissed.[1746] I hope to sail on Saturday …

224. *Alan I, Dublin, to Thomas, at his lodgings in Whitehall, 26 June 1714*

(1248/3/189–90)

After all the assurances which my late letters to you and my sister have given of my leaving this place by this nights pacquett boat at farthest, I find it impossible for me to perform my resolution; I have not finished my businesse, and if I had I really am soe wearied and dispirited with an insufferable weight of businesse this excessive hot and dry weather, that I cannot think but that lying stil a day or two is not only convenient but almost necessary to support me in any measure of health: but if I am living and well, I purpose (by Gods permission) to go by the boat which carryes Tuesdayes mail: but I think I made a promise much of this nature that I would begin my voyage this night at farthest. When I land you shal hear from me. Our weather is soe hot that we are hardly able to breath, and soe it hath been for a considerable time past, and the drowth is such that our springs are generally dryed up, few pumps have any water and the cattle are forced to go in many places eight or ten miles to drink. This day Ryley, Bourke and Carol were executed, with two other criminals: Many people beleived they would not suffer this day, the writ of execution directed to the Sherif of the County at large[1747] directing him to carry them from Newgate[1748] through the City to the gallows, which is near St Stephens Green in the County of the City, and to execute them there; and the writ carryes in it a mandate to the Sherifs of the City to be present att and assisting to the Sherif of the County in the execucion: Now there being either no Sherifs in the City, or none who will act as such, many thought the Sherif of the County would not (without assistance of the Sherifs of the City) execute them, and beleived that he would return his writ of execucion as formerly he had done, that for want of the City Sherifs attending and assisting he had not executed them. People too ruminated on what the fellow spoke the day when they were found guilty, that if they were hanged

[1746] Used to mean being sent away rather than being dismissed from office.

[1747] The county of Dublin, as opposed to the city, which was a county in its own right.

[1748] The largest and most important prison in Dublin, situated in the Cornmarket at the end of High Street, at the western end of the city, a considerable distance from St Stephen's Green. See Bernadette Doorly, 'Newgate Prison' in *The Gorgeous Mask: Dublin 1700–1850*, ed. David Dickson (Dublin, 1987), 121–31.

he would be hanged for them, which words seemed to import that fear or something else would influence some not to execute them: In short one sort of people were fearful least they should not be executed, which would have made their freinds insolent beyond enduring; and others seemed not to be very apprehensive of their suffering on the day they were to dye. But Mr Thornton the high Sherif of the County[1749] went yesterday to the Primate[1750] and Archbishop of Tuam (two of the Lords Justices)[1751] and as I hear carryed with him an affidavit or examination of threats given out that they should be rescued, if it was attempted to execute them: he desired an order from the Lords Justices for a Guard to assist him in conveying them to the place of execution and declared he would execute them if such guard were ordered.[1752] The Lords Justices conceived an order to that effect last night; I mean the two, for I think the Lord Chancellor was at Chappel Izod: and this morning every body in the Courts expected they would suffer, when the Attorney[1753] and Sollicitor[1754] and Cheif Baron[1755] were sent for out of Court, and as we hear since there either was a meeting of the Lords Justices and Councel, or of their Excellencyes, the Cheif Judges, and Queens Councel on this affair; the book of the City charter was sent for to consider I suppose what might be done in the City, the Sherifs of it not attending etc but between twelve and one it was resolved that a Guard should attend, and orders went accordingly; and about three they were carryed to execucion: there was a paper printed as their speech, before their death I am sure; calculated to insinuate that they went over only to gett bread, and to serve the French King, to support the story that hath been given out in many peoples hearings, that the Irish who were listed were not to serve the Pretender but to recruit some French regiments I mean in the French service which are composed of Irish. How well this consists with the evidence which I sent you over at large I leave you to judge. This day too one Carroll a brewer, of substance,[1756] who is committed on the same account was reported to be poisoned, but on examining the matter it seems only to have been a contrivance to try if his freinds could have prevailed to have had him bailed; I hear the proof is full against him, and the Sollicitor owned to me that he squeeked: soe as it might be of service somewhere that he were out of the way, and if he were allowed to take the air, I beleive we should never hear more of him then we doe of Sir John Hurly[1757] who was taken among others att the Hill of Hoath, but being permitted to ride to town rode clear away. I will conclude with two observacions: that in the Metropolis the Court of Queens Bench thought it necessary to have a Guard to secure these fellows, after they were convicted from the bar to the Gaol, and the Governement saw the same need of a

[1749]William Thornton (*d.* by 1733) of Finglas, Co. Dublin (Vicars, *Index*, 455).

[1750]Thomas Lindsay, formerly bishop of Killaloe and Raphoe, had been translated to Armagh in Jan. 1714.

[1751]John Vesey, who had been nominated as a lord justice together with Lindsay and Phipps.

[1752]The lords justices' version was that Thornton had asked for a guard because the city sheriffs refused to act, and he feared an attempt to rescue the prisoners (TNA, SP 63/370/44: lords justices to Bolingbroke, 29 June 1714).

[1753]Sir Richard Levinge.

[1754]Francis Bernard.

[1755]Robert Rochfort.

[1756]William Carroll (Ó Ciardha, *Ireland and the Jacobite Cause*, 142–3; *Ireland in the Stuart Papers,* ed. Patrick Fagan (2 vols, Dublin, 1995), ii, 63).

[1757]Sir John Hurley of Knocklong, Co. Limerick (John O'Hart, *The Irish and Anglo-Irish Landed Gentry* … (Dublin, 1884), 145).

Guard to secure their not being rescued in going to execucion.[1758] and that the house of Commons had some grounds when six months agoe they gave the world to understand men were listing for the Pretender,[1759] how ever unhappy they were not to obtain credit in time, but on the contrary to be called and looked on as ill affected for beleiving anything of the sort …

[1758] For details of various government precautions, see TNA, SP 63/370/82: Shrewsbury to Bolingbroke, 18 May 1714.

[1759] On 22 Dec. 1713 the Irish house of commons had examined a witness about reports of 'natives' being enlisted in Dublin for the service of the Pretender and had sent their informant off to speak to the lord chief justice of queen's bench (*CJI*, iii, 726).

Appendix 1: Brodrick Family Members and Connections Mentioned in the Text

Barry, James (1659–1717), of Rathcormac, Co. Cork, 1st s. of Redmond Barry of Rathcormac, and bro. of Catherine Barry, 1st w. of Alan I; m. (1) Mary, da. of Abraham Anselm of London, 2s. 1da. (2) Susanna, da. of John Townsend of Castletownsend, Co. Cork; MP [I] Rathcormac 1689, 1692–9, 1713–14, Dungarvan 1703–13, 1715–*d.*; capt. of foot by 1692, col. 1699.

Bettesworth, Richard (*d.* 1713) of White Rock and Ballydullea, Co. Cork, s. of Peter Bettesworth (*d.* 1707) of Ballydullea; m. 1688 Catherine Foulke, at least 1s.

Brodrick, Alan I (1656–1728), of Dublin, 2nd s. of St John I; cr. Baron Brodrick 1715, Viscount Midleton 1717; m. (1) by 1684, Catherine, da. of Redmond Barry of Rathcormac, Co. Cork, 1s. (2) 1695, Lucy Courthope (q.v.), 1s. 1da. (3) 1716, Anne Hill (q.v.), s.p.; MP [I] Cork 1692–10, Co. Cork 1713–14, and MP [GB] 1717–*d.*; recorder, Cork 1690–5, 3rd serjeant [I] 1690–2, solicitor-gen. [I] 1695–1704, privy councillor [I] 1695–1711, 1714–*d.*, Speaker of the house of commons [I] 1703–10, 1713–14, attorney-gen. [I] 1707–9, chief justice of queen's bench [I] 1709–11, lord chancellor [I] 1714–25, lord justice[I] 1717–19, 1719–21, 1722–3, 1724–5.

Brodrick, Alan II (1702–1747), 2nd but 1st surv. s. of Alan I by his 2nd w.; m. 1729, Lady Mary Capell (*d.* 1756), da. of Algernon, 2nd earl of Essex, 2s. (1 *d.v.p.*); commr of customs [GB] 1727–30, jt comptroller of army [GB] 1730.

Brodrick, Katherine (bef. 1665–1731), 1st and o. surv. da. of St John I; m. William Whitfield (c. 1658–1717), rector, St Martin's Ludgate 1691–1714, prebendary, St Paul's 1695, Canterbury 1710, vicar, St Giles Cripplegate, 1714–*d.*

Brodrick, Laurence (c.1670–1747), 6th but 5th surv. s. of St John I; m. 1710, Anne Humphreys, 2s. (1 *d.v.p.)* 3 da.(2 *d.v.p.*); vicar, Sandon, Herts.1697–1711, chaplain to house of commons [GB] 1708, prebendary of Westminster 1710–46, rector, Dauntsey, Wilts. 1712–14, Mixbury, Oxon. 1713–43, Turweston, Bucks.1713–41, Islip, Oxon., 1741–8.

Brodrick, St John I (1627–1712), of Ballyannan and Cahermone, Co. Cork, 4th s. of Sir Thomas Brodrick of Wandsworth, Surr.; knighted 1660; m. by 1653, Alice (*d.* 1691), da. of Randal Clayton of Thelwall, Chesh. and Mallow, Co. Cork, 6s (1 *d.v.p.*). 2 da. (1 *d.v.p.*); MP [I] Kinsale 1661–6, Co. Cork 1692–9; provost marshal, Munster 1661(life), commander of a troop of horse and co. of foot 1661–by 1679.

Brodrick, St John II (1659–1707), of the Middle Temple, 3rd s. of St John I; unm.; MP [I] Midleton 1695, 1703–7; queen's serjeant [E] 1705.

Brodrick, St John III (1684–1728), 1st s. of Alan I by his 1st w.; m. 1710, Anne Hill, jr (q.v.), 4 da.; MP [I] Castlemartyr 1709–13, Cork 1713–14, Co. Cork 1715–*d.*, and MP [GB] 1721–7; recorder, Cork 1708–*d.*, privy councillor [I] 1724–*d.*

Brodrick, Thomas (1654–1730), of Wandsworth, Surr. and Ballyannan, Co. Cork, 1st s. of St John I; m. Anne, da. of Alexander Pigott of Innishannon, Co. Cork,1s. *d.v.p.*; MP [I] Midleton 1692–3, 1715–27, Co. Cork 1695–1713 and MP [GB] 1713–27; comptroller of salt duties 1706–11, jt comptroller of army accounts 1708–11, privy councillor [I]1695–1711, 1714–27, [GB] 1714–*d.*

Brodrick, William (c.1666–aft. 1733), of Spanish Town, Jamaica and the Inner Temple, 5th but 4th surv. s. of St John I; m. (1) 1693, Hannah (*d.* 1703), wid. of Capt. John Toldervey and Major Thomas Ballard (2) by 1705, Ann (*d.* 1707), 1s. *d.v.p.*, 1da., (3) 1707, Sarah Ivey; attorney-gen. and judge admiral, Jamaica 1692–8, 1715, attorney-gen., Leeward Is. 1694, member of council, Jamaica 1695, speaker of house of assembly, Jamaica 1711–13, 2nd serjeant [I] 1718–21.

Clayton, Laurence (1655–1712), of Mallow, Co. Cork, s. of Randal Clayton of Mallow, cousin of Alan I, St John II and Thomas; m. (1) Catherine, da. of Sir Henry Tynte, 1s. *d.v.p.* (2) 1698, Ann Courthope (q.v.), 3s.; MP [I] Mallow 1692–*d.*; capt., Lesley's foot 1689, St George's foot 1689, queen's foot 1690–1.

Courthope, Ann, da. of Sir Peter Courthope (*d.* c. 1680) of Little Island, Co. Cork by his 2nd w. Elizabeth Giffard (*d.* c. 1694) and coh. to her bro. John Courthope (*d.* 1695); m. 1698 as his 2nd w., Laurence Clayton (q.v.).

Courthope, Lucy (*d.* 1703), da. of Sir Peter Courthope of Little Island, Co. Cork by his 2nd w., and coh. to her bro. John, sis. of Ann Courthope; m. 1695, as his 2nd w., Alan I, 1s. 1da.

Courthope, Martha (*d.* c. 1730), sis. of Sir Peter Courthope of Little Island, Co. Cork; unm.

Courthope, Rachel, da. of John Codrington of Codrington, Gloucs.; m. 1686, John Courthope (*d.* 1695) of Little Island, Co. Cork, s.p.

Hill, Anne (*d.* 1747), da. and eventual h. of Sir John Trevor (*d.* 1717) of Brynkinalt, Denbighs., Speaker of the house of commons [E]1685–7, 1690–5; m. (1) 1690, Michael Hill (1672–1699), of Hillsborough, Co. Down, MP [I] 1695–9, 2s. 1da. (2) Alan I, s.p.

Hill, Anne (b. aft. 1690), da. of Michael Hill of Hillsborough, Co. Down, and Anne Hill (q.v.); m. 1710, St John III, 4 da.

Meade, Robert (1653–aft.1707) of Kinsale, Co. Cork, 2nd s. of William Meade of Ballintober, Co. Cork, and bro. of Sir John Meade, MP [I] (for whom *see* Appendix 2); m. 1682, Frances, da. of Sir Peter Courthope of Little Island, Co. Cork by his 1st w. Catherine Daunt, and half-sis. of Anne and Lucy Courthope (qq.v.), 1s.1da.

Appendix 2: Members of the Irish House of Commons Mentioned in the Text

Addison, Joseph (1672–1719), of Sandy End, Fulham, Middx., St Margaret's, Westminster, and Bilton Hall, Warws., MP Cavan 1709–13 and MP [GB] 1708–9, 1710–*d.*; commr of appeals in excise [E] 1704–8, under-sec. of state [E] 1705–9, chief sec. [I] 1709–10, 1714–15, privy councillor [I] 1709–*d.*, keeper of the records in the Bermingham Tower, Dublin Castle 1709–19, sec. to lords justices [GB] 1714, lord of trade [GB] 1715–17, privy councillor [GB] 1717, sec. of state [GB] 1717–18.

Aldworth, Richard (1646–1707), of Stanlakes, Hurst St Nicholas, Wilts., and Newmarket, Co. Cork, MP TCD 1695–9; 2nd sec. to earl of Essex as ld. lieut. [I] 1672–7, chief sec. [I] 1693–6; privy councillor [I]1695–*d.*

Allen, John (1661–1726), of Stillorgan, Co. Dublin, MP Co. Dublin 1692–3, 1703–13, 1715–17, Co. Carlow 1695–9, Co. Wicklow 1713–14; privy councillor [I] 1714–*d.*; cr. Viscount Allen 1717.

Allen, Joshua (1685–1742), of Stillorgan, Co. Dublin, MP Co. Kildare 1709–26; s. of John Allen whom he suc. as 2nd Viscount Allen 1726.

Annesley, Arthur (c.1678–1737), of Farnborough, Hants., Bletchingdon, Oxon., and Knockgrenan, nr. Camolin, Co. Wexford, MP New Ross 1703–10 and MP [E & GB] 1702–10; gentleman of the privy chamber [E] 1689–1702, jt vice-treasurer and paymaster-gen. [I] 1710–16, privy councillor [GB] 1710–*d.*, [I] 1711–*d.*, lord justice [GB] 1714; suc. as 7th earl of Anglesey 1710.

Annesley, Francis (c.1653–1707), of Ballysonan, Co. Kildare, MP New Ross 1695–9.

Annesley, Francis (1663–1750), of Castlewellan, Co. Down, Lincoln's Inn Fields, Middx., and Thorganby, Yorks, MP Downpatrick 1695–1703, 1713–14 and MP [E & GB] 1705–15, 1722–34; commr of inquiry into Irish forfeited estates 1699–1700, trustee for sale of Irish forfeited estates 1700–3.

Annesley, Maurice (aft. 1653–1718), of Little Rath, Co. Kildare, MP Clonmines 1695–9; yr. bro. of Francis Annesley, MP New Ross.

Ashe, Thomas (1656–1722), of St John's, Co. Meath, MP Swords 1695–9, Clogher 1713–*d.*

Ashe, Thomas (bef. 1664–1721), of Ashfield, Co. Meath, MP Cavan 1692–1713.

Atkinson, Anthony (1681–1743), of Cangort, King's Co., MP St Johnstown (Co. Longford) 1711–13, Belfast 1713–14.

Badham, Brettridge (c.1678–1744), of Ballyheen, Co. Cork, MP Charleville 1713–14, Rathcormac 1743–*d.*; collector of customs and excise for Youghal and Dungarvan.

Barry, James, MP Rathcormac 1689, 1692–9, 1713–14, Dungarvan 1703–13, 1715–*d.*: *see* Appendix 1.

Barry, James (1661–1725), of Newtownbarry, Co.Wexford, MP Naas 1695–9, 1711–13, Kildare 1715–*d.*; jt clerk of the pipe [I] 1693–*d.*, jt prothonotary of common pleas [I] 1701–*d.*

Barton, William (bef.1665–1721), of Carrickmacross, Co. Monaghan, MP Co. Monaghan 1692–1713.

Bayly, Edward (1684–1741), of Mount Bagnall, Co. Louth, MP Newry 1705–14; cr. Bt 1730.

Beauchamp, John (bef. 1661–1745), of Ballyloughan, Co. Carlow, MP Old Leighlin 1695–9, 1713–*d.*, Thomastown 1703–13.

Bellew, Thomas (bef.1668–1746), MP Mullingar 1713–27; capt., Stewart's foot by 1693, Charlemont's foot 1696, half-pay 1698, major, Meredith's foot 1702, lieut.-col. by 1704.

Bellingham, Thomas (1646–1721), of Castle Bellingham, Co. Louth, MP Co Louth 1692–1713; colonel of his own regiment 1689–c.1690.

Bernard, Arthur (1666–by 1736), of Palace Anne, Co. Cork, MP Bandon 1713–14.

Bernard, Francis (1663–1731), of Castle Bernard, Co. Cork, MP Clonakilty 1692–3, Bandon 1695–1727; solicitor-gen. [I] 1711–14, prime serjeant [I] 1725–6, judge of common pleas [I] 1726–*d.*; eldest bro.of Arthur Bernard (*q.v.*).

Berry, William (c.1668–1739), of Wardenstown, Co. Meath, MP Enniscorthy 1703–13, 1715–*d.*, Duleek 1713–14; lieut., Inniskilling horse 1689, capt., St George's foot 1696, lieut.-col., Wolseley's horse by 1704.

Bingham, John (c.1655–1707), of Newbrook, Co. Mayo, MP Castlebar 1692–3, Co. Mayo 1695–1707.

Blenerhassett, John (1665–1709), of Ballyseedy, Co. Kerry, MP Tralee 1692–3, Dingle 1695–9, Co. Kerry 1703–*d.*

Blenerhassett, John (1691–1775), of Ballyseedy, Co. Kerry, MP Co. Kerry 1709-13, 1715–27, 1761–*d.*, Tralee 1713–14, 1727–60; 1st s. of John Blenerhassett (*q.v.*).

Bligh, Thomas (1654–1710), of Brittas, Co. Meath, MP Athboy 1692–3, Co. Meath 1695–*d.*; privy councillor [I] 1706–*d.*

Blundell, Sir Francis (1643–1707), 3rd Bt, of Blundell Manor, King's Co., MP King's Co. 1692–*d.*

Boyle, Hon. Henry (1669–1725), of Westminster, MP Co. Cork 1692–3 and MP [E & GB] 1689–90, 1692–1710; commr for public accts [E] 1695–7, lord of treasury [E] 1699–1702, privy councillor [E] 1701, chancellor of exchequer [E & GB] 1701–8, lord treasurer [I] 1704–15, sec. of state [GB] 1708–10, privy councillor [I] 1714, lord president [GB] 1721–*d.*; 2nd surviving s. of 1st Baron Clifford; cr. Baron Carleton [GB] 1714.

Boyle, Henry (1682–1764), of Castlemartyr , Co. Cork, MP Midleton 1707–13, Kilmallock 1713–14, Co. Cork 1715–56; Speaker of house of commons [I] 1733–56, chancellor of exchequer [I] 1733–5, privy councillor [I] 1733–*d.*, revenue commr [I] 1735–54, lord justice [I] with intervals 1734–*d.*; cr. earl of Shannon 1756.

Brabazon, Chaworth (1686–1763), Lord Brabazon, of Tara, Co. Meath, MP Co. Dublin 1713–14; privy councillor [I] 1716–*d.*; s. of 5th earl of Meath, whom he suc. as 6th earl 1715.

Brasier, Kilner (*d.* 1725), of Ray, Co. Donegal, MP Dundalk 1695–9, St Johnston (Co. Donegal),1703–13, Kilmallock 1715–*d.*; capt., Viscount Mountjoy's foot 1685, major, Peyton's foot 1689, lieut.-col. 1694, col. 20th foot 1706.

Brewster, Sir Francis (bef. 1642–1705), of Brewsterfield, Co. Kerry, MP Tuam 1692–9, Doneraile 1703–*d.*; commr of inquiry into Irish forfeited estates 1699.

Brewster, Francis (1667–aft. 1713), of Brewsterfield, Co. Kerry, MP Midleton 1695–9, Dingle 1703–13; s. of Sir Francis Brewster (*q.v.*).

Brodrick, Alan I: *see* Appendix 1.

Brodrick, St John II: *see* Appendix 1.

Brodrick, St John III: *see* Appendix 1.

Brodrick, Thomas: *see* Appendix 1.

Brownlow, Arthur (1645–1711), of Lurgan, Co. Armagh, MP Co. Armagh 1689, 1692–*d.*

Burgh, Thomas (1670–1730), of Oldtown, Co. Kildare, MP Naas 1713–*d.*; capt., royal regiment of foot 1692, engineer in king's own company 1696, surveyor-general [I] 1700–*d.*, lieut. of ordnance [I] 1706–14, lieut. col., 20th foot 1707–14.

Burton, Benjamin (bef. 1665–1728), of Dublin and Burton Hall, Co. Carlow, MP Dublin 1703–27.

Burton, Samuel (1687–1733), of Burton Hall, Co. Carlow, MP Sligo 1713–27, Dublin 1727–*d.*; 1st s. of Benjamin Burton (*q.v.*).

Bushe, Arthur (bef.1670–1731), of Dangan, Co. Kilkenny, MP Thomastown 1695–1714; sec.to revenue commrs [I], advocate-gen. [I] 1702–12, collector of Cork, 1693–8, jt customer, Dublin port 1711–27.

Butler, Pierce (1670–1732), of Garryhundon, Co. Carlow, MP Co. Carlow 1703–14; suc. fa. as 4th Bt 1704; privy councillor [I] 1712–27.

Butler, Theophilus (1669–1724),of Belturbet, Co. Cavan, MP Co. Cavan 1703–13, Belturbet 1713–14; jt clerk of the pells [I] 1678 (life), privy councillor [I] 1710–*d.*; cr. Baron Butler of Newtownbutler 1715.

Callaghan, Cornelius (c.1682–1742), of Shanbally, Co. Tipperary, MP Fethard (Co. Tipperary) 1713–14.

Campbell, Charles (bef. 1640–1725), of Donaghadee, Co. Down, MP Newtownards 1695–*d.*

Carter, Thomas (c.1650–1726), of Dublin and Robertstown, Co. Meath, MP Fethard (Co. Tipperary) 1695–9, Portarlington 1703–13; clerk of rules of king's bench [I], clerk of errors in exchequer [I].

Caulfeild, Hon. John (1661–1707), of Tullydowey, Co. Tyrone, MP Charlemont 1703–*d.*; col., Londonderry foot 1689, lieut.-col., Tiffan's regiment 1691; s. of 1st Viscount Charlemont.

Caulfeild, William (1665–1737), of Donamon, Co. Galway, MP Tulsk 1692–1714; 2nd serjeant [I] 1708–11, prime serjeant [I] 1714–15, judge of king's bench [I] 1715–34.

Chetwood, Benjamin (c.1655–1728), of Harristown, Co. Kildare, MP Harristown 1713–14; comptroller of customs, Limerick 1702–15, solicitor to revenue commrs. and clerk of the casual revenue and first fruits [I] by 1707–1715.

Christian, Maynard (1668–1714), of Waterford, MP Waterford 1703–*d.*

Christmas, Richard (1661–1723), of Whitfield, Co. Waterford, MP Waterford 1695–1713.

Christmas, Thomas (1687–1747), of Whitfield, Co. Waterford, MP Waterford 1713–*d.*; 1st s. of Richard Christmas (*q.v.*).

Clayton, Laurence: *see* Appendix 1.

Cliffe, John (1661–1728), of Mulrankin Hall, Co. Wexford, MP Bannow 1692–1727; 3rd serjeant [I] 1711–13, 2nd serjeant [I] 1713–14.

Coghill, Marmaduke (1673–1739), of Dublin and Drumcondra, Co. Dublin, MP Armagh 1692–1713, TCD 1713–*d.*; judge of prerogative court, Armagh 1699–*d.*; privy councillor [I] 1722–*d.*, revenue commr [I] 1729–35; chancellor of exchequer [I] 1735–*d.*

Coghlan, Joseph (c.1655–97), MP TCD 1689, Limerick 1692–*d.*

Conolly, William (1662–1729), of Capel St, Dublin and Castletown, Co. Kildare, MP Donegal 1692–9, Co. Londonderry 1703–*d.*; customer, Derry and Coleraine,1697–*d.*, revenue commr [I] 1709–10, 1714–*d.*, privy councillor [I] 1710–11, 1714–*d.*, Speaker of the house of commons [I] 1715–1729, lord justice [I] 1717–19,1719–21, 1722–4, 1726–7, 1728–*d.*

Conyngham, Henry (1664–1706), of Mount Charles, Co. Donegal, MP Killybegs 1692–3, Co. Donegal 1695–*d.*; capt., 9th foot 1688, lt-col. 1691, and in Echlin's regiment bef. 1693, col. 8th Hussars 1693, col of a regiment of dragoons 1693, brig.-gen. 1703, major-gen. 1704.

Corker, Edward (c.1680–1734), of Mucktown, Co. Dublin, MP Rathcormac 1713–14, Midleton 1715–27, Clonmines 1727–*d.*

Corry, James (1634–1718), of Castle Coole, Co. Fermanagh, MP Co. Fermanagh 1692–*d.*

Cox, Richard (1677–1725), of Dunmanway, Co. Cork, MP Tallow 1703–14, Clonakilty 1717–*d.*

Crowe, William (c.1657–1711), MP Blessington 1692–3, 1703–*d.*, TCD 1698–9; commr of appeals in revenue [I] 1706, master in chancery [I] 1706–10, customer, Waterford and New Ross 1704–10.

Dawson, Joshua (c.1660–1725), of Castle Dawson, Co. Londonderry and Dublin, MP Wicklow 1705–14; clerk in secretary's office [I] 1690–9; under-sec. [I] 1699–1714, 1st clerk of paper office [I] 1703–*d.*, comptroller of customs, Drogheda 1703–8, customer, Dublin port 1703–8.

Deane, Edward (1660–1717), of Gowran, Co. Kilkenny, MP Inistioge 1692–3, 1703–*d.*, Co. Dublin 1695–9.

Deane, Joseph (1674–1715), of Castlemartyr, Co. Cork, MP Co. Dublin 1703–14; chief baron of exchequer [I] 1714–*d.*, privy councillor [I] 1714–*d.*

Deane, Sir Mathew (c.1685–1747), 3rd Bt, of Dromore, Co. Cork, MP Charleville 1713–14, Co. Cork 1728–*d.*

Dering, Charles (1656–1719), of Dublin, MP Monaghan 1692–9, Carlingford 1703–13; deputy auditor-gen. [I] c.1692–1708, jt auditor-gen. [I] 1708–*d.*, privy councillor [I] by 1702–14.

Dillon, Sir John (bef. 1663–1708), of Lismullen, Co. Meath, MP Kells 1692–3, Co. Meath 1703–*d.*

Dixon, Robert (c.1664–1726), of Calverstown, Co. Kildare, MP Randalstown 1692–3, 1712–*d.*, Harristown 1703–13.

Dodington, George (c. 1662–1720), of Dodington, Somerset and Eastbury, Dorset, MP Charlemont 1707–13 and MP [E & GB] 1705–*d.*; commr for appeals in excise [E] 1679–1705, paymaster to treasurer of navy [E] 1695–9, chief sec. [I] 1707–8, privy councillor [I] 1707–*d.* lord of admiralty [GB] 1709–10, 1714–17, clerk of the pells [I] 1715–*d.*

Dopping, Samuel (1671–1720), of Dublin, MP Armagh 1695–14, TCD 1715–*d.*; privy councillor [I] 1711–14.

Echlin, Robert (1657–1724), of Monaghan and Purfleet, Essex, MP Monaghan 1695–9, Co. Monaghan 1703–13 and MP [GB] 1710–15; lieut., Viscount Mountjoy's foot 1685, lieut.-col., 6th dragoons 1689, colonel 1691–1715, brig.-gen.1703, major-gen. 1704, lieut.-gen. 1707.

Echlin, Robert (1674–1706), of Rush, Co. Dublin, MP Newtownards1692–3, Newry 1695–*d.*

Edgeworth, Henry (aft.1658–1720), of Lissard, Co. Longford, MP Mullingar 1703–13, Co. Longford 1713–14, St Johnstown (Co. Longford) 1715–*d.*; ensign, Newcomen's foot 1685, capt. Viscount Lisburne's foot 1689, capt. 1692, capt. Coldstream Guards 1692–1703, lt. col. after 1696, searcher, packer and gauger, Dublin 1691–1714.

Erle, Thomas (c.1650–1720), of Charborough, Dorset, MP Cork 1703–13 and MP [E & GB] 1679–81, 1685–7, 1689–1718; col. of foot 1689–98, 19th foot 1691–1709, brig.-gen. 1693, major-gen. 1696, lieut.-gen. 1703, gen. of foot 1711, c.-in-c. [I] 1701–5, privy councillor [I] 1701–*d.*, lord justice [I] 1702–3, lieut.-gen. of ordnance [E] 1705–12, 1714–18, privy councillor [GB] 1705, c.-in-c., land forces [E] 1708–12.

Evans, George (1655–1720), of Bulgaden Hall, Co. Limerick, MP Co. Limerick 1692–3, Askeaton 1695–9, Charleville1703–*d.*; privy councillor [I] 1717–*d.*

Evans, George (c.1680–1749), of Bulgaden Hall, Co. Limerick, MP Co. Limerick 1707–14, and MP [GB] 1715–27; privy councillor [I] 1715–45; 1st s. of George Evans (*q.v.*); cr. Baron Carbery 1715.

Eyre, Edward (1666–1739), of Galway, MP Castlebar 1695–9, Galway 1703–13, 1716–27.

Eyre, George (1680–1711), of Eyrecourt, Co. Galway, MP Banagher 1703–*d.*

Eyre, John (1659–1709), of Eyrecourt, Co. Galway, MP Co. Galway 1692–*d.*; fa. of George Eyre (*q.v.*).

Fitzgerald, Robert (1654–1718), of Corkbeg and Lisquinlane, Co. Cork, MP Youghal 1692–9, Castlemartyr 1703–13.

Fitzgerald, Robert (1671–1725), of Castle Dod, Co. Cork, MP Charleville 1703–13; 2nd serjeant [I] 1714–17, prime serjeant [I] 1717–*d.*

Flood, Francis (c.1660–1730), of Burnchurch, Co. Kilkenny, MP Callan 1703–5, 1713–27; lieut., Lord Granard's foot 1685, Coote's foot 1693, capt., Lord Charlemont's foot 1694.

Forster, John (1668–1720), of Dublin, MP Dublin 1703–14; recorder, Dublin 1701–14, counsel to revenue commrs [I] 1706, solicitor-gen. [I] 1709–10, attorney-gen. [I] 1710–11, chief justice of common pleas [I] 1714–*d.*, privy councillor [I] 1714–*d.*

Foulke, Robert (1663–1741), of Mallows, Co. Cork, MP Rathcormac 1692–9, Midleton 1703–13.

Fownes, Williagm (bef.1672–1735), of Islandbridge, Co. Dublin and Woodstock, Co. Kilkenny, MP Wicklow 1704–13; comptroller of customs, Youghal and Dungarvan 1693–1714, jt ranger of Phoenix Park, Dublin 1698–1704; knighted 1709, cr. Bt 1724.

Freke, George (bef. 1682–1730), of Upway, Dorset, MP Clonakilty 1703–27, Bandon 1727–*d.*; ensign, Erle's foot 1691, capt. 1696, lieut.-col., col. 1709, brig.-gen. 1711.

Freke, Percy (c.1644–1707), of Rathbarry, Co. Cork, MP Clonakilty 1692–9, Baltimore 1703–*d.*

Freke, Ralph (1675–1717), of Rathbarry, Co. Cork, MP Clonakilty 1703–*d.*; s. of Percy Freke (*q.v.*); cr. Bt 1713.

Gahan, Daniel (1671–1713), of Fishamble St., Dublin, MP Portarlington 1692–3, Rathcormac 1703–13; knighted 1705.

Gilbert, St Leger (bef. 1668–1737), of Kilminchy, Queen's Co., MP Maryborough 1692–1713, Old Leighlin 1713–27, commr of appeals in revenue [I] 1707–15.

Gore, Francis (bef. 1664–1724), of Clonroad, Buncraggy, Co. Clare, MP Ennis 1695–9, 1713–14, Co. Clare 1715–*d.*; capt., queen's regiment of dragoons 1691, Lord Fairfax's dragoons 1694, major 1696, lieut.-col.1699, col., queen's regiment of dragoons, brig.-gen. 1710.

Gore, George (1675–1753), of Tennalick, Co. Longford, MP Longford 1709–20; attorney-gen. [I] 1714–20, judge of common pleas [I] 1720–45.

Gorges, Richard (1662–1728), of Kilbrew House, Co. Meath, MP Charlemont 1692–3, Bandon 1703–13, Ratoath 1713–27; cornet of horse 1685,capt., Viscount Lisburne's regiment 1689, adjutant-gen. of forces [I] 1696, quartermaster-gen. [I] 1701, col. of foot regiment 1703, brig.-gen. 1704, col., 25th foot 1706, major-gen. of forces in Spain 1707, lieut.-gen. 1710.

Graydon, Alexander (c.1666–1739), of Killashee, Co. Kildare, MP Naas 1703–13, Harristown 1713–27.

Haltridge, John (1670–1725), of Dromore, Co. Down, MP Killyleagh 1703–*d.*

Hamilton, Gustavus (1642–1723), of Rosguile, Manorhamilton, Co. Leitrim, MP Co. Donegal 1692–1713, Strabane 1713–14; capt., Mountjoy's foot, 1685, privy councillor [I] 1685–8,1710–*d.*, colonel, 20th foot 1689–1706, brig.-gen. 1696, major-gen. 1706; cr. Baron Hamilton 1715, Viscount Boyne 1717.

Handcock, William (1654–1701), of Dublin, MP Boyle 1692–3, Dublin 1695–9; recorder of Dublin 1695–*d.*; knighted 1700.

Harman, Wentworth (bef. 1655–1714), of Bawn, Moyle, Co. Longford, MP Co. Longford 1695–9, Granard 1703–13; lieut., Irish Life Guards 1684–5, capt., battle-axe guards [I].

Harrison, Francis (1677–1725), of Dublin, Lisburn, Co. Antrim and Castlemartin, Co. Kildare, MP Knocktopher 1703–13, Lisburn 1713–14, Co. Carlow 1715–*d.*

Harrison, Michael (1669–1709), of Lisburn, Co. Antrim, MP Lisburn 1703–*d.*; capt., Hamilton's foot 1695; commissary-gen [I], clerk of the cheque [I] 1700–*d.*, muster-master gen. [I] 1700–*d.*; elder bro. of Francis Harrison (*q.v.*).

Hartstonge, Standish (1656–1705), of Talbot's Inch, Co. Kilkenny, MP Kilkenny 1695–*d.*

Hartstonge, Standish (c.1672–1751), of Bruff, Co. Limerick, MP Kilmallock 1695–9, Ratoath 1703–13, St Canice 1713–27; nephew of Standish Hartstonge (*q.v.*); suc. grandfather as 2nd Bt 1697.

Hawley, Henry (1657–1724), of Kinsale, Co. Cork, MP Kinsale 1703–*d.*; major, 19th foot 1689, lieut.-col. 1690, lieut.-col. 33rd foot 1691, Erle's foot 1695, gov., Kinsale 1701–*d.*

Hayes, John (1643–1705), of Great Russell Street, Bloomsbury, Middx., MP Thomastown 1692–3, Doneraile 1695–9 and MP [E] 1698–1700, 1701–2; comptroller-gen. of revenue [I] 1671–8.

Hayman, John (1664–1731), of Youghal, Co. Cork, MP Youghal 1703–13.

Hoare, Edward (c.1678–1765), of Dunkettle, Co. Cork, MP Cork 1710–27.

Hyde, Arthur (bef.1674–1720), of Castle Hyde, Co. Cork, MP Tralee1703–13, Midleton 1713–14, Youghal 1715–*d.*

Ingoldsby, Richard (bef. 1651–1712), of Ballybricken, Co. Limerick, MP Limerick 1703–*d.*; ensign, Hildyard's company 1678, lieut. 1680, lieut., Fairfax's foot 1685–8, major, Ingoldsby's foot 1689, col. 1689, col. Royal Welch Fusiliers 1693, brig.-gen. 1696, major-gen.1702, lieut.-gen. 1704, col., 18th foot 1705, major-gen. of ordnance [I] 1706, c.-in-c. [I] 1706–12, lord justice [I] 1709–10, 1710–11, 1711–12.

Jeffreys, Sir James (c.1650–1719), of Blarney Castle, Co. Cork, MP Lismore 1703–14; col. 1690, governor of Cork 1698–*d.*, brig.-gen.1704.

Jephson, Anthony (c.1689–1755), of Mallow Castle, Co. Cork, MP Mallow 1713–*d.*, cornet, Wharton's dragoons 1710, half-pay 1713, capt., Fielding's dragoons 1716, lieut.-col., Lord Doneraile's dragoons, 1716, col. 1740.

Jephson, John (1652–1724), MP Blessington 1703–*d.*; searcher, packer and gauger, Youghal and Dungarvan 1690–*d.*, customer, Dublin port 1690–2, commr of appeals in revenue [I] 1706.

Jephson, William (bef.1686–1716), of Mallow Castle, Co. Cork, MP Mallow 1713–16; capt.,Wittewrong's foot 1708–12, half-pay 1713; elder bro. of Anthony Jephson (*q.v.*).

Johnson, Robert (c.1657–1730), of Dublin, MP Trim 1697–9, Athboy 1703–4; baron of exchequer [I] 1704–14.

Jones, Edmond (bef. 1674–1700). MP Carlow 1695–9.

Jones, Edward (c.1637–95). MP Old Leighlin 1692–*d.*

Jones, Richard (1662–1729), of Dollardstown, Co. Meath, MP Donegal 1703–13; lieut., Townshend's regiment by 1712, half-pay 1712.

Jones, Thomas (1680–1716), of Osberstown, Co. Kildare, MP Kildare 1703–14.

Keating, Maurice (1664–1727), of Narraghmore, Co. Kildare, MP Athy 1695–*d.*

Keightley, Thomas (c.1650–1719), of Castlemartin, Co. Kildare, MP Inistioge 1695–9, Co. Kildare 1703–14; gentleman usher to Duke of York, 1672, revenue commr [I] 1692–1714, privy councillor [I] 1692–*d.*, commr for forfeited estates [I] 1693, lord justice [I] 1702–3, commr of great seal [I] 1710.

Kelly, Joseph (1673–1713), of Kellymount, Co. Kilkenny, MP Doneraile 1705–*d.*; commr of appeals in revenue [I] 1710–*d.*

King, John (1673–1721), of Boyle Abbey, Co. Roscommon, MP Boyle 1695–1714, Co. Roscommon 1715–*d.*; suc. as 2nd Bt 1708.

King, Robert (bef. 1677–1711), of Lissenhall, Co. Dublin, MP Lifford 1698–9, 1709–*d.*

Levinge, Sir Richard (1656–1724), of High Park, Mullalea, Co. Westmeath and Parwich, Derbys., MP Blessington 1692–3, Longford 1698–1713, Kilkenny 1713–14 and MP [E & GB] 1690–5, 1710–11; solicitor-gen. [I] 1690–5, 1704–9, Speaker, house of commons [I]1692–3, attorney-gen. [I]1711–14, chief justice, common pleas [I] 1720–*d.*, privy councillor [I] 1721–*d.*; cr. Bt 1704.

Ludlow, Peter (c.1685–1750), of Ardsallagh, Co. Meath, MP Dunleer 1713–14, Co. Meath 1719–*d.*

Ludlow, Stephen (bef. 1648–1721), of Ardsallagh, Co. Meath, MP Boyle 1692–3, Charlemont 1695–9, Dunleer 1703–13, 1715–*d.*, Co. Louth 1713–14; one of the six clerks in chancery [I] 1669–1711, revenue commr [I] 1711–14; fa. of Peter Ludlow (*q.v.*).

Luther, Henry (1667–1714), of Ballyboy, King's Co., MP Youghal 1703–14.

Macartney, George (1672–1757), of Lissanoure, Co. Antrim, MP Belfast 1692–3, 1715–*d.*, Limavady 1703–13, Donegal 1713–14.

Manley, Isaac (bef. 1682–1735), of Dublin and Manley Hall, Staffs., MP Downpatrick 1705–13, Limavady 1715–*d.*; postmaster-gen. [I] 1703–*d.*

Maxwell, Henry (1669–1730), of Finnebrogue, Co. Down, MP Bangor 1698–1713, Killybegs 1713–14, Donegal 1715–*d.*

May, Edward (bef. 1653–1710), of Mayfield, Co. Waterford, MP Gowran 1695–9; revenue commr II] 1690, commr for forfeited estates [I] 1695.

Maynard, Samuel (1656–1712), of Curryglass, Co. Cork, MP Tallow 1692–*d.*

Maynard, William (1690–1734), of Curryglass, Co. Cork, MP Tallow 1713–*d.*; collector of revenue, Cork 1717–*d.*; 1st s.of Samuel Maynard (*q.v.*).

Meade, Sir John (1642–1707), of Ballintober, Co. Cork, MP TCD 1689, Co. Tipperary 1692–*d.*; King's Counsel [I]1685; knighted 1678, cr. Bt 1703.

Medlycott, Thomas (1662–1738), of Dublin and Binfield, Berks., MP Kildare 1692–9, Clonmel 1703–13, Ballynakill 1713–14, Downpatrick 1715–27, Limavady 1728–*d.* and MP [E & GB] 1705–15, 1727–34; deputy steward of Westminster 1705–14, revenue commr [I] 1714–27, 1727–33.

Meredyth, Charles (bef. 1639–1710), of Newtown, Co. Meath, MP Co. Meath 1692–3, Kells 1695–*d.*

Meredyth, Richard (1657–1743), of Greenhills, Co.Kildare, MP Athy 1703–13.

Molesworth, Robert (1656–1725), of Brackenstown, Co. Dublin and Edlington, Yorks., MP Co. Dublin 1695–9, Swords 1703–14 and MP [E & GB] 1695–8, 1705–8, 1715–22; envoy extraordinary to Denmark 1689–92, privy councillor [I] 1697–Jan. 1714, Oct. 1714–*d.*; cr. Viscount Molesworth 1716.

Moore, Charles (1676–1714), Lord Moore, of Mellifont, Co. Louth, MP Drogheda 1692–1713; 1st s. (*d.v.p.*) of 3rd earl of Drogheda.

Moore, Sir Emmanuel (1685–1733), 3rd Bt, of Dunmore, Co. Cork, MP Downpatrick 1715–27.

Moore, John (bef. 1676–1725), of Croghan, King's Co., MP Philipstown 1703–13, King's Co. 1713–14; privy councillor [I] 1715–*d.*; cr. Baron Moore 1715.

Napper, James (c.1662–1719), of Loughcrew, Co. Meath, MP Athboy 1695–9, Trim 1703–13, Co. Meath 1715–*d.*; col. bef. 1711, brig. 1711.

Napper, William (1661–1708), of Loughcrew, Co. Meath, MP Trim 1695–*d.*; elder bro. of James Napper (*q.v.*).

Neave, William (c.1662–1713), of Killincarrig, Co. Wicklow, MP Tulsk 1692–*d*; 2nd serjeant [I] 1696–1708, prime serjeant [I] 1708–*d.*

Nutley, Richard (1673–1729), of Dublin, MP Lisburn 1703–11; judge of queen's bench [I] 1711–14.

O'Brien, Sir Donough (1642–1717), 1st Bt, of Dromoland, Co. Clare, MP Co. Clare 1692–1714; privy councillor [I] 170-4–14.

O'Brien, Lucius (c.1674–1717), of Leamaneigh, Co. Clare, MP Co. Clare 1703–14; s. (*d.v.p.*) of Sir Donough O'Brien (*q.v.*).

Ogle, Samuel (1659–1719), of Bowsden, Northumb., MP Belfast 1707–13 and MP [E & GB] 1690–1710; revenue commr [I] 1699–1714.

Oliver, Charles (1646–1706), of Castle Oliver, Co. Limerick, MP Midleton 1695–9, Co. Limerick 1703–*d.*; capt., Foulke's foot, 1690–aft. 1692.

Oliver, Robert (1674–1739), of Castle Oliver, Co. Limerick, MP Kilmallock 1703–13, 1727–*d*., Castlemartyr 1713–14, Co. Limerick 1715–27; s. of Charles Oliver (*q.v.*).

O'Neill, Charles (bef. 1676–1716), of Shane's Castle, Co. Antrim, MP Randalstown 1697–9, 1713–14, Bangor 1707–13; privy councillor [I] 1712–*d*.

Osborne, John (c.1641–92), of Stackallan, Co. Meath, MP Co. Meath 1692; 2nd serjeant [I] 1676, prime serjeant [I] 1680–7, 1690–2.

Pakenham, Sir Thomas (1651–1706), of Pakenham Hall, Co. Westmeath, MP Augher 1695–9; King's Counsel [I]1685–93, 2nd serjeant [I]1693–5, prime serjeant [I]1695–1705.

Palmer, William (1657–1726), of Dublin and Castlelackan, Co. Mayo, MP Castlebar 1695–1713; commr of appeals in revenue [I] 1693–1707; deputy clerk of privy council [I] 1695, 1697–1702, sec. to lords justices [I] 1696–7, 1701–3.

Parry, Benjamin (1672–1736), of Dublin, MP Killybegs 1703–13, Limavady 1713–14, Tallow 1715–27, Dungarvan 1727–*d*.; register of memorials of deeds, [I] 1707–*d*., privy councillor [I] 1714–*d*., keeper of Phoenix Park, Dublin 1722–*d*.

Pennefather, Kingsmill (1671–1735), of Newpark, Cashel, Co. Tipperary, MP Cashel 1703–14, Co. Tipperary 1715–*d*.

Peppard, James (bef. 1664–1725), of Milestown, Co. Louth, MP Swords 1703–13, Philipstown 1713–14, Granard 1715–*d*.

Perceval, Sir John (1683–1748), 5th Bt, of Burton House, Co. Cork, MP Co. Cork 1703–14 and MP [GB] 1727–34; privy councillor [I] 1704–*d*.; cr. Baron Perceval 1715, Viscount Perceval 1723, earl of Egmont 1733.

Philips, Chichester (bef. 1664–1728), of Drumcondra, Co. Dublin, MP Askeaton 1696–1713; ensign, Benjamin's foot 1672, lieut., Viscount Ranelagh's troop of horse 1675, capt., Viscount Mountjoy's foot 1685, Fairfax's regiment by 1689, earl of Meath's foot 1689.

Philips, William (*d*. 1734), of Dublin, MP Doneraile 1703–13; capt., Viscount Ikerrin's regiment 1704–6.

Pigott, Robert (1682–1730), of Dysart, Queen's Co., MP Maryborough 1703–*d*.; lieut., earl of Inchiquin's foot 1704, capt. 1712, major 1713, col. 1715.

Pollard, Walter (bef. 1641–1718), of Castlepollard, Co. Westmeath, MP Fore 1695–1713.

Ponsonby, William (1659–1724), of Bessborough, Co. Kilkenny, MP Co. Kilkenny 1692–1721; privy councillor [I] 1715–*d*.; cr. Baron Bessborough 1721, Viscount Duncannon 1723.

Power, Roger (bef. 1672–1707), of Lismore, Co. Waterford, MP Dungarvan 1703–*d*.

Pulteney, John (c.1661–1726), of St James's, Westminster, and Harefield, Middx., MP Wexford 1692–3, and MP [E & GB] 1695–1710; under-sec. of state[E] 1689–90, 1690–2, 1693–5, sec. to lords justices [I] 1690, chief sec. [I] 1692–3, clerk of council [I] 1692–*d*., chief clerk to master-gen. of ordnance [E] 1693–1702, clerk of deliveries [E] 1701–3, lord of trade [GB] 1707–11, commr of customs [E] 1714–22, surveyor-gen. of crown lands [E]1722–*d*.

Purdon, Bartholomew (1675–1737), of Ballyclogh, Co. Cork, MP Mallow 1699–1713, Doneraile 1713–14, Castlemartyr 1715–*d*.

Richardson, William (1656–1727), of Richhill, Co. Armagh, MP Co. Armagh 1692–3, 1715–*d*., Hillsborough 1703–13.

Riggs, Edward (c.1620–1706), of Riggsdale, Co. Cork, MP Bandon 1692–9.

Riggs, Edward (bef. 1686–1741), of Riggsdale, Co. Cork, MP Baltimore 1707–13, Bangor 1716–27, Limavady 1739–*d*.; revenue commr [I] 1733–*d*.; s. of Edward Riggs (*q.v.*).

Robinson, William (1644–1712), of Island Bridge, Dublin, and Sherwood, Co. Carlow, MP Knocktopher 1692–3, Wicklow 1695–9, TCD 1703–*d*.; surveyor-gen. [I] 1671–1700, keeper of parliament house [I] 1677–1712, dep. receiver-gen. and paymaster-gen. of forces [I] 1692–1703, privy councillor [I] by 1702; knighted 1702.

Rochfort, Robert (1652–1727), of Gaulstown, Co. Westmeath, MP Co. Westmeath 1692–1707; commr of great seal [I] 1690–3, Speaker, house of commons [I] 1695–9, attorney-gen. [I] 1695–1707, chief baron of exchequer [I] 1707–14, privy councillor [I] 1707–14.

Rogers, George (c.1650–1710), of Ballyknavin, Co. Tipperary and Ashgrove, Co.Cork, MP Lismore 1692–9.

Rogers, Robert (*d.* 1717), MP Cork, 1692–9; elder bro. of George Rogers (*q.v.*).

Rogerson, John (1676–1741), of Glasnevin, Co. Dublin, MP Granard 1713–14, Dublin 1715–27; recorder, Dublin 1714–27, solicitor-gen. [I] 1714–20, attorney-gen. [I] 1720–7, chief justice of king's bench [I] 1727–*d*., privy councillor [I] 1727–*d*.

Rose, Henry (1675–1743), of Mountpleasant and Morgans, Co. Limerick, MP Ardfert 1703–34; judge of king's bench [I] 1734–*d*.

St George, Sir George (bef. 1640–1713), of Dunmore, Co. Galway, MP Co. Galway 1695–9, Carrick-on-Shannon 1703–13; lieut., Lord Mountrath's horse 1661, capt., earl of Ardglass's horse 1686, col. of foot 1692, half-pay 1711.

St George, Sir George (c, 1640–1735), 2nd Bt, of Carrickdrumrusk, Co. Leitrim, MP Co. Roscommon 1692–14; vice-admiral, Connacht 1696–*d*., privy councillor [I], 1715–*d*.; cr. Baron St George 1715.

St George, Henry (1676–1723), of Woodsgift, Co. Kilkenny, MP Clogher 1703–13, Athlone 1715–*d*.

St George, Oliver (1661–1731), of Carrickdrumrusk, Co. Leitrim, MP Carrick-on-Shannon 1703–13, Dungannon 1713–*d*.; capt. of a troop of dragoons 1685, capt. queen's regiment of dragoons 1685–8, privy councillor [I] 1714–*d*.; nephew of Sir George St George, 2nd Bt. (*q.v.*).

St George, Richard (1670–1755), of Kilrush, Co. Kilkenny, MP Galway 1695–9, Carrick-on-Shannon 1715–*d*.; adjutant, St George's foot 1690, capt.1691, major, Lord Slane's foot 1708, lieut.-col. 1711, lieut.-col., Macartney's horse 1727, col. of foot regiment 1737; col. of dragoon regiment 1740, major-gen.1744, lieut.-gen.1747, major-gen. of staff [I] by 1755.

St Leger, Arthur (1657–1727), of Doneraile, Co. Cork, MP Doneraile, 1692–3; cr. Viscount Doneraile 1703.

St Leger, Sir John (1674–1743), of Capel St., Dublin and Grangemellon, Co. Kildare, MP Doneraile 1713–14; baron of exchequer [I] 1714–41; half-bro. of Arthur St Leger (*q.v.*).

Sandford, Henry (bef. 1671–1733), of Castlereagh, Co. Roscommon, MP Roscommon 1692–*d*.

Sankey, Nicholas (1657–1722), of Tennalick, Co. Longford, MP Lanesborough 1703–13; capt., Irish foot guards. bef. 1685–c.1687, col. of regiment of foot 1689–90, 39th foot 1703, brig.-gen. 1704, major-gen. 1707, lieut.-gen. 1710.

Saunders, Anderson (c.1653–1718), of Newtown Saunders, Co. Wicklow, MP Taghmon 1692–*d*.; one of the six clerks in Chancery [I] 1682–1715.

Saunders, Morley (1671–1737), of Saunders Grove, Co. Wicklow, MP Enniscorthy 1703–14; 2nd serjeant [I] 1711–13, prime serjeant [I] 1713–14; nephew of Anderson Saunders (*q.v.*).

Saunders, Richard (1679–1730), of Saunders Court, Co. Wexford, MP Taghmon 1703–13, 1715–*d.*, Wexford 1713–14; nephew of Anderson Saunders (*q.v.*) and cousin of Morley Saunders (*q.v.*).

Saunders, Robert (c.1654–1708), of Castle Saunders, Co. Cavan, MP Cavan 1692–*d.*; queen's serjeant [I] 1703–*d.*; brother of Anderson Saunders (*q.v.*), fa. of Morley Saunders (*q.v.*) and uncle of Richard Saunders (*q.v.*).

Savage, Philip (1644–1717), of Dublin, MP Co. Wexford 1692–1714; jt prothonotary of king's bench [I] 1671–7, chancellor of the exchequer [I] 1695–*d.*, privy councillor [I] by 1702–1710, 1711–14.

Silver, John (c.1665–1724), of Fountain, Co. Waterford, MP Rathcormac 1703–13.

Singleton, Edward (bef. 1653–1710), of Drogheda, Co. Louth, MP Drogheda 1692–*d.*

Sloane, James (1655–1704), of Boswell Court, Little Lincoln's Inn Fields, London, MP Killyleagh 1692–9 and MP [E] 1696–1700; sec. to chief justice in eyre, south of the Trent [E] 1697–1702.

Smyth, Boyle (bef. 1692–1730), of Headborough, Co. Waterford, MP Youghal 1713–14; lieut., earl of Barrymore's foot 1706, capt., Masham's horse 1708, major 1713, half-pay 1713.

Somerville, James (c.1664–1705), of Dublin, MP Dundalk 1703–*d.*

South, John (c.1669–1711), of Dublin, MP Newcastle 1703–*d.*; commr for stating accounts of army [I] by 1693, revenue commr [I] 1696–*d.*, keeper, Phoenix Park, Dublin (life).

Southwell, Edward (1671–1730), of Kings Weston, Gloucs., Kinsale, Co. Cork, and Spring Garden, Westminster, MP Kinsale 1692–9, 1713–*d.*, TCD 1703–13, and MP [E & GB] 1702–8, 1713–15; clerk of privy council [E] 1693–*d.*, jt prothonotary of common pleas [I] 1698–1717, judge of admiralty court and vice-admiral, Munster [I] 1699–*d.*, jt commr of privy seal [E] 1701–2, [GB] 1715, 1716, sec. of state [I] 1702–*d.*, privy councillor [I] 1702–*d.*, chief sec. [I] 1703–7, 1710–13, prothonotary of king's bench [I]1715–17.

Southwell, Sir Thomas (1665–1720), of Castlematrix, Co. Limerick, MP Co. Limerick 1695–1717; revenue commr [I] 1697–1714, 1714–*d.*, privy councillor [I] 1710–*d.*, [GB] 1714–*d.*; cr. Baron Southwell 1717.

Southwell, William (bef.1682–1720), of Dublin, MP Kinsale 1703–13, Castlemartyr 1713–14, Baltimore 1715–*d.*; lieut., Hamilton's foot 1693, capt.-lieut. 1694, major, Rivers' foot 1702, lieut.-col. 1703, col. of regiment of foot 1706–8, col., 6th foot 1714–*d.*, capt., battle-axe guards [I] 1714–*d.*

Spring, Francis (bef. 1660–1711), of Jigginstown, Co. Kildare, MP Naas 1703–11.

Stafford, Edmond Francis (c.1660/2–1724), of Mount Stafford, Brownstown, Co. Meath, MP Randalstown 1692–1713, Lisburn 1715–*d.*; lieut. under Schomberg's command 1689; capt., Leveson's horse 1699, Langston's horse 1706–aft. 1707.

Stanley, Sir John (1663–1744), of Grangegorman, Co. Dublin, MP Gorey 1713–14; commr for stamp duties [E] 1698–1700, commr of customs [GB] 1708–44, chief sec. [I] 1713–14, privy councillor [I] 1713–27, 1732–*d.*, surveyor-gen. of customs [I] 1732–*d.*

Steuart, William (1652–1726), of Hanover Sq., London, MP Co. Waterford 1703–14; ensign, Vaughan's foot 1673, lieut.1673, capt., Wheeler's foot 1678, major 1678, capt.,1st foot guards 1685, lieut.-col. 1687, col., 9th foot 1689, brig. 1690, privy councillor [I] 1696–*d.*, inspector of garrisons [I] 1696, major-gen. 1696, c.-in-c. [I] 1696–1701, 1712–14.

Stevenson, James (bef.1692–1738), of Dublin, MP Killyleagh 1713–14, 1727–*d*., Randalstown 1715–27.

Stewart, Hon. Richard (1677–1728), of Ballycastle, Co. Antrim, MP Co. Tyrone 1703–14, 1727–*d*., Strabane 1715–27; 2nd s. of 1st Viscount Mountjoy.

Stone, Richard (1674–1727), of Dublin, MP Limavady 1695–9; master in chancery [I] 1694–1714, surveyor-gen. [I] 1695–1714.

Stopford, James (1668–1721), of Courtown, Co. Wexford, MP Wexford 1703–13, Co. Wexford 1713–*d.*

Stratford, Edward (1664–1740), of Belan, Co. Kildare, MP Carysfort 1695–9, Baltinglass 1703–27, Harristown 1727–*d.*

Tenison, Henry (1667–1709), of Dillonstown, Co. Louth, MP Co. Monaghan 1695–9, Co. Louth 1703–*d*.; revenue commr [I] 1704–*d.*

Tynte, James: *see* Worth.

Upton, Clotworthy (1665–1725), of Castle Upton, Templepatrick, Co. Antrim, MP Newtownards 1695–9, Co. Antrim 1703–*d.*

Upton, Thomas (1677–1733), MP Antrim 1713–14, Co. Antrim 1716–27, Derry 1727–*d*.; King's Counsel [I] 1715, commr of appeals in revenue [I] 1717–*d*., counsel to barracks commrs [I] by 1721–*d*., customer, Derry and Coleraine 17230; younger bro. of Clotworthy Upton (*q.v.*).

Vernon, Sir Richard (1678–1725), 3rd Bt, of Hodner, Salop, MP Monaghan 1703–13; lieut., Coldstream Guards 1702; capt., duke of Ormond's horse by 1704–1710, lieut.col., Echlin's regiment, later Killigrew's 1710; a.-*d*.-c. to Ormond.

Wall, William (bef. 1690–1755), of Maryborough, Queen's Co., MP Maryborough 1713–*d*.; master in chancery [I] 1742–*d.*

Wandesford, Sir Christopher (1656–1707), 2nd Bt , of Kirklington, Yorks., and Castlecomer, Co. Kilkenny, MP St Canice 1692–*d.* and MP [E] 1679–81; privy councillor [I] 1695–*d*.; cr. Viscount Castlecomer 1707.

Warburton, Richard (1674–1747), of Donnycarney, Co. Dublin, MP Portarlington 1715–27, Ballynakill 1727–*d.*

Westgarth, William (bef. 1682–1710), of Dublin, MP Roscommon 1703–*d.*

Whitshed, William (1679–1727), of Dublin and Killincarrig, Co. Wicklow, MP Co. Wicklow 1703–14; solicitor-gen. [I] 1710–11, chief justice of king's bench [I] 1714–27, privy councillor [I] 1714–*d*., chief justice of common pleas [I] 1727–*d.*

Williamson, Sir Joseph (1633–1701), of Cobham Hall, Kent, MP Co. Clare 1692–3, Limerick 1695–9 and MP [E] 1669–81, 1685–7, 1690–*d*.; under-sec. of state [E] 1660–74, postmaster-gen. [E] 1667–85, clerk of privy council [E] 1672–4, sec. of state [E] 1674–9, lord of admiralty [E] 1674–9, privy councillor [E] 1674–9, 1696–*d*., privy councillor [I] 1681–5, 1694–*d*., ambassador extraordinary at The Hague 1697–9.

Wingfield, Edward (1659–1728), of Powerscourt, Co. Wicklow, MP Co. Sligo 1692–1713.

Wolseley, Richard (c.1655–1724), of Mount Arran, Co. Carlow, MP Carlow 1703–*d*.; capt., Wolseley's regiment 1689, half-pay 1690–1, capt., Viscount Windsor's regiment 1706.

Wolseley, William (1640–97), MP Longford 1692–*d*.; capt, 11th foot 1685, lieut.-col. 1688, col. 1689, col., Inniskilling horse 1689, brig. of a regiment of horse 1691, master-gen. of Ordnance [I] 1692–*d*., brig.-gen. 1696, lord justice [I] 1696; privy councillor [I] 1696–*d.*

Worth, James (1682–1758), of Old Bawn, Co. Dublin, and Dunlavin, Co. Wicklow, MP Rathcormac 1716–27, Youghal 1727–*d.*; privy councillor [I] 1715–*d.*; assumed the name of Tynte on inheriting estates.

Wych(e), Sir Cyril (c.1632–1707), of Westminster and Hockwold, Norf., MP TCD 1692–3 and MP [E] 1661–79, 1681 1685–7, 1702–5; one of the six clerks in Chancery [E] 1662–75, chief sec. [I] 1676–85, 1692–3, privy councillor [I] 1676, 1692–*d.*, lord justice [I] 1693–5.